D1229957

Reading

A Program o

Paul McKee

WITH THE ASSISTANCE C

Instruction for the Elementary School

INSTRUCTIONAL CONSULTANT, DENVER PUBLIC SCHOOLS

WILLIAM K. DURR MICHIGAN STATE UNIVERSITY

Houghton Mifflin Company · Boston

NEW YORK · ATLANTA · GENEVA, ILL. · DALLAS · PALO ALTO

WILMINGTON COLLEGE
Library
WILMINGTON N C

LB1573
.M169

The poem which appears on page 44 is reprinted by permission of the publisher, THE DENVER POST, and the author, William S. Corwin.

Copyright © 1966 by Houghton Mifflin Company. All rights reserved, including the right to reproduce this book or parts thereof in any form. Printed in the U.S.A.

Charles W Clark

6 26

35/60

3.1.67

To

S. G. M.

Preface/

THE SUBSTANCE of this volume is a detailed description and explanation of a carefully built program of instruction in reading for the elementary school. That suggested program is composed of what the author considers to be the best ideas gleaned from his forty years of experience in working with elementary school teachers and pupils in different parts of the United States, in teaching courses on instruction in reading to some fifteen thousand undergraduate and graduate students, in serving as instructional consultant to various city school systems, and in conducting and directing research on the teaching of reading. The first chapter gives you, the reader, a chance to gain some awareness of a few of the problems which the young child encounters in beginning to learn to read, and Chapter 2 lays part of the foundation of the suggested program as presented in the remaining chapters. Although the author certainly would follow the suggested program if he were once again teaching a child to read, he does not claim that the program cannot be improved or that all other programs are ineffective.

This volume is in no sense a revision or a rewriting of *The Teaching of Reading*, published in 1948 by Houghton Mifflin Company. Instead, it is an entirely new proposal of what the author at present believes the teaching of reading can and should be in any elementary school. It is not merely a group of writings on any or all topics that could be included in a book on the teaching of reading, nor is it an extended discourse on remedial reading. It is, rather, a detailed blueprint of what the author believes should be taught to practically all elementary school pupils and how the appropriate instruction can be carried on during those years. It is not a source to which the advanced student can turn to find summaries, evaluations, or even notations of all or much of the research which has been concerned with the teaching of reading. Other publications serve that purpose. This is not to say that the author has failed to use the results of research in building the suggested program. On the contrary, much research, most of which is not referred to in footnotes, lies behind many — but not all — of the included proposals. However, this research includes only those relatively few investigations which were concerned with instructional dilemmas that teachers actually face, which were directed at significant rather than trivial matters, which were designed and carried out with skill, and which are to be interpreted with insight into the pressing and unsolved problems of teaching children to read.

The author is indebted to many people — certain colleagues whose chief professional interest is the study of the teaching of reading, many elementary school reading consultants, teachers, principals, and pupils, a number of editors, some of his former graduate students, and close friends. He is grateful for the help and encouragement they have supplied during the years.

PAUL McKEE

GREELEY, COLORADO, 1966

Contents /

READING/

A Program of Instruction

for the Elementary School

part ONE / *Introduction*

chapter 1

Once Again You Begin
to Learn to Read!

It would be easy for you to understand the following sentence if you heard someone say it, but can you read it?

◦⊏+∧ ⦋⧧◦∨⊔ ⊇⧧◦ ⊔⧧ ∧⧧ ⬚⊗ꟽ∪ꞵ
∧⧧ ∧⊗+⦋⊏ + ⦋⊏∪∨⊔ ∧⧧ ⅂⊗+⊔?

Chances are, you couldn't read it because the words are composed of unfamiliar symbols which have been substituted for the English letters you know so well. If you were similarly acquainted with these strange symbols, you would know immediately that they stand for the familiar spoken words, *What could you do to begin to teach a child to read?*

One good way to acquire a few ideas needed for answering this question is to let yourself be placed in a position somewhat like that of the first-grade pupil as he uses a first preprimer.[1] In order to put you in this position, it is necessary to present you with a passage to read in which the letter symbols used — and so the forms of all the words — are strange to you, just as the words in the child's preprimer are strange to him. To the child who has never seen it before, *come* is just as strange as ⦋⧧⅋⊗ is to you, yet both are printed forms of the same word that

---

[1] Usually a modern series of readers provides for first-grade pupils a first preprimer, a second preprimer, a third preprimer, a primer, and a first reader — to be read in that order. Thus, ordinarily, a first preprimer is the first book that the pupil actually reads in school.

is so familiar in its spoken form. If you are willing to undertake this enlightening experience, just follow the directions given, think what you are learning, and think, too, of the answers to the questions asked.

In certain important ways, the passage you are going to read is much like the little stories or incidents that make up the content of a first pre-primer. Each printed word is one you know perfectly well when you hear it spoken; it stands for a meaning with which you are already familiar, and it is strange to you only in print. Each printed line is one you would understand easily if you heard it spoken, and the punctuation marks used are those found in any first preprimer. The pictures show the events that take place in the incident, and the printed lines tell what some person is saying to someone else, whether that person is one story character talking to another, or the author talking to you, the reader. The content may not greatly interest you, but in a very real sense it is representative of that found in many present-day preprimers.

Will it be harder for you to learn to read the passage than it is for the first-grade pupil to learn to read his first preprimer? Well, perhaps so. Since the passage contains a larger number of different words, presents a higher average number of new words per page, and provides fewer repetitions of each word than does a typical first preprimer, you may progress less rapidly than the child. Furthermore, since you will not be using a so-called workbook, you will not have the benefit of working your way through several types of exercises which would help you to fix in mind thoroughly certain things you need to know. Actually, however, your learning job may be easier for you than the first-grade child's is for him. After all, you have had years of experience in reading printed symbols; in general, you know what reading is. You already know that each printed line stands for a familiar spoken form, and that it is something which someone is saying. You are aware that each new word you meet makes sense with the other words and that it is a word you know well when you hear it spoken. You know that a printed word is made up of letters and that letters stand for sounds. You understand what is meant by the beginning of a printed word and perhaps what is meant by the beginning of a spoken word. Finally, you will be required to learn only one rather than two forms for each letter. Usually the child has none of these advantages.

Are you ready to begin? If so, look at the first word you will meet in the passage. Here it is:

$$= + \cup \delta \wedge$$

Just what is that odd-looking print? Simply a strange form that stands for one of the thousands of spoken words you already know. What is it that you don't know and need to know? Just which familiar spoken word is the one that this strange printed form stands for. What do you need to do? Certainly you do not have to figure out the pronunciation of the word. You already know that! You need merely to call the familiar spoken word — the pronunciation — to mind. But how can you do this? How can you, all by yourself, unlock a word that is strange to you only in print?

You can try using the context — the meaning of something being said — together with the sounds that some — but not all — of the letters in the word stand for. But before you can do this you need to know what those sounds are. To find that out, use the rows of items given below. The names of the objects in the pictures at the left of each row begin with the sound that the letter at the right stands for.

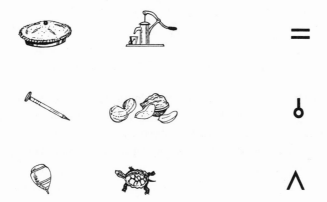

Now here in English is a line of context that you can use.[2] When you read the line and come to the strange word, think of a word that begins with the sound = stands for and that makes sense there. To make sure of the word, use either or both of the two other letter-sound associations you have just learned.

Please hand me that can of =+U♭∧.

What is the word? *Soup, peas, pears, milk* and several other words make sense with the context. But neither *soup* nor *milk* begins or ends with the right sound. *Peas* and *pears* begin with the right sound but end

[2] In introducing to pupils the first words in a first preprimer, the teacher would present the context orally.

with a wrong sound. *Pant, punt, point,* and *pent* begin and end with the right sounds, but none of those words makes sense with the context. Obviously, the strange word is *paint*. There is nothing else it could be. Notice that in unlocking the word, you used letter-sound associations only for consonants. You had not learned and did not need to know the letter-sound association for the two vowels ✛ and ∪. What told you the sound you needed to think there? Was it the context?

Have you fixed in mind the three letter-sound associations presented on page 5? You will need to do this so that you can use them in unlocking other words. Perhaps it will help you to fix the letter-sound associations in your mind if you familiarize yourself with key pictures on which the strange letter forms are superimposed. Notice that the name of the picture begins with the sound the letter stands for and that the shape of the letter and the picture are similar enough so that one suggests the other. Here are key pictures for =, ♦, and ∧.

path   note   tent

Before attempting to unlock the remaining words in the first five pages of the passage, you should learn eight more letter-sound associations. In each row below, the names of the objects in the two pictures at the left begin with the sound the letter at the right stands for. The key picture is at the end of the row.

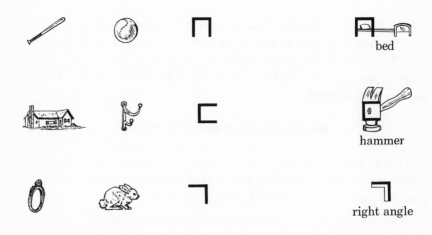

bed

hammer

right angle

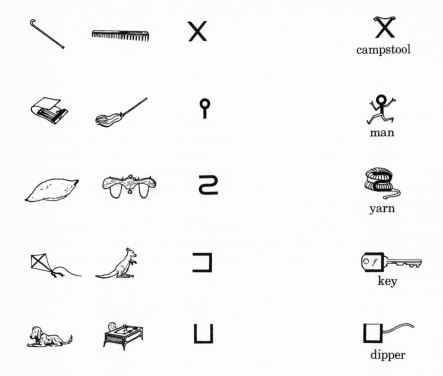

If you have observed the similarity between the form of each letter and the shape of the key picture to the point where they are fixed in your mind, you are ready to unlock the next five words you will meet in the passage. Whenever you come to a strange word in the following numbered lines, think of a word that begins with the sound the first letter stands for and that makes sense there. Use other letter sounds you know to make sure of the word. In order to keep yourself in the position of the beginning first-grade pupil as you work, do your best to avoid trying to fit a spelling you know to the strange printed form. Most first-grade pupils cannot do that, and neither you nor any of them needs to do it.

1. Mother has gone to town, but Dad is ⊏⊗⊓⊗. What is the word? How do you know it isn't *home*? *Hire*?
2. When will Mr. Black get here? Why doesn't he ✗╪ໆ⊗? What is the word? How do you know it isn't *arrive*? *Hurry*? *Comb*? *Care*?
3. Did Mr. Black come to see Mother and ⊇╪○? What is the word? How do you know it isn't *yes*? *Him*? *Dad*?

The remaining two words are the names of story characters. Since context is of little if any help in unlocking a proper name which cannot be used also as a common noun or some other part of speech, you will have to depend entirely upon letter-sound associations you have learned. Here are the two words:

◊⊗⊔   ⊐⊔Ƽ

The word above at the left is the name of a boy. What word that begins with the sound ◊ stands for and ends with the sound ⊔ stands for is a boy's name? How do you know it isn't *Ted? Nick? Fred?* The other word is the name of a girl. What word that begins with the sound ⊐ stands for and ends with the sound Ƽ stands for is a girl's name? How do you know it isn't *Kit? Min?*

Now try reading the first five pages of the passage. The first page is merely a title page with an appropriate illustration and a word which is the name of the incident. In reading each of the other pages, look first at the picture to observe the action taking place, to get the setting in which the lines of text are spoken, and to decide who is doing the talking. Then read the lines to find out what the story character is saying.

=+⊔◊∧

1

◊⊗Ц. ◊⊗Ц.

2

⊏⊗⊓⊗,◊⊗Ц.
⊏⊗⊓⊗. ⊏⊗⊓⊗.

3

X‡ᱼ⊗ ⊏⊗ᱤ⊗, ᱡ⊗∐.
X‡ᱼ⊗ ⊏⊗ᱤ⊗.

ᱭ‡ᱼ⊸ X‡ᱼ⊗ ⊏⊗ᱤ⊗, ⊐∐ᱼ.
ᱭ‡ᱼ⊸ X‡ᱼ⊗ ⊏⊗ᱤ⊗.

Well, how did you get along? Could you recognize instantly — without any puzzling — one or more of the six words that had been introduced to you, or did you have to unlock all of them again?[3] What could you do to fix each word form so well in mind that you could recognize it quickly either in context or in isolation? Would it help if, as you looked at the form, you said the word enough times to hear the sound of each of its letters for which you have learned the letter-sound association? Would writing the word help? Do you think you could ever learn to recognize a printed word just by its length, the outline of its form, some distinguishing visual characteristic it contains, or any combination of such items? Could you become so familiar with any printed word that you could recognize it merely by seeing it as a "whole" without noting any of its visual parts or without thinking the sound of any one of its letters? As you proceed through the rest of this book, answers to these questions will become more and more apparent to you. Bear in mind that what works or doesn't work for you might well apply to the first-grader as well.

Here are six more letter-sound associations you should learn so that you can unlock the strange words you will meet on pages 6–10 in the passage. Use each row of items just as you used the rows on pages 6 and 7.

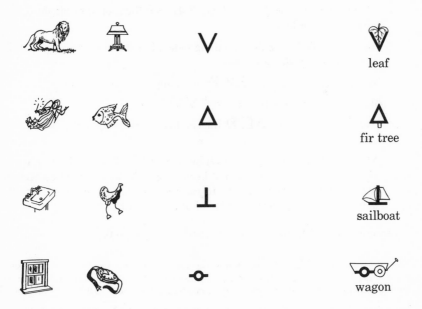

leaf

fir tree

sailboat

wagon

---

[3] It would not be surprising if you had to unlock all the words again. Lack of space does not permit giving the practice you need for learning to recognize any one of the words instantly.

wheelbarrow

thinker[4]

When you meet a strange word in each of the following numbered lines, think of a word that begins with the sound the first letter stands for and that makes sense there.[5] Use other letter sounds you know to make sure of the word.

1. I am trying to find my new skates that Dad gave me. Will you help me to V‡‡⌐ for them?

2. Jack can't whistle, but Sally X+◊.

3. Dick and Fred can't run as △+⊥∧ as the rest of the boys in Miss Brown's class.

4. The boys will come home when ⊶⊗ call them on the telephone this afternoon after lunch.

5. Betty said she had to do something today, but she didn't say ⊶⊏+∧ it was or where she was going.

6. It is so dark that I can't ⊥⊗⊗ anything.

7. Tom is trying to climb that ⊶+VV.

8. Where did you put ∧⊏⊗ bucket that I left out on the back porch last night?

9. Mary can't go to the party. Neither can U. (The word U is a one-letter word. Since you have not been taught the letter-sound association for that letter, it is necessary to tell you that the letter stands for the sound you hear at the beginning of *ice* and *idea*.)

Now continue with the passage by reading pages 6–10.

---

[4] In the passage, ∧⊏ always stands for the sound you hear at the beginning of *this* and *that*. That sound is not the one presented here simply because there is no picturable object which has a name beginning with that sound. However, the sound ∧⊏ stands for in *this* and *that* is so close to the sound ∧⊏ stands for in *thumb*, *thermometer*, and *thicket* that those letters should cause you no trouble in your reading if you are also using the context to help you think of a word which makes sense and which you know when you hear it.

[5] In 5 and 8, use the sound the first two letters stand for.

∨≠≠⊐. ∨≠≠⊐, ⊐∪Ⴎ.
∨≠≠⊐ ⊏⊗⊓⊗.

6

∨≠≠⊐. =+∪ჼ∧.
X+ჼ ⊂≠ᕈ =+∪ჼ∧, ⊐∪Ⴎ?

7

ᑌ ᗄ+ᒡ =+ᑌᒡᐱ, ᒡ⊗ᒣ.

ᑌ ᗄ+ᒡ =+ᑌᒡᐱ ᐃ+ᐯᐱ.

ᗄ+ᒡ ᘔᚲ° =+ᑌᒡᐱ ᐃ+ᐯᐱ?

8

ᑌ ᗄ+ᒡ =+ᑌᒡᐱ ᐃ+ᐯᐱ.

°ᒥ+ᐱ ᗄ+ᒡ °⊗ =+ᑌᒡᐱ?

9

V‡‡⌐, ♭⊗⊔.

⊥⊗⊗ ∧⊏⊗ ⚬+∨∨.

⚬⊗ ✕+♭ =+∪♭∧ ∧⊏⊗ ⚬+∨∨.

10

The experience you have had so far in using context and letter sounds together to unlock strange printed words makes it possible for you to think of answers to several important questions. What does using the context do for you? Of course it makes you call to mind a familiar meaning and simultaneously a familiar spoken word that makes sense. Does it make you reject quickly any familiar spoken word that doesn't make sense? What can the using of letter sounds do for you? Can they help you decide which of several spoken words that make sense is the right one? Does using the context and just the beginning sound stimulate you to reject quickly any word which begins with the right sound but doesn't make sense or which makes sense but doesn't begin with the right sound? Did you find that the beginning sound in itself suggested a word that made sense so that context and beginning sound seemed to work together simultaneously to enable you to unlock the strange printed word? Suppose there were two words that began with the same sound and ended with different sounds but both made sense. Could the context and just the beginning and ending sounds help you decide which word was the right one? Could the context and just the beginning sound, the ending sound, and a consonant sound within the word help you decide which of two spoken words that make sense, begin with the same sound, end with the same sound, but have different internal consonant sounds is the right word? Did you unlock any word that had in it one or more letters for which you had not been taught the letter-sound associations? What were those letters?

You will need to learn the following letter-sound association in order to unlock strange words in the last part of the passage. Use the row of items just as you used the rows on pages 6 and 7.

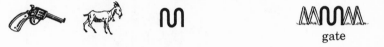

gate

Here are two of the nine strange words you will meet in the last pages of the passage. One of them is the single-letter word ✛. Since you have not been taught the letter-sound association for that letter, you must be told that it stands for the sound you hear at the beginning of *about* and *around*. The other word is ✛⌐⊗. It begins with the sound you hear at the beginning of *arm* and *ark*. Use the following numbered items to unlock the two words:

1. Jim's dog can climb ✛ wall but he can't stand on his hind legs or do any other tricks.
2. Do you know when Dad and Mother ✛⌐⊗ going to leave for their vacation in the mountains?

As you read the rest of the passage, do your best to unlock the remaining seven strange words. Remember that the spoken word you need to call to mind for each strange printed form is one which you know well when you hear it, which makes sense in the context on the page, and which contains sounds the consonants represent. Remember too that in order to snap the familiar spoken word into your consciousness, you will not need to use all of the letter-sound associations represented in the printed form.[6]

---

[6] No doubt you have noticed that in introducing strange printed words to you, the context has been presented in the familiar English alphabet rather than in the special one you have been using in reading the passage. This was done simply because you had had neither the time nor the practice necessary for becoming so familiar with the printed words that you could use them readily as context. In working with first-grade pupils while they are using a first preprimer, the various contexts the teacher uses are, for a time, spoken or read aloud by her, but as soon as pupils have a ready recognition of printed words with which suitable context can be made, that context is shown to pupils for them to read to themselves.

∪ ⊥⊗⊗ ∧⊏⊗ ⊶+∨∨.

⊶⊗ ⊶∪∨∨ =+∪ᓂ∧ ∧⊏⊗ ⊶+∨∨ ∆+⊥∧.

∧⊏⊗ ⊶+∨∨ ⊶∪∨∨ ∨ᖽᖨᖽᖨ⊐ ᗰᖽᖨᖽᖨ∪.

11

ᓂ⊗∪ ⊐∪ᕀ.

⊥∧ᖽᖨ=. ⊥∧ᖽᖨ=.

12

V‡‡⊃. V‡‡⊃.
⊶⊗ X+δ =+∪δ∧.
∧⊏⊗ ⊶+∨∨ ⊶∪∨∨ V‡‡⊃ ⋒‡‡⊔.
⊶⊗ +⊓⊗ ⋒‡‡⊔.

13

∧⊏⊗ ⊶+∨∨ ⊶∪∨∨ δ‡∧ V‡‡⊃ ⋒‡‡⊔.
⊇‡⊶ +⊓⊗ δ‡∧ ⋒‡‡⊔. ⊶‡⊇
⊇‡⊶ +⊓⊗ + የ⊗⊥⊤.

14

15

By reading the passage on the preceding pages and learning what you were asked to in this chapter, you have acquired two important assets that would be basic capital for you to use in reading independently other material printed in words composed of the letter forms used in the passage. One of these assets can be called your reading vocabulary. This vocabulary is composed of whatever words among the twenty-four different ones presented in the passage have become so familiar that you can recognize them quickly. The other asset is whatever beginning you have made in gaining control of a definite and effective technique for unlocking strange printed words independently. This technique consists of using (1) the context — the sense of what is being said — together with the beginning sound of the word and (2) only as many of the remaining letter sounds as are needed to make sure of the word. It is precisely this technique which the author believes should be taught to first-grade pupils as they are learning to read.

Your attention should be called to the fact that a procedure different from that followed in this chapter could have been used. With the so-called sight method of beginning to teach a child to read — a method widely used in American schools for decades — each strange word is introduced simply by showing the printed form and telling him what the familiar spoken word is. Under this method you would have been taught no letter-sound associations first, and you would have learned no technique to use in unlocking strange printed words independently. Perhaps if you had been taught by the sight method, and frequent repetition of each word had been supplied, you could have learned to recognize at least some of the words and could have read the passage. But by the time you had finished that reading, what assets would you have that would enable you to read independently other material printed in the same letter forms? Only a reading vocabulary composed of whatever words you had learned to recognize among the twenty-four. You would have developed no power to unlock strange words independently; consequently the additional reading you could have done on your own would have been limited to selections written within the limits of your reading vocabulary. In the author's judgment, failure to begin early to teach first-grade pupils a definite and effective technique for unlocking strange printed words independently is the chief — but by no means the only — objection to the use of the sight method. How much better it is to equip pupils just as soon as possible to read independently the many excellent books available for five-, six,- and seven-year-old boys and girls!

If the author had used a purely phonic method of beginning to teach a child to read — a method used in some American schools — he would have presented a rather large number of letter-sound associations in addition to those you learned. Then in introducing each new word, he would have shown you the printed form and directed you to note in that form individual letters and groups of letters from left to right, to think the sounds those letters stand for, and in some way to combine them to sound out the word, somewhat as you do in getting from a dictionary the pronunciation of a word you have not heard before. There is no doubt that the use of the purely phonic method, providing also for the repetition of each word, would have enabled you to get the episode read, to learn to recognize at least some of the words, and to begin to acquire a technique with which to unlock strange words in additional selections printed in the same letter forms. But the technique you would have begun to learn is one which, in failing to take advantage of the fact that you already know the pronunciation of the word, would have led you to belabor a given strange printed form, to get into the habit of wasting time by using more letter sounds than you need to use, and to learn to read simple material much too slowly.

You must not think that what you were asked to learn in this chapter represents everything first-grade pupils can be expected to learn by the time they have completed the use of a second preprimer, a third preprimer, a primer, a first reader, and the accompanying materials. As will be noticed in Chapters 4, 5, and 6, the author is convinced that most first-grade pupils can and should be expected, among other things, (1) to learn, through their basal readers, additional letter-sound associations for other consonants and endings, (2) to learn, through their basal readers, to recognize instantly several hundred different words, (3) to sharpen their skill in using together context and letter sounds sufficiently so that they can unlock independently almost any unfamiliar word that is strange to them only in print and that appears in reading matter intended for them, (4) to acquire, as a result of their independent reading, a substantial additional vocabulary of words they recognize instantly — perhaps as many as a thousand, depending on the amount of extra reading done, and (5) to learn to think for printed lines the voice intonations with which those lines would be spoken. Having acquired these assets, pupils will be in a position to gain from wide independent reading much of the information and enjoyment they need.

Are you wondering why you were asked to begin to learn to read all over again? Merely so that you would acquire a nodding acquaintance with just some of the problems the young child meets in beginning to learn to read and with some of the things his teacher needs to do. Keep these problems in mind and use the experience you gained through reading the preprimer passage to help you understand the proposals made in Chapters 3 through 6.

QUESTIONS TO BE ANSWERED

1. In what way is beginning to learn to read, as illustrated in Chapter 1, different from what you thought it was?

2. What technique did you learn to use in unlocking strange printed words independently? Of what help is context? Of what help are letter sounds?

3. Can you read the following words when you see them out of context?

     bass, bow, does, dove, lead, live
     read, row, sow, tear, wind, wound

4. How are you able to recognize the italicized words when you read them in the following sentences?

   a. When Johnny saw the *tears* in his coat, *tears* came to his eyes.
   b. I *read* the book last night. You can *read* it today.
   c. I can *live* till I find a *live* lizard.

5. When you were unlocking strange words in the passage, how much easier do you think your task would have been if you had learned the sounds with which the symbols for the vowels are associated?

6. Some of the sounds that the letter *o* stands for are illustrated by the following common words which occur early in children's reading:

come, home, gone, to

Can you think of any other sounds for which this letter stands?

7. How many different sounds can be associated with each of the following consonants?

f, g, j, k, l, m, n, p, s, t, x, z

8. As a a result of your experience in reading the passage presented on pages 8–19, to what extent would you agree with the following statements?

   a. In reading the printed form of the language that is thoroughly familiar to you in its spoken form, you seldom need to concern yourself with vowel sound relationships.

   b. You need not sound out all the elements in the strange printed form of a word that is familiar to you in speech, since you already know its pronunciation, and since, through context and a limited number of consonant sound clues, you can readily unlock that word.

   c. Most of the time spent in trying to teach children the relation of vowel letters to the sounds they stand for is wasted time which only leads to confusion and contributes little or nothing to the development of independent reading ability.

9. Which, if any, of the twenty-four different words in the passage presented on pages 8–19 did you learn to recognize quickly? What could you do to become so familiar with the others that you could recognize them instantly?

10. What weakness did the author assign to the use of the sight method? To the use of the purely phonic method? How does the way you were taught avoid these weaknesses?

11. What did you learn in this chapter that you think would be useful to you in beginning to teach a child to read?

chapter 2

Basic Considerations

It is the chief purpose of this volume to propose and describe in detail a program of instruction in reading for the elementary school. The main objectives of this program are (1) to help the child develop the power to read independently and (2) to stimulate him to build an abiding interest in reading a variety of worthy material on a wide range of topics. The program has evolved out of the author's years of experience with and study of the teaching of reading, the results of appropriate research, the contributing work of many people, and the success with which ingredients of the program have been used in teaching boys and girls to read. This is not to say that there is no need for strengthening the program at various points or that other programs now in operation are not effective.

The present chapter briefly discusses several matters basic to understanding the proposed program as it is described in Chapters 3 through 12. These are (1) certain characteristics of communication by means of language, (2) the school's offering in the use of English as a vehicle of communication, (3) the nature of the process of reading, (4) benefits that reading provides for people, and (5) an introduction to the program to be offered.

Certain Characteristics of Communication

Most human communication takes place through the medium of language. People talk and write in order to convey meanings and feelings to others. They listen and they read in order to understand what others

23

mean and how they feel. One may say that talking and writing constitute the broadcasting parts of communication by means of language and that listening and reading are the receiving parts of the process.

Language is entirely symbolic. In trying to convey a meaning through talking, the speaker does not say the meaning itself. He utters only sounds — the names or the pronunciations of words and the voice intonations — which he has chosen and arranged to stand for the meaning he intends.[1] No writer writes a meaning itself. He makes only marks — word forms, punctuation marks, and various typographical signals — selected and organized to represent his meaning. Many but not all of the breakdowns in communication — in the receiver's failure to understand the meaning intended by the broadcaster — arise from the fact that language is symbolic, that in any given expression the symbols are merely a cloak for the meaning intended and not the meaning itself, that the meaning lies more or less hidden behind the symbols, and that either the broadcaster is careless or inept in his choice and organization of symbols or the receiver simply does not have the power to use the symbols effectively as a vehicle of the intended meaning.

No broadcaster can give a meaning to a receiver in the sense that his talking or writing makes it unnecessary for the receiver to be mentally active in order to understand the intended meaning. The most the broadcaster can do is to choose and organize symbols so well that the expressions he uses faithfully represent his meaning and are among those the receiver is able to interpret. Then the receiver needs to construct — either think immediately or figure out — the meaning intended by the broadcaster. Sometimes the constructing is relatively easy; at other times, as this chapter explains later in considering the nature of the reading process, it is difficult.

Almost always the receiver makes some meaning for a given spoken or printed expression that a broadcaster presents to him. Sometimes that meaning is indeed far removed from the one intended by the broadcaster, as witnessed by many so-called boners, but even in such cases it is usually a meaning for which the expression could stand in some other context or situation. More often, however, the meaning the receiver makes lies somewhere between zero and perfection on a scale measuring the extent to which the receiver constructs the broadcaster's intended meaning. At times the meaning made is inexcusably vague, but not infrequently it is close enough to the intended meaning so that some com-

---

[1] Often, too, a speaker's gestures and facial expressions are indicators of his meaning, and these the listener sees rather than hears.

munication does take place.[2] But because the receiver's ability to make the intended meaning is dependent upon the inherent difficulty of that meaning, the clearness and correctness of the concepts the receiver has built through his experiences, his familiarity with the topic being presented, his interest in understanding what the broadcaster means, and even his hopes and prejudices, never is the meaning he makes exactly the same as, all of, or only that intended by the broadcaster. Nevertheless, obviously communication takes place only to the extent to which the receiver makes the meaning intended by the broadcaster, listening and reading are good only insofar as the receiver makes this meaning, and the degree of understanding for which a receiver should strive in his listening or reading is that which will enable him to satisfy the demands of the situation at the time and will serve him later as an effective tool in straight thinking and intelligent action. Less than this degree of understanding is vagueness — a source of bad judgments, false conclusions, and futile if not harmful action.

Three of the important relationships between spoken language and printed language should now be pointed out. *First,* any printed expression stands for the spoken form of that expression — both the word names and the voice intonations — as well as the meaning itself. Thus any piece of reading matter, small or large, is printed talk in the sense that it stands for sounds which the writer thought as he wrote the lines and which he probably would make in speaking the lines. Furthermore, in the same setting, the printed form and the spoken form of a given expression stand for exactly the same meaning. *Second,* any person has had several years of experience in making correct meaning for spoken language before he begins to learn to read, he continues through the years to listen to spoken language much more than he reads printed language, and from the very beginning he makes himself highly dependent upon the sounds which make up the spoken form of an expression for understanding that expression in print. *Third,* once one has established the correct associations between the symbols that constitute a given printed line and the spoken symbols the print represents, the mental process of making the meaning intended by the writer is essentially the same as that which would be

[2] For examples that show pupils' understanding of a writer's intended meaning, see Ernest Horn, *Methods of Instruction in the Social Studies* (Charles Scribner's Sons, New York, 1937) pp. 187–199; Paul McKee, *The Teaching of Reading in the Elementary School* (Houghton Mifflin Company, Boston, 1948), pp. 45–58. For similar examples pertaining to pupils' listening, see *Improving Our Instructional Talking,* Bulletin of the Ernest Horn Elementary School, Vol. 1, No. 1, Colorado State College, Greeley, Colorado, 1941.

required of him if he were listening to the writer speak what he has written. The uses to which these three facts should be put in the construction of materials and procedures for teaching reading will be made clear later in this volume.

The School's Offering

The modern elementary school provides instruction in a group of subjects or activities commonly called the language arts and sometimes labeled the English language arts. These arts are (1) *speaking,* including the school subjects known as composition, speech, and grammar, (2) *writing,* including the school subjects known as composition, spelling, grammar, and handwriting, (3) *listening,* and (4) *reading.* One of the fundamental purposes of the instruction offered is to help the pupil build the control of English which he needs in order to communicate effectively with others. Speaking and writing are taught so that he can acquire the power to convey his meanings and feelings to others. Listening and reading are taught so that he can acquire the power to arrive at the meanings and the feelings expressed to him by others in their talking and their writing.[3]

It is interesting to note here the order in which the child develops these four skills in English. His first bona fide use of the language is in listening to people talk; quite early in life, long before he enters school, he learns to understand much of the language he hears. A little later he begins to express ideas by speaking English that he has been hearing. At the age of five or six he begins to read, but the only printed English for which he can make correct meaning is the English which he already understands in his listening. Almost simultaneously he begins to express at least some of his ideas in writing — in, of course, the English that he understands in his listening or uses in his talking. Sound instruction in the language arts coincides with this order of development, taking advantage of what the child has learned about listening and talking before he comes to school.

It is possible for skillful teaching of speaking and writing to have a favorable effect upon the pupil's achievement in listening and reading. For example, the child who is made aware that in speaking he uses voice intonations to convey his meaning may be helped thereby to think as he reads, the voice intonations which are essential to his understanding of

---

[3] Actually spelling and handwriting are largely mechanical aspects of writing and have little to do with conveying the message that a writer undertakes to present to a reader.

what the characters in a story are saying. Teaching the pupil to punctuate his writing may help him to interpret punctuation marks when they appear as crucial indicators of meaning in his reading matter. The pupil who learns to keep to one topic in writing an informative paragraph will be at least partially equipped to decide, as he studies a piece of informative reading matter, what the topic of a given paragraph is.

Perhaps skillful teaching of listening and reading can have a favorable effect upon the pupil's achievement in speaking and writing. For example, learning certain letter-sound associations required for reading may help him to build the power to figure out independently the correct spelling of some important words. Possibly understanding why a story that he hears or reads is an intriguing tale may enable him to construct good stories of his own. Visualizing events and objects as he reads about them may lead him to learn to describe things so that his listeners or readers can visualize them. It is quite possible that the pupil who learns, in reading, how to study an informative paragraph and how to cope with a paragraph that is poorly organized acquires thereby some of the insight he needs for writing a good paragraph.

The points of contact just mentioned and others that could be identified among the language arts should not be misinterpreted by the teacher. The presence of such relationships does not necessarily mean that the language arts should be taught together as a "unified whole" or even as a single subject. It does not mean that the best instruction in listening and reading can teach the pupil to speak and write well or that effective teaching of speaking and writing can equip him to read and to understand any English he hears. It does not mean that the words to be taught in spelling, the grammatical constructions to be introduced in composition, or the expressions to be included in practice material in pronouncing words correctly are necessarily those found in the reading matter used. It does not mean that any given important part of any one of the language arts can be taught best in an incidental manner in connection with the teaching of any other language art. It does not mean that during or after the teaching of a story in reading, pupils should be asked to engage in speaking and writing activities, such as making reports, telling stories, or writing letters, merely because those activities can in some way be given a meager link with the content of the story. It does not mean that the teaching of a given item in any one of the language arts should be used as a springboard for having pupils engage in all sorts of activities pertaining to the other language arts. It is important to bear in mind, however, that in teaching a skill in one of the language arts any real and sensible point of contact between that skill and another skill in another language art should be made clear to the pupil and that he should be led to take advantage of the fact that the two skills reinforce each other.

The Nature of the Process of Reading

Some people seem to believe that the act of reading is a physical process rather than a mental one, that it is done with the eyes rather than the mind, that it is passive rather than active, and that the reader needs to exert little effort as he reads. Nothing could be farther from the truth. Actually, reading is very different from merely looking at printed lines in order to let the writer's meaning reveal itself. Understanding what a writer means by a given expression, short or long, is always an active mental process and at times a complicated one in which the reader must work diligently. The truth of this statement becomes apparent when one considers the following brief discussion of the reader's job in communicating with the writer by means of just a short printed passage:

The writer starts with a need or an urge to convey a certain meaning to the reader; it requires, we shall say, the use of a sentence as its vehicle. If the writer is considerate of whatever language limitations the reader may have and mindful of how easy it is to make a sentence that could be taken to have two or more meanings, that says something which is not intended, or that can be misinterpreted, he will construct his sentence with care. He will try hard to choose words, punctuation marks, and a sentence structure which comprise a simple, clear, and exact representation of the meaning he wants to convey and which enable if not encourage the reader to construct a meaning as close as possible to that intended by the writer.

When the writer has written his sentence with all the simplicity, clearness, and exactness he can muster, he has gone as far as he can in his attempt to impart his meaning to the reader. Then the reader must do whatever he needs to do in order to try to construct or make the meaning intended by the writer. If the sentence is one which he would understand easily in its spoken form, his task is *relatively* simple. At the most, he has to perform only three acts which are necessary for stimulating himself to think, or hear in "the ears of his mind," the familiar spoken language he would hear if someone said the sentence to him. These three acts are noted in the following paragraphs:

1. The reader must think instantly the familiar spoken words and consequently the meanings which are represented by the forms in the sentence — the words and groups of words — that already are familiar to him in print. Often this act is labeled *recognizing familiar printed words*.

2. If the sentence contains one or more words which are strange to him in print but familiar to him in spoken form, he must do whatever is necessary to call to mind the familiar spoken words and consequently the meanings for which the strange printed words stand. Often this act is labeled *unlocking strange printed words.*

3. He must think the voice intonations which the writer probably would use in speaking the sentence and which are essential to making the writer's intended meaning.

Assume now that the writer's sentence is *not* one which the reader would understand if he heard it spoken. Such a sentence might contain, for example, one or more of the following items, which could cause the reader serious difficulty and with which he would have to struggle in order to come close to the meaning intended by the writer:

1. A word or group of words for which the reader has no meaning.
2. A word or group of words for which the reader has one or more meanings but not the one intended.
3. A word that stands for a meaning the reader has but does not think first.
4. A use of a punctuation mark meant to keep the reader from misunderstanding but that is strange to the reader.
5. A figure of speech that is strange to the reader.
6. An arrangement of words (sentence structure) that is strange or misleading to the reader.

To read the sentence with adequate understanding, the reader needs to do more than perform the three acts mentioned above. In addition, he may have to find out what a given word means, debate with himself as to just which of several meanings a given word has, discard for a word a meaning he first thought of and decide what the intended meaning is, interpret a strange use of a punctuation mark, figure out what is meant by a strange figure of speech, or mentally put in a familiar sequence the words used in the sentence.

If the meaning that the writer wants to convey requires a paragraph or more, he will at least, besides making each sentence say exactly what he means in language that he believes the reader can interpret, (1) arrange the sentences in an order indicating the relationships he intends among those sentences and (2) place the paragraphs in a sequence that helps the reader in his attempt to understand what the passage as a whole is saying. Then the reader, in addition to making correct meaning for each sentence, will need to (1) sense quickly the relationships among the sentences in each paragraph and think the meaning of that paragraph as a unit and (2) think the relationship between the paragraphs and understand what the selection as a whole is saying. If the passage is highly informative and factual and the reader's purpose is to digest or study it thoroughly, he may also find it necessary to (1) decide whether meanings presented are pertinent to a given topic or question, (2) decide whether meanings included are important for the achieving of a given purpose, (3) judge the truthfulness of a given statement, (4) decide what the topic of a paragraph is, (5) decide whether a given statement is informative or emotive, and (6) establish retention of meanings.

To become a skillful and mature reader, particularly of material that would not be understood readily in spoken form, anyone needs to be aware of at least four pitfalls. First is the temptation to be satisfied with recognizing a word or group of words merely as a symbol which he has seen before and for which he can or does think or speak the pronunciation without understanding the meaning the symbol has in the setting in which it is used. Yielding to this temptation is often called verbalism, and in most cases it should be avoided vigorously. A good reader is a persistent demander of meaning; he expects to understand what he reads; he feels disturbed when he does not do so and spends time trying to arrive at the intended meaning. To do less is simply not to read.

A second possible obstacle is the almost unconscious tendency of the reader to permit the erroneous concepts he has built through his experiences, his likes and dislikes, his hopes and fears, and even his attitude toward the writer — if he knows him — to influence the meaning he makes for a passage. Such more or less fixed ideas can lead easily to the reader's misinterpretation of what the writer means, to his making whatever meaning he wishes, and to his "reading" into a passage notions which simply are not represented there. The practiced reader knows that, although there is nothing wrong with thinking of legitimate implications of the intended meaning, he must be on guard against the misleading influence which the tendency mentioned at the beginning of this paragraph can exert.

A third obstacle may be the lack of interest which the topic of the writer's passage has at the outset for the reader. That topic may be so foreign or remote to the reader's experience or interests that he has unusual difficulty in generating the drive or even in providing the attention needed for understanding what the writer means. There is only one thing for the reader to do in such a situation. If at all possible, he should keep on reading with the hope that soon the writer will so relate the topic to his experiences and interests that he can supply the needed drive.

If this does not happen, he should admit that the writer simply does not reach him and stop reading the passage.

The fourth obstacle is poor writing that may appear in a given printed passage. Examples of such writing are described in the numbered paragraphs that follow:

1. The passage presents a word or group of words that, in the context provided, does not say exactly what is intended. Thus *close to* is used when *behind* is meant, *few* when *four* is meant, *surprised* when *startled* is meant, *dark* when *cloudy* is meant, or *manage* when *control* is meant.

2. For a meaning that is familiar to the reader, the passage presents a word or group of words that is strange to him and does not explain that the strange symbol stands for the familiar meaning.

3. For a meaning that is strange to the reader, the passage presents a word or group of words that is familiar to him but does not explain the strange meaning.

4. On one page the passage uses one symbol for a given meaning and later uses another symbol for the same meaning, without sufficient clue to the fact that symbols are being shifted.

5. On one page the passage uses a symbol for a given meaning and soon thereafter uses the same symbol for another meaning, without letting the reader know that meanings are being shifted.

6. The passage presents a sentence structure which encourages mis-interpretation. For example, the sentence *By 1790 cotton had been planted along the Atlantic coast on only a narrow strip of land* is used when the intended meaning is *By 1790 cotton had been planted on only a narrow strip of land, along the Atlantic coast.*

7. The passage fails to use commas where they are needed to help the reader keep apart ideas which he should keep apart.

8. A paragraph includes one or more sentences that say nothing about the topic with which the paragraph started.

9. The order of the sentences in a given paragraph in the passage is such that misinterpretation of what is being said is encouraged.

There are several things that a reader may do to counteract the in-fluence of bits of poor writing. One is to find out what meaning a given symbol stands for in each instance. The others constitute what may be called a bit of "quarreling" with the reading matter itself: (1) thinking for a symbol used in a passage another, more exact symbol of what seems to be the intended meaning, (2) taking time to decide whether a symbol is being used with the same meaning it had before, (3) taking time to decide whether an expressed meaning is the same as that for which the same symbol was used before, (4) thinking a sentence structure which is different from that used in the passage and which says without ambiguity what the writer seems to be trying to say, (5) casting out of a paragraph any sentences that do not keep to the topic most of the sentences talk about, and (6) mentally putting in a different order the sentences presented in a paragraph.

Have you begun to feel that reading is always a very difficult thing to do? Such is not at all the case! Actually, except for the beginner, reading a passage composed entirely of English the reader would understand immediately if he heard it spoken is easy. But in reading passages which are heavily loaded with ideas to be weighed and related to one another and which contain expressions the reader would not understand if he heard them spoken, almost anyone must do a considerable amount of scratching and clawing in order to come close to the meaning intended by the writer. Even here the interested reader who has the skills necessary for doing this scratching and clawing does not have too hard a time. It is the reader lacking the required interest, background, or skills who finds the going unquestionably tough.

Keep in mind too that how completely you or any reader needs to understand the meaning intended by the writer depends largely upon the purpose for which the reading is being done. If that purpose is merely to pass the time away, to get only fun, or to enjoy just the "top" of a story, perfection certainly is not pressing. If the purpose is to digest the writer's intended meaning thoroughly and serious consequences set up by you or some other person are attached to whether or not you do this, as is the case in much so-called study reading and some leisure reading in and out of school, your need to understand the writer's meaning clearly and correctly is urgent.

Benefits That Reading Provides

For the child or the adult who can and does read with interest a wide variety of worthy printed matter, reading offers a large number of benefits. Some of them pertain to enjoyment, others to information of various types. Sometimes the reading of a given selection provides only pleasure, sometimes it provides only information, but often it supplies both.

The pleasure derived from reading may lie in (1) satisfying a mood, (2) enjoying a tale, (3) obtaining excitement, (4) idling time away, (5) gaining release from the stress of the day's work, (6) satisfying curiosity, (7) enjoying an author's constructions and style, (8) living vicariously a ready-made emotional experience, (9) opening up new interests or following old ones, or (10) escaping boredom or distracting the mind from irritating situations. Usually, but not always, the materials yielding such benefits are narrative rather than highly factual, are relatively light in nature, and include both prose and poetry.

The information that one acquires through reading may contribute to his development as a well-educated person and to his discharging of the many responsibilities he faces from day to day both as an individual and as a member of a group. Such information may pertain to (1) maintaining and improving personal and public health, (2) choosing and following a vocation, (3) establishing fruitful relations among the members of the family and maintaining the home as a center for one's friends, (4) gaining an acquaintance with and at times participating in the solving of social, economic, and political problems that confront the local community, the state, the nation, or the world, (5) building interests to follow in the wholesome use of leisure time, (6) acquiring traits inherent in strong ethical character, (7) maintaining pleasant relations with other people, (8) gaining religious or spiritual values, or (9) learning to appreciate the beauty and other aesthetic values that the world presents. Usually, but not always, the materials offering such benefits are factual in nature.

Special emphasis should be placed on the importance of reading as the major tool for acquiring the part of an education that the school offers and for continuing to educate oneself long after school days are over. While it is true that in most elementary schools the bulk of the instruction offered in the first grade and perhaps in the early part of the second grade is presented orally, printed matter soon becomes the chief medium in teaching elementary school history, geography, science, English, mathematics, literature, and other subjects. When one considers also the rapidly growing and highly desirable tendency of the secondary schools and colleges as well as the upper elementary school grades to foster more and more independent study and learning through intensive and wide reading in various subjects, the important role that reading plays in obtaining the education provided by the school is even more evident. Thus at almost any educational level the student must be able to understand, digest, and often react critically to what is said in his textbooks and the supplementary books he should use. This statement is supported by the results of numerous investigations of the relation between an individual's reading ability and his achievement in other school subjects.

By reading books and other materials that present significant messages in an intelligible manner the adult who reads well can do much to educate himself through the years after he leaves school. The benefits he can receive are listed on page 33, and particularly important in the list are those benefits which enrich his personal life, promote his vocational competence, contribute to the realization of his responsibilities as a citizen, and enable him to be a helpful influence in the home. Certainly it is difficult to see how life itself can be made more fruitful or enjoyable, how the cultural level of the nation can be strengthened and enriched, how democracy can be improved or even maintained, or how America can offer leadership of any desirable type if adults — the people who make decisions on critical issues — cannot or will not use reading to keep themselves informed year after year on what is happening in various fields of human endeavor. Indeed, what the world becomes or the direction that human life takes may depend upon how well educated the people become, and the depth and the breadth of their education is heavily influenced by the amount and quality of the reading they do. What has been said in this and the preceding paragraph should enable any teacher of reading to believe that helping pupils develop the power to read independently and to build an abiding interest in reading widely is extremely important to the educational achievement of boys and girls in school and the wisdom of the adult society.

Consider now one of the important relationships between listening and reading. Until the child begins to learn to read, the only way he can receive meaning through English is by listening to people talk. During the next two years or so, or until the pupil becomes quite skillful at thinking for printed lines the familiar spoken English for which they stand, listening is for him a more effective way to understand what is being said than reading. Probably this is one reason why instruction in the first grade and much of the second grade is predominantly oral. But actually, for most students at any level, most talk, even much of that used by teachers in their expositions, is composed of words and sentences chosen and organized on the spot and contains ambiguities and vagueness which make the meaning elusive to the listener. Furthermore, talk has only instantaneous existence; seldom can it be mulled over or even recalled accurately by the listener. Certainly, for example, no listener can be thinking of either the meaning or the significance of a sentence he has just heard and at the same time be listening to a sentence now being spoken.

From the third grade on, reading can and should provide advantages that listening cannot supply. As mentioned previously in this chapter, the composer of a well-written selection has taken the time to choose his symbols carefully, to avoid ambiguities and vagueness, to organize his ideas so well that the relationships between them are plain, and consequently to make his written message much more exact and adaptable to study than his spontaneous oral expression of that message could be. In reading the selection, the reader can take the writer's ideas at his own pace, reread if he finds it necessary to do so, ponder this or that sentence, and take the time to think critically about ideas the writer presents. It is in this sense that, for the individual who acquires the necessary skills, reading can become a much more effective means of receiving meaning through English than listening ever could be.

Perhaps space should be taken here to consider briefly some of the more obvious advantages and disadvantages of television as a means of instructing elementary school pupils. The range of topics which could be presented by means of television's static or moving pictures and the accompanying instructional talking — usually that of a so-called master teacher — is practically unlimited. Television can portray an event of educational value that is happening right now almost anywhere. It can give a clear demonstration of almost anything which can be demonstrated, such as a principle of science, a process in arithmetic, the making of a good paragraph, a session of a state legislature, or the launching of a ship. By presenting authentic events, objects, and actions that are remote to pupils in either time or space, it can provide the background of concepts needed for reading this or that selection. Insofar as television supplies motivation, it can stimulate pupils to read good non-fictional books on educationally valuable topics. A television presentation in which the accompanying instructional talk is quite simple may be particularly helpful to pupils with limited ability to receive meaning through print. Obviously, the number of pupils viewing any television presentation may be small or large, and all of them can get the same view from the same vantage point at the same time.

But the instructional talking that is part of a television presentation has only instantaneous existence, just as does that of any classroom teacher. Furthermore, the speaker talks at a rate which he judges to be best for all pupils who might see and hear the presentation, and he has no way of adjusting his tempo so that a given group of pupils could understand what he is saying. He has to assume that all pupils have the same background required for understanding and that the language constructions he uses are intelligible to all. Certainly he has no way of knowing from audience reaction whether his message is getting across. In addition, the audience — the pupils — must take the ideas presented at the rate of the teacher's talking. If a pupil does not understand something, if he misses an expression here and there, he cannot ask the teacher to explain or to go back. He has little if any opportunity to study, to reflect on, to analyze, or to evalute what is being said. Indeed, active participation by the pupil is difficult even though so-called feedback, which makes it possible for him to communicate with the television teacher, may be provided.

There is no question that carefully planned and skillfully portrayed television expositions of valuable topics have an important place in the teaching of elementary school pupils. But just what that place is or just what parts of the teaching television presentations can do best has yet to be determined. Certainly they cannot take the place of carefully planned oral explanations made by the classroom teacher who knows the background and language limitations of her particular pupils. Neither can they provide for the pupils' active participation, the give-and-take, the learning from others, and other values inherent in well-conducted group discussions. In no sense can they take the place of learning through direct experience. Least of all can they supplant reading as a means of independent study or as the chief tool for continuing one's education on innumerable topics long after his schooling has been completed. The individual who develops the power to read and a lasting interest in reading has the opportunity to respond with his deepest sense of values, to proceed at a tempo which is best for him, to reread and ponder, to take time to think of implications, to challenge the ideas of the writer, to receive inspiration, to wonder at the fitness and the power which printed words can have, and to teach himself.

An Introduction to the Proposed Program

At the time the English-speaking child enters kindergarten or first grade, he already understands the meaning of most of the English used in talking to him.[4] The only expressions, short or long, for which he can make adequate meaning and which now can be made intelligible to him in print are those included in this familiar spoken English. It seems reasonable to say, therefore, that the first extended efforts to teach him to read should be devoted to equipping him with the insights and skills required to make for printed lines the meaning he would make if he heard those lines spoken in the setting in which they appear. This teaching may be called the first major phase of instruction in reading.

Before long — usually a little more than two years — the child begins to encounter, in his reading of juveniles, children's magazines, textbooks, detailed informative books, and other printed matter, expressions which he would not understand readily if he heard them spoken, which can be

[4] This point is explained fully in Chapter 3.

called meaning difficulties, and with which he must do some scratching and clawing in order to come close to the meaning intended by the writer. At about the same time, he must also begin to use reading as an effective study tool in order to digest, evaluate, and in other ways react intelligently to much of what he is expected to learn in school and what he undertakes to learn on his own outside of school. The teaching which needs to be carried on so that the pupil can acquire the insights and skills required for coping with meaning difficulties, for studying effectively, and for reacting critically to questionable statements he reads is in addition to a needed continuation of the instruction referred to in the preceding paragraph. It can be called the second major phase of instruction in reading.

The program of instruction which this volume offers is organized on the basis of what is said in the two preceding paragraphs. The first major phase of instruction, assigned to the first grade and the second grade or, if preferred, to the latter part of the kindergarten, the first grade, and the second grade, is described in Chapters 3 through 6. Through the intelligent use of the appropriate parts of a series of basal readers, many suitable individual books of various types, magazines, newspapers, and pieces of reading matter constructed by the teacher, the instruction to be given is concerned chiefly with (1) teaching items judged to be basic to beginning to learn to read, (2) developing independence in unlocking strange printed words and skill in recognizing familiar printed words and groups of words, and (3) encouraging pupils to think, as they look at printed lines, the voice intonations essential to understanding just what those lines mean. The second major phase of instruction, assigned to Grades 3 through 6, is described in Chapters 7 through 12. Through the sensible use of appropriate parts of a series of basal readers, textbooks in social studies, science, and other content subjects, many individual books of the so-called literary type, many detailed informative books, and suitable magazines and newspapers, the instruction to be given is concerned chiefly with developing insights and skills needed for coping with meaning difficulties, for studying informative reading matter effectively, and for reacting critically to questionable statements read.

What has been said so far in this section emphasizes the importance of teaching required insights and skills. But the power to read independently includes other ingredients, particularly (1) an interest in topics presented by various types of reading matter and (2) a background of clear and correct although incomplete concepts which the reader must have in order to make adequate meaning for printed lines and many of which are to be developed through the skillful teaching of the various school subjects. Furthermore, in addition to the power to read, any pupil, in order to reap the maximum benefits of reading, must have an aggressive interest in reading a wide range of worthy material. Consequently, the role that concepts play in reading, various means of helping the pupil develop clear and correct concepts, ways of arousing his interest in reading on this or that topic, and procedures for stimulating him to broaden the scope of his reading material are discussed from time to time in various chapters and particularly in Chapters 7, 11, and 12.

The suggested program is to be carried on in accordance with the following propositions, which are based on what seem to the author to be the most pertinent facts presented by investigations of child development and of children's growth in reading and which are applied at various points in Chapters 3 through 12.

1. Apparently one may expect a pupil's progress in reading to be similar to and influenced by his general social, intellectual, emotional, and physical development. A relatively slow rate of learning to read may be no less than normal for the pupil whose rate of general development is slow, and a rapid rate of learning to read may be no more than normal for one whose rate of general development is rapid. At any given time, a pupil's level of achievement in reading can be expected to correspond with rather than differ widely from his general level of development. Thus what is considered a normal rate of learning and level of achievement in reading for one pupil may not be normal for another pupil. It is important to remember at this point that the data on the general development of children, used by some persons to forecast if not limit the progress which a pupil should be expected to make, were gathered through observations made of pupils in their environments as those environments were. No one knows either the rate or the amount of the social, intellectual, emotional, and physical growth that children could achieve if their environments provided the stimulations and opportunities needed for optimum development. It is quite possible that under the influence of such an advantageous environment, both in and out of school, the pupil's progress in reading could be much greater than it now is in many schools.

2. One should expect any pupil to vary from time to time in his rate of learning to read and in both the ease and the rate with which he gains control of a given reading skill. Consequently, the teacher should not be too disturbed by an occasional but brief slackening in a given pupil's learning and should use more patience, explanation, and time in teaching some items to that pupil than are needed for teaching other items.

3. The pupils within any class at any grade level will differ widely from one another in their level of achievement in reading, in their rate of learning to read, in the ease and speed with which they acquire a given skill, and in the particular deficiencies they have. Instead of striving to have all pupils reach a certain level of reading ability at a certain time, the teacher should center her attention on helping each pupil make the most progress that he can. This means that the teacher must continually adjust instruction to individual differences, discovering each pupil's deficiencies, supplying the particular teaching needed for removing those deficiencies, providing material which the pupil can read without too much difficulty, using whatever amount of detail is necessary for making the meaning and the correct use of a skill clear to the pupil, giving whatever amount of practice the pupil needs in order to acquire a given skill, and using patience and simple courtesy to actually help the pupil do the best he can.

4. There is no sound reason to assume that a pupil's lack of progress in reading is caused by social immaturity, physical immaturity, emotional immaturity, or relatively low intelligence and that the teacher's best course of action is merely to wait until he has reached a higher level of general maturity. Possibly some poor progress that some pupils make in reading should be thought of as a part of general immaturity, but other factors may be just as much if not more responsible for unsatisfactory achievement. One of these factors could very well be the lack of needed instruction or the low quality of the instruction which is provided. Obviously any physical disability which a pupil has and which may be interfering with his progress in reading, particularly a disability of the eyes or ears, should be referred to a competent physician.

5. Beginning early in the first grade and continuing through the elementary school years, one should expect the pupil who receives just a little encouragement to show an increasing interest in becoming an independent reader and in working as a member of a group. One important way of taking advantage of this interest is to give definite instruction which equips the pupil to read on his own rather than to depend on some older person to tell him what this or that word is or what this or that expression means. A second way is to allow the pupil to exercise increasing independence in choosing suitable selections to read by himself. A third way is to provide for group reading activities, for pupils to work together on projects which require reading, and for the class or group to set standards for and to evaluate group performances in certain types of reading activities.

6. The interests which first-grade pupils have in various aspects of their

immediate environment, in day-to-day activities, and in other matters which are quite concrete and real should be utilized in the selection or the construction of reading matter intended for those pupils. Furthermore, the known reading interests of pupils at subsequent grade levels should be used to implement the choice of selections with which to stimulate pupils in those grades to broaden the scope of their voluntary reading and to select what they read with increasing critical judgment.

7. Capital should be made of the fact that even at the first-grade level the great majority of pupils are able to reason within the limits of their experience and the data they observe and that they continue to grow during the school years in the ability to be objective, to note similarities and differences, to see relationships, to draw conclusions or make generalizations, to make judgments about cause and effect, and to think of implications of ideas presented in their reading matter. Certainly these pupils are quite capable of learning the skills needed for effective studying of informative material and for thinking critically about what they have read.

8. The available data pertaining to the mental age at which a pupil can or should begin to learn to read are both inconclusive and misleading. The early investigations of this problem, carried on more than thirty years ago, set this mental age at six or six and one-half years, and in some quarters today the teacher is not permitted or is unwilling to begin to teach any younger pupil to read. Later investigations set the mental age at no more than five. But it should be clear that the mental age, if any, which should be used as a guide in deciding when to begin to teach a given pupil to read depends a great deal upon what is to constitute the teaching. If beginning to teach a pupil to read consists in giving him a book — probably a first preprimer — having him look at each word as he is told what it is, and then asking him to read the lines, that is one thing. If it consists in giving the pupil the names and the sounds of letters, handing him a book, and asking him to sound out the words in order to read the lines, that is another thing. If it consists in teaching the pupil items that are essential to learning a definite and effective technique for discovering by himself what a given printed word is, as described in detail in the second part of the next chapter, that is still another thing. As matters stand today, no one knows the mental age that any boy or girl should attain before a skillful teacher should begin to teach him to read. One should remember also that the most suitable time for a given pupil to begin to read is determined not only by the youngster's mental age and the nature of the instruction he is to be given but also by how much he really wants to learn to read.

QUESTIONS TO BE ANSWERED

1. What are the two main objectives of this volume's proposed program of instruction in reading? Just what do you think is meant by the power to read independently? By an interest in reading and a taste for a wide variety of worthy material?

2. What are the four main ways in which people communicate by means of language? What is meant by the statement that language is symbolic?

3. Why is communication between a broadcaster and a receiver rarely if ever perfect?

4. What are the important relationships between spoken language and printed language?

5. What are the elementary school's four main offerings in teaching pupils to communicate by means of language? What is the function of each? In what ways can the teaching of one offering reinforce learning in another?

6. Under what circumstances is reading relatively simple? When is it relatively difficult?

7. What are some of the benefits that reading can provide for people? In what way does reading hold a unique place as a tool for self-education?

8. How can reading become a more effective method of receiving meaning than is listening? In what way can reading on a given topic be more effective than watching and listening to a television presentation on that topic?

9. What are the two main phases of the program of instruction in reading which this volume proposes? What are the differences between the two?

10. What are some of the characteristics of child development and children's growth in reading to be applied to this volume's proposed program in reading?

MORE TO READ

Burton, William, Clara Baker, and Grace Kemp, *Reading in Child Development*, Henry Holt & Co., Inc., New York, 1956, Chapters 1 and 4.

Durrell, Donald, *Improving Reading Instruction*, World Book Company, Yonkers-on-Hudson, N.Y., 1956, Chapter 14.

Encyclopedia of Educational Research, The Macmillan Co., New York, 1960, pp. 307–311, 744–750, 1088–1095, 1103–1105, 1114–1115.

Gray, Lillian, and Dora Reese, *Teaching Children to Read*, The Ronald Press Company, New York, 1957, Chapter 1.

Harris, Albert, *Effective Teaching of Reading*, David McKay Co., Inc., New York, 1962, Chapter 1.

Hildreth, Gertrude, *Teaching Reading*, Henry Holt & Co., Inc., New York, 1962, Chapters 1, 4.

McKim, Margaret, *Guiding Growth in Reading*, The Macmillan Co., New York, 1955, Chapter 1.

Smith, Henry, and Emerald Dechant, *Psychology in Teaching Reading*, Prentice-Hall, Inc., Englewood Cliffs, N.J., 1961, Chapter 2.

Strang, Ruth, *Helping Your Child Improve His Reading*, E. P. Dutton & Co., Inc., New York, 1962, Chapter 3.

Tinker, Miles, and Constance McCullough, *Teaching Elementary Reading*, Appleton-Century-Crofts, Inc., New York, 1962, Chapter 1.

Yoakam, Gerald, *Basal Reading Instruction*, McGraw-Hill Book Co., Inc., New York, 1955, Chapter 2.

THINGS TO DO

1. Make a list of purposes for which you have read during the past week. Compare that list with the lists of others in your class.

2. Make a list of types of printed material you find difficult to read. Then compose a paragraph that tells why you think your attempted reading is difficult.

3. Think of a recent lecture you heard an instructor give. Then make a list of advantages you think you would have had if you could have read what he had to say instead of listening to him talk. Make also a list of advantages you think you get from listening to a lecture that you might not get from reading that discourse.

4. List the ways in which reading can sometimes be more difficult for almost anyone than you had formerly supposed.

5. List specific purposes for which you think it would be profitable to use television presentations in teaching elementary school pupils. List also things you think should characterize those presentations.

part TWO/

The First

Major Phase of Instruction

I well remember my delight when first
The meaning of a printed sentence burst
Upon me; I had vaguely sensed a link
Between the symbols reproduced in ink
And what was read to me, but had not found,
The kinship of the letters and the sound;
Then suddenly the synthesis was clear,
And all at once I understood that here
Incorporated in these symbols lay
The language I was speaking every day.

WILLIAM S. CORWIN

chapter 3

An Approach to
First-Grade Reading

As stated in Chapter 2, the program of instruction in reading which this book proposes for the elementary school is divided into two main phases. The first phase, presented in Chapters 3 through 6, covers Grades 1 and 2 and is concerned with teaching the child to think, as he looks at printed lines, the familiar spoken language for which those lines stand and which he would understand if he listened to someone say them. The purpose of this chapter is (1) to describe certain assets which the English-speaking child[1] entering the first grade has already acquired through learning to understand spoken English, assets which will stand him in good stead in learning to read, (2) to offer detailed suggestions for teaching certain basic insights and skills which are preliminary to learning to read, and (3) to consider two other matters of importance in preparing the child for reading.

The Young Child's Assets

At the time the child enters the first grade, he has had at least four years of experience in listening to people talk. He can understand much of the English language when he hears it spoken and has acquired at

---

[1] From this point on, the term *child* or *pupil* is used with the assumption that the child or pupil understands readily most of the English spoken to him and that he speaks the language himself.

45

least seven important assets which need to be used advantageously and to the fullest in teaching him to read. The discussion that follows considers the nature of these assets and some of their uses.

1. Understanding Spoken Words

Any word has a spoken form, a printed form, and a meaning. The spoken form is simply the pronunciation which you hear when someone says the word correctly, which you speak in saying the word correctly, which comes to your mind when you think of the word, and which stands for the meaning. The printed form is nothing more than the group of letters which you see when you look at the word. It stands for both the spoken form and the meaning. The meaning is the sense in which either the spoken form or the printed form is used at the time.

It is obvious that the young child already has both a listening vocabulary and a speaking vocabulary as he approaches the task of learning to read. The former is composed of all the words for which he makes correct meaning when he hears them. The latter is made up of all the words which he uses with correct meaning when he says them. Except for a few printed words which older people may have taught the child or he has picked up on his own, he has no reading vocabulary. That will come as he learns to read, and at any given time it will consist of all the words he recognizes when he sees them.[2]

The listening vocabulary — if not the speaking vocabulary — of children up to six years of age is the basic source for words to include in first-grade reading matter. Each word in such printed material should be one for which first-grade pupils make correct meaning when they hear it spoken or which they use with correct meaning in their talking, and each time the word appears it should be used with a meaning already familiar to the pupils. If this suggestion is followed, only the printed form will be strange to the pupils when they first see the word. To learn to read it, they will only need to become well acquainted with the printed form. Since they already know the spoken form — the pronunciation — and consequently the meaning, the association between the two forms, *printed* and *spoken*, should be automatic. Whenever they see the printed form thereafter, they will immediately think the pronunciation and the meaning. If the word is chosen with the pupils' speaking and listening vocabularies in mind, the teacher will simply have to help the youngsters become well acquainted with the printed form and associate it with the pronunciation and the meaning. Otherwise the printed form of the word will be strange to the pupils and it will be im-

[2] Some people use the term *sight vocabulary* for our term *reading vocabulary*.

possible for them to convert it into its familiar spoken form. If the word should come from outside the speaking and listening vocabularies of the children, the teacher will need to teach not only the printed form but also the pronunciation and the meaning. Thus, limiting the selection of first-grade reading matter to words found in either the pupils' listening vocabulary or their speaking vocabulary will simplify the learning task of the pupils and the instructional task of the teacher.

Just what words make up the listening vocabulary of boys and girls at the time they enter the first grade? Just what words make up their speaking vocabulary? No one knows. Probably the number of words in the listening vocabulary is closer to ten thousand than to two thousand; probably it is somewhat larger than the number of words in the speaking vocabulary, and certainly it is much larger than the number of words the pupils will be expected to learn to read in the first grade. Although a few investigators have reported data on the words children use and respond to at or below the first-grade level,[3] important information on their speaking vocabulary and listening vocabulary is still lacking. There is at present an urgent need to discover (a) what words constitute the common listening vocabulary of children at the time they enter the first grade, (b) what words constitute their common speaking vocabulary, and (c) the different meanings they associate with each word included.[4] At

[3] See Madeline Horn, *A Study of the Vocabulary of Children Before Entering the First Grade* (International Kindergarten Union [now Association for Childhood Education], Washington, 1928); Robert Seashore, "The Importance of Vocabulary in Learning Language Skill," *Elementary English*, 25: 137–152 (March, 1948); Burleigh Shibles, "How Many Words Does a First Grade Child Know?" *Elementary English Journal*, 41: 42–47 (January, 1959); Madorah Smith, *An Investigation of the Development of the Sentence and the Extent of Vocabulary in Young Children*, University of Iowa Studies in Child Welfare III, No. 5, Iowa City, Iowa, 1926; Mary Smith, "Measurement of the Size of General English Vocabulary Through the Elementary Grades and High School," *Genetic Psychology Monographs*, 24: 311–345 (November, 1941). For examples of discussions of the young child's control of spoken language, see John Anderson, "The Development of Spoken Language," Thirty-Eighth Yearbook of the National Society for the Study of Education (Public School Publishing Company, Bloomington, Ill., 1939), Chapter X; John Carroll, "Language Development," *Encyclopedia of Educational Research* (The Macmillan Co., New York, 1960), pp. 744–752; Gertrude Hildreth, *Teaching Reading* (Henry Holt & Co., Inc., New York, 1958), pp. 50–62; Dorothea McCarthy, "Language Development in Children," *Manual of Child Psychology* (John Wiley & Sons, Inc., New York, 1954), Chapter X; Dorothea McCarthy, "Research in Language Development: Retrospect and Prospect," *Child Development Monographs*, Vol. XXIV, Serial No. 74, pp. 3–24 (1959).

[4] As will be noted later, these investigations should be extended so that the listening vocabulary and the speaking vocabulary are determined at different age and grade levels, including probably that of children who have reached the age of nine and have just completed the third grade. Investigations under way show that the number of meanings with which children under six years of age use a given word in talking is much larger than most people think.

the present time, anyone who needs to decide whether a word is suitable for first-grade reading matter can only (a) use as a checklist the words reported by Madeline Horn in the first reference listed in footnote 3 on page 47 or (b) base his judgment on his experience in noting young children's understanding as they listen to people talk and on his experience in listening to those children talk.

While the first-grade child is learning to read, just as you were when you used the episode in Chapter 1, he will quite often meet a word which he doesn't recognize. If the word is within his listening or speaking vocabulary, however, only the printed form will be strange to him. Nevertheless, in order to read the word, he will have to find out which familiar spoken word it stands for. How will he do so? If he is taught by the sight method, referred to in Chapter 1, he will simply listen to the teacher tell him what the word is. But, as everyone knows, this system cannot continue if the pupil is to become an independent reader in the sense that all by himself he can call to mind the familiar pronunciation for which a strange printed form stands. Sooner or later he will have to acquire a definite and effective technique to use in unlocking strange printed words independently. Teaching such a technique as early as possible in the first grade will soon enable the pupil to read much suitable material of increasing difficulty entirely on his own; consequently the development of a technique for unlocking strange printed words stands as one of the first-grade teacher's most important instructional activities.

But great care should be used in deciding what technique to teach. If the teacher does not take advantage of the fact that the pupil already knows the spoken form of the word and therefore has no need to find out its pronunciation, the technique she teaches may very well be what is often called detailed phonetic analysis. This means that the pupil will be taught to "figure out" the word by noting the individual letters or groups of letters in the strange printed form, thinking the sounds of those letters in order, and connecting or blending the sounds to arrive at the pronunciation. This is the "sounding out" method, essentially the same as the one you use in getting from a dictionary the pronunciation of a word you have not heard. On the other hand, if the teacher does take advantage of the fact that the pronunciation is already familiar to the pupil and that, through listening to people talk, he has become quite adept at using the meaning of what someone is saying to think of a familiar word that could come next,[5] she will teach him a technique he can use quickly as a trigger to snap the familiar pronunciation into his consciousness. A full descrip-

[5] An explanation of this point appears in the next section of this chapter.

tion of the technique the author believes should be taught to first-grade boys and girls and suggested procedures for teaching it appear in Chapter 4.

2. Skill in Using Spoken Context

Through listening to people talk, the young child has learned to expect any given word in a person's talking to make sense with what that person has just said. Even more significant, he has become quite skillful at using spoken context — the meaning of what someone is saying to him — to think of a word that could come next to make sense. You can easily check the validity of this statement by testing almost any four-year-old you know. For example, tell him that you are going to say something to him, that you are going to leave out the last word, and that you want him to give you any word which will make sense there. Then read aloud one or more of the following items:

1. Tommy sailed his boat on the _____.
2. Sally rode down the street on her _____.
3. Every night before he goes to bed, Sam drinks some _____.
4. I'll clean up the floor with a _____.

He will have no trouble in supplying one or more correct words for each item, even though he does not know he is using the context as a clue. He will give you such words as these:

1. lake, pond, river, sea, ocean, stream
2. bicycle, tricycle, pony, horse, scooter
3. water, lemonade, cocoa, milk
4. broom, cloth, sweeper, mop

The author has had no difficulty in eliciting correct responses from boys and girls no more than three years of age. Indeed, often children of that age use spoken context naturally to supply a word for which another person was groping as he talked.

What is the point of all this? Well, as already mentioned in this chapter, it is imperative that the first-grade pupil acquire as soon as possible a definite and effective technique which he can use to unlock strange printed words independently. Since the child can already use spoken context as a clue to a familiar missing word and since printed context is usually a clue to the familiar pronunciation for which a strange printed word stands, it seems reasonable to make the use of printed context a major part of the technique. What the child does not yet know about the use of context and will need to learn early in his reading is (a) that the strange word always makes sense with what he is reading and is a word he already knows when he hears it, (b) that he can use the meaning of what he is reading as a clue to the strange printed word just as he has used the meaning of what someone says to him as a clue to a missing spoken word, and (c) that any one of two or more familiar words may make sense with the meaning of what he is reading and in order to decide definitely which is the right word, he will need to use the sounds of one or more of the letters in the strange printed form.

3. Understanding of Spoken Sentences

There is little doubt that the young child understands the meaning of most of the sentences people use in talking to him. Of course, some of these sentences are simple in structure, but many are either compound or complex. Most of the latter are long enough so that if any one of them were printed in a book to be read by first-grade pupils it would take up two or three lines of type. So far as purpose is concerned, some of the sentences tell things and others ask things, and often the "telling" or "asking" is done in such a way that it shows strong feeling or gives a command. In some sentences the subject comes first, in some it comes between two parts of the predicate, and in some it comes last. If a sentence spoken to the child contains only words that are within his listening vocabulary and presents only word relationships that he has already learned to interpret, the effect of the structure of the sentence, the length of the sentence, or the placement of the subject in the sentence upon his understanding of either the meaning or the purpose of the sentence is probably quite negligible.

What sort of sentences should be included in reading matter to be used by first-grade pupils? At present most of the sentences are quite short, simple in structure, and so composed that the subjects come first. Certainly such elementary sentences are much less complicated than many which first-grade pupils understand easily in their listening and use in their own talking. Indeed, they are probably much more elementary than they need to be.[6] Perhaps the most fundamental question to be asked by anyone who is trying to decide whether a given sentence is to be included in first-grade reading matter is: Would the pupils understand this sentence if someone said it to them?

[6] Parenthetically, as one writer has pointed out, the overabundance of highly elementary sentences and the absence of more complicated sentences in first- and second-grade readers may be one reason for the apparent lack of growth in sentence structure in pupils' writing during the first two grades. See M. Lucile Harrison, "The Need for an Adequate Oral Language Program in the Kindergarten and Primary Grades," Elementary English Review, 8: 99–102 (March, 1942).

4. Skill in Noting Voice Intonations

Suppose that a friend of yours wants to convey an idea to you in one sentence. He can present the sentence in either spoken or written form. As stated in Chapter 2, the spoken form consists of the word pronunciations and the voice intonations — the emphases, the little pauses, and the inflections — used in speaking the sentence. The written form consists of the word forms and the punctuation marks used in writing the sentence. Of course the written form stands for exactly the same meaning as the spoken form, and if your friend writes the sentence, he no doubt hopes that as you read you will associate the very meaning with it that he would want you to make if you heard him speak the same sentence.

It is common knowledge that in order to understand just what is meant by a spoken sentence any listener must pay attention to the voice intonations of the speaker. To understand the importance of noting where the speaker places strongest emphasis, read the following sentence aloud six times, placing the most emphasis each time on the appropriately numbered word below the sentence:

Nancy didn't tell Chris about the big surprise we had for him.

1. Nancy   2. Chris   3. surprise   4. big   5. we   6. him

Didn't you make the following meanings as you heard yourself read the sentence, though not necessarily in the same order?

1. Nancy may have told Chris about a big surprise that someone else had for him, but not about the one that we had.
2. Nancy may have told someone about the big surprise we had for Chris, but she didn't tell him.
3. Nancy may have told Chris about the big surprise we had for someone else, but not about the one we had for him.
4. Someone may have told Chris about the big surprise we had for him, but Nancy didn't do the telling.
5. Nancy may have told Chris about one of the surprises we had for him, but not about the big one.
6. Nancy may have told Chris about something we had for him, but not about the surprise.

To get an idea of the importance of noting the little pauses which the speaker uses in saying a sentence, avoid making any little pause as you read the following sentence aloud to yourself:

We'll take ham sandwiches fruit salad hot chocolate cake and ice cream to the picnic.

What different things did the speaker say he would take to the picnic? As you read the sentence aloud again, make a little pause after *sandwiches, salad,* and *cake.* Now read the sentence aloud a third time, making a little pause after *ham, sandwiches, fruit, salad, chocolate,* and *cake.*

Through listening to people talk, the young child has become quite adept at paying needed attention to voice intonations. If you emphasize most the word *I* when you say to him, "I didn't see Sue's dog," he has no trouble in understanding that although someone else may have seen the dog, you didn't. If you emphasize most the word *see,* he knows you mean that you may have heard or heard of the dog, but you didn't see him. If you emphasize most the word *Sue's,* he does not think you mean that you saw one of Sue's other pets, but you didn't see her dog; he quickly gets the idea that you may have seen someone else's dog, but you didn't see Sue's. When you say to him, "Is that so," and use a rising inflection at the end, he knows among other things that you are asking a question and expect a reply. He does not think that you are merely making a comment about something he had previously said and do not expect an answer.

In understanding what a speaker means by a particular statement or question, the child — just like you and me — is very dependent upon voice intonations. For example, if you were to say something to him in such a way that you merely named the words without using emphasis, pause, or inflection anywhere — a highly artificial and very uncommon way of talking — he could not possibly understand exactly what you mean. To him the language you would use, with its lack of voice intonations, would be quite a strange one which he seldom if ever hears, and the best he could do with your sentence would be to consider which of whatever meanings occur to him might be the one you intend. If you were to speak a sentence without placing the most emphasis or without using a pause at the proper point in order to make your meaning clear, he would have serious difficulty in grasping that meaning. If you were to speak a sentence placing the most emphasis on a word that should not be stressed or making pauses where they should not be made, the meaning he would make is the meaning of what you said rather than the meaning you intend.

Just what are the lines which constitute the reading matter that is suitable for the first-grade pupil's use in learning to read? In a very real sense, they are simply printed familiar talk. Each line or sentence repre-

that what has already been said and what has already happened in the material he is reading will give him strong hints about how a given line probably sounded when a story character said it or how it would sound if he heard somebody say it correctly. Doing these three things will undoubtedly help the pupil acquire the basic understanding that reading a line is very different from just knowing the words in it or from engaging in the fruitless activity which many teachers have labeled word-calling.

5. Acquaintance with Letter Sounds

Although the young child does not know that the sounds in spoken words are what letters and groups of letters stand for, he is well acquainted with those sounds and has already distinguished them from one another. If such were not the case, he could not understand what people say to him, nor could he speak the language. Instead he would undoubtedly think that a word you said was some other word and he would not pronounce a word the same way twice.

If you wish to check on whether young children have already distinguished letter sounds from one another, use the following procedure in working with almost any four-year-old: *First*, show the child some familiar object, perhaps a book, and say, "What is this?" *Second*, after the child has answered, ask, "Did you say *cook?* What did you say?" Then note his reply. *Third*, say, "I think I heard what you said that time. You said *hook*." Notice again what the child's response is. *Fourth*, to try once more, say, "Why do you call it a *look?*" To continue your checking with other letter sounds, show the object named by the first word in each of the following rows, and use the remaining words in the row to raise your questions:

> spoon — moon, noon, prune, tune
> can — cab, cat, cap, car
> bib — bid, big, bill, bit
> pin — pan, pen, pain
> bat — beat, boat, bit, bite, boot

The fact that the child has already distinguished letter sounds from one another means that there is no need to acquaint him with those sounds and that giving him practice in noting the distinctions is likely to be useless. It certainly indicates also that he is already prepared to learn what is meant by the beginning of a spoken word and that, as soon as he learns the letter forms, he will be ready to establish letter-sound associations required for unlocking strange printed words independently.

sents somebody's conversation, whether that somebody is one story character talking to another or whether it is the author talking to the reader. Each line or sentence is one which the pupil would understand easily if he heard it spoken, which he has heard and understood time and again in his listening, and which he himself has used in talking. Each line or sentence stands for a group of word pronunciations and voice intonations already perfectly familiar to the pupil when he hears someone say it, and for him the only strangeness about the line is the new clothing — the printed form — in which the talking appears.

For the first-grade pupil, reading will consist almost entirely of using the printed lines to stimulate himself to think or "hear in his mind" the familiar spoken language for which they stand and which he would understand easily if he heard someone say them. As already indicated, an important part of what he will need to "hear in his mind" is voice intonation. Some but by no means all of the required pauses and inflections will be represented by punctuation marks, which the pupil can learn to interpret early and readily if their significance is made clear to him. However, few if any of the required emphases and none of the remaining pauses and inflections will be represented by special marks. Consequently the pupil will have to find other means for determining at what points to think the most emphasis and certain pauses and inflections.

Since the pupil will need to think correct voice intonations as he looks at printed lines, the teacher most certainly should do everything she can to help him. However, in view of the fact that for years he has been interpreting voice intonations used in talking, this task will not be so difficult as might appear. Only three simple actions are required. *First,* the fact that the pupil's reading matter stands for talk should be explained to him early. He must come to realize that the characters in his stories talk to one another just as he and his friends do and just as the characters in a comic strip do. He must also realize that sometimes lines tell things that the author is saying to him, and that by using "the ears of his mind" he can make a story character or an author talk to him. He must become aware that the lines at which he looks are nothing but the language which he has been hearing and understanding and speaking all his life. *Second,* the pupil should be encouraged persistently but patiently to think how the printed lines probably sounded when the story character said them or how they would sound if he heard somebody else say them, and always to be sure just who is saying the lines. He needs also to be encouraged to make the lines sound, as he reads aloud, exactly the way he thinks they probably sounded when the story character said them or as he himself would say them. *Third,* the pupil should be told early

6. Awareness of Natural Expressions

In the drawing on this page, Tommy Brown's mother is calling him to dinner. The illustration shows only two of the three lines she spoke in calling him.

TOMMY! TOMMY! DINNER IS READY.

No one knows what the third line was. Which of the following do you think is most probable? Why?

1. Come to me.
2. Come, come, come.
3. Come down now.
4. Come quickly.
5. Come, Tommy, come.
6. Hurry and come down.
7. Come down, down, down.
8. Come and get it.

Would you expect Mrs. Brown — or anyone else — to speak line 3, 4, 6, or 8 in the situation described? You probably would. Would you call each of those lines natural talk in that situation? Probably. Have you ever heard anyone say something similar to line 2 or line 7 in a situation such as the one described? Probably not. Are those lines natural talk? Of course not. Are lines 1 and 5 each more natural than either line 2 or line 7? Possibly, but not much.

In listening to people talk, the young child time and again has heard one or another of several different expressions that make sense in a given situation. Each expression he now considers to be natural in that situation and in some similar settings. There are other expressions, however, which he does not think of as being natural in those situations, even though he may recognize that they make sense in other situations.

As already stated, the first-grade pupil will need to realize early that his reading matter stands for talk, the very language he has been hearing and speaking for years. It will be difficult for him to acquire this insight, however, if his reading matter contains many expressions which he does not consider to be natural talk. Consequently, each line included in first-grade reading matter should ring true to him. There should be no lines that block his attempt to think the familiar spoken language for which the lines stand, invite him to believe that he does not need to understand everything his reading matter says, encourage him to engage in word-calling rather than reading, and stimulate him to think for a given printed word another one which he or almost anyone else would naturally expect at that point.

7. Attitude of Demanding Meaning

Have you ever heard a young child ask a speaker to explain the meaning of something that he — the speaker — has just said? Have you heard a child say something like *I don't understand what you mean, That doesn't make sense, Say that again,* or *What do you mean?* Of course you have! Such expressions show that the child has learned to expect the talking he hears to mean something. He is not satisfied with just hearing words pronounced; he actually wants to understand what is meant, and at times he is quite concerned about his failure to understand. In short, they show that the child has developed the attitude of demanding meaning as he listens to people talk.

As stated in Chapter 2, the extent to which anyone understands just what a printed line is saying depends a great deal upon the degree to which he demands meaning. It seems reasonable to propose, therefore, that in the first grade everything possible should be done to encourage the pupil to apply to his attempts at reading the same attitude of demanding meaning which he has developed so well through his experience in listening. For example, this fact should be pointed out to him early: printed language, like most talk, is supposed to mean something and he should always read to understand what is being said. His reading matter should have such a strong interest-pull that he will want to understand what is being said and will be eager to find out what happens next. The method of teaching used should hold him responsible for making correct meaning for the printed lines and should in no way give him the notion that merely knowing or pronouncing the words constitutes reading.

8. The Teacher's Recognition of the Assets

The first-grade teacher who takes advantage of her pupils' understanding of much of the spoken language they hear does not try to teach them what they already know, does not delay teaching them things they do not know and can learn easily right now, and encourages them to apply to their reading certain important things they have been using for years in their listening. Knowing that the pupils already have listening and speaking vocabularies, skill in understanding and speaking different types of sentences, and skill in distinguishing letter sounds from one another, she does not waste their time by having them engage in activities which are aimed only at developing those same vocabularies and skills.[7] Realizing (a) that her pupils already know how to use spoken context in order to think of a word that could come next to make sense and (b) that each strange word they will meet in their reading will be strange to them only in print, she begins as early as possible to teach them a definite and effective technique for unlocking strange words independently. Since this technique includes the use of context as one basic clue, it will not lead them into the habit of analyzing each strange word into all its phonetic elements, as they will have to do three or four years later when they learn to use a dictionary to get the pronunciation of a word they have not heard before. Understanding that her pupils need to learn to look upon their reading matter as familiar printed talk and that they are both dependent upon and capable of thinking voice intonations when interpreting language, she gives them only reading matter which is made up of natural talk. She encourages them to think, as they look at printed lines, of the sounds they believe they would hear if someone spoke the lines to them, and when the children read aloud, she asks them to read the lines as they would say them. Knowing that her pupils have acquired the attitude of demanding meaning in listening to language and that they can and need to apply this same attitude to their reading, she gives them reading matter with strong interest-pull. She helps them understand that reading matter is supposed to mean something, that they should always read for meaning, and that reading a printed line is much more than just

[7] Of course this statement does not apply to pupils who have little or no understanding of English when they hear it spoken. Obviously such pupils should learn to understand spoken English to a considerable extent and to speak the language with reasonable facility before anyone attempts to teach them to read. It is possible that non-English-speaking pupils should be taught to do with their natural languages the six things proposed on pages 58–81 in this chapter.

naming the words therein. This first-grade teacher is well aware that in having learned to understand spoken English her pupils have a major achievement to their credit. She makes the most of that achievement by using it to help the children quickly become much more independent and much more interested in reading than are most pupils at the completion of the first grade in most elementary schools.

Teaching Basic Insights and Skills

As will be explained in detail in Chapter 4, the technique which the author believes the pupil should be taught to follow in unlocking strange printed words independently requires him to use context and letter sounds together — just as you did in reading parts of Chapter 1 — as the two clues to the familiar spoken word for which a strange printed form stands. The teaching of the technique itself is to be initiated *early* in the first grade — in connection with beginning the use of the first pre-primer — and is to be continued in the second grade until the pupil has acquired sufficient skill to unlock almost any word which is strange to him only in print. However, before the use of the first preprimer and this teaching are begun, it is imperative that the pupil be equipped with certain insights and skills basic to the learning of the technique.

This preparatory instruction consists of six teaching activities: (1) providing practice in using spoken context, (2) providing practice in listening for beginning sounds, (3) providing practice in distinguishing letter forms from one another, (4) establishing letter-sound associations, (5) providing practice in using together spoken context and the beginning letter or letters to think a word that could come next, and (6) providing practice in using together spoken context and the beginning letter or letters to decide what the next word is. It is the purpose of most of the remainder of this chapter to describe and offer directions for carrying on these six teaching activities.[8]

1. Providing Practice in Using Spoken Context

Although pupils entering first grade are already quite skillful at using spoken context to call to mind a word that could come next to make sense, they do not yet know that with almost any context there is more than one word that will make sense. The following exercises are intended to make pupils aware of this simple fact. In each exercise, three dots

[8] Some persons may wish to call this preparatory instruction the developing of readiness for beginning reading, even though the teaching proposed here is quite different from that included in conventional reading readiness programs.

after a statement or question indicate that the teacher should give pupils time at that point to think or respond.

1. Find or make up several unrelated and uncompleted statements such as the following:

> Billy has gone to the grocery store to get some _____.
> Sally is helping her mother do the _____.
> When Sam called Mary, he asked her to come _____.
> Our dog likes to run and _____.
> We dressed up and went to the _____.
> We would rather play softball than _____.
> At breakfast I always eat _____.
> My skates are not _____.
> Let me carry the _____.
> I'll race you to the _____.

Then, when you are ready to read the items to pupils, say: "I am going to read some things to you, and in each of them I will leave out the last word. When I stop reading each time, think of a word that makes sense with what I have read. Listen now to the first thing I will read: Billy has gone to the grocery store to get some _____. . . . . What word did you think of? . . .

"Now listen to the next thing I will read: Sally is helping her mother do the _____. . . . . What word did you think of? . . ."

Proceed in the same manner with the remaining items in the exercise.

2. Find or make up several short and unrelated paragraphs such as:

> Sam had been playing in the mud. When he came into the house for lunch, his mother said, "Before you eat, you'll have to clean up. Use plenty of _____."

> Betty's mother needed some sugar before she could make the frosting for the birthday cake. She asked Betty to go to the store for some. Soon Betty came back with the sugar in a _____.

> Kathy's daddy was making her a new table. "Ouch!" he said. "I've hurt my thumb with that _____."

> As Dick was riding his bicycle down the front walk, he heard something. It was far away and the sound was hard to hear, but it kept coming closer and closer and getting louder and louder. Dick looked down the street. Around the corner came a _____.

Then when you are ready to read the items to pupils, say: "I am going to read some things to you, and in each of them I will leave out the last word. When I stop reading each time, think of a word that makes sense with what I have read. Listen now to the first thing I will read: Sam had been playing in the mud. When he came into the house for lunch, his mother said, 'Before you eat, you'll have to clean up. Use plenty of _____.' . . . What word did you think of? . . .

"Now listen to the next thing I will read: Betty's mother needed some sugar before she could make the frosting for the birthday cake. She asked Betty to go to the store for some. Soon Betty came back with the sugar in a _____. . . . What word did you think of? . . ."

Proceed in the same manner with the remaining items in the exercise.

3. Find or make several short and related paragraphs such as the following that together tell an incident:

> John's mother had invited some of his friends to come to a _____.
> For a while John and his friends played games and had a lot of fun. The game they liked most was _____.
> Then it was time to eat. They had sandwiches and soup and several other things that the boys and girls enjoyed. Finally Mother said, "Shut your eyes and don't open them until I tell you to do that." She tiptoed up to John and put in front of him a big birthday cake. On the cake were _____.
> The most exciting thing came last. Mother walked into the room pulling a new wagon. The wagon was full of _____.
> The present that John liked best was a _____.

Then, when you are ready to read the paragraphs to pupils, say: "I am going to read something to you, and every now and then I will stop. Each time I stop, think of a word that could come next to make sense with what I have read. Listen:" Then read the paragraphs, and each time you stop, wait a few seconds before asking: "What word did you think of? . . ."

4. Find a short story or part of a story that your pupils have not heard, and go over that material carefully to mark places at which you could expect pupils to supply a word that could come next to make sense. Then, when you are ready to read the material aloud, say: "I am going to read something to you, and every now and then I will stop. Each time I stop, think of a word that could come next to make sense with what I have read. Listen:" Then read the material and each time you stop, wait a few seconds before asking: "What word did you think of? . . ."

5. Have your pupils make items like those in the first exercise, on page 59, and use them as in a game with you and their classmates.

The following cautions should be kept in mind when making and using exercises like those just described:

First, in asking a pupil to say a word he has thought of, point or nod to him instead of calling on him by name. Sometimes hearing his name makes him forget the word he had thought of.

Second, as pupils name words, accept *any* word that makes sense with the context you read or said. There is no reason why a word given by a pupil must be a word you selected.

Third, although you no doubt could get from pupils for an item in an exercise a rather long list of correct words, such as *bread, butter, milk, crackers, potatoes, tomatoes, meat, lettuce, carrots,* and *apples* for the first one on page 59, do not stay with a given item until you have gotten all the suitable words you think the pupils know. Just three or four words — if not two — for each item are enough to make pupils realize that within almost any context any one of two or more words may make sense. The purpose of the exercises is not to give pupils practice in using words or to increase their listening and speaking vocabularies.

Fourth, if a pupil supplies a word that does not make sense with the context you read or said, be sure to have the group consider the fitness of that word.

Fifth, do not use any item for which only one word makes sense. Such an item does not provide the practice needed.

Sixth, make sure that the context you read or say contains only words pupils know well when they hear them spoken and tells only about topics with which they are familiar.

Seventh, after pupils have become aware that in almost any context any one of two or more words makes sense, you should drop the kind of practice that is illustrated by the exercises in this section. The children won't require much practice to begin with, and unnecessary work of this kind will be profitless for them.

Finally, give pupils all the practice they need in using spoken context alone before you undertake the instruction suggested in any of the five remaining teaching activities.

2. *Providing Practice in Listening for Beginning Sounds*

In order to use letter sounds in unlocking strange printed words or, for that matter, in recognizing familiar printed words, the pupil needs to be well acquainted with the ways in which those sounds work in words, to know the letter forms so well that he can distinguish them from one another instantly, and to have associated the forms of certain of the letters so thoroughly with the sounds for which they stand that when he sees the form of one of them he can think the sound quickly. It is the purpose of this section to consider just what has to be taught about letter sounds and to offer detailed suggestions for accomplishing it. Discussions of the teaching of letter forms and the establishing of letter-sound associations appear respectively on pages 70–73 and 73–77.

The letter sounds to be developed during the preparatory instruction are those for *b* as in *ball, c* as in *cat, d* as in *dog, f* as in *fun, g* as in *go, h* as in *him, j* as in *just, k* as in *kick, l* as in *land, m* as in *more, n* as in *not,*

p as in *pan, r* as in *run, s* as in *sat, t* as in *top, v* as in *very, w* as in *went*
y as in *yes, ch* as in *chin, sh* as in *shut, th* as in *think,* and *wh* as in *when.*[9]
But what do pupils need to be taught about these twenty-two consonant
sounds? As mentioned earlier, they certainly do not have to be introduced to or made acquainted with the sounds, and they already know
how to distinguish the sounds from one another. Since they will be taught
later that the sound to use first in unlocking a strange printed word is the
one at the beginning of the word, what they now need is to learn exactly what is meant by the *beginning of a spoken word* and to become
aware of the fact that these sounds occur at the *beginning* of spoken
words.[10]

The experience can be provided through the use of exercises which
afford practice in deciding whether given spoken words begin with the
same sound.[11] However, in order to make the learning job as easy as possible for the pupils, the twenty-two sounds should be presented in groups,
and the sounds in each group should be quite different from one another. The recommended grouping is:

Group 1: the sounds for *m, d, f,* hard *g*
Group 2: the sounds for *b, t, s*
Group 3: the sounds for *k, j, p, n,* hard *c*
Group 4: the sounds for *h, l, r, v, y*
Group 5: the sounds for *ch* as in *chum, sh,*
    th as in *thank, wh*

A description of illustrative exercises follows, with directions for their
use.[12] It should be understood that the practice is entirely oral, that letter
forms or printed words are not shown to pupils, and that no associations
are made between letter forms and the sounds for which they stand. In

[9] Reasons for using these consonant sounds rather than the sounds of vowels are
presented on page 74.

[10] If the reader doubts that pupils who are entering the first grade have already
distinguished the twenty-two consonant sounds from one another, let him ask almost
any three-year-old what his name is. When the child replies by saying, for example,
"Ted," ask, "Did you say Ned?" After he replies, ask, "Did you say Jed?" Again after
he replies, ask, "Did you say Red?" Notice what the child's replies are. If this
demonstration is not convincing, show the child a familiar object such as a chair and
ask him what it is. After he replies, ask, "Did you say hair?" After he replies, ask,
"Did you say pear?" Again, after he replies, ask, "Did you say bear?" Notice what
the child's replies are. Of course, if the reader were to ask the child, "Do chair and
hair begin with the same sound?" he probably would not know the right answer,
not because he confuses the sound of *ch* with the sound of *h*, but because he does not
understand what is meant by *begin with the same sound.*

[11] Some persons refer to this as practice in auditory discrimination.

[12] The author is indebted to M. Lucile Harrison for many of the exercises proposed
in this and other sections of the third chapter.

the description of each exercise, three dots indicate that time should be given there for pupils to think or to respond orally. Occasional parentheses enclose responses pupils can be expected to give.

a. Changing Sounds at the Beginning of Words

The two exercises presented under this heading are preliminary in nature. They are not concerned with any particular letter sound and are intended for use in introducing to pupils what is meant by the beginning of a spoken word.

1. Choose an object with a name which begins with a consonant sound, which is familiar to pupils, and which sounds the same as another familiar word except at the beginning. Among possibilities are a book, a ring, a mitten, and a coat. Then show the object — perhaps the book — to pupils and say, for example: "What is this? . . . Did you say *hook?* . . . Do *book* and *hook* sound exactly alike? . . . No, they do not. In what way do *book* and *hook* not sound alike? . . . That's right. The words *book* and *hook* do not start in the same way when we say them. They do not begin alike. They do not begin with the same sound.

Continue in the same manner with a ring, a mitten, a coat, and other familiar and available objects.

2. Think of two words which begin with different consonant sounds, which sound the same except at the beginning, which sound the same as other words except at the beginning, and which you will use as the first and last names of a fictitious boy or girl. Among possibilities are *Ted Sled, Jack Mack, Dick Stick, Ben Wren, Mark Park, Joe Bloe, Frank Bank, Bill Hill, Dan Mann, Dale Hale, Fay May, Jane Kane, Mary Carey, Ruth Booth, Sue Blue.* Then say: "I am thinking of a boy that we have not seen. His first name is Ted. I don't know what his last name is, so I'll make one up for him. I'll start the name so that it is different from Ted. Listen: Ted Sled. Are *Ted* and *Sled* the same word? . . . No, they are not. *Ted* and *Sled* do not start alike. They do not begin with the same sound. Now I'll make up another name for Ted and I'll start that name in a new way. Listen: Ted Bed. Are *Sled* and *Bed* the same word? . . . No, they are not. *Sled* and *Bed* are not alike at the beginning. Those words begin with different sounds. Can you make up another last name for Ted? Remember to use a new way to begin the name. . . ." Ask other pupils to give Ted other last names. When a pupil gives a correct response such as Dead, Fed, Head, Led, Ned, Red, Said, say, for example: "That's right. _____ and _____ do not start alike. They begin with different sounds. We say that they are not alike at the beginning."

Continue in the same manner so that pupils will learn what is meant by expressions you will be using, such as *begin alike, begins like, starts with the same sound, sound alike at the beginning, start differently, does not begin the same way.* In order to keep pupils' attention on the beginning of words, avoid using such expressions as *rhyme, sound alike at the end, ends with the same sound.*

Although the remaining exercises will be devoted to only the first group of consonant sounds, the same exercises are to be used with each of the other groups. It should be noted here also that in order to carry on most of these exercises for each sound, the teacher should have available small objects, miniatures of large objects, and pictures of objects that have names beginning with that sound. The small objects can be collected easily. The miniature objects, made of plastic, rubber, or metal, can be purchased for a nominal sum at variety stores. The pictures can be cut from magazines.[13] Following is a list of suggestions from which the objects themselves, miniatures, and pictures may be chosen for working with the first group of sounds:

m — mouse, mop, mailbox, monkey, magazine, man, mattress, meat, melon, milk, moon, mule, mitten, maid, matches, mailman, mirror

d — dog, deer, duck, doll, dart, desk, dime, dipper, dish, dollar, door

f — fish, football, fork, fox, farm, faucet, feather, fence, file, fire, fountain

g — goat, goose, girl, gun, gate, garden, gum

Ideally the teacher should collect at least four objects and four pictures for each sound in the first group before beginning most of the following exercises:

b. Noting That Given Spoken Words Begin with the Same Sound

1. On a low table put a box, about the size of a child's shoe box, and four small or miniature objects that have names which begin with the same sound as *me* and *my.* Among possibilities are mouse, matches (packet of), monkey, mitten. Then hold up any two of the objects, for example the matches and the mitten, and say: "Listen while I name these things. Matches. Mitten. The words *matches* and *mitten* start the same way. Listen to me name them again. Matches. Mitten. I'll put the matches and the mitten into this box together because matches and mitten begin with the same sound. Now let's see if these other things begin like *matches* and *mitten.*" Hold up a third object. "I'll say the names of the things I have put into the box and the name of this thing. Listen: Matches. Mitten. Mouse. *Mouse* begins like *matches* and *mitten,* so I'll put the mouse into the same box." Hold up the monkey. "Here is something else. What is it? . . . I'll say the names of all the things in the box and the name of this thing. Listen: Matches. Mitten. Mouse. Monkey. *Monkey* begins like *matches, mitten,* and *mouse,* so I'll put

[13] Suitable picture cards can be bought from various publishers.

the monkey with the others into the box. What can you tell me about the way *matches, mitten, mouse,* and *monkey* sound alike? . . ." (They all begin with the same sound.)

"Perhaps you can find other things to put into this box. Look for them at home. Remember that each of them must begin with the same sound as *matches, mitten, mouse,* and *monkey.*

2. On a low table put the box and four small or miniature objects that have names which begin with the same sound as *me* and *my.* Then hold up two of the objects, perhaps the monkey and the mouse, and say: "Listen to me name two things that begin with the same sound. Monkey. Mouse. *Monkey* and *mouse* begin with the same sound, so I'll put them into the box." Hold up the matches. "Listen to me name this thing. Matches. Does *matches* begin like *monkey* and *mouse?* . . . Yes, it does, so I'll put it into the box with the monkey and the mouse." Hold up the mitten. "Here is the mitten. Does *mitten* begin with the same sound as *matches, mouse,* and *monkey?* . . . Yes, it does. That is why I'll put it into the box."

Choose pupils who have brought objects that have names which begin with the same sound as *me* and *my.* Say to each of them in turn: "Please hold up and name what you brought to put into the box. . . . Let's ask the boys and girls whether _____ belongs in the box with the monkey, mouse, matches, and mitten. Does _____ begin with the same sound as *monkey, mouse, matches,* and *mitten?* . . . Yes, it does. We will put it into the box."

3. Have at hand four pictures of objects that have names which begin with the same sound as *me* and *my.* Possibilities are listed among appropriate items on page 64. Show the pictures one at a time to pupils and make sure they have in mind the name you will use for each picture. Then place one of the pictures, perhaps that of the moon, in a pocket chart or on a chalk rail and say to pupils: "What is this a picture of? . . ." Place a second picture beside that of the moon. "What is this a picture of? . . ." (Meat) "Listen while I say the names of these two pictures. Moon. Meat. The words *moon* and *meat* begin with the same sound. That is why we call them 'Begin Alikes.' " Place a third picture beside the first two. "What is this a picture of? . . ." (Man) "Does *man* begin with the same sound as *moon* and *meat?* . . . Is *man* another 'Begin Alike' word? . . ." Place the fourth picture beside the others. "What is this a picture of? . . ." (Milk) "Listen to me say the names of the four pictures. Moon. Meat. Man. Milk. What can you tell me about the way the four words begin? . . ." (They begin with the same sound; they start the same way.)

4. Have in mind four words that pupils know well and that begin with the same sound as *me* and *my.* Then say: "Listen while I say four words you know. Listen to hear how they all begin. *Make. Much. More. Mine.* What can you tell me about the way all those words begin? . . ." (They begin with the same sound; they start alike.)

At least the first or the third of the foregoing exercises should be used also with *d, f,* and hard *g,* the remaining sounds in the first group, before the more important and somewhat more complicated exercises to be described next are undertaken. For most pupils, it will not be necessary to use all four exercises with each of the three sounds. Probably exercise 3 is preferable to exercise 4.

c. Deciding Whether a Given Spoken Word
Begins with a Given Sound

1. Put two boxes on a low table and mix there four objects that have names which begin with one of the sounds in the first group and four objects that have names which begin with another sound in the same group. Possibilities are dog, matches, mitten, duck, doll, mouse, dish, monkey. Then hold up the dish and say: "Here is the dish. I will put it into this first box." Hold up the mouse. "Here is the mouse. Mouse and dish cannot go into the same box. . . . Who can tell me why? . . . That's right. *Mouse* does not begin with the same sound as *dish*. That is why I will put the mouse in this other box." Name a pupil and say: "Please come and choose one thing from the table. Think whether it begins like *mouse* or like *dish*. If it begins like *mouse*, put it into the box with the mouse. If it begins with the same sound as *dish*, put it into the box with the dish." Continue asking other pupils to do the same thing until all the objects are in the right boxes. If any pupil makes a mistake, say: "Listen while I name the things in this box and the thing you just put into the box. Mouse. Monkey. Matches. Mitten. Dog. Does dog belong in that box? . . . Where does it belong? . . . Why? . . ."

Repeat this exercise from time to time, using other combinations of two boxes and their objects, three boxes and their objects, and four boxes and their objects.

2. Distribute to pupils the objects that belong in two boxes so that each pupil has one object and the objects which have names beginning with the same sound are scattered through the group. Leave one object in each box, and place the boxes before pupils. Then say, for example: "There is a mouse left in this box. If you have something that begins with the same sound as *mouse*, come and put it into the box with the mouse. . . ." Name a pupil and say: "Please come to see what is in the box. If something is there that does not belong in the box, we'll give it back to the person who put it there. Maybe he can put it into the right box later." Have the pupil name the things in the box as he checks.

"There is a doll left in this other box. If you have something that begins like *doll*, come and put it into the box. . . ." Ask a pupil to check as before.

Repeat this exercise from time to time, using other combinations of two boxes and their objects, three boxes and their objects, and four boxes and their objects.[14]

---

[14] To label the boxes, paste a picture of something which has a name beginning with the appropriate sound on the outside of each box, but at this time do not use as a label the letter form representing the sound.

3. Suggest to pupils that they begin to make a large class scrapbook placing on each page pictures of objects they will collect having names that begin with the same sound. Choose one picture as a key picture for each page and place it in a frame at the top of the page. A key picture should be one that represents a familiar object and that usually is not called by any name other than the one which begins with the correct sound. Suitable key pictures for the first group of sounds are mouse, dog, fish, girl.

When a pupil finds a picture to place in the scrapbook and has decided on what page that picture belongs, his decision should be checked by the class or the teacher before he puts the picture into the book. New pages in the scrapbook should be started from time to time as the different beginning sounds are taken up.

Some teachers prefer to use a scrapbook for each sound simply because pupils bring too many pictures for the making of only one book. Others prefer to use a large chart for each group of pictured objects. Either plan will serve the purpose intended.

4. Place in mixed order on the chalk rail pictures that have names beginning with the same sound as *me* and *my* and the same sound as *do* and *did*. Then place in a pocket chart a picture, perhaps that of milk, which has a name that begins with the same sound as *me* and *my*. Say: "I will put the picture of the milk here. Now look at the pictures on the chalk rail and find something that begins like *milk*. . . . Put it in the chart to show that _____ begins like *milk*. They are 'Begin Alikes.' . . . Look at the pictures left on the chalk rail and find something else that begins like *milk* and _____. . . . Put _____ in the chart with the milk and the _____ to show that it begins like *milk* and _____. . . ." Continue in like manner until all the pictures with names that begin like *me* and *my* have been put into the pocket chart. Then say: "Who will name the 'Begin Alikes' that we have found and put into the chart? . . ."

Repeat this exercise from time to time, using other combinations of two sounds within the first group.

5. Place in the pocket chart any three pictures that have names beginning with the same sound as *me* and *my* and one picture that has a name beginning with the same sound as *do* and *did*. Then say: "Listen to me name these things. Moon. Melon. Dish. Man. Now say the names softly to yourself and think which one does not begin like the others. We will take that one away. . . . Which one should we take away? . . . Why should we take it away? . . ." Take the picture of the dish away. Remove also one of the other pictures and put in its place another that has a name beginning like *me* and *my*. Add a picture that has a name beginning like *do* and *did,* and proceed as before.

Repeat this exercise from time to time, using other combinations of two sounds within the first group.

6. Place in the pocket chart three rows of pictures so that in each row all except one have names which begin with the same sound. The rows may be as follows:

moon	man	dipper	meat
dog	fork	doll	door
fence	fish	fox	mirror

Then point to the top row and say: "Listen to me name the pictures in this first row. Moon. Man. Dipper. Meat. One does not begin like the others. Which one is that? . . . Put it on the chalk rail. Later we will find out in which row it belongs." Proceed in the same manner with the other rows. Then say: "Now let's decide where the pictures on the chalk rail belong. In what row shall we put the picture of the dipper? . . ." Proceed in the same manner to place the other two pictures correctly. Then say: "Say softly to yourself the names of the pictures in each row. . . . Do all the pictures in each row begin with the same sound? . . ."

Repeat this exercise from time to time, using other combinations of three sounds and all four sounds within the first group.

7. Shuffle the pictures for the first group of sounds and place them on the chalk rail. Mix the objects for the same sounds on a nearby table. Then say: "Name all these pictures softly to yourself. . . . Now I'll choose from the table one thing that begins like the names of some of the pictures. I'll put it in front of a picture that begins with the same sound." Put the matches in front of the picture of the man. "You can see that I put the matches in front of the man. I did that because *man* begins like *matches*. I could have put the matches in front of the moon, the meat, or the milk. They all begin with the same sound. Now we will take turns in getting something from the table and putting it in front of a picture that begins with the same sound. Who will be first? . . ." Continue until all the objects have been placed correctly.

8. Have in mind four words, three of which begin with the same sound as *me* and *my* and one of which begins with one of the other sounds in the first group. Then say: "Listen to me say four words. Listen for the word that does not begin like *me* and *my*. Much. More. Find. Make. Which word does not begin like *me and my?*"

Repeat this exercise from time to time, using other combinations of two sounds within the first group.

9. Choose some part of the classroom in which objects beginning with one or another of the sounds in the first group can be seen easily by pupils. Then say, for example: "Look at things near the piano. What do you see that begins like *mouse* and *milk?* . . ."

Repeat this exercise from time to time, using different combinations and other sounds in the first group.

10. Say: "Who can give me a word that begins with the same sound as *mop* and *man?* . . ." Repeat this exercise, using other sounds in the first group.

Attention should be called now to some important statements relative to providing pupils with practice in listening for beginning letter sounds: *First,* in speaking the crucial words used in any exercise, the beginning consonant sound may be elongated, but it should not be isolated from the rest of the word. Such isolating nearly always results in adding a short *u* sound to the sound of the consonant. The sound of *m* is not that of *muh*, the sound of *d* is not that of *duh*, the sound of *f* is not that of *fuh*, and the sound of *g* is not that of *guh*. The sound of each of those letters is the sound heard at the beginning of such words as *might, must, done, dart, fire, face, get, go.*

Second, wasting the pupil's time by continuing to provide him with practice in listening for beginning sounds after he understands what is meant by the beginning of a spoken word certainly should be avoided. To this end, the teacher should use only as many exercises as are necessary for helping the pupil develop this understanding, and pupils should be excused from further practice just as soon as they get the idea, no matter how early that may be. In working with even the first group of sounds, not all the exercises presented will be necessary for all pupils, and in working subsequently with each of the four remaining groups of sounds, all the exercises headed "Changing Sounds at the Beginning of Words," some of the exercises headed "Noting That Given Spoken Words Begin with the Same Sound," and some of the exercises headed "Deciding Whether a Given Spoken Word Begins with a Given Sound" should be omitted. The purpose of giving the pupil practice in listening for beginning sounds is *not* to teach him to distinguish those sounds from one another. The English-speaking child already does this automatically.

Third, it makes little if any difference whether the five groups of sounds are presented in the order indicated in this chapter. Any order will do. Neither does it matter whether the sounds within any one group are presented in the order in which they are listed.

Fourth, any exercise in the "Deciding Whether a Given Spoken Word Begins with a Given Sound" category may be undertaken as soon as the sounds to be used in that exercise have been worked with in the "Noting That Given Spoken Words Begin with the Same Sound" exercises.

Fifth, do not take all groups of letters through the "listening for beginning sounds" stage before proceeding to the next level with any one of them. Instead, when the pupils have had sufficient practice with the first group of sounds, move to the next level of instruction (to be described) with the same items. In like manner, after the children have practiced listening for beginning sounds with each of the other groups, that group should become the focal point of the next group of exercises.

Sixth, in working with the hard sound of *c* or the sound of *k*, any word which begins with that sound should be accepted from pupils, regardless of the beginning letter in the spelling of the word. Since there will be no letter names and no association of letter sound with letter form in the practice in listening for beginning sounds, there is no need for concern here about their spelling. Spoken words starting with the hard sound of *c* and the sound of *k* do, after all, begin with the same sound.

Seventh, the exercises presented in this section are merely illustrative. No doubt others would suffice just as well. Some of the so-called reading readiness programs that are part of contemporary series of basal readers supply profitable exercises in addition to those described here.

3. *Providing Practice in Distinguishing Letter Forms from One Another*

In order to use letter sounds in unlocking strange printed words or in recognizing familiar printed words, the pupil must be well acquainted with both the capital form and the small form of each of the twenty-six letters. At the time they enter first grade, some pupils know all the letter forms, others know some of the forms, and many know none of them. Obviously a given letter form should be taught only to those pupils who do not know it. Also, so far as instruction in first-grade reading is concerned, there is no need to teach the alphabetical order of the letters.

It is the purpose of this section to describe and give directions for carrying on certain exercises designed to make the pupil so familiar with the letter forms that he can readily distinguish them from one another.[15] Engaging in these exercises will teach the pupil the names of the letters. Knowledge of the names is important, not so much for success in first-grade reading, but because the names will soon be very useful to him in thinking and talking about similarities and differences in printed words.[16]

Probably the letters should be grouped so that any one group contains only letters which are not easily and frequently confused with one another. The grouping recommended here, quite similar to that proposed in the previous section, is:

Group I: M, U, D, F, I, G
Group II: W, E, S, T, B, X
Group III: P, A, N, C, K, J, Z
Group IV: H, O, V, R, L, Y, Q

[15] Some persons refer to the practice provided by these activities as practice in visual discrimination.

[16] It is true, however, that there is a close relationship between knowledge of the names of the letters and success in first-grade reading. See, for example, "Success in First Grade Reading," *Boston University Journal of Education,* Vol. 140, No. 3 (February, 1958), School of Education, Boston University, Boston, Massachusetts. Yet undoubtedly knowledge of letter names is a symptom rather than a cause of success.

Although the following exercises deal with only the first group of letters, it is understood that the same exercises, with appropriate adaptations, are to be used in working with each of the remaining three groups. Also, in order to carry on most of the exercises, the teacher will need to have available duplicate sets of printed letter cards. Other profitable exercises may also be found in the so-called reading readiness programs of contemporary series of basal readers.

1. Give a different capital letter card — M, U, D, F, I, G — to each of six pupils and make sure he holds the card so that the letter is right side up. Keep a duplicate of each card in your hand. Then place in the left end of the top pocket of a chart one of the cards in your hand, for example M, and say: "This is the letter M. We call it capital M. If you have capital M, come and place your card under mine in the chart as you name the letter. . . ." Place another letter, for example D, to the right of your first one in the chart. Name it as before and ask the pupil who has the same letter to place his card under yours. Then ask him to name the two different letters as he points to them. Continue in this manner until all the cards are placed in the chart. Repeat the activity, presenting the letters in a different order.

2. Pass out the capital letter cards — M, U, D, F, I, G — including duplicates. Then, without holding up a card, say: "I am looking for capital M. Everyone who has capital M may come and put the cards in the top pocket of the chart. . . . Now I am looking for capital D. Everyone who has capital D may come and put the cards here." Point to the second pocket in the chart. . . . "Who can name the two different letters we have here? . . ." Continue in the same manner, asking for different letters by name only. Repeat the activity, asking for the letters in a different order.

3. Place one each of the capital letter cards — M, U, D, F, I, G — in a horizontal row in the pocket chart. Then say: "Who will name these letters? Begin here." Point to the left end of the row. "And go this way." Move your hand to the right. . . . Shuffle the cards and place them in a different order in the chart. Then ask pupils to name them.

4. Place the capital letter cards — M, U, D, F, I, G — in the top pocket of a chart. Then say: "Listen while I point to and name each of these letters. Capital M. Capital U. Capital D. Capital F. Capital I. Capital G. Who will name them the way I did? . . ."

Hold up the letter card for small m. Then say: "This is the letter m too. We call it small m. It looks something like capital M."[17] Place small m under capital M in the chart. Continue in the same way with small u, d, f, i, g. Then remove the small letter cards, pass them out to pupils, and say: "Who has the small m? . . . Come and place it under capital M in the chart." Continue in the same manner until all the small letters have been placed

[17] In working with a small letter form that is quite different from the corresponding capital letter form, say instead: "It does not look like capital ———." Corresponding letter forms that are quite similar are those for c, k, o, p, s, v, w, x, z.

correctly in the chart. Then say: "Who will come to the chart and point to and name each of the small letters? . . ." Remove the capital letter cards. Say: "Who can name the small letters now? . . ."

5. Mix the capital letter cards and the small letter cards for *M, U, D, F, I, G.* Then distribute them so that each pupil in a small group has only one card. Ask pupils who have capital letter cards to stand before the class and hold the cards so that others may see the letters. Then ask pupils who have small letter cards to stand beside the person who has the capital letter with the same name. When all have found their partners, ask those with capital letter cards to hold their cards behind them, and ask those who have small letter cards to hold them up so that others may see the letters. Ask someone to name the small letters. Then ask those with capital letter cards to give them to pupils who have not had a turn. Pupils who still have small letter cards should exchange them. The new holders of the capital letter cards should then stand beside the person who has the small letter with the same name. Next, pupils holding small letter cards should give them to other pupils who have not had a turn, and the activity may be continued until all pupils have taken part.

A game called Letto can be played by pupils who need more practice in distinguishing letter forms from one another. A set of ten cards on each of which four rows of letter forms are printed will be needed. The numbered cards are as follows:

1.	O	G	C	X;	M	T	F	B;	S	D	A	U;	N	E	V	I
2.	P	G	D	Y;	M	Z	Q	E;	W	o	R	J;	L	U	H	N
3.	W	R	L	Q;	F	Z	M	Y;	N	R	P	K;	V	J	G	H
4.	A	t	O	I;	s	C	x	b;	X	K	T	a;	i	B	S	c
5.	R	n	M	u;	p	G	F	E;	e	f	r	N;	m	U	P	g
6.	Q	j	v	Z;	w	D	L	q;	z	x	d	H;	J	h	W	l
7.	Y	q	n	K;	e	P	f	U;	F	k	E	p;	u	N	Q	y
8.	d	V	l	J;	z	D	y	H;	W	j	v	L;	Y	h	Z	w
9.	U	p	B	v;	n	M	W	r;	R	u	P	N;	w	b	m	V
10.	b	m	v	p;	g	f	n	s;	t	d	z	w;	r	h	u	q

If only one set of cards is available, up to ten pupils may play the game, and there will be only one winner. If more sets are used, more pupils may play the game, and there will be more than one winner.

Each pupil who is to play the game should be given a Letto card and twelve or more small squares of paper with which to cover letters as they are called. To start the game, the teacher says something like this:

> When I say the name of a letter, look carefully at your card to see if that letter is there. If it is, cover it with one of the small squares of paper. Do not mark on the letter I name. If the letter is not on your card, look up and

wait to hear the name of the next letter to look for. When you have covered all the letters in one row, call "Letto." It may be a row across the card from left to right. It may be a row from top to bottom. If I say capital A, cover only the big A. Do not cover small a. If I say small a, cover only small a. Do not cover capital A.

Then the teacher should call one of the ten numbered rows of letters given below, waiting after naming each letter for pupils to find that letter. The number at the beginning of the row called will be the number of the winning pupil's card. All pupils will have covered some letters on their cards.

1. M–f–K–x–W–C–T–v–B–w–N–f
2. D–t–u–A–Q–E–o–b–H–j–S–r
3. V–r–a–J–s–n–I–H–c–p–Y–G
4. A–O–P–s–e–m–q–X–L–Z–k–i
5. R–U–z–M–d–h–l–y–u–X–g–n
6. j–N–U–D–g–n–T–B–x–r–O–h
7. F–t–e–k–v–C–I–E–y–l–q–p
8. J–X–b–H–f–z–R–u–L–d–s–w
9. B–n–t–W–p–G–v–K–P–o–c–m
10. r–M–S–h–A–Y–Z–a–u–Q–i–q

When the twelve letters in any numbered row have been called and the winner has responded, a check should be made to see that he actually did win. A quick way to do that is simply to ask for the number of his card. Any pupil who calls "Letto" before the last letter in the row has been called has made errors or has covered letters not called. The card of any pupil who indicates that he has won when he has not done so should be checked to show him what his errors are.

One caution should be mentioned relative to providing practice in distinguishing letter forms from one another. There is no necessity to continue such practice until the pupil has secured what may be called mastery of all the letter forms. The eighteen consonants b, c, d, f, g, h, j, k, l, m, n, p, r, s, t, v, w, and y are the most important for the pupil to know well before he begins actual reading. Lack of knowledge of the other letter forms can be taken care of later, after he has begun to learn to read.

4. Establishing Letter-Sound Associations

If the pupil is to use letter sounds in unlocking strange printed words and in recognizing familiar printed words, he must get the form of a given letter or group of letters so thoroughly associated with the sound or sounds for which it stands that whenever he sees the form he can think the sound instantly. Twenty-two letter-sound associations should be taught during the preparatory instruction. They are: *b*, hard *c*, *d*, *f*, hard *g*, *h*, *j*, *k*, *l*, *m*, *n*, *p*, *r*, *s* as in *saw*, *t*, *v*, *w*, *y* as in *yet*, *ch* as in *chop*, *sh*, *th* as in *thumb*, *wh* as in *where*.[18] The three chief reasons for teaching these twenty-two letter-sound associations for consonants rather than associations for vowels at this time are:

a. Most of the words which the pupil will meet in his reading begin with consonants. As stated in Chapter 1 and as will be illustrated in detail in Chapter 4, the technique the pupil will be taught to follow in unlocking strange printed words leads him to use first the beginning sound of the word with the context.

b. The consonants are relatively regular in the sounds they stand for. Fifteen of the twenty-two listed above usually stand for only one sound each. Those which stand for two or more sounds each are *c*, *g*, *s*, *y*, *ch*, *th*, and *wh*. Each of the single vowels stands for a number of different sounds. By learning to use first the twenty-two letter-sound associations for consonants rather than even just one for each of the single vowels, the pupil can acquire early the confidence he needs in his ability to unlock strange printed words independently.

c. As will be explained in Chapter 4, the first-grade pupil who knows letter-sound associations for consonants, who understands that each printed word in his reading matter is one which makes sense with the context and which he knows well when he hears it spoken, and who has some degree of control of the technique for unlocking strange printed words can get quite a lot of reading done on his own without having been taught any letter-sound associations for vowels. He cannot possibly read much if he knows letter-sound associations for vowels but does not know those for consonants.

As soon as the work in listening for beginning sounds and in distinguishing letter forms from one another has been completed for any one of the five groups of letters listed on page 62, the pupil is in a position to learn the letter-sound associations for that group. The instruction on any given item consists of (a) introducing the letter-sound association for that item and (b) giving the practice needed for fixing the association firmly in mind.[19] Although the description of the introducing of a letter-sound association refers only to the letter *m* and the descriptions of essential practice are limited to only the first of the five groups of letters, you should understand that the same type of introduction can be used with

[18] As will be noted in Chapter 4, other letter-sound associations are to be taught later in the first grade and in the second grade.

[19] Many persons refer to the teaching of letter-sound associations as the teaching of "phonics."

each of the remaining twenty-one items and that the same type of practice can be used in working with all of the remaining groups of letters.[20]

The materials needed for the proposed instruction include for each letter (a) pictures of objects with names beginning with the sound the letter stands for, (b) a card on which the small form of the letter is printed, (c) the box of objects with names beginning with the sound the letter stands for, and (d) a picture to serve as an aid in remembering the letter-sound association. This fourth item can be called, for want of a better name, a magic picture; it is simply a picture of an object which has a name beginning with the sound the letter stands for and on which the letter form has been superimposed. Here, for example, are possible magic pictures for the first group of letters:

a. Introducing a Letter-Sound Association

1. Place in a row in the pocket chart or on the chalk rail three pictures that have names which begin with the sound *m* stands for. Possible pictures are those of meat, milk, moon. Then point to the picture on the left and say: "Let's name these pictures, beginning here. . . What can you tell me about the way all the names begin? . . . That's right. They all begin with the same sound." Hold up the letter card for small *m*. "They all begin with the sound this letter stands for. What is the letter? . . . You can hear the sound *m* stands for at the beginning of *mitten, man, mop, much,* and *more.*"

Hold up the magic picture for *m*. "What is this a picture of? . . . (mice) What letter do you see in the picture? . . . If you remember that the letter *m* is in the picture of the mice, you can remember that *m* stands for the sound that you hear at the beginning of *mice.*" Hold up the letter card for *m*. "What picture do you think of when you see this letter? . . ."

2. Print small *m* on a piece of paper that can be fastened to the box containing objects which have names beginning with the sound *m* stands for. Then ask pupils to name objects as you take them one by one from the

[20] There are other good ways of introducing a letter-sound association and of giving the needed practice.

box and place them on a table. . . . Say: "What can you tell me about the way all the names begin? . . . Yes, they all begin with the same sound." Hold up the piece of paper, showing the letter *m*. "They all begin with the sound this letter stands for. What is this letter? . . . All the names begin with the sound the letter *m* stands for. That is why I'll fasten this paper to the box.

The two foregoing exercises should be used next to introduce the letter-sound associations for *d*, *f*, and *g*, the three remaining letters in the first group.

b. Giving Needed Practice

1. Place in the top row of a pocket chart the letter card for *m*. Put on the chalk rail any three pictures for *m*, one picture for *d*, one for *f*, and one for *g*, but do not use a magic picture. Then say: "Look at the letter in the chart. What picture do you think of when you see that letter? . . . (mice). Yes, you can hear the sound that letter stands for at the beginning of *mice*."

Point to the picture at the left on the chalk rail. Say: "Let's name these pictures, beginning here. . . . Who will come and put beside the letter in the chart a picture that begins with the sound the letter stands for? . . ." Continue in this way until all appropriate pictures have been placed in the chart.

Point to the remaining pictures on the rail. "Why did we not put any of these pictures in the chart? . . ."

Repeat the exercise, using the letter cards for *d*, *f*, and *g*.

2. Place at the left end of different pockets in the chart the letter cards for *m* and *d*. Put on the chalk rail three pictures for each letter, but do not use a magic picture. Then point to *m* and say: "Look at this letter. Now look at the pictures on the chalk rail and think what their names are. . . ." Point to *m*. "Who will come and put beside this letter a picture that begins with the sound the letter stands for? . . ." Point to *d*. "Look at this letter. Now look at the pictures on the chalk rail. Who will come and put beside the letter a picture that begins with the sound the letter stands for? . . ." Continue until all the pictures have been placed correctly in the chart.

Repeat the exercise, using in turn three letters and all four letters.

3. Place in mixed order in the chart three pictures for *m* and three for *d*. Hold up the letter card for *m* and say: "Who can find a picture that starts with the sound this letter stands for? . . ." Hold up the letter card for *d* and say: "Who can find a picture that begins with the sound this letter stands for? . . ." Continue in the same manner until all the pictures except one have been used. Then hold up both letter cards and say: "The last picture begins with the sound one of these letters stands for. Which letter is it? . . ."

Repeat the exercise, using three letters and all four letters.

4. Place on a table the two boxes that have been labeled *m* and *d* and mix there several *m* objects and several *d* objects. Ask one pupil after an-

other to choose an object and place it in the box on which is the letter that stands for the sound with which the name of the object begins. After one object has been placed in each box, do not let pupils see what is in the boxes.

Repeat the exercise, using three sets of objects and four sets of objects.

5. Place in the pocket chart three letter cards and the corresponding pictures. Here is an example:

m	milk	meat	dog
d	dog	fence	duck
f	mirror	football	fireman

Then say: "Look at the letter and the pictures in this first row." Point to milk. Does *milk* begin with the sound the letter at the beginning of the row stands for? . . ." Point to meat. "Does *meat* begin with the sound the letter stands for? . . ." Point to dog. "Does *dog* begin with the sound the letter stands for? . . . Who will put the picture of the dog with the letter that stands for the sound you hear at the beginning of *dog?* . . .

"Look at the letter and the pictures in the second row. Say the name of each picture softly to yourself. Think which pictures belong in that row because they begin with the sound the letter at the beginning of the row stands for. . . . Which pictures belong there? . . . Which picture does not belong in that row? . . . Why? . . . Who will put that picture in the right row? . . .

"Look at the letter and the pictures in the bottom row. Which pictures belong in that row? . . . Why? . . . Which picture does not belong in that row? . . . Why? . . . Who will put the picture in the right row? . . Now look again at the letter and the pictures in each row. Do all the pictures in each row begin with the sound the letter at the beginning of the row stands for? . . ."

Repeat the exercise, using three letters and four letters.

In using any of the activities headed "Giving Needed Practice" with the third group of letters — *p, n, c, k, j* as named on page 62 — do not include both *c* and *k*. At one time *c* should be used with *p, n,* and *j* in that activity. At another time *k* should be used with *p, n,* and *j.*

5. Providing Practice in Using Spoken Context and the Beginning Letter or Letters

Consider next the position of the pupil who understands that within almost any context two or more words make sense, who knows what is meant by the beginning of a spoken word, and who has learned the letter-sound associations for one or another of the groups of items listed on page 62. Within the limits of those items, that pupil is now ready to learn to use together spoken context and the beginning letter or letters to call to mind a word which makes sense and begins with the proper sound. The exercises described in this section will help him learn this.

Although the exercises suggested deal only with the first group of items — m, d, f, g — appropriate adaptations of the same exercises are to be used in working with each of the four remaining groups.

1. Find or make up unrelated sentences, each ending with a word that is familiar to the pupils in spoken form and that begins with the sound of m, d, f, or hard g. Make sure that each sentence could also end with another word beginning with some other sound. Here are examples:

I wanted to buy some candy, but I didn't have enough _____ (m).
Daddy has gone to the filling station to get some _____ (g).
We can go swimming here if the water isn't too _____ (d).
Sam has bought a birthday present for his _____ (f).
Tom wants to start the fire, but he can't find any _____ (m).
Each morning before Betty goes to school, she feeds her _____ (d).
How did you get that cut on your _____ (f)?
Did you use your money to buy some _____ (g)?

When you are ready to read the items to pupils, say: "I am going to read some things to you, and in each of them I will leave out the last word. Each time I stop, I will show you a letter. When I do that, think of a word that begins with the sound the letter stands for and makes sense with what I read. Listen now to the first thing I will read: I wanted to buy some candy, but I didn't have enough _____." Hold up the letter card for m or print m on the board. . . . "What word that begins with the sound this letter stands for makes sense with what I read? . . ." Accept any word that begins with the sound m stands for and makes sense with the context. If a pupil gives a word that makes sense but begins with the wrong sound or a word that does not make sense but begins with the right sound, have the group decide why that word is not correct. Continue in the same manner with the remaining items in the exercise.

Repeat this exercise, using in other sentences other words beginning with the sound of m, d, f, or hard g.

2. Find or compose a paragraph relating some common experience and containing words that begin with the sounds of m, d, f, and hard g. Here is an example:

Bob went to a big pet store to choose a pet for his birthday. What he really wanted was a small _____ (g). But the owner of the store told Bob that he didn't have one. Then Bob began to watch all the animals, birds, and fish. One animal was playing with an old shoe. That was a _____ (d). Another animal was climbing a rope. That was a _____ (m). Then suddenly Bob saw near a rock in a big tank something he knew he would like to have. It was a strange-looking _____ (f).

When you are ready to read to your pupils, say: "I am going to read something to you, and every once in awhile I will stop and show you a letter. When I do that, think of a word that begins with the sound the letter stands for and makes sense with what I have read. Listen now as I read: Bob went to a big pet store to choose a pet for his birthday. What he really wanted was a small _____." Hold up the letter card for g or print g on the board. . . . "What word did you think of? . . . But the owner of the store told Bob that he didn't have one. Then Bob began to watch all the animals, birds, and fish. One animal was playing with an old shoe. That was a _____." Hold up the letter card for d or print d on the board. . . . "What word did you think of? . . . Another animal was climbing a rope. That was a _____." Hold up the letter card for m or print m on the board. . . . "What word did you think of? . . . Then suddenly Bob saw near a rock in a big tank something he knew he would like to have. It was a strange-looking _____." Hold up the letter card for f or print f on the board. . . . "What word did you think of? . . ."

Accept for each blank in the paragraph any word that begins with the right sound and makes sense with the context. If a pupil gives a word that begins with the right sound but does not make sense or begins with a wrong sound but does make sense, have the group decide why it is not correct.

Repeat this exercise, using in other paragraphs other words beginning with the sounds of m, d, f, and hard g. Although in the example given above all the omitted words are at the ends of sentences, it is advisable that in other paragraphs some omitted words occur in different positions.

3. Find a short story which you believe your pupils will enjoy hearing and which contains familiar words beginning with the sounds of m, d, f, and hard g. Then choose such words at points where you believe it is all right to omit the words as you read the story to pupils and where another word which begins with a different sound would make sense.

When you are ready to read the story to pupils, say: "I am going to read a short story to you. Every once in awhile I will leave out a word and show you a letter. When I do that, think of a word which begins with the sound that letter stands for and makes sense with what I have read." Then begin the reading of the story. Each time you come to a word to be omitted, show pupils the letter with which the word begins and ask them to give you one or more words they thought of. Accept here any word that makes sense within the context and begins with the right sound, but if a word given begins with a wrong sound or does not make sense, have the group decide why that word is not correct.

Repeat the exercise, using in other stories other words that begin with the sounds of m, d, f, and hard g. It is unnecessary if not inadvisable for each omitted word to be at the end of a sentence.

6. Providing Practice in Using Spoken Context and a Printed Word

In the practice suggested in the preceding section, spoken context was given to the pupil, just the beginning letter was shown to him, and he was asked to think of a word which made sense with that context and began with the sound of that letter. The practice recommended in this section will give him spoken context and a printed word and ask him to use that context and the beginning letter to decide what the word is. Here the pupil will need to note the beginning letter in the word itself, and the teacher will need to make sure that the printed word used is the only word within the pupil's listening vocabulary which makes sense and begins with the right sound. Once again, although the following exercises make use of only the first group of items — *m, d, f, g* — appropriate adaptations of the same exercises can be used for each of the four remaining groups.

1. Find or make up unrelated sentences, each ending with a word that your pupils know when they hear it and that begins with the sound of *m, d, f,* or hard *g.* Be sure that the word at the end of each sentence is the only word within your pupils' listening vocabulary which begins with the right sound and makes sense and that the sentence could end with another word beginning with a different sound. Here are possibilities:

> Before I go to bed, I'll drink some _____ (*milk*).
> My toy car is broken, and it won't _____ (*go*).
> Let me have a shovel and help _____ (*dig*).
> Mary stumbled over that log and _____ (*fell*).
> Are those the new skates that you _____ (*got*)?
> Where did you put that toy airplane I _____ (*made*)?
> This one shoe is so tight that it hurts my _____ (*foot*).
> Shall I put the mashed potatoes in this _____ (*dish*)?

After you have printed on the board each sentence including its last word and are ready to read the lines to pupils, say: "Today you are going to help me read these lines. I will read aloud most of each line, but I will leave out the last word. When I do that, look at the last word and think of a word that begins with the right sound and makes sense with what I read. Listen now to the first line: Before I go to bed, I'll drink some _____." Point to milk. "To find out what this word is, think of a word that begins with the right sound and makes sense with what I read. . . . What is the word? . . . How do you know it isn't *mile?* . . . How do you know it isn't *lemonade?* . . ." Continue in the same manner with the remaining items in the exercise.

Repeat the exercise, using in other sentences other words which begin with the sounds of *m, d, f,* and hard *g.*

2. Find or compose a paragraph containing words that begin with the sounds of *m, d, f,* and hard *g.* Make sure that where each of those words appears, no other word in your pupils' listening vocabulary which begins with the same sound would make sense and some other word which begins with a different sound would make sense. Here is a possibility:

Mary has done a good job of teaching her dog to _____ (*mind*). That dog will bring to her just about anything she asks him to _____ (*get*). When Mary plays the piano and tells the dog what she wants him to do, he will stand on his hind legs and _____ (*dance*). If Mary tells him not to look while she hides, he sits up and puts his front paws across his _____ (*face*).

When you are ready to read the paragraph to your pupils, say: "I have something that you can help me read. I will read most of it aloud, but every once in awhile, I will leave out a word. Then I'll show you that word. When I do that, think of a word that begins with the right sound and makes sense with what I have read. Listen now as I read: Mary has done a good job of teaching her dog to _____." Print the word *mind* on the board or show it on a card. "Here is the word I left out. . . . What is it? . . . That dog will bring to her just about anything she asks him to _____." Print the word *get* on the board or show it on a card. "Here is the word. . . . What is it? . . . When Mary plays the piano and tells the dog what she wants him to do, he will stand on his hind legs and _____." Print the word *dance* on the board or show it on a card. "Here is the word. . . . What is it? . . . If Mary tells him not to look while she hides, he sits up and puts his front paws across his _____." Print the word *face* on the board or show it on a card. "Here is the word. . . . What is it? . . ."

Repeat the exercise, using in other paragraphs other words beginning with the sounds of *m, d, f,* and hard *g.* It will be advisable to have some of the words to be omitted elsewhere than at the ends of sentences.

3. Find a short story containing familiar words that begin with the sounds of *m, d, f,* and hard *g.* Then choose such words at points where you believe no other word in your pupils' listening vocabulary beginning with the same sound would make sense and some other word beginning with a different sound would make sense.

When you are ready to read the story to your pupils, say: "I have a little story that you can help me read. I'll read most of it aloud, but every once in awhile I will leave out a word. Then I'll show you that word. When I do that, think of a word that begins with the right sound and makes sense with what I have read." Then read the story. Each time you come to a word to be omitted, show it to your pupils and ask them to tell you what it is.

Repeat the exercise, using in other stories other words that begin with the sounds of *m, d, f,* and hard *g.* Try to have the words to be omitted in different positions in sentences.

7. Sequence and Time of Teaching

The foregoing section completes the description of the six teaching activities which make up the preparatory instruction proposed in this volume. It is appropriate, therefore, to present now a summary statement relative to the sequence of the teaching. In addition, the time when the teaching takes place has not yet been considered.

It is recommended that all teaching in using spoken context alone — the first of the six teaching activities — be completed first. Then one of the groups of items listed on page 00 should be used in the five remaining activities in the order in which those activities are described. Thus, for example, the first group of items should be used sequentially in listening for beginning sounds, in distinguishing letter forms from one another, in establishing letter-sound associations, in using together spoken context and the beginning letter, and in using together spoken context and a printed word. When this teaching has been completed, each of the four remaining groups of items should be used in turn in the same sequence.

In a school which has no kindergarten, the preparatory instruction should be carried on during the first month or two of the first grade, before the children begin a first preprimer. It should be given to all pupils who speak English but who have not yet learned the skills and insights that the instruction imparts. For pupils who do not speak English, who cannot understand the oral contexts to be spoken or read aloud by the teacher, or who have no acquaintance with the objects represented by the pictures and the miniatures, the instruction should be delayed until those pupils have acquired the language facility and background of concepts essential to success in learning what is to be taught. The teaching of reading itself, usually through the use of a first preprimer, should be undertaken immediately with pupils who are so advanced that they have little if anything to gain from participation in the six activities.

Experimental work carried on during recent years with four thousand pupils in the public schools of Denver, Colorado, has produced results pertinent to supplying the preparatory instruction in the kindergarten. Among these results are: (1) practically all English-speaking pupils who received the instruction in the kindergarten learned readily there the items which that instruction purports to teach and forgot very little during the immediately following summer; (2) at the end of the first grade, pupils who had received the instruction in the kindergarten were vastly superior — in both reading ability and the amount of material read voluntarily — to pupils who received the instruction in the early part of the first grade and to pupils who did not receive the instruction at all; (3) at the end of the second grade, the third grade, and the fourth grade, significant superiority was maintained by pupils who had received the instruction in the kindergarten and had been given in those later grades reading instruction that capitalized on what had been taught in the kindergarten and the first grade; and (4) at no time was the incidence of visual deficiencies or emotional disturbances among pupils who had received the instruction in the kindergarten less or greater than that found among other pupils.[21]

Whether the preparatory instruction is to be made a part of the kindergarten curriculum in a school system will depend largely upon the convictions of teachers and administrators in that system relative to what the educational offerings of a kindergarten should be and to the importance of giving pupils an early start in reading. If they believe that the kindergarten child's need for the kind of guidance that concentrates on social, emotional, and physical development is more crucial than his need for beginning to learn to read as soon as he enters the first grade, no doubt the preparatory instruction will be made a part of the first-grade program. If, on the other hand, they believe that the preparatory instruction itself can contribute to the child's intellectual and emotional development and that it is important for him to get an early start toward reading independently in the first grade, the preparatory instruction will take place in the kindergarten. Some schools have constructed and distributed carefully prepared guides for parents of preschool children to use in working at home on the six teaching activities that make up the preparatory instruction proposed in this chapter.[22] Data collected by the Denver schools on the effectiveness of parents' use of such a guide show clearly that the average child with a mental age of four and one-half learns readily the items developed by the preparatory instruction.[23]

The teacher giving the preparatory instruction in a kindergarten should avoid pushing the pupil to learn any faster than is necessary. Fifteen or twenty minutes of instruction a day over a period of four months or so seems to be sufficient to enable the great majority of pupils to complete the program satisfactorily. If during one or another of the six teaching activities a pupil shows lack of enthusiasm, tires, or fails in attempting something he has done successfully before, this should be taken as a sign that he needs a temporary change.

8. Evaluating Pupil Achievement

Some of the evaluation of the pupil's achievement in the items which the preparatory instruction offers can be made through the teacher's con-

[21] At the time of this writing, the Denver experiment has not been completed. Detailed reports on various aspects of the experiment will be published later.

[22] See, for example, Erma Rimmel and Gwendolyn Hurd, *Preparing Your Child for Reading* (Denver Public Schools, Denver, Colorado, 1962). Now published and distributed to educational television stations by Houghton Mifflin Company, Boston.

[23] *The Effectiveness of Parents in Helping Their Preschool Children to Begin to Read* (Denver Public Schools, Denver, Colorado, 1963).

stant observation of how successfully he responds in the various exercises. A more objective measurement, however, can be obtained by using a valid standardized test or a similar test which the teacher can make.[24] The following paragraphs describe such a test:

A good test could include two main parts. The first part, a survey that measures the pupil's ability to use together context and beginning sounds, would include both a test of skill in using spoken context and the beginning letter and a test of skill in using spoken context and a printed word. The second part, diagnostic in nature and useful in locating the particular difficulty of any pupil who fails to make a satisfactory score on the first part, would include a test on using spoken context alone, a test on listening for beginning consonant sounds, a test on distinguishing letter sounds from one another, and a test on the letter-sound associations for the twenty-two consonants. The pupil who makes a satisfactory score on the first part would not need to take any of the tests in the second part.

The test on using spoken context and the beginning letter could present a row of items for each of the twenty-two consonants. At the left of each row a consonant would be printed, and in the rest of the row pictures of four objects would be shown. Two objects would have names that begin with the sound of the letter at the left, and two would have names that begin with the sound of some other letter. The name of one object in each pair would make sense with context the teacher read aloud, and the other would not. In each row the pupil would be asked to draw a line under the picture with a name that began with the sound the letter at the left stood for and made sense with the context the teacher read. Such a row of items might look like this:

The context the teacher read aloud might be: *Mary went to the zoo to see a _____.*

The test on using spoken context and a printed word could present a row of items for each of the twenty-two consonants. At the left of each row a word would be printed, and in the rest of the row pictures of four

---

[24] *The Murphy-Durrell Diagnostic Reading Readiness Test* (World Book, Yonkers-on-Hudson, N.Y.) can be used to measure achievement in distinguishing beginning sounds from one another and in distinguishing letter forms from one another. A *Prereading Inventory* (Houghton Mifflin, Boston) was constructed expressly to measure pupil achievement in the preparatory instruction. None of the remaining standardized reading readiness tests can be used to measure that achievement.

objects would be shown. One of the objects would have the name printed at the left. Another would have a name which began with the same sound as the word printed at the left but which did not make sense with context that the teacher read aloud. A third would have a name which made sense with that context but began with the sound of another letter. The fourth would have a name which began with the same sound as the name of the third object but which did not make sense with the context. In each row, the pupil would be asked to draw a line under the object having the name printed at the left. Such a row of items might look like this:

hammer

The context the teacher read aloud might be: *Tommy hit his finger with a* _____.

The test on using spoken context alone could present ten or more rows of items, each showing pictures of four objects. Two of the objects would have names making sense with the context the teacher read aloud, and two of them would not. In each row, the pupil would be asked to draw a line under the two pictures with names that made sense with the context the teacher read. Such a row of items might look like this:

The context the teacher read might be: *Billy had so many things to take home from the store that he had to use a* _____.

The test on listening for beginning sounds could present for each of the twenty-two consonant sounds a box showing four pictures. Two of the pictures would have names beginning with the same sound, and two would have names beginning with a different sound. In each box, the pupil would be asked to draw a line between the two pictures with the names beginning with the same sound. Such a box might look like this:

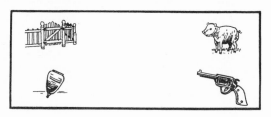

The test on distinguishing letter forms from one another could present three letters in each of twenty or more rows. In each row, the pupil would be asked to draw a line under the letter the teacher named.

The test on letter-sound associations could present for each of the twenty-two consonants a box with a consonant printed at the left and pictures of three objects shown at the right. One of the objects would have a name beginning with the sound the letter stands for. The other pictures would have names that began with other sounds. In each box, the pupil would be asked to draw a line from the letter to the picture with a name beginning with the sound the letter stands for. Such a box might look like this:

Two Other Matters of Importance

The author now proposes two additional teaching activities which can be considered preparatory to beginning to learn to read and which could foster pupils' success in reading during the time they spend in the first grade. One activity pertains to the early and overt teaching of certain printed words. The other is concerned with the teacher's reading aloud to the pupils.

1. Teaching Certain Words

The ten common words, *a, and, I, in, is, it, of, the, that,* and *to* make up about one-fourth of all printed English. Two distinct advantages could result from pupils' knowing the printed forms of these words well before they begin to read a first book, whether that book be a preprimer or some other publication. In the first place, pupils with this knowledge would possess quite a little of the capital they need for reading that book and other suitable materials. Second, authors and publishers of first-grade basal readers and accompanying books, realizing that beginning pupils already know these words, could use them without considering them "new vocabulary." They would thus be in a position to reduce considerably the rigid vocabulary control the schools now expect in such books and be free to produce first-grade basal readers and accompanying books with much more substance, literary value, and interest appeal than most first-grade reading matter now contains. Of course one could add to the ten words listed at the beginning of this paragraph other extremely common words — perhaps *an, at, are,* and *on* — but the number of words should be small enough so that the time when pupils begin to read books is not postponed unnecessarily.

The teaching of the ten or fourteen words can be carried on as a seventh activity immediately after the six which make up the preparatory instruction described on pages 58–81 have been completed. By that time pupils will have had considerable experience in learning letter-sound associations, will know that letters stand for sounds, and will have been given quite a bit of practice in using together spoken context and the beginning sound to think a word which makes sense with the context and begins with that sound. The teaching of the ten or fourteen words, then, needs to include only (a) a brief and simple explanation of the letter-sound associations for short *a,* short *i,* short *o, th* as in *that,* and of the words *a* and *I,* (b) introducing each word by printing it in context on the board, reading the context to the pupils, and having them unlock the word, and (c) providing practice the pupils need for learning to recognize the words instantly. The first two of these tasks can be carried on almost simultaneously, as the following suggestions illustrate:

1. Print the following line on the board:

Uncle Bill gave bicycles to Mary and me.

Then say: "You can help me read this line." Point to *and.* I will read all the words aloud except this one. With what letter does the word begin? . . . That *a* stands for the sound you hear at the beginning of *am* and *ant.* It is a sound the letter *a* often stands for. Now I will read all the other words. When I stop, think of a word which begins with that sound *a* stands for and makes sense here. Listen: Uncle Bill gave bicycles to Mary _____ me. . . . What is the word? . . ."

The same procedure can be used in introducing *at, are,* and *an.* Suitable context to print on the board for each of those words and words to use for helping explain the sound *a* stands for in each case follow:

at	Do you know where Dick is?
	He is not at home.
	and, am

>   *are*   I can not find my skates.
>   Do you know where they are?
>   arm, art

>   *an*   I have never taken a trip on an airplane.
>   and, at

2. Print the following lines on the board:

> I can not find my ball.
> Do you know where it is?

Then say: "You can help me read these lines." Point to *is*. "I will read all the words aloud except this one. With what letter does the word begin? . . . That *i* stands for the sound you hear at the beginning of *if* and *in*. It is a sound the letter *i* often stands for. Now I will read all the other words except this one. When I stop, think of a word which begins with that sound *i* stands for and makes sense here. Listen: I can not find my ball. Do you know where it _____? . . . What is the word? . . ."

The same procedure can be used in introducing *it* and *in*. Suitable context to print on the board for each of those words and words to use for helping explain the sound *i* stands for in each case follow:

>   *it*   I don't want this candy.
>   Do you want it?
>   is, if

>   *in*   The puppy was outside.
>   Did you let him in?
>   is, it

3. Print the following line on the board:

> Where is that old bat of mine?

Then say: "You can help me read this line." Point to *of*. I will read aloud all the words except this one. With what letter does the word begin? . . . That *o* stands for the sound you hear at the beginning of *on* and *odd*. It is a sound the letter *o* sometimes stands for. Now I will read all the other words. When I stop, think of a word which begins with that sound *o* stands for and makes sense here. Listen: Where is that old bat _____ mine? . . . What is the word? . . ."

You can use the same procedure in introducing the word *on*. Suitable context to print on the board and words to use for helping explain the sound *o* stands for are as follows:

> It is cold outside.
> Get your jacket and put it on.
> of, odd

4. Print the following lines on the board:

> This is my new bicycle.
> Would you like to ride?

Then say: "You can help me read these lines." Point to *to*. "I will read all the words aloud except this one. With what letter does the word begin? . . . You know the sound *t* stands for. Now I will read all the other words. When I stop, think of a word that begins with the sound *t* stands for and makes sense here. Listen: This is my new bicycle. Would you like _____ ride? . . . What is the word? . . ."

5. Print the following lines on the board:

> Tom can stand on his head.
> Can you do that?

Then say: "You can help me read these lines." Point to *that*. "I will read aloud all the words except this one. With what two letters does the word begin? . . . You know one sound that the letters *th* stand for. In this word they stand for a sound that is just a little different. It is the sound you hear at the beginning of *these* and *them*. Now I will read all the other words. When I stop, think of a word which begins with that sound *th* stands for and makes sense here. Listen: Tom can stand on his head. Can you do . . . ? . . . What is the word? . . ."

Use the same procedure in introducing the word *the*. Suitable context to print on the board and words to use for helping explain the sound *th* stands for are as follows:

> Can you throw this ball high in the air?
> this, that

6. Print the following lines on the board:

> My skates are lost.
> Do you have a pair?

Then say: "You can help me read these lines." Point to *a*. "I will read all the words except this one. This word has only one letter. What is that letter? . . . That *a* stands for the sound you hear at the beginning of *alone* and *about*. Now I will read the other words aloud. Think here a word that has that sound and makes sense. Listen: My skates are lost. Do you have ___ pair? . . . What is the word? . . ."

7. Print the following line on the board:

Jimmy is taller than I am.

Then say: "You can help me read this line." Point to *I*. "I will read all the words aloud except this one. This word has only one letter. What is that letter? . . . The word sounds just like the name of the letter. Now I will read all the other words. When I stop, use that sound to think of a word that makes sense here. Listen: Jimmy is taller than _____ am. . . . What is the word? . . ."

The following paragraphs offer suggestions for providing needed practice for learning to recognize the ten or fourteen words instantly:

1. Print sentences on the board, each of which contains one of the words you have introduced. Have pupils help you read each sentence aloud by naming the appropriate word, just as they did when you introduced the word.

2. As soon as three or more of the words have been introduced, print those words in column form on the board and ask pupils to name words to which you point and to point to words which you name. Keep adding to and checking with the list on the board as you introduce additional words.

3. Use one or more of the exercises headed "Finding the right word," "Selecting the word named," "Fishing," "Playing Wordo," and "Using a word wheel" on pages 128–130 in Chapter 4.

2. Reading Aloud to Pupils

Certainly it is to be hoped that pupils will read on their own many suitable juveniles during the time they are in the first grade. These books can begin to acquaint pupils with a variety of beginning reading matter and can open up to them some of the values which, as stated in Chapter 2, are attached to reading. They can also provide the realistic practice pupils need in order to make rapid progress in learning to read independently.

As noted earlier in this chapter, practically all pupils entering the first grade already possess the control of spoken English which they need in order to read first-grade basal readers. Further, the great majority of these boys and girls already have a strong desire to learn to read. But these assets do not guarantee that pupils have sufficient control of the spoken form of some English expressions and language constructions which they will encounter in many of the juvenile books they should be encouraged to read. Neither do these assets give assurance that pupils already have the acquaintance they need with the types of vicarious experiences which are portrayed in books intended for young readers and which could stimulate their interest in reading such books on their own. Lack of control of some spoken English and of acquaintance with what juveniles have to offer is to be expected particularly in the case of the pupil whose environment before entering the first grade exposed him to spoken English which in the main was trite and commonplace and gave him little if any contact with the content of children's books.

It is recommended, therefore, that the teacher do a considerable amount of oral reading of suitable juveniles to pupils during the months when the preparatory instruction is under way. Surely such reading done well and with enthusiasm can expose pupils to somewhat unfamiliar language constructions found in juveniles and to the satisfactions to be derived from reading such books. The books named in the following list are suitable for the purpose indicated. It is to be understood clearly, of course, that the author can give no guarantee that any of the books will be in print at any given future date.

Anderson, Neil, *Freckle Face,* Crowell, 1957.
Bannon, Laura, *Red Mittens,* Houghton Mifflin, 1946.
Bannon, Laura, *The Scary Thing,* Houghton Mifflin, 1956.
Barr, Cathrine, *Sammy Seal of the Circus,* Oxford, 1955.
Beatty, Hetty Burlingame, *Little Wild Horse,* Houghton Mifflin, 1949.
Beim, Jerrold, *Andy and the School Bus,* Morrow, 1947.
Beim, Jerrold, *Country Mailman,* Morrow, 1958.
Beim, Jerrold, *Danny and the Dog Doctor,* Morrow, 1950.
Beim, Lorraine and Jerrold, *The Little Igloo,* Harcourt, Brace, 1941.
Bradbury, Bianca, *Muggins,* Houghton Mifflin, 1944.
Bradbury, Bianca, *Mutt,* Houghton Mifflin, 1956.
Brown, Margaret Wise, *The Runaway Bunny,* Harper, 1942.
Brown, Myra Berry, *Flower Girl,* Watts, 1961.
Brown, Myra Berry, *Somebody's Pup,* Watts, 1961.
Carter, Katharine J., *Willie Waddle,* Steck, 1959.
Chalmers, Mary, *Boats Finds a House,* Harper, 1958.
Chalmers, Mary, *Kevin,* Harper, 1957.
Chalmers, Mary, *Mr. Cat's Wonderful Surprise,* Harper, 1961.
Child Study Association of America, *Read Me Another Story,* Crowell, 1949.
Child Study Association of America, *Read Me More Stories,* Crowell, 1951.
Child Study Association of America, *Read to Me Again,* Crowell, 1961.
Child Study Association of America, *Read-to-Me Storybook,* Crowell, 1947.
Felt, Sue, *Contrary Woodrow,* Doubleday, 1958.
Fiedler, Jean, *The Green Thumb Story,* Holiday, 1952.
Flack, Marjorie, *Angus and the Cat,* Doubleday, 1931.
Flack, Marjorie, *Angus and the Ducks,* Doubleday, 1930.
Flack, Marjorie, *Angus Lost,* Doubleday, 1932.

Flack, Marjorie, *Ask Mr. Bear*, Macmillan, 1958.

Flack, Marjorie, *Wait for William*, Houghton Mifflin, 1935.

Flack, Marjorie, *William and His Kitten*, Houghton Mifflin, 1940.

Georgiady, Nicholas P., and Romano, Louis G., *Gertie the Duck*, Follett, 1959.

Guilfoile, Elizabeth, *Nobody Listens to Andrew*, Follett, 1957.

Hastings, Evelyn, *Big New School*, Follett, 1959.

Hoban, Russell, *Herman the Loser*, Harper, 1961.

Hoff, Carol, *The Four Friends*, Follett, 1958.

Johnson, Crockett, *The Blue Ribbon Puppies*, Harper, 1958.

Joslin, Sesyle, *Brave Baby Elephant*, Harcourt, Brace, 1960.

King, Patricia, *Mabel the Whale*, Follett, 1958.

Krasilovsky, Phyllis, *Scaredy Cat*, Macmillan, 1959.

Lattin, Anne, *Peter's Policeman*, Follett, 1958.

Lenski, Lois, *Big Little Davy*, Oxford, 1956.

Lenski, Lois, *Davy and His Dog*, Walck, 1957.

Lenski, Lois, *A Dog Came to School*, Walck, 1955.

Lenski, Lois, *Surprise for Davy*, Walck, 1947.

Lindman, Maj, *Flicka, Ricka, Dicka and the Big Red Hen*, Whitman, 1960.

Lindman, Maj, *Flicka, Ricka, Dicka Go to Market*, Whitman, 1958.

Marino, Dorothy, *Fuzzy and Alfred*, Watts, 1961.

Marino Dorothy, *Good-bye Thunderstorm*, Lippincott, 1958.

Marsh, Corina, *Flippy's Flashlight*, Dutton, 1959.

Meeks, Esther K., *The Hill That Grew*, Follett, 1959.

Meeks, Esther K., *Something New at the Zoo*, Follett, 1957.

Miller, Alice P., *The Little Store on the Corner*, Abelard-Schuman, 1961.

Nordlie, Ruth, *A Dog for Susie*, Children's Press, 1960.

Norton, Natalie, *A Little Old Man*, Rand McNally, 1959.

Olds, Helen, *Miss Hattie and the Monkey*, Follett, 1958.

Olds, Helen, *The Silver Button*, Knopf, 1958.

Petersham, Maud and Miska, *The Circus Baby*, Macmillan, 1950.

Schlein, Miriam, *Little Rabbit, the High Jumper*, William R. Scott, 1957.

Shorthall, Leonard, *John and His Thumbs*, Morrow, 1961.

Slobodkina, Esphyr, *Caps for Sale*, William R. Scott, 1947.

Slobodkina, Esphyr, *The Wonderful Feast*, Lothrop, Lee & Shepard, 1955.

Stevenson, Carol Dornfeld, *Stubborn Binnder*, Reilly & Lee, 1961.

Thayer, Jane, *Andy and His Fine Friends*, Morrow, 1960.

Thayer, Jane, *A Little Dog Called Kitty*, Morrow, 1961.

Thayer, Jane, *Little Monkey*, Morrow, 1959.

Thayer, Jane, *The Puppy Who Wanted a Boy*, Morrow, 1958.

Thayer, Jane, *Sandy and the Seventeen Balloons*, Morrow, 1955.

Thayer, Jane, *Where's Andy?* Morrow, 1954.

Tresselt, Alvin, *Wake Up, City!* Lothrop, Lee & Shepard, 1957.

Tresselt, Alvin, *Wake Up, Farm!* Lothrop, Lee & Shepard, 1955.

Vreeken, Elizabeth, *The Boy Who Would Not Say His Name*, Follett, 1959.

Woods, Ruth, *Little Quack*, Follett, 1961.

QUESTIONS TO BE ANSWERED

1. What assets possessed by the child should be used in the teaching of first-grade reading? In what ways can each asset be used?

2. What are the teaching activities which make up the preparatory instruction proposed in this chapter? What advantage will the pupil who gets this instruction have?

3. What is the purpose of giving pupils practice in using spoken context alone to think a word that could come next? Why should any exercise on this skill not include an item in which only one word in the pupil's listening vocabulary could make sense? What other cautions should be observed in giving the practice?

4. What is the purpose of giving practice in listening for beginning sounds? What main types of exercises are to be used in giving the practice? What cautions are to be observed? Why is practice in listening for beginning sounds likely to be more profitable than practice in listening for rhyming sounds?

5. What is the purpose of giving practice in distinguishing letter forms from one another? Why are the names of the letters to be taught? What caution is to be observed in giving the practice?

6. What letter-sound associations are to be taught? How can the teaching of a given letter-sound association be done? In what way can the magic picture help?

7. What is the purpose of giving practice in using together spoken context and the beginning letter? In using together spoken context and the printed word? What must the pupil do in the latter type of practice that he does not need to do in the former? What particular caution must be observed in giving the latter type of practice?

8. What advantage is attached to giving the preparatory instruction in the kindergarten instead of in the first grade? Under what circumstances would you not give it there?

9. What advantages could result from teaching the ten or fourteen words before pupils begin to read the first book?

10. Why should the teacher read suitable juveniles to pupils during the time when the preparatory instruction is being carried on?

MORE TO READ

Anderson, Irving, and Walter Dearborn, *The Psychology of Teaching Reading,* The Ronald Press Company, New York, 1952, Chapter 2.

Bond, Guy, and Eva Wagner, *Teaching the Child to Read,* The Macmillan Co., New York, 1950, Chapters V, VI, VII.

Dechant, Emerald, *Improving the Teaching of Reading*, Prentice-Hall, Inc., Englewood Cliffs, N.J., 1964, Chapter 7.

Durrell, Donald, *Improving Reading Instruction*, World Book Company, Yonkers-on-Hudson, N.Y., 1956, Chapters 3, 4.

————, and Alice Nicholson, "Preschool and Kindergarten Experience," *Sixtieth Yearbook of the National Society for the Study of Education, Part I*, University of Chicago Press, Chicago, 1961, pp. 257–269.

Gans, Roma, *Common Sense in Teaching Reading*, The Bobbs-Merrill Company, Inc., Indianapolis, 1963, Chapters 2, 3, 4.

Harris, Albert, *Effective Teaching of Reading*, David McKay Co., Inc., New York, 1962, Chapter 2.

Heilman, Arthur, *Principles and Practices of Teaching Reading*, Charles E. Merrill Books, Inc., Columbus, Ohio, 1961, Chapter 2.

Hildreth, Gertrude, *Teaching Reading*, Henry Holt & Co., Inc., New York, 1962, Chapter 9.

McCracken, Glenn, *The Right to Learn*, Henry Regnery Co., Chicago, 1959, Chapter 5.

McKim, Margaret, *Guiding Growth in Reading*, The Macmillan Co., New York, 1955, Chapters 3, 4.

Russell, David, *Children Learn to Read*, Ginn & Company, Boston, 1962, Chapter 6.

Spache, George, *Toward Better Reading*, The Garrard Press, Champaign, Ill., 1963, Chapter 1.

Tinker, Miles, and Constance McCullough, *Teaching Elementary Reading*, Appleton-Century-Crofts, Inc., New York, 1962, Chapters 3, 4, 5.

Yoakam Gerald, *Basal Reading Instruction*, McGraw-Hill Book Co., Inc., New York, 1955, Chapter 7.

THINGS TO DO

1. The preparatory instruction proposed in this chapter can be called a program in reading readiness. To find out what some other such program proposes, examine (a) the teacher's edition of the pupil's readiness book and the accompanying supplementary material which constitute the readiness program offered by a contemporary series of basal readers, or (b) one of the references listed above, or (c) the course of study in reading issued by a city school system. Decide which things suggested by the material you examine do not need to be taught to English-speaking pupils and what things not included you think should be included.

2. Make a list of things which are not included in the preparatory instruction proposed in this chapter but which you think should be taught in order to get English-speaking pupils ready for first-grade reading. Keep in mind that

each thing you list should be one which has a direct bearing upon learning to read and which is something pupils do not yet know. Write your justification for including each thing you put into your list.

3. Write directions, statements, questions, and items you would include in one of the following:
   a. An exercise in listening for beginning sounds.
   b. An exercise in distinguishing letter forms from one another.
   c. Teaching a letter-sound association.
   d. An exercise in using context and the beginning letter.
   e. An exercise in using context and a printed word.

4. Choose one of the six teaching activities described in this chapter. Construct a test with which to measure pupil achievement in what that activity is supposed to teach.

5. Make a list of things you would do with pupils who do not understand spoken English before giving them the preparatory instruction proposed in this chapter.

6. Find in a children's library juveniles which are not included in the list given in this chapter but which you would read to pupils before they begin to read.

chapter 4

Unlocking and Recognizing Printed Words

The teaching of reading itself to any pupil should be initiated just as soon as he has acquired the insights and skills with which the preparatory instruction described in Chapter 3 can provide him. In the first and second grades, this teaching, directed at equipping the pupil to think as he looks at printed lines the familiar spoken language for which those lines stand, can be organized into three main instructional activities that are to be carried on simultaneously: (1) developing the power to unlock and recognize printed words, (2) using the selections in the basal readers, and (3) providing for additional reading. The present chapter considers the first of these activities. The two remaining activities will be discussed in Chapters 5 and 6 respectively.

The instructional program proposed in this volume for the first and second grades is to be carried on through the intelligent use of (1) the preprimers, the primer, the first reader, the second readers, and their accompanying materials, all of which are a part of one or another series of basal readers, (2) a wide variety of other suitable books, and (3) pieces of reading matter built by the teacher. The basal readers and their accompanying materials will identify for the teacher at least some of the items that need to be taught and offer definite suggestions relative to the timing of and procedures pertinent to the teaching of those items. They will also supply the pupil with the opportunity to get a considerable amount of practice in reading and stimulate his development of an interest in reading different types of materials. The other suitable books and the reading matter built by the teacher will offer the pupil material that can give him needed additional practice in reading and extend his interest in reading a wide variety of worthy material.

While these materials are being used, a major responsibility of the teacher is to help the pupil learn to unlock strange printed words independently and to recognize familiar printed words instantly. In this volume the term *unlock* stands for the mental act the pupil performs in order to call to mind the familiar spoken word represented by the printed form which is strange to him *only* in the sense that he has not seen it before, has forgotten it completely, or has not yet gained sufficient acquaintance with it to permit him to think the spoken word instantly. The term *recognize,* meaning to know again, stands for the mental act the pupil performs in order to think instantly — without any puzzling whatsoever — the familiar spoken word represented by a printed form which is also thoroughly familiar to him. Although investigations have discovered aids with which pupils attack printed words,[1] the studies do not show just what aids pupils should be taught to use in unlocking and recognizing printed words, and no one knows what differences do or should exist between the skillful unlocking of a strange printed word and the skillful recognizing of a familiar printed word. While it may be idle to search for such differences, inasmuch as familiarity is usually a matter of degree, it is quite possible that they pertain largely to the amount of time required for and the number of word elements used in performing the act. In any case, the important points to be kept in mind are (1) that the pupil's development of the power to unlock strange printed words independently is essential to his reading of any selection which contains even a few words he has not yet learned to recognize in a flash, (2) that his acquisition of the power to recognize familiar printed words instantly is a prerequisite for his reading with satisfaction and reasonable speed any reading matter intended for him, and (3) that most assuredly instruction in reading in the first and second grades should include the teaching of a definite procedure to follow in unlocking strange printed words independently and the giving of practice needed for learning to recognize familiar printed words instantly.

[1] For examples of summarizing statements of results of such investigations, see Arthur Gates, *The Improvement of Reading* (The Macmillan Co., New York, 1947), Chapter 7, Gerald Yoakam, *Basal Reading Instruction* (McGraw-Hill Book Co., Inc., New York, 1955), pp. 47–49.

Unlocking Strange Printed Words

Before considering what to teach a pupil so that he will be able to unlock strange printed words independently, let us reiterate certain points presented in preceding chapters. Each strange word which the first- or second-grade pupil encounters in reading a selection intended for his use is strange to him *only* in print. He already knows both the meaning and the pronunciation of the word, and he has thoroughly associated that meaning with the pronunciation. What he does not know and needs to find out is which of the thousands of words he already knows in spoken form is the one the strange printed word stands for. To make this discovery all by himself, he does not need to learn the meaning or figure out what the pronunciation is. All he needs to do is call to mind the familiar spoken word and consequently the meaning for which the strange printed form stands.[2]

To do this the pupil needs to use the aids that are most helpful to him. One is the context, the sense of what words and groups of words that come before, after, or both before and after the strange word are saying. You used this aid to great advantage in unlocking strange printed words as you read the preprimer passage in Chapter 1. From your experience you know that the skillful use of context, based on the normal use of language and the pupil's experience in listening to people talk, can make him think one or more meanings and simultaneously one or more familiar spoken words, each of which makes sense with what is being said, can encourage him to read for meaning rather than for just word names, and can shorten the time he requires for unlocking the word. But you also know that the situation in which a strange printed word can be unlocked by using context alone is rare indeed, that as a rule any one of two or more words makes sense in a given context, that context is of no help in unlocking many proper names, that once in a great while context is too weak to provide any clue to the strange word, and that context cannot be used in unlocking a strange word when that word stands alone. Thus, while context is a fundamental and essential aid which the pupil most assuredly should be taught to use, he should never be encouraged to use it all by itself in unlocking any strange word. He needs to gain

---

[2] Since each strange word presented in reading matter suitable for the first- or second-grade pupil is within his listening vocabulary, the matter of coping with a word that is strange in pronunciation or meaning or both is in no sense a part of the problem under discussion here. What to teach a pupil later so that he can get by himself the meaning and/or the pronunciation of a word not yet within his listening vocabulary will be discussed in Chapter 8.

control of some other aid which will provide the help that the context cannot supply.

Other possible aids are those which help the pupil analyze the strange word itself at least in some degree. One such aid is the sounds that individual letters and groups of letters stand for in the strange word — sounds represented by consonants, vowels, certain endings or some other common syllables. You used sounds which consonants stand for when you read the preprimer passage, and you learned that letter sounds can enable the pupil to decide which of two or more words that make sense with the context is the right one for a given strange form. But because you used context too and you already knew the word in spoken form, you did not need to pay attention to all or even many of the elements in the strange form, and you did not need to sound out each word. Although the sounds of letters and groups of letters are essential to unlocking any strange printed word, the pupil must be taught always to use this aid simultaneously with the context, except in the case of proper names or any other word when it stands alone, and to use only as many of the sounds represented in a given strange word as he needs to. To encourage him to use only the sounds of letters and groups of letters in unlocking any strange printed word, other than a proper name, in connected discourse is to invite him to use more time and more sounds than he needs to and to learn to read slowly and laboriously.

Some pupils have been taught to use short familiar words in longer words. It is true, of course, that many but by no means all of the strange printed words which the first- or second-grade pupil is likely to meet — including one-syllable words, variants, compound words, and other words of more than one syllable — do contain short words that may be familiar and that could be used in unlocking the strange words. Thus, for example, *short* contains *or,* *carpet* contains *car* and *pet,* *doing* contains *do,* *sidewalk* contains *side* and *walk,* and *continue* contains *on,* *tin,* and *in.* But often the pronunciations of the short words lead away from rather than to the unlocking of the strange words. *On* and *one* do that in *bone;* *break* and *fast* in *breakfast;* *pa, pat,* and *tie* in *patient;* and *fat, at, the, he,* and *her* in *father.* Anyone who is interested in getting some idea of the possible usefulness of this aid to a pupil in reading a given book should examine all the strange words in the book, note how many of them contain short familiar words, list for each strange word all the short familiar words within it, and decide how many of the familiar words have a pronunciation which leads to the pronunciation of the strange word and how many do not. Unpublished data compiled by the author indicate that teaching the pupil to unlock a given strange word by looking for familiar short words in it and using the pronunciations of the short words is highly questionable. It is chiefly for this reason that such teaching is not recommended here.

Some pupils have been taught to substitute parts of familiar printed words. Thus, for example, to unlock the strange printed word *shop*, the pupil is expected to note *sh* in *shop*, recall a familiar printed word that begins with those letters, perhaps *shut*, think the sound *sh* has in *shut*, note the *op* in *shop*, recall a familiar printed word that ends with the letters *op*, perhaps *hop*, think the sound those letters stand for in *hop*, and combine the sounds thought to arrive at *shop*. It is the author's experience that only a relatively small number of pupils can learn to apply this roundabout aid, that its use consumes an unreasonable amount of time, that to be successful with it the pupil must have considerable acquaintance with the spelling of the words he recalls, and that pupils who use it stop doing so as soon as they have been taught to use letter-sound associations directly. For these reasons the teaching of this aid is not recommended here.

Some persons have proposed that the pupil should be taught to use as aids (1) the general configuration or outline of the form of the strange printed word, such as ⬜ for *found* and ⬜ for *drop*, (2) any so-called striking characteristic in the form, such as its length, the dot in *i*, the cross in *t*, the tail in *y*, descending letters or ascending letters, and (3) any so-called unique patterns of letters in the form. But at best these aids can help only with words that the pupil has seen at least once and are, therefore, means of recognizing familiar words. Furthermore, any general configuration bears little if any relation to the familiar pronunciation that needs to be called to mind, can usually stand for any one of many words within the pupil's listening vocabulary (*lady* and *baby*, for example), and as a rule can suggest one or more familiar spoken words which it does not represent rather than the one it does stand for. A "striking" characteristic or a "unique" pattern of letters appears in so many different words that it also is not sufficiently distinguishing. The author's experience in working with first- and second-grade pupils has convinced him that the pupil who has learned to use context and letter sounds together in unlocking strange printed words does not need to resort to the aids just presented; teaching him to do so is likely to be futile.

Some writers have insisted that the pupil needs to gain control of many aids so that he can use a versatile attack. No doubt those aids include (1) the context, (2) the sounds of letters and groups of letters, (3) familiar small words within the strange word, (4) substitution of parts of familiar printed words, sound elements which he knows well and can transfer with little difficulty, (5) general configuration, (6) striking characteristics, and (7) unique patterns of letters. Apparently these writers believe that certain aids are more useful in unlocking some words than others, and that in attacking a word the pupil first needs to observe the form and decide which aid or aids to try immediately, then, if these do not suffice, try other aids.

It is the contention of the author that the pupil should be taught to use only two aids in unlocking all strange printed words: (1) the context and (2) the sounds that letters and groups of letters stand for in the word — often called phonics. To unlock any strange word, except some proper nouns, when it appears in connected discourse, the pupil should always use the two aids together, never either one alone. If he understands clearly what he is trying to do and realizes that each strange word is one which makes sense with what the lines are saying and which he already knows when he hears it, his use of the context and the beginning sound together will suggest to him quickly two or more words that fit the context and begin with the right sound. Immediately his use of one or more additional sounds will enable him to decide which of the suggested words is the right one. At times the only additional sound needed will be the final sound in the word. Sometimes one or more sounds within the word will be required also. For any given strange word, the number of letter sounds the pupil will need to use from among those represented in the word will depend almost entirely upon the strength of the context in which the word appears, but rarely will he need to use all of them. To unlock any strange word which stands alone or is any one of certain proper names, the pupil will have to depend entirely upon letter sounds.

The instruction to be provided so that the pupil can develop the power to unlock strange printed words independently includes (1) the teaching of letter-sound associations and (2) the teaching of a definite and effective technique to follow in using context and letter sounds together to unlock such words. The discussion moves now to a consideration of these tasks, each of which is to be carried on as part of the day-to-day use of the basal readers.[3]

1. Teaching Letter-Sound Associations

The great bulk of the first-grade or second-grade pupil's reading matter is the connected discourse which makes up the content of his first-grade and second-grade readers, the many juveniles he will read, suitable newspapers and magazines, and selections the teacher may prepare. Almost

[3] How the instruction described on the following pages is to be fitted into the use of the basal readers will be explained in Chapter 5.

always, in such material, each strange word appears in context which is strong enough to serve as a clue to the familiar spoken form of the word. Hence, as will be demonstrated later, the pupil needs to know and use in unlocking the word few if any letter-sound associations other than those for the included consonants. The remainder of the pupil's reading matter consists of little pieces, so to speak, in which individual strange words stand alone or more or less alone out of helpful verbal context — as on a traffic sign or a sign on a building, in a list of people's names, items to be obtained at a store, or jobs to be done, or in the short title of a story as listed in the table of contents of a book or a magazine. To unlock a strange word in such a setting, often but not always the pupil will need to know and use letter-sound associations other than those for the included consonants. Thus it is important that the selection of letter-sound associations to be taught include all those which are most helpful, whether the strange words to be unlocked appear in connected discourse or as items without helpful verbal context. Yet teaching the pupil the relatively few letter-sound associations he needs for economically unlocking strange words as they appear in connected discourse has much more to do with promoting his growth in reading than does teaching him all the associations he might need for unlocking such words when they stand more or less alone.

One group of letter-sound associations to be taught are those for *b*, hard *c*, soft *c*, *d*, *f*, hard *g*, soft *g*, *h*, *j*, *k*, *l*, *m*, *n*, *p*, *qu*, *r*, *s* as in *see*, *s* as in *his*, *t*, *v*, *w*, *y* as in *yet*, *z*, *ch* as in *chop*, *sh*, *th* as in *thumb*, *th* as in *them*, and *wh* as in *where*. Knowing each of these twenty-eight associations well and using it wherever needed is absolutely essential to unlocking strange words, regardless of their setting. The teaching of twenty-two of the listed associations was part of the preparatory instruction described in Chapter 3. Of the remaining six — soft *c* as in *cent*, soft *g* as in *gentle*, *qu* as in *quick*, *z* as in *zoo*, *s* as in *his*, and *th* as in *this* — the first four are by far the most important and certainly should be taught early in the first grade. Quite probably most pupils — surely those who know that each strange word is one which makes sense with what they have read so far and which they already know how to pronounce — will teach themselves, as they read, the association for *s* as in *his* and the association for *th* as in *this*. Indeed, it is difficult to think that any pupil who has learned to read for meaning and has established the association for *s* as in *see* but not the association for *s* as in *his* will fail to switch quickly in his thinking from the former to the latter sound upon encountering the strange word *was* in his reading of connected discourse. The same point applies to the encountering of the strange word *than* by the pupil who knows the association for *th* as in *thumb* but not the association for *th* as in *this*. If he cannot or does not do this simple switching, he has not grasped the significance of the fact that his reading matter stands for familiar spoken language.

A second group of letter-sound associations that the pupil can learn to some advantage is made up of those for (1) common endings which are added to base words to make variants and (2) other common syllables. The most important endings are *ing* as in *walking*, *ed* as in *talked*, *ed* as in *wanted*, *ed* as in *drowned*, *er* as in *faster*, *ly* as in *tightly*, *est* as in *tallest*, *es* as in *bushes*, *y* as in *cooky*, *less* as in *friendless*, *ness* as in *kindness*, *ful* as in *careful*, *en* as in *beaten*, *ment* as in *amusement*, and *able* as in *comfortable*. Other important common syllables are *tion* as in *mention*, *un* as in *unopened*, *dis* as in *dislike*, *mis* as in *misplace*, *re* as in *repay*, *com* as in *complete*, *de* as in *decide*, *im* as in *improve*, *con* as in *confess*, *ex* as in *excuse*, *pre* as in *prepare*, and *le* added to consonants to make *ble, cle, dle, fle gle, kle, ple, tle* as in *bubble, bicycle, candle, ruffle, eagle, ankle, sample, kettle*. The chief reason for the pupil's knowing associations for common endings and other syllables is simply that it will enable him to use larger pronounceable elements than those represented by single consonants and speech consonants in unlocking strange words. The associations for the commonest endings should be taught in the first grade. Those for the remaining endings and the common syllables may be reserved for the second grade.

A third group of letter-sound associations which the pupil will need to know, particularly for unlocking strange words as they stand more or less alone out of helpful context, is made up of some of those which could be taught for vowels — the unreliables or undependables. Each of the five single vowels stands for many different sounds, and most vowel combinations, such as *ou* or *ai*, stand for several different sounds. Because at the present time the question of what to do about teaching letter-sound associations for vowels as part of instruction in beginning reading is unsettled and highly arguable, awaiting the results of conclusive research on the validity of such teaching, certain statements are in order before tentative recommendations concerning the letter-sound associations to be taught for vowels are presented. These statements are based on the author's experience in working with many first-grade pupils who had been taught *only* the letter-sound associations for *consonants*, who had come to understand that in unlocking a strange word they were merely calling to mind the right familiar spoken word, and who realized that each strange word is one which makes sense with what they are reading and which they already know very well how to pronounce.

First, time and time again the author has found that in reading connected discourse first-grade pupils can unlock strange words easily without knowing any of the letter-sound associations represented by vowels in those words. They did this as they read an unfamiliar primer story in which blanks had been substituted for the vowels in the strange words. They did it also in reading such isolated sentences as the following:

1. Mary left her new j–ck–t at our house.
2. Why did Jack paint his w–g–n red?
3. Mother said that you and your fr–nd may go to the show with us.
4. Billy took his bicycle to the r–p–r shop this morning.

If you think that the pupils were able to unlock the strange words *jacket, wagon, friend,* and *repair* because they knew how to spell those words, you are mistaken. All they did was to apply the skill they had acquired in using context and consonant sounds together to call to mind the familiar spoken words for which the strange printed forms stand. Actually, the pupils could not spell the words later when they were asked to do so.

Parenthetically, it should be added that these first-grade pupils had no trouble reading an unfamiliar primer story in which all the words included were familiar to them in print and a blank was substituted for each vowel sound in each word. Perhaps you can do much the same in reading the passage that follows, even though merely your habit of seeing vowels in printed words will make you read more slowly than is your custom. To help you resist the temptation to try to fit a spelling you know to each word in the passage, a blank is substituted for each vowel sound, whether that sound is represented in English spelling by one letter or by two letters, and no mark is used for silent *e.* As you read, think for each blank the vowel *sound* — not the letter or letters — that the context and the consonant sounds tell you to think there.

Th– w–dd–ng w–s t– t–k pl–c –n th– M–th–d–st Ch–rch
–t s–v–n –'cl–ck –n th– –v–n–ng, –nd –s –ll th– p–pl –n
th– v–llag h–d b–n –nv–t–d, M–th–r s–d, "W–'d b–tt–r b– th–r
s–n –ft–r f–v –f w– w–nt t– g–t – s–t." –v–n th–n
th– ch–rch w–s –lm–st f–ll, –nd w– t–k – s–t n–r th– b–ck.
W– g–rls w–r th– p–nk dr–ss–s w–th th– sh–rrd y–ks –nd
sl–vs th–t M–th–r h–d s–t –p l–t t– f–n–sh f–r –s, –nd
sh– h–d –n – f–n g–n th–t sh– h–dn't –v–n w–rn t– ch–rch
y–t.

Th– ch–rch sm–lld l–vl–, j–st l–k – f–n–r–l. Th– fl–r–st h–d
t–k–n b–dspr–ngs –nd t–rnd th–m –n –nd f–r – b–ckgr–nd,

–nd c–v–rd th–m w–th l–l–s –nd f–rns. –t b–th –nds –f
–ch p– w–s – b–q–t –f f–v l–l–s t–d w–th – wh–t s–t–n
r–bb–n, –nd th–r w–r h–ndr–ds –f wh–t c–ndls gl–m–ng –ll
–r–nd –s.
   Th– –rg–n b–g–n pl–ng, –nd s–n th– br–d p–ssd th– p– wh–r
w– s–t. Th–r sh– w–nt, fl–t–ng –n h–r f–th–r's –rm
–nd l–k–ng j–st l–k – dr–m. Th–n w– s– s–mth–ng th–t
t–rnd –r bl–d t– –cw–t–r. C–m–ng –l–ng b–h–nd th– br–d,
h–ld–ng th– tr–n h–gh –n th– –r w–r –ld M–tt– –nd l–ttl
S–s–, r–g–d w–th s–l–mn–t–. Th– br–d h–d br–ght th–m
t– th– ch–rch t– –rr–ng h–r tr–n s– –t w–ld str–m –t j–st
r–ght, b–t th– h–d n–t –nd–rst–d, –nd h–r th– c–m b–h–nd
h–r, k–p–ng st–p w–th th– m–s–c –nd h–ld–ng th– tr–n –l–ft.[4]

Second, what is it that tells any pupil or even you what sound to think for the omitted vowel or vowels in each of the numbered sentences that follow? Is it the form of the vowel? Is it your ability to spot in a word a group of letters you call a digraph or a diphthong? Is it some rule about deciding what sound to think for a vowel under such and such circumstances? Is it the context? Do the sounds of the consonants help?

 1. Dick ate that whole watermelon, and now he says he feels awfully f–ll.
 2. Please f–ll this cup with water.
 3. Nancy broke her arm when she f–ll out of the tree.
 4. Don't let that new dish of mine f–ll.
 5. If Tom doesn't do better at school, he may f–l to pass this year.
 6. Uncle Frank has gone to the barn to see your horse and her new f–l.
 7. Can you f–l cold air coming through that door?
 8. You can't f–l me with that trick.
 9. A f–l was called on Joe.
10. Mr. Brown has a wooden duck that he uses as a f–l.
11. You should let that f–l roast longer.

Third, the author has repeatedly found that, in unlocking in helpful context a strange word containing several vowels, pupils who know how to use consonant sounds with the context switch easily from a first-thought wrong sound for each vowel to the sounds the vowels have in the familiar word to be called to mind. Thus in unlocking the strange word *automobile* in the sentence *The next time we take that trip, we'll go by automobile,* pupils who were told to think first for each vowel the short *u* sound as in *until* switched quickly to the vowel sounds in *automobile.* To the question of how they knew the word was *automobile* and the

---

[4] This passage is an adaptation of paragraphs on pp. 118–119 of *Smile Please,* by Mildred Topp (Houghton Mifflin Company, Boston, 1948). Used by permission.

vowels have the sounds they do have, the consensus of replies was, "That word makes sense there, and it has in it the sounds of those consonants. The letters you called vowels must have the sounds they have in *automobile*. What other sounds could they have there?" Once again let it be said that the pupil who cannot or does not do this simple switching just does not understand the significance of the fact that his reading matter stands for familiar spoken language.

Fourth, some time ago the author became interested in finding out whether first-grade pupils — who are taught during the year letter-sound associations for consonants only and who have ample practice in using together the context and those associations to unlock strange words — teach themselves any of the letter-sound associations for vowels as they engage in whatever reading they do. To get a preliminary answer to this question, a test covering twenty-four such associations was given to more than 600 first-grade pupils at the end of the school year. The testing checked each pupil three times on the following associations: (a) the short sound of each of the five single vowels, (b) the long sound of each of the five single vowels, (c) *ai* as in *rain, ea* as in *meat, oo* as in *boot, ow* as in *town, ie* as in *thief, ea* as in *head, ou* as in *loud, au* as in *caught, ow* as in *low, ay* as in *hay, oa* as in *boat, ie* as in *cried, oo* as in *look, ee* as in *need.* In scoring the test, an incorrect response on any of the three checkings on a given association was taken to mean that the pupil had not learned that association. Some pupils made perfect scores, and some made three correct responses for less than half of the associations checked. More than half of the pupils responded correctly three times for seventeen associations.

Fifth, suppose now that a mother sends her six-year-old child to a store with the following list of items he is to bring home. She does not name the items to him, and the child knows no letter-sound associations for vowels. Only the word in which vowels have been omitted as presented here is strange to him:

> butter
> cookies
> the s–p you like

What is that strange word? Soup? Soap? With very little if any context and only the consonant sounds to use, the child can't possibly unlock the word. To decide that it is *soap*, he must know a letter-sound association for the *oa* which would be there or perhaps, as a sound not to use, an association for *ou*. To decide that it is *soup*, he must know an association for the *ou* which would be there or perhaps, as a sound not to use, an association for *oa*.

Suppose also that in the table of contents in a book or magazine the same child sees the story title "No Water in the Pool" and that the last word in the title is strange to him. With such meager context and only the consonant sounds to use, the child can't possibly choose between *Pool* and *Pail*. To decide right then that it is *Pool*, he must know a letter-sound association for *oo* or perhaps an association for *ai*.

Suppose again that in reading a story the same child encounters the boy's name *Tom* and that both this name and the name *Tim* are strange to him only in print. Since context never provides help for unlocking the name of a person and the child has here only the consonant associations to work with, he cannot decide that the word is *Tom* instead of *Tim* without knowing a letter-sound association for *o* or perhaps *i*.

Could the child unlock the strange italicized word in the following isolated sentence in a letter received from a friend?

I like to play with the toy *ship* my Dad got for me.

The answer is *no*. He could not tell whether the word is *ship, shop,* or *sheep*.

Is it ever helpful for the pupil to break a strange printed word into its syllables? If so, he should learn what letters are vowels and what sounds are vowel sounds. The number of vowel sounds in a word is a strong clue to the number of syllables in that word.

Keep in mind too that some but not most of the strange words that the first-grade or second-grade pupil will meet in his reading begin with a vowel or a vowel combination. As will be explained later in this chapter, the technique which the pupil is to be taught to follow in unlocking any strange word encourages him to use, first and together, the context and the beginning sound of the word. To apply this technique to strange words which begin with a vowel or a vowel combination, he must be acquainted with a few letter-sound associations for those letters.

The foregoing statements present examples of situations in which the pupil needs to know some letter-sound associations for vowels in order to unlock strange words. The statements do not imply that the teaching of such associations is to be neglected. Neither do they suggest that the instruction must be as elaborate or as complicated as it is in many schools.

Sixth, it is very easy to overload instruction pertaining to letter-sound associations for vowels with the teaching of questionable items and the performing of futile activities which the pupil who reads for meaning and who knows the associations for consonants simply does not need to know or perform in order to unlock the strange words in his reading of connected discourse. Examples of some of these practices follow:

a. Teaching several associations — not just two — for each single vowel as thoroughly as the associations for consonants should be taught. When the pupil encounters the strange word *about, call, care,* or *asked,* for example, and thinks first for the *a* the short sound or the long sound, he has little if any trouble in shifting quickly to the sound that letter has in the familiar spoken word called for by the context and the consonants.

b. Teaching several associations for most of the commonest vowel combinations and teaching associations for relatively rare vowel combinations as thoroughly as associations for consonants should be taught.

c. Having the pupil examine printed words to see if they contain examples of what he has been told are digraphs or diphthongs.

d. Having the pupil change the vowel or vowels in a given familiar word to make another word. Here, for example, the pupil is shown the familiar word *boat* and is asked to remove the vowels and put in their place the vowels needed to make the word *beat.* This sort of thing is spelling, not reading.

e. Having the pupil memorize and try to apply rules — often many in number, complicated in nature, and highly questionable in validity — which are supposed to tell him what sounds to think for vowels.

f. Encouraging the pupil to always take time to use what he has been taught about vowels or to pay close attention to each vowel in his attempt to unlock a strange word.

Is the pupil who receives such elaborate instruction expected to use in unlocking strange words what the instruction purports to convey? If not, what is its purpose? If the pupil is encouraged to use and actually does use that knowledge in unlocking strange words, what would he do to unlock in the following lines the word *astronaut,* which is strange to him only in print?

> The space ship will take off tomorrow.
> No one knows who the astronaut will be.

Would the pupil (a) note the first *a,* recall the rule *If you don't know what sound to use for a vowel, try the short sound first, and if that sound doesn't work try the long sound,* and decide what sound to try, (b) note the *o,* recall the same rule, and decide what sound to try, and (c) note the *au,* think that it is a diphthong, recall either a rule he has been taught about sounds to think for diphthongs or the rule *When two vowels go walking, the first one does the talking,* and decide what sound to try? Any pupil who does this sort of thing has made a start in learning to belabor a strange word as he unlocks it and to spend more time and effort than he needs to in performing the relatively simple task of calling to mind the familiar spoken word which the strange form represents. One wonders if the pupil would not be better off if with *astronaut,* as perhaps with many other words, he thought for each vowel the short *a* sound, the short *e* sound, the short *u* or schwa sound, or almost any other vowel sound. Would the combination of that sound and the consonant sounds he hears in his mind be close enough to the spoken form of the word so that, with the context, he would think, "Oh, sure. It has to be *astronaut*"? Perhaps one should be thankful that the vowels are as unreliable as they are, for this condition, presented truthfully to the pupil who uses context and only consonant sounds correctly, can encourage him to read for meaning rather than word pronunciations.

From what source springs the practice of including in the teaching of reading so much about vowels that, as intimated by the six lettered paragraphs just presented, the pupil is expected to learn a mass of confusing letter-sound associations, many of which he no doubt will acquire on his own just through experience in reading, and is overburdened with technical names and numerous rules of doubtful validity? Is it the notion that the pupil's task in unlocking strange words is much the same as the job which anyone faces in getting from a dictionary the pronunciation of a word he does not already know how to pronounce and that the purpose in teaching letter-sound associations is to give him the tools he will need to figure out the pronunciations of the strange words? The notion is sheer nonsense. Unlocking a strange word is very different from getting a pronunciation from a dictionary. Since the pupil already knows how to pronounce the strange words he will encounter in his reading matter, he has no need to learn how to figure out their pronunciations. Is it felt that one purpose of teaching beginning reading is to improve the pupil's spelling? Well, spelling is much tougher than beginning reading, the demand for knowing exactly what letter or letters to write for a vowel sound in a word is much more severe than is the demand for knowing exactly what sound to think for a vowel in a printed word, and it is almost impossible to teach about vowels what might be profitable for purposes of spelling without doing serious damage to the teaching of reading itself.

The paragraphs that follow present the author's recommendations pertaining to what the pupil should learn about letter-sound associations for vowels:

a. Very early in the first grade — certainly in connection with the reading of the first preprimer — the pupil should be told that the letters *a, e, i, o,* and *u* are called vowels, that each vowel stands for many different sounds, but that for the time being he does not need to be concerned about knowing what those sounds are.

b. A little later, by using either spoken context or familiar printed context, the teacher should present sentences containing a strange word in which blanks are substituted for vowels. Unlocking each strange word will lead the pupil to see that he can decide what this or that word is by using the context and just the consonant sounds. What to do and say in directing the pupil to unlock each strange word will be discussed later in this chapter.

c. Soon the teacher should present the same strange word — maybe f–ll — with the vowel omitted, in several different contexts, and the pupil should be asked to decide what the word is in each context. This will enable him to learn that usually the context tells him what sound to think for a vowel.

d. Throughout the first grade, as will be explained more fully later, needed but only appropriate letter-sound associations for vowels should be presented to the pupil in connection with the introduction of each new word which begins with a vowel. Thus, for example, in introducing the new word *above,* the teacher may say, "With what letter does this new word begin? . . . That's right. In this word, the *a* stands for the sound you hear at the beginning of *alone* and *about*. That sound is one that the letter *a* sometimes stands for, and it is a sound you will often use for the letter *a*." This sort of presentation, simple though it is, will suffice for introducing a few associations for each of the single vowels.

e. Early in Grade 2, if not before, the teacher should make the pupil aware that the weak context which he will meet once in a great while in his reading does not tell him what sound to think for a vowel in a strange word, that often he cannot decide just what word a given strange word in a list is by using only the included consonant sounds, and that these are reasons why he needs to know letter-sound associations for vowels. This can be done by using sentences such as *I like to play with my toy ship* and lists of familiar words in which, for example, a strange word such as *soup* or *cup* appears.

f. Then, if the pupil has not yet learned certain letter-sound associations for vowels, the following items — and only those items — should be taught thoroughly to him over a period of time: short *a* as in *bad,* long *a* as in *cake,* short *e* as in *met,* long *e* as in *me,* short *i* as in *lip,* long *i* as in *bite,* short *o* as in *hot,* long *o* as in *fold,* short *u* as in *cup,* long *u* as in *tube* or *cube, ai* as in *nail, ea* as in *meat, ea* as in *head, ee* as in *need, oa* as in *boat, oo* as in *look, oo* as in *room, ow* as in *row, ow* as in *cow, ou* as in *out, oi* as in *boil, ay* as in *lay, aw* as in *crawl, au* as in *auto, ie* as in *cried, ie* as in *field*.

Teaching a letter-sound association consists of two main parts: (a) presenting the association and (b) providing practice needed for fixing the association in mind and for learning to use it, if needed, in various positions in words. The discussion now considers the first of these two parts.

a. Presenting an Association

Because the pupil, through learning the twenty-two consonant associations included in the preparatory instruction described in Chapter 3, must have acquired the generalization that letters and groups of letters stand for sounds, the presentation of the associations listed on page 102, 103, and 110 need not be lengthy, detailed, or elaborate. The pupil's attention is merely called to the letter or group of letters in two or more familiar printed words, and he notes that the letter or group of letters stands for the same sound in each word. At times one or more additional important statements are made. In order to avoid wasting the pupil's time by trying to teach him an association he already knows, the presentation may include at the beginning a brief, simple checking on that association.

By showing one way to present the association for soft *c* and the association for *qu*, the two numbered passages which follow, addressed to you, the reader, illustrate how the associations for soft *c*, soft *g, qu, z, th* as in *this,* and *s* as in *his* can be introduced. It is understood that presenting the association for *s* as in *his* will require the use of words which end in *s* standing for the *z* sound.

1. Show the pupil one or more rows of three or more words that rhyme and that you think he does not know in print. One word in each row must begin with *c* standing for the soft sound, and the others should begin with different consonants standing for other sounds. The following rows are examples:

cell	dell	quell
hinder	tinder	cinder
flinch	cinch	winch

Then, without telling the pupil what the words are, say to him: "In each row, draw a line under the word that you think begins with the sound you hear at the beginning of *circus* and *cement*. . . ." If the pupil makes the correct response in each row, there is no need to teach him the letter-sound association for soft *c*. If he makes an incorrect response in any row, present that association as suggested in the next paragraph.

Print on the board two or more words which the pupil already knows in print and which begin with *c* standing for the soft sound, perhaps *cent* and *city*. Then say: "With what letter does each of these words begin? . . . You know these words. Let's say them together and listen for the sound they begin with. . . . Do the words begin with the same sound? . . . In what two ways do the words begin alike? . . . That's right. All the words begin with the letter *c*, and they all begin with the same sound. That sound is a sound that the letter *c* sometimes stands for. We call it the soft *c* sound. It is a sound you know for the letter *s*. You hear the soft *c* sound at the beginning of *cent, city, circus, cement, center,* and *certain.*"

2. Show the pupil one or more rows of three or more words that rhyme and that you think he does not know in print. One word in each row must begin with *qu*, and others should begin with different consonants standing for other sounds. The following are examples:

quest	crest	jest
flip	grip	quip
saint	quaint	taint

Then without telling the pupil what the words are, say to him: "In each row, draw a line under the word that you think begins with the same sound as *quilt* and *quiet*. . . ." If the pupil makes the correct response in each row, there is no need to teach him the letter-sound association for *qu*. If he makes an incorrect response in any row, present that association as suggested in the next paragraph.

Print on the board two or more words which the pupil already knows in print and which begin with *qu*, perhaps *quick* and *quiet*. Then say: "With what two letters does each of these words begin? . . . You know these words. Let's say them together and listen for the sound they begin with. . . . Do the words begin with the same sound? . . . In what two ways do the words begin alike? . . . That's right. All the words begin with the letters *qu*, and they all begin with the same sound. That sound is the sound that *qu* stands for. You hear that sound at the beginning of *quick, quiet, quilt, queer,* and *quart.*"

Perhaps a statement should be made here relative to the presentation of associations for consonant blends such as *bl, br, cl, cr, dr, fl, fr, gl, gr, pl, pr, sc, scr, shr, sk, sl, sm, sn, sp, spl, spr, squ, st, str, sw, thr, tr, tw, wr* which were not included among the consonant associations on page 102. The sound that each of these items stands for is a quick blending of the sounds of the individual letters which make up the item. Since the pupil who has learned *qu* and what the preparatory instruction purports to teach already knows the letter-sound association for each of the individual letters in a given consonant blend, there is no need to present to him as a separate and new item the letter-sound association for that blend. However, when the first new word which begins with a consonant blend, for example *street*, is introduced, his attention should be called to the letters *str*, he should be reminded that he already knows the sound each of the letters stands for, and he should be told that when those letters come together in this order in a word, they stand for the sound he hears at the beginning of *strap*, *straight*, and *strike*.

By showing one way of presenting the association for *ed* as in *talked*, the two paragraphs that follow illustrate the procedure to be followed with the fifteen associations for common endings included in the list on page 103:

Show the pupil one or more rows of three or more words that are variants of the same base word and that you think he does not know in print. One word in each row must end with *ed* standing for the sound which that ending has in *talked*. The following are examples:

sacking	sacker	sacked
balk	balked	balker
quenched	quenching	quenches

Then, without telling the pupil what the words are, say to him: "In each row, draw a line under the word that you think ends with the same sound as *talked* and *walked*. . . ." If the pupil makes a correct response in each row, there is no need to teach him the letter-sound association for *ed* as in *talked*. If he makes an incorrect response in any row, present that association as suggested in the next paragraph.

Print on the board two or more words which the pupil knows in print and which end with *ed* standing for the sound that ending has in *talked*, perhaps *talked* and *walked*. Then say: "With what two letters does each of these words end? . . . You know these words. Let's say them together and listen for the sound at the end of each of them. . . . Do all the words end with the same sound? . . . In what two ways do all the words end alike? . . . That's right. They all end with the letters *ed*, and they all end with the same sound. That sound is the sound that the letters *ed* sometimes stand for at the end of a word. You hear that sound at the end of *talked*, *walked*, *backed*, *faked*, *raked*, and *winked*."

The following presentation of the letter-sound association for the syllable *mis* can be used as a model for the presentation of any of the thirteen associations for common syllables included in the list on page 103, except the one for *tion* and the one for *le* with a preceding consonant:

Show the pupil one or more rows of three or more words that begin with the same letter and that you think he does not know in print. One word in each row must begin with the common syllable *mis*. The following are examples:

missive	motive	massive
material	melody	misdeal
memento	misquote	mosquito

Then, without telling the pupil what the words are, say: "In each row, draw a line under the word which you think begins with the same syllable sound as *mistake* and *mislay*. . . ." If the pupil makes an incorrect response in any row, present the association for the syllable *mis* as suggested in the next paragraph.

Print on the board two or more words beginning with the syllable *mis* which the pupils know in print, perhaps *mistake* and *misplace*. Then say: "With what three letters does this word begin? . . . You know these words. Let's say them and listen for the sound that the first three letters stand for in each word. . . . Do all the words have the same sound for the first three letters? . . . In what two ways do the words begin alike? . . . That's right. They all begin with the letters *mis*, and they all begin with the same sound. That is the sound the syllable *mis* stands for in words. You hear that sound at the beginning of *mistake, mislay, miscount, mislead, misspell,* and *mistook*."

In some schools it has been the custom to teach the pupil (1) the relation between the number of vowel sounds in a word and the number of syllables in that word and (2) at least two if not more rules for determining what are the syllables in a word. This knowledge is supposed to be used in unlocking strange printed words. The author has no serious objection to letting the pupil know that usually the number of syllables in a word is the same as the number of vowel sounds in that word. But rarely, if ever, has he found that any pupil who has learned to use together context and letter-sound associations for consonants and a few other items needs to use a knowledge of rules of syllabication in order to call to mind the familiar spoken word for which a given strange printed word stands. Consequently this volume does not recommend that the pupil be taught to use syllabication rules as aids in unlocking words which are strange only in print. Possibly those rules may be useful to him now in recognizing familiar words and later in figuring out a pronunciation for a word that is strange to him in both form and pronunciation. Yet in the latter case, certainly he should use also a dictionary to find out whether the pronunciation he figured out is correct, as explained in Chapter 8.

To present any one of the ten associations for single vowels included in the list on page 110, one can proceed according to the following presentation of the association for short *a*. It is understood that, when an association for the long sound of any single vowel is taught, the pupil will be told that this sound is the same as the name of the letter.

Show the pupil one or more numbered rows of three or more words that are alike except for the vowels and that you think the pupil does not know in print and cannot spell. One word in each row must contain the letter *a* standing for the short sound. The following are possibilities:

1. crimp	cramp	crump
2. flack	fleck	flick
3. sip	sop	sap

Then, without telling the pupil what the words are, say: "Look at the words in row 1. Draw a line under the word that you think is *cramp*. . . . Look at the words in row 2. Draw a line under the word that you think is *flack*. . . . Look at row number 3. Draw a line under the word that you think is *sap*. . . ." If the pupil makes an incorrect response in any row, present the association for short *a* as suggested in the two paragraphs that follow.

Print on the board two or more words which the pupil knows in print and which begin with the letter *a* standing for the short *a* sound, perhaps *and* and *at*. Then say: "With what letter does each of these words begin? . . . You know these words. Let's say them together and listen for the sound they all begin with. . . . Do all the words begin with the same sound? . . . In what two ways do the words begin alike? . . . That's right. They all begin with the letter *a*, and they all begin with the same sound. We call that sound the short *a* sound. It is a sound that *a* often stands for in words, and you hear it at the beginning of *add, after, an, am, as,* and *act*."

Print on the board two or more words which the pupil knows in print and which have in the middle the letter *a* standing for the short *a* sound, perhaps *bad* and *can*. Then say: "What letter do you see in the middle of each of these words? . . . You know these words. Let's say them together and listen for the sound in the middle of each of them. . . . Do all the words have the same sound in the middle? . . . In what two ways are the words alike in the middle? . . . That's right. They all have the letter *a* in the middle, and they all have the same sound in the middle. That sound is the short *a* sound, and you hear it in the middle of *can, bad, cap, dad, fan, ham, pan, ran,* and *tack*."

By showing one way to teach the association for the vowel combination *ai* as in *rain*, the two paragraphs that follow illustrate the presentation of the sixteen associations for vowel combinations included in the list on page 111:

Show the pupil one or more numbered rows of three or more words that are alike except for the vowel combination included and that you think the pupil does not know in print and cannot spell. One word in each row should contain the vowel combination *ai*. The following are possibilities:

1. lain	loon	loan
2. stead	staid	steed
3. bawl	boil	bail

Then, without telling the pupil what the words are, say: "Look at the words in row 1. Draw a line under the word that you think is *lain*. . . . Look at the words in row 2. Draw a line under the word that you think is *staid*. . . . Look at the words in row 3. Draw a line under the word that you think is *bail*. . . ." If the pupil makes an incorrect response in any row, present the association for *ai* as suggested by the following paragraph.

Print on the board two or more words which the pupil knows in print and which contain in the middle the vowel combination *ai*, perhaps *rain* and *fail*. Then say: "What two letters do you see in the middle of each of these words? . . . You know these words. Let's say them together and listen for the sound in the middle of each of them. . . . Do all the words have the same sound in the middle? . . . In what two ways are the words alike in the middle? . . . That's right. They all have the letters *ai* in the middle, and they all have the same sound in the middle. That sound is a sound that the letters *ai* sometimes stand for. You hear that sound in the middle of *rain, fail, pain, rail, mail,* and *pail*."

b. Providing Needed Practice

The teaching of letter-sound associations includes more than merely presenting those associations to the pupil. In addition, practice which will enable him to fix them in mind and learn to use the appropriate ones in different positions in words should be provided. Of course the best type of practice will be supplied by the reading the pupil does in his basal readers and in numerous other books. Special practice which some pupils may need can be provided by substitution exercises.

In one type of substitution exercise, the pupil is shown a familiar printed word that ends with a consonant. Then that consonant is replaced by others for which the letter-sound associations have been presented, making words which are strange to the pupil in print but familiar to him in spoken form, and the pupil is asked what the strange words are. The following paragraph describes such an exercise:

Place on the board a word which the pupil knows in print, perhaps *did* Then say: "What is this word? . . . You can use part of the word *did* and some letter sounds you know to make other words. Watch what I do to the end of *did*." Change final *d* to *g*. Say: "What did I do? . . . You know a sound that *g* sounds for. What is the new word? . . . Watch what I do to the end of *dig*." Change *g* to *m*. Say: "What did I do? . . . You know the sound that *m* stands for. What is the new word? . . . Watch what I do to the end of *dim*." Change *m* to *ll*. Say: "What did I do? . . . You know the sound that *l* stands for. What is the new word? . . . Watch what I do to the end of *dill*." Change *ll* to *p*. Say: "What did I do? . . . You know the sound that *p* stands for. What is the new word? . . . Watch what I do to the end of *dip*." Change *p* to *sh*. Say: "What did I do? . . . You know the sound that *sh* stands for. What is the new word? . . ."

A second type of exercise is like the first except that consonants are substituted within the word. Thus, for example, a familiar word such as *leading* can be printed on the board. Then substitutions of *n, p, f, k,* and *v* can be made in turn within the word to form the strange words *leaning, leaping, leafing, leaking,* and *leaving,* and the pupil can be asked what each strange word is.

In a third type of exercise, endings for which letter-sound associations have been taught are added to a familiar base word to make strange variants. For example, the familiar word *talk* can be printed on the board. Then the endings *ed, ing,* and *er* can be added in turn to make the strange words *talked, talking, talker,* and the pupil can be asked to decide what each variant is.

In a fourth type of exercise, a familiar printed word beginning with a consonant is printed on the board and other consonants, for which letter-sound associations have been presented, are substituted at the beginning to make words strange to the pupil in print but familiar to him in spoken form. Because the pupil has learned, through the preparatory instruction described in Chapter 3, twenty-two letter-sound associations for consonants, it is recommended that the substitutions made in this exercise be limited to others, namely soft *c*, soft *g*, *qu*, *th* as in *them, z,* and the consonant blends. Thus the familiar word *take* may be printed on the board and *br, fl, qu, sn,* and *st* substituted in turn to make *brake, flake, quake, snake,* and *stake*.

Six points should be kept in mind relative to the using of any substitution exercise. *First,* only pupils who need the practice the exercise supplies should be asked to take part in it. *Second,* each starting word must be one which the pupil knows in print. *Third,* each letter or group of letters substituted must be one for which the letter-sound association has been presented. *Fourth,* in replying to the question *What did I do?* the pupil should name the letter taken away and the letter substituted instead of giving a vague answer such as *Changed the beginning of the word* or *Took away one letter and put another in its place. Fifth,* each word made by a substitution must be a word that is unfamiliar in print to the pupil.

Sixth, there is no reason to hold the pupil responsible for remembering the words made through substitutions. The purpose of a substitution exercise is not that of teaching those words.

Other exercises, varieties of which appear in the workbooks and the teacher's guides accompanying basal readers, can help the pupil fix in mind letter-sound associations that have been presented. The following items give a general description of what at least some of the exercises ask the pupil to do:

1. Choose from among a group of pictures those with names which begin with the sound a supplied consonant letter or group of letters stands for.

2. Choose from among several consonant letters or groups of letters the one that stands for the sound with which the name of a supplied picture begins.

3. Choose from a group of familiar printed words those beginning with the same sound as the name of a supplied picture.

4. Choose from among consonant letters or groups of letters the one that stands for the sound with which two or more words spoken by the teacher begin.

5. Choose from among words spoken by the teacher those which have in them in one position or another the sound represented by a consonant letter or group of letters.

6. Think of and speak words which begin with the sound that a supplied printed letter or group of letters stands for.

7. Decide which of several words spoken by the teacher contain a shown syllable.

8. Decide which group of letters in a printed word is a syllable spoken by the teacher.

9. Match syllables in different familiar printed words.

The teacher can construct simple tests to duplicate and use any time in making an inventory of the letter-sound associations which the pupil has learned and of those which he does not yet know:[5]

> To make a test on consonants, print a numbered row of words for each association to be checked, such as the following for *b:*
>
> 1. hump   pump   dump   bump

[5] Instead of making tests, the teacher may wish to use *The McKee Inventory of Phonetic Skill* (Houghton Mifflin Company, Boston, Mass.). Test One of this inventory includes associations for most of the consonants and for a few of the endings. Test Two includes associations for most of the consonants, endings, and vowels. Test Three includes associations for all the consonants, endings, vowels, and syllables.

All the words in each row should be exactly alike except for the beginning consonant, and each word should be strange in print to the pupil. In each row, the pupil is to mark the word that begins with the sound which is to be checked by the row and which you will supply by naming other words beginning with the sound. Thus in using row 1 to check on *b*, you can direct the pupil by saying, "Find row number 1. Look at the words in that row. Draw a line under the word that begins with the same sound as *band* and *book*."

To make a test on endings, print a numbered row of words for each association to be checked, such as the following for *ing:*

    1. guessed   guessing   guesser   guesses

All the words in each row must be variants of a given base word and should be strange in print to the pupil. In each row, the pupil is to mark the word that has the ending which is to be checked by the row and which you will supply by naming other words having that ending. Thus in using row 1 to check on *ing*, you can direct the pupil by saying, "Find row number 1. Look at the words in that row. Draw a line under the word that ends with the sound you hear at the end of *helping* and *looking*."

To make a test on syllables, print a numbered row of words for each association to be checked, such as the following for *tion* and *com:*

    1. attention   attentive   attendant   attended
    2. candid   cemented   compute   cauldron

All the words in each row should be strange in print to the pupil. In each row, the pupil is to mark the word that contains the syllable sound which is to be checked by the row and which you will supply by naming other words containing that sound. Thus in using row 1 to check on *tion* and row 2 to check on *com*, you can direct the pupil by saying, "Look at the words in row number 1. Draw a line under the word that ends with the same syllable sound you hear at the end of *mention* and *action*. . . . Look at the words in row 2. Draw a line under the word that begins with the same syllable sound you hear at the beginning of *common* and *compare*."

To make a test on vowels, print a numbered row of words for each association to be checked, such as the following for short *e:*

    1. punt   pent   pint   pant

All the words in each row sould be alike except for the vowel, and each word must be one which is strange in print to the pupil and which he does not know how to spell. In each row, the pupil is to mark the word that contains the vowel sound which is to be checked by the row and which is in the word you will name. Thus in using row 1 to check on short *e*, you can direct the pupil by saying, "Look at the words in row number 1. Draw a line under the word that you think is *pent*."

2. Teaching the Technique

A mastery of letter-sound associations will not in itself equip the pupil to unlock strange printed words economically. With only that knowledge, he is likely to be unaware of how to use those associations economically, to attack a strange word at almost any point in the word, to miss the advantage that comes from using first the context and the beginning sound of the word, to use more letter sounds than he needs to use, and to read for word names rather than meaning. In addition to mastering letter-sound associations the pupil must gain control of a definite and effective technique to follow in using context and letter sounds together to unlock strange words.

The technique to be taught is simply that of using first and together the context and the beginning sound of the word and then *only* as many of the remaining sounds as are needed to make sure of the word. By using the context, the few letter-sound associations for consonants you were taught in Chapter 1 and four other associations the author will give you, unlock the strange words in the following short passages and you will refresh your memory about how this technique can work. When you come to each strange word, think of a word you know that begins with the sound the ,first letter or letters stand for and makes sense there. Use only as many other letter sounds as you need to make sure of the word.

a. The first passage is as follows:

"Mary," said Mother, "your Aunt Sue just called. I'm going over to see her, and there is some work I wish you would do before I come ⊓+✕⊐. Those glasses I washed aren't as ✕∨⊗+⌐ as they should be. Will you wash them again?"

What is ⊓+✕⊐? How do you know it isn't *home?* What other word if any that begins with the right sound could it be? Did you need to use the letter-sound association for the last letter to decide what the word is? Did you need to know the association for the vowel? Here is an example of that rare situation in which the pupil who uses the context would need to use only the beginning sound to call to mind the right word.

What is ✕∨⊗+⌐? How do you know it isn't *shiny?* What other word that begins with the right sound could it be? *Clean?* Did you need to use the letter-sound association for the last letter to make sure of the word? The association for the vowel combination? Here is a case in which the pupil who uses the context would need to use only the beginning sound and the ending sound to decide what the word is.

b. The second letter in the first strange word in the following passage is a vowel that stands for the sound you know for short *a*. The last three letters in the other strange word are an ending that stands for the sound you know for *ing*. Knowing that association may save time for you.

"I'll do it, Mother, just as soon as I pick some apples from that tree by the old ⚬+∨∨," said Mary. "Is Aunt Sue ⚬‡┐┐Ɔ∪ᵟ爪 about our going away?"

What is ⚬+∨∨? How do you know it isn't *bush*? What other word that begins with the right sound and ends with the right sound could it be? *Well*? Here is an example of that rather uncommon situation in which insufficiently strong context would make it necessary for the pupil to use the letter-sound association for the vowel in order to make sure of the word.

What is ⚬‡┐┐Ɔ∪ᵟ爪? How do you know it isn't *fretting*? *Wondering*? Of what help was using the letter-sound association for *r* to you?

c. In the second strange word in the next passage, the first three letters are a syllable that stands for the sound you know for *com*. The last four letters are a syllable that stands for the sound you know for *tion*. Perhaps knowing those associations will save time for you.

"I don't know, Mary," replied Mother. "The children were making so much ✕∨+∧∧⊗┐ that I could hardly hear your aunt. When I get there, I'll find out what all the ✕‡ᵖᵖ‡∧∪‡ᵟ is about."

What is ✕∨+∧∧⊗┐ ? How do you know it isn't *racket*? What other word that begins with the right sound could it be? *Clamor*? In what way did using the letter-sound association for *t* help you?

What is ✕‡ᵖᵖ‡∧∪‡ᵟ ? How do you know it isn't *commitment*?

The technique is to be taught through directive statements that, as will be explained in Chapter 5, the first- or second-grade teacher can use from time to time in introducing to the pupil some or all of the strange words in the selections to be read immediately by him in the basal reader. But these important directive statements cannot be made if introducing a given strange word consists of (a) showing the pupil the word by itself and telling him what it is, (b) presenting the word to him in familiar context, telling him what the word is, and having him read the line or lines, or (c) showing him the word by itself and having him sound it out. Consequently, as will be noted in detail in Chapter 5, each strange word is to be presented to the pupil in context, and the teacher is to direct him to use the context and the beginning sound to think a word which makes sense and begins with the right sound and to use only as many of the remaining sounds as he needs to make sure of the word. In the very beginning — probably while the first preprimer is being used — the context will be read aloud by the teacher from the board or a chart and the strange word included there but omitted by the teacher in her oral reading will be needed to complete what she says. But as soon as possible the context will be composed of words which the pupil by that time knows in print and will be shown with the strange word for him to read to himself. Although the directive statements made by the teacher will vary now and then according to the nature of the word being introduced and the letter-sound associations which have been taught up to that time, they will enable the pupil to learn to attack any strange word by using letter sounds economically with the context.[6]

Occasional special exercises in using letter sounds economically with context to unlock strange printed words can contribute to the teaching of the technique. The total array of such exercises from the beginning of the first grade to the close of the second grade should include items which are constructed so that the pupil, in unlocking the strange word, needs to use — or in the case of an ending or syllable simply can use — the context, the beginning sound, and (a) only the final sound, (b) only the final sound and one or more consonant sounds within the word, (c) the final sound and the sound of a vowel within the word, (d) the sound of the ending, and (e) the sound of one or more syllables. Here are correspondingly lettered examples of such items:

a. Can you help me mend this broken ✕⊏+∪⌐ ?

b. Where did you put that ⊓+♦♦⊗⌐ I made?

c. Mary has gone to get some ⊥‡⊸= at the store.

d. The old man who lives there seems to be so △⌐∪⊗♦⊔∨⊗⊥⊥ .

e. Billy was pretty ⊸♦✕‡♀△‡⌐∧+⊓∨⊗ on that long ride.

How do you know that the strange words are not in turn (a) *chain*, (b) *batter*, (c) *salt* or *soap*, (d) *friendly*, (e) *unhappy?*

To be helpful at any given time, a single exercise must be of such a nature that the letter-sound associations needed for unlocking the strange

---

[6] Illustrations of directive statements appear in Chapter 5.

word in each item are among those which have already been presented. At the beginning of the first grade, the teacher will need to read the context aloud, omitting the shown strange word. Later the context should be printed and shown with the strange word for the pupil to read to himself. The directive statements the teacher will use to teach the technique are much like those used in introducing strange words to be encountered in reading the selections in the basal reader.

Recognizing Familiar Printed Words

During the time that the pupil spends in the first and second grades, he encounters possibly two thousand different words in his basal readers and whatever additional words appear in the selections he reads outside those books. Most of these words have permanent value for him because they will appear frequently year after year in selections he attempts to read. In order to become a good reader in the sense that he reacts to printed lines with satisfaction, relative ease, and a reasonable degree of speed, he must become so familiar with the words that he can recognize them in a flash, without any puzzling whatsoever. If the pupil fails to acquire such familiarity, he will read slowly and ploddingly, unlocking time and again words that he should be recognizing instantly, and very probably he will not learn to like to read.

How does a good reader recognize a familiar printed word? Because this act occurs so quickly, no doubt within a fraction of a second, because so many things flash into the mind at once, and because tools needed for a valid study of the matter do not exist, no one actually knows the answer to this question. However, some writers have insisted that a good reader recognizes a familiar word *as a whole*. Without explaining just what is meant by the expression *as a whole,* they imply that the pupil can and should learn to do the same thing.

Recognizing a word *as a whole* may mean knowing what the word is by seeing only its general configuration, without noting or perhaps being conscious of any of its letters or without thinking the sound which one or another of those letters or groups of letters stands for. Can you do that by using these configurations of words you know well in print?

1.   2.   3.   4.

Of course, by trying to fit letter forms into each of the four configurations, you can think of several words it does *not* stand for. But which word — *butter, father, farther, talks, beckon, lettuce* — does configuration 1 stand for? Which word — *some, cone, mouse, noise, mamma* — does configuration 2 stand for? Which word — *going, young, pant, jump, query* — does configuration 3 stand for? Which word — *breakfast, handiest, fruitful, blueblood* — does configuration 4 stand for? You have no way of knowing. Just what words included in first-grade and second-grade reading matter have configurations so distinctive that they can be used to recognize the words as they stand alone?[7]

Perhaps, in the following sentences, you can use together the context and just the general configuration to recognize the word which the configuration stands for and which you know well in print:

1. What did you do with that new ⬜ I brought home? (Is the word *book, fork,* or *tool?*)
2. Let me carry those ⬜ for you. (Is the word *bundles, letters, bottles,* or *further?*)
3. Fred is the one who did all the ⬜ while we carried the boxes. (Is the word *pulling, puffing, yelling,* or *grunting?*)
4. Do you want both cereal and ⬜ for breakfast? (What could the word be except *eggs?*)

Do you think you could read a sentence readily if all its words were represented by general configurations? Try the following lines:

While a mature reader who has had years and years of practice in reading, who can think quickly of one or more letters that could fit into a general configuration, who knows quite a bit about the spelling of words, and who knows the sounds the letters stand for might be able to recognize *some* words just by their configurations in *some* contexts, the number of such words would no doubt be quite small, and the number of words which he could recognize in *any* context would be even smaller. (How many words were you able to recognize from the configurations above? You may have recognized some of them, but it would be almost impossible to figure out the entire sentence, *Bright and early the next morning the two boys hurried to the circus grounds,* without knowing something about the context in which it appears.) Probably the best that can be expected from most general configurations is the suggesting

[7] Some first-grade and second-grade teachers give pupils practice in (1) deciding which of several general configurations stands for a named word they have met in reading and (2) naming the word that a given configuration stands for and that they have had in reading. A few writers have recommended that in order to promote the pupil's skill in word recognition, the vocabulary of preprimers should be composed of words with configurations which vary greatly from one another.

of a word or words which make sense with the context but which are not the word the configuration stands for. It is the contention of the author that expecting first-grade and second-grade pupils to learn to recognize words by their general configurations, either as the words stand alone or as they appear in contexts, is asking too much, and that attempts to teach pupils to do so may very well prove to be fruitless.

Possibly recognizing a word as a whole means knowing what the word is at a single glance which is so brief — one-tenth of a second or less — that further movement of the eyes is not permitted. Unquestionably, as reported in several investigations, good readers do this with some words in some contexts, but there is nothing in the connotation or the investigations themselves providing a valid explanation of how they do it. Of course it is to be hoped that pupils will learn to recognize with such rapidity many familiar printed words in various contexts.

Recognizing a word as a whole may mean knowing what the word is by using only one or a very few of its parts to suggest the whole. A part used may be the initial letter or group of letters, the final letter or group of letters, or a letter or group of letters which in some way, perhaps by its ascending or descending form, stands out as a lead to the whole word. The using of a part includes noting its form and thinking the sound for which it stands. This the pupil most certainly should learn to do.

While in recognizing a printed word the good reader may see first the general configuration of the word, he must in addition, the author believes, note almost simultaneously one or more of its letters and think the sound which that part or those parts stand for. Consequently, it is proposed here that the pupil be taught to recognize familiar words by using together context and letter sounds, the same two aids recommended for use in unlocking strange words. As stated previously, the difference between unlocking a given strange word and recognizing that word when once it has become familiar is a matter of the amount of time and the number of letter sounds used.

The remainder of this chapter offers suggestions for helping the first-grade or second-grade pupil become so familiar with the printed words which constitute the vocabulary of his basal readers that he can recognize those words instantly.[8] These suggestions are concerned with (1) helping the pupil note in words certain parts that are likely to be useful in recognizing those words, (2) providing the pupil with much suitable reading

[8] There is no implication here that the pupil does not need to learn to recognize other words which he encounters in reading outside the basal readers. On the contrary, he should learn to recognize any word which has immediate and permanent value for him in the sense that it appears frequently in reading matter he will use in both the immediate and distant future. The immediate value of a word is indicated by its inclusion in such word lists as A. I. Gates, *A Reading Vocabulary for the*

matter that contains the words, and (3) using special exercises designed to help the pupil fix the word forms in mind. It is imperative for the teacher to realize that some words are much harder to learn to recognize than others, that patience will be needed when the pupil cannot recognize today a word that he seemed to know well yesterday, that some pupils will need many more contacts with a given word than other pupils will require, that all pupils will not need to use all the exercises suggested, and that the teacher is the one who must decide which exercises to use with a given pupil or group of pupils.

1. Helping the Pupil Note Useful Parts

As will be explained in Chapter 5, teaching a selection or part of a selection in a preprimer, the primer, the first reader, or a second reader in a basal series includes introducing new words which the pupil will encounter as he later reads that material.[9] Immediately after a given new word has been introduced and the pupil has unlocked it,[10] certain things should be done to call his attention to parts which can be useful to him in recognizing the word. A useful part may be the beginning letter or letters, the final letter or letters, or one or a group of ascending or descending letters within the word.

One way of pointing out useful parts is to have the pupil listen for their sounds as he looks at the word and pronounces it. For example, with the new word *mother,* which has just been introduced and unlocked, the teacher may say to pupils: "What did you tell me this word is? . . . With what letter does *mother* begin? . . . Let's say *mother* together and listen for the sound *m* stands for at the beginning. . . . With what letter does *mother* end? . . . Let's say *mother* again and listen for the sound *r* stands for at the end. . . . What two tall letters do you see together in the word? . . . Let's say *mother* once more and listen for the sound *th* stands for. . . . What do you think can help you remember the word *mother* the next time you see it?" . . .

A second way of pointing out useful parts is to have the pupil copy the word by printing or typing it on a sheet of paper. The purpose here is not to teach him the spelling of the word but rather to focus his atten-

---

Primary Grades (Teachers College, Columbia University, New York, 1935); C. R. Stone, *Progress in Primary Reading* (Webster Publishing Company, 1951), pp. 107–130; Helen Knipp, *Basic Vocabulary, Phrases, and Sentences for Early Reading Instruction* (Keystone View Company, Meadville, Pa., 1952). The best indication of the permanent value of a word is its placement in E. L. Thorndike and I. Lorge, *A Teacher's Word Book of 30,000 Words* (Teachers College, Columbia University, New York, 1944).

[9] The term *new word* is used here to refer to a word which the pupil has not yet encountered in the readers.

[10] A recommended procedure for introducing new words is presented in Chapter 5.

tion upon one or more parts. Preliminary data collected by the author show that first-grade pupils who copied the new words when they were first presented during the time a certain preprimer was being used were able to recognize more of the words later in their reading than were first-grade pupils who did not copy the words.

2. Providing Much Suitable Reading Material

Although a basal reader — each preprimer, the primer, the first reader, and each second reader — repeats several times every new word it presents, the amount of practice so provided is not sufficient to enable many pupils to learn to recognize many of those words instantly. Probably the most effective and certainly the most realistic way to offer the pupil needed additional practice is to supply him with much easy reading material which has a strong interest-pull, which he can read by himself, and which contains the new words. This material is often found in individual story books accompanying the basal reader and having a vocabulary composed entirely of words the reader has presented. Other suitable books are juveniles written for first-grade and second-grade boys and girls. These may or may not accompany the reader. Their vocabulary is made up largely of words previously presented in the reader but contains some strange words the pupil is equipped to unlock independently. The selection and use of such books is discussed in Chapter 6.

During the time that a given basal reader is being used, the teacher can and should construct pieces of reading matter for the pupil to read to himself, written in a vocabulary composed largely of words the reader has presented. This material includes experience charts, notices for the day, assignments to classroom duties, news items, weather reports, directions, announcements, questions to be answered, summaries of class discussions, rules for situations, and short stories that are not available in a form the pupil can read. The construction and use of these and other pieces of so-called homemade material is discussed in Chapter 6.

3. Using Special Exercises

A variety of special exercises can be used to help the pupil learn to recognize instantly, in and out of context, words which have been presented in the basal readers.[11] Detailed exercises appear in the manuals and the workbooks accompanying basal readers.[12]

[11] The words of greatest importance to learn to recognize out of context are among those frequently used as nouns and those used as verbs.

[12] For other illustrations and other exercises, see David Russell and Ella Karp, *Reading Aids Through the Grades* (Teachers College, Columbia University, New York, 1959).

Naming and Pointing to Words. The teacher prints individual words on the board. Then she asks the pupil to name words to which she points and to point to words which she names.

Distinguishing Words from Others Which Look Much Like Them. The teacher prints on the board a number of individual words, any one of which looks much like one or more of the others. Then she asks the pupil to name each word. If the pupil confuses two words, she prints those words one above the other and asks the pupil to point out or note the difference or differences between them.

Reading New Sentences. The pupil is asked to read a group of sentences which he has not seen before and which contains the words he needs practice on. Then the teacher raises questions to check on the pupil's comprehension of the sentences.

Building New Sentences. The teacher places on the chalk rail individual word cards with which sentences the pupil has not seen can be built. Then she asks the pupil to choose the right cards to make short sentences she speaks. As he chooses the cards, they are placed in correct order in a pocket chart. Then the pupil is asked to read the sentence.

Choosing the Right Word. The pupil is given individual printed sentences each of which contains a blank where a word is left out. Below each sentence are three words that look somewhat alike. The pupil is asked to choose the one word among the three that makes sense in the blank.

Finding the Right Word. A sheet of paper on which several different words appear a number of times is given to the pupil. Then he is directed to underline a given word and all its repetitions with a certain colored crayon, to underline another word and all its repetitions with another colored crayon, to underline a third word and all its repetitions with still another colored crayon, and so on. Usually the group of words printed on the paper includes some words not to be underlined.

Selecting the Word Named. A sheet of paper on which numbered rows of words are printed is given to the pupil. Then the teacher asks him to underline the one word she names in each row. Preferably each row should contain only words that look somewhat alike.

Fishing. A paper clip is fastened to each of several word cards, and the cards are then placed face down on a table. The pupil "fishes" for a card, using a short stick from one end of which hangs a small horseshoe magnet attached to a string. When he "catches" a card, he is expected to name the word printed on it. If he cannot do so, the card is returned to the table. This game can be played by several pupils at a time, each pupil taking his turn at "fishing."

Playing Wordo. Cards 5″ × 7½″ are cut from oak tag, and each card is marked off to contain 25 boxes, each 1″ × 1½″. Twenty-five words on which practice is needed are then printed in the boxes, but in a different order on each card. One card is given to each pupil to use in playing Wordo, a game much like Letto as described on pages 72–73. As the teacher names words one at a time, pupils use slips of paper to cover the words on their cards. The first pupil to cover all the words in any column or row without having made a mistake in recognizing those words wins the game.

Choosing Words to Answer Questions. The pupil is given a list of printed questions. Below each question are four words which look somewhat alike, but only three of them are answers to the question. The pupil is asked to draw a line under the three words that are answers.

Using a Word Wheel. A word wheel can be made by cutting a large disk from oak tag, printing on it radially from the center to the rim words on which practice is needed, drawing on the left side of a wider and heavier piece of material (to be used as a backing) a short arrow that points toward the center, and fastening the wheel and the backing together at the center by means of a large two-pronged metal pin so that the wheel can be spun. The pupil is expected to name the word to which the arrow points when the wheel stops spinning.

Choosing the Pictured Object a Word Represents. The pupil is given a group of sentences including a word on which practice is needed and accompanied by a few pictures of objects. The pupil is asked to mark the picture of the object represented by the word being checked.

Using Pictures to Answer Questions. The pupil is given a group of questions that contain words needing attention, that are accompanied by a picture, and that can be answered by *Yes* or *No* according to what the picture shows. The pupil is asked to answer each question by underlining *Yes* or *No* according to what the picture shows.

Choosing Sentences. The pupil is given a group of sentences accompanied by a picture and containing words on which practice is needed. Only one or some of the sentences tell about the picture. The pupil is expected to mark the particular sentences which do so.

Matching Pictures and Sentences. The pupil is given a number of pictures and several groups of sentences that contain words needing attention. He is then asked to match each group of sentences with the picture it tells about.

Making Judgments. The pupil is given a group of sentences containing words on which practice is needed and directing him to mark an item in an accompanying picture to show whether something suggested by the sentences is true.

Following Directions. The pupil is given a group of sentences containing words needing attention and directing him to do something, such as marking or coloring, to items in an accompanying picture.

Selecting the Right Answer. The pupil is given a picture, a question, and a few suggested answers containing words needing attention. He must choose the right answer according to what the picture shows.

Choosing Words That Answer. The pupil is given a question and suggested answers that are words needing attention. Only some of the words are correct answers. The pupil is asked to mark those.[13]

A few cautions pertaining to the use of special exercises in word recognition should be kept in mind. *First,* in recognizing individual words out of context, the pupil tends to think or utter a falling pitch at the end of each word, a voice intonation which usually he should not make in reading those words in connected discourse and which possibly encourages word-calling. Furthermore, recognizing words in connected discourse is a much more frequent and crucial need than is recognizing those words as they stand alone. Consequently, most of the practice on a word needing attention should be given in exercises which present the word in context. *Second,* to maintain the pupil's interest in working on

[13] The special exercises just described are only illustrative. Additional types appear in other professional writings. See, for example, Donald Durrell, *Improving Reading Instruction* (World Book Company, Yonkers-on-Hudson, New York, 1956), Chapter 10.

exercises, a variety of types should be used during the school year. *Third,* the exercises should be adjusted to individual needs. There is no point in having a pupil work out an exercise which presents only words he already knows well. Some pupils will need more exercises on a given group of words than will other pupils. Some exercises are more helpful to slow-learning pupils than to average or fast-learning pupils. *Fourth,* many of the exercises should be used only with words that present persistent difficulty for the pupil.

To increase the speed with which first-grade and second-grade pupils recognize words they have encountered, some teachers use commercially manufactured devices such as a tachistoscope, a reading accelerator, or the Metronoscope. A tachistoscope is simply a projector that can expose words or groups of words at different degrees of speed — as rapidly as ⅟₁₅₀ of a second — on film strips or, in some cases, on lantern slides.[14] A reading accelerator presents reading matter at a preset speed. A bar or shutter comes down a page of typed or printed matter, covering lines as it moves.[15] The Metronoscope, usable with groups of pupils, and the Junior Metronoscope, suitable for individual use, offer practice in recognizing familiar words as printed lines are exposed rapidly one after the other.[16] At present no one knows whether the practice provided by one or more of these machines is more effective in establishing skill in recognizing familiar printed words than is the practice supplied by reading many easy books which contain the words and which offer a strong interest-pull for pupils.

Notes on Initial Teaching Alphabet

During recent years the serious attention of persons much concerned with the nature of instruction in beginning reading has been attracted to a topic that is pertinent to the pupil's task in unlocking and recognizing words which are strange to him only in print. This topic is commonly known as Initial Teaching Alphabet, sometimes called augmented Roman.

Initial Teaching Alphabet — often labeled i/t/a — is simply an orthographic device proposed for use only in the beginning stage of instruction in reading. It is made up of forty-four symbols which take the place of

[14] Directions for making simple tachistoscopes that expose words and phrases on cards are given in *ibid.,* pp. 200–201.

[15] See, for example, *The S.R.A. Reading Accelerator* (Science Research Associates, Chicago, Ill.)

[16] The Metronoscope and the Junior Metronoscope are distributed by the American Optical Company, Southbridge, Massachusetts.

the twenty-six letters of the conventional English alphabet; each symbol stands for one and only one sound. Twenty-four of the symbols are duplicates of conventional English letters, fourteen look somewhat like a joining of two conventional letters, and the remaining six are more or less "new." The capital form of each of the forty-four symbols is simply an enlargement of the lower case form, and there is only one printed form for each word. The basic contribution of Initial Teaching Alphabet is said to be the eliminating of whatever confusion and frustration may arise for the pupil from the fact that in conventional English (1) each letter may be printed in two or more forms, (2) each word may be presented in two or more printed forms, (3) many sounds can be spelled in several different ways, and particularly (4) certain letters and groups of letters — notably each single vowel and each vowel combination — stand for two or more sounds. It is quite clear that Initial Teaching Alphabet itself is in no sense a system or method of instruction in beginning reading. Being merely a new array of letter forms, it could be used in printing the material to be read by the pupil as he learns under the stimulation of any system.

Initial Teaching Alphabet was constructed by Sir James Pittman, and was first widely used in 1960 in England to teach beginning reading to four- and five-year-old children. Today in the United States, it is used in kindergarten or first grade in certain schools in more than half the states, and in some quarters it is applied in working with remedial reading cases and in teaching illiterate adults to read. In general, wherever it is used in kindergarten or first-grade, the pupil learns the letter-sound association for the forty-four symbols, comes to rely on these associations as his chief if not only aid in unlocking strange words, accomplishes quite a large amount of reading of teacher-made and commercially prepared material printed in the forty-four symbols, and often, but not always, learns to write words in those symbols. At or near the beginning of the second school year the pupil turns completely to the reading of material printed in conventional English and applies to the unlocking of strange words the skill in using letter-sound associations and the insight into the nature of reading which he has acquired through his use of Initial Teaching Alphabet. Printed reports indicate that this transfer which the pupil is expected to make is not so formidable as some people have anticipated.[17]

[17] For a description of the nature and use of Initial Teaching Alphabet, see John Downing, *The Initial Teaching Alphabet Explained and Illustrated* (The Macmillan Co., New York, 1964); John Downing, "The Augmented Roman Alphabet for Learning to Read," *The Reading Teacher*, March, 1963, pp. 325–336; John Downing, "The i/t/a Reading Experiment," *The Reading Teacher*, November, 1964, pp. 105–110; and *The Story of i/t/a* and other bulletins issued and distributed by i/t/a Publications, 20 East 46th Street, New York.

The sponsors of Initial Teaching Alphabet and teachers who have experimented with it point out certain benefits attached to its use with kindergarten or first-grade pupils. One of the major advantages is the feeling of security with the letter-sound associations that it gives the pupil and the confidence that he quickly acquires in his ability to attack reading matter containing strange words. Another is the interest in reading which it enables the pupil to build soon and the large amount of voluntary and independent reading that he consequently does. A subsidiary benefit is the improvement of the pupil's interest and skill in spelling, speech, and creative writing. One would expect the correct use of any good system of instruction in beginning reading which presents only the twenty-six conventional letters rather than Initial Teaching Alphabet to produce the same benefits.

That kindergarten or first-grade pupils can begin to learn to read and read a good deal quite early with the use of Initial Teaching Alphabet is beyond question. But inherent in this use are certain highly questionable attitudes and ideas, most of which spring from an unwarranted concern about the fact that some letters and groups of letters in conventional English stand for two or more sounds. The same attitudes, by the way, apply to the use of *Words in Color*[18] and any purely phonic approach. The four statements which follow identify the most important of these questionable matters:

1. A denial of, an unwillingness to capitalize on, or at least a failure to recognize the simple fact that the pupil already knows the pronunciation of each strange word and that the only thing he does not know and needs to find out is which of the many words familiar to him in spoken form is the one represented by the strange printed form.
2. The notion that the pupil's task in unlocking a strange word consists of figuring out the pronunciation of the word and that instruction in beginning reading includes teaching him how to pronounce the words he encounters.
3. The belief that in order to unlock a strange word the pupil needs to know well each letter-sound association represented in the word, and that he should be taught to unlock each strange word by sounding it out through the use of most if not all the associations represented therein.

[18] *Words in Color* was developed by Dr. Caleb Gattegno, a British educator. It is used today in certain localities in the United States to teach beginning reading to first grade pupils, remedial cases in reading, and illiterate adults. A different color is used to stand for each of twenty vowel sounds and twenty-seven consonant sounds, regardless of the way in which the sound is spelled.

4. The notion that what the pupil could be taught profitably about letter-sound associations for vowels as a part of instruction in spelling is also what he needs to know about those associations in order to do well in beginning reading.

There are no data to show that the use of Initial Teaching Alphabet in kindergarten or first grade produces results superior in any sense to those obtained with conventional letter forms in the instructional program offered in Chapters 3, 4, 5, and 6 of this volume. Indeed, it is the author's contention that there is no need for using Initial Teaching Alphabet instead of the letter forms of conventional English if the pupil (1) understands from the very beginning that each strange word is one which makes sense with the context and which he knows well when he hears it spoken, (2) masters the letter-sound associations for the consonants and is taught to use them with the context as clues in unlocking strange words, and (3) receives about the nature and function of vowels exactly and only the instruction which this chapter has suggested.

QUESTIONS TO BE ANSWERED

1. In what one way is a strange word in reading matter prepared for first-grade or second-grade pupils strange to them? What advantages are attached to the fact that such a word is strange in only this way?

2. What is meant by the expression *unlocking a strange printed word?* What two aids does this volume recommend the pupil be taught to use in unlocking strange words? What weaknesses does it assign to other aids described?

3. Of what help in unlocking strange words is the context? Of what help are letter sounds? In unlocking a strange word in connected discourse, why do the sounds of all the letters or groups of letters in the word rarely need to be used?

4. What groups of letter-sound associations need to be taught? Which associations are assigned to the preparatory instruction? Which are to be taught during the time that basal readers are being used in the first grade? Which are to be taught while second-grade readers are being used? In what ways can too much emphasis be placed upon the teaching of letter-sound associations for vowels?

5. How can a letter-sound association be presented to pupils? What can be done to help pupils establish that association?

6. What is the technique which this volume recommends that pupils be taught to follow in unlocking strange words? How is the technique to be taught?

7. What can be done to help pupils learn to recognize familiar words instantly? How can useful parts in a printed word be pointed out? Why is the providing of much suitable reading matter which contains words pupils have encountered probably the best way to give needed practice? What can this reading matter be?

8. What cautions should be observed in using special exercises in word recognition? Why is practice in recognizing words in context preferable to practice in recognizing those words in isolation? Which of the exercises described provide practice in recognizing words in context?

MORE TO READ

Anderson, Irving, and Walter Dearborn, *The Psychology of Teaching Reading*, The Ronald Press Company, New York, 1952, Chapter 5.

Botel, Morton, *How to Teach Reading*, Follett Publishing Company, Chicago, 1962, Chapter 5.

Dechant, Emerald, *Improving the Teaching of Reading*, Prentice-Hall Inc., Englewood Cliffs, N.J., 1964, Chapters 10, 11.

Dolch, Edward, *Teaching Primary Reading*, Garrard Press, Champaign, Ill., 3rd ed., 1960, Chapters 1, 2.

Durkin, Dolores, *Phonics and the Teaching of Reading*, Teachers College, Columbia University, New York, 1962.

Durrell, Donald, *Improving Reading Instruction*, World Book Company, Yonkers-on-Hudson, N.Y., 1956, Chapter 10.

Gans, Roma, *Common Sense in Teaching Reading*, The Bobbs-Merrill Company, Inc., Indianapolis, 1963, Chapter 8.

Gray, W. S., *On Their Own in Reading*, Scott, Foresman & Company, Chicago, rev. ed., 1960.

Harris, Albert, *Effective Teaching of Reading*, David McKay Co., Inc., New York, 1962, Chapter 8.

Heilman, Arthur, *Principles and Practices of Teaching Reading*, Charles E. Merrill Books, Inc., Columbus, Ohio, 1961, Chapters 6, 7.

Hildreth, Gertrude, *Teaching Reading*, Henry Holt & Co., Inc., New York, 1962, Chapters 6, 7, 15.

Smith, Henry, and Emerald Dechant, *Psychology in Teaching Reading*, Prentice-Hall, Inc., Englewood Cliffs, N.J., 1961, Chapter 7.

Spache, George, *Toward Better Reading*, The Garrard Press, Champaign, Ill., 1963, Chapter 13.

Tinker, Miles, and Constance McCullough, *Teaching Elementary Reading*, Appleton-Century-Crofts, Inc., New York, 1962, Chapters 3, 4, 5.

Yoakam, Gerald, *Basal Reading Instruction*, McGraw-Hill Book Co., Inc., New York, 1955, Chapter 8.

THINGS TO DO

1. Examine the teacher's edition of a basal primer, a first reader, or a second reader to get the answer to one or more of the following questions:
   a. What letter-sound associations are to be taught during the time that the reader is being used?
   b. What different aids for unlocking strange words are pupils to be taught to use?
   c. What technique, if any, for unlocking strange words are pupils to be taught to follow?
   d. What suggestions are provided for giving pupils practice needed for learning to recognize familiar words instantly?

2. Write directions, including statements and questions to be spoken aloud to pupils, for presenting the letter-sound association for one of the following:
   a. An ending you choose.
   b. A single vowel or vowel combination you choose.
   c. A syllable you choose.

3. Assume that your first-grade pupils have learned the letter-sound associations for consonants and vowels and that in a selection the pupils read today the word *pan* appeared as a new word. Write directions for a substitution exercise that could be used with that word to give pupils practice in fixing the letter-sound associations in mind and learning to use them in some position other than the beginning of words. Since you have no way of knowing what words the pupils would have learned to recognize, you must assume that each word made in the exercise will be new to them.

4. In the back of a basal first reader or second reader examine the list of words presented in that book. Find out how many of those words could be unlocked by a pupil who follows the procedure of looking for short familiar words in strange words. Assume that any short word you find will be familiar to the pupil.

5. Draw general configurations for the words listed in the back of a primer. Then decide how many of those configurations are so different from others that they could be used as a reliable aid in either unlocking or recognizing the words in context.

6. Read thoroughly what is said about developing independence in unlocking and recognizing printed words in one of the references listed above. Then write out statements which contrast the point of view presented in that reference with the point of view given in this chapter.

chapter 5

Using First-Grade and Second-Grade Basal Readers

As stated at the beginning of Chapter 4, the instruction which this volume proposes for the first two grades in reading itself is to be initiated just as soon as the preparatory work has been completed. That instruction is to be carried on through the effective use of (1) first-grade and second-grade readers that are parts of a series of basal readers, (2) suitable individual books, magazines, and newspapers, and (3) pieces of reading matter prepared by the teacher. It is the purpose of this chapter to describe the effective use of the first-grade and second-grade basal readers. The use of the other material will be discussed in Chapter Six.

No part of the foregoing paragraph implies that all first-grade and second-grade teachers must use basal readers in order to provide their pupils with the needed instruction in reading. It is conceivable that even from the very beginning in the first grade a skillful teacher could do quite an acceptable job under a plan of individualized reading. This would mean that at any given time each pupil could use instead of a basal reader a book of his choice that he could actually read and that might or might not be the same as the book being used by some other pupil; all pupils would be stimulated to develop an interest in reading a variety of material; each pupil could progress at his own rate and work on only his own deficiencies; and all kinds of individual differences would be cared for adequately.[1] Under the best instruction by means of individualized reading, the teacher (1) is fully aware of what constitutes the teaching of reading in the first and second grades, (2) has clearly in mind the skills that can and should be taught, (3) possesses control of effective ways of teaching those skills, (4) is in a position to do much of this teaching individually, (5) is able to select and make available to pupils a wide variety of books which they can read and with which she is thoroughly familiar, and (6) has the time and willingness to undertake the work in which parents of her twenty or more pupils would engage if each parent used a different book to teach his youngster to read. Although the time may come when the conditions just mentioned exist in most schools, certainly such is not yet the case. It is chiefly for this reason that the instruction proposed in this volume includes the use of basal readers.

What the Basal Materials Are

The basal materials are (1) the readers, which are to be read by the pupil, (2) the teacher's guides, which program the instruction to be carried on by the teacher while the readers are being used, (3) the workbooks, which provide the pupil with practice on skills being taught, and (4) the supplementary equipment, which is to be used by the teacher in providing the instruction.

The readers are the first preprimer, the second preprimer, the third preprimer, the primer, the first reader, the first second-grade reader, and the second second-grade reader. They are parts of a series of basal readers and are to be read in the order indicated. Each preprimer contains several short stories or episodes. The primer, the first reader, and each second-grade reader contains a number of stories and may or may not include a few poems and one or more informative selections. Other features of these books will be noted later in the chapter.

A teacher's guide accompanies each reader. Among other things, that guide should (1) offer definite suggestions for handling each selection in the reader and (2) provide in periodic installments a detailed description of the instruction which needs to be carried on while the reader is being used and which is directed at helping the pupil acquire the power to read independently. Usually the suggestions for handling each selection pertain to the teacher's presentation of the selection to the pupil, the

[1] For a description of individualized reading, see Walter Barbe, *Educator's Guide to Personalized Reading Instruction* (Prentice-Hall, Inc., Englewood Cliffs, N.J., 1961); Jeannette Veach, *Individualizing Your Reading Program* (G. P. Putnam's Sons, New York, 1959); and Helen Darrow and V. M. Howes, *Approaches to Individualized Reading* (Appleton-Century-Crofts, New York, 1960).

introduction to the pupil of new words he will encounter in the selection, the provision for him to read the selection silently, the use of questions and statements to foster a discussion of the selection, and the stimulation of the pupil to do whatever oral reading of the selection could be profitable for him. The description of the instruction to be carried on identifies the skills to be taught, arranges the teaching of those skills in a suitable sequence, explains in detail effective procedures to be used in doing the teaching, provides exercises needed for helping the pupil establish the skills, and offers exercises for use in caring for individual differences. A more detailed statement of items appearing in such a description is presented later in this chapter.

Usually the basal materials include one workbook for the preprimers and one for each of the four remaining readers. Each workbook, to be used by the pupil along with the reader it accompanies, is composed of (1) an array of exercises providing practice on skills that have been introduced in the reader or through the instruction programmed in the teacher's guide and (2) perhaps occasional comprehension tests. If each exercise is used by the pupil after the skill with which it is concerned has been introduced, and if the teacher carefully checks the pupil's responses in the exercise and makes sure that he understands why a mistake he has made is a mistake, the workbook can be of considerable value. It locates the pupil's deficiencies, helps him acquire needed skills, and relieves some of the weaknesses of group instruction.

The supplementary equipment includes such items as word cards, a pocket chart, tests, film strips, and perhaps a big book which presents on large pages the first thirty-two pages or so of the first preprimer. Each item may be used by the teacher in providing the instruction scheduled in the teacher's guides, as will be noted later in the chapter.

In using basal materials, the big job of the teacher is to carry on the instruction which is directed at helping the pupil acquire the power to read independently and which is programmed in the teacher's guides. This instruction consists largely but not entirely in (1) teaching certain letter-sound associations, (2) teaching the technique to be used in unlocking strange printed words, (3) providing practice needed for learning to recognize familiar printed words instantly, and (4) stimulating the pupil to think, as he looks at printed lines, the voice intonations required for understanding what those lines mean. Unfortunately a few first-grade and second-grade teachers tend to skip the instruction just mentioned. Their use of basal materials, they feel, needs to consist merely in introducing to the pupil the selections in the reader, telling him what each new word is, having him read the selections silently and perhaps orally, talking over the selections with the pupil, and possibly giving him comprehension exercises on the content of the selections. The same teachers tend to measure their success in teaching by the number of books the pupil reads, regardless of how he gets the reading done, and they often fret about whether a given group of pupils at a given time will be as far along in the readers as a similar group was at the same time the preceding year. It would be much more to the point if these teachers measured their success by the degree of power to read independently which the pupil has developed up to a given time and if, in order to give the basal materials a reasonable chance to yield the best results possible, they would carry on the instruction programmed in the teacher's guides.

Choosing the Preprimers

The first preprimer, the second preprimer, and the third preprimer should be chosen with considerable care. Four important points are to be emphasized:

1. Each selection should possess an interest-pull so strong that the pupil will want to read the next page to see what happens and will want to finish the selection to see how things turn out. Probably it should be a story which, like any good story that has been told or read to the pupil, presents a problematic situation the pupil can sense, gives hints of how things may turn out but maintains suspense, and provides a solution which may or may not be a surprise to the pupil. The accompanying pictures will show the events or action of the story, and the lines of print will represent what the story characters say to one another. Unfortunately, many selections in some preprimers are so barren in interest-pull that no sane person would choose one of them to read to a young child who asks for a story, they cannot provide the satisfaction which the pupil has been hoping he would get when he begins to read, the pupil's reading itself consists largely of the mere matching of printed forms with the familiar spoken words the forms stand for, and the content contributes little if anything to the pupil's acquisition of an abiding interest in reading.

2. The content of each selection should be familiar to the pupil in the sense that it deals only with ideas or concepts which he has acquired. This does not mean that each selection should be one which has been read to the pupil or which tells him only things he already knows. It insists merely that the printed lines present content for which the pupil can make correct meaning.

3. Each selection must possess substance that makes the selection worth reading in its own right. There is simply no place for the inane, banal,

and insipid *Tom can see the dog. Can Dick see the dog?* type of content that characterizes some preprimers.

4. To help the pupil learn early that his reading matter stands for talk — simply the language that for years he has been speaking and has been understanding in his listening — the text should possess certain characteristics of his familiar spoken English. *First,* each word should be one which is included in his speaking vocabulary or his listening vocabulary, and it should be used with a meaning he already knows. *Second,* each line should be one which he would understand readily if someone said it to him. *Third,* each expression should be natural talk in the sense that it is something people would say in the situation depicted. *Finally,* each page, without using quotation marks and such expressions as *said Fred,* should be so constructed that the pupil all by himself can know readily which story character is saying a given line or group of lines.

Of course other points should be considered. Each word included in a preprimer should have both immediate and permanent value for the pupil in that it appears frequently in printed matter he will be reading soon and in various types of material he will read later. To insure that the pupil will get a reasonable amount of reading done with relative ease on each page in a preprimer, the number of new words on a page should be low,[2] and some pages should present no new words. Several repetitions of each word should be provided here and there in various settings so that the pupil can practice learning to recognize the word, but such repetitions must not produce the unnatural language found in some preprimers. The pictures in a preprimer should possess unquestionable art quality, present objects and persons in realistic colors and forms, and stimulate the pupil to read the accompanying printed lines. The binding should be sufficiently strong to withstand rough handling, the cover should be attractive in color and design, and the pages should be white, nonglossy, opaque, and big enough to permit a generous use of pictures. A satisfactory size of type is 16 point.

The Grouping of Pupils

To determine the reading status of pupils at the beginning of a school year, the first-grade teacher may give her class a test similar to that described on pages 84–86 in Chapter 3. In addition, she should digest

---

[2] The preparatory instruction described in Chapter 3 and the teacher's introducing of new words as illustrated later in the present chapter equip the pupil with considerable control of the technique to be followed in unlocking strange printed words independently. As will be explained in Chapter 6, the pupil's acquisition of this

whatever appropriate information she can get from the pupils' previous school records, if any, from statements made by parents, and from pupils' attempt to read preprimer material. By means of such a simple survey, she may find her class to be made up of one or more of the following:

1. Pupils who have had some experience in actual reading in the kindergarten, at home, or elsewhere.
2. Pupils who have learned to a satisfactory degree what the preparatory instruction described in Chapter 3 purports to teach but who have not yet begun to read.
3. Pupils who have accomplished some but not a satisfactory amount of the learning offered by the preparatory instruction.
4. English-speaking pupils who have had none of the preparatory instruction.
5. Pupils who do not yet understand spoken English to the degree needed for undertaking the learning offered by the preparatory instruction.

Some of the pupils who have had experience in reading will have been through the preparatory instruction in the kindergarten and will now have some control of the technique to be followed in unlocking strange words. They may be grouped together and given suitable instruction through the use of a preprimer, the primer, or the first reader, whichever fits best their present level of reading ability. Other pupils who have had experience in reading will be able to read only passages which are composed entirely of the words they already know in print; they will not know letter-sound associations for consonants and they will have no control of the technique mentioned above. Such pupils may be grouped together for the preparatory instruction and at the same time may be supplied with books which, because the text is composed of only familiar printed words, they can read on their own.

Pupils who have learned to a satisfactory degree what the preparatory instruction offers but who have not yet begun to read may be grouped together, and for them beginning instruction in reading should be initiated immediately. It can be provided through the correct use of the first preprimer, the second preprimer, and the third preprimer, with their accompanying materials, in the order indicated.

Pupils who have not yet learned enough of what the preparatory instruction offers may be grouped together and given first the parts of that

---

control suggests that new standards should be used in deciding what makes a word new and in judging the difficulty of the vocabulary of a passage. There may no longer be any need to hold to the thirty-year-old custom of permitting the use of only one so-called new word per page.

instruction that will equip them with the particular items they have not yet learned. Immediately following the completion of this work, the teaching of reading itself should be initiated, through the correct use of the preprimers and their accompanying materials in the proper order.

Pupils who have had none of the preparatory instruction may be grouped together and given all of that instruction, regardless of the amount of time required. When this teaching has been completed, the use of the preprimers and their accompanying materials in the proper order should begin.

Pupils who do not yet understand spoken English should first be given instruction which will equip them with that skill. Then the preparatory instruction should be undertaken and completed, followed by the use of the preprimers and their accompanying materials.

Probably most entering first-grade classes will consist only of (1) pupils who have learned to a satisfactory degree what the preparatory instruction offers and who may be grouped together to receive immediately instruction in reading itself, (2) pupils who have learned some but not enough of what the preparatory instruction offers, who may be grouped together to receive the further preparatory instruction needed, and who, upon completion of that work, should be introduced immediately to instruction in reading, and (3) pupils who have had none of the preparatory instruction, who may be grouped together to receive that instruction, and who, upon completion of this work, should be introduced immediately to instruction in reading. It is imperative, however, that the teacher keep in mind at least two important points about all grouping of pupils. *First*, since there will be within each group wide individual differences in the sense that different pupils will need different amounts of instruction and practice on almost any given item, the teacher will have to discover the particular abilities and deficiencies of each pupil and provide him with the appropriate instruction. *Second*, since the pupils within any one group will progress at different rates rather than move along in unison as they acquire the power to read independently, the groups should be kept elastic so that a given pupil may be transferred from one group to another when his achievement and needs indicate that such transfer will be profitable for him.

Using the Preprimers

In approximately forty-eight or sixty-four pages, each preprimer offers a number of short stories. As proposed by the teacher's guide, the work to be done by the teacher in connection with the use of part or all of each selection is concerned with at least (1) introducing the selection to the pupil, (2) having him read the selection and take part in a discussion of its content, and (3) giving him practice in appropriate reading skills. To illustrate the carrying on of this work with a given group of pupils, the following discussion presents first a brief description of the first six pages, pages 39–44, of a story in a hypothetical first preprimer and then a somewhat detailed explanation of the jobs to be done in connection with them. The explanation is presented under the purely arbitrary headings "Getting Ready to Read," "Reading and Talking," and "Practicing Reading Skills."

The first page of the story, page 39, in the hypothetical preprimer is the title page. In the picture, Tom and Mary, characters in previous stories, are close to the back porch of a house and are tugging at the padlocked lid of a small tin box. The box lies just in front of latticework which extends down from the bottom of the porch floor to within six inches of the ground. A garden rake lies nearby. The one line of text on the page is the title of the story, stands for something the author of the story is saying to the pupil, and contains no words which the pupil has not encountered so far in his reading of the preprimer. That line is as follows:

What Is in the Box?

The big picture on page 40 shows Tom on his hands and knees, looking through the latticework. Mary stands nearby, talking to him. In a smaller picture at the right and near the bottom of the page, Tom and Mary are in much the same position, but Tom is looking up at Mary and talking to her. The lines of text contain the one new word *reach* and are as follows:

Can you get the ball, Tom?
Can you get it?

The ball is here, Mary.
I can not reach it.

The big picture on page 41 shows Tom sitting on the ground in front of the latticework looking up at Mary, who is handing him a rake and talking to him. In the small picture, Tom has the rake in hand, is pointing under the porch, and is looking at Mary and talking to her. The lines of text include the one new word *rake* and are as follows:

Here is the rake.
Can you reach the ball with it?

I will get it with the rake.
You will see.

In the one picture on page 42, Tom has pulled the rake from under the porch, bringing the ball with it. Tom is pointing to the ball and is talking to Mary, who stands nearby. On the ground just under the latticework is the small padlocked tin box, unnoticed by Tom and Mary. The lines of text include the one new word *Ben* and are:

> Here is the ball, Mary.
> Now you can play with it.
> Ben can play ball, too.
> Get Ben to play with you.

The one picture on page 43 shows Mary bending down and pointing to the box under the latticework. Tom is standing nearby, looking at Mary as she talks. The lines of text include the one new word *open* and are:

> Look, Tom!
> Here is a box!
> The box is not open.
> What is in it?

The big picture on page 44 shows Tom and Mary kneeling on the ground with their hands on the box. Mary is looking at Tom and talking to him. In the smaller picture, Tom has started to walk away, but has turned to talk to Mary, who is still kneeling over the box as she looks at him. The text includes the one new word *hurry* and is as follows:

> Open the box, Tom!
> Open it! Hurry!
> I want to see what is in it.
>
> I will hurry.
> We will get the box open, Mary.
> We will see what is in it.

1. Getting Ready to Read

The work that the teacher needs to do before her pupils start to read a selection or part of a selection in a preprimer consists usually in (a) providing the pupils with the slight motivation needed for *beginning* to read the selection and (b) introducing the new words they will encounter in their reading of the selection. At times these two tasks are interwoven and can be performed simultaneously. Usually they are to be carried on separately, in either order.

If the material to be read is an entire story or the first part of a story, arousal of interest in beginning to read the selection can be initiated merely by the teacher's directing the pupils' attention to the title of the story, to what is happening in the first one or two pictures, and to a consideration of what the story may be about and what may happen. If the material to be read is another part of a story, interest may be stimulated through the use of statements and questions which help the pupils recall main events that have happened so far in the story and which will enable them to think of what may happen next or how the story might end. In either case, the teacher should remember that her efforts are directed at stimulating the pupils just to begin their reading. There is little if anything she can do to help them build a sustained interest which equals the lasting motivation inherent in the reading of the story itself, and only a minimum amount of time is required to develop the slight motivation the pupils need for beginning to read the selection. Such preliminary activities as having pupils tell of experiences which could be related to those portrayed in the story, having them collect, display, and talk about pictures of events similar to those presented by the story, and trying to help them build a background which is needed for reading the selection with adequate meaning but which they certainly already possess are likely to waste time more profitably spent in actually reading the selection.

The following paragraph presents statements and questions the teacher could use to provide the motivation pupils need for beginning to read the six preprimer pages described on pages 144–145:

> Open your books to this page I am showing you. It is page 39. . . . Here is the beginning of a story we will start to read today. You know the boy and girl in the picture. Who are they? . . . What are Tom and Mary doing? . . . Where do you think they could have found that box? . . . The line of print on this page is the name of the story. It is something that the person who wrote the story is saying to you. You know all these words. What is the name of the story? . . . What do you think the story could be about? . . . What do you think could be in the box? . . . Maybe we'll find out what the answer is as we read the story. Close your books now. We need to find out what the new words in the story are.

Why does the teacher need to introduce the new words before the pupils begin to read a given selection? So that they will know what the words are when they meet them in the selection and presumably thereby can get it read? Probably that is a laudable reason, but certainly it is not the most important one. The significant reason is simply this: It is through the using of correct directional statements and penetrating questions in introducing new words that the teacher can best equip pupils with the definite, economical, and effective technique to be followed in unlocking strange printed words. As stated previously, the technique is that of using first and together the context and the beginning sound of the word and then only as many of the remaining letter sounds as are needed for making sure of the word.

Using as examples the five new words — *reach, rake, hurry, open, Ben* — that appear on the preprimer pages described on pages 144–145, the material which follows this paragraph illustrates good procedure for introducing new words to pupils who have learned the twenty-two letter-sound associations taught through the preparatory instruction. Because, as proposed in Chapter 4, introducing new words in the first and second grades includes checking and presenting letter-sound associations other than the twenty-two taught as part of the preparatory instruction, and because the associations for long *o* and for *y* as in *pretty* have not yet been taught in the use of the hypothetical preprimer, the introducing of *open* and *hurry* include at the beginning the checking and the presenting of those associations. Three dots indicate that the teacher should pause there to wait for pupils to think or to respond orally. Occasional parentheses enclose responses which may be expected from pupils.

Print the following lines on the board or use word cards to build them in pocket chart:

> The box is too high.
> I can not reach it.

Point to *reach*. Say: "Here is a word we will meet in our story. Let's find out what it is. With what letter does the word begin? . . . You know the sound that *r* stands for. What other letters in the word do you know the sound for? . . . Read the lines to yourself. Think of a word that makes sense here and begins with the sound *r* stands for. Use the other letter sound you know to make sure of the word. . . . What is the word? . . . How do you know it isn't *rich*? Betty? . . . (*Rich* doesn't make sense with the other words.) How do you know it isn't *touch*? Joe? . . . (*Touch* doesn't begin with the sound *r* stands for.) How do you know it isn't *read*? Ann? . . . (*Read* doesn't end with the sound *ch* stands for.) Who will read the lines aloud for us? . . ."

Point to *reach*. "What is this word? . . . Let's say *reach* together and listen for the sound *r* stands for at the beginning. . . . Let's say *reach* again and listen for the sound *ch* stands for at the end. . . ."

Print the following lines on the board or use word cards to build them in the pocket chart:

> I can help you in the yard.
> I can rake it.

Point to *rake*. Say: "Here is another word you may not know, but you can find out what it is. With what letter does the word begin? . . . You know the sound that *r* stands for. What other letter in the word do you know the sound for? . . . Read the lines to yourself. Think of a word that makes sense here and begins with the sound *r* stands for. Use the other letter sound you know to make sure of the word. . . . What is the word? . . . How do you know it isn't *rock*? Ben? . . . (*Rock* doesn't make sense with the other words.) How do you know it isn't *mow*? Helen? . . . (*Mow* doesn't begin with the sound *r* stands for; *mow* doesn't end with the sound *k* stands for.) Who will read the lines aloud for us? . . ."

Point to *rake*. "What is this word? . . . Let's say the word together and listen for the sound *r* stands for at the beginning. . . . Let's say *rake* again and listen for the sound *k* stands for at the end. . . ."

Print the following line on the board or use word cards to build it in the pocket chart:

Tom will play ball with Ben.

Point to *Ben*. Say: "This word is the name of a boy in the story. With what letter does it begin? . . . You know the sound that *B* stands for. What other letter in the word do you know the sound for? . . . What word do you know that is a name of a boy, begins with the sound *B* stands for, and ends with the sound *n* stands for? . . . What is the word? . . . How do you know it isn't *Bun*? Dick? . . . (*Bun* isn't a name for a boy.) How do you know it isn't *Don*? Sue? . . . (*Don* doesn't begin with the sound *B* stands for.) Who will read the line aloud for us? . . ."

Point to *Ben*. "What is this word? . . . Let's say *Ben* together and listen for the sound *B* stands for at the beginning. . . . Let's say *Ben* again and listen for the sound *n* stands for at the end. . . ."

Print the following lines on the board or use word cards to build them in the pocket chart:

It is too hot in here.
Open the door, Tom.

Print on the board also the following columns of numbered words:

1. ever   1. omit
2. over   2. admit
3. aver   3. edit

Point to the first column. Say: "Look at the three numbered words in this column. Think which word begins with the same sound as *only* and *obey*. . . . What is the number of the word that begins with the same sound as *only* and *obey*? . . ." Point to the second column. "Look at the three numbered words in this column. Think which word begins with the same sound as *ocean* and *old*. . . . What is the number of the word that begins with the same sound as *ocean* and *old*? . . ."

If pupils did not answer correctly both questions in the preceding paragraph, point to *open* in the sentence on the board. "With what letter does this word begin? . . . That *o* stands for the sound you hear at the beginning of *only, obey, ocean,* and *old.* It is a sound the letter *o* sometimes stands for, and it is the same as the name of the letter. We call it the long sound of *o.*" If pupils did answer correctly the two questions in the preceding paragraph, omit this step and proceed with the next paragraph.

Point to *open* in the sentence on the board. "Let's find out what this word is. With what letter does it begin? . . . You know a sound that *o* stands for. What other letters in the word do you know sounds for? . . . Read the lines to yourself. Think of a word that makes sense here and begins with a sound *o* stands for. . . . Use other letter sounds you know to make sure of the word. . . . What is the word? . . . How do you know it isn't *own*? Sally? . . . (*Own* doesn't make sense with the other words.) How do you know it isn't *shut*? Ben? . . . (*Shut* doesn't begin like *over* and *only*.) Who will read the lines aloud for us? . . ."

Point to *open*. "What is this word? . . . Let's say *open* together and listen for the sound *n* stands for at the end. . . . Let's say *open* again and listen for the sound *p* stands for. . . ."

Print the following lines on the board or use word cards to build them in the pocket chart:

> I can not play now.
> I am in a hurry to get home.

Print on the board also the following columns of numbered words:

1. handle	1. counter
2. handsome	2. county
3. handy	3. countless

Point to the first column. Say: "Look at the three numbered words in this column. Think which word ends with the same sound as *pretty* and *sticky*. . . . What is the number of the word that ends with the same sound as *pretty* and *sticky*? . . ." Point to the second column. "Look at the three numbered words in this column. . . . Which word ends with the same sound as *funny* and *beauty*? . . ."

If pupils did not answer correctly both questions in the preceding paragraph, point to *hurry* in the sentence on the board. "With what letter does this word end? . . . That *y* stands for the sound you hear at the end of *pretty, sticky, funny,* and *beauty.* It is a sound that *y* often stands for at the end of a word." If pupils did answer correctly the two questions in the preceding paragraph, omit this step and proceed with the next paragraph.

Point to *hurry* in the sentence on the board. "Let's find out what this word is. With what letter does the word begin? . . . You know the sound that *h* stands for. What other letters in the word do you know sounds for? . . . Read the lines to yourself. Think of a word that makes sense here and begins with the sound *h* stands for. Use other letter sounds you know to make sure of the word. . . . What is the word? . . . How do you know it isn't *honey*? Tom? . . . (*Honey* doesn't make sense with the other words.) How do you know it isn't *rush*? Mary? . . . (*Rush* doesn't begin with the sound *h* stands for.) Who will read the lines aloud for us? . . ."

Point to *hurry*. "What is this word? . . . Let's say *hurry* together and listen for the sound *h* stands for at the beginning. . . . Let's say *hurry* once more and listen for the sound *r* stands for. . . . Let's say *hurry* again and listen for the sound *y* stands for at the end. . . ."

A perusal of the preceding introductions of five words shows that in introducing a new word the teacher takes certain definite steps. In order, these steps, in addition to the occasional checking and presenting of a letter-sound association which has not yet been taught, are as follows:

a. Presenting the new word in context and merely pointing out that word to the pupils.

b. Asking questions which call pupils' attention to the beginning sound of the word and to other familiar sounds in the word.

c. Making statements which give pupils directions to follow in unlocking the word.

d. Asking pupils to name the new word and to tell how they know it is not some other word.

e. Asking pupils to read the new word aloud in the context in which it is presented.

f. Having pupils listen for the sounds of certain letters in the new word as they look at and say the word.

Certain matters not apparent in this listing should now be made clear. *First,* the contexts in which new words are presented (a) must be composed only of words which the pupils already know well in spoken form if not in print, (b) should be constructed in such a way that in a number of word introductions the new words appear in different positions in the contexts, (c) must be natural language, and (d) must be weak enough so that in any given case the context itself suggests at least two possibilities for the new word and makes it necessary for pupils to use letter sounds in unlocking it. During the time that the first half or so of the first preprimer is being used, and indeed occasionally while the subsequent preprimers are being read, the context used in presenting a new word must be read aloud by the teacher, simply because the pupils will not yet have enough words in their reading vocabulary to make suitable printed context they can read to themselves. In such case the new word may have to be the last word in what the teacher says, and the procedure she uses will vary somewhat from that given on page 147 for introducing the new words *reach* and *rake*. A description of one good procedure to use in introducing a word in spoken context is as follows:

Print the following lines on the board:

> Billy could not get the kite out of the tree.
> It was higher than he could reach.

Point to *reach*. Say: "Here is a word we will need to know when we read our story. Let's find out what it is. With what letter does it begin? . . . You know the sound that *r* stands for. What other letters in the word do you know a sound for? . . . I am going to read aloud all the words in these two lines except this last one. When I stop, think of a word that makes sense here and begins with the sound *r* stands for. Use the other letter sound you know to make sure of the word. Listen: Billy could not get the kite out of the tree. It was higher than he could _____. . . . What is the word? . . . How do you know it isn't *rich?* Bobby? . . . (*Rich* doesn't make sense with the other words.) How do you know it isn't *climb?* Ann? . . . (*Climb* doesn't begin with the sound *r* stands for.)"

Point to *reach*. "What is this word? . . . Let's say *reach* together and listen for the sound *r* stands for at the beginning. . . . Let's say *reach* again and listen for the sound *ch* stands for at the end. . . ."

Second, if a word begins with a letter or group of letters for which the needed letter-sound association has not been but needs to be taught, the checking and presenting of that association can be made a preliminary step in the introduction of the word. This procedure was illustrated in the introduction of *open* on page 148. If a word beginning with a letter or group of letters for which the letter-sound association has been taught ends with or contains in a medial position a letter or group of letters for which the needed letter-sound association has not been presented, the checking and presenting of that association can be made a preliminary step in the introduction of the word. This was illustrated in the introduction of *hurry* on page 148. If a word beginning with a letter or group of letters for which the letter-sound association has been taught ends with and contains in a medial position a letter or group of letters for which the needed letter-sound association has not been presented, the checking and presenting of one of those associations can be a preliminary step in the introduction of the word.

Third, asking pupils to note consonant sounds in the word other than the beginning sound should not be omitted. It encourages them to get into the habit of using these letter sounds in addition to the beginning sound of the word in unlocking strange words.

Fourth, the statements which give directions for unlocking the new words must be used persistently. It is the teacher's making of these statements and the pupils' following of the directions the statements give which teach the technique to be followed in unlocking strange words.

Fifth, the questions asking the pupils to tell how they know the new word is not some other word are also quite important. They make pupils aware of just how the context can help them, how letter sounds can help them, and how easy it is to make mistakes if they do not use these two aids together. One of the questions should propose a word that begins with the right sound but does not make sense, another should propose a word that makes sense but does not begin with the right sound, and a third a word that makes sense, begins with the right sound, but ends with a wrong sound. If possible, and after letter-sound associations for at least some vowels have been taught, a fourth question may suggest a word that makes sense, begins with the right sound, ends with the right sound, but has within it a wrong sound, whether for a consonant or for a vowel. Any word proposed by a question must be one which the pupils know in spoken form but do not know in printed form.

Sixth, after pupils have unlocked the new word, the teacher asks one or more of them to read the context sentences aloud. This provides a bit of initial practice in recognizing the word in ordinary reading matter.

Seventh, although asking pupils to listen for certain letter sounds as they look at the new word and say it is not part of the actual introduction of that word, it can point out to pupils certain characteristics of the word which may help them in their later recognition of the word. Probably those sounds should include the beginning sound, the final sound, and, if appropriate, the sound of ascending or descending letters within the word.

Eighth, since context is of no aid in unlocking some proper nouns, pupils should not be asked to use this aid here. They are led instead to depend upon letter sounds alone and perhaps an occasional helpful statement such as *This word is the name of a boy* or *This word is the name of a town.* However, the new word is presented in context for one or more pupils to read aloud after it has been unlocked.

Ninth, in order for pupils to make rapid growth in acquiring the technique to be followed in unlocking strange words, every new word in the three preprimers — even the very first word in the first preprimer — should be introduced according to procedures described in the foregoing discussion. As will be explained later, only some of the new words appearing in any given selection in the primer and the first reader will need to be introduced before pupils begin to read that selection.

2. Reading and Talking

Once the pupils have been motivated to begin reading a given selection or part of a selection in a preprimer and the new words have been introduced, the reading should be undertaken immediately. Usually activities here may be organized into three simple steps, in which pupils (a) note the events shown by the pictures and read the accompanying printed lines silently, (b) discuss what the pages say, and (c) read the lines orally. Although the teacher may have her pupils do all three of these things with one page before moving to the next, such procedure is not necessary in working with a group of what are commonly called "faster" pupils. Quite possibly the latter may first read silently a small number of pages at the end of which is a break in the story, then talk over what they have read, and go on to the oral reading of the pages.

The following material, covering one at a time the last five of the six preprimer pages described on pages 144–145, illustrates the work mentioned above. Presumably presentation of the title page of the preprimer story, as given on page 144, has been completed.

Page 40

Silent Reading. Show and point to page 40 in the preprimer. Say: "Open your books to this page. It is page 40. Now we will begin to read our story. Look at the big picture. What is Tom doing? . . . What do you think he could be looking for? . . . Is Mary talking to Tom? . . . How do you know? . . . Now look at the small picture. Is Tom talking to Mary? . . . What could he be telling her? . . . You'll find out soon what he is saying. Read all the lines on the page to yourself. Think how they sounded when Tom and Mary talked. Find out what Tom's trouble is. . . ."

Talking. "What was Tom looking for? Joe? . . . Why couldn't he get the ball? Ann? . . . How do you think the ball got under the porch? Bob? . . . How do you think Tom could get the ball? Martha? . . ."

Oral Reading. "Now read aloud the lines that tell what Mary said to Tom. Make the lines sound just the way you think they did when Mary said them. Betty? . . . Will you read the same lines, Jerry? Read them just as you would say them. . . . Now read what Tom said. Try to make us hear him talking. Mark? . . . Will you read the same lines, Sue? . . . Now turn to page 41. . . ."

Page 41

Silent Reading. "Look at the big picture. What is Mary doing? . . . What do you think Tom will do with the rake? . . . Who is doing the talking in this picture? . . . How do you know? . . . Look at the small picture. What is happening there? . . . Is Tom talking to Mary? . . . Read all the lines on the page to yourself. Think how they sounded when Mary and Tom talked. Find out whether Tom thought he could get the ball with the rake. . . ."

Talking. "Why did Mary hand Tom the rake? Alice? . . . Did Tom think he could get the ball with the rake? Jerry? . . . What else might Tom use to try to get the ball? Ben? . . ."

Oral Reading. "Read aloud the lines that tell what Mary said to Tom. Make them sound just the way you think they did when Mary said them. Bert? . . . Now read what Tom said. Make the lines talk. Billy? . . . Let's hear you read the same lines, Sue. . . . Turn to page 42. . . ."

Page 42

Silent Reading. "What is happening in this picture? . . . Who do you think is doing the talking? . . . How do you know? . . . Can you tell whether Tom or Mary has seen the box yet . . . Read all the lines to yourself. Think how they sounded when Tom said them. Find out whether Tom is going to play ball with Mary. . . ."

Talking. "Is Tom going to play ball with Mary? Joe? . . . How do you know? . . . Who might Ben be? Alice? . . . Who do you think will see the box first? Jerry? . . ."

Oral Reading. "Read all the lines aloud. Make them sound just as you think they did when Tom said them. Mark? . . . Will you read the same lines. Read them just as you would say them. Betty? . . . Turn to page 43. . . ."

Page 43

Silent Reading. "Look at the picture. What has Mary found? . . . How do you think she feels? . . . Who is doing the talking on this page? . . . Read the lines to yourself. Think how they sounded when Mary said them. . . ."

Talking. "Is the box still locked? Billy? . . . How would you open that box? Sally? . . ."

Oral Reading. "Will you read all the lines aloud? Remember that Mary is excited. Read the lines just as you would say them if you were excited. Betty? . . . You read the same lines, Bobby. . . . Turn to page 44. . . ."

Page 44

Silent Reading. "Look at the big picture. What do you think Tom and Mary want to do? . . . Is Mary talking to Tom? . . . Look at the small picture. Where do you suppose Tom is going? . . . Is Tom talking to Mary? . . . Read the lines to yourself. Think how they sounded when Tom and Mary talked. . . ."

Talking. "What does Mary want Tom to do? Tom? . . . Why do you think that Mary is in such a hurry? Sue? . . . What do you think Tom is going to do? Ben? . . ."

Oral Reading. "Read aloud what Mary said to Tom. Read the lines just the way you would say them if you were Mary. Martha? . . . Will you read the same lines, Betty? . . . Now read aloud the lines that tell what Tom said. Read them so that you will show just what Tom meant. Jerry? . . .

Will you read the same lines, Sue? . . . How do you think Tom will get the box open? Ben? . . . We'll find out about that when we read the next part of the story."

Several important points relative to the work just described need to be emphasized. *First,* since the pictures in a preprimer story tell the events or action of the story and provide much of the setting in which the story characters speak the lines of the printed text, it is usually essential that pupils "read" at least the main picture on a given page before they read the accompanying lines. This "reading" consists in noting what is happening rather than merely deciding what objects, characters, or locale are shown. The questions given under "Silent Reading" for each of the five preprimer pages referred to in the foregoing material are intended to stimulate pupils' reading of the picture or pictures on that page and to help them see there what they need to see in order to follow the action of the story.

Second, although it is possible for the teacher to set a purpose for the pupils' silent reading of a given page or group of pages, it is not always necessary to do so. However, in deciding what if any purpose to set, it should be remembered that usually the purpose the pupils already have is simply the sensible and natural one of finding out what happens next. Certainly any purpose set by the teacher should promote the pupils' achievement of their purpose instead of asking them to find out about some minor or extraneous matter.

Third, as intimated in Chapter 3, any printed line in a preprimer stands for sounds — the names of the words *and* the voice intonations — which are the spoken form of the line that the pupil would understand readily if he heard someone say it. In reading the line silently, the pupil's task is essentially to "turn" the printed form into the familiar spoken form so that he "hears in the ears of his mind" the sounds he would actually hear if the line were read aloud or spoken.[3] The "turning" necessarily includes thinking not only the names of the words but also the voice intonations — the emphases, inflections, and little pauses — with which the line was or would be spoken in the situation depicted. Failure to think the required intonations invariably results in misunderstanding what the line says.

From the very beginning, a basic task of the teacher is to make the pupil aware that each line in his reading matter is something which someone is saying to somebody else, that it is something he himself has said and often has heard and understood, that when he reads a line it is

[3] There is no intimation here that the pupil must or should say the words to himself.

important for him to know just who is saying the line, and that he needs to take time as he looks at a line to think, according to what has happened so far in the story, how it probably would sound if he could hear the story character or the storyteller — whoever it may be — actually speak the line. In directing pupils to read a given page silently, the establishment of this needed awareness can be furthered by a directive statement such as *Think how the lines sounded when* _____ *said them, Make the lines talk to you,* or *Remember that* _____ *is quite angry.* Of course such a statement is not called for in directing the silent reading of every page, but it should be made frequently enough so that pupils begin to realize what silent reading is and that their reading matter is the language they have been speaking and hearing all their lives.

Fourth, the questions to use in encouraging the discussion which usually should follow the pupils' silent reading should be selected with considerable care. Instead of merely determining pupils' comprehension of the lines, the questions should be concerned with helping pupils enjoy the story, understand its main thread, and react to matters portrayed therein by making judgments, drawing conclusions, and thinking of implications not stated in the printed matter. Even during the time when pupils are reading the preprimers, most of them are quite capable of doing to at least some degree the so-called critical thinking implied here.

Fifth, in reading a given line or group of lines orally, the pupil's chief job is to say the words with the voice intonations required for portraying just what they are intended to mean. Merely naming the words in a line — word-calling — or using incorrect voice intonations is by no means reading that line. Word-calling is caused much more by the pupil's not understanding that his reading matter stands for talk than by his unfamiliarity with the printed forms of the words, and an unusual degree of patience is necessary in pleasantly encouraging the pupil time after time to read lines as he would say them. Such encouragement can be inherent in a directive statement, such as *Read the lines so that they sound just as you think they did when* _____ *said them, Make the lines talk to us,* or *Read the lines the way you would say them if you were the person in the story.* No doubt on occasion the teacher will have to ask a pupil several times to read the same lines aloud again until what he utters comes close to the talk for which the lines stand.

There is no need to have each pupil read each preprimer page aloud, but he should be given enough opportunities to read orally so that he can begin to get a correct idea of what oral reading is and to acquire skill in orally expressing ideas presented by printed lines. Whenever a pupil reads aloud an excerpt from a preprimer, the group or class —

who have already read the excerpt silently — should listen primarily to hear whether the reader expresses the meaning that the excerpt stands for.

Sixth, if a pupil in his silent reading of a page encounters a word he does not know in print, the teacher need not tell him what the word is. Instead, working with the pupil individually, she should raise questions which stimulate him to use context and letter sounds he knows to decide by himself what the word is. If the context in which the word appears is not of sufficient help, the teacher may use either the context she used in introducing the word or whatever spoken context she judges to be suitable. If in his oral reading the pupil encounters a word he does not know, the teacher should tell him the word so that the reading can go forward immediately for his listeners to hear, but he should be given soon the practice he needs for learning to recognize the word.

3. Practicing Reading Skills

Up to this point the discussion of the use of the preprimers has been concerned only with the teacher's task in getting pupils ready to read a given selection or part of a selection and in having them read and talk over its content. Although this work includes the presenting of letter-sound associations not taught as part of the preparatory instruction described in Chapter 3 and, through the introducing of new words, the giving of some practice in using the technique to be followed in unlocking strange words, additional practice should be directed at helping the pupil develop the power to read independently. This additional practice is concerned with (a) recognizing the new words presented in the selection, (b) fixing in mind letter-sound associations that have just been presented and learning to use them in different positions in words, and (c) using the technique for unlocking strange words.

a. Practice in Recognizing Words

As explained in Chapter 4, the practice needed is inherent, not only in the pupil's reading of much suitable material outside the basal reader, but also in the use of various types of exercises which give opportunities to respond to the new words both as individual items outside of context and as parts of connected discourse. In one exercise that provides practice outside of context the teacher prints the new words on the board along with other previously introduced words of somewhat similar appearance and asks pupils to respond to each word. Thus, in working with the five new words presented on the preprimer pages described on pages 144–145, the teacher might print the following words on the board:

rake	See
open	hurry
over	reach
here	Ben

Then she may ask pupils to name words as she points to them, to point to words which she names, and to explain by referring to letter sounds how they know a given word is what it is. If a pupil confuses one word with another, she may print the two words one above the other and raise questions which help the pupil note the differences between them.

In an exercise that provides practice in recognizing the new words in connected discourse the teacher prints on the board a group or groups of sentences composed of familiar words and the new words and asks pupils to read the lines. Thus, in working with the five new words presented on the preprimer pages described on pages 144–145, the teacher might use the following sentences:

I will hurry and get the ball now.
We can play ball with Ben.

Can you reach the can?
Can you get it open?

Here is the rake.
I can get it.

Other suitable exercises were described briefly on pages 128–130 in Chapter 4 and do not need to be repeated here. Specific examples of these and other types of exercises can be found in the workbooks and some of the teachers' guides which accompany the preprimers of different series of basal readers.

b. Practice for Fixing Letter-Sound Associations in Mind

Usually one or more of the new words presented in a preprimer selection can be used in making substitution exercises for fixing in mind letter-sound associations that have been presented and learning to use them in different positions in words. In any given substitution exercise, as described in some detail in Chapter 4, the teacher (1) prints one of the new words on the board again and asks pupils to name it, (2) substitutes for a letter or group of letters in the word another letter or group of letters for which the letter-sound association has been introduced, making a word which the pupils know in spoken form but do not yet know in print, and (3) asks pupils to name the word made. Care must be used here to see that no letter or group of letters substituted is one for which the letter-sound association has not yet been taught and that no word made is one which is unfamiliar to pupils in spoken form or familiar to them in printed form. Since pupils already know well twenty-two letter-sound associations for consonants and have had ample practice in using them at the beginning of words, there is no need to use those particular items in any exercise in which substitutions are made at the beginnings of words.

Each of the five new words on the preprimer pages described on pages 144–145 could be used in one or more substitution exercises. Assuming that letter-sound associations for some consonant blends, soft *c*, soft *g*, short *i*, *oa*, *th* as in *this*, short *u*, short *a*, and certain endings have been presented to pupils, those exercises are as follows:

Starting with *reach* (1) substitute in turn *bl* and *pr* for *r* to make *bleach* and *preach;* (2) substitute in turn *d, l, m, p,* and *ch* to make *read, real, ream, reap;* (3) substitute in turn *i* and *oa* for *ea* to make *rich* and *roach;* (4) add in turn *es, ing, ed* to make *reaches, reaching, reached.*

Starting with *rake* (1) substitute in turn, *br, fl, sn* for *r* to make *brake, flake, snake;* (2) substitute in turn *c, g, t, v* for *k* to make *race, rage, rate, rave.*

Starting with *Ben* (1) substitute in turn *th, wh, wr* for *B* to make *then, when, wren;* (2) substitute in turn *i* and *u* for *e* to make *Bin* and *Bun* (3) substitute in turn *d, g, ll, st, t, th* to make *Bed, Beg, Bell, Best, Bet, Beth.*

Starting with *open*, add in turn *s, ed, ly, er, ing* to make *opens, opened, openly, opener, opening.*

Starting with *hurry* (1) substitute in turn *fl* and *sc* to make *flurry* and *scurry;* (2) substitute *ff* for *rr* to make *huffy;* (3) substitute *a* for *u* to make *harry.*

Other examples of substitution exercises and additional types of exercises for helping pupils fix in mind letter-sound associations that have been presented and use them in different positions in words appear in some of the teacher's guides and workbooks which accompany the preprimers of different series of basal readers.

c. Practice in Unlocking Strange Words

It is true that the teacher's introducing of the new words presented in the selections of the preprimers, as proposed on pages 146–152, provides the pupil with directed practice he needs for learning the technique to be followed in unlocking strange words and that he can and should get a considerable amount of additional but undirected practice by reading independently other suitable materials, including those described in

Chapter Six. However, if the pupil needs further directed practice, the teacher can supply it through exercises in which, under her direction, he unlocks strange words just as he does in the introducing of new words.

These exercises were described in Chapter 4 and no detailed repetition is required here. In general, for each of several items in an exercise, the teacher will simply print the strange word in context on the board, point to the word, and say, perhaps, "Let's find out what this word is. With what letter (letters) does it begin? . . . You know the sound that ____ stands for. What other letters in the word do you know sounds for? . . . I will read aloud all the words except this one. When I stop, think of a word that begins with that sound — stands for and makes sense here. Listen: [Reads the line.] What is the word? How do you know it isn't _____? How do you know it isn't _____?"

One or more items in an exercise may be of such a nature that the pupil can unlock the strange word by using the context and chiefly the beginning sound. Here are examples:

1. We need to build a hotter fire. Get some more _____ (wood). How do you know it isn't *water?* . . . How do you know it isn't *sticks?* . . .
2. We can get to the store before dark. It isn't very _____ (far). How do you know it isn't *late?* . . . How do you know it isn't *fan?* . . .

Before letter-sound associations for vowels have been taught, an exercise may include items which require the pupil to use the final consonant sound in order not to mistake the strange word for another word which begins with the same sound and makes sense. The following are illustrative:

1. My old doll is worn out. She has no arms or _____ (hair). How do you know it isn't *head?* . . .
2. Mother wants to cook the potatoes now. I have to get her a _____ (pot). How do you know it isn't *pan?* . . .

Before letter-sound associations for vowels have been taught, an exercise may include items which require the pupil to use a medial consonant sound in order not to mistake the strange word for another word which makes sense, begins with the same sound, and ends with the same sound. The following are illustrative:

1. Look at the potatoes on the stove and see if they are _____ (burning). How do you know it isn't *boiling?* . . .

2. I'll go to the barn and gather the eggs in this _____ (*basket*). How do you know it isn't *bucket?* . . .

3. Little Bobby doesn't want to eat his _____ (*supper*). How do you know it isn't *sucker?* . . .

After letter-sound associations for vowels have been taught, an exercise should include items which require the pupil to use a vowel sound in order not to mistake the strange word for another word that makes sense, begins with the same sound, and ends with the same sound. The following are illustrative:

1. Where did you get those old _____ (*socks*)? How do you know it isn't *sacks?* . . .

2. Be careful, Dick. That's a pretty heavy _____ (*load*). How do you know it isn't *lid?* . . .

The strange word presented by any given item in an exercise must be one which the pupil already knows in spoken form. The word suggested by a question asking the pupil to tell how he knows the strange word isn't that word should be one which the pupil knows in spoken form but does not know in print. If the pupil's reading vocabulary contains words needed for making suitable context for a given item, there is no reason why the teacher should not have the pupil read that context to himself.

Using the Primer and the First Reader

The primer and the first reader, each containing approximately 190 pages, contain short stories and perhaps a few poems. As with the preprimers, the pupil's reading matter in these books is composed only of language which he already understands in spoken form. Beginning early in the primer and continuing through the first reader, as the pupil's reading vocabulary expands and permits the use of more and more different printed words, the number of lines on a page increases, the stories become longer, and the pictures, instead of telling by themselves much of the action in those stories, enrich the text by illustrating events, actions, and situations mentioned or implied by the printed lines. The work to be done by the teacher with a selection or part of a selection in each reader is programmed by the teacher's guide which accompanies the reader and, as in the case of that proposed for each preprimer, is concerned with (1) getting ready to read, (2) reading and talking, and (3) practicing reading skills.

1. Getting Ready to Read

Getting pupils ready to read something in the primer or the first reader, like getting them ready to use selections in the preprimers, consists in (1) stimulating their interest in beginning to read the selection and (2) introducing new words presented in the reading matter. To stimulate interest in beginning to read an entire selection or just its first part, it is necessary only to have them notice the title and the first few pictures in order to think what the story could be about and what might happen. If the material to be read is the second or some later part of the selection, merely having pupils recall what has happened so far and consider what may happen next or how things might turn out is sufficient. Since pupils usually possess the background required for reading a given selection or a part of a selection with adequate meaning, rarely if ever will the teacher have to attempt to provide that background. Most teacher's guides that accompany primers and first readers have suggestions for doing the stimulating proposed in this paragraph.

In order to provide pupils with further directed practice they need for learning to use the technique to be followed in unlocking strange words and in order to present new letter-sound associations, the teacher should introduce most of the new words that appear in a given selection in the primer and some of those that appear in a given selection in the first reader. But because pupils also need considerable experience in following the technique by themselves, without any direction from the teacher and as they are reading along, some of the new words in a selection in the primer or the first reader should not be introduced. Each new word not to be introduced is one that the teacher does not require for presenting a letter-sound association, that in the selection itself appears in context with a sufficiently strong clue to the word, and that contains a number of letters or groups of letters for which the letter-sound associations have been taught. Procedures to be followed in introducing new words are those described on pages 146–152. Some teacher's guides accompanying primers and first readers provide detailed suggestions for and contexts to be used in introducing new words and distinguish between the words to be introduced and those not to be introduced.

2. Reading and Talking

As with the use of a given selection or part of a selection in a preprimer, the teacher's work here consists in (a) having pupils read several pages silently, (b) stimulating group discussion of what is said on those pages, and (c) having pupils read the pages orally. As pupils progress through their reading of the primer and the first reader, the number of pages to be read silently before the discussion and the oral reading are undertaken can be increased gradually. The need to "read" the pictures before starting to read the text becomes less and less pronounced, and the teacher may or may not set a purpose for the silent reading. Most certainly, in directing pupils to read a group of pages silently, the teacher should continue to encourage them to think, as they look at the lines, how those lines probably sounded when they were spoken. Any help she gives a pupil who meets a difficulty in his silent reading should be in the form, not of the answer to his problem, but of questions which stimulate him to recall what he needs in order to figure out all by himself what the answer is.

The discussion following the silent reading should help pupils enjoy the story being told as well as serve as a means for finding out whether they have understood what the pages say. To this end, comments made and questions raised by the teacher should stimulate pupils to keep the main thread of the story in mind, to clarify and organize ideas presented in the story, to almost see the sights, hear the sounds, and feel the feelings portrayed by the story, and to express their reactions to events, situations, and bits of behavior depicted in the story. Many questions asked by the teacher should give pupils opportunity to do the critical thinking inherent in making judgments and drawing conclusions which are not stated in the story but are based on things that happen and things that are said therein.

There is no need to have every pupil read all or part of every page aloud or to have all the lines on the page read aloud. Usually it is sufficient to have some pupils read aloud lines on this or that page, to have other pupils read aloud lines on another page, and to have pupils read aloud on any given page only the lines most suitable for oral reading. In directing a pupil to read orally, the teacher certainly should encourage him to read the lines so that they sound the way he thinks they probably did when the story character said them. In order to get a reproduction of the particular voice intonations required for showing just what the lines mean, it often may be necessary to have one pupil read them several times or to have different pupils try to read them as they ought to be read.

3. Practicing Reading Skills

The practice to be given on appropriate reading skills while the primer and the first reader are being used is concerned with helping pupils to (a) develop skill in recognizing words, (b) fix in mind letter-sound associations that have been presented and learn to use them in different positions in words, and (c) increase their control of the technique to be followed in unlocking strange words. As will be noted in the following paragraphs, this practice is largely an extension of that offered in connection with the use of the preprimers.

Practice in recognizing words both in and out of context needs to be provided frequently from time to time. Exercises to be used are those described on pages 128–130 in Chapter 4.

The practice needed for fixing in mind letter-sound associations that have been presented and for using those associations in different positions in words can be provided through the use of the different types of substitution exercises which were described on pages 116–117 and 158–159 and which supply substitutions at the beginning, at the end, and within words.

Special exercises which give directed practice in using the technique to be followed in unlocking strange words should be continued. Such exercises were described on pages 160–161. Some items in exercises to be used while the primer and the first reader are being read should be so constructed that the pupil must use the final consonant sound in order to distinguish the word from another word that begins with the same sound and makes sense in the context. Other items should require him to use a sound within the word in order to distinguish it from another word that begins with the same sound, ends with the same sound, and makes sense in the context.

Using Second-Grade Readers

Most series of basal readers include a first second-grade reader, a second second-grade reader, and a teacher's guide and a workbook that accompany each reader. In approximately 250 pages, each reader presents short stories, several poems, and a few informative articles. All selections are composed of language the pupils would understand readily if they heard it spoken. Each teacher's guide programs the instruction to be given during the time the reader it accompanies is being used. Each workbook contains practice exercises on skills to be taught.

The instruction to be given in connection with the use of a given group of pages in either of the second-grade readers pertains to (1) getting ready to read, (2) reading and talking, and (3) practicing reading skills. Brief comments on these three tasks follow:

1. Getting pupils ready to read a given group of pages includes (a) providing the slight motivating push which they may need for beginning

to read those pages and (b) introducing the relatively few new words that should be introduced. The motivation can be provided by the means described on page 162 for use with selections in the primer and the first reader. The only new words to be introduced are those that are needed for presenting letter-sound associations which have not been presented and that, because of the weakness of the contexts in which the words appear in the selection and the pupils' lack of acquaintance with needed letter-sound associations, the teacher believes the pupils cannot unlock as they read the pages to themselves. Each such word should be introduced according to suggestions given on pages 146–152. Rarely if ever is the teacher called upon to provide pupils with the background needed for reading the pages with adequate meaning.

2. The number of pages to be read and talked over by the teacher and the pupils before moving to the next group of pages may be larger than that used when the first reader was being read. The teacher may or may not set a purpose for the pupils' silent reading of the pages, but she should encourage the pupils to think, as they look at the lines, how the lines probably would sound if they heard them spoken. The group discussion that follows the silent reading should stimulate them to keep in mind the main events in what was read, to enjoy the story being told, to clear up any misunderstanding, to express their reactions to events, behavior, and story characters, and to use what the pages say in making judgments, drawing conclusions, and considering implications. In directing pupils to read orally, the teacher should encourage them to read the lines the way they would say them, and in most of the oral reading pupils should assume the parts of story characters and read aloud the lines those characters say, while others in the group listen to think whether the oral reading expresses the meaning intended by the story characters.

3. From the beginning and continuing through the year, second-grade pupils should do so much independent reading of suitable materials outside the basal reader — books, magazines, and newspapers — that they will get all the practice they require in using skills which have to be refined. But pupils who need special practice should continue with exercises suggested as appropriate for first-grade pupils. Exercises suitable for developing skill in recognizing words are described on pages 128–130. Exercises to be used for fixing in mind letter-sound associations presented in the second grade — mainly those for syllables — are described on pages 116–117. Exercises concerned with increasing control of the technique to be followed in unlocking strange words are quite similar to those described on pages 160–161 and should emphasize the importance of paying attention to consonant sounds wherever they occur

in words. In any exercise of the type just named, some items should be of such a nature that the pupil must use the final consonant sound in order not to mistake the word for some other word which makes sense and begins with the right sound. Others should require him to use one or more consonant sounds within the word to keep from mistaking that word for another word which makes sense, begins with the same sound, and ends with the same sound.

A Note on the Use of Workbooks

The teaching of most of the skills which this volume proposes as part of the instructional program for the first and second grades includes, among other things, the providing of sufficient practice for the pupil in the use of the skills. Much of this needed practice can and should come through the pupil's application of these skills to the reading he does in and outside the basal readers, but possibly the amount of practice supplied thereby will not be sufficient to enable some pupils to make the progress they can make in getting the skills established. That is why the use of special exercises which are in addition to those already described and provide concentrated practice on specific skills is recommended.

How can a school get the additional special exercises that first-grade and second-grade pupils may need to use? So far as the author knows, there are only two main ways of doing this. One way is to have the teacher herself, the principal, a supervisory official, or a curriculum expert make them. The other is to purchase them — probably in the form of workbooks — from publishers whose authors have established considerable ability to construct good practice material. Since most teachers and perhaps school officials simply do not have the time and perhaps the inclination to make good practice material, purchasing good workbooks is probably the wiser course to follow.

As stated on page 138, the preprimers and each of the remaining basal readers is accompanied by a workbook providing special exercises on skills that have been introduced either in the reader or by the teacher, as proposed in the teacher's guide. Usually the teacher's edition of the workbook has a key to each exercise and directions for setting the pupil to work on that exercise. If the teacher has the pupil use each exercise only after the skill it is concerned with has been introduced, if that exercise pertains to a skill not yet mastered, if the teacher makes sure that the pupil understands how to proceed in working on the exercise, if she sees to it that his responses in the exercise are carefully checked, and if she takes time to be sure that he understands why each mistake he makes is a mistake, the workbook can be quite helpful in relieving weaknesses inherent in group instruction, in providing the pupil with needed practice, in making him aware of his progress, in locating his particular deficiencies, and in pointing out where reteaching is in order. In situations where these conditions do not or cannot exist, the pupil's use of a workbook is likely to be for him nothing more than mere busy work which almost any parent could assign.

Supplementary Equipment

On page 139, word cards, the pocket chart, film strips, the big book, and tests were listed as supplementary equipment for carrying on the instruction proposed for the first two grades. In most series of basal readers the word cards number 150 or so. On each card is printed one of the words that make up the vocabulary of the preprimers and the primer. The cards can be used in introducing new words and in supplying practice in recognizing familiar words in and out of context, as proposed by exercises described on pages 128–130. The pocket chart is simply a piece of material, made perhaps of heavy cardboard and oak tag and measuring about $3\frac{1}{2}' \times 2\frac{1}{2}'$, that can be hung on an easel or the wall and that has a number of wide pockets into which word cards can be placed for use in introducing new words and in giving practice in word recognition. Film strips provide instruction and practice in listening for beginning sounds, distinguishing letter forms from one another, associating letter forms and sounds, and unlocking strange words. The big book, possibly $2\frac{1}{2}' \times 2'$ in size, reproduces on large pages and in large print the first thirty-two pages or so of the first preprimer. It is used by some first-grade teachers to have pupils read a given group of pages before they reread the same pages in their individual copies of the first preprimer. The tests that accompany the basal readers usually are standardized and may provide at various stages measures of such important matters as the pupil's reading aptitude, his knowledge of letter-sound associations, and his skill in noting similarities and differences in letter sounds, in unlocking strange words, and in comprehending the meaning of short passages.[4]

Most of the standardized tests available for use in determining first-

[4] See, for example, *The McKee Inventory of Phonetic Skills, Tests One, Two, and Three;* James Stroud and Albert Hieronymus, *Primary Reading Profiles, Level One and Level Two;* Albert Reilly, *Basic Reading Test, Grade One, Grade Two.* All these tests are published by Houghton Mifflin Company, Boston, Massachusetts.

grade and second-grade pupils' achievement in reading are more general than those just mentioned and are concerned chiefly with the measurement of skill in word recognition and in comprehension of short passages. In selecting tests for this purpose, the teacher may wish to consider the following:

California Reading Tests. Lower Primary, Grades 1, 2, word recognition, comprehension; Primary, Grades 3, 4, word recognition and comprehension. California Test Bureau, 5916 Hollywood Boulevard, Los Angeles 28, California.

Chicago Reading Tests. Test A, Grades 1, 2, word recognition, comprehension; Test B, Grades 2–4, comprehension, rate. E. M. Hale and Company, Eau Claire, Wisconsin.

Detroit Reading Tests. Test 1, Grade 2; Test 2, Grade 3, comprehension. Harcourt, Brace, & World, Inc., 750 Third Avenue, New York 17, New York.

Detroit Word Recognition Test. Grades 1–3, word and phrase recognition. Harcourt, Brace, & World, Inc., 750 Third Avenue, New York 17, New York.

Developmental Reading Tests. Primer, word recognition, comprehension; Lower Primary, word recognition, comprehension. Meredith Publishing Company, 1716 Locust Street, Des Moines, Iowa.

Dolch Basic Sight Word Test. Recognition of 220 common words. Garrard Press, Champaign, Illinois.

Durrell-Sullivan Reading Capacity and Achievement Tests. Primary, Grades 2–4, word recognition, comprehension. Harcourt, Brace, & World, Inc., 750 Third Avenue, New York 17, New York.

Gates Reading Tests. Primary, Grades 1, 2, word recognition, comprehension; Advanced Primary, Grades 2, 3, word recognition, comprehension. Bureau of Publications, Teachers College, Columbia University, 525 West 120 Street, New York 27, New York.

Haggerty Reading Examination. Sigma I Grades 1–3, word recognition, comprehension. Harcourt, Brace, & World, Inc., 750 Third Avenue, New York 17, New York.

Metropolitan Achievement Tests. Primary I Battery, Grade 1, word and phrase recognition, word meaning, numbers; Battery II, Grade 2, word recognition, comprehension, arithmetic, spelling. Harcourt, Brace, and World, Inc., 750 Third Avenue, New York 17, New York.

SRA Achievement Series: Reading. Grades 1, 2, word recognition, comprehension; Grades 2–4, word recognition, comprehension. Science Research Associates, 259 East Erie Street, Chicago 11, Illinois.

Stanford Achievement Tests. Primary Battery, Grades 1–3, word meaning, comprehension, spelling, arithmetic. Harcourt, Brace & World, Inc., 750 Third Avenue, New York 17, New York.

Williams Primary Reading Tests. Grade 1, word recognition, comprehension; Grades 2, 3, word recognition, comprehension. Public School Publishing Company, Bloomington, Illinois.

Providing for Group and Individual Differences

If the first-grade teacher or the second-grade teacher organizes her class into two or more groups for the purpose of instruction in reading through the use of the basal readers, all the teaching proposed in this chapter should be well fitted to the needs and the ability of each group. The following paragraphs point out some of the general adjustments that may be necessary:

In "Getting Ready to Read," more time may have to be spent with one group of pupils than with another in raising suitable questions, calling attention to what the first few pictures show, and getting comments and queries from pupils in order to provide motivation for beginning to read a selection or part of a selection. Starting with the primer and continuing through the second-grade readers, the teacher will find that more of the new words in a selection need to be introduced to one group of pupils than should be introduced to another group.

In "Reading and Talking," one group of pupils may be able to read silently a larger number of pages than another group should attempt before moving to the discussing and oral reading of those pages, and certainly one group can cover in fewer reading periods the reading and talking to be done with a selection than can another group. More of the questions used in a discussion with one group can be of the penetrating type that asks for critical thinking than probably should be used with another group. The teacher will need to exercise much more patient perseverance with one group than another in getting pupils to read lines aloud with the required voice intonations.

In "Practicing Reading Skills," one group of pupils may need to be given all the practice in all the items previously discussed, including (1) the practice in word recognition, (2) the practice inherent in substitution exercises, and (3) the practice in unlocking strange words. Another group may need the proposed practice in only some of these items. Furthermore, the amount of practice given in each of the three categories to each group should vary according to the group's need. Obviously each group should be given only practice which teaches something the pupils in that group do not yet know, and no group should be given practice on any item which the pupils in that group have already mastered. There is no place here for mere busy work.

The pages immediately following briefly describe exercises that can help provide for individual differences. Each exercise can be constructed to fit the particular basal readers the pupils are using and, with variations in content, can be used time and again at different stages by first-grade and second-grade pupils. Some of the exercises require participation by the teacher; others supply seatwork. The latter can be duplicated for several pupils' use. Certain exercises should be used only by slower pupils, some can be used by average pupils, and others should be used only by pupils who are "ahead of the game." While the teacher is the best judge of which exercises are best suited to this or that pupil's needs, no one should be asked to practice something he has already mastered.

Reading New Words in New Context. Print a number of sentences on a sheet of paper. In each sentence, one word should be a word that was new in a selection just read. All other words should be words that the pupil knows well in print and should make a context in which he has not seen the new word. Have the pupil read each sentence aloud.

Context and Sound Riddles. Print on the board and point to a consonant, perhaps *t*, for which the letter-sound association has been introduced. Then say: "I will give you a riddle. You think of a word that begins with the sound this letter stands for and is an answer to my riddle. Listen: What do you dry your hands on after you have washed them? . . . What do you have on each foot? . . . What do you use for chewing? . . . What come to your eyes when you cry? . . ." In each case, accept any word that begins with the right sound and makes sense. Repeat, using other consonants and riddles.

Associating Letters and Sounds. Paste on cards pictures of objects with names beginning with consonants for which letter-sound associations have been introduced. Then make sure the pupil knows the name you have in mind for each picture. For each consonant to be used, supply the pupil with an envelope on which that consonant has been printed. Mix the cards in front of the pupil. Then have him place in each envelope the cards with the pictures that have names beginning with the sound the consonant on the envelope stands for.

Matching Pictures and Sounds. At the top of a paper print a consonant, perhaps *m*, for which the letter-sound association has been introduced. Draw on the paper objects that have names beginning with consonants, including some that begin with *m*. Have the pupil mark pictures beginning with the sound the letter on the paper stands for. Repeat, using other letters and objects. To expand this exercise, draw scattered pictures, print a column of different letters down the middle of the paper, and have the pupil put a line from each picture to the right letter.

Building New Sentences. On the chalk rail place cards that show words which have been introduced and which can be used to make short sentences. Have the pupil select and arrange in the pocket chart the cards needed to make a sentence you speak. Repeat, using other sentences. Have the pupil read aloud the sentences in the chart.

Matching Consonant Sounds. On a paper draw pictures that have names beginning with different consonants for which the letter-sound associations have been introduced. Below each picture print two familiar printed words. One word should begin with the same sound as the name of the picture; the other should not. Have the pupil mark the word which begins with the same sound as the name of the picture.

Finding the New Words. On a paper print several boxes similar to the following:

	ball	here	Mary	rake
rake	reach	rake	play	open
	with	will	rake	what
	rake	see	Ben	box

At the left of each box print a word that was new in a selection just read. All the other words in the box should be words that have been introduced. Have the pupil mark every word that is the same as the word at the left.

Choosing the Right Word. On a paper print several numbered items such as the following:

> 1. Ben can play _____ with me.
>   will   ball   rake

Explain that in each item a word is missing where the dash is and that only one of the three words below the line would make sense in the blank. Have the pupil mark that word.

Finding Words That Begin Alike. On a paper print several boxes in each of which at the left you draw a picture that has a name beginning with a consonant for which the letter-sound association has been introduced. To the right of the picture print three rows of words that have been introduced. Have the pupil name the pictures. Then have him mark each word that begins with the same sound as the name of the picture. To expand this exercise, draw three pictures at the top of a paper and print a number of words below them. Direct the pupil to draw a circle around one picture, a line under another, and two lines under the third. Then have him mark each word correspondingly.

Reviewing Words. On a paper print several numbered rows of words which have been introduced. Have the pupil mark in each row the one word you name for that row. Name a different word for each row.

Making Words Make Sense. At the left of a paper print a column of the first parts of sentences. At the right, print in a different order the last parts of those sentences. Have the pupil draw a line from each first part to the correct second part. Each word on the paper should be one that has been introduced.

Making Substitutions. On the board print a word that has been introduced. Then say: "What is this word? . . . I am going to say a jingle, but I'll leave out the last word. When I stop, you give me a word to finish the jingle. The word you give me must rhyme with *rake* and begin with a letter I'll show you. Listen: Take the *r* away from *rake*." (Erase the *r* and put *b* in its place.) "Put in *b* and you have _____. What is the word? . . ." Repeat, using other words and letters.

Using Context and Letter Sounds. On a paper print several numbered items such as the following:

1. Ben will not come _____ to the party.
        tack   back   sack

Each word in the numbered line should be a word the pupil knows in print. Only one of the three words below the line should be familiar in print, and it should not be the one which makes sense in the numbered line. The two strange words should be just like the familiar word except at the beginning, and only one of them should make sense in the blank space. Explain to the pupil that he knows one of the three words, that the other two are strange to him and that he will need to use what he knows about letter sounds to decide what those two words are. Have the pupil mark the word that makes sense in the numbered line.

Choosing Picture Cards. On the chalk rail place picture cards that have names beginning with different consonant sounds for which the letter-sound associations have been introduced. Then have the pupil select the card that begins with the sound a letter you name stands for. Repeat, naming other letters.

Classifying Words by Sounds. On 3″ × 5″ cards print words — one to a card — that have been introduced. Supply the pupil with several envelopes, on each of which is pasted a picture that has a name beginning with a letter for which the letter-sound association has been introduced. Have the pupil place each card in the envelope with the picture the name of which begins with the same sound as the word on the card.

Discriminating Among Words. On the board print words which have been introduced and which the pupil confuses with one another. Have the pupil name words to which you point and point to words which you name. If he mistakes a word for one of the others, print the two words one above the other and have him tell you what the differences are.

Matching Letters and Sounds. Print several letters in a row on the board. Give the pupil picture cards, one for each letter. Have him place on the chalk rail under each letter the picture which begins with the sound the letter stands for.

Recognizing Individual Words. Print on the board five or six words introduced in a selection just read and underline each word with different colored chalk. Give the pupil a paper on which are printed a number of words that have been introduced, including several repetitions of each word on the board. Have the pupil draw under each repetition a line of the same color as that under the same word on the board.

Finding in Context Words That Begin Alike. Draw on the board four objects that have names beginning with different letters for which the letter-sound associations have been taught. Underline each sketch with a different colored chalk. Give the pupil a paper on which are printed numbered sentences made of words which have been introduced and containing a number of words beginning with the same sound as the names of the sketches. Have the pupil draw under each such word a line of the same color as that under the corresponding sketch on the board.

Finding Words That End with the Same Sound. Give the pupil a paper on which are printed several rows of words, each of which is a word that has been introduced and some of which end with the same consonant, perhaps *t*. Then say: "Say each word softly to yourself. If a word ends with the same sound as *cat* and *nut*, draw a line under it." This exercise can be expanded by drawing sketches on the board, drawing a line of a different color under each sketch, and having the pupil draw a line of the right color under each correct word.

Unlocking Strange Words. On a paper print several sentences, each containing only one strange word. That word must begin with a letter for which the letter-sound association has been taught. Say to the pupil: "Read these sentences to yourself. When you come to a word you do not know, think of a word that begins with the right sound and makes sense there. Use other letter sounds you know in the word to help you." Have the pupil tell you what each strange word is.

Copying Words. If the pupil has unusual difficulty in learning to recognize a given word, print that word on the board. Then have the pupil print a copy of the word as he says it to himself. Do not require him to learn the spelling of the word.

Making Letter-Sound Associations. Give each of several pupils a card bearing a letter for which the letter-sound association has been introduced. Have a leader show picture cards, one by one. As a picture card is shown, the pupil who holds the letter which stands for the sound at the beginning of the name of the picture takes the picture card.

Reviewing Letter-Sound Associations. Print on the board three words that are strange in print, perhaps *clap, strap,* and *nap.* Then ask; "Which of these words begins with the same sound as *stream?* . . . Which begins with the same sound as *clown?* . . .

Choosing Opposites. On a paper print a numbered list of items such as the following:

1. Ben has to stay <u>in</u> the house.
   He can not come out to play.

All the words in each item should be words that have been introduced. One word in the first line should be underlined. A word that means about the opposite of the underlined word should be used in the second line. First explain to the pupil what is meant by *opposite*, using perhaps *big* and *little* to do so. Then have him read the items to himself and underline in each the word in the second line that means about the opposite of the underlined word in the first line.

Classifying Words. On a paper print several numbered groups of words such as the following:

1	2	3
dog	meat	boy
red	cake	run
cat	play	girl

Each word should be a word that has been introduced. In each group, two words should go together in the sense that they are in the same category, such as the names of colors, animals, foods, clothes, games, or what not. The third word should be one that does not belong in the same category. Use the first group of words to explain to the pupil, what is meant by words' going together. Then tell him to mark in each remaining group the one word that does not belong there.

Recognizing Vowels. On a paper print several words that have been introduced. Have the pupil mark the vowels in each word.

Finding Words That Have the Same Vowel Sounds. On a paper print several words that have been introduced. Some should be words in which the short sound of a given vowel is used; others should be words in which the long sound of that vowel is used. Have the pupil mark the words in which a given sound — the long or the short sound — is used.

Choosing the Right Meaning. On a paper print several numbered items such as the following:

1. Get me a <u>glass</u> of water.
   _____ Ben broke the <u>glass</u> in the window.
   _____ Put the milk in this <u>glass</u>.

All the words in each item should be words that have been introduced. One of the words in the first line is underlined. In one of the last two lines, that same word is underlined and is used with the same meaning it has in the first line; in the other, it is underlined but is used with a different meaning. After explaining this to the pupil, direct him to mark the line in which the underlined word has the same meaning it has in the first line.

Choosing the Right Answer. On a paper print a list of questions, each of which is made up of words that have been introduced and which the pupil can answer by *Yes* or *No.* Opposite each question, print *Yes* and *No.* Have the pupil read each question to himself and mark the answer he thinks is right.

Associating Vowels and Sounds. Print a vowel combination on the board, perhaps *oa.* Then say: "As I say three words to you, listen for the word that has in it a sound these letters stand for." Then say three words, only one of which has the *oa* sound, perhaps *meal, boat, nail.* Have the pupil tell what the word is. Repeat, using other vowel combinations and words.

Using Vowel Sounds. Print on the board three or more words which are strange in print, which begin and end alike, but which have a different medial vowel sound, perhaps *mean, main, moan, moon.* Call the pupil's attention to the fact that all the words begin and end alike, but that the vowels in the word are different. Then ask him to tell one by one what three of the words are. Right after he tells what one of the words is and before he names another, have him tell how he knows the word he named isn't one of the other words that you name. Repeat, using other appropriate words.

Notes on Linguistics

Linguistics is the scientific study of language, and persons who engage in this work are called linguists. In general, up to the present time, linguists have reported chiefly their findings pertaining to (1) the smallest sound or speech elements — called phonemes — which are significant in the language and which are somewhat more exact and less elaborate than the sound elements commonly called phonics, (2) prefixes, suffixes, base words, and word form changes including variants, each of which — called a morpheme — is made up of phonemes and carries meaning, (3) patterns or structures in which morphemes are arranged or ordered to make phrases, clauses, and sentences, (4) the parts that words and groups of words play in these expressions, and (5) voice intonations, sometimes called the melodies of the language.[5] Within the scope of elementary school instruction, linguistics has influenced most the teaching of sentence structure, grammar, and the so-called parts of speech as part of the offering in English in Grades 3 through 6. In quite recent years, however, some linguists have set forth certain basic propositions and suggestions pertaining to instruction in reading.[6] Using little of the

[5] Groups of linguists differ much from one another in the terminology they use to describe the findings of linguistics and in their interpretations of those findings.

[6] Persons interested in what linguistics offers for the improvement of instruction in reading should read at least the volume by Carl LeFevre and that by Charles Fries, both of which are identified among the books listed at the end of this chapter.

terminology peculiar to linguistics and without adhering to the views of any particular group of linguists, the numbered sections that follow give the author's arbitrary descriptions[7] of and offer his comments on only those particular propositions and suggestions which he believes are most pertinent to the teaching of reading in Grades 1 and 2.[8] It is to be noted that (1) these propositions are concerned chiefly with *helping the pupil learn to think and when advisable to reproduce for printed lines the familiar spoken language and consequently the meanings which those lines represent,* a basic provision that Chapters 2, 3, and 4 emphasized time and again and that for some years has been incorporated in several reading programs, (2) up to the present time linguistics has provided, not a system of instruction in reading, but rather a body of valid information about the nature, structural properties, and operations of language, (3) becoming acquainted with some aspect of this nature and certain of these properties and operations can help the pupil learn to read well, and (4) practically all the specific suggestions pertaining to instruction can be carried out in connection with the use of basal readers.

1. Language is basically oral and is composed of sounds which talkers utter and at least some of the facial expressions and bodily movements they use as they talk. In general, the making of the sounds themselves includes (a) the pronouncing of words, all of which play different parts, most of which appear in one or another of different positions, and some of which take different forms from time to time in order to fit grammatically in what is being said, (b) the ordering or arranging of individual words to make groups of words — nouns and their modifiers, verbs and their modifiers, phrases, clauses, and particularly sentences — that are the significant units in carrying meaning and that often are called structures, and (c) the using of voice intonations. By the time the English-speaking pupil enters the first grade, he is well acquainted with many of these words, structures, and intonations in the sense that he uses them readily to express his ideas in talking and understands the

---

Of interest also are most of the articles included in the December, 1964, issue of *The Reading Teacher*. It is well to keep in mind here that linguists do not agree fully in either their identification of or the proposals they make for using possible contributions of linguistics to the teaching of reading.

[7] No doubt some linguists will take exception to the meagerness and possible inexactness of one or more of these descriptions. All inaccuracies should be charged to the author.

[8] It is not to be inferred here that findings of linguistics apply to the teaching of reading in only Grades 1 and 2. Some applications for later grades are noted in Chapters 8 and 9.

meanings which they are intended to convey, even though he is not aware of and does not need to know just what parts the different words are playing, the positions they have or the forms they take, or just what the structures and intonations are.

Reading matter is simply a printed code that stands for spoken language and that has the function of stimulating the reader to think or recall (a) the pronunciations, structures, and intonations which make up the spoken form, and simultaneously (b) the meaning for which those items stand. In any piece of printed connected discourse, individual words stand for pronunciations, play different parts, and signal relationships between words, and the groups of words — sentences or not — represent language structures. Some but by no means all of the voice intonations that would be heard in the spoken form of the discourse are indicated by punctuation marks and occasional special typographical signs. Whatever facial expressions and bodily movements one could observe in listening to the lines being spoken are not represented at all, except perhaps by unusually well constructed pictures which may accompany the printed text.

That the author agrees with statements made in the two preceding paragraphs should be obvious. Various explanations and applications of them were made repeatedly in Chapters 2, 3, 4, and 5. Among the most important of these applications are the following recommendations:

a. All reading matter used in teaching beginning reading must be composed of words, structures, and intonations — language — that stand there for the same meanings with which the pupil uses them in his talking and listening.

b. Very early the pupil must be made aware of the fact that his reading matter stands for talk which is already familiar to him.

c. The teaching of reading to any given pupil should not be undertaken until he has become adept at using in his talking and interpreting in his listening the very words, language structures, and intonations which he will encounter in his reading matter.

2. The voice intonations that a person uses in talking are chiefly (a) the stress which he places on one or more words, (b) the pitch or pitches at which he utters a word or group of words, and (c) the junctures and terminals with which he makes breaks and stops in his talk. Stress may be heavy, medium, light, or weak. Pitch may be normal, low, high, or highest. Open junctures separate words, groups of words, or the syllables within a word, and terminals denote finality or conclusion at the ends of expressions. Stress, pitch, and junctures or terminals are used more or less together, are indicators of the talker's intended meanings, and must

be interpreted by the listener who wants to understand what is being said.

Usually a talker places heavy or medium stress on only one word in a sentence or other structure — commonly the last word — and utters that word with a falling pitch. Much the same terminal with a falling pitch concludes (a) any statement that consists of only one word and answers a question and (b) most longer statements, commands, requests, and many questions, particularly questions that begin with *What, Where, Who, Why,* or *Which.* Questions that often end with a rising-pitch terminal are those which result from turning statements into questions, those which ask for repetitions of statements just made or express strong feelings such as amazement, impatience, disbelief, or relief, and short questions which begin with forms of *be, do,* or *have.* Within a sentence, relative stress and pitch together indicate whether a word such as *record* names something or expresses action, whether a sequence of letters such as *r, o, u, n, d, u, p* is doing the work of a noun or the work of a verb and an accompanying adverb, and whether a sequence such as *b, l, u, e, b, i, r, d* is playing the part of a compound noun or the parts of a noun and an accompanying adjective. In addition, within a sentence, junctures and terminals accompanied by a slight rise in pitch indicate items that make up a series, the introductory *Yes* or *No* in an answer to a question, that someone is being spoken to, the end of an introductory phrase or clause, and the setting off of a non-restrictive clause.

No one questions the pupil's need to interpret the voice intonations that are an important part of the familiar spoken language represented by the printed lines of his reading matter. As explained in Chapters 2 and 3 and illustrated in this chapter, such interpreting is an essential part of the pupil's work in "turning" the printed lines into their familiar spoken form, is required for his making of correct meaning for those lines, and prevents his placing on each word in a sentence the heavy or medium stress with a falling-pitch terminal that results in mere word-calling. In reading silently, the interpreting that the pupil needs to do is the thinking of the particular heavy and medium stresses, pitches, and junctures or terminals at the points he would hear them if the lines were spoken. In reading orally, it consists in uttering these intonations where they need to be expressed in order to reproduce the spoken language for which the lines stand. It is important to understand here that in order to do all this interpreting, the pupil does *not* need to know either the elaborate intricacies of voice intonations as reported by linguists, only a few of which are mentioned in the preceding paragraph, or the linguistic terminology used by linguists in describing those intonations.

Perhaps it should be pointed out also that most of the ideas about the nature and use of voice intonations as reported by linguists have their origin in analyses of individual sentences outside connected discourse. Yet surely the act of thinking the strongest stress on the right word or the correct pitch at the right point is to be directed just as much by what has happened and what has been said as reported by the context up to that point as by the structure of the sentence itself. It can be just as damaging to read a selection sentence by sentence as it is to read a sentence word by word.

Actually, to interpret voice intonations in reading, the pupil needs only an awareness of the following:

a. That in his talking he emphasizes some words more than others, uses different pitches at different points, and makes stops to help others understand what he means, and that his reading matter stands for talk which is already familiar to him and which includes emphases, pitches, and stops as well as the names of words.

b. That in order to understand what the printed lines of his reading matter are saying, he must think the voice intonations which his experience in talking and listening leads him to believe he would hear if he heard the lines being spoken. That in reading a selection the commas, periods, question marks, exclamation marks, boldface type, and full caps can help him think a few needed voice intonations, but for the most part he must let what he has read so far tell him where to think the most emphasis and what pitch to think at this or that point.

The statements that follow offer suggestions for helping the pupil gain the awareness just explained. Procedures described by the first six statements are basic in teaching all pupils. Those described by the last three statements can be useful in working further with any pupil for whom the other procedures do not suffice and for whom the realization that print stands for talk and that in reading he must think the required voice intonations as well as the names of the words does not break through as easily and quickly as it should.

1. In beginning the use of the first preprimer, explain to the pupil that in each story in his book the story characters talk to one another just as he talks to people and they talk to him, that the pictures in the story show what is happening and the printed lines tell what the story characters say to one another, that to understand the story he needs to think as he looks at each line how that line would sound if he heard the story character say it, and that in this way he can make the story characters talk to him. From then on, as illustrated in this chapter, when you ask the pupil to read lines silently, keep encouraging him to think how those lines would sound if he

heard them spoken. When you ask him to read lines aloud, keep encouraging him to read those lines as he would say them.

2. Be sure to introduce each new word in context rather than by itself. No one thinks for an isolated word the voice intonations he needs to think in reading that word in connected discourse.

3. From time to time as you are reading aloud to the pupil, stop just before a short speech by a story character, tell the pupil that you are going to read aloud in three different ways what the story character said, and ask him to decide which way shows best what the story character meant when he spoke. Then read the sentence once in a word-calling way, a second time with the most emphasis on the right word, and a third time with the most emphasis on a wrong word. Also from time to time as you are reading aloud, stop just before a short speech that a story character makes and that is composed of words the pupil knows in print. Then print the line on the board and ask the pupil to read it aloud, placing the most emphasis on the word which he thinks the story character emphasized most when he spoke. After the pupil has read the sentence with correct stress, point out that, in his reading of a story, what has happened and what has been said so far in the story tells him where to think the most emphasis on words that come later. It can be helpful also to print on the board from time to time a short sentence made up of words the pupil knows in print and, without giving hints as to needed emphasis, ask him to show how he would read the sentence aloud if he means this, if he means that, and if he means something else. Such a sentence might be *Jack has not seen the book,* and your directions might be "Read it to show that you mean someone else may have seen the book but Jack didn't," "Read it to show that you mean Jack may have seen something else but not the book," and "Read it to show that you mean Jack may have heard about the book but he hasn't seen it."

4. In using the first preprimer, when the situation arises point out and name the period at the end of a simple statement, request, or command. Explain that when people talk they say different words with different pitches or voices, that a voice may be medium, high, or low, that the voice may fall a little or rise a little at the end of a word, and that a period tells him to think a falling voice and a stop at the end of the word which comes just before it. As the situations warrant, follow the same procedure to explain that usually a question mark tells him to think a slightly falling voice and a stop at the end of the word which comes just before it, that an exclamation mark tells him to think the words which come just before it as being spoken with strong feeling, and that a comma inside a sentence tells him to think a slight change in voice and a short stop at the end of the word just before it. In addition, as the need appears, proceed in a similar manner to explain that sometimes a question mark tells him to think a slightly rising voice and a stop at the end of the word which comes just before it, and that when a word is printed in heavy black type or in full capital letters he should think that word with strong emphasis. In doing the teaching suggested in this paragraph, it is important to avoid giving the pupil the idea that he should think

a rising pitch at the end of any question and a short stop only when he sees a comma. In continuing with the use of the first preprimer and subsequent books, expect the pupil to read periods, commas, question marks, and exclamation marks as you have explained.

5. Make sure always that the pupil has read lines silently before you ask him to read those lines aloud. The silent reading enables him to gain some acquaintance with the voice intonations he needs to use. This acquaintance in turn helps to prevent his oral reading of the lines later without the required intonations.

6. To provide most of the practice the pupil needs for learning to recognize words and groups of words instantly, make provision for him to read much suitable connected discourse, as suggested in Chapter Four and explained more fully in Chapter Six. Do not depend much upon having him use instead numerous exercises in which he responds to individual words as they stand alone. In responding to any word as it stands alone, anyone has a strong tendency to use a falling-pitch terminal at the end of the word, and much practice in doing this can encourage the pupil to engage in word-calling as he attempts to read connected discourse.

7. Very early — certainly no later than the time during which the first preprimer is being used — print on the board from time to time a short sentence which the pupil has just spoken. Read the sentence to him, using the same intonations he used. Then have the pupil "read" the sentence aloud, even though his response may be a mere reciting from memory of what you and he said. Explain that the print on the board stands for the sounds he made when he spoke the sentence. Doing this can help the pupil realize that what he says can be put into print and that print stands for talk. Often the simplest types of selections made by the teacher and described in Chapter 6 can be used for this purpose.

8. Very early, print on the board from time to time a short sentence that the pupil has just spoken and that is composed of words he knows well in print. Explain to the pupil that when he talks he speaks some words with more emphasis or force than others to help people understand just what he means. Ask him to say the sentence again without looking at the print on the board and note which word he speaks with the most emphasis. Then ask him to read the sentence aloud, emphasizing most the same word he so emphasized when he spoke the sentence.

9. Very early, print on the board four short sentences which are composed of words that the pupil knows well in print, which are things story characters might say, and which end with the correct punctuation mark. One sentence should be a simple statement, the second a request or command, the third a question which does not take a rising-pitch terminal at the end, and the fourth should contain commas used to separate structures — perhaps items in a series — from one another. Explain to the pupil that when he talks he speaks different words with what we call different pitches or voices and that a pitch or voice may be medium, high, or low and may fall or rise or stay much the same when he makes a stop in his talking. Taking each of

the first three sentences one at a time, ask the pupil to listen as you read it aloud to hear whether your voice goes up a little or goes down a little when you say the last word. As you read each sentence, use a falling-pitch terminal. Then ask the pupil to read the same sentence aloud and let his voice fall just as you did. After the three sentences have been so read, point out and name the punctuation mark at the end of each and explain that, in reading a sentence which ends with a period and often a sentence which ends with a question mark, he needs to think a falling voice and a stop at the end of the last word. When you read the fourth sentence aloud, use a slightly rising pitch and a short stop in saying the word which comes just before each comma, and use a falling pitch and a stop in saying the last word in the sentence. After the pupil has read the sentence aloud, using the same intonations you did, point out and name the commas and explain that usually a comma tells him to think the word just before it with a slightly rising pitch and a short stop.

3. At the time the pupil enters the first grade, he uses in his talking and understands in his listening a wide variety of declarative sentences which, according to the ordering or arranging of the words and groups of words they contain, exemplify one or another of four basic sentence patterns. Symbols often used in making simple formulas to describe these patterns are N, standing for a word or group of words that is doing the work of a noun; V, standing for a word or group of words that is doing the work of a verb; Lv, standing for a linking verb such as a form of *be*; A, standing for an expression that is doing the work of an adjective; and Ad, standing for a word or group of words that is doing the work of an adverb. It is understood here that (a) a group of words which is doing the work of a noun, whether that group appears as the subject of a sentence or in the complementing position after the verb, includes the head word being used to name something, whatever article may come before it, the one or more adjectives which may intervene, or even a prepositional phrase, and (b) a group of words which is doing the work of a verb includes the verb and whatever accompanying adverbs are used, whether they be single words or prepositional phrases. The five paragraphs that follow present the simplest examples of the four basic patterns and some of their variations:

One pattern is *N V*. Examples are *Tom skates* and *The gate swings*. In talking, however, the pupil usually speaks a verb group rather than the simple form of the verb, so that he says *Tom is skating* and *The gate is swinging*. Furthermore, this pattern usually includes at the end an adverb or an adjective, to make *Tom skates well* and *The gate is swinging open*, and often it is expanded by a prepositional phrase to make *Tom skates at the lake* and *The gate is swinging open on those rusty hinges*.

A second pattern is *N V N*. Examples are *Mary makes candy* and *The boys played softball*. Often this pattern is expanded by adverbs or prepositional phrases to make, for example, *Mary makes candy often* and *The boys played softball in the park*.

A third pattern is *N Lv N*. Examples are *Buster is a dog* and *Tom was a clown*. Often the pattern varies to make *N Lv A*, as in *Buster is sleepy*, and *N Lv Ad*, as in *Tom is at the park*.

The fourth pattern is *N V N N*. Examples are *Tom named his dog Buster* and *Tom gives Buster meat*. At times in this pattern a word or group of words that plays the part of an adjective is used in place of the final noun, to make, for example, *Tom painted the fence white*.

Most sentences that the pupil uses in talking are variations of one or another of the four basic patterns. For example, adjectives, adverbs, and prepositional phrases are inserted or added to make longer declarative sentences. Questions are composed (1) by inverting nouns and forms of *be* and *have*, symbolized by *Lv N* as in *Am I?* or *Has it?*, (2) by using at the beginning such a word as *What, Who*, or *Where* with a form of *be*, symbolized by *Lv N* as in *Where is he?* or *What are they?*, (3) by using a form of *do* to make *vN V* as in *Does Tom Skate?*, *vN V N* as in *Did Tom find Buster?*, *vN V N N* as in *Does Tom give Buster meat?*, *vN V A* as in *Does Tom feel sick?*, and (4) by using a form of *be* at the beginning to make *Lv N N* as in *Is Buster a pest?*, *Lv N A* as in *Is Tom strong?*, *Lv N Ad* as in *Was Buster here?* Sentences using passive voice are composed (1) by inverting word order and inserting a form of *be* to make *N vV* as in *The book was read*, or with the insertion of *by* to make *N vV N* as in *The book was read by Tom*, and (2) by inverting word order and inserting a form of *be* to make *N vV* as in *The dog was fed*, and by inserting also the word *by* to make *N vV N* as in *The dog was fed by Tom* or *N vV N N* as in *The dog was fed meat by Tom*. The expressions *There is, There are*, and *It is* or *It's* are often used to begin variations of *N V* and *N Lv* patterns.

The meaning-carrying structures in printed connected discourse are not so much the individual words themselves as the groups of words that are the sentences, the noun groups, the verb groups, and the prepositional phrases within sentences, and the expressions that are not sentences but that by themselves do the work of sentences in conversations. The meaning of any one of these structures is the meaning that the structure as a unit represents. In no sense is this meaning that which could result from thinking a meaning for each included word by itself or from adding to a meaning of the first word a meaning of the second word, a meaning of the third word, and so on. Actually each of most of the individual words in connected discourse plays a relatively minor role by itself. According to the context in which it appears, it shifts this way and that in its meaning, in its function, in the voice intonations with which it should be thought, and at times in its form. Consequently, if the pupil in his silent reading is not to enclose each word by itself within a mental box, so to speak, and is to avoid word-calling in his oral reading, he must think the meaning-carrying structures as units, just as he thinks them in his talking and listening.

There are two or three hundred frequently used words that stand for little if any meaning by themselves. They are called structure words.[9] Of particular importance among the structure words are the markers, those used most often as the beginnings of meaning-carrying structures in and out of sentences. The words *a, an,* and *the* in particular and such words as *your, few, much, this, several, any, another, my, his, these, both,* and *many* are often used as noun markers, indicating the beginning of a group of words that includes at least the marker itself, a noun, and whatever modifiers the noun may have. The forms of *be, have,* and *do,* often called helping words in connection with the teaching of grammar, and words such as *can, must, will, would, may, do, get, keep,* and *need* are used frequently as verb markers, indicating the beginning of a group of words that includes at least the marker itself, a main verb, and whatever modifiers the verb may have. The words *in, to, on, at, with, by, about, from, up, down, for, around, beside, over, near, along, across,* and others, commonly labeled prepositions, often mark the beginning of the structure called a phrase. Among the words frequently used as markers to indicate the beginning of a clause and at times the relation of that clause to the rest of the sentence in which it appears are *who, when, if, although, so, which, why, as, after, that, since, unless,* and *before.* Appearing often as markers that indicate the beginning of a question are *What, Where, Why, When, Which, How, Who, Whose.* Generally in talking, a marker is given a light or a weak stress. Among the exceptions to this are the speaking of *a* or *the* with heavy stress and the long sound, rather than the normal schwa sound of the vowel, to portray emphatic and often selective intention and the use of forms of *be, have,* and *do* with heavy stress to show defense against or rebuttal of something which has just been said. So far as reading is concerned, the most important thing about any marker is that it can be a signal to the reader that here is beginning a group of words which he needs to think as a unit, just as he would hear those words being spoken in talk.

The author has no quarrel with the idea that the sentences the pupil speaks and understands in his listening are constructed according to different patterns, that linguistic formulas can be used in explaining these patterns, that certain structure words are often used to signal the

[9] For a list of structure words, see Chapter Six in Carl LeFevre's *Linguistics and the Teaching of Reading* (McGraw-Hill Book Co., Inc., New York, 1964).

beginning of groups of words which are meaning-carrying structures, and that the pupil must learn to read each such structure as a unit instead of thinking each individual word within the structure by itself. But he does object seriously to the recommendation or at least the inference, made by some linguists, that equipping the first-grade or second-grade pupil to read well material suited to his use should include teaching him what nouns, noun groups, verbs, verb groups, adverbs, adjectives, prepositional phrases, and markers are and do; explaining what a sentence is and what the different basic sentence patterns are; having him apply linguistic formulas to describe sentences he has read; and encouraging him to think as he meets a structure within a printed sentence just what work that structure is doing. To the author, this recommendation or inference is close to plain nonsense. Many first-grade and second-grade pupils who know nothing about the structure of the sentences included in their reading matter, or who do not sense that structure as they read, understand very well indeed what those sentences say. Furthermore, in the author's experience, carrying out the foregoing recommendation contributes little if anything to the pupil's comprehension of the sentences. There is as yet no sound reason to believe that, as some linguists suggest, the meaning and the structure of any given sentence are one and the same and knowledge of the structure is necessary to or insures the reader's comprehension of what the sentence says. As evidenced by the influence of the various contexts in which a sentence may appear, the meaning of that sentence depends as much on what surrounds it as on its own structure. Perhaps it is unfortunate that the linguists' investigations of the operations of the language have been largely limited to the study of sentences as they stand more or less alone and of individual words and groups of words as they function in those sentences.

It is the contention of the author that, so far as reading is concerned, about all the knowledge which the pupil needs to acquire relative to sentence patterns and words used as markers is an awareness that (a) in the sentences in his reading matter the order of the words and groups of words is the same as that which he uses in speaking such sentences, (b) to read well he must often think together rather than one by one the words which make up a group of words, just as he thinks that group in his talking and listening, and (c) certain words are often used to tell him that here is beginning a group of words which he needs to think together rather than one by one. Some of the specific suggestions presented on page 186 and those given in the statements that follow are applicable to developing this awareness. Suggestions offered in the first seven statements refer to the teaching of all pupils. Those in the remaining statements may be used in working with pupils who need additional help. Quite probably the last four of the latter suggestions are much more applicable to the teaching of written composition than to the teaching of reading.

1. As implied previously in this chapter, be sure that all reading matter to be used by the pupil is composed entirely of sentences and other structures which he already uses in his talking and understands in his listening and that the words and groups of words within each sentence are arranged in an order which is familiar to him.

2. Very early, explain by illustration to the pupil that the left edge of a printed line is the beginning of the line and that in reading, he begins at the left, moves from left to right across the whole line, down one line and back to the left of that line, across the whole line, down again and back to the beginning of the next line, and so on. To avoid giving the pupil the impression that the end of any line is also the end of a meaning-carrying structure, it is probably advisable not to talk much about the right edge of a line as the end of that line.

3. Introduce each new word in context so that the pupil unlocks it as a part of a meaning-carrying structure. To introduce as a marker each new word often so used, be sure that the context is one in which the word works as a marker in the usual position of a marker. Introducing a marker out of context, or with context in which it does not occupy the usual position of a marker, always requires the pupil to think that word with intonations different from those needed for reading the word as the beginning of a group of words to be thought as a unit.

4. After you have introduced a few markers of a given type — noun markers, verb markers, or prepositional phrase markers — print on the board a few short sentences composed of words the pupil knows in print and containing at least one word used as a marker of that type. Print each sentence so that the different groups of words to be read as units in the sentence are separated by spaces wider than those you would normally use in printing the sentence. Explain to the pupil that usually a sentence is made up of groups of words and that he needs to read the words in each group together, just as he says them when he talks. In using the first sentence, tell him to listen as you point to each group and read it aloud as a group, and have him read each group aloud right after you have done so. Then point to and name each word used as a marker in the sentence. Tell the pupil that in stories he will read usually any one of those words is the beginning of a group of words, and that to read that group he should read the words together, just as he would say them. Finally, print the sentence on the board without using the wide spacing between the groups of words and have the pupil read the sentence aloud. Follow the same procedure with each sentence on the board.

5. From time to time as you ask the pupil to read lines silently, encourage him to think how they would sound if he heard someone say them. When

you ask him to read lines aloud, encourage him to read them as he would say them.

6. Make sure that the pupil has read lines silently before you ask him to read those lines aloud. The silent reading enables him to note the groups of words which he needs to think as units and helps prevent word-calling of the words in those groups when he reads the lines aloud.

7. To provide most of the practice which the pupil needs for learning to recognize words and groups of words instantly, have him read much suitable reading matter, as described in Chapter 6. Using instead special word recognition exercises in which the pupil responds to individual and unrelated words as they stand alone gives him no practice in reading meaning-carrying structures as units, cannot help him become aware of the relation between printed lines and talk, and is likely to encourage him to respond to lines silently and orally as though they were composed of lists of words arranged in column form. Yet it must be remembered that probably some pupils need the additional practice on some words which such special exercises supply.

8. Print on the board in column form several prepositional phrases, noun groups, or verb groups, each of which is composed of words the pupil knows well in print. Point to the first word in the first group and explain that this word is often used at the beginning of a group of words in stories he will read and that in such a group he should read the words together, just as he would say them. Tell the pupil to listen as you read the group aloud. Then ask him to read it aloud just as you did. Finally, add words to the group so that you have on the board a sentence composed of words the pupil knows in print and ask him to read the sentence aloud. Treat each of the other groups of words in the same manner. The same general procedure may be followed in working with simple clauses, such as *after we ate, that we played, before mother came.*

9. Provide the pupil with a copy of a short selection that is composed of words he knows well in print and that contains only three or four sentences in which several markers are used. Have him tell you what words in each sentence need to be read together, just as he would say them. Then have him read the sentences aloud. Often short selections made by the teacher and described in Chapter 6 can be used for this purpose.

10. On the board print a short sentence that is an example of one of the four basic patterns and that is composed of words the pupil knows in print. Have the pupil read the sentence aloud. Then point to and name a word used there as a noun and ask him to tell you another word he could put in its place to make sense. Do the same with the main verb. If the sentence contains a prepositional phrase, do the same with it so that, for example, *Tom found his wagon in the park* becomes *The girl lost her doll at the lake.*

11. On the board print a simple sentence that is composed of words the pupil knows in print and is an example of one of the four basic sentence patterns, perhaps *That girl ran.* Then, by inserting and possibly adding words, show the pupil that you can make, for example, *That little girl ran quickly into her house.* Print another simple sentence of the same pattern, and this time ask the pupil to give you words he can add to say something that makes

sense. Then print his sentence on the board and ask him to try to read it aloud.

12. Print on the board in column form and in incorrect order groups of words which the pupil knows in print and which, when arranged in correct order, make a short sentence of one of the four basic patterns. Ask the pupil to read each group and to tell you the sentence he can make out of the groups. Then print the sentence on the board and have the pupil read it aloud.

13. Print on the board in a row and with space between them only the markers you have thought in a short sentence. What you print might look like this: The ＿＿＿ ＿＿＿ a ＿＿＿ to the ＿＿＿. Ask the pupil to give you words that fit in the blanks to say something which makes sense. Here you could get from the pupil such examples as *The boy took a friend to the party* and *The little girl took a rag doll to the park.* Print the pupil's sentence on the board and ask him to try to read it aloud.

4. Many words take different forms to fit grammatically and at times to express correct meaning in what is being said. A noun can be singular or plural. The plural of many nouns is formed by adding *s* to the singular form, and in these cases the *s* may stand for one or another of three slightly different sounds, depending upon the sound of the immediately preceding consonant or vowel. The plural of some nouns is formed by adding the common ending *es* to the singular form. Some plural forms such as *women, feet, children,* and *mice* are described as irregular, and in forming plurals such as *babies* and *ponies,* the *y* in the singular form is changed to *ies* or to *i* before adding *es.* Adding *'s* to singular nouns and *s'* or sometimes just *'* to plural nouns makes the corresponding possessive forms. The possessive form of a noun often plays the part of an adjective in a noun group, and the *'s* stands for the same sound as the final *s* in the plural form of the noun.

A verb can be singular or plural as called for by the number of the subject. Third person singular subjects often call for verb forms ending in *s,* and the past tense of many regular verbs ends in *ed,* that ending representing one or another of the three sounds noted in Chapter 4. A verb has five parts, commonly called the base form, the third person singular, the past, the present participle, and the past participle. For some verbs all five parts are different, as in *drive, drives, drove, driving,* and *driven.* A few verbs have the same form for three of the five parts, as in *shut, shuts, shut, shutting,* and *shut.* Most verbs have four forms in the five parts, as in *stay, stays, stayed, staying,* and *stayed.* Among the verbs which take four forms are a few in which the vowel sound is changed and *t* is added to make the past and the past participle, as in *keep, keeps, kept, keeping,* and *kept;* a few in which final *d* is changed to *t*, as in *send, sends, sent, sending,* and *sent;* and a few in which the vowel and the final consonant are changed for the same purpose, as in *think, thinks, thought, thinking,* and *thought.* Some simple words are often used as verbs to pair with other simple words used as adverbs rather than prepositions in making units that express action, such as *look out, put on, give up, come in, get over,* and *pull through.* As LeFevre points out,[10] when a noun follows a verb in a sentence which is symbolized by *N V N* and which uses such a pair, the adverbs may be placed just after the verb or just after the noun, as in *Tom put on a coat* and *Tom put a coat on,* but if a pronoun takes the place of a noun, the pronoun should be used between the verb and the adverb: *Jack took it in* is talk; *Jack took in it* is not. Attention is called also to the fact that in using a verb-adverb pair, the position of the adverb indicates the intended meaning. *We pulled through it* means something quite different from *We pulled it through.*

Adjectives can be inflected to make what are commonly called the comparative and the superlative forms. Thus the common endings *er* and *est* are added to the base form of many short words, as in *kind, kinder,* and *kindest.* In inflecting longer adjectives, usually the words *more* and *most,* as in *beautiful, more beautiful,* and *most beautiful,* precede the base form. A few adjectives, particularly *good, bad,* and *little* take quite different forms in their inflection. Some adjectives are a combining of a noun and a final syllable or a verb and a final syllable, as in *careful, headed, beaten, thoughtless,* and *childish.* Some quite common words such as *fast, slow, late, hard,* and *early* have exactly the same form when used as adjectives and when used as adverbs. The ending *ly* occurs often at the end of adverbs and sometimes at the end of adjectives.

So far as the author can determine, the fact that words take different forms in the pupil's reading matter has little significance in the teaching of beginning reading. Surely this fact does not mean that the pupil should be taught such matters as the meaning of singular and plural, the different ways in which plurals are formed, the different letter-sound associations for final *s* in plurals, the meaning of agreement in number between subject and verb, what the different parts of verbs are, or what adjectives and adverbs are and do and how they are formed. The pupil already uses in his talking and interprets correctly in his listening all the word forms that he will encounter in his reading matter, and if he is taught carefully what Chapter 4 and this chapter have recommended, he will have no trouble in thinking for a given printed form of a word the correct corresponding spoken form.

[10] See *ibid.,* p. 156.

There are, however, a few points which probably need to be emphasized. They are explained in the paragraphs that follow. The suggestions given in the first three paragraphs are to be followed in teaching all pupils. Those offered by the remaining paragraphs are much more pertinent to the teaching of written composition, including spelling, than to the teaching of reading.

1. Introduce each new word in context which presents the word as doing there the same work it performs in the material to be read immediately. Thus, for example, if the new word *ride* is used as a noun in the material to be read, introduce it in context in which it does the work of a noun, not the work of a verb.

2. In introducing a new word, put in context whatever form of that word is the one which the pupil will encounter in the material to be read immediately. Thus, for example, if the new word is *carry*, introduce that word itself, not *carries, carried,* or *carrying*.

3. In introducing the first new word in which an apostrophe is used to show possession, explain that this mark is called an apostrophe and that often an apostrophe is used to show that what the word names has or owns something. In introducing the first new word which is a contraction, explain that the word is a short way of printing two words, name the two words, point out the apostrophe, and explain that the apostrophe is used to show where letters are left out in printing the word in a short way.

4. Print on the board in column form a few words which the pupil knows in print, which are commonly used as verbs, and to each of which the ending *er* can be added to make a noun that names any doer of the action represented by the verb. Words you might print are *play, work, dig, kick, run, fly, call, sleep.* Point to and name the first word. Then to start a second column, print at the right the noun form, perhaps *player,* name that word, and explain that it is a name for anyone who plays and that you have made it by adding the ending *er* to the word *play.* Ask the pupil to use the ending *er* to give you the correct words you need for filling in the second column. There is no need here to call the words in the first column verbs and those in the second column nouns or to center the pupil's attention on variations you make in the spelling of some of the verbs to print the corresponding nouns.

5. Print in a column on the board several words which the pupil knows in print, which are commonly used as nouns, and which have forms often used as adjectives. Words you might print are *trick, string, wood, boy,* and *back.* Point to and name the first word. Then to start a second column, print at the right of the first word the adjective form, perhaps *tricky,* name that word, and explain that it is often used to describe someone or something and that you made it by adding *y* to *trick.* Explain further to the pupil that he can add the sound of a letter or group of letters he knows to each word in the first column to make a word that describes someone or something. Ask him to give you words he can think of. Words you could get may be *stringy, wooden, boyish,* and *backward.*

6. Print on the board a few words which the pupil knows in print and which are commonly used as adjectives, perhaps *sweet, quiet, noisy,* and *cheerful.* Point to and name the first word, explain that *sweet* is often used to describe someone or something, and as you print on the board a short sentence made up of words the pupil knows in print, perhaps *Tom likes sweet apples,* say: "In this sentence the word *sweet* describes the apples." Print *sweetly* to the right of *sweet* in the column on the board, point to and name that word, and explain that you made *sweetly* by adding *ly* to *sweet* and that *sweetly* is often used to tell how someone does something. As you print on the board a short sentence made up of words the pupil knows in print, perhaps *Mary sings sweetly,* say: "You can see that in this sentence, *sweetly* tells how Mary sings." Fill in the second column with the corresponding adverbs, perhaps *quietly, noisily,* and *cheerfully.* Then for each word in the first column, ask the pupil to tell something in which he uses that word to describe a person or a thing. For each word in the second column, ask him to use that word in telling you how a person does or did something.

5. In analyzing spoken language, some linguists have paid particular attention to the smallest basic sounds used in uttering words. Each of these sounds is called a phoneme and is distinguished in the sense that it differs markedly from all the others. In a phonemic alphabet — and there is more than one set of printed symbols so named — each basic sound element is represented by one and only one printed symbol, and each symbol stands for one and only one phoneme. Usually such an alphabet includes some English letter forms which stand for phonemes that are sounds they represent in conventional print, including, for example, *b, d, f, g* as in *gate, h, k, l, m, n, p, r, s* as in *see, t, v, w, y* as in *yet, z* as in *zoo, e* as in *met, i* as in *lip,* and *u* as in *put.* Other conventional letters and certain "new" symbols stand for other phonemes, including, for example, those represented by *th* as in *thank, th* as in *this, j, s* as in *his,* short *a, o* as in *cot, ch* as in *chill, sh,* the schwa sound for different single vowel letters and combinations of vowel letters, *wh* as in *where,* and *wh* as in *who.* So far as the author knows, no beginning reading matter printed in a phonemic alphabet has been provided for the pupil's use, but if and when it is and if the pupil who uses it is expected or required to learn all the corresponding letter-sound associations, that material may well be open to the criticisms which, in Chapter 4, were directed at the use of Initial Teaching Alphabet.

Beginning reading materials that are based on certain phonemic principles and that in one way or another place such emphasis on letter-sound associations for vowels and consonants have made their appearance. Many but not all of these materials present to the pupil at the beginning and for some time only simple words which are regular in the sense that each included letter stands for what is said to be the regular sound the letter represents, as, for example, in *can, Dan, fan, man, Nan, pan, ran, tan; bed, fed, led, Ned, red, Ted;* and *cot, Dot, got, hot, lot, not, pot.* Sentences provided for the pupil to read are built out of such words. Irregular words are presented to the pupil after he has learned the regular words thoroughly and are used with previously learned regular words to make printed lines for him to read.[11] It is the author's contention that in general practically all these materials place far too much emphasis upon letter-sound associations for vowels and provide in the pupil's first books reading matter which does not stand for familiar talk and which is more insipid and barren than is the content of most contemporary preprimers and primers, now so vehemently criticized for lack of interest appeal and substance by some linguists themselves.

Much work remains to be done before anyone can possibly know all the aspects of language structure which can enhance the pupil's comprehension in reading and just when and how these aspects can and should be taught. Yet the author believes that appropriate findings of linguistics should be applied to the teaching of beginning reading now and that any system of instruction should be linguistic in the sense that it is in line with those particular findings. Certainly all reading matter to be used by the pupil should be composed entirely of language in which the individual words, groups of words, structures within sentences, and sentences themselves are among those he already interprets with ease in spoken form, and the pupil himself must be made aware of the fact that this material stands for talk which is familiar to him. Furthermore, he must be encouraged to think as he observes printed lines the voice intonations which are a part of that talk, and he must be taught to think as a unit the words which make up each meaning-carrying structure, just as he does in his talking and listening. In addition, he must learn that the arrangement of words and groups of words in the sentences included in his reading matter is the order which he uses in his talking and understands in his listening. In reading any given sentence, he must sense between the words and between the groups of words the correct relationships he would sense if he heard that sentence spoken. Any one of these aspects of linguistics should be introduced in such a way that the pupil looks upon it as an aid to his comprehension of what his reading matter says rather than as a mere ingredient in the structure of the language.

There is one very real danger to be avoided vigorously in applying

---

[11] What is probably the most extreme example of this sort of material appears in L. Bloomfield and C. Barnhart, *Let's Read* (Wayne State University Press, Detroit, Mich., 1961).

findings of linguistics to the teaching of beginning reading. It is the danger of engaging in practices which can encourage the first-grade or second-grade pupil to center his attention, as he reads, on form and structure rather than on meaning and content and can lead him to conclude that reading is much more analytical and difficult and much less satisfying than it is or should be. Such practices, illustrated by the items which follow, probably grow out of the highly questionable notion (a) that the pupil's possession of at least some acquaintance with the operations of the language is essential to or a guarantee of the comprehension of the sentences included in his reading matter, or (b) that, as a part of his reading of such a sentence, he should think what the forms, positions, and functions of included words and groups of words are or what the syntactical structure of the sentence is:[12]

a. Teaching the pupil the intricacies of voice intonations as reported by linguists.
b. Teaching the pupil what the basic sentence patterns are, encouraging him to think as he reads any sentence the particular pattern it follows, and having him decide after the reading of a selection just which pattern is represented by each different sentence.
c. Teaching the pupil what nouns, verbs, adjectives, adverbs, noun groups, and verb groups are, how changes in the forms of nouns and verbs are made, and how adjectives and adverbs are inflected.
d. Constructing and using beginning reading matter which, although sound in some aspects of linguistics, certainly does not stand for familiar talk and lacks substance and interest appeal.

QUESTIONS TO BE ANSWERED

1. Why has the author included the use of basal readers as part of the instructional program this volume proposes for the first and second grades? What things should be true before the teacher is in a position to do well without the use of basal readers?

2. What are the different pieces of equipment included in the basal materials for the first and second grades? What does each provide?

3. What points should be kept in mind in choosing preprimers? Why is each of those items important?

---

[12] This statement does not deny the possibility that at later grade levels the pupil's thinking of sentence structure may help him work his way through to the intended meaning of a sentence which at first was to him a rather complicated puzzle.

4. What different groups of pupils may the first-grade teacher need to form? What are the advantages of such grouping?

5. What are the three main divisions into which the instruction to be carried on in using a selection in a basal reader can be organized? Why should the third division not be omitted?

6. What two main jobs does the teacher need to do in "Getting Ready to Read"? How can the needed motivation be provided?

7. What is the main reason for the teacher's introducing of new words the pupils will meet in a selection? In general, what should the teacher's introducing of a new word include? What cautions should be observed?

8. What things are particularly important to keep in mind about the work to be done in "Reading and Talking"?

9. What different jobs make up the instruction included in "Teaching Reading Skills"? Why is each of these jobs important?

10. In what ways does the using of a primer and a first reader differ from the using of the preprimers? The using of the second-grade readers from the using of the first reader?

11. In using basal readers, what provisions may the teacher need to make for differences between groups of pupils?

12. What aspects of linguistics, if any, were applied in the instruction described in Chapters 3 and 4 and in pages 140–165 of the present chapter? What other aspects of linguistics would you apply to the teaching of reading in Grades 1 and 2? Why? Which aspects would you not apply? Why?

MORE TO READ

Anderson, Irving, and Walter Dearborn, *The Psychology of Teaching Reading,* The Ronald Press Company, New York, 1952, Chapter 6.

Bond, Guy, and Eva Wagner, *Teaching the Child to Read,* The Macmillan Co., New York, 1950, Chapters VIII, X.

Dechant, Emerald, *Improving the Teaching of Reading,* Prentice-Hall, Inc., Englewood Cliffs, N.J., 1964 Chapter 9.

Durrell, Donald, *Improving Reading Instruction,* World Book Company, Yonkers-on-Hudson, N.Y., 1956, Chapters 2, 6.

Fries, Charles, *Linguistics and Reading,* Holt, Rinehart, & Winston, Inc., New York, 1963.

Gans, Roma, *Common Sense in Teaching Reading,* The Bobbs-Merrill Company, Inc., Indianapolis, 1963, Chapters 5, 6.

Harris, Albert, *Effective Teaching of Reading,* David McKay Co., Inc., New York, 1962, Chapters 3, 4.

Heilman, Arthur, *Principles and Practices of Teaching Reading*, Charles E. Merrill Books, Inc., Columbus, Ohio, 1961, Chapters 3, 4, 5, 7.

Hildreth, Gertrude, *Teaching Reading*, Henry Holt & Co., Inc., New York, 1962, Chapters 10, 12, 14.

LeFevre, Carl, *Linguistics and the Teaching of Reading*, McGraw-Hill Book Co., Inc., New York, 1964.

McKim, Margaret, *Guiding Growth in Reading*, The Macmillan Co., New York, 1955, Chapters V–IX.

Russell, David, *Children Learn to Read*, Ginn & Company, Boston, 1962, Chapters 7, 10.

Spache, George, *Toward Better Reading*, The Garrard Press, Champaign, Ill., 1963, Chapter 2.

Yoakam, Gerald, *Basal Reading Instruction*, McGraw-Hill Book Co., Inc., New York, 1955, Chapter 5.

THINGS TO DO

1. Examine the preprimers that are parts of a series of basal readers and decide how well they meet the standards which this volume proposes for use in selecting preprimers.

2. Read a selection in a primer. Then write out (a) what you would do and say to stimulate pupils to begin to read that selection and (b) what you would do and the statements and questions you would use to introduce three of the new words in that selection.

3. Read a selection in a first reader. Then write out what you would do and say to provide for "Reading and Talking" in connection with the use of a group of pages in that selection.

4. Get the teacher's guide for any first-grade or second-grade basal reader and read therein what is said about the teaching of reading skills that is to be carried on in connection with the use of any selection you choose. Decide (a) what parts of that instruction you think are not but should have been included in the author's "Practicing Reading Skills" and (2) what part of the author's "Practicing Reading Skills" you think are not but should have been included in the guide.

5. Examine a workbook that accompanies a first-grade or second-grade basal reader and make a list of the different skills on which it provides practice.

6. Decide which of the exercises described on pages 170–175 you would give to (a) a pupil who needs extra practice in recognizing words that have been introduced, (b) a pupil who needs more practice in associating letters and sounds, (c) a pupil who needs extra practice in unlocking strange words, (d) a fast-moving pupil.

7. Choose any skill which you think a first-grade pupil should be taught. Make an exercise which would give him practice in using that skill.

8. In a teacher's guide which accompanies a first-grade or second-grade basal reader examine and list the different things it would expect you to do in using a selection. Decide which if any of those things have nothing to do with teaching the pupil to read.

9. Examine the first-grade and second-grade readers and the accompanying teacher's guides of any modern series of basal readers to discover what if any applications of linguistics are made therein.

chapter 6

Providing for

Additional Reading

Chapter 5 described the instruction that can be provided through the effective use of the first-grade and the second-grade readers which are parts of a basal series. But even when that teaching is excellent, the pupil's reading of only those few books and perhaps the accompanying workbooks cannot provide him with enough practice to build the degree of power to read independently which he can be expected to develop in the first two grades. Neither can that reading, exposing him as it usually does to only a relatively small number of very short stories, an occasional poem, and an array of exercises on reading skills, offer all the content needed for stimulating and feeding his interest in reading a wide variety of worthy material or for putting him in touch with reading matter which tells of things he wants to know about. It is imperative, therefore, that from almost the very beginning of the first grade the pupil's reading of the basal readers be supplemented by his simultaneous and independent reading of additional materials. This chapter will consider the nature and use of such additional materials. In general, they are composed of (1) selections prepared by the teacher and (2) various books and certain magazines and newspapers issued by publishers.

Selections Prepared by the Teacher

Selections that the teacher can prepare may be classified arbitrarily as (1) special words, (2) short passages — including such items as

197

posters, rules, plans, assignments to duties, directions, pieces of news, jokes, riddles, reports, stories or humorous incidents, and original verses — and (3) longer selections, including a class newspaper, experience charts, and adapted stories. All these types of reading matter can and probably should be presented to first-grade pupils. In the second grade only those which provide benefits that pupils do not gain from their reading of many individual books and appropriate magazines and newspapers should be used.

1. Special Words

The first-grade pupil will frequently encounter, in and out of school, the need for reading certain words which may not occur in his basal readers and which, for want of a more precise term, can be called special words. Among these words may be his name, the first names of his classmates, the name of his school, street, town or city, the names of the days of the week, special days, months, colors, pieces of equipment such as *pencil, paper,* and *crayon* that printed directions will ask him to use, and directive words such as WALK, STOP, GO, IN, and OUT. Any such word that the pupil does not already know in print should be introduced to him if and when he needs to become acquainted with it.

No doubt the quickest and easiest way to introduce any of these special words to the pupil is to show the form on the board or a card, tell him what the familiar spoken word is, and have him say that word as he looks at the form. But this procedure makes no contribution to his acquisition of skill in unlocking independently words which are strange to him only in print or to his acceptance of the fact that he should expect to unlock strange words on his own. Consequently it is recommended that each special word listed in the preceding paragraph be introduced the same way new words in the basal readers are introduced.

Any special word may be introduced as soon as the twenty-two consonant letter-sound associations included in the preparatory instruction described in Chapter 3 have been taught. The name of a person, a street, a town, or a school may be presented with no context, as illustrated on page 148. If the word begins with or contains elsewhere a letter or group of letters for which the needed letter-sound association has not yet been learned and that association is essential to unlocking the word—perhaps the *A* in *Ann,* the *Ph* in *Phillip,* the *O* in *Oberlin,* the *E* in *Elm,* the *Ch* in *Chicago,* the *g* in *Roger,* or the *y* in *Sally* — the teacher should present that association as part of her introduction of the word. Furthermore, if the word contains a silent consonant — possibly the *p* in *Camp-*

bell or the *h* in *Beulah* — the pupil, before he attempts to unlock the word, should be told that the letter (or letters) has no sound in the word. In introducing the name of a person, a school, a street, or a town, the teacher may print the word on the board, tell the pupil that it is the name of a ————, call his attention to the beginning sound and other sounds he knows in the word, and direct him to think of a word which is a name for a ————, begins with the right sound, and has in it sounds other letters in the word stand for.

Any directive word or the name of a day of the week, a special day, a month, a color, or a piece of equipment may be introduced with spoken context, as described on page 147. The following items show respectively suitable spoken context to be used in introducing such words:

1. Billy's foot is so sore that he can't _____ (*walk*).
2. We will have a fire drill next _____ (*Monday*).
3. Are you going to Sally's party on _____ (*Halloween*)?
4. Those flowers will bloom next _____ (*June*).
5. Joe will color the picture _____ (*brown*).
6. Betty has broken her _____ (*pencil*).

The following points should be kept in mind when introducing any directive word or the name of a day of the week, a special day, a month, a color, or a piece of equipment:

a. The introducing of any one of these words should follow the steps described on pages 151–152.

b. If the context is sufficiently strong and if the pupil understands what he is doing in his attempts to unlock strange words, the fact that he has not yet had presented to him the letter-sound associations for *s* as in *his*, *y* as in *sky*, and *y* as in *pretty* should cause him no trouble in deciding that the names *Tuesday, Wednesday, Thursday*, the name *July*, the name of any day of the week, or the names *January* and *February* are those names.

c. It may be necessary as a preliminary part of the introductions of some words to present letter-sound associations which have not yet been taught. Possibilities are those for *c* in *December* and *pencil*, *Ch* in *Christmas*, *O* in *October*, and *Au* in *August*.

d. With some words it may be necessary to tell the pupil that a given letter has no sound in those words. Possibilities are the first *d* and the second *e* in *Wednesday* and the *y* in *May*.

The teacher must decide which of the special words she introduces have such permanent value for the pupil in reading that he needs to learn to recognize them instantly. Then she should provide the practice he needs in order to establish the required familiarity with those printed forms. If the reading of the various materials described in the remainder of this chapter does not supply all the needed practice, the special exercises described on pages 128–130 may be used also.

2. Short Passages

Certainly by the time the pupil has read the first two preprimers and a few individual books to be discussed later in this chapter and has had some special words introduced to him, he will have learned to recognize at least 100 different words and will have acquired considerable skill in unlocking strange words independently. With this capital at hand, he is in a position to read to himself simple short passages which the teacher may prepare in connection with various school activities. Many of these passages will be composed by pupils and edited by the teacher and, as is true of some of the longer selections to be described, can help the pupil understand that things he says can be put into print for others to read and that in a very real sense reading matter is printed talk. It is understood that in using any given passage the teacher will expect pupils to read it to themselves; she will *not* first read it to them.

From time to time posters with pictures that illustrate and lines of text that pertain to different important topics can be made and exhibited for first-grade pupils to read. A poster may be concerned with a safety rule, hygiene, manners, a coming event, playground rules, or almost any worthy topic of current interest. The picture may be cut from an old magazine or newspaper by a pupil or the teacher or may be drawn and colored by one or more pupils. The accompanying text may be suggested by pupils and, if necessary, edited by the teacher,[1] and it should be printed below the picture by the teacher. The following lines are typical of pieces of text used on posters:

> We look for cars before we cross streets.
> Listen to what people say to you.
> Put waste paper in the basket.
> We wash our hands before we eat.
> Book Week starts next Monday.

Every now and then some situation which arises in school suggests a need for pupils to set up a list of standards or rules pertaining to their future behavior: conduct in the halls, participation in group discussions, things to do in the classroom before school starts, behavior in the school

[1] The nature of the teacher's editing of the short passages described in this section is discussed on pages 203–204.

library, care of school equipment, respect for the rights of others, ways of being helpful at home, or things to do in reading to others. By initiating group discussion of a given situation and the need, the teacher can encourage pupils to suggest items for her to print on the board in making the list. As soon as she has edited the list, she may make a copy and place it on the bulletin board for pupils to read. The following lists were made by a first-grade class:

Telling Others About a Book You Read

Show the book and some of its pictures.
Tell who wrote the book.
Tell a little of what the book is about.
Tell whether you liked the book and why.

Walking to and from School

Obey traffic signs and signals.
Do not walk in water.
Watch where you are going.
Do not damage lawns or flowers.
Give others room to pass.

At times a group or class of first-grade pupils must make plans with the teacher for carrying out some activity such as giving a party or taking an excursion. During a class discussion in which the plans are to be made, the teacher may print on the board a list of things the pupils say they need to do. If the list does not require editing when it has been completed, she may have the pupils read it immediately. If it does, she may complete that work and make a copy of the revised list to place on the bulletin board for pupils to read. Here is a list of things one first-grade class said they would do to prepare for a party they had decided to give:

Things to Do for Our Party

We must decide when to give the party
We must choose people to greet guests and serve food.
We must decide what food to serve.
We must plan a program.
We must write invitations.

Many first-grade teachers make daily or weekly assignments of duties to be performed by different pupils in the classroom. After such an assignment has been made orally, the teacher may print a copy and place it on the bulletin board for pupils to read. An example follows:

> Today is Monday.
> Dick and Betty will pass the books.
> Sally will feed the bird.
> Fred will water the plants.
> Ann and Mark will collect the papers.

Instead of giving simple directions orally, the teacher can print those items for pupils to read. Thus such one-sentence directions as *Hang smocks here, Put story books back on the shelves,* and *Get drawing paper here* can be printed on long cards to be put up and allowed to remain as long as needed at appropriate places in the classroom. Other directives such as *It is time to put on your wraps, We will go to lunch now,* or *Bring pencils and workbooks to the reading corner* may be printed on the board for pupils to read in preparation for some activity.

Each morning one or more news items may be posted on the classroom bulletin board or printed on a chalkboard section reserved for that purpose. Often the teacher may need to supply all the news items for a given day, but certainly pupils should be encouraged to tell the teacher items which they think will interest the class and which she can include among those to be displayed. The following news items appeared one morning on the chalkboard in a first-grade classroom:

> Today is Friday.
> It is November 19.
> The new snow is three inches deep.
> Tom will come back to school next Monday.
> We will go to assembly at half-past ten today.
> The third-grade class will give a play there.

The teacher can give pupils considerable satisfaction by providing each of them at different times during the year with a duplicate sheet on which are printed a number of short jokes and riddles that she thinks the pupils have not heard and can read. Although many of the items included on each sheet issued will be supplied by the teacher, pupils can tell her jokes and riddles which they think the class will enjoy and which she can include in a forthcoming issue. The items that follow appeared with six others on a duplicate sheet prepared by one first-grade teacher:

> Tom: Billy lost his dog Bozo. He put an ad in the
>   paper about it last week.

Dick: Has Bozo come home yet?
Tom: No, not yet. I don't think that dog can read.

What stands on three legs in mud?[2]

In many first-grade and second-grade classes the teaching of English makes provision for pupils to give short oral reports, to tell short stories or humorous incidents, and to compose and recite original verses. In giving a report, the pupil tells about something that he has done or heard or that has happened to him or to someone he knows. A story or humorous incident he tells is usually one which has been told or read to him. A verse he composes and recites usually follows a pattern of rhythm and rhyme the teacher has presented through a poem she has read to the class. Some reports, stories, and verses given orally to the class by pupils are worth putting into print so that boys and girls who enjoyed them may later read them from duplicate sheets, from the classroom bulletin board, or perhaps from a book which the teacher has made by placing a number of sheets in a binder and giving it a title such as "Things We Have Told." The items that follow were composed and given orally to the class by first-grade pupils and later appeared in print on the classroom bulletin board.

Daddy took me fishing last Saturday. We went out on the lake in a boat. We had no luck at all. It was a good thing Mother did not depend upon us to catch fish for dinner that night.

Yesterday my little brother played all day with a balloon our Uncle Jack gave him. It is shaped like a pig. Last night he dreamed he was flying around on the back of a pig. Then the balloon broke and he started to fall. He woke up when he landed with a big bump near the bed.

> I watch the heavy snowflakes fall
> And hope they will not stay.
> I want to take my bat and ball
> And go outside to play.

Often, before presenting a poster, a set of standards or rules, a plan, a news item, a joke, or a riddle as a piece of material for pupils to read to themselves, the teacher will need to edit what pupils have suggested orally for the text. The same is true of the talking a pupil does in giving a report, in telling a story or humorous incident, or in reciting an original verse which the teacher decides later to put into print. Editing may

[2] The answer is *m*.

include the shortening of a sentence, the removing of ambiguity, the correcting of a grammatical error, the eliminating of repetition, or the changing of the order in which the words of a sentence or sentences are arranged. It will pay close attention to the vocabulary which makes up the text and will substitute whatever words should be substituted. Surely if pupils are to read a given short passage and to get from it needed practice in recognizing words, most of the words used in that passage should be already well known to them in print. But it must be remembered that by this time pupils who completed the preparatory instruction described in Chapter 3 and received the instruction carried on while the first two preprimers were being used have learned letter-sound associations for just about all the consonants, the short and long single vowels, and some endings, have learned to use consonant sounds in different positions in words, and have acquired considerable skill in using the technique for unlocking strange words. Thus a short passage may include now and then a word which is strange to the pupils but which they are equipped to unlock independently as they read the passage. In fact the total array of short passages used should include quite a number of strange words so that pupils can practice unlocking strange words independently and so that their reading of those passages can contribute to the growth of their reading vocabulary. The points made in this paragraph relative to the vocabulary of certain short passages apply also to the teacher's composing of directions and assignments to duties.

3. Longer Selections

A class newspaper prepared, duplicated, and issued periodically by the teacher and given to the pupils to read and take home can provide them with needed practice in reading, stimulate their interest in reading different types of selections, and help establish good relations between parents and the school. Each issue may contain news items, announcements of coming events at school, short informative articles on topics of interest to pupils, short jokes, puzzles, choice reports, stories, and verses given orally by pupils at school, and other suitable items. While the teacher can and should compose many of the passages to be included, pupils should be encouraged to tell her news items, jokes, puzzles, riddles, and whatever else they think would help make the paper interesting to others. She can edit these items for publication. In the editing and in composing passages for the paper, the teacher should make use of the vocabulary standards mentioned on this page.

In the latter part of the first grade some teachers make and use experience charts to provide pupils with reading matter. The content of such a chart is actually a record of some experience the pupils have had and is made up of lines dictated by them to the teacher. Usually the teacher first prints the lines on the board as the pupils dictate them. Later she edits the lines, applies the vocabulary standards mentioned on page 204, and prints the lines on large sheets of paper which she hangs on an easel or elsewhere for pupils to read to themselves. The following is the content of an experience chart prepared for one group of first-grade pupils:

> Yesterday we visited the creamery.
> Some of our mothers took us there in cars.
> Mr. Clark took us through the creamery.
> We watched one man make butter.
> We watched a machine separate cream from milk.
> We found out where buttermilk comes from.
> We saw men load cartons of milk in trucks.
> Mr. Clark gave each of us some milk to drink.

Attention is called to the fact that for many years first-grade teachers used experience charts rather than preprimers as material with which to *begin* to teach pupils to read. But when used for *that* purpose, such a chart has important disadvantages. *First,* since all the pupils already know what the chart says, they can have little if any demand for meaning as they look at the lines, and their interest is almost always limited to the mere matching of printed forms with the spoken words for which they stand. *Second,* the number of different words presented by almost any chart is so large that the teacher is almost forced into using the sight method, and the pupils cannot pay enough of the right kind of attention to each word to become sufficiently acquainted with its form. *Third,* because the pupils heard the lines spoken just a short time ago, they are tempted to recite groups of words here and there from memory and to think that this act is reading. No statement in this paragraph implies that experience charts resulting from pupils' desire to make and read records of experiences they enjoyed should not be used in the latter part of the first grade, after those pupils have acquired the reading vocabulary and the skill in unlocking strange words independently which they must have in order to actually read the charts.

Probably the very best piece of material that the teacher could prepare for pupils to read to themselves is her adaptation of a good short story which is not available in a form for her pupils to read, which she knows well, and which she thinks they would enjoy. In writing the adaptation, the teacher should retain as many of the ideas in the original story as possible. Most of the words she uses should be words that the pupils already know well in print. But, let it be repeated once again, since the pupils have been learning to unlock strange words independently, she should not hesitate to include every now and then a word which is strange only in print and which she knows her pupils are equipped to unlock. It would be a good thing for many pupils if skillful teachers adapted more unavailable stories than they do now.

Books, Magazines, and Newspapers

No doubt certain materials issued by publishers offer the best content for first-grade and second-grade pupils to read in addition to their basal readers. Books, monthly magazines, and weekly newspapers are prepared with unusual care for the use of boys and girls at these levels and offer much more variety of content and much more interest-pull than can selections prepared by the teacher. These publications can contribute much to the pupil's development of an abiding interest in reading a wide variety of material, to his acquisition of the power to read independently, and to his introduction to the values attached to reading.

1. The Selection of Books

The individual books to be made available for pupils to read on their own should be selected with care. Some of these books are issued by the education departments of publishing companies, were prepared especially as reading matter supplementary to this or that series of basal readers, and are fitted carefully to different levels in the instructional program offered by those readers. Most of the books are issued by trade departments of publishing companies, are commonly called juveniles, and have no connection whatsoever with any series of basal readers. Some of the books are essentially informative in their intent and may be read by pupils for information as well as pleasure, but most of them are purely recreational in their intent and should be read by pupils entirely for enjoyment. The remainder of this section presents five standards for choosing the particular books to be supplied.

First, each book should possess literary merit in the sense that it is well written, and it should present content that is worth reading. It may report actual experiences, episodes, or incidents as is the case with authentic history, biography, travel, science, and some poetry. It may be true to life in the sense that, although it makes no attempt to report actual occurrences, it does, as illustrated by good fiction and some poetry, portray things that could happen. It may make no pretense of being anything other than fanciful and present only straightforward nonsense, humor, or make-believe. Not included here is any book which pretends to report actual occurrences or to portray matters that are true to life but does neither.

Second, each book should have such a strong interest-pull that at any given point the content itself makes the pupil want to read on in order to find out what happens next, to see how things turn out, or to get answers to questions he wants answered. In brief, the book must be fun for the pupil to read.

Third, each word in the book's vocabulary must be one for which the pupil already knows the needed meaning when he hears the word spoken, and each sentence must be one which he would understand readily if he heard someone say it. This means that the English the book presents must be composed entirely of expressions for which the pupil would make correct meaning if someone read the lines to him.

Fourth, the total array of books to be made available to a given group or class should cover a wide range according to type, pupils' immediate interests, and peoples and countries. In addition to so-called classics, that array should include picture books with a small amount of text, contemporary fiction, poetry, nonsense, legend, history, science, fairy tales, travel, biography, fables, folk tales, and other worthy writings intended for boys and girls from six to nine or more years of age. The books should also tell about a variety of topics so that each pupil can be tempted to read in order to satisfy one or another of his immediate interests or so that at any given time he can find one or more selections pertinent to what he wants to read about. Furthermore, the books should offer the pupil an introduction to the peoples and customs of different countries as well as illuminate for him his immediate environment and other aspects of American life.

Fifth, in order to fit with the range of reading ability that exists among the members of almost any first-grade or second-grade class at any particular time and that most certainly will increase as continuing instruction in reading permits the individual pupil to progress at his own rate, the total array of books must cover a wide range of reading difficulty. Certainly beginning no later than the time when first-grade pupils finish reading the preprimers and continuing through the remainder of that grade and all the second grade, the books should include some which even the poorest reader in the group can read with ease, some which challenge the best reader, and for each pupil some which he can read easily and some which make him stretch his power to read independently. Of course the pupil who up to any one time has been taught entirely by the sight method and who has not yet developed the power to unlock strange words independently can read with the satisfaction to which he is entitled only those very few books with a vocabulary limited to words he has already met several times in print. But in addition to such books, which, of course, do provide needed practice in word recognition, the pupil who is being or has been taught to unlock strange words on his own can read many other books that present every now and then words that are new to him in print. Indeed, the author has found many first-grade pupils who, having been given the preparatory instruction described in Chapter 3 and part of the instruction outlined in Chapters 4 and 5, were reading by the end of the school year many books commonly considered to be third-grade reading matter. All this implies strongly that the instructional programs offered by some basal readers limit greatly both the number and the nature of the books which should be made available for pupils to read on their own, that programs offered by other series open early to pupils much more of the wealth of children's literature, and that at any given time the selecting of the individual books must take into account the extent to which the instructional program offered by the basal readers being used has so far equipped pupils to unlock strange words independently.

Of the more than thirty formulas that have been developed for measuring the reading difficulty of a book,[3] only a few are applicable to at least some of the books which are judged subjectively to be suitable for pupils in one or another of Grades 1 through 4 and which one would expect to make available for first-grade and second-grade pupils to read on their own. Prominent among these few are the formulas devised by Spache,[4] Wheeler and Smith,[5] Dale and Chall,[6] and Yoakam.[7] In applying these formulas to a book, one examines some of the passages it contains to determine the relative commonness and frequency of each word as provided by a valid word list, perhaps the Thorndike list,[8] the average length of the sentences, and in some cases the number of simple sentences in relation to the number of complex sentences. Thus the application of this or that formula to a given book can yield some sort of index of

---

[3] Some of these formulas are described at a more appropriate place in Chapter 12.

[4] George Spache, "A New Readability Formula for Primary-Grade Reading Materials," *Elementary School Journal*, 53: 410–413 (March, 1953).

[5] Lester Wheeler and Edwin Smith, "A Practical Readability Formula for the Classroom Teacher in the Primary Grades," *Elementary English*, 31: 397–399 (November, 1954).

[6] Edgar Dale and Jeanne Chall, "A Formula for Predicting Readability," *Educational Research Bulletin*, Ohio State University, Columbus, Ohio, 27: 11–20 (January, 1948).

[7] Gerald Yoakam, "The Yoakam Readability Formula," *Basal Reading Instruction* (McGraw-Hill Book Co. Inc., New York, 1955), pp. 329–340.

[8] E. L. Thorndike and I. Lorge, *A Teacher's Wordbook of 30,000 Words* (Bureau of Publications, Teachers College, Columbia University, New York, 1944).

reading difficulty which, among other things, indicates approximately the lowest grade level at which most pupils presumably are able to read this book.

There are three main reasons why the author does not recommend that the first-grade or second-grade teacher apply to a book any of the available formulas in order to decide whether that book is too difficult for this or that pupil or a group of pupils to read on their own. *First,* among the various factors which no formula considers and which one would expect to affect the reading difficulty that a given book holds for this or that pupil[9] are the desire he has for reading on the topic the book tells about and the interest appeal of the text for him. Any good teacher knows that high interest in getting a certain book read can be of much help to a pupil in overcoming many reading difficulties the text presents. She knows also that for him it can be a serious error to give up on his reading the book if he really wants to find out what it says.

Second, since each word and each sentence in a given book to be made available to first-grade or second-grade pupils is one which they would understand if the lines were read to them and since any word included could be difficult only in the sense that it is strange just in print, the criterion used by each formula to determine the vocabulary difficulty of that book is questionable. Surely, although one would expect inter-mediate-grade pupils to know in print more high-frequency than low-frequency words as reported in word lists, the words *bawl, cab, chew, clown, fatten, gravy, hitch, jam,* or others of low-frequency rating in the Thorndike list or any other list are not difficult for the first-grade or second-grade pupil who through the reading he has done has come to know them well in print. Similarly, the words *because, before, case, charge, die, fact, figure, length,* or any others with a high-frequency rating may be difficult for the pupil who has not yet met them in print. Furthermore, while any strange word the book contains has some diffi-culty for the pupil who has developed little if any power to unlock strange words independently, it has much less difficulty for the pupil who has learned to use to at least some degree the technique recommended in Chapter 4 for unlocking strange words on his own. Thus it would seem that in order to determine the vocabulary difficulty which this or that book has at a given time for a given pupil, one should have a clear idea of just what words the pupil already knows in print, the extent to which he is now equipped to unlock strange words independently, what differ-ent words make up the vocabulary of the book, and the nature of the strange words included and of the settings in which they appear.

[9] These factors are noted in Chapter 12.

Third, even though a publisher of children's books can apply a formula to one or another of them in order to get its approximate grade level difficulty to report to school people, the time which a first-grade or second-grade teacher would consume in making such application to even some of the books she should provide for her pupils simply cannot be justified and is not to be taken from that needed for carrying on important instructional activities. All that she needs to do to decide at any time whether a book is too difficult for a given pupil or group of pupils to read can be done in a relatively short time. She merely thinks of answers to the following questions as she herself reads the book:

1. Is this book one I think the pupil would enjoy?
2. Are the great majority of the different words in the book among those he already knows in print?
3. Are most of the strange words separated far enough from one another so that he will have a chance to use context as a clue in unlocking each of them?
4. Are the contexts in which most of the strange words appear strong enough so that they serve as clues to those words?
5. Do most of the strange words begin with letters and have in them other letters for which I have taught the needed letter-sound associations?
6. Are most of the strange words phonetically regular in the sense that, so far as I can tell, the letters they contain stand for sounds they often stand for?

By using these questions, the teacher will be basing her decision on her subjective judgment of the book's interest appeal and the extent to which her instructional program in reading has so far equipped the pupil to recognize the familiar words and unlock the strange words the book contains, whether that program is or is not one offered by a series of basal readers. If the teacher's answers to all six questions are in the affirmative, she should introduce the book to the pupil and give him a chance to read it.

It is important for the teacher to know what suitable juveniles are in print or are forthcoming, what they are about, and what competent judges think of them. This information she can acquire by paying attention to the catalogues and seasonal bulletins which are issued from time to time by publishers of children's books and which will be sent upon request, by referring to useful book lists and book indexes, by reading contemporary reviews of children's books, by noting the listings of certain book clubs, and by listening to the judgments expressed by children's librarians. Among the most useful book lists and indexes are *A Basic Book Collec-*

tion for Elementary Grades,[10] *Adventuring with Books,*[11] *Best Books for Children,*[12] *Bibliography of Books for Children,*[13] *Books They Can Really Read,* [14] *Children's Books for $1.25 or Less,*[15] *Good Books for Children,*[16] and *Subject Index to Books for Primary Grades.*[17] Reviews of contemporary books for children are supplied from time to time by several different publications including bulletins of the Center for Children's Books,[18] bulletins of various state departments of education, children's book sections of newspapers, particularly the *New York Herald Tribune* and the *New York Times,* and the periodicals *Junior Libraries,*[19] *Saturday Review,*[20] *Elementary English,*[21] *School Library Journal,*[22] and the *Horn Book.*[23] Book clubs which offer publications suitable for first-grade and second-grade pupils are Lucky Book Club,[24] Junior Literary Guild,[25] Weekly Reader Children's Book Club,[26] and Young Folks Book Club.[27]

No doubt the teacher who knows what words her pupils know in print and how far those pupils have progressed in developing skill in unlocking strange words independently can judge best the reading difficulty which this or that book holds for her pupils at any one time. But she may need help with other matters pertaining to the selection of books. If she feels she cannot judge whether a book is well written, whether it tells of a topic her pupils probably will like to read about, whether it has carried strong interest appeal for other pupils of the same age as hers, whether the offering of books she has available for pupils is well balanced — or if she is not in a position to find for herself books she should examine or to keep abreast of new publications as they come from the press — she should solicit the aid of a competent children's librarian.

[10] Compiled by Miriam Mathes and issued by the American Library Association, Chicago, 1960.

[11] National Council of Teachers of English, Champaign, Illinois, 1956.

[12] Compiled by Mary Turner and issued by R. R. Bowker Co., New York, 1961.

[13] Association for Childhood Education International, Washington, 1957.

[14] Prepared by Elvajean Hall and Katherine Torrant and published by Campbell and Hall, Boston, 1958.

[15] Association for Childhood Education International, Washington, 1959.

[16] Prepared by Mary Eakin and published by University of Chicago Press, Chicago, 1959.

[17] Prepared by Mary Eakin and Eleanor Merritt and published by the American Library Association, Chicago, 1961.

[18] The Center for Children's Books, University of Chicago, Chicago.

[19] Issued by R. R. Bowker Co., New York.

[20] Saturday Review Company, New York.

[21] National Council of Teachers of English, Champaign, Illinois.

[22] American Library Association, Chicago.

[23] Horn Book, Inc., Boston.

[24] Scholastic Magazines, Inc., New York.

[25] Junior Literary Guild, Garden City, N.Y.

[26] Weekly Reader, Columbus, Ohio.

[27] Young Folks Book Club, Brooklyn, N.Y.

2. *The Use of the Books*

In order to stimulate first-grade or second-grade pupils to read the books provided for their use and to gain maximum benefits from that reading, certain conditions should exist and different pertinent activities should be carried on in the classroom.

a. The Teacher's Enthusiasm

It is most helpful if the teacher herself has or develops an enthusiasm for children's books. This enthusiasm, which most certainly many pupils will catch from the teacher's demeanor as she presents and talks about the books, is acquired by becoming well acquainted with children's literature and by building a devotion to introducing to pupils the values offered by these writings. It will show itself largely in the sincerity with which the teacher entices rather than drives pupils into reading individual books on their own and makes the provisions and carries on the activities described in the following paragraphs.

b. The Classroom Library

The books to be made available to pupils during the year may be borrowed from the school library, the town or city public library, perhaps the county library, individual pupils' collections, and the teacher's personal supply. They should be set up as a classroom library which must be kept elastic in the sense that every now and then books which pupils have read are returned to their owners and other volumes which they have not read are added. The shelves on which the books are placed, even though they be merely plain boards separated a foot or more from one another by several piled bricks, should be low enough so that pupils can reach the books easily. Sections of shelves may be labeled according to the topics the books tell about: *Animals, Adventure, Science, Fairy Tales, Toys, Humor, True Stories,* and *Machines,* for instance. Near the bookshelves a table and several chairs may be placed to make what is commonly called a reading corner. Here, at odd times during the day, pupils may read or browse in books they select from the shelves. Book jackets, posters that pertain to books read, and pupils' drawings illustrating events told about in different books can be displayed to lure to those books pupils who have not yet looked at them and to help make the classroom library attractive.

Special attention is called to the recommendation that at any given time the classroom library must cover such a wide range of reading difficulty and topics that each pupil can find, often with the teacher's guidance, one or more books which he can read and which satisfy his immediate interests or tell of topics he wants to read about. Suggestions for estimating the reading difficulty of a given book were given on page 210. Instead of relying upon the results of the numerous investigations of children's interests, the teacher should seriously try to find out what the present and worthy interests of her particular pupils are. This she can do by administering orally and individually an interest questionnaire[28] or, preferably, by observing her pupils, listening to their conversations, noting what they say in their short oral reports about their hobbies and activities, and paying close attention to the replies each pupil gives when she asks what he likes to do and what he would like to read about.

c. Provision for Time

The daily schedule should provide a definite period of time for activities which, as described in sections *d* through *i*, can stimulate pupils to read on their own books supplied by the classroom library. For any given pupil or group of pupils, that period may be in addition to times set aside for the continuing instruction programmed by the basal readers. Since, as recommended several times in Chapter 5, any pupil is to receive only the parts of that instruction which teach him things he does not yet know, and since there is no particular date when this or that pupil should finish a given basal reader, the needed period can and often should be for at least some pupils one of those ordinarily assigned to the use of that reader.

d. Free Silent Reading

Throughout the school year, many of the periods referred to in the first sentence of the preceding paragraph should be devoted to free silent reading. In this activity one or more pupils are encouraged to go to the classroom library, to select one or more books, and to sit at the table in the reading corner or at their desks to browse in or read those books to themselves, much as people do at home or in a public library. It is understood that at times the teacher, knowing a pupil's reading ability and the reading difficulty of the books, will need to help him choose a book which she believes will appeal to him and which he can read. If, while reading to himself, a pupil asks what a certain word is, the teacher, instead of giving him the answer, should note the beginning sound and a few

[28] See, for example, Albert Harris, *How to Increase Reading Ability* (David McKay Co., Inc., New York, 4th ed., 1961), pp. 478, 480–481, and Paul Witty, *Reading in Modern Education* (D. C. Heath & Company, Boston, 1949), pp. 208–214, 302–307. For a brief and simple interest questionnaire, see Albert Harris, *Effective Teaching of Reading* (David McKay Co., Inc., New York, 1962), p. 293.

of the other sounds in the word, read to herself a few lines that come before and after the word, and then ask questions which will stimulate him to use what he already knows about unlocking strange words. For additional free silent reading, each pupil should be encouraged to keep at his desk or to get from the classroom library a book to read whenever he finishes an assignment early and to take home books to read after school hours.

e. Oral Reading by the Teacher

The first-grade or second-grade teacher should spend considerable time reading to her pupils intriguing short stories and poems that they will enjoy[29] and other types of good writings with which she is so familiar that in her reading she can alter her speed, use the inflections, emphases, and pauses, and create the atmosphere essential to making the lines sound as the author probably intended them to. This reading not only helps to increase pupils' listening vocabulary and extend their acquaintance with different types of sentence structure, but makes them aware of the types of content juvenile literature can offer them and stimulates their interest in getting similar selections to read to themselves. If, after the teacher's reading of a selection, the pupils wish to talk over with her what the selection told, they should be encouraged to do so, but this making of comments and raising of queries centered around pupils' reactions should never include either quizzing by the teacher or her assigning chores which have little if anything to do with enjoying the selection.

f. Oral Reading by Pupils

It is to be expected that a pupil, while reading to himself at school, at home, at a children's library, or elsewhere, will sometimes find a short story, a part of a story, a poem, a piece of information, an anecdote, or some other passage which he thinks is particularly good and would like to read to the rest of the class. Each pupil should understand that when this happens to him, he is to show the passage to the teacher, who certainly in most cases will make provision for him to prepare well for his oral reading and then read to the class. Similarly, at times the teacher may have a few pupils who have read to themselves a particularly good

[29] A compiled list of poems for which various investigations of children's choices in poetry show that first-grade and second-grade pupils have strong preference appears in Ernest Horn, *Poetry for Primary Children*, Extension Bulletin 776 (State University of Iowa, Iowa City, Iowa, 1961). For suggestions on presenting poetry to young children, read May Arbuthnot, *Time for Poetry* (Scott, Foresman & Company, Chicago, 1952) and Miriam Ruber, *Story and Verse for Children* (The Macmillan Co., New York, 1955).

story assume the character parts in the story and, after careful preparation, read the lines spoken by those characters to the class, with the teacher herself reading aloud the lines not spoken by the story characters. It is in situations such as these, with the audience not having at hand what is read aloud, that a pupil has a sound reason for reading well orally and the listeners have a realistic purpose for listening, two features which are difficult to obtain when, as with the use of the basal reader, each pupil in the group has already read silently what is to be read aloud. Possibly before pupils undertake the two types of oral reading recommended in this paragraph, the teacher may want to have them list standards to follow in reading orally and, now and then during the year after a given oral reading session has been completed, apply those standards in evaluating their performances.

g. Book Introductions

Every so often the teacher should use the time period proposed in section *c* on page 213 to introduce to pupils one or a few books which they have not read, which she thinks they will enjoy reading to themselves, and which are available for their use. In introducing a book, probably the teacher should show the book and some of its pictures, tell a little of what it is about and who one or more of its main characters are, read aloud one interesting part of the book, and explain where — usually but not always from what library — pupils can borrow the book. Once pupils understand that the purpose in giving a book introduction is to tell just enough so that others can decide whether or not they wish to read the book, the time should be used now and then for having pupils introduce to the class books they but not most of the class have read. Before initiating book introductions by pupils, the teacher should have the class make a list of standards pertaining to what the group likes to have a person do and tell in introducing a book to them. That list no doubt should include, besides at least some of the items mentioned above, telling whether or not the book is a good one and why. If the teacher is concerned about having pupils improve the quality of their book introductions as the year goes on, she can have the class use the list of standards periodically to evaluate, not as individual performances but as a group of items, the introductions which pupils give from time to time.

h. Panel Discussions

There is profit in having a small group of pupils who have read a given book carry on, with the teacher, an informal panel discussion of that book in front of the other members of the class. Here the teacher as chairman will direct the discussion so that what the pupils on the panel say expresses their reaction to the book and their feelings about this or that character or event. She will not resort to a mere quizzing to find out whether or not those pupils have read the book. If the book discussed has not been read by the rest of the class, care must be taken lest the talking be so detailed that those other pupils will have no need to read the book. If the entire class *has* read the book it makes no difference how detailed the panel's talking is as long as it does not produce boredom.

i. Additional Activities

Other things the teacher can have pupils do to stimulate their interest in reading books are keeping records of books read, making reproductions of small portions of books read, and engaging in somewhat specialized activities. As recommended by Harris,[30] an individual record may be (1) simply one or more sheets of paper on which are given the name of each book the pupil has read, perhaps the number of pages the book contains, and possibly the dates when the pupil started and finished his reading of the book, or (2) a paper showing the pupil's drawing or the teacher's duplication of a picture of a few empty bookshelves in which, for each book the pupil reads, he draws and colors the shelf edge of a book. A class record can be made by (1) placing after each pupil's name on a large sheet of chart paper small folded papers, each of which represents and gives the title of a book the pupil has read, or (2) placing on a paper cover made to fit a given book the names of pupils who have read that book. Reproductions of small portions of a book read can be made by having pupils draw and place on the bulletin board a strip of pictures depicting an episode, use puppets to show a scene in which pupils speak character parts, pantomime actions as someone reads a scene aloud, dramatize a scene with different pupils taking assigned roles, and show a scene on a shadow screen. The somewhat specialized activities include putting on a book fair, having a book parade in which pupils wear costumes to represent story characters, attending story hours at town and school libraries, and giving a program for parents at which pupils tell about books they have read.

j. Encouragement to Read More Advanced Books and to Read on More Topics

It is almost obvious that the teacher should be doing continually whatever she can (1) to encourage pupils to read books which are of higher quality, more maturity, and somewhat greater difficulty than those they

[30] Albert Harris, *Effective Teaching of Reading*, pp. 297–299.

have read on a given topic, and (2) to arouse their interest in reading on topics about which they have done as yet little if any reading. For pupils who have read on a given topic only simple books of little import, the teacher can at times provide for the introduction of more advanced books which she knows carry interest appeal and offer increasingly greater substance and a larger amount of text. Usually the introduction of such a book should be made by the teacher in the manner described on page 215. Sometimes it can be made by a pupil who has read and enjoyed the book. Occasionally it is sufficient to display the book's jacket and to place the book on the table in the reading corner. To entice pupils into reading books on a topic in which they have as yet little or no interest — perhaps pioneer life, rockets, ships, wild animals, Indians, jet airplanes, sports, or what not — and on which suitable books are available, that topic should first be presented to the pupils. The teacher can talk and perhaps show pictures and objects about the topic, read aloud an intriguing passage on it, or take the pupils on an excursion to see items pertaining to it. Or she may open up a topic by having a pupil who is informed on and has enthusiasm for it tell the class interesting things he knows about it. When once a topic has been presented, the pupils should be encouraged to raise questions about it which they want answered. Then the teacher may introduce books which they can read and which tell at least part of what they want to know. Of course no teacher can do the things proposed in this paragraph unless she has the more advanced books needed, suitable books on unexplored topics, and considerable enthusiasm for introducing new topics for the pupils to read about.

k. Suggestions to Parents

It is not uncommon for parents of first-grade and second-grade pupils to ask the teacher what they can do to stimulate their children to read books. When this happens, certainly the teacher can recommend a source or two from which a parent can get help in choosing books for his child.[31] She can also suggest that a shelf of books for the child be started at home, that the parent read to the child, that the parent read to himself frequently in the presence of the child so that the latter can realize that there must be some value in reading, and that each week a time be set aside when members of the family, including the child, read aloud to one another. In addition she can propose that the parent organize a neighborhood book club for children in which the members exchange books with one another, that the parent cooperate with other adults in taking book

---

[31] See Nancy Larrick, A *Parent's Guide to Children's Reading* (Doubleday & Company, Inc., New York, 1957), and *Let's Read Together* (American Library Association, Chicago, 1960).

club members to events at the children's library, and that the parent introduce to the child's class at school new books for children to read.

3. Magazines and Newspapers

The children's magazines in which first-grade and second-grade pupils will find selections they can read are *Child Life*,[32] *Children's Playmate Magazine*,[33] *Humpty Dumpty's Magazine*,[34] and *Jack and Jill*.[35] These periodicals contain short stories, short informative articles, pictures, puzzles, games, poems, children's original compositions, and other types of selections. If it is not practicable for the classroom library to supply a copy of each monthly issue of one or another of these periodicals, it is to be hoped that the school library will provide copies of most of them for pupils to read to themselves.

The weekly newspapers published for first-grade and second-grade pupils are *News Pilot, News Ranger, My Weekly Reader 1*, and *My Weekly Reader 2*.[36] These publications offer informative pictures and short articles pertaining to contemporary events and objects, strip cartoons, puzzles, jokes, exercises on appropriate reading skills, and other items. A teacher's manual accompanies each issue of each newspaper. In many schools pupils themselves subscribe to one or another of the newspapers and use each issue as the teacher directs in her teaching of reading, social studies, and science.

QUESTIONS TO BE ANSWERED

1. What are the reasons why the teacher should see to it that pupils do much reading on their own simultaneously with and in addition to their reading of the basal readers?

2. What are some of the pieces of reading matter the teacher can prepare? Why will she need to edit most of these selections, and what should constitute that editing?

---

[32] Published at Review Publishing Co., 1100 Waterway Blvd., Indianapolis, Indiana.
[33] Published at 6529 Union Ave., Cleveland, Ohio.
[34] Published by The Better Reading Foundation, Inc., 52 Vanderbilt Avenue, New York, New York.
[35] Published by Curtis Publishing Company, Independence Square, Philadelphia, Pennsylvania.
[36] *News Pilot* is geared to most first-grade pupils, *News Ranger* to most second-grade pupils. Both are published by Scholastic Magazines, Inc., 50 West 44th Street, New York, New York. *My Weekly Reader 1* is geared to most first-grade pupils, *My Weekly Reader 2* to most second-grade pupils. Both are published by American Education Publications, Columbus, Ohio.

3. Which types of selections prepared by the teacher do you think are most profitable to pupils? Why?

4. What standards should be applied to the selection of individual books to be made available for pupils to read on their own? Why is each standard important?

5. How can the teacher estimate the reading difficulty of a given book? What must she know about the vocabulary of that book? In what way does the selection of a book depend upon the instructional program offered by the basal readers being used or by the teacher herself?

6. How can the teacher get some idea of what topics her pupils would like to read about?

7. What are some of the sources to which the teacher can turn to get help in choosing books for the classroom library? How can she keep abreast of new publications as they come from the press?

8. What conditions should exist and what activities should be carried on in the classroom to stimulate pupils to read books on their own? In which activities would you have pupils engage most often? Why?

9. What benefit if any do you think pupils get from reading selections prepared by the teacher but do not get from their reading of books? What benefits do you think they get from their reading of books but cannot get from reading selections prepared by the teacher?

MORE TO READ

Arbuthnot, May, *Children and Books,* Scott, Foresman & Company, Chicago, 1957.

Bond, Guy, and Eva Wagner, *Teaching the Child to Read,* The Macmillan Co., New York, 1950, Chapter 15.

Dawson, Mildred, and Harry Bamman, *Fundamentals of Basic Reading Instruction, Longmans, Green,* & Co., Inc., New York, 1959, Chapter 8.

Gray, Lillian, and Dora Reese, *Teaching Children to Read,* The Ronald Press Company, New York, 1957, pp. 408–428.

Harris, Albert, *Effective Teaching of Reading,* David McKay Co., Inc., Chapter 13.

Hildreth, Gertrude, *Teaching Reading,* Henry Holt & Co., Inc., New York, 1962, Chapters 21, 22.

Larrick, Nancy, *A Teacher's Guide to Children's Books,* Charles E. Merrill Books, Inc., Columbus, Ohio, 1960.

Let's Read Together, American Library Association, Chicago, 1960.

Russell, David, *Children Learn to Read,* Ginn & Company, Boston, 1962, Chapter 12.

Spache, George, *Good Reading for Poor Readers*, The Garrard Press, Champaign, Ill., 1960.

Tooze, Ruth, *Your Children Want to Read*, Prentice-Hall, Inc., Englewood Cliffs, N.J., 1957.

THINGS TO DO

1. Assume that a group of first-grade pupils have learned to recognize in print any 60 common words you choose, that they have learned letter-sound associations for all the consonants, and that they have acquired some skill in using the technique to be followed in unlocking strange words. Then, after you have become acquainted with the type of writing used in almost any primer, write, in the 60 words you chose and some other words, a good short story which you know well and which you would give to the pupils mentioned above to read to themselves.

2. In a children's library find a simple book you think a first-grade pupil can and would like to read. Then make a list of more advanced books which you find on the same topic and which you would introduce to that pupil from time to time as his reading ability increases.

3. Choose any topic you think second-grade pupils may not be interested in reading about. Then write in some detail a statement of just what you would do to get them interested in reading about that topic.

4. Choose any five topics which you think second-grade pupils would be interested in reading about. Then go to a children's library to find there several books which you think those pupils could read on each topic. Make a list of the books you find.

5. Go to an elementary school to read a second-grade newspaper Then write a statement of just what you would do to make fullest use of that paper with a class.

6. Go to a children's library and look through a magazine intended for first-grade pupils. List the selections you think they could read, and write a statement of how you would use the magazine in the classroom.

7. Get a book written for teachers that contains an explanation of what the teaching of reading in the first grade according to an individualized or personalized plan is. Read that explanation carefully. Then write a statement which explains why you would or would not use that plan with first-grade pupils instead of using basal readers and providing for the additional reading suggested in this chapter.

part THREE /

The Second
Major Phase of Instruction

chapter 7

Introduction to the Program
for Grades 3 Through 6

As stated in Chapter 2, the program of instruction in reading proposed in this volume is divided into two main phases. The first phase, assigned to the first and second grades and described in detail in Chapters 3 through 6, is concerned primarily with helping the pupil develop the insights and skills he needs in order to make for printed lines which stand for familiar spoken English the meaning he would make if someone said or read the lines to him. If the teaching carried on during these two school years is done so well that the pupil acquires (1) control of the technique to be followed in unlocking strange words, (2) skill in recognizing instantly several thousand familiar words, (3) skill in thinking required voice intonations as he looks at printed lines, and (4) strong interest in reading about a variety of topics on which suitable material has been prepared for him, by the close of the second grade he should be able to read independently almost anything which is composed entirely of English he already understands in spoken form.

The second phase of the program is assigned to Grades 3 through 6 and is to be described in Chapters 7 through 12. It is the purpose of the present chapter to (1) offer criticisms of contemporary instruction in reading in these grades, (2) introduce the instruction which this volume's program suggests for them, (3) propose certain preliminary testing and teaching to be done at the beginning of each grade, (4) explain the place and the use of basal reading materials in the instruction to be given, and (5) comment on the grouping of pupils.

Criticisms of Contemporary Instruction

The author's observations of the classroom activities that teachers say constitute their teaching of reading, the discussions that Chapter 2 presents on most but not all the topics it includes, and data that will be noted in later chapters suggest five main criticisms which can be directed at the contemporary teaching of reading in Grades 3 through 6. To any given school, none, only some, or all of these criticisms may be applicable, but each of them is real in the sense that it is no figment of anybody's imagination and can be applied legitimately to at least some schools. No criticism is to be regarded lightly by the instructional staff of any school.

First, far too little attention is paid to the definite teaching of insights and skills that the pupil must possess in order to do well the various types of reading he is expected to do and should do both in and out of school. In some schools such skills have not even been identified and no teaching of any of them occurs except that which may take place feebly, incidentally, and almost unconsciously through the teacher's proper use of questions raised in group or class discussions of selections read in the basal reader. In other schools the teacher, without having done anything beforehand to help the pupil acquire an understanding of the meaning, the importance, and the correct use of a given skill, may admonish him to use that skill whenever he needs to in his reading. In addition, she may have him work out special exercises which supply directed practice in using the skill. But it is difficult to see how this mere admonishing and this premature providing of practice constitute by themselves the teaching of a skill or how such impotent substitutes for competent instruction can possibly equip the pupil to read the numerous books and other publications he must read in order to gain most of the benefits which reading offers.

Second, it is not at all uncommon to find the teaching of social studies, science, and other content subjects to be of such a nature that it encourages the pupil to engage in a small amount of sloppy reading in order to get his lessons. Unfocalized assignments which fail to direct the pupil's attention to and arouse in him no curiosity about particular problems or questions to be considered tempt him to read with only the vaguest purposes, with little concern for what his reading matter is saying, and without applying appropriate reading skills he has been taught. When the teacher fails to help the pupil build beforehand the background which his textbook itself does not supply and which he needs in order to understand what the book says, she invites him to resort to verbalism — to be satisfied by thinking the names without the meaning of words at which he looks — and to develop the notion that there is such a thing as reading a line without understanding what it means. Limiting the pupil's reading on a given topic or question to what a textbook says about it can dampen whatever interest he may have in the topic and deny him both the practice and the substance he could get by reading also other books that could illuminate and amplify the textbook's statements. Class discussions that do not hold the pupil responsible for accurately reporting information he has read on a given topic, that do not clarify statements which he saw in print and repeats but does not understand, and that allow the pupil to present in a disorganized form the information he has surely do not encourage him to use certain reading skills he has been taught or to read further on the topic under discussion.

Third, in many classrooms the provision made for arousing in pupils an abiding interest in reading on their own a variety of material on a wide range of topics certainly is inadequate. Many trade books, many school books, several magazines, and other publications of varied reading difficulty and interests to which pupils should be exposed simply are not made available. Furthermore, many teachers' acquaintance with and interest in children's literature are so shallow and their opportunities for acquiring those assets are so few and barren that they do not possess and cannot acquire within a reasonable time either the substance or the enthusiasm which are almost essential to stimulating pupils to read. In addition, at least some of the classroom activities meant to excite pupils' interest in reading are so unenticing and require so much belaboring and remembering of the content of selections that almost any pupil's chances of acquiring a distaste for reading are just as good as his chances for developing an interest in finding out what books say.

Fourth, the teaching of oral reading is often neglected or handled in a perfunctory manner. It fails to take into account the fact that the oral reading of a given passage is more difficult than and something in addition to the silent reading of the same passage. Seldom are pupils made aware of what constitutes good oral reading, and on few occasions are they given the time and opportunity they need in order to prepare to read well to others a selection or part of a selection they have enjoyed and would like to share with their classmates. Many pupils, even by the time they are in the sixth grade, have not yet learned that printed lines stand for spoken language, that what they read stands for talking which story characters do or which the author himself had in mind, and that in reading to others one needs to read lines as he would say them under the circumstances depicted. Most of the opportunities pupils are given for reading to others are those in which they take turns reading aloud short parts of selections the group or class has already read silently in the basal reader. They therefore provide the oral reader with little motivation for getting the story or message across to his listeners. Under the conditions mentioned in this paragraph it is little wonder that many pupils when reading to others find it difficult to avoid boring their audiences.

Fifth, adjustments of instruction to the individual pupil which should be made in any classroom are often omitted. Usually the books available for pupils to read on their own are not of sufficient scope in either range of reading difficulty or variety of interests so that each pupil has at hand enough material which he can and wants to read. Testing that should be done to determine which pupils have already learned this or that skill or which skills this or that pupil has not yet acquired is neglected. At a given grade level, instruction on items which the pupil has already learned but which are supposed to be introduced at that level is rehashed, instruction on items he was supposed to have learned in a preceding grade but does not yet know is not given, and instruction on items which he needs and could learn now but which are supposed to be taught in a later grade is withheld. Time and again, a pupil who has already learned an item sufficiently well is required to work out practice exercises on that item, and practice he needs on items he has not yet learned is not provided. In some quarters attempts made to discover a pupil's deficiencies which keep him from doing well in his reading or which have made him a so-called remedial case are not fruitful, and the relatively simple instruction which could put him on his feet, so to speak, is not undertaken. The fact that often the gifted pupil is not supplied with the advanced reading matter he could handle on his own is almost too obvious to mention.

Some of the weaknesses noted in the preceding paragraphs may spring from the notion that reading can be taught effectively in Grades 3 through 6 by the correct use of only basal reading materials.[1] This is a delusion. In the first place, such materials provide only some of the help required for giving competent instruction in appropriate reading skills. With a few exceptions, the pupil's reader itself, usually nothing more than a small anthology or group of selections for him to read, contains no lessons or

[1] The purpose and nature of the pupil's reader or readers, the accompanying workbooks, the teacher's guides or manuals, and the specialized pieces of equipment which make up a set of basal reading materials at a given grade level will be explained later in this chapter.

passages that introduce reading skills to be acquired. The aid which most basal materials do supply on the teaching of reading skills consists almost entirely of (1) pages in the pupil's accompanying workbook that give practice in using skills and (2) proposals in the teacher's guide that admonish the teacher to do something about a given skill, provide suggestions to be followed in introducing skills, or offer questions for class discussions which require the pupil to have used a skill in order to respond correctly. Second, teaching social studies and other content subjects in such a way as to reinforce what has been taught in reading is a part of instruction in those content subjects and is not and cannot be a responsibility of the basal reading materials. Third, the selections offered by any reader, no matter what they are, are just a drop in the bucket compared to the number and variety of selections to which pupils should be exposed during a school year. Finally, while the pupil's workbook, the teacher's guide, and certain pieces of specialized equipment accompanying a basal reader may supply some aids that can be used in providing for individual differences, no basal reading materials do or can offer all the help the teacher needs in order to make all the adjustments of instruction to the individual pupil which should be made.

It is unfortunate that some teachers in Grades 3 through 6 tend to limit their teaching of reading to that which may occur through using one or more readers in a questionable way or perhaps as just a story book with a given group or class. Almost invariably this activity, consuming 150 or more of 180 so-called reading periods available during a school year, consists in doing only the following things:

1. Arousing pupils' interest in reading a selection in the reader, telling them what each new word in the selection is, at times building background the pupils need for reading the selection, and perhaps setting a purpose with which pupils are to do the reading.
2. Having pupils read the selection silently and, when asked to do so, telling this or that pupil something that solves a problem he has.
3. Providing for group discussion which may be nothing more than a rehashing of what the selection says and in which the teacher uses questions to find out whether pupils comprehended what they apparently read.
4. Having pupils read part or all of the selection aloud.
5. Having pupils use workbook exercises, which more often than not pertain only to the content of the selection.
6. Relating the selection to other types of school work, often called enrichment.

While parts of these six performances may occasionally enhance pupils' progress in reading, surely, with their failure to provide instruction in appropriate reading skills, to offer realistic opportunities for pupils to read to others, and to stimulate each pupil to read on his own, they fall far short of what should be the teaching of reading in any given grade or during any extended period of time.

Introduction to the Proposed Instruction

As stated at the beginning of Chapter 2, the two main objectives of this volume's suggested program of instruction in reading are (1) to help the pupil develop the power to read independently and (2) to stimulate him to build an abiding interest in reading a variety of worthy material on a wide range of topics. Of the instruction assigned to the first and second grades, the part directed at the first objective and described in Chapters 3 through 5 is concerned with helping the pupil acquire the insights and skills he needs in order to read independently the relatively simple English he already understands in spoken form. The part directed at the second objective and described in Chapter 6 is concerned with providing the material, the opportunities, and the incentives the pupil needs in order to begin to build some interest in reading various types of selections on several different topics.

Three main teaching activities, named in the numbered paragraphs that follow immediately, constitute the instruction in reading which this volume proposes for Grades 3 through 6. The first is devoted to the fulfillment of the first objective, the second to both objectives, and the third to the second objective.

1. *Teaching insights and skills that the pupil must possess in order to cope with meaning difficulties presented in much of his reading matter by expressions he does not understand yet in spoken form, to study informative reading matter effectively, and to react critically to questionable statements he has read.* All of this instruction is concerned with the problem of enabling the pupil to make reading more effective as a means of receiving meaning through language than listening is or can be and to use reading as a means of educating himself. The discussions offered in Chapters 8, 9, and 10 identify and explain the particular items to be taught and give detailed suggestions for teaching them.

2. *Teaching social studies and the other content subjects in a way which reinforces insights and skills taught in reading itself, which develops concepts needed for reading passages pertaining to those subjects,*

and which stimulates pupils to read on their own much material on topics presented by the same subjects. This activity is described in detail in Chapter 11.

3. Providing materials and classroom experiences which will entice pupils into reading on their own the numerous worthy juveniles and other publications intended for their use. Sometimes called the teaching of children's literature or recreatory reading, this activity is the subject of Chapter 12.

Preliminary Testing and Teaching

Any pupil in one or another of the grades under discussion will encounter in his reading quite a number of words which he understands when he hears them spoken but which as yet are strange to him in print. If he is to do much independent reading, he must unlock these words all by himself, just as first-grade and second-grade pupils unlock such words included in the selections they read. While one certainly should expect the great majority of pupils entering Grade 3 or any higher grade to be adept at unlocking words which are strange to them only in print, some youngsters are not as skillful at doing this job as they can or should be. These particular pupils should be identified early in the school year and helped to improve.

The first thing to do is to test all pupils in a given class on the letter-sound associations they should have learned in the first two grades. The material that follows presents such a test, covering the associations for consonants, vowels, and common endings and other syllables. Each part of the test, without its accompanying explanation and directions for the teacher, may be duplicated so that every pupil has a copy to use as the teacher administers that part to the entire class at one time. Presumably all the words used in each part of the test are words which the pupils do not know in print.

Part I: Consonants

Name of Pupil _____

1. wield	yield	bield	14. jest	zest	quest
2. squid	grid	quid	15. barrow	harrow	marrow
3. bier	tier	kier	16. rector	vector	sector
4. whence	thence	hence	17. foil	roil	coil
5. callow	fallow	hallow	18. hart	tart	mart
6. clime	prime	chime	19. kine	dine	thine
7. purge	gurge	surge	20. firth	girth	mirth

8. heckle	sheckle	speckle	21. nard	bard	pard
9. mite	cite	rite	22. foist	joist	moist
10. rally	tally	dally	23. vend	rend	fend
11. bode	lode	mode	24. dusk	husk	tusk
12. phane	vane	thane	25. sane	bane	wane
13. bicker	dicker	flicker	26. vender	gender	render
	27. lore	yore	gore		

Explanation and directions for the teacher: Each of the 27 rows in Part I is to be used in testing on only one association, and in the order in which the rows are listed. The associations to be checked are those for: (1) *b*, (2)*qu*, (3) *k*, (4) *wh*, (5) hard *c*, (6) *ch* as in *chap*, (7) *p*, (8) *sh*, (9) soft *c*, (10) *r*, (11) *l*, (12) *th* as in *thank*, (13) *d*, (14) *z*, (15) *m*, (16) *s* as in *sit*, (17) *f*, (18) *t*, (19) *th* as in *that*, (20) hard *g*, (21) *n*, (22) *j*, (23) *v*, (24) *h*, (25) *w*, (26) soft *g*, (27) *y*. All the words in each row sound exactly alike except at the beginning and presumably are words the pupil does not know in print. In working with each row, the pupil's task will be to draw a line under the one word which you will name. It is suggested that before administering the test you make sure of the correct pronunciation of each word you will name.

To administer the test, proceed as follows: Give a copy of the rows of words to each pupil to be tested. Then say: "Today we are going to find out whether you know what sounds certain consonants stand for. You can see that there are 27 rows of words on your paper. In each row, there are three words that sound exactly alike except at the beginning. I will ask you to draw a line under just one of the words in each row. Now look at row number 1. Draw a line under the word that you think is *bield*." Repeat the word. . . . "Look at the words in row number 2. Draw a line under the word that you think is *quid*." Repeat the word. . . . "Look at the words in row 3. Draw a line under the word that you think is *kier*." . . .

Continue in the same manner with the remaining 24 rows. The words to name for those rows are as follows: (4) *whence*, (5) *callow*, (6) *chime*, (7) *purge*, (8) *sheckle*, (9) *cite*, (10) *rally*, (11) *lode*, (12) *thane*, (13) *dicker*, (14) *zest*, (15) *marrow*, (16) *sector*, (17) *foil*, (18) *tart*, (19) *thine*, (20) *girth*, (21) *nard*, (22) *joist*, (23) *vend*, (24) *husk*, (25) *wane*, (26) *gender*, (27) *yore*.

Part II: Vowels

Name of Pupil _____

1. dint	dent	daunt	14. braw	brew	brow
2. brawl	brail	broil	15. rave	rove	rive
3. bide	bode	bade	16. haw	hoe	hie
4. bleat	bluet	bloat	17. ply	ploy	plea

5. crotch	cratch	crutch	18. trey	troy	trow
6. mewl	maul	moil	19. stele	stile	stale
7. crimp	cramp	crump	20. peon	peen	pawn
8. reek	roak	rook	21. mute	mite	mote
9. slag	slug	slog	22. lien	loon	loin
10. cowl	coil	caul	23. hied	hoed	heed
11. bun	bin	ban	24. tread	treed	tried
12. plait	pleat	plight	25. bawl	boil	bail
13. vile	vole	vale	26. beet	bait	bout
	27. bray	brew	braw		

Explanation and directions for the teacher: Each of the 27 rows in Part II is to be used in testing on only one association, and in the order in which the rows are listed. The associations to be checked are those for: (1) short *e*, (2) *oi* as in *boil*, (3) long *i*, (4) *oa* as in *coat*, (5) short *o*, (6) *au* as in *caught*, (7) short *a*, (8) *oo* as in *look*, (9) short *u*, (10) *ow* as in *cow*, (11) short *i*, (12) *ea* as in *meat*, (13) long *a*, (14) *ew* as in *few*, (15) long *o*, (16) *ie* as in *fried*, (17) *y* as in *type*, (18) *ow* as in *blow*, (19) long *e*, (20) *aw* as in *lawn*, (21) long *u* as in *mute*, (22) *oo* as in *room*, (23) *ee* as in *feet*, (24) *ea* as in *head*, (25) *ai* as in *main*, (26) *ou* as in *loud*, (27) *ay* as in *play*. In working with each row, the pupil's task will be to draw a line under the one word which you will name.

To administer the test, proceed as follows: Give a copy of the rows of words to each pupil to be tested. Then say: "Today we are going to find out whether you know what sounds vowels and certain vowel combinations stand for. You can see that there are 27 numbered rows of words on your paper. In each row are three words that sound alike except for the vowel sound in each word. I will ask you to draw a line under just one of the words in each row. Now look at the words in row number 1. Draw a line under the word that you think is *dent*." (Sound *e* as in *met*.) Repeat the word. . . . "Look at the words in row number 2. Draw a line under the word that you think is *broil*." (Sound *oi* as in *soil*.) Repeat the word. . . . "Look at the words in row 3. Draw a line under the word that you think is *bide*." (Sound *i* as in *mine*.) Repeat the word. . . .

Continue in the same manner with the remaining 24 rows. The words to name for those rows are as follows: (4) *bloat* (sound *oa* as in *coat*), (5) *crotch* (sound *o* as in *bomb*), (6) *maul* (sound *au* as in *laud*), (7) *cramp* (sound *a* as in *cap*), (8) *rook* (sound *oo* as in *look*), (9) *slug* (sound *u* as in *cub*), (10) *cowl* (sound *ow* as in *frown*), (11) *bin* (sound *i* as in *tin*), (12) *pleat* (sound *ea* as in *meat*), (13) *vale* (sound *a* as in *safe*), (14) *brew* (sound *ew* as in *few*), (15) *rove* (sound *o* as in *cove*), (16) *hie* (sound *ie* as in *tie*), (17) *ply* (sound *y* as in *try*), (18) *trow* (sound *ow* as in *know*), (19) *stele* (sound the first *e* as in *he*; the second *e* is silent), (20) *pawn* (sound *aw* as in *lawn*), (21) *mute* (sound *u* as in *tube*), (22) *loon* (sound *oo* as in *room*), (23) *heed* (sound *ee* as in *feel*), (24) *tread* (sound *ea* as in *head*), (25) *bail* (sound *ai* as in *sail*), (26) *bout* (sound *ou* as in *couch*), (27) *bray* (sound *ay* as in *hay*).

Part III: Common Endings and Other Syllables

Name of pupil _____

1. abates	abating	abated
2. cherishes	cherished	cherishing
3. grapple	grappler	grappled
4. absolves	absolving	absolved
5. variably	variable	variability
6. dolefully	dolefulness	doleful
7. defector	defection	defective
8. banisher	banished	banishing
9. bounty	bountied	bounteous
10. blustering	blustery	blustered
11. grieving	grievance	grievant
12. fondler	fondly	fondle
13. blandisher	blandishment	blandished
14. vainer	vainest	vainly
15. grosser	grossed	grossing
16. beholding	beholder	beholden
17. lavishing	lavishly	lavishness
18. shiftless	shifty	shiftiness
19. frailty	frailly	frailness
20. revest	rivet	russet
21. impact	intact	iliac
22. proceed	precede	primmed
23. umbrage	usage	unbrace
24. duress	depress	digress
25. missive	motive	massive
26. camphor	conspire	comprise
27. desolation	dilatation	dissolution
28. expansive	evasive	effective
29. camphor	computer	conjure
30. pertain	profane	preface

Explanation and directions for the teacher: Each of the 30 rows in Part III is to be used in testing on only one association, and in the order in which the rows are listed. The associations to be checked are those for: (1) *ed* as in *wanted*, (2) *es* as in *bushes*, (3) *ple* as in *sample*, (4) *ed* as in *ordered*, (5) *able* as in *comfortable*, (6) *ful* as in *careful*, (7) *tion* as in *mention*, (8) *ed* as in *walked*, (9) *ty* as in *county*, (10) *y* as in *snowy*, (11) *ing* as in *going*, (12) *dle* as in *candle*, (13) *ment* as in *pavement*, (14) *est* as in *coldest*, (15) *er* as in *safer*, (16) *en* as in *beaten*, (17) *ness* as in *kindness*, (18) *less* as in *fearless*, (19) *ly* as in *fairly*, (20) *re* as in *replant*, (21) *im* as in *improve*, (22) *pre* as in *prepare*, (23) *un* as in *unopen*, (24) *de* as in *depart*, (25) *mis* as in *misplace*, (26) *con* as in *conduct*, (27) *dis* as in *dislike*, (28) *ex* as in *excuse*, (29) *com* as in *compare*,

(30) *per* as in *perfect.* In working with rows 1 through 19, the pupil's task will be to draw a line under the one word which you will name. In working with rows 20 through 30, his task will be to draw a line under the one word which begins with the same syllable sound as two words you will name.

To administer the test, proceed as follows: Give a copy of the rows of words to each pupil to be tested. Then say: "Today we are going to find out whether you know what sounds certain common endings and other common syllables stand for. You can see that there are 30 rows of words on your paper. In each of rows 1 through 19, there are three words that sound alike, except for the sound at the end of each word. In each of those rows, I will ask you to draw a line under the one word which I will name. Look at the words in row 1. Draw a line under the word which you think is *abated.*" (Sound *ed* as in *wanted.*) Repeat the word. . . . "Look at the words in row number 2. Draw a line under the word that you think is *cherishes.*" (Sound *es* as in *bushes.*) Repeat the word. . . . "Look at the words in row 3. Draw a line under the word that you think is *grapple.*" (Sound *ple* as in *sample.*) Repeat the word. . . .

Continue in the same manner with rows 4 through 19. The words to name for those rows are as follows: (4) *absolved* (sound *ed* as in *ordered*), (5) *variable* (sound *able* as in *portable*), (6) *doleful* (sound *ful* as in *careful*), (7) *defection* (sound *tion* as in *mention*), (8) *banished* (sound *ed* as in *walked*), (9) *bounty* (sound *ty* as in *county*), (10) *blustery* (sound *y* as in *mighty*), (11) *grieving* (sound *ing* as in *going*), (12) *fondle* (sound *dle* as in *candle*), (13) *blandishment* (sound *ment* as in *pavement*), (14) *vainest* (sound *est* as in *coldest*), (15) *grosser* (sound *er* as in *safer*), (16) *beholden* (sound *en* as in *spoken*), (17) *lavishness* (sound *ness* as in *kindness*), (18) *shiftless* (sound *less* as in *fearless*), (19) *frailly* (sound *ly* as in *fairly*).

When you are ready to use row 20, say: "In each of the rows that are left on your paper, I will ask you to draw a line under the one word which begins with the same syllable sound as two other words I will name. Look at row number 20. Draw a line under the word that begins with the same syllable sound as *repel* and *request.*" Repeat the words. . . . "Look at row number 21. Draw a line under the word that begins with the same syllable sound as *impart* and *imbibe.*" Repeat the words. . . . "Look at row 22. Draw a line under the word that begins with the same syllable sound as *preside* and *prevail.*" Repeat the words. . . .

Continue in the same manner with rows 23 through 30. Words to name for each of those rows are as follows: (23) *unstable, uncertain,* (24) *desist, delete,* (25) *mislay, misfit,* (26) *convex, contend,* (27) *dismay, disrupt,* (28) *extent, expend,* (29) *compete, compel,* (30) *perforce, pernicious.*

In scoring each pupil's test to determine just which letter-sound associations he does not yet know sufficiently well, the teacher should check any row in which the pupil underlined a wrong item, even though he may have underlined also in that row the one correct item. Then for each association a list of pupils who do not know that association can be made. To avoid wasting any pupil's time by trying to teach him something he already knows, the teacher, in giving the instruction needed on any given letter-sound association, should work with only those pupils who do not yet know that association.

To teach one or more pupils a letter-sound association for any given consonant, the following procedure — using here as an illustration the teaching of the association for *m* — may be used:

Print on the board two words which begin with *m* and which the pupil knows well in print, perhaps *make* and *mine*. Point to the words. Then say: "You know these words. With what letter do they both begin? . . . Now let's say the two words to hear whether they begin with the same sound. . . . Do the two words begin with the same sound? . . . In what two ways do the words begin alike? . . . (They both begin with the letter *m*, and they both begin with the same sound.) The sound that you hear at the beginning of *make* and *mine* is the sound that *m* usually stands for wherever you see it in a word. You can hear that sound at the beginning of *map, meat must, more,* and *miss*. What are some other words you know that begin with the sound *m* stands for? . . ."

To teach one or more pupils a letter-sound association for any given single vowel, the following two-step procedure — using here as an illustration the teaching of the association for short *a* — may be used.

Step 1: Print on the board two monosyllabic words which begin with the letter *a* and the short sound of that vowel and which the pupil knows in print, perhaps *am* and *at*. Point to the words. Then say: "You know these words. With what letter do they both begin? . . . Now let's say the two words and listen to hear whether they begin with the same sound. . . . Do the two words begin with the same sound? . . . In what two ways do the words begin alike? . . . (They both begin with the letter *a*, and they both begin with the same sound.) The sound you hear at the beginning of *am* and *at* is a sound the letter *a* often stands for. We call it the short sound of *a*. You can hear that sound at the beginning of *add, an, as, ashes, absent*. What are some other words you know that begin with the short sound of *a*? . . ."

Step 2: Print on the board two monosyllabic words in which the letter *a* standing for the short sound appears in the middle and which the pupil knows in print, perhaps *bad* and *pan*. Then say: "You know these words. What letter is in the middle of each of them? . . . Now let's say the two words to hear whether they have the same sound in the middle? . . . In what two ways are the words alike? . . . (They both have the letter *a* in the middle, and they both have the same sound in the middle.) That sound is a sound that the letter *a* often stands for in the middle of a word. You can hear that sound in the middle of *dad, rat, can, lap, ham*. What do we call that sound? . . ."

The following procedure — using as an illustration the teaching of the association for *ea* as in *meat* — can be used in teaching a letter-sound association for any vowel combination:

Print on the board two monosyllabic words in which the vowel combination *ea* standing for the long *e* sound appears in the middle and which the pupil knows in print, perhaps *meat* and *bean*. Point to the words. Then say: "You know these words. What two letters are in the middle of each of them? . . . Now let's say the two words and listen to hear whether they have the same sound in the middle. . . . Do the two words have the same sound in the middle? . . . In what two ways are the words alike? . . . (They both have the letters *ea* in the middle, and they both have the same sound in the middle.) That sound is one that the letters *ea* often stand for when they come in that order in a word. You hear that sound in *beat, deal, lean, meal, neat*."

The following procedure — using as an illustration the teaching of the association for *tion* — can be used in teaching an association for any ending or other common syllable:

Print on the board two words which end in *tion* and which the pupil knows in print, perhaps *mention* and *action*. Point to the words. Then say: "You know these words. With what four letters do they end? . . . Now let's say the two words to hear whether they both end with the same sound. . . . Do the two words end with the same sound? . . . In what two ways do the words end alike? . . . (They both end with the letters *tion*, and they both end with the same sound.) That sound is the sound the letters *tion* usually stand for in a word. You can hear that sound in *action, mention, position, notion, attention, pronunciation*."

Note: In teaching a letter-sound association for a group of letters that is a beginning syllable, the teacher should print on the board two words which *begin* with that group of letters and which the pupil knows in print. In talking with the pupil, she should refer to the *beginning* letters and the *beginning* sound of the words.

In helping a pupil in the third grade or a higher grade become adept at unlocking independently words that are strange to him only in print, it is not sufficient merely to teach him important letter-sound associations he does not know. The teacher must give him also a considerable amount of directed practice in using the technique to be followed in unlocking such words. As explained and illustrated in detail on pages 120–123, this technique consists in using first and together the context and the beginning sound of the word and then only as many of the remaining sounds as are needed for making sure of the word.

To provide the needed practice, the teacher should choose a number of words — perhaps fifteen or more — that are strange to the pupil in print and that begin with a letter or group of letters and contain other letters and groups of letters for which the pupil has learned letter-sound associations. Then the teacher should introduce the words one at a time in printed context, just as the first-grade teacher introduces new words to her pupils, using the directive statements and questions which do the teaching of the technique, as in the following introduction of the supposedly strange word *depends*. Other examples of word introductions were given on pages 147–150.

Print the following lines on the board:

> My little sister can't do much for herself.
> She depends on me for help.

Point to *depends*. Then say: "You know all these words except this one. With what letter does the word begin? . . . You know the sound that d stands for. What are some of the other letters in the word you know sounds for? . . . To find out what the word is, read the lines to yourself. Think here a word that begins with the right sound and makes sense with the other words. Use other letter sounds you know in the word to make sure just what it is. . . .

"What is the word? . . . How do you know it isn't *relies?* . . . How do you know it isn't *leans?* . . . How do you know it isn't *defends?* . . ."

The teacher may find that introducing the fifteen or more strange words does not give the pupil all the directed practice he needs for learning to follow the technique. In this case additional words which are strange to the pupil only in print should be introduced to him in the same manner. They may or may not be among those he will encounter in reading the basal reader or some other book.

Using Basal Reading Materials

It is common practice in Grades 3 through 6 to try in large part to teach reading to a given group or class by using, poorly or well, a set of basal reading materials. Generally these materials include the pupil's reader, the pupil's accompanying workbook, the teacher's guide or manual, and whatever associated film strips, tests, "read-by-yourself" books, and other supplementary equipment are available. The reader itself is essentially a collection of perhaps seventy-five or more passages for pupils to read more or less under the direction of the teacher and usually contains quite a number of short stories, most of them adaptations of writings by authors of juveniles, a few informative articles, several short poems, a play or two, scattered puzzles, jokes, and anecdotes, and in a few cases a small number of lessons which introduce reading skills to be taught. The pupil's workbook provides exercises on reading skills that have been introduced or, as in some instances, comprehension checks on some of the selections presented in the reader. The teacher's guide programs the instruction to be given during the time the reader is being used and offers suggestions for handling each selection with a given group or class.[2]

No one knows how long the basal reading materials will occupy the prominent place that they now have. Certainly it is possible that for pupils who have learned what is offered by the instruction proposed in this volume for Grades 1 and 2, the effective use of very different equipment could yield greater profit than is usually the outcome of even the best use of basal materials. This equipment might include, among other things, (1) a pupil's textbook which provides only carefully planned instruction and practice in important reading skills, such as that described in Chapters 8 through 10, and which makes no attempt to supply stories and other types of selections as a basal reader now does, (2) a teacher's guide which programs the instruction to be given through the use of the pupil's textbook, explains the system of the teaching of reading to be followed, and supplies helpful suggestions for stimulating pupils to use in other school work appropriate items they have learned in reading, and (3) a very large number of individually bound, well-written, and appealing selections which cover a wide range of interests, which fit well with the pupil's continuing progress in developing the power to read independently, and from which each pupil will choose what he is to read at almost any given time. For effective handling of such equipment the teacher could use reading periods for teaching reading skills, for enabling each pupil to read on his own numerous worthy selections he can and wants to read, and for carrying on group or class discussions and other activities. In the latter, pupils could tell their classmates about selections they had read, and pupils who had read a given selection could exchange their ideas about it in a manner conducive to building interest in books. Such an offering should do much to eliminate most of the practices which, commonly attached to the ordinary use of basal materials, require all pupils to read the same selections, often insist upon pupils' questionable rehashing of what they have read, and may permit if not encourage perfunctory and somewhat unrealistic oral reading by pupils.

But basal materials have been with us for many years, and they are widely used as a main director of what the teaching of reading is to be.

[2] The purposes of the film strips, the tests, and the "read-by-yourself" books will be noted later in this section.

Correctly used they have made and can make an important contribution to pupils' progress in reading. In any case, they are not likely to go away soon. Furthermore, the equipment described briefly in the preceding paragraph simply is not yet available in acceptable form. It is imperative, therefore, that the teacher who uses basal materials proceed in a way which will enable them to yield for each pupil the greatest benefit they can. This is the reason space is given in this volume to a discussion of their use in Grades 3 through 6.

Usually most of the suggestions offered by the teacher's guide that accompanies a basal reader are organized around the selections presented by the reader itself and pertain to certain instructional activities. These activities can be labeled arbitrarily (1) preparing pupils for the reading of a selection, (2) having pupils read and talk over the selection, (3) developing appropriate reading skills, and (4) providing for individual differences.

1. Preparing for Reading

To prepare pupils for reading one or another of the selections in a basal reader, the teacher may need to perform three tasks: (a) introducing new words the pupils will encounter in their reading of the selection,[3] (b) supplying background which pupils do not have and will need for understanding what the selection says, and (c) providing the slight motivating push which will stimulate pupils to want to begin to read the selection. Probably the third task should be undertaken to at least some small extent in presenting any selection to any group of pupils. As will be explained later, how much time is to be devoted to either or both of the first two tasks depends upon the particular group of pupils being taught and the nature of the selection to be read.

Consider first the matter of introducing to pupils new words they will encounter in the selection. No doubt the pupils already know some of these words in print.[4] The remaining new words are strange to them in one way or another. Most of them are strange only in print, just as are all the strange words included in reading matter suitable for first-grade and second-grade pupils. Some of them are strange only in meaning, in the sense that although the pupils have at least one meaning for the word when they see it in print and know which familiar spoken word the printed form stands for, they do not have the particular meaning they need in order to read the word in the setting in which it appears in the

---

[3] The term *new words* refers to those words which have not appeared heretofore in the series of basal readers and are now used for the first time in the selection to be read.

[4] Possibly pupils acquired this familiarity through the reading they did on their own outside the basal readers they used in previous grades.

selection. It is only in this way that the word *file* in the following passage may be strange to most fourth-grade pupils:

> Suddenly a rabbit leaped from under a bush at the far end of the fence and scampered over the hill. Then for a mile or more, Dick and his father followed the *file* across the snow-covered fields.

The rest of the strange words are strange in form, pronunciation, and meaning, as illustrated by the italicized word in the following sentence:

> Slowly the old man came up the hill, carrying the heavy *fustian* across his shoulder.

What the teacher needs to do first is to examine the new words that the selection presents[5] and decide which ones probably are strange to her pupils and in just what way.

It is a serious error to introduce to pupils who have gained control of the technique to be followed in unlocking strange words, as explained in Chapters 4 and 5, new words which are strange to them only in print. One should expect these particular pupils to unlock the words independently as they meet them in their reading of the selection. The procedure described on page 236 should be used in introducing to pupils who have not acquired this control several — but only several — of these words. The directed practice that such introductions give can help these pupils acquire the skill they do not yet have and need for unlocking independently words which are strange to them only in print.

Any new word that is strange only in meaning presents quite a different problem. The pupils already know which familiar spoken word the printed form stands for and they have at least one meaning for the word, but they do not know the particular meaning the word has in the setting in which it is used in the selection to be read. Such a word should not be introduced if the pupils have already learned how to use context to get the needed meaning of a word[6] and the context contains the needed helpful parts, or if the pupils have learned how to use a dictionary to get the meaning of a word.[7] Instead the pupils should be expected to use

---

[5] Usually a basal reader includes at the back a list of the new words presented in each selection.

[6] As will be explained in Chapter 8, this use of context is quite different from that which the pupil should make in unlocking words that are strange only in print. The instruction which pupils need so that they can become adept at using context to get the meaning of a word is considered in the same chapter.

[7] The instruction that pupils need for learning to use a dictionary to get the meaning of a word is considered in Chapter 8. Usually a basal reader includes a small dictionary at the back.

one or both of these aids to get the needed meaning by themselves. If neither of the conditions just mentioned exists, the teacher should introduce the word by (a) showing the form to the pupils, (b) asking them to tell what the word is, and then (c) explaining to them what the particular meaning is that the word stands for in the selection to be read.

Any new word that is strange in form, meaning, and pronunciation constitutes a somewhat complicated problem. The pupils have no acquaintance with the form of the word. The spoken word for which the form stands is not within their listening vocabulary or their speaking vocabulary, and consequently they have no meaning for the word. Such a word should not be introduced if the pupils have already learned to use context to get the meaning of a word and the context in which the word appears in the selection provides the needed helpful parts, or if they have learned how to use a dictionary to get both the meaning and the pronunciation of a word. Instead one should expect such pupils to use both these aids to get first the meaning of the word, and then the pronunciation, if it is actually needed,[8] when they meet the word in their reading of the selection. If the conditions just mentioned do not exist, the teacher should introduce the word, but since the pupils know neither the meaning nor the spoken word for which the form stands, the procedure described on page 236 must not be used. It will suffice if the teacher (a) prints the word on the board for the pupils to see, (b) asks them to use what they know about letter sounds to try to pronounce the word, (c) if necessary gives them the correct pronunciation of the word, and (d) explains the meaning the word stands for in the selection to be read.

Begin now to think about the matter of supplying background which pupils may need in order to read a given selection. As implied in Chapter 2 and as will be explained more fully in Chapter 8, both the quality and the quantity of the meaning which any person makes in reading the symbols that constitute a given printed passage depend a great deal upon the extent to which he himself has already experienced directly or vicariously what the passage tells about. Thus, for example, a pupil who has lived on a cattle ranch in the West, who knows something about the habits and idiosyncrasies of cattle, and who has seen cattle roundups can make much more clear and correct meaning in reading about a cattle stampede than can a pupil who as yet knows nothing about such matters. Similarly, a pupil who knows nothing about the purposes and nature of lighthouses cannot possibly make for a story about the adventures a boy

---

[8] It is possible to read a word without being able to pronounce it. The chief reason why the pupil needs to learn the pronunciation of a word is so that he can speak it correctly in his oral reading or talking and can recognize it when he hears other people speak it.

has when he is alone in his father's lighthouse during a storm either the quality or the quantity of the meaning that could be made by a pupil who has lived along the northern Atlantic coast and has visited a lighthouse and learned something about its operation.

Some of the selections in almost any basal reader tell about topics which are quite remote from pupils in either time or space or both and of which they have seen, heard, or read little if anything. Unless such a selection itself provides the background needed for understanding and enjoying the selection reasonably well, provision must be made for supplying that background in some other way. Occasionally the pupil's reader prefaces a selection with a short informative article and explanatory pictures. More frequently the teacher's guide offers suggestions which encourage the teacher to build the needed background herself by using appropriate pictures, objects, simple oral explanations, oral reading, movies, excursions, and perhaps other aids. Sometimes the suggestions the guide offers for working with pupils who already have a considerable amount of background are either different from or much less elaborate than those it proposes for working with pupils who are not so well informed.

It is true that the extent and the nature of the background which needs to be provided for a given group of pupils depend almost entirely upon the amount of appropriate knowledge those pupils already possess. But supplying background which pupils simply do not need for reading a selection is a waste of time that those pupils probably could spend more profitably in actually reading the selection. Some time ago the author was invited by a fourth-grade teacher to observe for two successive reading periods the building of background supposedly needed by pupils who lived in a small village and who, in the third period, were to read a short story in a basal reader. The story explains that a poor farmer with an unusually strong affection for animals brings home from town, much to his wife's dismay, a convalescing elephant for which a small circus owner has persuaded him to provide a temporary home. The farmer's children overcome their mother's disapproval of the project by having the elephant do several pieces of difficult work which she has wanted done for a long time. During the two reading periods the author observed, the teacher, by talking, reading aloud, showing and explaining pictures, and having individual pupils tell what they knew, attempted to acquaint the pupils with the differences between Indian elephants and African elephants, how wild elephants are captured, how elephants are trained, the work that elephants do, how elephants are cared for in zoos, how elephants care for their young, and what pachyderms are. Surely no one needs to know this much or all that there is to know about elephants in order to read with a reasonable amount of understanding and enjoyment either the word *elephant* or what the elephant did in the story. Probably, since the story itself presented pictures of an elephant and showed him doing one of the pieces of work that he did, the only background that almost any pupil would need would be some understanding of the work elephants can do and what kinds of heavy work they could be expected to do on a farm.

Stimulating pupils to want to begin to read a given selection in a basal reader need not be an elaborate and time-consuming matter. Usually a selection has at its beginning a picture or two, a title, and a few intriguing or "teasing" lines which, with the teacher's suitable comments and questions (often suggested by the teacher's guide), can provide the required motivation in only a minute or so. It is important to remember here that the motivation needed is just that small amount which will make pupils want to begin the reading. The motivation for reading a good selection through to the end comes from the reading itself, with the ideas given by one page making pupils want to read the next. If the selection has little or no interest-pull, there is nothing any teacher can do to motivate pupils to continue what must be to them a spiritless job of plodding through a banal passage.

2. Reading and Discussing

As soon as the teacher has completed the preparatory tasks, the pupils may be directed to begin their silent reading of the selection. If the particular group of pupils being taught can read the entire selection in one sitting, certainly they should be permitted and directed to do so. In case pupils need two or more sittings for doing this amount of reading, the teacher will need to name a natural break in the selection as the point at which to end the reading for the first sitting. The teacher may or may not set a purpose with which pupils are to do the silent reading, but any purpose that is set should pertain to some major matter and should fit well with the pupils' normal desire to find out what happens next or how things turn out.[9] Occasionally, as a part of the direction to silent reading, the teacher should remind pupils to think, as they look at the lines, how those lines probably would sound if they heard someone say them. During the silent reading the teacher may help any pupil who encounters a difficulty he is sure he cannot handle, but, instead of answering his problem for him, she should raise questions which stimulate him to recall things he knows and can use to overcome the difficulty himself.

[9] If a given group of pupils takes two sittings for the silent reading of a selection, the teacher may need to have those pupils recall main events told in the first part of the selection and possibly to set a purpose for the reading of the second part before the pupils begin the second part.

Helping pupils to carry on the right kind of group discussion following their silent reading can increase their enjoyment of the selection. But questions raised here by the teacher must do more than instigate a mere rehashing of the selection and serve only as checks on pupils' comprehension of what the selection says. Usually any needed checking of comprehension is inherent in more profitable questions which stimulate pupils to share their reactions to and feelings about the selection or one or another of its events or characters, which illuminate story situations and conversations to be read aloud later, which encourage pupils to consider implications, if any, that the selection suggests, to make judgments, to draw conclusions, and to react critically to debatable statements they have read. Although it is sometimes profitable in the discussion to help pupils consider a moral value portrayed by the selection, care must be taken to see that questions and comments do not lead to the making of snap judgments which a pupil in the group can use to agitate an emotional conflict he has. The author saw this happen when a third-grade girl, already finding it difficult to like her father because of the abominable treatment she received from him, heard her classmates' affirmative replies to the teacher's questions: "Does the story show that Sally loved her father? Do you think that a boy or a girl who doesn't love his father is an ungrateful person?"

Although the most realistic and motivating situations for oral reading by pupils occur in connection with the teaching of children's literature, as will be noted in Chapter 12, it is not uncommon for the teacher, following a group discussion of a selection in the basal reader, to have pupils read parts or all of that selection aloud. Actually there is little if any need for this practice. Preferably almost any poem should be read aloud by individual pupils, or in unison by the group, or perhaps by the teacher. A play may or may not be dramatized or read aloud by pupils assuming character parts, largely according to the wish of the group. One or more parts which pupils select from a story may be read aloud, with different pupils reading different characters' speeches and the rest of the group listening (books closed) to hear the readers' interpretations of the lines. In the various oral reading situations, the teacher should encourage the pupils now and then to read lines as they would say them or to make them sound as they think they did when the story characters said them, or perhaps as the writer would say them, in the circumstances depicted. To be avoided in all provision for oral reading is a procedure which, somewhat like that followed in a barbershop, asks different pupils to read aloud and in the order in which they appear the various paragraphs that make up a selection.

3. Developing Reading Skills

Only some of the reading periods assigned to the use of basal reading materials during a school year should be devoted to preparing pupils for reading selections in the basal reader and having them read and talk over such passages. Other periods so assigned should be used for teaching reading skills, which compose a major and most important part of the program of instruction offered by the basal materials and which are exemplified by the skills described in Chapters 8 through 10. The teaching to be done in these other periods may consist in any one or more of the following:

1. Introducing a given skill — such as using context to get the meaning of a word, interpreting metaphor, deciding what the topic of a paragraph is — by using a lesson provided for that purpose in the pupil's reader itself, or by following suggestions supplied for the same purpose in the teacher's guide.
2. Having pupils reconsider here and there in a selection just read one or more points at which their use of a skill previously introduced was needed in order to interpret expressions correctly.
3. Having pupils work out one or more exercises which, as supplied by the accompanying workbook or the teacher's guide, give directed practice in using a skill that has been introduced.

Some teachers in Grades 3 through 6 often omit this teaching of skills which the basal materials propose. But such omission, probably born of the teacher's desire to devote most of her effort to using the reader itself as just a story book, makes instruction in reading at those grade levels lopsided, disregards the pupils' need to develop the power to read independently, and fails to give the program of instruction offered by the basal reading materials a chance to do for pupils the best it can. Of course care must be taken to see that no pupil's time is wasted by trying to teach him a skill he has already acquired.

4. Providing for Individual Differences

Usually the aids which a set of basal reading materials supplies for providing for individual differences consist largely but not entirely of (1) a variety of exercises on reading skills and (2) individual supplementary or "read-by-yourself" books and recommendations of other books. The exercises, supplied by the pupil's workbook, the teacher's guide, or both, are fitted to different levels of reading ability and provide practice on skills that have been introduced. Some exercises are intended for only those pupils who need extra practice on a given skill, some are fitted to the so-called average pupil's needs, and others require the best readers to stretch the relatively high degree of power they possess. In using the exercises, it is imperative that the teacher select for each pupil one or more that give him practice he needs and require no pupil to work out any exercise which does not sharpen a skill he ought to refine.

The individual "read-by-yourself" books, still all too few in number, are especially prepared to fit well at different levels of reading ability with the program of instruction offered by the basal materials and provide selections for pupils to read on their own. Recommendations of other books that are by no means as closely associated with the basal materials usually appear in the teacher's guide. Often they refer to writings which, in one way or another, are somewhat similar to selections in the basal reader, which are appropriate to different levels of reading ability, and which may be read independently by pupils just for pleasure or for working out some individual project that may or may not be suggested by the teacher's guide. It should be understood that usually the reading difficulty level indicated for a book is at best only the estimate of some person or persons who know the book and that at any time a book recommended may no longer be in print.

5. Concluding Notes

In working with a given selection in a basal reader, about how much time should one expect to spend on the teaching suggested in the four numbered sections just presented? If the group of pupils being taught is of so-called average background and reading ability, usually the teacher can expect to complete in one reading period the instruction proposed under both "Preparing for Reading" and "Reading and Discussing."[10] The teaching suggested under "Developing Reading Skills" will require the use of a second reading period, but always this instruction should be given only to pupils who have not yet built needed control of the skill or skills to be taught. Suggestions given under "Providing for Individual Differences" are to be carried out, not necessarily in any given reading period, but for this or that pupil at any time the teacher may choose.

Sharp adjustments of this time schedule will be called for at certain points according to the pupils being taught. If their background is relatively meager and their reading ability less than average, the teacher can expect to use considerably more time than that indicated in the preceding paragraph to introduce more of the new words, to provide for reading and discussing the selection, and to develop reading skills. If their background and reading ability are superior, much less time should

---

[10] If the selection itself is unusually long, a second reading period may be required for reading and discussing a second part of that selection.

be used in introducing new words (if any), in reading and discussing the selection, and in developing reading skills than is required when teaching an average group. It is particularly these so-called superior pupils who, more than any others, should be sharpening their reading skills, discovering and feeding new interests, and extending their experiences by reading on their own a very large number of individual books.

Film strips and tests that are parts of or accompany basal reading materials were mentioned on page 236. Usually the film strips either introduce or supply practice in using one or another of the reading skills included in the program offered by the basal materials and can be viewed by an entire class, a small group, or an individual pupil. The tests, sometimes called basic tests or unit tests, are intended for periodic use in determining pupils' recognition vocabulary, skill in unlocking strange words, sentence comprehension and paragraph comprehension, and control of certain skills including some of those to be discussed in Chapters 8, 9, and 10.

In selecting one or more standardized tests to use in determining the reading achievement of pupils in Grades 3 through 6, the teacher may wish to consider the following:

Iowa Every-Pupil Tests of Basic Skills. Elementary, Grades 3–5; Advanced, Grades 5–9. Tests vocabulary, paragraph comprehension, reading-study skills. Houghton Mifflin Company Test Department, 110 Tremont Street, Boston, Massachusetts.

Iowa Tests of Basic Skills. Grades 3–9. Tests vocabulary, comprehension, reading-study skills. Houghton Mifflin Company Test Department, 110 Tremont Street, Boston, Massachusetts.

Iowa Silent Reading Tests. Elementary Test, Grades 4–8. Tests word meaning, rate, comprehension, and locating information. Harcourt, Brace & World, Inc., 750 Third Avenue, New York, New York.

Gates Reading Tests. Advanced Primary, Grade 3. Tests word recognition, paragraph comprehension. Basic Reading Test, Grades 3–8. Tests word recognition, comprehension, reading for specific purposes. Bureau of Publications, Teachers College, Columbia University, New York, New York.

Stanford Achievement Tests. Elementary Reading Test, Grades 3–4. Tests word meaning and paragraph comprehension. Intermediate Reading Test, Grades 5–6. Tests word meaning and paragraph comprehension. Harcourt, Brace & World, Inc., 750 Third Avenue, New York, New York.

Durrell-Sullivan Reading Capacity and Achievement Tests. Intermediate, Grades 3–6. Tests vocabulary and comprehension. Harcourt, Brace & World, Inc., 750 Third Avenue, New York, New York.

Nelson Silent Reading Test. Grades 3–9. Tests vocabulary and paragraph comprehension. Houghton Mifflin Company Test Department, 110 Tremont Street, Boston, Massachusetts.

California Reading Tests. Primary, Grades 3–4; Elementary, Grades 4–6. Tests vocabulary and comprehension. California Test Bureau, 5916 Hollywood Boulevard, Los Angeles, California.

Metropolitan Achievement Tests. Elementary Reading, Grades 3–4. Tests vocabulary and comprehension. Intermediate Reading, Grades 5–6. Tests vocabulary and comprehension. Harcourt, Brace & World, Inc., 750 Third Avenue, New York, New York.

SRA Achievement Series: Reading. Grades 3–4. Tests vocabulary and comprehension. Grades 4–6. Tests vocabulary, comprehension, reading-study skills. Science Research Associates, Inc., 259 East Erie Street, Chicago, Illinois.

Diagnostic Reading Tests. Lower Level, Grades 4–6. Tests vocabulary word attack, comprehension, rate. Committee on Diagnostic Reading Tests, Mountain Home, North Carolina.

Comments on the Grouping of Pupils

Most but not quite all of what is said or written about the grouping of pupils in Grades 3 through 6 for purposes of instruction in reading pertains to pupils' ability to read the selections in basal readers. Presumably the selections in any such book intended for use primarily at a given grade level can be read with relative ease by pupils whose reading ability is judged to be at, slightly below, or somewhat above that grade level. At the same time they present occasionally the difficulties needed for stimulating pupils' continued growth in the power to read independently. But, as all pertinent data show, the range of the general reading ability of all pupils at this or that grade level in almost any school is wide indeed, covering at least six years. For example, in Grade 4 the poorest reader will read at the level of the average second-grade pupil and the best reader at the level of the average eighth-grade pupil. This means, among other things, that of the pupils enrolled in any grade in a given school some can read with unusual ease the selections in a basal reader prepared for that grade, many can read those passages with just the amount of puzzling needed for increasing their reading ability, and others cannot possibly read them at all. Obviously, if basal readers are to have a part in supplying pupils with reading material, each pupil, whatever his grade level, should use a reader which he can read with enough ease to get a good deal of what its selections offer.

To try to establish what are supposed to be favorable teaching and learning conditions for pupils' reading of selections in basal readers, many schools use (1) one or another of several types of homogeneous grouping which the administration sets up in order to assign pupils to classes, or (2) the teacher's homogeneous grouping of pupils within a class. Here are two examples of the first grouping system:

1. A school which enrolls enough pupils so that two or more classes can or should be formed at each grade level ranks all the pupils at that level according to their achievement in various school subjects, if not in reading alone, as indicated by standardized test scores and perhaps teachers' ratings. Then only pupils whose general achievement or reading levels are most alike are assigned to a given class.

2. A school which may or may not assign pupils to homerooms on the basis of achievement levels ranks all its pupils in Grades 3 through 6 according to general reading ability as indicated by standardized test scores and perhaps teachers' ratings. Then to each of several classes are assigned only pupils who, regardless of the grades in which they are enrolled, have levels of reading ability which are most alike.

When either of these or any other type of administrative homogeneous grouping is in force in a large school, each class can use a basal reader which most if not all the pupils can read with relative ease, no matter for what grade level that book is primarily intended, and the teacher can be one who is well equipped to teach reading at that particular level. While it is true that almost any type of homogeneous grouping by the administration reduces the range of reading ability within a given class, in no sense does it eliminate the teacher's responsibility to fulfill the need for individual instruction which still exists in that class. Certainly such grouping does not release the teacher of an above-average class from the need to stimulate her pupils to read many books on their own. Neither does it discharge the responsibility that the teacher of any below-average class has for teaching reading skills, the lack of which, probably as much as any other one thing, accounts for the failure of those pupils to read as well as they can be taught to read.

Whether the administration does or does not apply some type of homogeneous grouping as a means of assigning pupils to classes, the teacher of any class is likely to group within that class, particularly if all the pupils are not at or above the normal grade level of reading ability. In some situations only two groups are formed, one made up of pupils who can and the other of pupils who cannot read without serious trouble the basal reader intended for use primarily in that grade. The higher group uses that basal reader, the lower group an easier basal reader at or below the grade level. The teacher provides for much independent reading by the higher group, spends considerable time teaching reading skills to the lower group, and supplies special materials for and individual help to the few pupils who have trouble keeping up with the lower group. In other situations, the teacher forms three groups, one for below-average pupils, one for average pupils, and one for above-average pupils. If the range of general reading ability within the entire class is relatively small, the teacher may use with each group a basal reader intended primarily for that grade, devoting much more patience to and providing more time and detail for the lowest group than the highest and giving much individual help to the poorest readers in the lowest group. If the range of reading ability is relatively large, it is common practice to use with the highest group and the average group a basal reader intended for the grade in which those pupils are and to supply the lowest group with an easier reader at or below grade level. While the number of groups to be formed depends upon the range of reading ability within the class and the teacher's willingness to handle different groups, no amount of grouping removes the need for giving extra help to the slowest pupils individually and for stimulating pupils of superior ability to read an unusually large amount of advanced material on their own. Sometimes the author wonders whether carrying on effectively the instruction which this volume recommends for Grades 1 and 2 and using skillfully in Grades 3 through 6 the materials described briefly on page 237 would make unnecessary most of the extensive grouping that many schools now set up at those later grade levels.

Soon after the opening of a school term or year, the teacher who plans to form reading groups within a class will need to decide in just what group each pupil should be placed and at just what grade level the basal reader which that pupil is to use should be. The following paragraphs addressed to the teacher give directive statements some or all of which may help in making this decision:

1. Examine each pupils' school record to get evaluations made of his reading ability during the previous school year and reported there as standardized test scores and teacher's ratings.

2. Check each pupil's ability to read the basal reader intended for use primarily at the grade level in which he is enrolled. First have all pupils open their copies of the reader to the beginning of a selection that is near the front of the book and that you know well, and present this selection to them much as described on pages 238–242, but without introducing any words. Then have each pupil read aloud several sentences that you assign to him alone. As he reads, note such items as the quickness with which he recognizes words, his skill in unlocking words that are strange to him only in print, his use of correct voice intonations, his repeating or misnaming of words, and whether or not he reads with unusual slowness. If a pupil tells you that he does not know what this or that word is, encourage him then and there to use context and letter sounds to try to unlock it, but if he cannot do this, tell him what the word is so that he can continue his reading. On the following day, present to all the pupils another story near the beginning of the reader, have them read part or all of it silently, and note the time used by each pupil in doing the reading. When the reading

is finished, have all the pupils write answers to a comprehension test you have made to cover important points made in the material read. Pupils who exhibit little if any trouble in their oral reading and in responding correctly to the items in the comprehension test may be placed temporarily in the average or the above-average group and may be expected to read with relative ease the basal reader used in doing the checking. By using the basal reader for the next lower grade to make the same testings on both oral and silent reading,[11] the teacher may further check pupils she feels should be started in the low group.

3. Give each pupil an informal reading inventory. First get two copies of each basal reader for Grades 2 through 6 that are parts of a basal series and that the pupil has not read, and choose from each book two selections to be used respectively in checking his oral reading and his silent reading. Then, beginning with a book that is well below what you think the level of the pupil's reading ability is, have him read aloud a passage of 100 or 200 words from one of the selections as you listen and go along with him in your copy of the book. Note the time he consumes in doing the oral reading and also the items mentioned in the preceding paragraph as matters to be observed in such reading. Use part or all of the other chosen selection to check his silent reading, noting the time the reading consumes and, after the reading is finished, using oral or written questions to check his comprehension. If the pupil has little trouble in his oral and silent reading, continue in order with readers intended for higher grade levels until his performances show that the book being used at the time is too difficult. Then assume that he can read with sufficient ease the next lowest reader in the series and place him temporarily in a group of pupils who will use that reader or another of just about the same reading difficulty level.

4. Give each pupil a standardized reading test on which his performance tells you what the grade level of his general reading ability is. Use the test results to help you choose the level of the basal reader he can read with relative ease and the group in which to place him temporarily.[12]

In working with any group, the teacher, in addition to having the pupils read selections in a basal reader, will give them instruction in appropriate reading skills and will make provision for them to read on

[11] This paragraph gives a somewhat different description and a slight variation of a procedure recommended in Albert Harris, *Effective Teaching of Reading*, pp. 119–120.

[12] Among the tests used commonly for this purpose are: (1) *California Reading Tests*, Primary, Grades 3–4; Elementary, Grades 4–6, California Test Bureau, Los Angeles, California; (2) *Iowa Every-Pupil Tests of Basic Skills*, Elementary, Grades 3–5; Advanced, Grades 5–9, Houghton Mifflin Company, Boston, Massachusetts; (3) *Iowa Tests of Basic Skills*, Grades 3–9, Houghton Mifflin Company, Boston, Massachusetts; (4) *Iowa Silent Reading Tests*, Elementary Test, Grades 4–8, Harcourt, Brace & World, Inc., New York; (5) *Metropolitan Reading Tests*, Elementary Reading, Grades 3–4; Intermediate Reading, Grades 5–6; Advanced Reading, Grades 7–8, Harcourt, Brace & World, Inc., New York; (6) *Stanford Achievement Tests*, Elementary Reading Test, Grades 3–4; Intermediate Reading Test, Grades 5–6; Advanced Reading Test, Grades 7–9, Harcourt, Brace & World, Inc., New York.

their own whatever books are suitable for and available to them. Because the different pupils in the group will learn skills at different rates and will respond with different degrees of enthusiasm to stimulations to independent reading, they will not maintain for long whatever degree of homogeneity was the basis for the forming of the group. This fact, together with mistakes the teacher may have made in placing pupils, explains why all grouping for the purpose of reading selections in basal readers must be kept elastic in the sense that a pupil can be moved from one group to another whenever such transfer promises to be profitable for him. In considering any such transfer, it is important to take into account the pupil's attitude toward the move. Some pupils are helped by moving to a lower group in which they feel they can succeed without being under constant pressure, and others feel that they can make reasonable progress under the stimulation they expect to receive by working with a higher group.

Grouping pupils for the reading of selections in basal readers is not the only type of grouping that can or should be provided within a given class. Very probably the teacher will find it advantageous to form now and then a special group which includes from different basal reader groups those pupils who need in common extra help in some important matter pertaining to reading. Usually that help consists of extra instruction or practice in using a certain group of letter-sound associations, using the technique to be followed in unlocking strange words, recognizing words which have proved to be troublesome or distinguishing from one another words frequently confused, thinking correct voice intonations, reading with accurate comprehension, comprehending with reasonable speed, or using any one or another of the skills described in Chapters 8, 9, and 10. The number of special groups to be organized at any one time depends largely upon the amount of help and time the teacher has for providing the extra instruction, but certainly any such group should be discontinued just as soon as the disability toward which that instruction is directed has been eradicated.

QUESTIONS TO BE ANSWERED

1. What criticisms of the teaching of reading in Grades 3 through 6 does this chapter offer? What have you seen happen in a classroom that supports or denies one or another of those criticisms?

2. What three main teaching activities constitute the instruction in reading which this volume proposes for Grades 3 through 6? Why is each of them important? What parts of this teaching do you think you did not receive

when you were a pupil in the elementary school? Which part do you think is most neglected today?

3. What is the purpose of the preliminary testing? What preliminary teaching may need to be done and why?

4. What are some of the weaknesses attached to the use of basal reading materials in Grades 3 through 6? What things that a teacher may do or fail to do constitute using basal materials poorly?

5. What materials might be substituted for basal materials? In what ways might the use of these materials be more profitable than the use of basal materials?

6. Which of the new words presented by a selection in a basal reader should be introduced to pupils before they begin to read that selection? Why?

7. Why might the teacher need to provide background for pupils before they begin to read a selection in a basal reader? What warning needs to be observed here?

8. What should characterize the group discussion of a selection read in a basal reader? What provision, if any, should be made for pupils' oral reading of a selection?

9. Why do you think some teachers omit the teaching of reading skills which basal reading materials propose as a major part of their instructional program and which the pupils have not acquired?

10. What provisions can be made for the grouping of pupils for instruction in reading? What can a teacher do to determine a pupil's placement at the beginning of a school term?

MORE TO READ

DeBoer, John, and Martha Dallmann, *The Teaching of Reading*, Holt, Rinehart, & Winston, Inc., New York, 1958, Chapters 14, 15.

Dechant, Emerald, *Improving the Teaching of Reading*, Prentice-Hall, Inc., Englewood Cliffs, N.J., 1964, Chapter 9.

"Development In and Through Reading," *Sixtieth Yearbook of the National Society for the Study of Education, Part I*, University of Chicago Press, Chicago, 1961, Chapter XVI.

Durrell, Donald, *Improving Reading Instruction*, World Book Company, Yonkers-on-Hudson, N.Y., 1956, Chapters 5, 7.

Gans, Roma, *Common Sense in Teaching Reading*, The Bobbs-Merrill Company, Inc., Indianapolis, 1963, Chapter 9.

Gray, Lillian, and Dora Reese, *Teaching Children to Read*, The Ronald Press Company, New York, 1957, Chapter 9.

Harris, Albert, *Effective Teaching of Reading*, David McKay Co., Inc., New York, 1962, Chapters 5, 6, 7.

Heilman, Arthur, *Principles and Practices of Teaching Reading*, Charles E. Merrill Books, Inc., Columbus, Ohio, 1961, Chapter 8.

Hildreth, Gertrude, *Teaching Reading*, Henry Holt & Co., Inc., New York, 1962, Chapters 17, 19.

McKim, Margaret, *Guiding Growth in Reading in the Modern Elementary School*, The Macmillan Co., New York, 1955, Chapters 10, 11, 13.

Russell, David, *Children Learn to Read*, Ginn & Company, Boston, 1962, Chapter 8.

Spache, George, *Toward Better Reading*, The Garrard Press, Champaign, Ill., 1963, Chapter 7.

THINGS TO DO

1. Write out what you would do and say to teach the letter-sound association for any consonant, single vowel, vowel combination, or common syllable you choose other than those used as illustrations in this chapter.

2. Write out what you would do and say in introducing one word to give pupils practice in using the technique to be followed in unlocking strange words.

3. Find in a dictionary a word you think most fourth grade pupils do not know in print, do not know how to pronounce, and have no meaning for. Write statements that tell when you would not introduce that word if it appeared in a selection to be read by pupils, when you would introduce it, and what you would do and say in making the introduction.

4. Examine any intermediate grade basal reader and its accompanying workbook and teacher's guide. Find out what reading skills these materials suggest be taught.

5. Examine the teacher's guide for any intermediate grade reader to find out what suggestions it gives for providing pupils with background for reading one or another of the selections the reader contains.

6. Talk with an intermediate grade teacher to find out just what is done in her school about grouping pupils for instruction in reading.

chapter 8

Coping with
Meaning Difficulties

Think again of the task that the first-grade or second-grade pupil must perform in order to read printed matter which is suited to his use. Actually, once he catches on to the idea that this material stands for talk which is familiar to him, that each line represents something someone is saying, that each word is one which he knows when he hears it and which makes sense with what he is reading, and that he can make printed lines talk to him, this task is fairly simple. Entirely free of the necessity of struggling with any language expressions that are not yet familiar to him in spoken form, the pupil needs only to unlock the relatively few words which are strange only in print, recognize instantly the numerous familiar words and groups of words, and think the required voice intonations. As implied in Chapter 2, these three acts are the chief vehicles for reaching the goal of thinking in "the ears of his mind" the familiar spoken language represented by the printed lines that are his reading matter.

While it is true that the material to be read by the pupil in Grades 3 through 6 contains passages composed entirely of language he already understands in spoken form, what he undertakes is considerably more complicated than the task described in the preceding paragraph. One — but not the only — main reason for this increase in difficulty[1] is the fact

[1] The other main reason is explained near the beginning of Chapter 9.

that his story books, textbooks, other informative books, newspapers, and magazines present rather frequently bits of language which easily entice him into misunderstanding what is being said and which require him at times to think diligently in order to come close to the sense intended by the writer. These particular trouble spots can be called meaning difficulties.

Some meaning difficulties are expressions and language constructions which the pupil would not understand if they were read to him and which are problematic for him in both his listening and his reading. Examples of such difficulties are:

1. A word or group of words which stands for a meaning the pupil does not have or, perhaps more exactly, has not yet attached to that word or group of words.
2. A word having several meanings already familiar to the pupil but used in a setting or manner which makes his selection of the particular and familiar meaning needed somewhat puzzling.
3. An unfamiliar figure of speech.
4. A strange or rare arrangement of words within a sentence.
5. Vague if not misleading indications of relationships the writer intends the sentences in an informative paragraph to have with one another.
6. A summary statement unaccompanied by details which the pupil does not have but needs in order to make that statement mean what it is intended to mean.
7. A short or long expression that, for its correct interpretation, requires the pupil to possess one or more concepts which are somewhat broad, which are remote in either time or space or both to his experience, and which are fruits of a background that he simply does not have and that the reading matter itself does not supply.

Other meaning difficulties — unfamiliar but crucial uses of punctuation marks and the use of the dash, italics, boldface type, full caps, a row of dots, and other typographical signals — are peculiar to printed matter and require the pupil to have had more than just a little experience in interpreting that form of the language. True, all these and additional meaning difficulties demand that the pupil do a considerable amount of sharp reasoning or problem solving in order to understand just what his reading matter is saying. Yet their occurrence at reasonable intervals, accompanied by needed aids, is imperative to his learning to use reading as the vehicle of pleasure and information that it can be for him. To be emphasized also at this point is the proposition that the solution to the pupil's problem in handling meaning difficulties lies in teaching him what he needs in order to cope with those matters; merely substituting for them appropriate language which he already understands in spoken form contributes nothing to his further development of the power to read independently.

The ability of many pupils to cope with meaning difficulties they encounter in their reading is inexcusably low, much lower than most teachers think. And because questions on standardized tests of reading comprehension are as general and unpenetrating as they are, it is often lower than the scores made on such tests show it to be. Indeed, many of the meanings which pupils make in their reading, particularly their interpretations of what their textbooks in the content subjects say, are almost unbelievably vague, far removed from the sense intended by the writer, and certainly much less clear and correct than they must be if satisfactory communication between the writer and the reader is to take place. In addition, pupils often do not possess a strong demand for correct meaning — an attitude which seems to be basic to success in doing much of their reading — and their willingness to substitute verbalism for adequate understanding of what they attempt to read tends to increase as the grade level advances. All these harsh statements are warranted by the quality of verbal responses and overt but non-verbal responses given by numerous average and above-average pupils in various localities to probing questions asked to discover the meanings they made in reading passages intended for their use.[2] The statements also emphasize the author's contention that the reading of a passage is good only insofar as the reader understands what the lines say, and that responsibility for most of the pupil's inability to cope with meaning difficulties can be charged to the failure of most elementary schools to equip him to handle those problems satisfactorily.

Part of the trouble that any pupil has in dealing with meaning difficulties can be attributed to his lack of experience — often called background — which would have enabled him to build concepts and the sense of relationships essential to his reading. No doubt some of the trouble results from his lack of interest in the topics presented by his reading matter and in finding out what the printed lines say. Surely some of it occurs simply because he does not possess certain insights and skills by

[2] Space cannot be given in this volume to a presentation of details of these investigations. For examples of details reported in studies made years ago see Ernest Horn, *Methods of Instruction in the Social Studies* (Charles Scribner's Sons, New York, 1937), Chapter V; Paul McKee, *The Teaching of Reading in the Elementary School* (Houghton Mifflin Company, Boston, 1948), Chapter 3; and Paul McKee, *Language in the Elementary School*, (Houghton Mifflin Company, Boston, 1939), pp. 21–24.

means of which he could cope independently with at least some of the meaning difficulties he encounters. A detailed discussion of the teacher's role in helping the pupil build needed background appears in Chapter 11. What can be done to stimulate his interest in topics to be read about and in finding out what passages say is considered in Chapters 11 and 12. It is the sole purpose of the present chapter to discuss the teaching of insights and skills which he needs in order to cope with certain meaning difficulties independently. For want of a better term, these insights and skills can be called items.

The author holds no brief for his selection of the particular items taken up in this chapter. It is based entirely on his belief that these items can be especially useful to the pupil for the purpose indicated and on the success with which they have been taught. No doubt other persons could name other items which they believe are of equal or greater importance and would omit one or more of those suggested here. It is unfortunate that almost fifty years of research in the teaching of reading has not produced a valid statement of the insights and skills which are of unquestioned importance to the pupil in coping with meaning difficulties.

The particular items to be considered in this chapter are (1) using context, (2) using a dictionary, (3) interpreting punctuation marks and certain typographical signals, (4) interpreting metaphor, (5) sensing the relationship that sentences have with one another, (6) thinking correct stress, and (7) visualizing. Each item refers to a major skill and whatever insights are basic to or accompany the correct use of that skill. All the items are useful in making correct meaning for both narrative selections and informative passages, regardless of the purpose for which the reading is being done. Since the first, third, fourth, fifth and sixth items pertain to ways in which language operates, they are fundamentally aspects of linguistics.

Preliminary attention is called now to the proposition that effective teaching of each of the seven items consists in carrying on at least two main instructional activities. The first of these can be called *introducing the item* and includes (1) making the pupil aware of the meaning and importance of the skill, (2) illustrating correct use of the skill, (3) by some means — perhaps group discussion — enabling the pupil to find out whether he understands how the skill is used correctly, and (4) giving initial practice in using the skill. The second activity can be called *providing practice in using the skill.* This practice can be supplied intermittently during the school year by having the pupil use suitable practice exercises, by making provision for him to apply the skill in appropriate aspects of all school work, and by getting him to do much suitable reading on his own. Each of the principal sections that make up most of the remainder of this chapter first presents an explanation of the nature of an item and then illustrates or explains fully the two main instructional activities for teaching it.

Using Context

As you read the following passage, you will encounter a word which has been placed there deliberately with the hope that it is strange to you in form, meaning, and pronunciation and that when you meet it you will be able to think then and there only very little if any meaning for it. If this is what happens in your case, use other expressions in the passage which are familiar to you, wherever they may be, to try to teach yourself what the meaning of the word is. Don't be concerned at this point about whether a pronunciation you may think for the word is correct.

> "Have you heard from Mark yet, Emily?" asked Mr. Carter. "How is he getting along in Paris? Is he having a good time, just as he does everywhere?"
>
> "I have heard nothing since we received the cable on the day he arrived," replied Mrs. Carter, "but he's so apolaustic that I'm sure he will enjoy every minute of his stay there. I do hope, Fred, that he won't let his studies at the university slide and spend all his time seeing the sights of the city and its environs."
>
> "Oh, come now," said Mr. Carter. "He'll probably get along all right this year. Sometimes I think both you and I would be better off today if we had insisted upon getting more fun out of life."

Now, let's assume that when you first encountered *apolaustic*, you thought little if any meaning for that word. What could you have done with other expressions in the passage to teach yourself what its meaning is? To begin with, you know from the way Mrs. Carter used the word that it refers to a trait or characteristic of Mark's. Is there anything in the last part of the first sentence of Mrs. Carter's speech that gives you a hint of what the trait is? Could the trait be fun-loving? What trait does the first part of the last sentence in Mrs. Carter's speech suggest? Negligence? What trait does the last part of that same sentence suggest? Can you get any help from the first two sentences in Mr. Carter's first speech? Does the last sentence in the same speech give you the idea that Mark is a person who persists in having a good time? Does the first sentence in Mrs. Carter's speech hint that Mark is an inconsiderate or procrastinating person? What help if any does the last sentence in the passage give you? Which of the following expressions tells best the meaning you think *apolaustic* stands for?

1. thoughtless	3. devoted to enjoyment	5. curious
2. profligate	4. transient	6. procrastinating

As you read the next passage, you will encounter a word which has been placed there deliberately with the hope that, although you know its pronunciation well and have one or more meanings for it, none of those meanings makes sense in the passage and you will not be able to think then and there what the particular needed meaning is. If this is what happens in your case, use other expressions in the passage which are already familiar to you, wherever they may be, to try to teach yourself that meaning.

After fishing for almost an hour in the same spot without getting even a nibble, Charlie gave up in disgust. "I can't figure out what's wrong," he muttered to himself as he reeled in his line. "Old Zeke said that there are always salmon here. Maybe they don't like this favorite fly of mine. I'll move to another spot and try my luck there." Then he opened his tin box, took out the baker Zeke had given him just that morning to use for salmon, fastened it to his leader, and began to walk upstream.

The word in question is *baker*. Which of the following expressions tells best the particular meaning you think it has here?

1. a small fish used as bait	4. a fly colored red and blue
2. a double-barbed fishing hook	5. a fly used in catching salmon
3. a South American bird	6. a strong fishing line

Which if any of the following words and groups of words that appear in the passage helped you decide what particular meaning *baker* stands for?

1. fishing	4. opened his tin box
2. fastened it to his leader	5. leader
3. fly	6. salmon

Whenever you meet in your reading a word that is strange to you in meaning, you can look here and there in the passage for other expressions which give you hints of or explain the meaning of the word. Such helpful parts may appear before, after, or both before and after the strange word. Any one of them may be a single word, a phrase, a sentence, a synonym, an appositive, a parenthetical statement, an outright definition, or some other language construction. True, you will make errors now and then in the sense that the meaning you teach yourself is incorrect or not sufficiently close to the sense intended by the writer, but continued practice will sharpen your skill. Furthermore, often what you are reading will contain no helpful parts, and you will be left stranded, as it were, unable to think the meaning you need in order to understand the passage. When this happens — and it will — your chief recourse is the use of a good dictionary. Right now, if you are not sure that the meanings you taught yourself to think respectively for *apolaustic* and *baker* are sufficiently close to the sense which the author of the two passages intended, look up these words in an unabridged dictionary and, if necessary, alter the decisions you made.

Often you need to read a very common word for which you already have several different meanings, and at times you may need to think carefully in order to decide just which of those familiar meanings to assign to that word. Here, for example, are ten of the various meanings which no doubt you know for the word *show:*

1. convince	6. lead or conduct
2. explain	7. plead
3. point out	8. prove
4. grant	9. indicate by record
5. put in sight	10. reveal or disclose

Which do you think *show* stands for in each of the following sentences?

1. The evidence given at the trial today did not show that Mr. Brown was guilty.
2. Did the district attorney show how the accident happened?
3. Did he show the judge the photographs that were taken?
4. Yes, but those pictures did not show anything he did not already know.
5. No witness was able to show the jury that the collision had been planned.
6. Didn't the defense attorney show that someone could have tampered with Mr. Brown's brakes?
7. Didn't the broken clock in Mr. Brown's car show anything?
8. The district attorney's summation will show cause for a verdict of not guilty.
9. If the jury convicts Mr. Brown, perhaps the judge will show him some mercy.

Can you think of any reading situation in which your understanding of a passage would be seriously marred if you thought for *show* meaning

8 when you should have thought meaning 1, meaning 3 when you should have thought meaning 6, or meaning 5 when you should have thought meaning 10? Do you believe that making this type of error in reading any common word ever could make much difference? Sometimes the elementary school pupil is trapped into misunderstanding what printed lines say by his ready acceptance of and clinging to the first familiar meaning which pops into his mind for a common word and by his failure to consider at all other meanings he knows for the word.

When you read the passage containing the word *apolaustic* — for which you had little if any meaning — you used the familiar meanings of other words in the passage to teach yourself what it means or, perhaps more exactly, to inform yourself that a meaning you already knew when expressed in other words is the meaning for which *apolaustic* stands. When you read the passage containing the word *baker* — for which you already had a few meanings but not the particular one needed — you used the familiar meanings of other words in the passage to teach yourself an additional meaning for *baker* or, perhaps more exactly, to inform yourself that a meaning you recognized when expressed in other words is one of the meanings for which *baker* can stand. When you read each of the sentences containing the word *show* — for which you already had the needed and several other meanings — you used the sense of other words in that sentence to decide just which familiar meaning to think for *show*. Engaging in any one of these acts can be called using the context to figure out the meaning of a word.

Is there a difference between (1) using context in figuring out what the meaning of a word is and (2) using context in unlocking a word which is strange only in print? There certainly is! In the first situation, the reader uses context (1) as an explainer of a meaning which as yet is unfamiliar to him or, more commonly, as a reporter of the unfamiliar fact that a meaning he knows when expressed in other words is the meaning of a given word, or (2) as a determiner of which of several familiar meanings is the one he needs to think for a given word. In the latter situation, as described in Chapter 4, the reader uses context as a clue which, along with his use of a few letter sounds, stimulates him to call to mind simultaneously both the familiar spoken form and the familiar meaning of a given word. It is important to understand the distinction between the two main uses of context simply because the teaching of either use is quite different from that of the other.

One of the meaning difficulties that the pupil encounters now and then in his reading is a word which is strange to him in meaning. That word may be one for which he can think little if any meaning at the time, just as *apolaustic* was to you. It may be a word for which he can think immediately one or more meanings but not the particular meaning needed, just as *baker* was for you. To overcome this difficulty, surely the most normal thing for the pupil to try first is to use the context to teach himself the meaning of the word, but he cannot do so if he is unable to spot and use helpful parts provided in the context.[3] Since investigations show that lack of skill in using context for this purpose is quite prevalent among elementary school pupils and since such use of context is the chief means for increasing vocabulary through reading, there is good reason to recommend that the teaching of this skill be a part of instruction in reading in Grades 3 through 6. Inasmuch as words which are strange in meaning do and should begin to appear in third-grade reading matter, it is recommended further that this teaching be initiated in Grade 3 and continued and expanded as needed by the pupil in each succeeding grade.

It is not enough merely to tell the pupil that sometimes in his reading he will meet a word which is strange to him in meaning and that when this happens he should use the sense of other words in the passage to try to decide what the word means. It is not enough merely to have the pupil work out special exercises which, since they offer no explanation of the problem, give him only practice in using the skill. As stated earlier in this chapter, the teaching should include at least (1) introducing the item to the pupil and (2) providing practice in using the skill.

1. Introducing the Item

One way of introducing the use of context as the explainer of the meaning of a word is to teach a definite lesson which, among other things, (a) helps the pupil develop an understanding of what is meant by using context for that purpose, (b) illustrates for him correct use of the skill, (c) provides means by which he can find out whether he understands how the skill is used correctly, and (d) gives him initial practice in using the skill. Possibly one such lesson should present a word which is strange to the pupil in form, meaning, and pronunciation, as *apolaustic* was to you, and a second lesson should present a word which is strange to him only in meaning, as *baker* was to you. The following material, addressed to the pupil as a member of a group or class and presenting a word presumably of the first type, is merely illustrative of what a lesson could be like and is not offered here as a model or a finished product to be used

---

[3] Even though a given context may provide no helpful parts, the pupil should first try to use context. What he should be taught to do when he discovers that a context contains no helpful parts is explained later in this chapter.

in teaching any particular group of pupils at any given grade level.

To read and think over

Sometimes when you are reading along, you will come to a word for which you cannot think right then any meaning that makes sense. How can you try to find out all by yourself what that word means?

You can try to teach yourself what the meaning of the word is. That is what Billy Ford did with the word *menagerie* when he was reading the part of a story that follows:

Sally and her father arrived at the circus grounds a full hour before the time when the big show would begin.

"We're here early, Sally," said Mr. Brown. "What would you like to do before it is time for us to go into the big tent?"

"Could we go to see some of the animals that will be in the big show?" asked Sally. "Do you know where they are?"

"Look over there," said Mr. Brown, pointing to a green tent not far away. "Do you see all the people going in and out of that tent? The menagerie is in there. Let's find out what they have in that collection."

Inside the green tent, locked in cages, were lions, tigers, leopards, and many other wild animals. As Sally and her father walked along with the crowd to look at them, she would stop now and then in front of a cage to talk with a guard who stood nearby. Always she would ask him what tricks the animals in that cage would do in the big show.

When Billy first saw the word *menagerie,* he did not know what it meant. But he remembered that Sally had asked about seeing the animals, and he learned from what Mr. Brown said that the menagerie was in a tent and perhaps was some kind of collection. Quickly he looked over again what he had read so far, but he found there no other words that gave him hints of what *menagerie* meant. Then from the next paragraph, he learned that in the tent Mr. Brown and Sally found caged wild animals, a crowd of people, and guards. "Sally and her father wouldn't go into that tent just to see the crowd and the guards," he thought. "*Menagerie* must mean a collection of caged wild animals."

What Billy did can be called using the context to figure out the meaning of a word. He used the meanings of other words and groups of words in the story to teach himself the meaning of *menagerie.*

When you meet a printed word for which you cannot think right then a meaning that makes sense, do what Billy did. The parts of the context that can help you may come before, after, or both before and after the strange word. A helpful part may be a word or a group of words.

Sometimes you may find that the context has no helpful parts which you can use to teach yourself what a word means. When that happens, how would you find out what the meaning is?

Talking together

Help your class answer these questions:

1. What is meant by using the context to figure out the meaning of a word?
2. What may the helpful parts of the context be? Where may they appear?
3. What helpful parts did Billy use to figure out the meaning of *menagerie?*
4. When the context does not give the help you need, what would you do next to get the meaning of a word?[4]

To do by yourself

Read the next part of the story to yourself. If you meet a word for which you cannot think right then a meaning that makes sense, use the context to help you.

One of the clowns and a monkey in the big show kept Sally laughing much of the time. The clown had filled one of his coat pockets with peanuts, and the monkey kept pilfering some of them from time to time when he thought the clown wasn't looking. Sometimes the clown would see the monkey doing that, and he would become very angry and chase the little animal back and forth in front of the stands. But the monkey was too fast and quick for the clown, and often the clown would sit down to rest. Then the monkey would try to placate him by showering him with water from a hose. That did no good at all. The clown just kept on being upset.

Working together

Did you use the context to try to figure out the meaning of *pilfering?* If you did, help others in your class decide which of the following words or groups of words tells best what that meaning is:

1. taking   2. stealing little by little   3. eating rapidly

Did you use the context to try to figure out the meaning of *placate?* If you did, help others in your class decide which of the following words or groups of words tells best what that meaning is:

1. make wet   2. tease   3. calm down

If you are asked to do so, tell what parts of the context you used to figure out the meaning of each word.

Several points relative to the construction and use of a lesson such as that just presented need to be emphasized. *First,* the part labeled "To read and think over" is to be read by the pupil in order to develop some

---

[4] If such a lesson as this is being taught before the pupil has learned how to use a dictionary to get the meaning of a word, a good answer to question 4 is one that implies *I would ask someone to tell me what the meaning is.*

understanding of (a) the meaning and value of using context as an explainer of the meaning of a word and (b) the correct use of that skill. The word to which the context is being applied in this part must be strange to the pupil in meaning, although it may or may not be strange in either form or pronunciation or both. *Second,* the part labeled "Talking together" should not be omitted. The questions given there for group discussion can help both the pupil and the teacher discover whether the former has acquired some understanding of how context is used correctly. *Third,* the part labeled "To do by yourself," to be read and worked out by the pupil individually, provides him with initial practice in using context to figure out the meaning of one or more words. Each of those words must be strange to him in meaning. *Fourth,* the part labeled "Working together" enables both the pupil and the teacher to find out whether the former has acquired some degree of power in using context to figure out the meaning of a word and helps the pupil learn things to do and errors to avoid in applying the skill. *Fifth,* each word used in the lesson, other than those few to which the use of context is to be applied, should be familiar to the pupil in form, pronunciation, and meaning, and each sentence, except the few containing the crucial words, should be one which he understands easily and quickly in print. *Sixth,* no great concern needs to be shown when the pupil has figured out the meaning of a word but does not know the pronunciation of that word. If, at the time this situation arises, he has already learned how to use a dictionary to get the pronunciation of a word, he should turn to that source. If he has not yet done this learning, the teacher shall tell him what the pronunciation is. Usually it does little good to direct him to use what he knows about letter sounds to figure out the pronunciation. When the word is not within his listening vocabulary, as is often the case, he could not possibly know whether the pronunciation he figured out is correct.

Introducing the use of context as a means of figuring out the meaning of a word does not require the construction and use of a lesson such as that offered in the preceding pages. For example, the teacher could instead (a) find in a printed selection a passage containing a word that is strange to the pupil in meaning and including parts that explain the word's meaning, (b) present the passage to the pupil and go through it with him, much as the first part of the illustrative lesson did, (c) raise questions much like those which the lesson provided for group discussion, (d) find and have the pupil use for initial practice another passage containing one or more words that are strange in meaning and supplying helpful parts, and (e) check the results of the initial practice. No matter what procedure the teacher may use in introducing the skill and regardless of whether that procedure includes more or less detail than is implied by the illustrative lesson, surely it should be directed at all the goals which that lesson purports to attain.

It is doubtful that an extensive lesson is necessary for teaching the pupil that many very common words — such as *get, good, make, take,* or *show* — stand for many different familiar meanings, that words work in this way, that at times in his reading he may need to think carefully in order to decide just which of those meanings is intended, and that it is the context which tells him what his decision should be. It should suffice to present several such words to the pupil one at a time together with several of its familiar meanings, provide sentences in which the word is used with some or all those meanings, and ask him to tell which meaning the word stands for in each sentence and explain how and why he made his decision. The following material is illustrative:

The word *take* has several different meanings. Here are ten of them:

1.	feel	6.	grasp or hold on to
2.	have	7.	do or make
3.	accept	8.	rent
4.	choose	9.	use or make use of
5.	carry	10.	require

Which meaning does *take* stand for in each of the following sentences?

1. Will you take these packages home for me?
2. Mother said she would take a taxi home.
3. Mr. Fox wouldn't take any pay for mowing our yard.
4. It will take a lot of patience to do that job well.
5. Joe's little sister always takes his hand when they cross a busy street together.
6. Betty said she would take my picture with her new camera.
7. Are you going to take a long vacation next summer?
8. Mother will take the loss of her watch pretty hard.
9. Which road shall we take to the city?
10. We are going to take a cabin in the mountains again next summer.

2. Providing Practice in Using the Skill

There are three main ways of providing the pupil with practice in using context to figure out the meaning of a word. One of these is largely a matter of stimulating him to read on his own much material which presents now and then a word that is strange in meaning and that is accompanied by helpful parts explaining the needed meaning. This provision is discussed in Chapters 11 and 12 as a part of the teaching of social studies and other content subjects and of children's literature.

A second way is that of providing opportunities for the pupil to use the skill in connection with reading he is expected to do in other appropriate school work. As the teacher plans to have the pupil read a selection in a reader or any other textbook, she should look through the selection to see whether it contains a word which is strange in meaning to the pupil. If it does, and if the word is accompanied by helpful parts, certainly she should not explain the meaning before the pupil begins his reading. Instead, she should give him the chance to use the context to figure out the meaning all by himself. In addition, from time to time after the pupil has read a selection containing a word which is strange in meaning and is accompanied by helpful parts, the teacher should ask him to tell what meaning he figured out for the word and to explain how or why he made the decision he did.

The third way is that of having the pupil work out occasionally a special exercise which gives practice in using the skill. Some workbooks that accompany some basal readers provide such exercises. The following material, addressed to the pupil, is illustrative:

Read to yourself each of the numbered paragraphs that follow. If you meet a word for which you cannot think right then a meaning that makes sense, use the context to help you.

1

Half way up the wooded hills stood an old log cabin. There, far from the village and the homes of other people, Caleb Stone had lived as a recluse for almost twenty years. The old gentleman seldom came to the village to talk with friends he had known long ago, and no longer were any of them interested in visiting him on the hill. No one seemed to know why Caleb had left his fine house in the village to live alone in the old cabin. But Tom and Joe had seen Caleb a few times, and they felt that there was a mystery about him which kept making them more and more curious.

Draw a line under the group of words below that tells best what you think *recluse* means:

1. a person who is disliked
2. an angry person
3. a person who lives away from others
4. a man who has no wife

2

Mary's little brother had a small blanket that he loved so much he tried to keep it with him all the time. At night he took it to bed with him, and if he happened to forget it, he wouldn't go to sleep until somebody brought it to him. He always took it along when he went outdoors to play, no matter what the weather was like. Then he draggled it over the snow, the wet grass, or the vacant lot across the street where the boys and girls in the neighborhood play. Usually his mother had to wash the blanket every day.

Draw a line under the word or group of words below that tells best what you think *draggled* means:

1. pulled
2. made wet and dirty by dragging

3. tore or ripped by dragging
4. used in play

3

Of the two boys in the family, Dick was by far the more even tempered. Very seldom did he become angry, not even at times when others thought he had good reason to do so. But Harry, the older son, was quite irascible. He would fly off the handle quickly at almost any little happening that didn't please him. If Ben, the boy who had just moved into the house next door, had known this about Harry, the trouble that burst on the neighborhood early the next morning probably never would have occurred.

Draw a line under the word or group of words below that tells best what you think *irascible* means:

1. unfriendly
2. hard to get along with

3. thoughtless
4. quick to become angry

Using a Dictionary

As stated in the preceding section, sometimes a given context which contains a word strange to you in meaning does not provide the helpful parts needed to figure out for the word a meaning sufficiently close to the sense intended by the writer. In presenting the words *abstersion* and *balked,* the two paragraphs that follow may be illustrative:

Actually Sarah Conners was indeed a good woman, utterly devoted to her family and friends and always willing to lend a hand to anyone in the village who needed it. But her continual abstersion annoyed her husband Jake and no doubt accounted for his failure to bring his friends to the home. Sarah, who was quite proud of the home and her accomplishments, never understood this and every now and then asked Jake why he behaved as he did. Always Jake would brush the question aside and begin to talk about some other matter he knew would interest Sarah.

All week long Jim had been sick in bed, and to the disappointment of the family, he was getting no better. He did not sleep well, continued to complain about the pain in his back, and still balked at his food. Old Dr. Hoyt said that if Jim's condition did not improve soon, he would call in a specialist from the city.

You know that under the circumstances mentioned above you can use a good dictionary to get the meaning you need. But consider for just a moment what you need to know and do in order to use that source easily and quickly. Would you need to know alphabetical order so well that you could open a dictionary at or close to the listed words which begin with the same letter as the word you are looking for, use the guide words on the page you see first to decide whether the word you are looking for could be on that page, decide in which direction you should turn pages to find the one on which the word would be listed, and when you have found the right page and noted there a listed word, decide in which direction you should go in the column to find the word you are looking for? Should you read all the definitions or meanings the dictionary you are using gives? Which of those meanings should you choose?

Often a pupil finds in his reading that a given context which contains a word strange to him in meaning does not provide the helpful parts he needs for figuring out its meaning. When that happens, he too can use a good dictionary — if he knows how. The remainder of this section is concerned with teaching the pupil how to use a dictionary to get the meaning of a word. This teaching, consisting in introducing the item to the pupil and giving him practice in using the skill, includes much more than merely admonishing him to use a dictionary whenever he needs to and having him work out special exercises which, without explaining the problem, give him only practice in using the skill. It is recommended here that the teaching be initiated through the use of a simple dictionary with average or advanced third-grade pupils and that it be continued and expanded as needed in each subsequent grade.

1. Introducing the Item

The following material, addressed to the pupil as a member of a group or class, constitutes a definite lesson which introduces to him the use of a dictionary as a source of the meanings of words. Its parts and their purposes are much the same as those of the lesson on the use of context presented on pages 263–264. It is merely illustrative and is not offered as a finished product to be used with any particular group of pupils.

To read and think over

You know that sometimes you can figure out the meaning of a strange word by using the context in which you meet the word. But when the context does not give the help you need, you should try to get the meaning all by yourself in some other way. That is one reason why you should learn how to use a dictionary.

A good dictionary lists many words and tells you what their meanings are. Look at the dictionary page below [see following page]. There you can see that words included in the dictionary list are printed in heavy black type and are placed furthest to the left in each column. The meanings given for each word are numbered and come right after that word.

All the words in a dictionary list are placed in the order of the letters of the alphabet. First come all the words that begin with *a*. Then come all those that begin with *b*. The words that begin with *c* come next, and so on through the *z* words, which are the last words in the list.

You can see that in a dictionary list the words *coat* and *cupboard* would be among the words which begin with *c*. Which word would come first? The

---

bit

bit (bit), 1. The part of a bridle that is put into a horse's mouth. 2. The part of a key which enters and works a lock. 3. The cutting edge of a tool. 4. A tool made for drilling or boring. 5. A small piece or quantity of anything; a little; as a *bit* of food, a *bit* of work.

bite (bīt), 1. To seize and pierce with the teeth; as to *bite* an apple; to hurt with the teeth or with any part joined with the mouth; as insects *bite*. 2. To smart; to sting; as pepper *bites* the mouth. 3. A sting, such as that of an insect. 4. The amount taken by the teeth or the mouth at one time; as a *bite* of food.

bit·ing (bīt′ing), 1. That bites; as a *biting* dog. 2. Sharp, cutting; as *biting* remarks.

bit·ter (bit′ər), 1. Sharp and unpleasant to the taste. 2. Harsh or cutting; as *bitter* insults. 3. Painful; arising from anger, distress, or sorrow; as *bitter* tears.

bit·tern (bit′ərn), A brownish marsh bird which has a loud booming cry.

bi·tu·men (bə·tü′mən), A mineral that can easily be set on fire, such as tar.

blackboard

bi·tu·mi·nous (bə·tü·mə·nəs), Containing bitumen.

bi·valve (bī′valv), An animal such as a clam or an oyster that has a shell which is divided into two parts that are hinged on one side and can open or shut.

bi·year·ly (bī·yir′lē), Taking place twice a year.

bi·zarre (bə·zär′), Strange or unusual in form, color, and so on; as *bizarre* dress, *bizarre* designs.

blab (blab), To talk freely and carelessly; especially to tell secrets.

black (blak), 1. Of the color of coal. 2. Very dark; as a *black* night. 3. Having dark hair, skin, and eyes. 4. Dirty; as *black* with dirt. 5. Black clothes; as dressed in *black*. 6. To make black.

black·ber·ry (blak′ber·ē), 1. The black, berry-like fruit of several kinds of bramble bushes. 2. Any bush that bears these berries.

black·bird (blak′bərd), One of a number of birds so called because the males are largely black, as the rusty *blackbird* and red-winged *blackbird*.

black·board (blak′bōrd), Any dark, smooth surface, such as one of slate, used for writing, drawing, and so on with chalk or crayons.

---

add, āte, ärm; end, hē, hėr; in, īce; hot, gō, cȯrn; up, pu̇t, rüle, yü = u in use; oil, out; ə = a in about and total, e in silent and maker, i in pencil, o in contain, u in circus; think, this; zh = s in pleasure; y = y in yes.

From Paul McKee, Annie McCowen, M. Lucile Harrison, Elizabeth Lehr, and William K. Durr, *High Roads*, Fourth Edition (Houghton Mifflin Company, Boston, 1966), p. 100. Used by permission.

second letter in each word tells you. Since *o* comes before *u* in the alphabet, *coat* comes before *cupboard* in the dictionary list. Which word comes first in a dictionary list, *hull* or *hilt?* Why?

Which word would come first in the dictionary list, *donkey* or *double?* When the first two letters in each word are the same, the third letter in each word tells you. Since *n* comes before *u* in the alphabet, *donkey* comes before *double* in the dictionary list. Which word comes first in the dictionary list, *golf* or *goat?* Why?

Think of a dictionary as having a first part, a middle part, and a last part. To which part would you open the book to find the word *lantern* in the dictionary list? Each of the words *venture, oriole, axle?* Why?

Look again at the dictionary page above [opposite page]. Do you see the words *bit* and *blackboard* at the top of the page? They are called guide words. Notice too that the first guide word, *bit,* is the first word in the dictionary list on the page and that the second guide word, *blackboard,* is the last word in the list. All the other words listed on the page come in alphabetical order after *bit* and before *blackboard.*

You can use the guide words on a dictionary page to decide quickly whether a word you are looking for is listed on that page. If your word comes between the two guide words in alphabetical order, it will be on that page unless the dictionary you are using does not list it at all. If your word comes before the first guide word in alphabetical order and the dictionary lists it, it will be on some page which comes before the one you are looking at. If your word comes after the second guide word and the dictionary lists it, it will be on some page which comes after the one you are looking at.

Suppose that you opened a dictionary to a page on which the guide words are *game* and *get.* Why or why not would you expect to find on that page each of the following words? *Gate, gem, gander, geyser.*

Sometimes a dictionary gives only one meaning for a word. Often, however, more than one meaning is given. Notice the different meanings that the dictionary page you saw gives for the word *bit.*

If a dictionary gives more than one meaning for a word that you look up, be sure to read all those meanings. Then choose the one which makes the most sense in the sentence in which you met the word.

When you meet in your reading a word for which you cannot think right then a meaning that makes sense, try first to use the context to teach yourself what the meaning is. If the context does not give the help you need, use a good dictionary.

Talking together

Help your class answer these questions:

1. When you are reading along and meet a word for which you cannot think right away a meaning that makes sense, what should you try to do first to get the meaning you need? If you cannot get the meaning in that way, What should you do next?

2. In what order are the words in a dictionary list placed? Would *cabin* come after *deal?* Why or why not? Would *hilt* come before *hull?* Why or why not? Would *goat* come before *golf?* Why or why not?

3. To which part would you open a dictionary to find *oriole? Venture? Axle? Lantern?*

4. How can the guide words on a dictionary page help you?

5. In a certain dictionary the guide words on one page are *game* and *get.* Which of the following words would you expect to find on that page? *Gander, gate, geyser, gem, gable, gelatin.* To find each word which you think would not be on the page, would you turn pages toward the front of the dictionary? Toward the back?

6. When you use a dictionary to get the meaning of a word you met in your reading, why should you read all the meanings given? Which meaning should you choose?

To do by yourself

The word *bit* or *bitter* is used in each of the numbered sentences that follow. Use the dictionary page you saw to help you decide which meaning that word has in each sentence.

1. Here is the bit to use for making a hole as big as you need.
2. Tom said some bitter things about the team when he was not allowed to play in the baseball game.
3. The notches on that bit are not like those on the key for the front door.
4. Dad will have to sharpen the bit of his ax before he can chop down that old tree.
5. Sally's feelings about the election of officers in our club are pretty bitter.

Number a paper from 1 through 5 to stand for the five sentences you just read. After each number, write the number of the meaning you chose from the dictionary page for *bit* or *bitter* in that sentence.

If you are asked to do so, read aloud the numbers of the meanings you chose. If you made a mistake in choosing a meaning, find out why it is a mistake.

Probably the amount of instruction suggested by the foregoing illustrative lesson is greater than that to which some groups of pupils should be exposed in one reading period. It is expected, therefore, that the teacher will make whatever adjustments are necessary to fit the amount taught in a period to the background and ability of the pupils. Possibly, for example, in some situations a first lesson should be limited to the teaching of alphabetical order, a second lesson to the use of guide words, and a third lesson to the selection of the needed meaning. Each such lesson should include from each section which the illustrative lesson labels "To read and think over," "Talking together," and "To do by yourself" expansions of only those points appropriate to the purpose of that lesson. Each lesson can be presented in print for the pupil to read to himself or, except for the sample dictionary page, it can be presented to him orally.

Attention is called parenthetically to the fact that the illustrative lesson includes nothing concerned with teaching the pupil how to use a dictionary to get the pronunciation of a word which he does not already know how to pronounce. It is true that the pupil can read such a word in the sense that he thinks the meaning for which it stands, just as you no doubt have read foreign names in newspapers, magazines, and novels, and as you may have read years ago such proper names as Penelope, Williamette, and Stephen, without knowing how to pronounce them. Nevertheless there are times when the pupil needs to use such a word in his talking or oral reading, and since he certainly should not depend upon his knowledge of letter sounds or phonics as a tool for figuring out the pronunciation, he needs to gain control of a reliable means of getting that pronunciation independently. This is the chief reason why he needs to learn how to use a dictionary to get the pronunciation of a word. The following illustrative lesson, addressed to the pupil and constructed with the assumption that he has already learned alphabetical order and the use of guide words, suggests what needs to be taught:

To read and think over

One day when Jack was reading a short story about a family that had several pets, he decided that it would be a good tale to read to his class. Then he came to a paragraph that told how the neighbors treated the pets. In that paragraph, he met the word *benignant*.

Jack did not know what the word meant, and when he tried to use the context to teach himself what the meaning is, he could not find there the help he needed. Also, he did not know whether the pronunciation he had thought for *benignant* was correct. These are the reasons why Jack looked up the word in a dictionary.

When Jack found the word in the dictionary this is what he saw:

be·nig·nant (bē·nig′nənt), 1. gracious. 2. kind. 3. pleasant.
4. favorable.

Quickly Jack decided that the second meaning was the one which made the most sense in the paragraph in which he met the word. Then he figured out what the correct pronunciation of *benignant* is. He did this by using what are called the special spelling and the list of key words.

The special spelling of a word listed in a dictionary is shown in parentheses right after that word. You can see that the special spelling of *benignant* is bē·nig′nənt.

In any good dictionary, usually at the bottom of each or every other page, are rows of words called key words. They show what sounds to give vowels and certain other letters in the special spelling. They are words that you already know how to pronounce, and they may look something like this:

add, āte, ärm; end, hē, hėr; in, īce; hot, gō, côrn; up, pút, rüle, yü = u in use; oil, out; ə = a in about and total, e in silent and maker, i in pencil, o in contain, u in circus; think, ~~this~~; zh = s in pleasure; y = y in yes.

In the special spelling of *benignant,* the first syllable looks like this: bē. Notice the little mark above the e. In what key word is the letter e marked in the same way? Yes, in *he.* This means that the e in the first syllable of *benignant* is to be pronounced just like the e in *he,* which you already know how to pronounce.

Look at the second syllable in bē·nig′nənt. Notice that the i in that syllable is not marked. In what key word is the letter i not marked? Yes, in *in.* This means that the i in the second syllable of *benignant* is to be pronounced just like the i in *in.*

Do you see the mark (ə) in the last syllable of bē·nig′nənt? The key words tell you that ə stands for a sound you often use for vowels in different words. That sound is the short u sound you hear in *untie* and *unlock,* and it is the sound a has in *benignant.*

The mark (′) after the second syllable in bē·nig′nənt is called an accent mark. A syllable that has an accent mark is to be pronounced with more force than a syllable which has no accent mark. When you pronounce *tablet,* you accent the first syllable. When you pronounce *tomatoes,* you accent the second syllable.

Can you pronounce *benignant* correctly now? Practice saying it to yourself until you can pronounce it easily.

Talking together

Help your class answer these questions:

1. Where is the special spelling shown for a word listed in a dictionary?
2. What does the special spelling of a word show?
3. How can you find out what sounds to use for certain letters in the word?
4. What does an accent mark tell you?

To do by yourself

If you do not know the meaning or the correct pronunciation of any one or more of the underlined words in the following sentences, use a dictionary to get that meaning and that pronunciation:

1. We have never seen a underline{bittern} in this part of the United States.
2. What kind of coal contains the most underline{bitumen}?
3. Sometimes people use underline{bivalves} in making soup.
4. Years ago many people burned underline{bituminous} coal in furnaces to heat their homes.

5. The street parade in our town on the Fourth of July was a rather <u>bizarre</u> performance.

When you are asked to do so, read one or more of the sentences aloud. If you make a mistake in pronouncing any one of the five words, find out what that mistake is and correct it.[5]

The foregoing illustrative lesson does not provide for teaching the pupil any given system of diacritical marking or set of diacritical marks. Since the different systems and sets used in different dictionaries vary, such teaching is likely to be futile. The important thing for the pupil to learn about using a dictionary to get the pronunciation of a word is a procedure to follow in using the special spellings of words with the key words which make up whatever pronunciation key a dictionary offers. It is such a procedure that the illustrative lesson purports to teach.

2. Providing Practice in Using the Skill

No doubt ways of providing the pupil with the practice he needs in order to become skillful in using a dictionary to get either the meaning or the pronunciation of a strange word, or both, should be utilized. One such is to have him read to himself a great deal of intriguing material which contains here and there a word that stands for a strange meaning not explained adequately by the context and that he does not already know how to pronounce. Hand in hand with this should go a persistent encouraging of the pupil to prepare to read to the class passages that he has enjoyed and thinks the others would like to hear. When the pupil is reading a selection which has a strong interest-pull and which presents such words occasionally and the pupil himself possesses a strong demand for meaning in his silent reading and a sincere desire to get the message and enjoyment across to others through good oral reading of that selection, he has a normal and potent motivation for using a dictionary.

A second way of providing needed practice is to give the pupil a chance to use in his reading in all appropriate school work what the introductory lessons have presented to him. Thus, after these lessons have been taught, the teacher in introducing a story to be read in a reader will not explain the meanings or give the pronunciations of words that are strange to the pupil in either meaning or pronunciation or both. Similarly, in making reading assignments in social studies, science, and

---

[5] The particular words underlined in this section of the lesson are used there so that, if necessary, the pupil can refer to the sample dictionary page shown on page 270 instead of making use of a dictionary itself. Of course any words the teacher chooses could be used in other sentences, provided those words are words which the pupil does not know how to pronounce and provided he has a dictionary at hand.

any other appropriate subject, the teacher will avoid giving meanings and pronunciations of strange words included in the material to be read. Instead, in all these situations the pupil will be given the chance to do with each strange word what the introductory lessons have directed him to do. This means that he is to be encouraged to proceed as follows in coping with a word which is strange to him in either pronunciation or meaning or both:

1. First, try to use the context to figure out the meaning of the word.
2. If the context does not give the needed help, use a dictionary to find out what the word means.
3. Use a dictionary to get the pronunciation of the word.

Special practice exercises, provided by workbooks which accompany some basal readers or constructed by the teacher, can be used to give needed practice. There is no need to provide here detailed examples of such exercises. The short descriptive statements that follow should suffice to make clear the nature and purpose of the most useful types:

1. Exercises in which the pupil arranges in alphabetical order given words found commonly in children's dictionaries. Such exercises vary in difficulty in the sense that some require the pupil in making his decisions to use only the first letter of the given words, some require him to use the second letter, and some require his use of the third letter.
2. Exercises in which the pupil decides which words in a given list would be listed on a dictionary page if the guide words on that page were two given words. Sometimes these exercises also ask the pupil to show in what direction he would turn pages in a dictionary to find words that are in the list but would not be found on the given dictionary page.
3. Exercises in which the pupil chooses from among the meanings that a dictionary offers for a given word the particular meaning which the word has in each of several different sentences.
4. Exercises in which the pupil uses a dictionary pronunciation key to figure out the pronunciations of given strange words.

Interpreting Punctuation Marks and Certain Typographical Signals

Do you have any trouble in interpreting each of the following sentences spoken by story characters?

1. If you can't help my young friends the cabin will not be built this summer.

2. I will bring fruit salad lettuce sandwiches chocolate pie ice cream and lemonade to the picnic.

3. Finishing an important job in woodworking is what Joe should learn to do.

4. If more of us don't learn to drive the new car will prove to be a poor investment for the family.

In sentence 1, is the story character talking to his young friends, or is he talking to someone else about helping his young friends? You have no way of knowing. But since you know what to think for commas, you would have had no trouble in interpreting the sentence if it had been written like this:

If you can't help, my young friends, the cabin will not be built this summer.

In sentence 2, just what and how many items is the story character saying that he will bring to the picnic? You can't possibly tell. He could be naming five, six, seven, eight, or nine items. You would have had no trouble in thinking quickly just what the story character meant if the sentence had been written like this:

I will bring fruit, salad, lettuce sandwiches, chocolate pie, ice cream, and lemonade to the picnic.

In sentence 3, is the story character saying that Joe should learn to complete an important job that he starts in woodworking? You would not have thought that if the sentence had been written like this:

Finishing, an important job in woodworking, is what Joe should learn to do.

No doubt you interpreted sentence 4 correctly as soon as you overcame one little difficulty. As you read the sentence the first time, it was very natural for you to connect the meaning of the expression *to drive* with the meaning of the expression *the new car*. Then you met immediately the word *will*, which made no sense with the thought you had in mind. Did you then start over and, with your experience in making sense for printed English, think a comma right after the word *drive*? Of course you could have interpreted the sentence much more quickly than you did if it had been written like this:

If more of us don't learn to drive, the new car will prove to be a poor investment for the family.

Possibly right now you are thinking, "So what? Any competent author uses commas where they are needed to help the reader understand just what he means. No reader meets the problems presented by the four numbered sentences." Well, if that is what you are thinking, you are half right and half wrong. It is true that the competent author uses within sentences commas he should use to help the reader think the relationships between ideas he must think and to keep apart ideas he must keep apart in order to understand just what the author means. But unfortunately, more elementary school pupils than is commonly thought do not know how to pay the attention to commas that is required for doing this thinking and keeping apart. Consequently they often misunderstand or achieve only vague understanding of the author's intended meaning. There is here no implication that all uses of commas or of a comma to set off the names of persons spoken to as in sentence 1, items in a series as in sentence 2, an appositive as in sentence 3, or a dependent clause as in sentence 4 are crucial indicators of the intended meaning. In many sentences, the meanings of the words themselves make the use of the comma unnecessary for this purpose. Yet sentences like the numbered four do occur in children's reading matter, and when they do, they present serious meaning difficulties for the pupil who fails to think what the commas tell him to think.

In reading the conversations carried on by the characters in a story, you often meet expressions which end with an exclamation mark. What does that mark tell you to think? Just that the expression it accompanies was spoken with strong feeling? Would it increase your understanding or enjoyment of the story if you thought a specific feeling — perhaps anger, fear, sarcasm, disbelief, surprise, or whatever particular feeling the author is trying to present? What would tell you which specific feeling is the correct one to think?

Now think what the next sentence says:

1. Have you seen the boys slide on the ice at the lake?

Does the following sentence mean the same thing to you?

2. Have you seen the boys' slide on the ice at the lake?

What meaning would you have thought for sentence 2 if you did not know what to think for that apostrophe, or if you had developed the habit of disregarding punctuation marks, apostrophes, and other typographical signals?

In reading the following passage, what relationship if any do you think between the part that comes before the colon and the part that comes after it?

> The colonists faced several difficulties during the first winter in New England: a shortage of food, trouble with the Indians, extremely cold weather, and severe sickness.

Suppose that in reading a story you come to a conversation being carried on by Mr. Smith and Mr. Brown. The first paragraph in the conversation begins with quotation marks and the author tells you that Mr. Smith is talking, but there are no quotation marks at the end of the paragraph. The very next paragraph begins with quotation marks. Which of the two story characters is saying that second paragraph?

What do the quotation marks in the next sentence tell you?

> I was right in the middle of "Mary's Garden" when the doorbell rang.

When you are reading along and come to an expression printed in italics, boldface type, or full caps, what does the use of that special type tell you to do in thinking that expression?

Sometimes in a story you will find a row of dots or a dash after something that a story character starts to say but does not finish. Does that row of dots or the dash mean that the speaker is being interrupted by either someone who starts to talk or something that happens?

Many of the uses of punctuation marks in children's reading matter serve little if any purpose in helping the pupil understand just what the author means. But other uses of punctuation marks in certain situations and the use of such typographical signals as special type, the apostrophe of possession, and a row of dots play an important role in the pupil's attempt to arrive at the author's intended meaning. That elementary school pupils should learn to think for these marks and signals what they need to think as they meet them in their reading is beyond question, and fortunately some pupils do this learning by themselves. Perhaps the fact that quite a number of pupils in Grades 3 through 6 do not know what to think for crucial uses of punctuation marks or have developed the habit of disregarding these symbols can be accounted for by the customary locking of the teaching of punctuation marks within instruction in written composition. Yet it may be merely a result of the quaint notion that what needs to be taught about punctuation marks for purposes of reading is exactly the same or much like what needs to be taught about those marks for purposes of writing.

The following statements constitute a recommendation concerning what needs to be taught to uninformed pupils about paying attention to punctuation marks and certain typographical signals in their reading matter:

1. The use of a period as a signal to think there the falling inflection that people use at the end of a spoken statement. The use of a question mark as a signal to think there the falling, and sometimes rising, inflection that people use at the end of a spoken question. These simple matters should have been explained early in the first grade.

2. The use of an exclamation mark as a signal to think of the foregoing expression as being said with a certain strong feeling. Included here should be an explanation to the effect that it is what has happened or what has been said so far in the passage which indicates the particular strong feeling to be thought.

3. The use of a comma as a signal to think there the short pause needed for keeping apart the items in a series, for separating an appositive or the names of persons addressed from the rest of the sentence, and for keeping the sense of an introductory dependent clause separated from the sense of the immediately following words. There is no need here to talk to pupils about the comma in a series, the comma of appositive, the comma of address, or the comma following an introductory dependent clause.

4. The use of a dash between words as a signal to think there a pause which is a little longer than the pause to be thought for a comma.

5. The use of a dash or a row of dots before the end of a story character's speech as a sign that another speaker or some event has interrupted the speech or that the speaker has decided not to finish it.

6. The use of a colon as a signal to think that what is coming next explains what has just been said.

7. The use of an apostrophe as a signal to think possession.

8. The use of italics, boldface type, or full caps as a signal to think with strong emphasis the expression so printed.

9. The use of quotation marks as a sign that a given expression is the name of a story, song, or poem.

10. The absence of quotation marks at the end of all but the last paragraph of a story character's speech.

1. Introducing the Item

Most uses of punctuation marks and typographical signals can be introduced to the pupil merely by calling his attention to those uses as they appear in material being read and explaining then and there what the marks direct him to think. For example, the teacher can introduce the interpretation of an exclamation mark by asking the pupil to note that mark at the end of something said by a story character — Nancy in this case — in a story being read and by saying something like this: "We call that mark an exclamation mark. Often you will find it at the end of something a character in a story says. It tells you to think of the story character as saying what he said with some strong feeling such as anger, fear, surprise, excitement, or disbelief. But to really understand and enjoy what is going on in the story, you will need to think the right strong feeling. With what strong feeling do you think Nancy said what she said? . . . How do you know? . . . What is it that tells you just which strong feeling to think for an exclamation mark in a story? . . . That's right. What has happened or what has been said so far in the story tells you." Surely some similar but appropriate procedure can be followed in introducing the thinking for a colon, a dash, italics, boldface type, full caps, and quotation marks enclosing a title. The interpretation of other punctuation marks, particularly that of certain uses of the comma, may require the use of a definite lesson.

The following illustrative lesson, addressed to the pupil as a member of a group or class, is concerned with teaching the need for paying attention to commas that appear within sentences and what to think for those marks when reading. The parts of the lesson and their purposes are much the same as those of the lessons which appeared previously in this chapter. In no sense is the lesson itself a finished product to be used in teaching any given group of pupils.

To read and think over

As you try to read the following sentence, think how many boys are to be in the class play and what the names of those boys are:

Bill James Tom Sidney Joe Gale and Sam are the boys who will be in the class play.

How many boys are to be in the class play? You can't be sure. The answer could be four, five, six, or seven.

Now read the same sentence again as it is printed below. When you come to each comma, make a little pause there as you think what is being said. Doing that will help you think the meaning you would get if you heard someone say the sentence.

Bill, James, Tom Sidney, Joe Gale, and Sam are the boys who will be in the class play.

Are you sure now how many boys are to be in the play and just what their names are? Are there five? Are their names Bill and James and Tom Sidney and Joe Gale and Sam? If that is what you decided, the little pause you made for each comma helped you think the right meaning for the sentence.

Now try to decide what the next sentence says and who is being spoken to:

If you will drive Aunt Mary we can all go to the fair.

Is the person who spoke that sentence talking to Aunt Mary or to someone else? You can't be sure.

To read the same sentence as it is printed below, make a little pause for each comma as you think what is being said. Doing that will help you think the meaning you would get if you heard someone say the sentence.

If you will drive, Aunt Mary, we can all go to the fair.

Did you decide that the person who spoke the sentence was talking to Aunt Mary instead of to someone else? If you did, the little pauses you made for the commas helped you think the right meaning for the sentence.

Here is another sentence for you to try to read:

Teaching a job to be done in school is something that Miss Brown does easily.

Which of the two explanations that follow tells what the sentence means?

1. Teaching is a job which is to be done in school and which Miss Brown does easily.
2. Teaching a job which is to be done by pupils in school is something that Miss Brown does easily.

You can't be sure. Either explanation could be right.

To read the same sentence as it is printed below, make a little pause for each comma as you think what is being said:

Teaching, a job to be done in school, is something that Miss Brown does easily.

Often in your reading, you will meet one or more commas inside a sentence. To help you understand just what the sentence means, make a little pause for each comma as you think what is being said.

Talking together

Help your class answer these questions:

1. Which of the two explanations gives the meaning of the sentence that tells about Miss Brown and has commas in it? How do you know?
2. Why do you think an author uses commas inside sentences in his writing?
3. What should you do when you meet a comma inside a sentence? Why?

To do by yourself

Think of answers to the numbered questions that follow:

1. Who is being spoken to in the sentence that comes next, Tom Carr or someone else?

   Why don't you wait here and see, Tom Carr, if you think the teams are going to play this morning?

2. Just what things does the next sentence say that the boys will bring to the class picnic?

   The boys will bring sugar cookies, ham, sandwiches, fruit, cake, and iced tea to the class picnic.

3. Does the next sentence mean that memorizing something which she doesn't enjoy is hard work for Sally?

   Memorizing, something that she doesn't enjoy, is hard work for Sally.

   Number a paper from 1 through 3. After each number, write your answer to the question which has the same number.

   If you are asked to do so, read your answers aloud. If you made a mistake, find out why it is a mistake.

Introducing the interpretation of use of punctuation marks and typographical signals in reading can and should be initiated at the third-grade level, and it is to be continued and expanded as needed at each subsequent grade level, whether or not it is done by means of a definite lesson. Possibly for some groups of pupils the amount of instruction which any given lesson provides should be less than that suggested by the foregoing illustrative lesson. Certainly in any definite lesson presented in print, all words used should be among those which make up the pupil's reading vocabulary.

2. Providing Practice in Using the Skill

There are three chief ways of providing the pupil with the practice he needs in order to become skillful at interpreting punctuation marks and typographical signals. *First,* the teacher can entice the pupil into reading a variety of much suitable material which is so intriguing that he will be motivated to interpret such marks and signals as he needs to do so. *Second,* from time to time, after the pupil has read a given selection in a reader, the social studies or science text, or any other book, the teacher can ask him to explain the meaning of an expression which he would have misunderstood if he failed to interpret the accompanying mark or marks correctly. *Finally,* special exercises, including some to be found in workbooks that accompany some basal readers, may be used. The following statements describe briefly some different types of such exercises:

1. An exercise in which the pupil is asked to decide just what items are named in each of several sentences. Each sentence must list several items separated by commas. The names of the items listed in each sentence must be of such a nature that interpretation of the commas is required for deciding just what those items are.
2. An exercise in which the pupil is asked to decide for each sentence included just who is being spoken to. Each sentence must be of such a nature that interpretation of the one or two commas included is required for making the needed decision.
3. An exercise in which each sentence included contains an appositive set off by commas, and the words used are of such a nature that the commas must be interpreted in order to keep from misunderstanding what the sentence says. The pupil is asked to decide which of two or more given meanings each sentence has.
4. An exercise in which each sentence included contains an introductory dependent clause, and the words used are of such a nature that an omitted comma is needed in order to read the sentence quickly at the first attempt. The pupil is asked to place a comma where it is needed for so reading each sentence.
5. An exercise in which the pupil is asked to decide for each of several sentences whether words enclosed by commas explain something that comes just before the first comma, name persons or things spoken to, or are items in a list of people or things.
6. An exercise which presents late in a conversation several exclamation marks. The pupil is asked to decide with just what strong feeling each exclamation was spoken.
7. An exercise in which each sentence included contains a possessive indicated by an apostrophe, and the words used are of such a nature that the apostrophe must be interpreted in order to keep from misunderstanding what the sentence says. The pupil is asked to decide which of two given meanings each sentence has.
8. An exercise in which each of several short passages contains commas or dashes, and three possible interpretations of each excerpt are provided. The pupil is asked to choose the correct explanation. Each excerpt must be of such a nature that the interpretation of the commas or dashes is required for making the choice.
9. An exercise which presents in a conversation a few uses of boldface

type, full caps, or italics to indicate words to be thought with strong emphasis. For each such item, the pupil is asked to choose between two interpretations, one being the meaning he would get if he thought the indicated emphasis and the other being a meaning he could get if he failed to think that emphasis.

10. An exercise presenting a conversation in which speeches of one or more characters are composed of two paragraphs. In each such case, the pupil is asked to decide which character is speaking the second paragraph.

11. An exercise which is mixed in the sense that it contains one or more uses of several items named in the preceding descriptions.

It is understood that special exercises such as those just described are to be used only by pupils who need the practice and that all words used in any exercise should be among those making up the pupils' present reading vocabulary.

Interpreting Metaphor

Just what meaning do you think the italicized expression in the following passage is intended to convey?

> Once the two older children were off to school, Mrs. Clark dressed her two-year-old son Tommy and took him into the kitchen. There she placed on the low table before him a bowl of cooked oatmeal, and hopefully urged him to begin eating his breakfast. Then she walked across the room to her counter tops and began kneading dough to make the fresh home-made bread she had promised the family for dinner that evening.
>
> Tommy, watching his mother at work, apparently became fascinated by her activity, and soon began to move his small fists here and there in the oatmeal. Attracted by the noise of Tommy's bowl sliding back and forth across the table, Mrs. Clark looked up to see what was going on. Then she laughed, and exclaimed, "Oh, Tommy! *You're a monkey!* That oatmeal was to be part of your breakfast!"

The expression *You're a monkey* is a metaphor, a saying in which one person or one thing — perhaps a boy, an object, a situation, or an activity — is given the name of something else which it isn't. In the preceding passage Mrs. Clark said that her young son was a monkey. Since you have some acquaintance with the nature of metaphor, you know that the words *a monkey* mean something other than what they seem to say, that Mrs. Clark did not mean her son actually was a monkey, that no doubt she meant Tommy was in some way like or had one or another of the characteristics of a monkey, and that the words *a monkey* stand for that way or characteristic. But just what is that way or characteristic? Is it silly? Is it mischievous? Playful? Tampering? Imitative? Stupid? Troublemaking? Mean? Cute? How do you know? To read this simple metaphor, you must do more than decide that the words *a monkey* are those words and call to mind the animal for which they often stand. In addition, you need to think quickly of characteristics that a monkey and a small boy can have in common and choose for the meaning of the words *a monkey* the one or more which fit best in the context or setting. This comparing and choosing requires some degree of reasoning, even though that reasoning may be completed very quickly indeed.

You encounter innumerable figures of speech in your reading, including metaphors, similes, personifications, hyperboles, and other types of figurative language. Many of these you use with sense in your talking and interpret readily in your listening, and insofar as they are now a seasoned part of your equipment for carrying on oral communication with people, they cause you little if any difficulty in your reading. No doubt the following items, most of them metaphors used in talking about situations and activities, are examples of figures of speech that, though what they describe is not stated, you have learned to interpret almost instantly through your years of experience in listening to people talk:

walking on air	wind him around her finger
turn over a new leaf	get your back up
puts a finger in every pie	make a mountain out of a molehill
let grass grow under his feet	stuck to his last
toe the line	beating about the bush
let the cat out of the bag	barking up the wrong tree
pick a bone with him	skating on thin ice
pulled in his horns	tend to her knitting
brought down the house	drove the nail home
holding the bag	make head or tail
pulling my leg	eating his heart out
put her foot into it	poking his nose into

Yet you will meet also in printed matter metaphors for which your experience in listening to people talk has not taught you the meaning required at the time and which you certainly will want to try to interpret. Sometimes the interpreting is relatively easy, perhaps as easy as that which you did in reading *a monkey*. In such situations you will find that it is much enhanced by (1) noting just what is being given the name of something else which it isn't and just what that something else is, (2) thinking of ways in which the two things could be alike, and (3) choosing for the meaning the way which fits best with the context in which the metaphor appears. At other times the interpreting may be quite difficult, as when the writer, in using what is sometimes called a metonymy or a synecdoche rather than a strictly simple metaphor, does not state what is being given the name of something else. The italicized expressions in the following sentence are examples:

> During the crisis through which our great nation has just passed, this candidate for public office stood strong and firm against *the jackals* shrieking on *the outer walls* of the republic.

Quite possibly the difficulty may lie in your lack of sufficient knowledge of the thing being given the name of something else and of this something else so that you cannot think of ways in which the two can be alike or of characteristics they can have in common. Under these circumstances you cannot possibly do the reasoning necessary for reading the metaphor until you first acquire the background needed for making the intended comparison.

Several investigations have shown that (1) textbooks in the content subjects and story books intended for pupils in Grades 3 through 6 contain a very large number of figures of speech, (2) many of these expressions are unfamiliar metaphors, (3) some of these metaphors are of the simpler type in which the thing being given the name of something else is clearly stated and for which the pupil already has the background required for making the needed comparison, (4) the remaining unfamiliar metaphors are of the more difficult type in which the thing being given the name of something else is not stated or for which the pupil does not possess the required background, and (5) figures of speech constitute a serious difficulty for the pupil in his reading, and of all types of such expressions the unfamiliar metaphor is the most difficult. Does this make you wonder why a writer in preparing reading matter for the child of elementary school age uses metaphors which are unfamiliar to his prospective readers and which are of the more difficult type? Why, for example, if a writer means *The rogues' carefully laid plans to use the power of the church in gaining the king's authority was destroyed by a sudden declaration of war*, does he write instead *The rogues' carefully laid plans to use the bishops' robe in gaining the crown was swept to the four winds by a sudden declaration of war?* Is the latter more expressive or forceful than the former? Does it have more literary merit? Does it sound more pleasant? Be all this as it may, metaphor — simple or intricate — is a highly useful ornament which serves as a delightful if subtle portrayer of meaning and feeling in language, which often lends lifeblood, so to speak, to the printed page, and which is a permanent part of the language that the pupil must learn to read. Surely one responsibility of instruction in reading is to help the pupil interpret such forceful expression.

1. Introducing the Item

Consider first the matter of helping the pupil learn how to interpret the simple type of unfamiliar metaphor in which the person or thing being given the name of something else is stated clearly and for which the pupil has the background required for making the needed comparison. Here the teacher can use a definite lesson that makes the pupil aware of the nature and function of a metaphor, introduces to him a procedure to follow in figuring out what such an expression means, checks his acquaintance with the procedure, and gives him a bit of initial practice in interpreting simple metaphor. The following material, addressed to the pupil, is in no sense a finished product to be used with any given group of pupils, but it does illustrate a type of lesson which can be used with third-grade pupils and in each succeeding grade as needed. The purposes and parts of the illustrative lesson are much the same as those of similar lessons which have appeared previously in this chapter.

To read and think over

Mr. Brown was sitting in the living room, reading the newspaper before dinner. His nine-year-old son Billy was there too, moving here and then there and never settling down, not even for two minutes. Finally Mr. Brown spoke. "Billy, what is the matter with you?" he asked. "You're a grasshopper this evening. Why don't you get something to do and sit still for awhile?"

When Mr. Brown spoke, he said that Billy was a grasshopper. Of course, he did not mean that Billy was a real grasshopper. He just gave him that name to show that Billy was like a grasshopper in some way. When people talk, they often give one person or thing the name of something else to show that the person or thing is in some way like that something else. Doing this can make the talking interesting.

To read the words *a grasshopper* in what Mr. Brown said, you need to do more than decide that the words are those words. You must think of ways in which a boy — Billy — and a grasshopper can be alike. Then you should choose for the meaning of the words *a grasshopper* the way which makes the most sense in what you read.

In what ways can a boy and a grasshopper be alike? Can they both be hungry? Can they both make noise? Can they both be pests? Can they both keep moving from place to place? Can they both jump, see, hear, or be busy or dangerous? Which of these ways do you think Mr. Brown meant when he used the words *a grasshopper?* How do you know?

Often in your reading you will find one person or thing being given the name of something else. To decide just what that name means, do these things:

1. First, make sure that you know just who or what is being given the name of something else and just what that something else is.

2. Next, think of ways in which the two things can be alike.

3. Choose for the meaning the way which makes the most sense in what you are reading.

Talking together

Help your class answer these questions:

1. What do you think Mr. Brown meant when he said that Billy was a grasshopper? What makes you think so?
2. Why would a person who writes a story for you to read give one person or thing the name of something else?
3. What can you do to help you decide what is meant when one person or thing mentioned in a story is given the name of something else?

To do by yourself

In each numbered paragraph that follows, one person or thing is given the name of something else. Just what meaning do you think that name stands for?

1

"Betty, your bedroom is a jungle," said Mrs. Carter to her young daughter. "I could hardly walk through it this morning. You simply must pick up things and put them away after school today."

2

"You should have heard our program at school today, Mother," said Sally. "That Nancy Barr certainly is a nightingale. I never heard her do as well before."

3

"That paper route Jack has will be a gold mine for him," said Mark. "It is in a neighborhood that is growing. He should have no trouble in getting new customers."

If you are asked to do so, tell what you think Mrs. Carter meant when she said the bedroom was a jungle, what Sally meant when she said Nancy was a nightingale, and what Mark meant when he said the paper route would be a gold mine. Tell why you think each meaning you chose is a good one.

Three points pertaining to the nature of any lesson to be used in introducing the interpretation of the simple type of unfamiliar metaphor should be emphasized. First, the metaphor used in doing the explaining presented in the first part of the foregoing material and the metaphors used in giving the initial practice proposed by the last part must be unfamiliar to the pupil. Second, in the case of each metaphor used, the pupil must be sufficiently acquainted with both the person or thing being given the name of something else and that something else, so that he can think of characteristics they can have in common. Third, if the lesson is to be read by the pupil, all words therein should be among those which make up his present reading vocabulary.

How can the teacher help the pupil understand the more difficult type of unfamiliar metaphor in which the person or thing being given the name of something else is not stated or for which he does not have the background required for making the needed comparison? It will do no good to first encourage him to use here the procedure which the illustrative lesson suggested for interpreting the simpler type of unfamiliar metaphor. About the best the teacher can do is to handle each such difficult expression at the time it appears as a part of a selection the pupil reads. If the unfamiliar metaphor thus encountered is difficult in the sense that the person or thing being given the name of something else is not stated, possibly like one or more of those listed on page 286, the teacher can either (a) tell the pupil what meaning the expression stands for or (b) identify for him just what is being given the name of something else and then ask him to apply the procedure he has been taught to use in interpreting the simpler type of unfamiliar metaphor. If the metaphor is difficult in the sense that the pupil lacks the background required for making the needed comparison, the teacher can either (a) tell him what meaning the expression stands for or (b) give him the required background of information and then ask him to apply the procedure he has been taught to use in interpreting simple metaphor. Expecting most elementary school pupils to interpret all on their own the difficult type of unfamiliar metaphor is expecting too much.

2. Providing Practice in Using the Skill

For the pupil who has acquired the attitude of demanding meaning in his reading and who has received competent instruction in how to cope with the simpler type of unfamiliar metaphor, the most fruitful practice in interpreting such expressions is inherent in his reading of much suitable and intriguing material. Further practice is provided when the teacher, in discussing with the pupil a selection that has been read, asks him occasionally to tell what is meant by one or another of the simple unfamiliar metaphors presented in the selection and to explain why he thinks the meaning he chose is a good one. Special exercises, each containing items similar to the numbered paragraphs included in the last part of the illustrative lesson on page 289, may be used also with the pupil who needs the practice they provide. Examples of such exercises appear in the workbooks that accompany some basal readers.

Sensing the Relationship That Sentences Have with One Another

During a baseball game, the members of a team play different parts or positions. People call these parts by certain names — shortstop, right field, catcher, first base, and so on. By the time the game is over, two or more persons, one at a time, may have played the same part.

In a sense it is much the same with the sentences that make up an informative paragraph. Those sentences play different parts in carrying the message that the paragraph as a unit is intended to convey, even though people use no particular names in thinking or talking about the parts. Usually but not always one of the sentences, wherever it appears, may be a so-called topic sentence; it announces what the paragraph talks about. One or more sentences may explain or illustrate what the topic sentence says. Still other sentences may present examples or applications of ideas offered by one or more of the explanatory sentences. Sometimes one of the sentences is merely a commenting sentence in that it offers, more or less parenthetically, the writer's opinion of or reaction to the substance of one or more of the other sentences but in no way explains or exemplifies any other included sentence. Rarely if ever is the meaning of the paragraph as a unit the sense of sentence 1, plus the sense of sentence 2, plus the sense of sentence 3, plus the sense of sentence 4, and so on. Usually that meaning is inherent and perhaps somewhat hidden in the relationship which the writer intends the included sentences to have with one another.

Often when you read an informative paragraph, you need to understand what it is saying as a unit, and consequently you must sense the relationship of its sentences. Sometimes this sensing is quite easy, particularly when the paragraph contains a topic sentence, when it is well organized either deductively or inductively, and when its sentences start with expressions like *First, In the second place, For example,* or *Then too,* which signals the relationship between one sentence and another. Probably you will find that the relationship which the sentences in the following paragraph have with one another just falls into your lap, so to speak, as you read the paragraph only once. The sentences are numbered so that later the author can talk about them conveniently.

1. The large fireplace that was such an important part of the roomy kitchen in the early colonial home had three main uses. 2. The long logs burning there provided the only heat for the entire house during the cold days and nights of winter. 3. In addition, all the cooking was done in or near the open fireplace. 4. Corn was roasted in the hot ashes. 5. An iron rack, called a crane, that was fastened to one of the walls of the fireplace and extended over the burning logs, held suspended there pots and kettles which contained vegetables and other foods. 6. Meat was roasted on a pointed iron rod, called a spit, which was fastened to one wall of the fireplace and extended over the flames. 7. In the earliest days, someone had to turn the meat on the spit every now and then so that it would roast evenly. 8. Later, different devices were invented and used to keep the spit turning all the time until the meat was roasted. 9. Bread and pastries were baked in a small metal oven that was built into the stonework at one side of the fireplace. 10. Finally, the fireplace supplied in its immediate area a sort of social center where the family and sometimes their friends gathered on winter nights to talk and enjoy companionship.

Sentence 1 is a topic sentence in that it tells you what the whole paragraph is going to be about. After you had read that sentence, did you think immediately, "This paragraph is going to tell me three main uses of the colonial fireplace"? Then did you continue your reading to try to find out what those three uses are? If so, you made a sensible start. Did sentence 2 give you one main use? Did sentence 3 give you another main use? Did sentence 4 give you the third main use? If not what part is that sentence playing? Are sentences 5 and 6 playing the same part as sentence 4? What other sentence is playing the same part? What part are sentences 7 and 8 playing? What sentence gives you the third main use of the fireplace?

Does the following arrangement of the numbers of the sentences show the relationship that you think those sentences have with one another? Here the indenting of one number under another means that the sentence represented by the indented number explains, illustrates, or exemplifies the sentence represented by the number under which the indenting occurs, and it is understood that numbers which form a perpendicular column stand for sentences that are playing the same part coordinately.

1.
    2.
    3.
        4.
        5.
        6.
            7.
            8.
        9.
    10.

When, as sometimes happens, an informative paragraph contains no topic sentence, or its topic sentence is not the first one, or the arrangement of the included sentences does not permit you to think quickly during a first reading the part each sentence is playing, sensing the relationship among the sentences can be difficult. In such a situation, you may need to do a considerable amount of weighing and classifying of ideas, and this reasoning may require you to engage in an analytical second or even third reading of the paragraph. You may meet this sort of situation in working with the paragraph that follows. If you wish, number the sentences consecutively and write the numbers in an arrangement that shows the relationship you figure out.

Colonial children engaged in different games and sports. Boys and girls both played tag, croquet, and chess. The boys took part in wrestling, boxing, racing, and swimming contests. Young men and girls had time for fun too. They held husking bees at which, along with the husking of corn, there was much singing and dancing. During the winter, ice skating and sleighing were popular with these young folk. Indeed people of all ages in most of the colonies had various ways of amusing themselves. Even the adults found time for play. The men and women held dances and gave receptions, teas, and card parties. A favorite recreation of the older men was bowling or playing ten pins on smooth green lawns. One game that the boys played was much like the game we call soccer.

To show the relationship which you think the sentences in the foregoing paragraph have with one another, what changes would you make in the following incorrect arrangement of the numbers standing for those sentences?

1.
    2.
    3.
  4.
    5.
    6.
  7.
    8.
    9.
    10.
11.

Investigations have shown that intermediate-grade pupils have difficulty sensing the relationship of sentences in an informative paragraph. Particularly troublesome to them is a paragraph which has no topic sentence, which presents a topic sentence elsewhere than at the beginning, or in which the sentences are arranged in a somewhat illogical order. These pupils tend to be sentence readers in that, although they may understand sufficiently well what each sentence says standing by itself, they build a mental fence around that sentence and thereby shut out thinking the relationship it has with one or more other sentences, which they must sense in order to understand what the paragraph as a unit is saying. It does little if any good to say here that much of the pupil's difficulty would be eliminated if each informative paragraph intended for his use were organized so that its first sentence was a topic sentence, the opening words in some sentences were transitional expressions pointing out the relationship to be thought, and the sentences were placed in a clearly logical order — *and if* the pupil were fully aware of the significance of these simple readability standards.[6] Actually many well-constructed paragraphs included in the pupil's informative reading matter do not meet all these standards, but surely such paragraphs are and will continue to be a part of the language he must learn to read. That is why the task of equipping him to cope with such paragraphs should be a part of instruction in reading, beginning in Grade 4 and continuing as needed in each succeeding grade.

1. Introducing the Item

A definite lesson can be used to introduce the sensing of the relationship among the sentences of an informative paragraph. Such a lesson will

---

[6] It is true that the pupil would be helped considerably here if he knew how to decide what the topic of an informative paragraph is. A discussion of the meaning and the teaching of this skill appears in Chapter 9.

make the pupil aware of the nature and importance of this act, suggest a procedure for working with a paragraph which is somewhat puzzling, and give him initial practice in using the procedure. The material that follows is illustrative of such a lesson, but it is not offered for use with any particular group of pupils. The parts and purposes of the material are much the same as those of illustrative lessons presented previously in this chapter.

To read and think over

The players on a baseball team play different parts during a game. The names of some of those parts are pitcher, center field, and second base. Before the game is ended, more than one player may play the same part. To understand what the whole team does in a game, you must know what each player is doing and how he helps or works with the other players.

It is much the same with the different sentences in a paragraph that gives you information on a topic. The sentences play different parts, and more than one sentence may play the same part. To understand what the whole paragraph is saying, you need to think how each sentence helps or works with the other sentences.

To learn just what this means, read the following paragraph and try to think how the sentences help or work with one another. The sentences are numbered so that you can think about them easily.

1. Many years ago, pioneer women in the West used corn in making three main kinds of food. 2. One of these was hominy, something like the hominy you may eat now and then. 3. To make this popular food, the pioneer housewife first boiled shelled corn in water containing lye until the skins came off the grains. 4. Then she poured off the lye water and boiled the grains in plain water several times to remove all the lye. 5. Finally she boiled the lye free and skinless grains for several hours until they became hominy. 6. Another popular food was parched corn. 7. Grains of corn were fried in a big skillet containing a large amount of fat until they became brown and crisp. 8. Then the remaining fat was poured off, and the grains were salted. 9. Several different breads or cakes were made with ground corn. 10. Corn pone was a sweet raised bread baked in a large skillet, much as you may have seen a big pancake baked. 11. Corn dodgers were small cakes made of stiff batter mixed with small bits of brown crisp pork and fried with fat in a skillet. 12. Hoecake, much like corn pone, was baked on the blade of a garden hoe.

When you read sentence 1, did you think that the paragraph was going to tell you what the three main kinds of food were that pioneer women made with corn? Then did you read on to find out what those kinds of food were? If you did these things, you made a good start in thinking how the sentences in the paragraph work together.

Sentence 1 tells you what the whole paragraph talks about. That is why we can call it a *topic sentence*.

What are the numbers of the sentences that tell you what the three main kinds of food were? Yes, they are 2, 6, and 9. Each of these sentences helps to explain or gives an example of what sentence 1 says. If you wanted to write the numbers of all four sentences to show how they work together in the paragraph, those numbers should look like this:

1.
   2.
   6.
   9.

By indenting the numbers 2, 6, and 9 under the number 1, you show that you think each of sentences 2, 6, and 9 names a main kind of food and explains or gives an example of what sentence 1 tells about. By placing the numbers 2, 6, and 9 in a straight column, you show that each of those sentences is playing the same part in the paragraph.

What part is sentence 3 playing? Sentence 4? Sentence 5? Each of these sentences tells one thing that the housewife did in making hominy. In this way they give you ideas that explain sentence 2, and each of them plays the same part in the paragraph. If you were to put these numbers in your list, they should look like this:

1.
   2.
      3.
      4.
      5.
   6.
   9.

You can see that each of sentences 7 and 8 tells one thing that was done in making parched corn. In this way they give you ideas that explain sentence 6, and each of them plays the same part in the paragraph. Each of sentences 10, 11, and 12 gives you ideas that explain sentence 9. If you were to put these numbers into your list so that you have a sort of picture to show how all the sentences in the paragraph work together, they should look like this:

1.
   2.
      3.
      4.
      5.

6.
   7.
   8.
9.
   10
   11.
   12.

Sometimes you will need to read carefully a paragraph in which the topic sentence is not the first sentence. When that happens, you may need to work pretty hard to think how the different sentences work together to tell what the whole paragraph says.

Just what part do you think each sentence in the following paragraph is playing?

1. The settlers in the West needed cleared land on which to grow crops. 2. They also needed material for building houses and furniture. 3. So they kept cutting away the forests. 4. Great fires destroyed many of our forests. 5. The use of new inventions such as the telephone and the telegraph kept demanding more and more wood. 6. These are reasons why less than one-half of the forests we once had in the United States are still here.

When you read sentence 1, did you think that the paragraph was going to tell you how the settlers cleared the land or what the needs of the settlers were? Probably you had good reason to think either of those things. But if you did, your reading of sentence 4 told you that you had made a mistake. What is the number of the topic sentence, the one which tells you what the whole paragraph talks about? Yes, it is 6. The whole paragraph tells you reasons why less than half our forests remain. Since you now know that, read the paragraph again to find out what those reasons are.

Does the following list of numbers show how you think some of the sentences in the paragraph work together?

6.
   3.
   4.
   5.

Where would you put the numbers for sentences 1 and 2?

Often as you read a paragraph only once, you will think right then just how the sentences work together. If this does not happen as you read a given paragraph the first time, do these things to help you figure out how the sentences work together to tell what the whole paragraph says:

1. Number the sentences in the order which they have in the paragraph.

2. Decide which sentence you think is the topic sentence.

3. Read the paragraph again to decide what part each sentence is playing, and write each number in its correct place in a list to show how you think the sentences work together.

Talking together

Help your class answer these questions:

1. In what way are the sentences in a paragraph that gives you information on a topic like the players on a baseball team, a basketball team, or a football team?
2. Why would you need to think how the sentences in a paragraph work with one another?
3. What does the topic sentence in a paragraph do?
4. When might it be pretty hard for you to think how the sentences in a paragraph work together?
5. Just where would you put the numbers for sentences 1 and 2 in the list for the paragraph that tells why we lost many of our forests?
6. What can you do to help you figure out how the sentences in a paragraph work together to tell what the whole paragraph says?

To do by yourself

On a sheet of paper, write a list of the numbers of the sentences in the following paragraph so that your list shows how you think those sentences work together to tell what the whole paragraph says:

1. Some settlers who moved from the East to the West many years ago came because they could get new rich land at little cost. 2. Often this land was free, just for the taking. 3. Sometimes the price was no higher than one dollar an acre. 4. Other settlers came to escape trouble. 5. Such trouble may have been hard times that made it difficult to earn a living in the East. 6. It may have been illness which could not be overcome in the eastern climate. 7. A number of people joined the settlers to provide service to them. 8. Among these were ministers and doctors. 9. Then too there were traders who traveled from settlement to settlement selling all kinds of goods. 10. Thus there were several reasons why people from the East settled in the West to make new homes for themselves.

If you are asked to do so, write your list of numbers on the board. Then find out whether others in the class think your list is correct. If you made a mistake in placing a number in your list, find out why it is a mistake.

Several matters pertaining to the foregoing material need to be pointed out. *First*, the instruction suggested under "To read and think over" is much too extensive to be covered in one class period with almost any group of pupils. It is recommended, therefore, that a first period be used for providing the instruction suggested up to the beginning of the eleventh paragraph and for group discussion of only the first three questions listed under "Talking together." A second class period can be used for providing the remainder of the instruction suggested under "To read and think over," for group discussion of the remaining questions listed under "Talking together," and for the section labeled "To do by yourself." *Second,* if the teacher prefers to acquaint the pupil with a standard outline form and its nomenclature to use instead of the Arabic numbers the author used for sentences, there is no reason why this should not be done. It should be kept in mind, however, that the simple numbering of the sentences and the correct arranging of those numbers in a list serves just as well and with less burden than any standard outline form as a means of helping the pupil figure out the relationship which the sentences have with one another and as a record of the thinking he does. *Third,* the material makes no effort to teach the pupil how to work with an informative paragraph which contains no topic sentence. This matter can be delayed until the teacher undertakes instruction in how to decide what the topic of a paragraph is. *Fourth,* the paragraph used as an illustration in explaining what is meant by sensing the relationship of the sentences in an informative paragraph must be simple in that its first sentence is the topic sentence, some sentences begin with transitional expressions pointing up relationships, and all the sentences are arranged in a clearly logical order.

2. Providing Practice in Using the Skill

As mentioned previously, often the pupil will sense almost automatically as he reads an informative paragraph the relationship which its sentences have with one another. At other times he will need to take time to figure it out. That is why the pupil should be encouraged now and then to use the procedure suggested in the illustrative material whenever he needs to do so in his reading of textbooks in social studies, science, and other content subjects and of other informative books. The practice he gets in following the counsel given by such encouragement should enable him to acquire sufficient control of the procedure so that he can learn to read on his own informative paragraphs which are somewhat puzzling to him.

The pupil who needs additional practice can use special exercises, each presenting an informative paragraph to be figured out, which appear in workbooks that accompany some basal readers. Some of the exercises ask the pupil to use a standard outline form in portraying his thinking of the relationship of the sentences within a paragraph. Others do not.

Thinking Correct Stress

Sometime when you start to watch a television play, press in hard enough on the tragus of each ear so that you cannot hear the actors' talking. As you continue to look at the players' actions and note their facial expressions and gestures, try to imagine what they are saying. Then in a minute or two, open your ears to hear what is being said, and think how well the talking you imagined fits with what you are hearing and seeing now. This may help you realize even more clearly than you do at present the contribution that hearing the actors' talking makes to your understanding and enjoyment of the play.

When you read, it is helpful to keep in mind that each printed line stands for talk: something which one story character is saying to one or more other characters or which the writer is saying to you, the reader. You can see the print — the words, the punctuation marks, the typographical signals — but since the book has no sound track to carry the oral expression itself, you cannot hear the line being spoken. Yet to understand clearly what the print is saying, you should try to imagine or hear in the "ears of your mind" how the talking would sound if you actually heard the story character, or possibly the writer, speak the line.

This imagining is essential to your thinking the spoken language for which the print stands and which, assuming the absence of any expression strange to you in oral form, makes sense to you. It includes "hearing" not only the names of words but also the voice intonations — the stress, the inflections, and the little pauses — with which the story character or the writer spoke or would speak the line in the situation depicted. You must think the most stress on the words the writer no doubt emphasized as he wrote them and hopes you will too as you read them.

Except for occasional italics, boldface type, or full caps, the words or groups of words to be stressed in the reading of a passage is rarely indicated by print. Thus the rapid selection of such expression is almost entirely a responsibility of the reader himself. The choices he makes depend largely upon his careful application of what has been said and what has happened so far and upon his acquaintance with the emphases used in speaking in different situations.

Are you interested in discovering that the meanings you make in reading a given passage are determined at least partially by your thinking the most stress on certain words and groups of words rather than others? If so, read the following six paragraphs, trying to think the most stress on only the words printed in boldface type:[7]

---

[7] These paragraphs are a slight adaptation of the first seven paragraphs on pp. 28–30 in *Smile Please*, by Mildred Topp (Houghton Mifflin Company, Boston, 1948).

Grandpa was an old Union soldier. When he was **nineteen** years old he joined the **army** instead of going to **college** as his **older** brothers had done. They were all **captains** and **majors**, but **Grandpa** was **just** a private, and fought four years in the 1st West Virginia Infantry without a **scratch** or a **promotion.**

When the war was **over**, Grandpa went out to **Illinois** with the **rest** of the Whites. The boys who had been in the **army homesteaded** land, and the others **bought** it, in Mason County. After Grandpa had picked out a nice **farm** to homestead, and built a **house**, he began looking for a **wife.**

One Saturday afternoon when he had ridden to a German settlement to buy some **seed** corn, a terrible **rain** came up. Grandpa spent the **night** with a German farmer, and went to **church** with him the next **day.** Grandpa said, "A **German** from Pennsylvania had **started** that church, just like **John the Baptist** from Jerusalem **started** the **Baptist** Church." Grandpa was just a plain **Scotch Presbyterian,** and he had never seen **anything like** that German church. "The **men** sat on **one** side," Grandpa said, "and the **women** on the **other.** And running down the **middle** aisle was a tall **partition.** You couldn't see **over** it, even if you **stood up.** It was **supposed** to help the men and women keep their **minds** off each other during church anyway."

He **loved** to tell about that **first day** he saw **Grandma.** "If she hadn't been in the **choir** I would have **missed** her on account of that **consarned wall.** But **there** she **was,** sitting up in the **choir** in a **pretty brown silk** dress with a **sassy** bustle and a brown bonnet with pink flowers underneath the brim. She was **just** eighteen years old and **pretty** as a **peach.**

"The sermon and songs were all in **German,** which I couldn't understand a **word** of. So for two hours I didn't have a thing to **do** but **make eyes** at your **grandma.** By the time church was **out,** I had **decided** to make her the **mother** of my **children.** I found out that her name was Barbara Ellenberger, and that she was going to **marry** a rich young German farmer, **Fritz Noodle-man,** the next **week.** It made my flesh **crawl** to think about the sweet little thing being **saddled** with **such** a name as Mrs. Noodleman. So the night **before** she was to **marry** him, I borrowed a red-wheeled rubber-tired buggy from my rich brother **Davy,** and ran **off** with her. She **wasn't** very **hard** to persuade. Noodleman was **fat,** and **I** was a **fine figure** of a man, so she did just the **usual** backing off. Davy was a State Senator **and** a **Justice** of the **Peace,** so **he** married us, and invited us to stay at **his** house that **night.**

"The next day when we went back to get her **things,** we found her pappy in a high German **rage.** He spoke **seven** languages, and he was **yelling** at me in **all** of them. He wouldn't **let** your grandma have the **wedding** clothes **she** had made to marry **Fritz** with, **nor** her dowry. It took the old man a **week** to cool off, and **make** his **peace** with the Noodlemans. Then he **invited** us home for Sunday **dinner.**"

The following expressions appeared in the foregoing passage. As you read them again, think the most stress on only the words that are printed in boldface type. Then decide whether the meaning you make this time for that expression is the same as the meaning you made for the same expression when you read it the first time.

1. Grandpa was an **old Union** soldier. (the first sentence in the passage)
2. The **boys** who had been in the army homesteaded **land,** and the others bought it, in **Mason** County. (the second sentence in the second paragraph)
3. After Grandpa had **picked out** a nice farm to homestead, and **built** a house, he began **looking** for a wife. (the last sentence in the second paragraph)
4. Grandpa was just a **plain** Scotch Presbyterian, and **he** had never seen anything like **that** German church. (the fourth sentence in the third paragraph)
5. **But** there **she** was, sitting **up** in the choir in a pretty brown silk **dress.** (from the third sentence in the fourth paragraph)
6. She was just **eighteen** years old. (from the last sentence in the fourth paragraph)
7. **I** had decided to make her the mother of **my** children. (from the third sentence in the fifth paragraph)
8. I borrowed a red-wheeled rubber-tired buggy from my **rich** brother Davy, and ran off **with** her. (from the sixth sentence in the fifth paragraph)
9. Davy was a **State Senator** and a Justice of the Peace, so he married **us,** and invited us to stay at his house **that** night. (the last sentence in the fifth paragraph)
10. We found her pappy in a **high** German rage. (from the first sentence in the last paragraph)
11. He **wouldn't** let your grandma have the wedding clothes she had **made** to **marry** Fritz with, nor **her** dowry. (the third sentence in the last paragraph)

Was the meaning you made during your second reading of any of the expressions different from the meaning you made when you read them the first time? It should have been. Just which word or words you think the most stress on can often make such a difference. Are you wondering which of the two meanings you thought for any of the expressions is closer to the meaning intended by the writer? This is futile. With the possible exception of item 2, you couldn't possibly know without having first read the context provided by the first twenty-seven pages in the book from which the passage was taken.

Actually the pupil who has had the instruction proposed in this volume for first and second grades should have acquired considerable skill in thinking the most stress on the words and groups of words which he should so emphasize. Yet several investigations have shown that quite a large number of pupils in Grades 3 through 6 misunderstand here and there what they are reading because of their failure to think the most stress at the points where it is needed. By and large such pupils do not realize that reading matter stands for talk, do not know that printed lines stand for voice intonations as well as the names of words, and do not understand that reading is almost entirely a matter of thinking for the printed lines the familiar sounds they would hear if the lines were spoken. That their ability to think correct stress can be improved by a relatively small amount of appropriate instruction has been demonstrated by the investigations referred to above. Consequently it is recommended here that this instruction be provided for third-grade pupils who need it and that it be continued as required in each subsequent grade.

1. Introducing the Item

The act of thinking correct stress can be introduced through the use of a definite lesson which explains the meaning and importance of the act, illustrates correct use of the skill, and provides initial practice in thinking correct stress. The following material, addressed to the pupil, is illustrative of such a lesson, but it is not intended as a finished product for use with any given group of pupils:

To read and think over

When you talk, you emphasize some words more than others. You do this by saying those words in a higher, louder, or even lower voice, or by taking a longer time to say them than you use in saying the other words. By emphasizing some words more than others, you help people understand just what you mean.

When other people talk to you, they emphasize some words more than others. By doing this, they help you understand just what they mean.

The three numbered sentences that follow use exactly the same words, but you can make each sentence mean something different from the others by thinking the most emphasis on the word printed in heavy black type in that sentence. As you do that now, think how each sentence differs in meaning from the others.

1. **Mary** won't be at school tomorrow.
2. Mary won't be at **school** tomorrow.
3. Mary won't be at school **tomorrow.**

When you emphasized **Mary** in the first sentence, you made the sentence mean that although other people may be at school tomorrow, Mary won't be there. When you emphasized **school** in the second sentence, you made the sentence mean that although Mary may be somewhere else tomorrow, she won't be at school. When you emphasized **tomorrow** in the third sentence, you made the sentence mean that although Mary may be at school some other time, she won't be there tomorrow.

Each printed line that you look at stands for something that someone is saying. It may be something that one person in a story is saying to one or more other persons in the story. It may be something that one person in the story is saying to himself. It may be something that the person who wrote the story is saying to you.

When you read a story, do you think how the lines that the people in the story say and the lines that the person who wrote the story says would sound if you heard those people talking? Try to do that now as you read the part of a story that follows:

Bill Rogers was excited. "But, Tommy," he exclaimed, "think of the prizes and what fun it would be!"

"Oh, the prizes are great, and I'd like to enter the race. But I can't spend money on new wheels and the other things I'd need to make a soap box racer," answered Tommy.

Bill looked disappointed. He wanted Tommy White to be in the Soap Box Derby. "We'll think of some way for you to make a racer," he said. "Come on over to my house now and look at my plans for the Red Streak."

Tommy was eleven years old and was old enough this year to enter the Soap Box Derby. Bill was thirteen. He had raced before.

Over at Bill's house, the boys looked at the plans for Bill's Red Streak.

"Isn't it a dandy?" asked Bill.

"The plans look all right," agreed Tommy, "but what makes you think that it'll go faster than any other racer?"

"Well," said Bill, "Tony won the race last year. He told me that the important thing is to make a good plan before you begin to build. With these plans I'm sure I can make a winner."

On his way home, Tommy thought over Bill's plans for the Red Streak.

"Bill will have a good-looking racer," he said to himself, "but I wonder if it will be fast. I don't think Bill has paid enough attention to stream-lining. I'll bet I could draw plans for a faster racer than the Red Streak."

The part of a story you just read is printed again below. The particular words which Billy and Tommy probably emphasized most in their talking and which the person who wrote the story would probably emphasize most in talking to you are printed in heavy black type. As you read all the lines again, think the most emphasis on only those words.

Bill Rogers was excited. "But, **Tommy**," he exclaimed, "think of the **prizes** and what **fun** it would be!"

"Oh, the prizes are **great,** and I'd **like** to enter the race. But I **can't** spend money on new **wheels** and the **other** things I'd need to make a **soap box racer,**" answered Tommy.

Bill looked **disappointed. He wanted** Tommy White to be in the Soap Box Derby. "We'll think of **some way** for you to make a racer," he said. "Come on over to **my** house **now** and look at my **plans** for the **Red Streak.**"

Tommy was **eleven** years old and was old enough **this** year to **enter** the Soap Box Derby. Bill was **thirteen.** He had raced **before.**

Over at **Bill's** house, the boys **looked** at the plans for Bill's Red Streak.

"Isn't is a **dandy?**" asked Bill.

The **plans** look all right," agreed Tommy, "but **what** makes you think it'll go **faster** than **any other** racer?"

"Well," said Bill, "**Tony** won the race last year. He **told** me that the **important** thing is to make a **good** plan before you **begin** to build. With **these** plans **I'm sure** I can make a winner."

On his way **home,** Tommy **thought over** Bill's plans for the Red Streak. "Bill will have a **good-looking** racer," he said to himself, "but I wonder if it will be **fast.** I don't think Bill has paid enough **attention** to **stream-lining.** I'll bet **I** could draw plans for a **faster** racer than the Red Streak."

Did thinking the most emphasis on the words printed in heavy black type help you understand and enjoy the part of a story? Of course it did!

When you read, the print itself usually will not show you which words you should emphasize most as you think what is being said. You will have to decide what those words are all by yourself. To do this, think what has already been said and what has already happened in the story.

Talking together

Help your class answer these questions:

1. Why do people emphasize some of the words they use when they talk? How do they do this emphasizing? In what way does their emphasis help you when you listen?
2. Why is it important for you to think emphasis on some of the words when you read?
3. How can you decide which word or words to emphasize as you think what a printed sentence is saying?

To do by yourself

As you read the next part of the story about Tommy and Bill, think which words you should emphasize most to understand what is being said:

The next evening Tommy's mother looked up from her mending and said, "Tommy, what are you up to? You haven't said a word all evening. And what have you been putting on that paper?"

Tommy grinned. "Soap Box Derby comes next month," he answered. "Bill has plans for a racer, and I thought I could make better plans than his. I know I can't build a racer, but I'd like to give it a try."

"Why can't you build a racer?" asked Mrs. White. "You're very good at making things."

"It would cost too much," answered Tommy. "The wheels would cost a lot."

"Aren't there any old wheels in the cellar that you could use?" asked his mother.

"I suppose I could use the wheels off my old wagon," Tommy replied. "I know that wheels sold just for Soap Box Derby racers are much better, but those old wheels might be strong enough. I could call my car Wagon Wheeler."

"You'd enjoy making a racer," said his mother. "Why don't you try?"

For a few minutes Tommy just sat thinking. "I'll need some metal axles and a steering wheel," he said. "Maybe I could find them at Minelli's Junk Yard. I could use that heavy cardboard in the cellar for the outside."

"Mr. Minelli probably would let you work for him to pay for what you need," suggested Mrs. White.

"I think he would, at that," said Tommy. "His place needs a lot of straightening-up. I'll ask him tomorrow."

If you are asked to do so, read aloud some of the lines you just read. Emphasize most the words on which you thought the most emphasis when you read the lines to yourself.

2. Providing Practice in Using the Skill

Once the pupil understands the meaning and importance of thinking correct stress in his reading, the practice he needs in order to develop the habit of doing such thinking will come best through his reading of much suitable and intriguing material. In addition, the teacher should encourage him from time to time to think as he reads silently the emphasis he believes he would hear if he heard the lines being spoken. Such encouragement can be a part of assignments which direct him to read to himself pages in a basal reader, and certainly it should be included in providing him the ample time he should have now and then to prepare to read well to others a selection or part of a selection he has enjoyed and thinks they would like to hear. Finally, special exercises which ask him to mark in selections the words he believes should be thought with the most emphasis may be used. Examples of such exercises appear in workbooks that accompany some basal readers.

Visualizing

Sometime when you are waiting for the immediate start of a television showing of a play for which you do not already know the setting, the plot, the events, the story characters, or the actors, close your eyes. As you listen to the actors' talking and hear other noises that are a part of the play, try to imagine pictures of the events which are taking place, the location of and the objects surrounding the action, and the movements, appearance, facial expressions, and gestures of the actors. In a minute or two open your eyes to see what the screen is showing, and think how well the pictures you imagined fit with what you are seeing and hearing now. Doing all this can help you realize the contribution that seeing the events, the performers and their actions, and the setting makes to your understanding and enjoyment of the play.

Pictures sometimes accompany the text of a story. Some of them show small or instantaneous parts of events. Some show what story characters look like in a given situation or at a given time. Others show places and objects that the story tells about. Most if not all of the pictures are intended to help you understand and enjoy the story. Whether or not they do so depends much upon the care with which you observe and use them for that purpose.

No printed story can present pictures of every event, person, place, or thing that it tells about. But, as you read the text, you can make pictures in your mind to go with what the words say: ones that portray just an instantaneous bit of action, an object of some importance in the story, a story character expressing joy, fear, or some other strong emotion, or perhaps a corral, a hotel lobby, or the inside of a jet plane that is a setting. Often you will find that the picture you imagine for an item when you first read about it will need to be altered as you read on and the text tells you to add this to or subtract that from the picture. Sometimes the picture will be a sort of continuous one, a moving picture as it were, covering a complete event, a series of happenings, or even the full action of the entire story. While certainly you should not expect any picture you imagine for printed lines to be exactly like that which any other reader imagines for the same lines, you should try to make yours fit well with what the lines say in the sense that it includes most of their substance and does not contain anything not mentioned in or implied by the text.

As you read the following passage, think now and then what the pictures you are making in your mind look like:[8]

It was raining the next day when I came in from school, and my feet were wet. Mother made me put on some dry stockings and old summer slippers while my shoes dried. I was looking out of the window wishing it would stop raining, when I noticed a wagonload of cotton stuck in the mud in the street at the end of the bridge. The wagon had two nice mules hitched to it, and it was so heavy and the mud was so deep, that the mules couldn't pull

[8] This material is a slight adaptation of paragraphs on pp. 249–252 in *ibid*. Used here by permission.

it up onto the bridge. The driver was whipping the mules, and they were straining with all their might, but they could not budge the wagon.

I stood at the window and watched the man beat the mules as long as I could stand it; then I ran down the steps and out on the sidewalk in the rain. I shouted at the man, "Stop whipping those mules! They're doing the best they can." But he kept right on, and the wagon sank deeper and deeper into the mud. The mules were in a lather, and blood was running out of their mouths where the bit cut them.

It was more than I could bear, and I waded out into the street after him. The sticky mud pulled both my slippers off, but I went on anyway. When I reached the wagon, the driver was so busy beating the mules he didn't know I was there, until I grabbed his right arm. I jerked his hand down and sank my teeth into it. He let out a howl and tried to shake me off, but I kept on biting, even after he had dropped the whip.

Finally he tore me loose and grabbed me by the back of the neck. He reached down into the mud and got the whip, yelling, "Why, you little she-devil! I'll show you!"

He drew back to hit me, but I was too mad to be scared. All I wanted to do was to keep on biting him. He struck me once, with the handle of the whip, then a voice thundered, "Drop that whip, or I'll shoot you!"

There on the sidewalk stood Mr. Garner, holding a dripping umbrella in one hand and a pistol in the other. Mr. Garner was the finest lawyer in the Delta, but he had so many enemies because of the murder cases he was always trying that he had gotten permission from the sheriff to carry a pistol. I had always planned to call him in to save me from being hanged, if I murdered anybody. But I had never thought of his saving me from being beaten to death.

Now he shouted, "Pick up that child and bring her to the sidewalk." I didn't want the driver to pick me up; but Mr. Garner still had his pistol out, and I had to let him. When he dumped me down on the sidewalk, Mr. Garner said, "Are you hurt?" And I answered, "No, sir. He was too close to me to hit me hard." Mr. Garner said, "You run upstairs to your mother, and get some dry clothes on. I'm going to find out who those mules belong to, and swear out a warrant for this fellow's arrest. Precede me to the office, sir." And he marched the wagon driver down the street.

When I came in, soaking wet and muddy all over, with no shoes on and a red welt on my arm, Mother put on the teakettle and made me take a hot bath, and gave me a hot lemonade, "so I wouldn't catch my death." Then she talked to me a long time about the evils of high temper. She said, "Getting mad and fighting never gets you anywhere, except in trouble. You simply must quit biting people. This is two people you have bitten in two days. If you keep it up, you may get a ring in your nose, like the cannibals in darkest Africa."

Did you imagine a picture to go with the first two sentences in the foregoing passage? If so, what did you put into it? What did you put into the picture you imagined for the rest of the first paragraph? Was there any picture you imagined for certain lines that did not need to change as you read on? For what group of sentences or paragraphs, if any, did you imagine a sort of moving picture in which you saw events happen one after the other? Did the pictures you imagined as you read help you understand or enjoy what the lines said?

In general the available data on elementary school pupils' use of imagery in reading show that (1) the correlation between reading achievement as measured by standardized tests and the amount of imagery used in reading certain passages is low, (2) pupils vary greatly in the amount of imagery they use and in their ability to imagine pictures to go with what they read, (3) imagery of outdoor scenes is more commonly and frequently used than imagery of indoor scenes, and imagery of objects is more commonly and frequently used than imagery of people, (4) imagery is used more by primary-grade pupils than by intermediate-grade pupils, and (5) girls use more imagery than boys. But these survey data provide no answers to such questions as: Just what characterizes imagined pictures that fit well with printed lines in this or that story? Can the pupil learn to imagine such pictures and can his ability to do so be improved? Does the pupil who is skillful at imagining pictures that fit well with stories understand or enjoy those tales more than does the pupil who is not so skillful? What should constitute instruction which seeks to improve the pupil's ability to imagine pictures that fit well with stories he reads? No one knows the answers to these questions, and until they are answered with a clear negation, even though the data be gathered by means of today's crude tools for measuring imagery, the author recommends strongly that serious effort be made to improve the pupil's ability to imagine helpful pictures. Such effort may be initiated in the third grade and should be continued as needed in each subsequent grade.

1. Introducing the Item

The following material, addressed to the pupil, illustrates instruction that might be undertaken in introducing the possible need for imagining pictures which fit well with stories he reads. It is not offered as a model for use with any given group of pupils.

To read and think over

Often there are pictures in a story that you read. Some of those pictures show parts of events that happen in the story. Some of them show what people in the story look like. Others show places and objects that the story tells about.

Almost all the pictures that come with a story can help you understand and enjoy the story. If you look at them to see what they have to tell, they can help you see clearly the events, persons, places, and objects in the story. Sometimes they can even help you feel how the people in the story feel.

No story can have pictures that show every event, person, place, or object that it tells about. But as you read, you can make pictures in your mind to go with what the words say about those people and things. Each picture you make in your mind should have in it most of what the words say about the event, person, place, or object you are trying to imagine, and it should not have in it anything which does not fit well with what the words say. If you will practice making pictures in your mind as you read, you may understand and enjoy stories even more than you do now.

Below is a part of a story. As you read it, try to imagine a picture that goes well with the words which tell about the burning house and what the firemen did.

Ben came running up right after the fire truck had arrived. Then he just stood there watching the fire and hoping, I suppose, that the old house would be saved. Smoke was pouring from all the upstairs windows on the front, and small tongues of flames licked at the sides of the roof above the broken panes. A tall ladder had been placed under one of the windows, and a fireman was climbing into one of the rooms to fight the fire from the inside. Two other firemen stood on the ground, shooting streams of water from big hoses onto the roof and through the open windows into the upstairs. I felt a little sad about the whole thing when I remembered that Ben's family had lived there for years and years until just a few weeks ago.

Which of the two scenes pictured below [and on the opposite page] is most like the one you imagined? Why do you think so?

Talking together

Help your class answer these questions:

1. How can the pictures that come with a story you read help you?
2. What can you do about other pictures so that you will understand or enjoy a story as much as you can?
3. What things should be true about a picture you imagine?
4. Which of the two pictures about the fire is most like the picture you imagined? Why do you think so?

To do by yourself

As you read the next paragraph, try to imagine a picture that goes well with the words that tell how the damaged house looked the next morning:

I had to go home before Ben did, and didn't get to see how things turned out at the fire. But the next morning, Mary and I stopped there on our way to school to see what damage had been done. The firemen had stretched a heavy rope around the small lot to warn people to stay away from the smoldering timbers, but I could see all I wanted to see. The whole roof had fallen in, and the front porch was burned away. Most of the wood on the front and the two sides was gone, and there the old charred frame stood by itself, except for the walls still standing at the back. I couldn't remember such a bad fire happening in our town before, and I was a little disappointed when no one there could tell us how it started.

If you are asked to do so, tell what the picture you imagined looked like. Listen as others tell what they put into the pictures they imagined. Help

your class decide in what ways the pictures told about do or do not fit well with what the words say.

The foregoing material considers the imagining of only a single picture to depict a part of one short event and one object as reported by a small group of lines. It makes no effort to present either the problem of altering a picture as the reading of immediately subsequent lines might demand or the problem of imagining a moving picture to go with a series of related events. Other pieces of instruction can be used later to introduce these two additional problems. Preferably any instruction should make use of pictures in color rather than black and white drawings, and certainly anything presented to the pupil in print for him to read to himself should contain only words that are among those in his present reading vocabulary.

2. Providing Practice in Using the Skill

By reading much juvenile fiction which appeals to his interests and is suited to his level of reading ability, the pupil who has received instruction similar to that just illustrated can get a large amount of useful practice in imagining good pictures to go with stories he reads. In addition, the teacher will find that now and then, after the pupil has read a given short selection in which a particularly interesting group of lines is unaccompanied by a picture in the selection itself, it is helpful to have him tell about the picture he imagined to go with those lines. Workbooks that accompany some basal readers include special exercises in which the pupil is asked to choose from among two or three pictures the one most like the picture he imagined to go with a group of lines included in the passage presented by the exercise.

A Concluding Statement

The present chapter has considered the teaching of seven items — insights and skills — which are an important part of the equipment that pupils in Grades 3 through 6 require in order to cope independently with certain meaning difficulties presented by their reading matter. That such instruction is sorely needed is evidenced by the inability of these pupils to understand sufficiently well what they attempt to read in story books, textbooks, and other material intended for their use. It is to be hoped that teachers will make the instruction suggested by the illustrative lessons a definite part of their teaching of reading. Even though the necessary instructional material may not be supplied by the basal reader being used, definite periods should be set aside for providing this instruction, just as such times are reserved for presenting, for example, operations in mathematics. Merely naming a given skill for the pupils and admonishing them to use it or merely having pupils work out practice exercises in using the skill must not be substituted for the needed introductory instruction, and every effort should be made to encourage pupils to do on their own the large amount of suitable reading which in itself usually can supply the practice required for gaining adequate control of the skills.

QUESTIONS TO BE ANSWERED

1. In what way can the intermediate-grade pupil's task in reading be more difficult than that of the pupil in Grade 1 or grade 2?

2. What are some of the meaning difficulties which pupils encounter in their reading? To what factors can lack of ability to deal with meaning difficulties be attributed?

3. What seven items does this chapter suggest be taught to pupils so that they can cope independently with certain meaning difficulties? Of what two main teaching activities does the instruction to be given in each of these items consist?

4. What is the purpose of introducing each item to the pupil? How can practice in using each item be supplied?

5. Each of most illustrative lessons in this chapter contains three main parts. What is the purpose of each part?

6. What value that a pupil could get from learning to use context to figure out the meaning of a word do you consider to be most important? What is the difference between using context to figure out the meaning of a word and using context in unlocking words which are strange only in print?

7. What things might you need to teach so that a pupil learns how to use a dictionary to get the meaning of a word? Under what circumstances should a pupil use a dictionary to get the meaning of a word he encounters in his reading?

8. What punctuation marks do you think are most likely to cause the pupil difficulty? Under what circumstances would you use a definite lesson to introduce the interpretation of punctuation marks? In what other way might you introduce it?

9. What is the technique that this chapter suggests be taught to the pupil so that he can interpret simple unfamiliar metaphors? Under what circumstances will the pupil be unable to make this technique work? What should be done about other unfamiliar metaphors?

10. In what way may it be difficult for the pupil to understand the meaning of an informative paragraph even though he understands what each sentence itself says? What is the technique which this chapter suggests the pupil be taught so that he can work out the meaning of such a paragraph?

11. What is the main trouble with the intermediate-grade pupil who does not think needed stress in his reading? What can you do to help him?

12. What can you do to help pupils learn to imagine good pictures to go with stories they read?

13. If conditions were such that you could teach only three of the seven items discussed in this chapter, which three would you choose? Why?

14. What, if anything, did you learn from this chapter to help you with your reading?

MORE TO READ

Burton, William, Clara Baker, and Grace Kemp, *Reading in Child Development*, Henry Holt & Co., Inc., New York, Chapter 9.

Dechant, Emerald, *Improving the Teaching of Reading*, Prentice-Hall, Inc., Englewood Cliffs, N.J., 1964, Chapters 12, 13, 14.

Durrell, Donald, *Improving Reading Instruction*, World Book Company, Yonkers-on-Hudson, N.Y., 1956, Chapter 12.

Gans, Roma, *Common Sense in Teaching Reading*, The Bobbs-Merrill Company, Inc., Indianapolis, 1963, Chapters 10, 11.

Harris, Albert, *Effective Teaching of Reading*, David McKay Co., Inc., New York, 1962, Chapter 11.

Horn, Ernest, *Methods of Instruction in the Social Studies*, Charles Scribner's Sons, New York, 1937. Chapter V.

McKee, Paul, *The Teaching of Reading in the Elementary School*, Houghton Mifflin Company, Boston, 1958, Chapter 3 and pp. 319–334, 386–398.

McKim, Margaret, *Guiding Growth in Reading*, The Macmillan Co., New York, 1955, Chapter 12.

Russell, David, *Children Learn to Read*, Ginn & Company, Boston, 1962, Chapter 9.

Smith, Henry, and Emerald Dechant, *Psychology in Teaching Reading*, Prentice-Hall, Inc., Englewood Cliffs, N.J., 1961, Chapter 10.

Spache, George, *Toward Better Reading*, The Garrard Press, Champaign, Ill., 1963, Chapters, 4, 20.

Yoakam, Gerald, *Basal Reading Instruction*, McGraw-Hill Book Co., Inc., New York, 1955, Chapter 10.

THINGS TO DO

1. Get any basal reader, the accompanying teacher's guide, and the pupil's workbook intended for use at a given grade level above Grade 2 and no higher than Grade 6. Examine these materials to discover the instruction

they provide in coping with meaning difficulties and to note in which book it is given.

2. Not all of the meaning difficulties which pupils encounter in reading are discussed in this chapter. Examine other books on the teaching of reading to find out what some of these other difficulties are.

3. Choose any one of the seven items discussed in this chapter. Then make a list of the different things you would do to teach that item as completely as you think you should to pupils at any grade level you choose.

4. Choose any one of the seven items except the using of context. Then make an exercise to give practice in using that item to pupils at whatever grade level you choose.

5. Write out a statement telling in some detail what you would do to discover which pupils in a class need instruction in one or another of the seven items.

6. Choose any one of the seven items and make the material you think you would need for checking a pupil's ability to use that item.

chapter 9

Studying
Informative Material

As noted earlier, most reading material prepared for first and second grade pupils is narrative rather than factual and is intended not so much to convey information as to give fun or pleasure. Out of school, the first- or second-grade pupil rarely reads highly factual material in order to digest information on some topic, question, or problem. Furthermore, during these years, most school instruction in social studies, science, English, mathematics, and other subjects comes through the teacher's oral explanations and demonstrations, and the pupil should not be expected to read such informative material extensively.

But in Grades 3 through 6 much of the reading matter both in and out of school is highly factual in content and style, and is to be read, not as a story should be read, but as a conveyor of information to be thoroughly digested. Thus reading now becomes not only a source of pleasure but increasingly a tool or medium for studying printed content which has to be learned well. This increase in the so-called study type of reading, and the fact that such reading is more complicated than the reading of narrative, constitute one reason why reading in Grades 3 through 6 is more difficult than in Grades 1 and 2.[1]

---

[1] Another reason for increased difficulty in reading was given near the beginning of Chapter 8.

It is true that effective study of informative material demands insights and skills which, as described in Chapters 4, 5, 7, and 8, are essential to reading lines that stand for only language already familiar to him in spoken form and to coping with certain meaning difficulties presented by other lines. But since effective studying requires more than merely understanding what the lines say, the pupil will need to apply other insights and skills which, in the sense that they are rarely if ever required for the reading of narrative, are somewhat peculiar to this studying. The additional insights and skills pertain to locating information on a given topic or question, selecting from material read ideas pertinent to a given purpose, evaluating or reacting critically to questionable statements that have been read, and organizing ideas presented by reading matter. All this requires the pupil to do a considerable amount of sharp reasoning on which to base crucial judgments and in itself is much of what he needs for studying effectively during his remaining school days and for continuing his education independently long after those days are past.

It is the purpose of this chapter and Chapter 10 to consider the teaching of the additional insights and skills mentioned in the preceding paragraph. For want of a better term, they can be called items. Those to be taken up in this chapter are concerned with locating information on a given topic or question, selecting from material read ideas pertinent to a given purpose, and organizing ideas presented by reading matter. Chapter 10 will address itself to evaluating or reacting critically to questionable statements that have been read. The two chapters make no claim to covering all the items which are somewhat peculiar to the study type of reading. No doubt some persons could name other items not included in these discussions which they believe are of much importance.

The particular items to be discussed in this chapter are (1) using the index of a book, (2) locating quickly on a page information referred to by the index, (3) selecting ideas for a given purpose, (4) deciding what the topic of a paragraph is, (5) outlining an informative selection, (6) organizing notes made during study, and (7) interpreting graphs. Each of these seven items refers to a major skill and whatever insights are basic to or accompany correct use of that skill. All of them are highly useful in studying informative material effectively, in or out of school. Since the fourth and fifth items in particular pertain to ways in which the language operates, they are basically aspects of linguistics.

The teaching of each item consists in (1) introducing that item to the pupil and (2) providing additional practice in using the skill. The introducing of an item includes making the pupil aware of the meaning and importance of the skill, illustrating correct use of the skill, using some means for pupil and teacher to find out whether the former understands how to use the skill correctly, and giving a bit of initial practice in using the skill. The additional practice can be supplied intermittently during the school year by teaching social studies, science, and other subjects in a way which gives the pupil persistent and ample opportunity to use the skill in his study of those subjects and by using as needed special practice exercises. Each of the main sections which make up most of the remainder of this chapter first presents an explanation of the nature of one of the seven items and then illustrates or explains fully the teaching of that item. Any definite lesson included merely illustrates the introducing of an item and is not offered as a finished product to be used in teaching any given group of pupils.

Using the Index of a Book

There are times when you need to locate in a factual book information which it supplies on a particular topic, question, or problem. If the book you plan to use is a typical informative book rather than a set of encyclopedia or other general reference books in which the volumes are lettered alphabetically, how do you find out which pages in the book give the information you are looking for? Do you first look over the table of contents to find there a chapter title or section title which indicates that the information you want is given in that chapter or section, and then, after finding the beginning of the chapter or section itself, keep turning pages until you come to the one or more which you think will help you? Probably you do not use this procedure, but it is followed by many people who do not know how to use that most helpful aid, the index.

Think now of things that anyone needs to know and do in order to use the index of a book skillfully. What would you add to or subtract from the following list?

1. Where the index is. Where is it in a typical informative book, in a yearbook such as the *World Almanac*, in a set of encyclopedias that has an index?
2. What the material that makes up an index is and how it is arranged. What are main topics and how are they indicated and arranged? What are subtopics and how are they arranged? What do the numbers after the topics tell?
3. What word or words to look for among the main topics. Is such a word — commonly called a key word — always included in the topic or question on which information is to be located? Why might you need to use more than one key word?

4. How to find quickly a word in a list arranged in alphabetical order.
5. How to choose the right subtopic. Under what circumstances could this possibly be a problem?
6. The meaning of certain marks, including the dash between page numbers, boldface type, brackets, the word *Fig.*, the comma, the semicolon, and the designating letters *d, m, p, t.* What, for example, is the difference in meaning between the page references 20–22 and 20, 21, 22?
7. The meaning of the *See* cross reference and the *See also* cross reference.

Out of school, the pupil often needs to find information in connection with one or another of his activities. In many schools, the various content subjects are and should be taught in such a way that the pupil is required to locate by himself data to be considered later in class discussions. Thus there is good reason to teach the use of the index of a book in order to equip the pupil to study informative material effectively. Such teaching may begin in the third grade and should be continued and expanded as needed in each subsequent grade.

1. Introducing the Item

The following material, addressed to the pupil, illustrates instruction which probably should be included in introducing the use of an index. The different parts and their purposes are much the same as those in the illustrative lessons presented in Chapter 8.

To read and think over

How do you find the information that a book has on a given topic or a question you want answered? Do you open the book just anywhere and keep turning pages to the left or right until you come to the information you want? There is no need for you to use that slow way of finding what you are looking for. Instead, you can use the index that is at the back of most books you use in studying.

Look at the part of the index of a book on the next page. The words printed in heavy black type and furthest to the left in each column are called *main topics.* They name people and things that the book tells about, and they are arranged in the order of the letters in the alphabet.

When you use the index of a book to help you find the information the book gives on some topic or question, you must decide what word to look for among the main topics. We call that word a *key word.* Always try to choose a key word that names what your topic or question talks about.

Sometimes the key word to use for a question is in that question. What word would you use as a key word for each of these questions?

1. What are the different uses of automobiles?
2. What did the first bicycles look like?

Sometimes there may be in a question more than one word which you should use as a key word. For example, take the question *How does climate affect travel?* If you used only the word *climate* as a key word, you might miss some of the information the book gives. That is why you may need to use the word *travel* also as a key word.

What two words would you use as key words for each of the following questions?

4. Is coal mined in Illinois?
5. How is radio used in fighting crime?

Africa, automobiles in, 219; bridges, 255; burdens carried by men, 314; burros, 331; railroads, 182, 185; roads, 210; wagons, 293

Airplanes, first, 8, 9 *p*; how controlled in the air, 15; how supported in the air, 16; how they came to be, 10–14; uses of, 63–72

Airports, in mid-ocean, 97–98; in the United States, 70–72; on airmail routes, 65

Automobiles, different uses for, 217–219; how they came to be, 221–224; how they helped to improve roads, 207; increase in production, 227, 228 *t;* what the first ones were like, 224–226

Balloons, first crossing of the Atlantic, 87; first crossing of the English Channel, 89; first successful dirigible, 83; hot air, 74–78

Bicycles, how their use helped to improve roads, 206; how they came to be, 250; used in many parts of the world, 214

Boats, ancient, 411–412; native, in different parts of the world, 418–420

Bridges, built by natives, 255–258; famous, 249–252; importance of, 111, 243

Burros, in the United States, 189–191; work they do, 208, 314–315, 386

Canals, George Washington's interest in, 2; in China, 350, 419; in Europe, 384, 385; in the United States, 380

Cargoes, how loaded and unloaded on ships, 382, 401; kinds of, 356–358, 362, 382, 401, 406, 409

Cars, early railroad, 105, 136; electric, 236–237; modern railroad, 109–117. *See also* Pullman cars

Chicago, great railroad center, 117, 118 *m;* reached by foreign planes, 47; reached by ocean liners, 383

Coke, *see* Fuel

Dirigible balloons, advantages of, 96; defined, 182; early experiments with, 83; how brought to earth, 92–94; how managed in the air, 91; modern, 85; uses for, 96

Dog teams, of the Eskimos, 303; used by Arctic explorers, 59

Donkeys, in China, 333; in Egypt, 333; in Mexico, 293; in Sicily, 295; on lower slopes of the Andes, 352. *See also* Burros

Drags, used by the Indians, 299

Drawbridges, 244

Dredges, in a busy harbor, 363

Dry lands, Sahara Desert, 186; 345–349; transportation in, 344

Dugouts, in ancient times, 411; in Central America and Africa, 412; made by American Indians, 411

6. Why is cement used in building bridges?

Sometimes a word you need to use as a key word is not in the question. For example, take the question *In what states are the most peaches and apples grown?* If the index did not list the words *peaches* and *apples* among its main topics, would you decide that the book gave no information you needed? You should not do that. You might get the help you need by using the word *fruits* as a key word.

Suppose that an index you are using does not have among its main topics either of the italicized words in each of the following sentences. What other word that is not in the question would you try to use as a key word?

7. For what purposes are *tin* and *copper* used?
8. Are both *wheat* and *corn* grown in the same places?

Look again at the part of an index on the preceding page and find the main topic *Airplanes*. After it you can see five groups of words. They are *first, how controlled in the air, how supported in the air, how they came to be, uses of*. Each of these groups of words is called a *subtopic*. The subtopics show what the book tells about the main topic *Airplanes*. In some indexes, the subtopics are arranged in the order of the letters of the alphabet. In others, they are arranged in the order in which they are talked about in the book.

After each subtopic are one or more numbers. Each of them is the number of a page on which information is given about that subtopic. A dash between two numbers, such as *63–72*, means that information on the subtopic begins somewhere on page 63 and ends somewhere on page 72. In some indexes the letter *m, p,* or *t* is used after a page number to tell you that on the page is a map, a picture, or a table.

What subtopic in the part of an index you looked at would you use to find information on each of these questions?

1. How are cargoes loaded on ships?
2. In what ways were the first bicycles different from those we use today?

It is easy to choose the right subtopic to use for the first question, because one or more important words in the question are also in the subtopic. It is not so easy to choose the right subtopic for the second question, because none of the important words in the question are in the subtopic. You need to look at all the subtopics that come after the main topic **Bicycles** and try to decide which is the best one to try. Probably the subtopic *how they came to be* is the one to use.

Find the main topic **Coke** in the part of an index. No subtopics come after that topic, but you will find there the words "*See* Fuel." Those word mean that by using the main topic **Fuel** you may be able to find the information you want about coke.

Find the main topic **Donkeys** in the part of an index. After the subtopics you can see the words "*See also* Burros." Those words mean that by looking under the main topic **Burros** you can find where to look for other information about donkeys.

Talking together

Help your class answer these questions:

1. How can using an index help you find information on a topic or question?
2. How are the main topics in an index arranged? In what ways may the subtopics be arranged?
3. What are good answers to the first eight numbered questions you were asked in the first part of this lesson?
4. Why may you often need to use more than one key word to find the information that a book gives on a question?
5. Why may it sometimes be harder to choose the right subtopic than it is at other times?
6. What does the dash between two page numbers tell you? What does the word *See* tell you? What do the words *See also* tell you?

To do by yourself

On what pages listed in the part of an index would you expect to find information on each of the following questions? Write and number your answers on a sheet of paper.

1. What are some of the main canals in the United States?
2. What heavy loads do men in Africa carry?
3. Were more automobiles made in the United States in 1964 than in 1960?
4. In what countries in Europe are bicycles commonly used?
5. Where were the first airplane flights made?
6. What improvements have been made in railway cars?
7. What are the main airports in Chicago?
8. What were the first balloon flights over large bodies of water?

If you are asked to do so, read aloud the answers you wrote for some of the questions. If you made a mistake in any answer, find out why it is a mistake.

Attention is called to several matters pertaining to the foregoing material. *First,* the suggested instruction provided under "To read and think over" omits the teaching of alphabetical order. If, at the time the use of the index is introduced the pupil has not yet learned this order at least to the extent suggested in the illustrative lesson on the use of a dictionary,[2] the appropriate instruction should be included. *Second,* no doubt in most cases the instruction suggested under "To read and think over" is too extensive to cover in one lesson. A first lesson can be limited to the teaching of alphabetical order, if necessary, a second to teaching only the selection of key words to look for among main topics, and a third to instruction in choosing correct subtopics. Obviously, if such a division

[2] See p. 268 in Chapter 8.

is made, the work provided under "Talking together" and "To do by yourself" in each of the three lessons must be adjusted to the instruction therein. *Third*, if the suggested instruction is to be given to the pupil in printed form for him to read to himself, it must be easier to read than that provided by the illustrative material, particularly at the third- and fourth-grade levels. *Fourth*, preferably the instruction should be based on the index of a book being used by the pupil at the time rather than on the part of an index included in the illustrative material. Quite possibly at the third-grade level it may be profitable to begin the instruction with an index that is only a main-topic index.

The index of an informative book is unquestionably the fundamental tool to be taught for use in locating information quickly and accurately on a given topic or question. Yet there are in addition more or less special aids and specialized sources that should be introduced to the pupil at appropriate levels and times as he progresses through Grades 4, 5, and 6. Special aids provide references to books and magazines that give information on various topics, and they include (1) the card catalogue, (2) the *Children's Catalogue*, (3) special indexes such as *Subject Index to Poetry*, and (4) the *Readers' Guide*. The specialized sources provide information itself on various topics, and they include (1) an encyclopedia such as *The World Book*, (2) an atlas, (3) a yearbook such as *The World Almanac*, (4) bound volumes of magazines, and (5) biographical dictionaries such as *Who's Who in America, American Men of Science,* and *Junior Book of Authors*. Both the card catalogue and *Children's Catalogue* can be useful to the pupil in finding in the school library books which supply information to be studied in the content subjects[3] and juveniles which are to be read as children's literature.[4] The *Readers' Guide* can be helpful to the more advanced pupils in finding magazine selections which satisfy the same purposes. The pupil's use of an authentic encyclopedia that he can read, an atlas, and the *World Almanac* is almost indispensable to his study of many topics included in social studies and science.[5] Bibliographical dictionaries such as *Who's Who in America* and *American Men of Science* serve as sources for checking on the validity of printed statements read.[6] *Subject Index to Poetry* and *Junior Book of Authors* can help the pupil who is exposed to competent instruction in children's literature.[7]

[3] See Chapter 11.
[4] See Chapter 12.
[5] See Chapter 11.
[6] See Chapter 10.
[7] See Chapter 12.

Responsibility for teaching the use of the index of an informative book lies unquestionably with the regular classroom teacher. In a school without a librarian the responsibility for teaching the use of whatever special aids and specialized sources are available must be assigned to the same person. In a school having a librarian, instruction in the use of those aids and sources usually is undertaken by that person and is carried on during occasional so-called library periods. Whoever introduces a given special aid or specialized source to the pupil should be aware of and acquaint him with important specific matters which are essential to its use. The reasonably but not fully complete listings given in the following paragraphs offer illustrations of such matters:

The card catalogue: (1) the purpose and value of the card catalogue, (2) the meaning and use of the letters on the front of the drawers, (3) the purpose and use of the guide cards, (4) choosing one or more words to use as key words, (5) finding a word in a list arranged in alphabetical order, (6) the meaning of each piece of printed matter on and the purpose of an author card, a title card, and a subject card, (7) the meaning and use of cross reference cards.

An encyclopedia: (1) the purpose and nature of an encyclopedia, (2) the meaning and purpose of the guide letter or letters on the cover of each volume, (3) the meaning and use of guide words, (4) choosing one or more words to use as key words, (5) finding a word in a list arranged in alphabetical order, (6) the use of cross references, (7) interpreting maps, tables, and graphs, (8) the purpose of bibliographies at the end of articles, (9) location of the index in an encyclopedia that has an index.

2. Providing Practice in Using the Skill

Practice in using the index of an informative book comes best through working out reading assignments in social studies, science, and other content subjects. As explained fully in Chapter 11, each such assignment consists of one or more questions on which the pupil himself is to find in one or more books the information he needs to study, and by its very nature that assignment provides opportunities for getting required practice in using the index of a book. Even when the only book available for the study of a given content subject is the textbook, the problem or question assignment can still be made. Obviously no pupil can get the practice he needs by assignments to reading which name pages or sections to be studied. It is to be hoped, too, that in Grades 5 and 6 assignments to reading in the content subjects will give the pupil ample opportunity to use whatever special aids and specialized sources are available and have been introduced to him.

Special exercises which appear in workbooks accompanying some basal readers or which the teacher may construct can give the pupil practice on specific matters pertaining to using the index of a book. The following list describes such exercises:[8]

1. An exercise in which the pupil is asked to arrange listed words in alphabetical order.
2. An exercise in which the pupil is asked to choose for each of several listed questions the one included word he would use as a key word to look for among main topics.
3. An exercise in which the pupil is asked to choose for each of several listed questions the one included word other than the underlined word he would use as a key word.
4. An exercise in which the pupil is asked to name for each of several listed questions an unincluded word he would use as a key word.
5. An exercise in which the pupil is asked to choose for each of several listed questions the subtopic he would use from a shown part of an index, with the right subtopic including important words used in the question.
6. An exercise in which the pupil is asked to choose for each of several listed questions the subtopic he would choose from a shown part of an index, with the right subtopic not including important words used in the question.
7. An exercise which asks the pupil to name for each of several listed questions the numbers of the pages to which, as indicated by a shown part of an index, he would turn to get information on that question.
8. An exercise which asks the pupil to indicate for each of several listed questions what he would do to get information on that question through the use of cross references given in a shown part of an index.
9. An exercise which through the use of several listed questions asks the pupil to respond correctly to the dash between two page numbers, the word *Fig.*, and the designating letters *m, p, t* in a shown part of an index.

Locating Information Quickly on a Page

Sometimes, in telling which pages in a book supply information on a given topic or question, the index of that book shows a dash between two

[8] For illustrations of these exercises, see Paul McKee, *The Teaching of Reading in the Elementary School* (Houghton Mifflin Company, Boston, 1948), pp. 442–449.

number, such as 25–27. This means that the information referred to begins somewhere on page 25 and takes up all of page 26 and the first part if not all of page 27. At other times the index shows commas between page numbers, such as 25, 26, 27. This means that the information referred to appears along with other information on each of pages 25, 26, and 27. In the first case, the index does not tell you just where on page 25 the information begins. In the second case, it does not tell you just which lines on pages 25, 26, and 27 supply the information.

Some but by no means most informative books offer printed labels to help you find quickly on a page the particular lines with the information to which the index refers. Sometimes the labels are side headings, printed in the margins of pages, and each heading is supposed to name the topic which the lines beside and below it tell about. Sometimes each label is a line or sentence, printed in boldface or italic type as the first line or sentence in a paragraph or a small group of paragraphs, that is supposed to name the topic which the lines immediately following it tell about. Usually, however, no such labels are provided in the book, or often those which do appear are so undiscriminating or unlimiting that they do not provide the help needed. Consequently, you yourself often must find quickly on a page all the particular lines that supply the information to which the index referred.

How do you go about doing this? To discover the answer to this query, try to find quickly whatever information the following material gives on the question *What did the first towns of the Massachusetts Bay Colony look like?* As you proceed, think just what you are doing to find the particular lines you need.

In 1630 John Winthrop and a group of Puritan followers left England and sailed across the Atlantic Ocean to the town of Salem, which other Puritans had already built in what is now Massachusetts. But the newcomers did not stay long there. Instead they soon sailed south along the coast until they came to a bay into which flowed a river that some years before John Smith had named the Charles. It was beside this river that they built a town which they named Charlestown, one of the first settlements in the Massachusetts Bay Colony chartered by King Charles.

Just across the Charles River was a narrow neck of land which was much higher than the low swampy land of Charlestown and which could be defended easily against enemies. Here William Blackstone had lived alone for some years. Once Blackstone learned to know and like the Puritans in Charlestown, he asked them to build new homes near his. This many of the Puritans did, and the new town they built there was named Boston.

During the first year after the founding of Boston, more than a thousand

Puritans arrived in the Massachusetts Bay Colony from England. By 1640 the population of the Colony had grown to more than 20,000, and many new towns including Cambridge, Dorchester, and Roxbury were built near Boston. Thus the number of inhabitants in the Massachusetts Bay Colony increased rapidly as more and more Puritans arrived from England.

Today, in cities which were once some of the first little towns in the Massachusetts Bay Colony, one can still find parks or areas called commons in which statues and historical markers and monuments stand and musical entertainments and art exhibits are held. In early colonial days, each of these commons was a large vacant field which formed the center of a town and which was often used in proper seasons for the grazing of livestock. Usually the church and a meeting house, often but not always the same building, faced the common. On each side of the common were the settlers' homes.

Some of the Puritans who lived in the Massachusetts Bay Colony made their living by farming, even though the land was not highly productive. Some were fishermen, who caught cod, haddock, and other fish that were plentiful in the waters along the coast. Others were lumbermen, woodworkers, and shipbuilders. A few became unusually skillful at weaving, furniture making, and metal working. Some of those who traded with business firms in foreign countries made small fortunes.

In the foregoing passage, the only information about the appearance of the first towns in the Massachusetts Bay Colony is contained in the last three sentences in the fourth paragraph. How did you find that out? Starting with the first sentence in the first paragraph, did you carefully read every sentence in all the material and, as you came to the end of each sentence, decide then and there whether it gave information you needed? If so, didn't you find this procedure prolonged and wasteful of time and effort? Did you first assume that the first sentence in each paragraph was a topic sentence in that it announced what the paragraph told about, then read just that first sentence, decide at once whether it introduced information you needed, and if so, read the rest of the paragraph — and if not, skip the remaining lines of the paragraph? If you proceeded in this way, you may have missed the lines you needed. Instead of using either of these procedures, you may have first chosen a key word or words such as *towns, Massachusetts Bay Colony,* or *looked like,* glanced here and there among the lines to find the word or words, and, each time you found one, read the lines close to it. If this is what you did, you may have found yourself reading lines which contained none of the information you needed. The best but not infallible procedure which the author knows for finding quickly on a page all the particular lines giving the information referred to by the index of a book is the following: (1) Read the first two or three sentences in the first paragraph on the page and decide whether one or more of them give needed information. If they do, read the rest of the same paragraph to get whatever additional and appropriate information is offered. If none of the first sentences give needed information, skip the rest of the paragraph. (2) Follow the same plan in working with each of the remaining paragraphs on the page.

How do uninstructed pupils find on a page the information which the index of a book has told them is somewhere there? Some of them, instead of trying to find quickly the particular lines needed, begin at the top of the page, read every line on the page, and decide as they do so whether it is a crucial one. Others first employ some ineffective device, usually one which they themselves have picked up for use in so-called skimming, to locate what they think are the crucial lines and then read only those. Both procedures are often wasteful of the pupil's time and effort and lead him into studying lines he does not need to study or missing lines he should study. That is why the author recommends that the pupil be taught to use the procedure explained in the last part of the preceding paragraph. Instruction may begin in the third grade and should be continued and expanded as needed in each subsequent grade.

1. Introducing the Item

The following material, addressed to the pupil, illustrates instruction in finding quickly on a page information which he needs to study and to which the index of a book has referred him:

To read and think over

> Somewhere in the five paragraphs that come next is information that answers the question *In what ways were the first wheels that people made not very good?* Find that information as quickly as you can. The lines in the paragraphs are numbered so that you can talk about them easily later.

> 1. In the early days of our country, the colonists used sledges in moving
> 2. heavy loads over rough ground. A sledge was a big box set on wooden
> 3. runners. Usually it was pulled by oxen because the loads were too
> 4. heavy for horses to drag along rough ground. Today sledges are still
> 5. used in different parts of the world.
> 6. Do you wonder how thousands of years ago someone got the idea of
> 7. making wheels to use instead of runners? Perhaps one day a man was
> 8. trying to move a heavy load along the ground when a small branch of
> 9. a tree got caught under the runners of his sledge. As the man kept
> 10. pulling and pushing, suddenly his load moved forward a little distance

11. quite easily. Then the round branch rolled out behind the sledge, and
12. possibly the man thought that this piece of round wood had helped
13. him for a moment. After this, he probably used such a roller in moving
14. all heavy loads on his sledge.
15.   Soon the man thought of fastening the roller to the bottom of his
16. sledge so that it would keep turning and carry the load without rolling
17. from under the sledge. This he did by cutting two slices of wood
18. from the end of a log, pegging one of them to each end of a sort of
19. axle, and fastening the axle all the way across the bottom of the sledge.
20. Now the man had a cart with two wheels that could keep turning, but
21. because the axle was fastened as it was, he could not make the cart
22. turn a corner. Soon he learned to fasten the axle at only the center of
23. the bottom of the sledge. Then not only did the wheels keep turning
24. as he pulled the sledge along, but he could steer it around a corner.
25.   Each of these first wheels was nothing more than a circle of solid
26. wood with a hole in the middle that fitted over one end of the axle.
27. The wheels were very heavy and clumsy, and they were not nearly as
28. strong as they needed to be to keep from breaking easily. Then, too,
29. large pieces would split off as the wheels jerked sideways or ran against
30. big rocks. Because the rims themselves were wood, they wore out
31. quickly. As time went on, people learned to make a stronger wheel by
32. cutting wedges out of the solid circle and leaving only spokes that ran
33. from the hub at the center to the rim at the outer part of the circle.
34.   It took thousands of years for men to make iron strips and bend
35. them and nail them to the wooden rims of wheels. Then many years
36. later, solid rubber tires were invented. Wheels you ride on today have
37. tires made of rubber filled with air that makes a sort of cushion.

Think now how you found the lines that tell ways in which the first wheels people made were not very good. Did you read every line in each paragraph carefully and then decide whether it gave information on the question? If you did, you spent much more time than you needed to spend in finding the information you needed.

You know that the index of a book tells you the number of a page on which to look for information on a given topic or question. But the index does not tell you just which lines on the page give that information. To find those lines quickly, follow this plan in working with each paragraph as you come to it:

1. Read the first two or three sentences of the paragraph and decide whether one or more of them are giving information you need. If they are not, do not take time to read the rest of the paragraph. Go right on to the next paragraph.

2. If the first two or three sentences give information you need, read the rest of the paragraph to try to get more information on your topic or question.

Talking together

Help your class answer these questions:

1. What are the numbers of the lines that tell ways in which the first wheels people made were not very good?
2. How did you find those lines?
3. When you want to find quickly on a page the lines that give information you need, why is it not a good plan to read carefully all the lines in each paragraph? What is a good plan to follow?

To do by yourself

Somewhere in the four paragraphs that follow is information that answers the question *What were the first school buildings in America like?* Find that information as quickly as you can. The lines in the paragraphs are numbered so that you can talk about them easily later.

1.   The first public schools in America were established by Puritans who
2.   settled in what is now Massachusetts. These schools were not nearly
3.   as good as those we have today. Usually the teacher was a man who
4.   was not well educated, even for those days. If he happened to be also
5.   a harsh person, he punished severely those pupils who did not learn as
6.   easily as he thought they should.
7.   The only subjects taught regularly in the first schools were reading,
8.   writing, and arithmetic. Studying music, art, social studies, science,
9.   and other subjects you have now was thought to be useless. Textbooks
10.   were rare. The pupils used first a sort of wooden paddle, called the
11.   *Hornbook,* on which the alphabet and the numbers from 1 through 9
12.   were printed. Then they used the *New England Primer,* which con-
13.   tained the letters of the alphabet and a picture and a little verse to go
14.   with each letter.
15.   Do you think that your school building is quite a comfortable one in
16.   which to be? Each of the first Puritan school buildings was a one-room
17.   log cabin that often had a dirt floor. The pupils had no desks but sat
18.   on long wooden benches while reading, listening to the teacher talk,
19.   and answering his questions. In winter, the building was often cold,
20.   since the only heat came from wood burning in the one fireplace.
21.   These first schools were supported by money that the people paid
22.   as taxes. Parents of children who attended the schools paid more of
23.   the expenses than did people who had no children of school age.

If you are asked to do so, tell the numbers of the lines that give information on the question. Then explain how you found that information.

It is not necessary that the instruction provided by the foregoing illustrative material be given to the pupil in printed form for him to read to

himself. If it is to be given orally by the teacher, the two passages —
such as those included under "To read by yourself" and "To do by yourself" — which the pupil must read can be taken from an informative book
being used by him at the time. It is understood that if the instruction is
given to the pupil in printed form, the reading matter included must be
made up almost entirely of words he already knows well in print.

2. Providing Practice in Using the Skill

Whether the pupil gets in school the practice he needs in finding
quickly on a page the particular lines that supply information on a given
topic or problem depends much upon the nature of the reading assignments and the class discussions in social studies, science, and other
content subjects. The assignments should consist of questions or problems
on which the pupil is to get information from one or more books; they
should not be merely the naming of pages or sections to be read without
the guidance which such questions or problems provide. Class discussions should be such that the pupil is encouraged and expected persistently to contribute to the consideration of a given topic or question
only information which is pertinent to it.

Additional practice may be supplied through the use of special exercises that appear in some workbooks accompanying basal readers or that
the teacher herself constructs. Each exercise should ask the pupil to find
the particular lines or sentences in a passage which give information on a
certain topic or question. Often, in such an exercise, the crucial lines or
sentences should not all appear in the same paragraph.

Selecting Ideas for a Given Purpose

Sometimes you read an informative passage for a specific purpose: (1)
to decide what the main idea of the passage is, (2) to get all the details
which the passage gives on some topic it includes, (3) to decide which
points included in the passage are most appropriate for you to use in a
given situation, (4) to draw a conclusion based on but not supplied by
one or more statements included in the passage, or (5) to decide which
of the included ideas you need to retain for making a report to others, for
taking part in a discussion, or perhaps for taking a test. Some writers
have suggested additional purposes: to get the sequence of events, to
anticipate outcome, to get directions for performing some activity. But
the first two of these additional purposes pertain chiefly to the reading
of narrative rather than informative material and, since both sequence
of events and outcome are clearly stated in such material — except in a

few writings like "The Lady and the Tiger" — are purposes for which you rarely need to read. The third additional purpose is merely an example of getting details. Consequently this section considers only the five purposes listed at the beginning of this paragraph.

What does the expression *the main idea of a passage* mean to you? Apparently to some persons it is merely another name for the subject that the passage talks about. To others it means the principal point which the writer makes about that subject. Thus to some people the main idea of a given group of paragraphs is *How the Indians cared for their sick;* to others it is *The Indians used queer ways of caring for their sick.* Actually you need to read a passage to determine what its subject is only if that passage — perhaps a part of a chapter or article — has no title or heading, or when the supplied title or heading is so vague or misleading that it does not tell you what the subject is. Sometimes in such a situation you can decide what the subject is just by taking in and generalizing quickly about groups of words here and there as you scan the lines rather hastily. At other times you may need to read each paragraph carefully[9] and then choose for the subject of the passage the one thing all the paragraphs talk about.[10] To decide on the principal point that the writer makes about the subject of his passage, you may need to note carefully just what each paragraph says about the subject and sense the chief characteristic which it assigns to the subject. Doing this may or may not be easy, and it may consume either little or much time and mental effort.

Except in using some sets of printed directions, rarely do you need to read a passage to get all the details given therein on the subject of that passage. Much more common is your need to read such a passage to get all the details it offers on one or another of the topics it includes. To read for this purpose, you should first try to locate quickly the particular paragraph or lines which give the needed details, as described on pages 327–328 in this chapter, and then read those lines as carefully as you must to understand the details and fix them in mind.

Assume that you want to glean from a certain passage the points which will be most appropriate for you to use in some particular situation you must meet, such as giving a talk. Among the points that are pertinent to your topic may be, for example, (1) those which you think will be most entertaining to the audience, (2) those which you believe give information the audience wants, (3) those which you think the audience does not already know, and (4) those which you believe are most important for

9 See pp. 341–344.
10 See p. 352.

anyone to know. You yourself must decide just which of these or other criteria you will use in selecting the points which are most appropriate to the situation. To read a passage for this purpose, you should first try to locate quickly the lines giving ideas pertinent to your topic, read the lines carefully enough to understand the ideas they present, judge these ideas according to your chosen criterion and, if the time allotted to your talking is short, weigh them one against the other to determine their relative value for inclusion in your talk.

Often when you read a passage, you draw a conclusion or think a generalization which is not stated in the passage but is based on points you find there. Thus you may note the following points about the status of reading in the American colonies: (1) reading was a favorite amusement, (2) there were few books and no public libraries, (3) people who owned books read and reread them and allowed their friends to borrow them, (4) there were no daily newspapers, but weekly newspapers were common, (5) almanacs were published annually and were found in almost every home, and (6) one chief reason for the establishment of the first public schools was to make provision for children to learn to read. Then you may proceed to draw one or more of the following or other conclusions: (1) most of the colonists were able to read, (2) reading was encouraged by the colonists, (3) the colonists did not do much reading, and (4) reading matter was much more scarce in colonial days than it is now. To read a passage in order to draw a conclusion based on its statements, one must find and make correct meaning for all the pertinent points on both sides of the fence, so to speak, and then weigh the pros and cons carefully. Rarely is this reasoning simple, and often its difficulty is evidenced by the somewhat weird conclusions people draw now and then from their reading of informative material.

When you read a passage as part of your preparation for giving a talk, for taking part in a discussion, for taking a test such as that required in obtaining a driver's license, or for performing some other activity, you must decide which of the included ideas you need to retain. Usually such ideas are among but identical with only some of those which, as explained on page 332, are appropriate to the situation to be met, and you yourself must select the appropriate points that are important enough so that you should remember them. In your case, as a rule, selecting is relatively easy, if for no other reason than that you are the person who chooses the ideas you need to remember. As will be noted in Chapter 11, it is not so simple for the pupil. Unfortunately, the ideas he needs to remember for engaging in class recitations and for passing tests usually are selected by someone else and are not made known to him beforehand.

Although the pupil meets situations outside of school in which he has to select ideas from informative reading matter for one or another of the five purposes just discussed, the most frequent and crucial demands placed upon him for doing this occur in connection with school work. The various questions which make up a reading assignment in social studies, science, or some other content subject constitute one such demand, often without the pupil's awareness of its presence. The pupil may be asked to read a given passage to decide what its main idea is — *main idea* referring to the principal point that the writer makes about the subject of the passage. Or he may be asked to get all the details which this or that passage offers on a topic it includes. Or he may be asked to draw a conclusion based on statements in a passage. A second demand occurs when the pupil, in preparing a report to be given in a certain situation, for example, needs to decide which ideas in a passage are most appropriate to that situation. A third demand appears whenever the pupil, in studying for a test, say, to be prepared by the teacher, must decide — or more often than not make his best guess at — just which ideas, if any, in this or that passage he needs to retain for passing the test. Other demands arise with the use of workbook exercises giving the pupil practice in selecting ideas for the different purposes and the use of standardized reading tests measuring his skill in reading for those purposes.

The instruction which most schools provide as a means of helping the pupil learn to select ideas for any of the five purposes is much too feeble. Rarely does it include making the meaning of the purpose clear to the pupil and acquainting him with what he should do in order to select from a passage the ideas which fit that purpose. Usually the instruction is limited to (1) asking, in group discussions of selections that have already been read in basal readers or other books, questions which require the pupil to recall ideas that fit the purpose and (2) using workbook exercises which give practice only in selecting from supplied passages ideas pertinent to that purpose. To consider these two activities as being synonymous with teaching the pupil to read for a given purpose is questionable to say the least.

Instruction which seeks to equip the pupil to select ideas for a given purpose from an informative passage will be introduced by explaining the meaning of the purpose, characterizing the way the reading should be done, illustrating correct use of the skill, and providing a small amount of initial practice in using the skill. In addition, it will supply further practice from time to time during the school year. Such instruction can begin in the third grade with one of the specific purposes which is judged to be most suitable and should be expanded as needed in each subsequent grade.

1. Introducing the Item

Space does not permit providing here all the material needed in introducing the selection of ideas for all five purposes. Therefore, the following material, addressed to the pupil, illustrates only the introducing of the selection of ideas which are most appropriate for the pupil to use in a given situation:

To read and think over

For some time the boys and girls in Miss Blake's class had been studying how the American Indians lived years ago. One of the questions which they had read about and talked over was *What kinds of houses did the Indians build?* The paragraphs that follow tell all the answers that the boys and girls said they had found for the question:

The Pueblo Indians used bricks in building their houses. The bricks were made of adobe, which is a mixture of clay, ashes, and straw. The walls of each house were built thick enough so that the inside would stay cool. Some adobe houses had many rooms.

Indians who lived on the plains built different kinds of houses. Some were made of long heavy grass, and others were just large holes in the earth with soil piled up to make the sides and top above the ground. The most common house on the plains was the tepee, which was made of buffalo skins and poles and shaped like an ice cream cone turned upside down.

In the eastern part of the country, the Indians built houses called Long Houses. Such a house was large enough to hold many families, and each family had one room. The house was made of large pieces of bark fastened to a frame built with poles.

The Seminole Indians built houses by putting grass and leaves over a frame that was made of tree branches and shaped something like a dome. The summer houses of the Sac and Fox Indians were made of bark. Their winter homes were made of large pieces of woven grass placed on frames that were shaped much like those used by the Seminoles.

The boys and girls decided that the class could spend no more time in getting other answers for the question. Yet they wanted more answers than they had found. That is why they asked Joe to get information which they did not already know about Indian houses and tell it to them later.

The paragraphs that follow are those which Joe found on a page in a book. The sentences are numbered so that you can think about them easily. Which sentences give ideas that Joe should tell to the class? Why do you think so?

1. All Indians had straight black hair and small brown eyes, and most of them painted their faces. 2. But the different tribes did not look exactly alike. 3. The people of some tribes were short, and those of other tribes were tall. 4. Some tribes were light tan in color, and some had skin the color of dark copper. 5. Each tribe wore clothing that was somewhat different from that used by other tribes.

6. The house that the Indians who lived in the plains built most often was the tepee. 7. It was made of buffalo skins and poles. 8. Sometimes the poles were more than twenty feet long, and after the bark was taken off, three of them were tied together a few feet from the top and spread out at the bottom on the ground. 9. Then the other poles were fastened to the main three as they stood upright. 10. To make the cover, the buffalo skins were fastened together and shaped to fit over the poles. 11. Loops of skin were used to fasten the cover to the poles. 12. Each tepee had a hole at the top to let smoke out and an opening for a door at the bottom.

13. The Iroquois Indians built houses that were called Long Houses, and each of them was made of large sheets of bark fastened to a pole frame. 14. Sometimes one of these houses would be 200 feet long and about twelve feet wide. 15. There was a hall down the middle of the house with fireplaces for cooking placed here and there and a door at each end covered with skins. 16. Along the sides of the hall were many rooms that had walls of skins sewed together.

17. The Indians made three main kinds of boats. 18. Some were canoes made of birch bark and a framework of wood. 19. Others were made of hides and frameworks shaped like canoes and large tubs. 20. Still others were made by digging out long logs until they had the shape of a canoe.

When Joe read the page, his purpose was to choose from the paragraphs all the information given there that the class did not already have about the kinds of houses the Indians built. Since the first five sentences and the last four sentences give no information about those houses, he did not choose any of the ideas in those sentences. Do you know why Joe did not choose any of the information given in sentences 6, 7, and 13?

Sometimes you will need to read a page to choose from the paragraphs given there the ideas which will fit best in a talk or a report you are to give. Those ideas may be only the points which you think will entertain your listeners most, only the points which you think are most important to know about the subject of your talk, or only the points which your listeners do not already know about your subject. Whenever you need to read a page for this purpose, do these things:

1. First, find quickly on the page the lines which give information on the subject of your talk.

2. Next, read those lines carefully to find out what they say about your subject.

3. Then, choose only those ideas which fit well with the reason for giving your talk.

Talking together

Help your class answer these questions:

1. What purpose did Joe have for reading the page that gave information on the kinds of houses the Indians built?
2. Why did Joe not choose ideas given in sentences 6, 7, and 13? Why did he choose the ideas given in the other sentences in the second and third paragraphs?
3. What can you do to choose from a given page the ideas which fit best in a talk or a report you are to give?

To do by yourself

Suppose that you were asked to give a talk as part of a program for parents and that the subject of your talk was to be "How the Indians Made Fire." What sentences in the following paragraphs give ideas that you would use in your talk because you think they would interest your listeners most? The sentences are numbered so that you can talk about them easily later.

1. The Indians used almost as many ways of cooking food as we do today. 2. Fish, meats, vegetables, and nuts were roasted. 3. Bread made of meal obtained by grinding seeds, corn, and berries was baked. 4. Meats and fish were broiled and smoked, and meats and vegetables were boiled.

5. Since the Indians had no matches, they used other means to make fire. 6. Sometimes they rubbed the flat sides of two sticks against each other until they became so hot that they caught on fire. 7. Sometimes they made a small pile of dry leaves and grass and then struck two rocks together to make sparks fly into the grass and leaves. 8. Later they learned from white men to make sparks by using instead a very hard rock called flint and a piece of steel.

9. Often the Indians used a wooden drill to make fire. 10. The drill was a flat block of soft wood with small holes in it and a round stick of hard wood pointed at one end. 11. To make a fire, dry leaves or grass was placed around one of the holes, the pointed end of the stick was placed in the hole, and then the stick was turned rapidly until the edges of the hole became so hot that the leaves or grass caught fire. 12. Sometimes the Indian turned the stick by rubbing the palms of his hands back and forth against it. 13. Sometimes he wound a skin strap around the stick and then held the top of the stick against his chest as he pulled the ends of the strap back and forth. 14. The best way the Indian had for turning the stick rapidly was to wind the loose string of a bow around the stick twice, hold the top of the stick lightly with one hand, and pull the bow back and forth.

15. Only some Indians had ovens in which to do their baking, and these were made of clay. 16. Usually bread was baked on flat stones placed over a fire. 17. Roasting was done in hot ashes, and meat was broiled over an open fire.

On a sheet of paper, write the numbers of the sentences you chose. Do not expect the numbers you write to be exactly the same as those that others write.

If you are asked to do so, read aloud the numbers that you wrote. If someone reads numbers that you did not write, find out why he chose the sentences which have those numbers.

2. Providing Practice in Using the Skill

The teaching of various school subjects can and no doubt should provide opportunities for the pupil to get needed practice in selecting ideas for the five specific purposes which this section has considered. As will be noted in Chapter 11, some of the various questions which constitute reading assignments made during the school year in social studies, science, and other content subjects can by their very nature direct the pupil to decide what the main idea of a passage is, to get all the details which a passage gives on a topic it includes, and to draw a conclusion based on but not provided by one or more of the statements included in a passage. In the teaching of English, one or more of the questions which the pupil is encouraged to write out as a guide in gathering information for a report can require him to select ideas which are most appropriate for his use. Questions provided by the teacher as a guide for the pupil's reviewing or preparing for a test can enable him to get practice in deciding which ideas in a passage need to be retained. Additional practice in selecting ideas for this or that purpose can be given through the use of appropriate special exercises included in workbooks which accompany some basal readers.

Several investigations have shown clearly that giving the pupil practice in listening to decide what the main idea of a passage is, to get all the details in a passage on a topic it includes, and to draw a conclusion based on statements made in a passage improves his ability to read for these same purposes. Thus, since the reasoning which anyone must do in listening for these purposes is the same as that which he must do in reading for the same purposes, some of the needed practice can be given orally. From time to time the teacher can profitably ask the pupil to decide, as a short passage is read to him, what its main idea is, to get all the details offered on a topic included in the passage, or to draw a conclusion based on statements therein. Indeed, there is reason to believe that using very short passages to give first-grade and second-grade pupils practice in listening for these purposes lays a good foundation for their learning to read for the same purposes at later grade levels.

Deciding What the Topic of a Paragraph Is

You know that an informative selection — perhaps an article or a chapter or part of a chapter in a book — tells about a subject and that the sentences which make up the selection are arranged to make paragraphs. You know, too, that the writer's ideas play different parts in the selection. Some, the main points that the writer makes about the subject, can be called the main topics in the selection. Others support, explain, or illustrate the main topics and consequently can be called the subtopics in the selection. Still others are offered as examples or explanations that lend meaning to the subtopics; they can be called details. If the selection is well organized, each paragraph talks about only one topic, and that topic may serve in the entire selection as a main topic, a subtopic, or a detail.

Do you ever need to study an informative selection so well that you think out the relationship which the writer intends the included ideas to have with one another and get those ideas fixed in mind for your later use in taking part in a discussion, in giving a talk, in taking a test, in making something, or in carrying on some other activity? Of course you do! But just what constitutes your studying? To get some idea of what you do, think of answers to the questions which follow:

1. Do you read the entire selection only once, without doing anything else and without having in mind beforehand questions to be answered by the selection, much as you read a short story or some other narrative passage just for fun? Several investigations have shown that although this undirected single reading is commonly used, it is a very ineffective procedure for the study of informative material. When you use it, you will do much better than average if, immediately after reading a selection, you understand and can recall one-third of the ideas which are presented by that selection and which you did not know beforehand. Three weeks later, you will do well if you can recall one-tenth of those ideas.

2. Do you merely reread the selection one, two, or even three times, without doing anything else and without having in mind questions to be answered by the selection? Investigations have shown that such rereadings add little more than 6 per cent to the results obtained by the undirected single reading mentioned in the preceding paragraph.

3. Do you first use the title of the selection, whatever subheadings or side headings are provided, or perhaps the topics of paragraphs to help you think of questions which you expect the material to answer and then read to get answers to them? Investigations have shown that the

comprehension and retention which the school pupil obtains from a single undirected reading or rereading can be increased by his use of questions which, as formulated beforehand by the teacher or by both him and the teacher, guide his attention during the reading. Yet no one knows what value, if any, is attached to only your formulating and using such questions as guides for study of an informative selection.

4. As you read the selection, do you underline or mark in some other way portions which you think are important to clinch and, when the reading is finished, reread the marked portions as many times as you think necessary? The value of this marking and self-directed rereading has yet to be determined. If and when you use it, do your marks point up topics of paragraphs?

5. As you read the selection, do you write out questions pertaining to portions which you think are important to clinch and, when the reading is finished, try to recall the ideas that answer those questions? If you cannot do this recalling, do you reread the crucial portions? The value of this procedure is not yet known. If and when you use it, are any of the answers to your questions the topics of paragraphs?

6. As you read or after you have read the selection, do you write out a summary which answers questions you had in mind at the time of your reading or which states the main points that the selection gives about its subject? Investigations have shown that this procedure is superior to either the undirected single reading or mere rereadings. If and when you use it, do any of the statements in your summary give topics of paragraphs?

7. As you read or after you have read the selection, do you make notes — not in outline form — on the ideas it contains? If you have no questions in mind to be answered as you read, on what points do you make notes? Strange as it may seem, the value of making such notes has not been determined. Yet, judging by the extent to which people cling to this procedure, one would expect it to be of considerable value to the person who has learned what points to make notes on and how to make good notes. If and when you make such notes, do any of them state the topics of paragraphs?

8. As you read or after you have read the selection, do you make an outline of the ideas it contains? Investigations show that, for the person who knows how to determine what the main topics, the subtopics, and the details in a selection are and who can place those points in an arrangement which shows their correct relationship, this procedure is much superior to other procedures mentioned here. If and when you make an outline of the ideas presented by a selection, do you ever need to decide what the topic of a paragraph is? Why?

Statements and questions in the preceding material emphasize the proposition that deciding what the topics of paragraphs are can be important in studying an informative selection. Those topics may be points which you need to mark or think of questions about in order to direct your rereading or which you should include in your writing of a summary of the selection. Most important, paragraph topics are often good points on which to make enumerated notes in a form that is not an outline. Their use as main topics, subtopics, or details, as the case may be, is essential to making an outline of the ideas the selection contains.

Consider now what is meant by the term *the topic of a paragraph*. As you read the following lines, think what each sentence is talking about:

The first airplane flight from Europe to America was made in 1928 by the monoplane Bremen. The fliers were two Germans named Koehl and von Huenfeld and an Irishman named Fitzmaurice. After leaving the coast of Ireland, they encountered no trouble until the airplane ran into a heavy fog near the end of the flight. But when the fliers saw a lighthouse which told them that they had reached their destination, they brought the airplane down on the small island near New Foundland where that beacon stood. The entire flight was made in thirty-four hours.

Can you decide what one thing every sentence in the foregoing paragraph talks about? Certainly. The first sentence tells you when and by what *the first airplane flight from Europe to America* was made. The second sentence tells you who the fliers were on *the first airplane flight from Europe to America*. The third sentence tells you that there was no trouble on *the first airplane flight from Europe to America* until the airplane ran into heavy fog. The fourth sentence tells you when and where *the first airplane flight from Europe to America* reached its destination. The fifth sentence tells you the amount of time taken to make *the first airplane flight from Europe to America*. That topic — *the first airplane flight from Europe to America* — is the topic of the paragraph.

Any informative paragraph that is well organized talks about only one thing, and it is called the topic of the paragraph. Every sentence in the paragraph tells or asks something about that one and same topic.

As mentioned in Chapter 8, an informative paragraph usually — but not always — contains a sentence which announces or even names the topic of the paragraph as it says something about that topic. Sometimes the sentence — often called the topic sentence — is the first one in the paragraph, as in the paragraph you just read about the first airplane flight from Europe to America, the paragraph on page 292 about the uses of the kitchen fireplace in the early colonial home, and the paragraph on page 295 about the foods which pioneer women made with corn. Sometimes the topic sentence is the last sentence in or one near the middle of the paragraph. It is the last sentence in the paragraph on page 297 telling why less than half the forests we once had remain and in the paragraph on page 298 telling why people who lived in the East settled in the West. The topic sentence is the seventh of the eleven sentences in the paragraph on page 293 that talks about the ways people in the colonies amused themselves.

It is relatively simple to decide what the topic of a paragraph is when the first sentence is a topic sentence. At the very beginning of your reading of the paragraph, this sentence introduces the topic and, even though you can't be sure yet that such is the case, you note easily as you read on that each of the remaining sentences says something about the same thing. Thus by the time you have read the paragraph only once, the topic has fallen into your lap, so to speak. In this case, that first sentence is somewhat like a caller who, when you answer his knock at the door, tells you indirectly by the very first thing he says, after introducing himself, "This is what I am going to talk to you about."

It is not so easy to decide what the topic of a paragraph is when the topic sentence is the last sentence. Consider, for example, the paragraph which is made up of six numbered sentences printed in small type on page 297. The first sentence tells you that the settlers needed clear land, and here — if in some way you have acquired the quaint notion that the first sentence in a paragraph always tells what the topic of the paragraph is — you might be entitled to think, "The topic of this paragraph is *the needs of the settlers,* or perhaps *why the settlers needed cleared land,* or even *how the settlers cleared land.*" As the second sentence tells you that the settlers needed material for building houses and furniture, you may think, "Oh sure, the topic is *the needs of the settlers.*" Then the third sentence says that the settlers kept cutting away the forests, and perhaps you think, "It's still all right. This is simply one thing the settlers did to clear land and get material they needed." But the fourth sentence says that great fires destroyed forests, and since this has nothing to do with the needs of the settlers, you have to think, "I don't know yet what the topic is." You are still left uncertain by the fifth sentence as it tells you that the use of inventions kept demanding more wood. Then almost but not quite out of a clear sky, the last sentence tells you what the topic is. In this case, that last sentence — the topic sentence — is somewhat like a caller who, when you answer his knock at the door, does not let you know immediately what he is going to talk about but instead tells you several different things and then at the end says something which tells you indirectly, "This is what I have talked to you about." Possibly you can decide what the topic is by reading such a paragraph only once, but probably you will need to read it two or three times before you can make that decision.

Nor is it easy to decide what the topic of a paragraph is when the topic sentence is near the middle. Consider, for example, the paragraph printed in small type on page 293. The first three sentences could easily make you think that the topic is *colonial children's games and sports.* The next three sentences could make you broaden that idea so that a possible topic becomes *how colonial boys, girls, and young people entertained themselves.* Then the next sentence tells you that colonial people of all ages had various ways of amusing themselves, and the two sentences which follow immediately give examples of what adults did to this end. That seventh sentence — the topic sentence — is somewhat like a caller who, when you answer his knock at the door, first tells you several different things about something, then says indirectly, "What I am talking to you about is this, which you may not have realized, and I have a few more things to say about it," and finally adds other points about the topic. Perhaps now and then you can decide what the topic is by reading such a paragraph only once, but often you may need to read it two or three times in order to make that decision.

It can be difficult to decide what the topic of a paragraph is when there is no topic sentence. Consider, for example, a selection which carries the title or subject "Some Interesting Characteristics of Cats" and includes the following paragraph among others:

> Cats are from fourteen to sixteen inches long. They have soft fur, and they can see well in very dim light. They walk so quietly that you cannot hear them. They have five toes on each front foot and four on each hind foot. Each toe has a sharp claw that can be drawn back into a sheath. A full-grown cat has thirty teeth.

You can see that every sentence in the foregoing paragraph says something about cats, but the topic *cats* is quite broad, and when you recall what the title or subject of the entire selection is, you know that *cats* cannot possibly be the topic of the paragraph. But what is that topic? To answer this question, you need to figure out some appropriate generalization that is not announced in the paragraph itself. Can you think of some division of the title or subject of the selection which could be a generalization of what the sentences in the paragraph say? Could that generalization be "physical characteristics of cats"? Why or why not?

When you need to decide what the topic of an informative paragraph is and cannot do that just by reading the paragraph only once, how do you reach your decision? Probably there is no one best way of doing this. But do not depend much upon finding the topic sentence and choosing as the topic of the paragraph the thing which that sentence talks about. Instead, take each sentence one at a time and think, not what it says, but what it talks about; if you wish, write that point down. Then figure out what one thing all the sentences talk about. Usually that will be the topic of the paragraph.

Sometimes in your study of an informative selection you will encounter a paragraph that, instead of keeping to one topic, talks about two or more topics.[11] What are the different topics in the following paragraph that is part of a selection entitled "The First Railroad Cars in the United States"?

Soon after the first railroad tracks were laid in the United States, someone built a treadmill on a small flat car and set a horse to walking on it. The treadmill was like an endless chain connected to the wheels of the car so that as the horse walked, the wheels went around and moved the car forward on the track. The passengers sat on benches in another open car that was behind the car which carried the treadmill, the horse, and the driver. On the trial trip, a cow that was grazing near the track charged the cars, upset them, and sent the frightened passengers rolling down an embankment. That was why the inventor gave up the idea of using treadmill cars. Another early railroad car was the sailing car. This was a bowl-shaped basket in which the passengers sat and which had a mast and sails like those of a small boat. The wind moved the car on its wheels along the track.

You can see that the foregoing paragraph talks about two topics: (1) the treadmill car and (2) the sailing car. It is clear, too, that neither one should be called *the* topic *of* the paragraph. Yet one of them — the one to which most of the ideas in the paragraph pertain — can be called the *main* topic *in* the paragraph. What is it?

When you need to make a note on or place in an outline a point for a paragraph that talks about two or more topics, on what will you make that note or point? Sometimes your choice will depend much upon the subject for which you are making notes or an outline. Usually, however, the note or point should be on the main topic in the paragraph.

The instruction to be given so that the pupil learns how to decide what

[11] Actually such a composition is a paragraph in form only. In the interests of enhancing communication it should have been written as two paragraphs, each talking about only one topic.

the topic of an informative paragraph is consists of much more than merely telling him that the topic of a paragraph is what the paragraph talks about and then having him work out special exercises in which he is expected to decide what the topics of paragraphs are. Surely the introducing of the item should at least acquaint the pupil with what is meant by the topic of a paragraph and with a procedure to follow in making the needed generalization, illustrate the correct use of the procedure, and give him a bit of initial practice in using the skill. Furthermore, opportunities for additional practice in using the skill should be provided during the school year. Such instruction can begin in the fourth if not the third grade with simple and well-organized paragraphs and certainly should be expanded in each subsequent grade.

1. Introducing the Item

The following material, addressed to the pupil, illustrates teaching which can introduce to him the skill of deciding what the topic of a paragraph is:

To read and think over

Most of the pages which you study are printed in groups of sentences that are called paragraphs. It is easy to tell one paragraph from another because the first line of each paragraph begins a little further to the right than the other lines do. But often the most important thing for you to figure out about a paragraph is the one thing which all its sentences are talking about.

Try now to think what each sentence in the following paragraph is talking about. The sentences are numbered so that you can think about them easily later.

1. An elephant's foot is almost round. 2. Elephants found in India have five nails on each front foot and four on each hind foot. 3. Those found in Africa have four nails on each front foot and five on each hind foot. 4. Under the bones of each foot is a pad that acts as a cushion. 5. An elephant's great weight of several tons makes his feet swell as he stands, but when he holds a foot up or lies down, the swelling goes down.

Sentence 1 tells the shape of *an elephant's foot.* Sentences 2 and 3 tell the number of nails on *an elephant's foot.* Sentence 4 tells that there is a pad on *an elephant's foot.* Sentence 5 tells what makes *an elephant's foot* swell and when that swelling goes down. You can see that every sentence in the paragraph says something about *an elephant's foot.*

Any good paragraph that you need to study talks about only one thing. We call that one thing *the topic of the paragraph.* Every sentence in the paragraph tells or asks something about that topic. The topic of the paragraph you just read is *an elephant's foot.*

Sometimes right after you have read a paragraph only once, you will know quickly what its topic is. When that does not happen and you need to decide what the topic is, do these things:

1. Read the first sentence again and think what it is talking about. Write down a word or group of words that names what the sentence is talking about.
2. Do the same things for each of the other sentences in the paragraph.
3. Then look at the groups of words you have written and decide what one thing they all name. Usually that one thing will be the topic of the paragraph.

Can you decide what the topic of the following paragraph is?

To capture wild elephants, men often use tame elephants, horns, and a large pen made of heavy logs. After the pen is built, a tame elephant is placed inside to act as a lure to the wild beasts. Then men who are called beaters and who are riding tame elephants surround a wild herd. There the beaters set up a great racket by blowing horns and yelling. The frightened herd begins to move and is chased into the pen. When the wild elephants have quieted down, men enter the pen and tie stout ropes around each animal so that it is helpless.

Which of the following groups of words is the topic of the paragraph?

1. The work that elephants do   3. How wild elephants are captured
2. How elephants are tamed   4. The uses of tame elephants

Whenever you study one or more pages, do you ever need to make notes on what you read? If so, what points do you make notes on? Keep in mind that often paragraph topics are good points to make notes on.

Talking together

Help your class answer these questions:

1. What is meant by the topic of a paragraph? Why is *an elephant's foot* the topic of the paragraph that has five numbered sentences?
2. When you do not know what the topic of a paragraph is just by reading that paragraph once, what can you do to decide what the topic is?
3. You have read a paragraph in which one sentence says that beaters make a racket by blowing horns and yelling. Which of the four numbered groups of words listed after that paragraph is the topic? Why is each of the other three groups of words not the topic?
4. In what way can paragraph topics be useful to you in making notes as you study?

To do by yourself

What is the topic of the paragraph that follows?

Traveling on our first steam trains was not comfortable. Because the seats in the passenger cars had no springs or cushions, people were tossed roughly up and down. When the brakes were put on, the train lurched and swayed and the passengers were jolted this way and that. Each time the train stopped, there was much clanking and bumping as each car slid against the one just ahead of it. Instead of glass, leather curtains were used on the windows and doors to keep out the rain, snow, and wind. One or two coal stoves were used in each car, but people who sat near them became too hot and those who sat farther away almost froze. After dark, the only light was that given by oil lamps.

Think now of a good way to state the topic of the paragraph. Then, if you are asked to do so, tell what you think the topic is. If the topic you name is not the right one, find out why it is not right.

Particular attention is called to the fact that the foregoing material includes no instruction pertaining to the type of paragraph which talks about two or more topics. Such introductory instruction can and should be supplied subsequently, perhaps at the fifth-grade level if not sooner. It should include (a) using an appropriate paragraph to show the pupil that sometimes he will encounter a paragraph which talks about two or more topics, (b) explaining that no one of the topics in such a paragraph can be called *the* topic *of* the paragraph, but that the particular topic on which the paragraph gives the most ideas can be called the *main* topic *in* the paragraph, (c) explaining that, when the pupil needs to make a note for such a paragraph, usually this note should be on the main topic, and (d) giving him a little practice in deciding what the main topic is in a paragraph that talks about two or more topics. To be emphasized also at this time is the proposition that if all or part of the introductory instruction on paragraph topics is to be presented in printed form for the pupil to read to himself, all the reading matter used should be composed of words which are within his present reading vocabulary.

2. Providing Practice in Using the Skill

To help the pupil get the practice he needs in deciding what the topics of paragraphs are, one should remind him now and then that as he studies his reading assignments in social studies and other content subjects he may need to make notes from which he can talk later in class discussions, and that often good points on which to make notes are the topics of paragraphs. It is helpful also if some of the questions which make up such assignments require him to decide what the topics of paragraphs are. In addition, special exercises, such as some of those which are included in workbooks that accompany basal readers or which the teacher can construct, may be used. Each exercise, presenting one or more paragraphs, may ask the pupil to do one or another of the following things for each paragraph:

1. To choose from several topics listed below the paragraph the one which is the topic of the paragraph.
2. To choose from several questions listed below the paragraph the one for which the answer is the whole rather than just part of the paragraph.
3. To write out a question which is answered by the whole paragraph rather than by just part of it.
4. To figure out and state in written form the topic of the paragraph.
5. To figure out and state in written form the topic of each paragraph in a selection that has a title and that consists of two or more paragraphs.

Outlining an Informative Selection

In studying an informative selection, do you ever make and use a written outline of ideas contained in it? Making such an outline — assuming that it turns out to be a faithful representative of the substance of the selection — can help you figure out the relationship which the writer intends the ideas to have with one another, and often it will do much to fix those ideas in your mind. Once the outline is made, you can use it immediately or later to review quickly the content of the selection, and subsequently it can be a reminder to which you refer when giving a talk or taking part in a discussion on the subject that the selection tells about.

As stated earlier in this chapter, any informative selection tells about a subject. In doing so, it may give (1) ideas which are the main points made therein about the subject and which can be called *main topics*, (2) ideas which support, illustrate, explain, exemplify, or limit main topics and which can be called *subtopics*, and sometimes but not always (3) ideas which in one way or another amplify subtopics and which can be called *details*. A written outline of ideas included in a given selection is a presentation of that selection's main topics, subtopics, and details in a form which shows their interrelationships. Usually in the outline itself words or groups of words which stand for those different ideas are given correspondingly the same names. The making of the outline requires one to (1) choose for its main topics, subtopics, and details the particular ideas which play those same parts in the selection itself and (2) write in correct form words or groups of words which stand for the chosen ideas. An explanatory illustration of correct form, referring to a hypothetical brief selection that contains only two main topics, appears below. Notice which points are indented and under what they are indented as well as where Roman numerals, capital letters, Arabic numerals, and periods are used. Parentheses used here would not appear in an actual outline.

(Subject of the Selection)

I. (Statement of the first main topic)
    A. (Statement of the first subtopic pertaining to the first main topic)
        1. (Statement of the first detail pertaining to the first subtopic)
        2. (Statement of the second detail pertaining to the first subtopic)
    B. (Statement of the second subtopic pertaining to the first main topic)
        1. (Statement of the first detail pertaining to the second subtopic)
        2. (Statement of the second detail pertaining to the second subtopic)
        3. (Statement of the third detail pertaining to the second subtopic)

II. (Statement of the second main topic)
    A. (Statement of the first subtopic pertaining to the second main topic)
        1. (Statement of the first detail pertaining to the first subtopic)
        2. (Statement of the second detail pertaining to the first subtopic)
    B. (Statement of the second subtopic pertaining to the second main topic)
        1. (Statement of the first detail pertaining to the second subtopic)
        2. (Statement of the second detail pertaining to the second subtopic)
    C. (Statement of the third subtopic pertaining to the second main topic)
        1. (Statement of the first detail pertaining to the third subtopic)
        2. (Statement of the second detail pertaining to the third subtopic)
        3. (Statement of the third detail pertaining to the third subtopic)

Just how do you go about making an outline of ideas included in a selection? If you don't know, take time now to outline the brief and simple selection that follows, noting your procedure as you do so.

Enemies of Trees

Man himself is one of the chief enemies of trees. He cuts them down to get lumber for constructing buildings and all sorts of articles that contain wood. Sometimes this cutting is done to clear land on which to grow crops. By failing to put out campfires and by being careless with lighted matches and cigarettes, people start fires which destroy forests.

Insects of many kinds do much damage to trees. In particular, beetles cut pathways under the bark which break down the tree's circulatory system. Sometimes these same beetles carry on their feet spores of a mushroom-like plant which get under the bark of the tree and grow there to make a choking network of threads. Tent caterpillars eat the leaves of trees and infect their bark.

Diseases destroy many trees. Among the most common of these are Dutch Elm disease, birch dieback, chestnut blight, white-pine blister rust, and oak wilt. Since 1930 the Dutch Elm disease has spread almost entirely across the United States. It is controlled best by destroying the diseased trees.

How did you proceed in making your outline? Did you read through the entire selection before you began writing? Why or why not? Did you write words or groups of words to stand for main topics, subtopics, and details immediately as you came to those points in your reading? Did you reread the selection after you had made the outline? Why or why not? Did you read the selection once to get the main topics, a second time to get the subtopics, and a third time to get the details? In any case, how did you know just what kind of point — a main topic, a subtopic, or a detail — this or that idea in the selection was?

In making an outline of ideas included in a selection, many people have trouble deciding which ideas are main topics, which are subtopics, and which are details. Often they choose for main topics ideas which the person who wrote the selection intends as subtopics, and sometimes they choose for subtopics ideas which the writer intends as main topics or ideas which he intends as details. The result of making these and similar mistakes in thinking the relationships among the ideas in the selection is an outline which misrepresents the substance of the selection. If you think you may have made one or more such mistakes in outlining the ideas in "Enemies of Trees," make another outline of the same selection. This time, use in order the following suggestions, which, basically, are applicable in making an outline of almost any selection:

1. Read the title of the selection and think of a question which you expect the selection to answer about that title or subject. Your question may ask *How, Who, Why, What, In what way, When, Where,* or *For what reasons.* Possibly the first question you choose will not be the best one, but if it isn't, you will know that soon after you begin to read and you will sense quickly then what the best question is.

2. Read the selection to get the answers to your question. Those answers are the main topics for your outline. Write a word or group of words to stand for each of them in your outline form, leaving space for possible subtopics and details.

3. To test your choice of main topics, see if you can use each of them

with the same word or group of words in the title to think a statement which makes sense. If you can, your choice of main topics is probably correct. Thus if you chose for main topics (a) *Men,* (b) *Insects,* and (c) *Diseases,* you can think the statements (a) *Men* are an *enemy of trees,* (b) *Insects* are an *enemy of trees,* and (c) *Diseases* are an *enemy of trees.*

4. Read your first main topic and think of a question which you expect the selection to answer about it. That question may ask *How, Why, Who, What, In what way, When, Where,* or *For what reasons.*

5. Read as much of the selection as you must to get the answers to your question. Those answers are the subtopics to be indented under the first main topic in your outline. Write a word or group of words to stand for each of them, leaving space for possible details.

6. To test your choice of subtopics, see if you can use each of them with the main topic and the same word or words in the title to think a statement which makes sense. If you can, your choice of subtopics is probably correct. Thus if you chose for subtopics (a) *Cut them down,* and (b) *Start forest fires,* you can think the statements (a) *Men* are an *enemy of trees* because they *cut them down,* and (b) *Men* are an *enemy of trees* because they *start forest fires.*

7. Repeat steps 4, 5, and 6 above to get the subtopics for each of your remaining main topics.

8. Read the first subtopic under your first main topic and think of a question which you expect the selection to answer about that subtopic. The question may ask *How, Who, Why, What, In what way, For what reasons, When,* or *Where.*

9. Read as much of the selection as you must to get the answers to your question. Those answers are the details to be indented under the first subtopic you listed for the first main topic in your outline, but keep in mind here that the selection may contain no details for a given subtopic. Write a word or group of words to stand for each detail.

10. To test your choice of details, see if you can use each of them with the subtopic and the main topic and the same word or group of words in the title to think a statement which makes sense. Thus if you chose for details (a) *To get lumber,* and (b) *To clear land,* you can think the statements (a) *Men* are an *enemy of trees* because they *cut them down to get lumber,* and (b) *Men* are an *enemy of trees* because they *cut them down to clear land.*

11. Repeat steps 8, 9, and 10 to get whatever details, if any, the selection gives for each of your remaining subtopics.

At times you may want to make an outline of ideas in a selection which has no title. When that happens, you will first need to decide what the subject of the selection is. To do this, read the selection to find out what the topic of each paragraph is, and then figure out what one thing all the topics tell about. That one thing will be the subject of the selection. Then, to make your outline, follow the suggestions given in the preceding numbered paragraphs.

That pupils in Grades 5 and 6 should be made acquainted with the value of outlining an informative selection as a means of studying that material and should be taught how to make such an outline is beyond question. But the strong emphasis that contemporary instruction pertaining to this matter places upon the pupil's adhering to an outline form that is mechanically correct must be shifted to his choosing the right ideas to be stated in the outline as main topics, subtopics, and details. After all, the really important thing in making an outline is thinking the relationship which the writer of the selection intends the ideas to have with one another, and it is the pupil's choosing of ideas to serve as main topics, subtopics, and details that indicates the extent to which his thinking of that relationship is correct. So far as the outline form itself is concerned, only the pupil's indenting and labeling indicate his thinking of relationships, and minor matters — such as (1) beginning each main topic, subtopic, and detail with a capital letter, (2) placing a period after each Roman numeral, capital letter, and Arabic numeral, (3) keeping in a straight column the periods which come after these labels in a given set, and (4) using the same grammatical construction at the beginning of each entry in a set of topics — are mere conventions that have little if anything to do with showing what the pupil's thinking of relationships is. Emphasizing these minor matters in any way almost inevitably leads the pupil to draw false conclusions about the purpose, value, and ingredients of a good outline.

The instruction needed can be initiated at the fourth-grade level and should be expanded in each subsequent grade. Perhaps in the fourth grade the teaching should be limited to the choosing and recording of main topics. In the fifth grade the choosing and recording of subtopics and details may be added, but instruction pertaining to details may be reserved for sixth grade if such is judged to be preferable. Any instruction in making an outline of a selection should follow rather than precede that concerned with teaching the pupil how to decide what the topic of a paragraph is.

1. Introducing the Item

The following material, addressed to the pupil, is illustrative of teaching which can be done to introduce the making of an outline. It is concerned with the choosing and recording of only main topics and subtopics.

To read and think over

A group of paragraphs that gives information about a subject can be called an article. Such an article may be a chapter or just a part of a chapter in a book.

Sometimes you need to study an article so well that you understand clearly and remember ideas which it gives. Making an outline of those ideas can help you do that studying. Later you can use your outline to review the ideas quickly or to help you recall them as you give a talk or take part in a discussion about the subject of the article.

The ideas that an article gives play different parts. Some of these ideas are the main points that the article gives about its subject, and we call them the *main topics* in the article. Other ideas tell about the main topics, and we call these ideas the *subtopics* in the article. In making an outline of ideas in an article, you must decide just which of those ideas are the main topics and which are the subtopics.

Let's start now to make an outline of ideas in the article that begins right after the next paragraph. To do this, write now at the top of a sheet of paper the title of the article. Use capital letters where you see them.

The title you just wrote is the subject of the article, and it gives a hint of what you can expect the main topics in the article to be. To find out what those main topics are, first think of a question which you expect the article to answer about its subject. A good question to ask this time is *What things do animals supply for us?* Now read the article to get answers to your question.

Some Things That Animals Supply for Us

Some animals supply a great deal of pleasure for us. Many people enjoy the friendship they get from all kinds of pets, including cats, dogs, and horses. Some persons get excitement from watching horse races and from hunting wild animals.

Several animals supply us with food. Much of the meat we eat is the flesh of beef cattle, calves, hogs, pigs, and lambs. Some of it comes from rabbits, deer, elk, and even bears and buffalo. Most of our milk comes from cows. Now and then some people drink goats' milk.

Do you know what labor animals supply? Here and there in the world, horses, mules, camels, and elephants carry people and goods on their backs.

Most of the same animals and others, including large dogs, reindeer, oxen, and yaks, pull vehicles such as wagons, carts, sledges, and farm machinery. Tame elephants drag and lift heavy loads.

Material used in making much of our clothing comes from animals. The hides of cattle, pigs, and sheep are tanned to make leather for shoes, gloves, belts, and jackets. Some cloth is made of sheep's wool. The furs of wild animals such as the muskrat, mink, seal, fox, squirrel, beaver, ermine, and sable are used to make coats, jackets, and neckpieces.

What answers did you get for the question *What things do animals supply for us?* The answers are (1) *Pleasure,* (2) *Food,* (3) *Labor,* and (4) *Material for clothing.* These four answers are the main topics in the article, and they will be the main topics in your outline.

Now write a list of the four main topics under the subject on your paper. Put the right Roman numeral and a period — I. II. III. IV. — in front of each main topic. Begin each main topic with a capital letter. Be sure to leave space between each main topic and the one which comes below it so that you can write in later the subtopics which you will find in the article and which belong in your outline.

Would you like to find out whether your main topics are correct? To do this, see if you can use each of them with the *same* word or group of words in the subject to think a statement which makes sense.

Did you think of such a statement? You could have thought these four, in each of which the right main topic and the same group of words in the subject is used: (1) *Animals supply pleasure for us,* (2) *Animals supply food for us,* (3) *Animals supply labor for us,* and (4) *Animals supply material for clothing for us.*

Now let's find out what the subtopics in the article are that tell about the first main topic. To do this, first read that main topic and think of a question you expect the article to answer about it. A good question to ask this time is *What is the pleasure that animals supply for us?* Now read as much of the article as you must to get the answers to your question.

What answers did you get for your question? The answers are (1) *Friendship* and (2) *Excitement.* These two answers are the subtopics that the article uses to tell about the main topic *Pleasure,* and they will be the subtopics for that main topic in your outline.

List each of the two subtopics under the first main topic in your outline. To do this, write and indent under the main topic the right capital letter and period. After that letter and period, write the correct subtopic. Begin that subtopic with a capital letter.

To find out whether your subtopics are correct, see if you can use each of them with the main topic and the *same* word or group of words in the subject to think a statement which makes sense. Statements you could think are (1) *Friendship is a pleasure that animals supply for us* and (2) *Excitement is a pleasure which animals supply for us.*

Notice that the four main topics in your outline are also the topics of the four paragraphs in the article. Often when you outline an article, the topic of a given paragraph will be a main topic in the outline. Sometimes, however, the topic of a paragraph in the article will be a subtopic in the outline.

So far, your outline should look much like this:

Some Things That Animals Supply Us

I. Pleasure
   A. Friendship
   B. Excitement
II. Food

III. Labor

IV. Material for Clothing

Your outline is not yet complete. The article contains two subtopics that tell about the second main topic, three subtopics that tell about the third main topic, and three subtopics that tell about the fourth main topic. All these eight subtopics should be put into the outline.

Take time now to find out what these subtopics are and put them into your outline. To do this, take each of the last three main topics, one at a time, and follow these suggestions:

First, read the main topic and think of a question which you expect the article to answer about that topic. Your question may ask *What, How, Why, Who, Where, When,* or something else you may think of.

Second, read as much of the article as you must to get the answers to your question. Those answers are the ideas to use in your outline as subtopics for the main topic.

Third, list the subtopics under the right main topic in your outline. Sometimes you will need to use only one word to name a subtopic. At other times you will need to use two or more words. Indent and place in front of each subtopic the right capital letter and a period. Begin each subtopic with a capital letter.

Fourth, test your choice of subtopics. To do this, see if you can use each of them with the main topic and the *same* word or group of words in the subject to think a statement which makes sense. If you can do this, the ideas you chose for subtopics are probably correct.

Talking together

Help your class answer these questions:

1. How can making an outline help you in studying an article?
2. What part do the main topics in an article play? What part do the subtopics play?
3. What two things should you do to find out what the main topics in an article are?

4. What should you remember to do in writing the main topics in an outline? How can you find out whether the ideas you chose for main topics are correct?
5. What two things should you do to find out what the subtopics are that an article gives for each of its main topics?
6. What should you remember to do in writing the subtopics in an outline? How can you find out whether the ideas you chose for subtopics to go with a given main topic are correct?
7. What are the subtopics for the second main topic in the outline? For the third main topic? For the fourth main topic?

To do by yourself

On a sheet of paper, make an outline of the main topics and the subtopics in the article that follows. Use what you have learned about choosing ideas for main topics and ideas for subtopics.

Entertainment for Pioneer Adults in the Schoolhouse

Many years ago in almost any pioneer settlement in the West, the men and women used the schoolhouse in the evenings as a place in which to hold entertainments for themselves. One of these entertainments was what they called a singing school. Here they had fun learning to sing the popular songs of their time. Their holding of singing contests between two groups of singers always attracted a crowd. Persons who did not want to learn to sing but who came to the contest were the judges.

Spelldowns were very popular. In a spelldown two leaders chose up sides. Someone, often the schoolmaster, pronounced the words to be spelled. Usually each person called on spelled his word by syllables. For example, if he were asked to spell *horrified,* he would say, "Horrified. H-o-r, hor, r-i, ri, f-i-e-d, fied, horrified." The winner of the spelldown was the person who misspelled no words.

Play-party games in which the people sang as they danced were a favorite entertainment. Among the most popular of these games were *Skip to My Lou, Miller Boy,* and *Old Dan Tucker.* Perhaps you have heard the tune and words of one of these songs.

If you are asked to do so, name one of the main topics and its subtopics in your outline. If you made a mistake, find out why it is a mistake. Tell also what statements you thought to find out whether the ideas you chose for one of your main topics and its subtopics are correct.[12]

---

[12] Note to the teacher: Satisfactory statements for the first main topic and its subtopics are (a) *Learning to sing popular songs* at *singing school* was an *entertainment for pioneer adults,* (b) *Holding singing contests at singing schools* was an *entertainment for pioneer adults.* Such statements for the second main topic and its subtopics are (a) An *entertainment for pioneer adults* was *spelldowns* in which *leaders chose up sides,* (b) An *entertainment for pioneer adults* was *spelldowns* in which *someone pronounced words to be spelled,* (c) An *entertainment for pioneer adults* was *spelldowns* in which *each person spelled by syllables,* (d) An *entertain-*

Attention is called to several points pertaining to the foregoing illustrative material. *First,* the instruction provided therein is too extensive to be covered in one reading period. Probably one such period should be used for doing only the teaching proposed under "To read and think over." The discussion suggested under "Talking together" can be completed in a second period. A third period may be used for the outlining scheduled under "To do by yourself" and for the checking suggested there.

Second, any articles used in explaining to the pupil what outlining is and in giving him initial practice in making an outline must be well-organized compositions. If the instruction is to be presented to the pupil in printed form for him to read to himself, it should be composed entirely of words included in his present reading vocabulary.

Third, it is imperative to retain the emphasis the illustrative material places on teaching a procedure to follow in deciding which ideas in an article are the main topics and which ideas are subtopics. This procedure — essentially (a) thinking a question which the article can be expected to answer about its subject, (b) reading the article to find answers to that question, (c) thinking a question which the article can be expected to answer about a given main topic, (d) reading the article to get answers to that question, and (e) testing choices of ideas for main topics and for subtopics in the outline — can improve the pupil's skill in thinking the relationship which the writer of an article intends the ideas included therein to have with one another. Deleting the teaching of such a procedure from instruction in outlining limits that instruction almost entirely to the consideration of a correct form to be used in making an outline.

Fourth, the illustrative material makes no reference to what the pupil should do when he needs to outline ideas in an article that has no title. If and when the teacher has reason to believe that such a situation will arise soon, a procedure to follow should be explained to the pupil. It will consist in (a) reading the entire selection to decide what the topic of each paragraph is, (b) figuring out what one thing all the topics tell about, (c) using that one thing as the subject of the article, and then (d) choosing the ideas to serve as main topics and subtopics in the outline.

---

ment *for pioneer adults* was *spelldowns* in which the *winner was the person who misspelled no words.* Statements for the third main topic and its subtopics are (a) *Skip to My Lou* was one of the *play-party games* that were an *entertainment for pioneer adults,* (b) *Miller Boy* was one of the *play-party games* that were an *entertainment for pioneer adults.* (c) *Old Dan Tucker* was one of the *play-party games* that were an *entertainment for pioneer adults.* In each case, other satisfactory statements could be thought.

Fifth, the illustrative material includes nothing on choosing ideas to use as details in an outline. When instruction on that matter is undertaken, it should explain to the pupil that in order to choose for each subtopic whatever details the article gives about that subtopic he should first read the subtopic, think of a question which he expects the article to answer about it, and then read as much of the article as he must to get the answers. It should explain also that the answers he gets are the details to be placed under the subtopic in the outline, indented and preceded by the right Arabic number and a period, and that each detail begins with a capital letter. This instruction is not complete until the pupil is shown that he can test his choice of details by using each of them one at a time with the subtopic *and* the main topic *and* the *same* word or groups of words in the subject to think a statement which makes sense.

Sixth, the illustrative material does not explain that sometimes an article gives no subtopics for a certain main topic or no details for a certain subtopic. Obviously this simple fact should be made clear to him. Another point omitted from the illustrative material is the fact that sometimes an article has only one subtopic for a given main topic or only one detail for a given subtopic. Whether the pupil is taught to write the one subtopic as a part of the statement of the main topic or to place it as the only subtopic under the main topic is of little if any consequence. The same judgment refers to the placing of the one detail. The important thing here is whether the pupil knows just what main topic the one subtopic tells about and what the relation between those two ideas is, and whether or not he knows just what subtopic the one detail tells about and what the relationship between those two ideas is.

2. Providing Practice in Using the Skill

The additional practice which the pupil needs in order to become skillful at outlining ideas included in an informative selection can be provided in connection with the teaching of social studies, any other content subject, and English. After the introductory teaching has been completed, he should be encouraged to use outlining as a means of studying articles in social studies or science. Furthermore, it should be made clear to him that whenever he undertakes to contribute in class discussion a body of information on any given topic or question, such information should be well organized, and that he may do his talking from an outline he has made. Instruction in English which includes teaching the pupil how to prepare and give reports should encourage him to write out each report as part of its preparation and later to make an outline of it to which he can refer as he gives the report orally.

Special exercises, including those which appear in workbooks accompanying basal readers and those which the teacher herself constructs, may be used as needed. The brief list which follows describes such exercises. Obviously, any exercise used should ask the pupil to do only what the introductory teaching completed up to that time has taught him to do.

a. An exercise which provides first an informative selection that has a title. Below the title is an outline form which includes the title and only the Roman numerals needed to indicate the number of main topics in the selection. The pupil's only job is to choose and write the main topics.

b. An exercise like *a* above except that no outline form is provided. The pupil's only job is to write the title and choose and write only the main topics.

c. An exercise like *a* above except that the outline form provided includes statements of the main topics and only the capital letters needed to indicate the number of subtopics in the selection. The pupil's only job is to choose and write the subtopics.

d. An exercise like *a* above except that no outline form is provided. The pupil's job is to write the title, choose and write the main topics, and choose and write the subtopics.

e. An exercise like *d* above except that the selection has no title.

f. An exercise like *a* above except that the outline form provided includes statements of the main topics, the subtopics, and only the Arabic numerals needed to indicate the number of details in the selection. The pupil's only job is to choose and write the details.

g. An exercise like *a* above except that no outline form is provided. The pupil's job is to write the title and choose and write the main topics, the subtopics, and the details.

h. An exercise like *g* above except that the selection has no title.

It is relatively easy to make an outline of ideas in an informative selection which is well organized. Such a selection has a title stating clearly what its subject is. Each paragraph talks about only one topic, whether that topic turns out to be a main topic, a subtopic, or a detail in the outline. Right after the selection begins to talk about a main topic, a subtopic, or a detail, it tells all it has to say about that idea before beginning to tell about some other idea. If the subject is one which refers to a sequence of events, all the sentences and paragraphs are arranged in an order which follows that sequence faithfully. It is much more difficult to make an outline of ideas in a selection which is not well organized in any one or more of these respects. Statements in this paragraph are offered as a plea to the teacher to exercise much patience when the pupil attempts to outline informative selections which are not well organized.

Organizing Notes

Do you ever need to gather ideas from two or more books and arrange them so that you have at hand an organized body of information to use in writing a paper, giving a talk, or taking part in a discussion? If so, what procedure do you follow? Do you (1) make an outline of the ideas in each book and then (2) in some way try to combine the outlines? This procedure can be cumbersome and wasteful of time and effort. Do you (1) make notes — not in outline form — on ideas in one book, then (2), using each of the other books one at a time, add to your list other notes which stand for either (a) all the other ideas on the subject in the other book or (b) only amplifications the other book offers of ideas already represented in your list, and (3) finally make an outline of ideas from your complete list of notes? This procedure can make your notes unnecessarily repetitive or severely limit the scope of the information they contain. One effective procedure is as follows:

First, make notes — not in outline form — on ideas which one of the books gives on the subject. Number each note with an Arabic numeral, beginning with 1. These numbers will help you identify each separate note easily as you examine the entire list later.

Second, add other notes on ideas which another book gives on the subject and which are *not* already represented in your list. Number these additional notes, beginning with the Arabic numeral that comes right after the last one already in your list.

Third, repeat the second step in using a third, a fourth, or any additional book.

Finally, make an outline of ideas which your completed list of notes gives.

The procedure just described includes (1) selecting from informative reading matter ideas which pertain to a given subject and which have not already been chosen, (2) writing notes on those ideas, and (3) making an outline of ideas which the notes contain. The first of these three steps was considered on pages 335–338 as a part of instruction in reading. The second, an aspect of written composition, should be a part of instruction in English and does not need to be discussed here. The notes themselves make up a piece of informative reading matter, and the outlining of ideas they present surely is a part of the study type of reading with which this chapter is concerned.[13]

Usually the notes that anyone writes in following the procedure recommended in preceding paragraphs are disconnected and mixed up. Transition words that could point up relationships among ideas often are not used, and the numbered words and groups of words, written in the order in which the ideas they represent were found, are illogically arranged. Yet the notes form something much like an informative selection in the sense that some of the ideas are main topics which tell about the subject, probably some are subtopics which tell about main topics, and possibly some are details which tell about subtopics. It is the two conditions mentioned in the second sentence of this paragraph which make choosing from a set of notes ideas to use as main topics, subtopics, and details in an outline somewhat more difficult than is choosing such ideas for the same purpose from an informative selection that is well written.

The set of notes that follows tells about the subject "Some Occupations of Colonial Craftsmen." In outlining its content, which ideas would you use for main topics, subtopics, and details?

1. Making furniture important work. Windsor chairs and gateleg tables for living-room furniture. Big mahogany table for dining room. Straight chairs to match table.
2. Different kinds of clocks made. Grandfather clocks favorite.
3. High four-poster beds for bedroom. Also cradles made of wicker or wood.
4. Making metalware. Pewter used in making tableware. Also lamps.
5. Living-room upholstered chairs made. Big cupboard for dining room.
6. Much silverware made. Pitchers, platters, bowls.
7. Brassware articles, including doorknockers and andirons.
8. Cuckoo clocks and banjo clocks common.
9. Tall secretaries made for living room. Had desk with pigeonholes, drawers, lid. Bookshelves below desk. Drawers below.
10. Silver saltshakers and tumblers.
11. Highboys and lowboys for bedroom furniture.
12. Mantelpiece clocks of different shapes and sizes. Brass used in making bowls. Also feet for furniture legs.

[13] The remainder of this discussion is concerned with making an outline of ideas included in a set of unorganized notes and should be read only *after* pp. 348–360, which consider the outlining of ideas in a well-organized informative selection.

Do the ideas you chose fit the following outline form?

I.			III.	
	A.			A.
		1.			1.
		2.			2.
		3.		B.
		4.			1.
	B.			2.
		1.			3.
		2.			4.
		3.			5.
	C.			C.
		1.			1.
		2.			2.
		3.			3.
		4.			4.
II.				
	A.			
	B.			
	C.			
	D.			

If this form seems unsuited to outlining ideas presented by the notes, try again to choose ideas for main topics, subtopics, and details. This time, use in order the following directions, which, you will note, are much like those you used on pages 350–351 in making an outline of ideas in an informative selection:

1. Think of a question which you expect the notes to answer about the subject to which the notes refer. Remember that your question may ask *What, Why, Who, How, Where, When,* or something else you think of. Then read *all* the notes to get answers to your question. Those answers are the ideas to use as main topics. Cross out in the notes the words or group of words that stand for those topics so that you will not try to choose the same ideas again.

2. Think of a question which you expect the notes to answer about the *first* main topic. Then read all the words that are not crossed out in the notes to get answers to your question. Those answers are the ideas to use as subtopics for the first main topic. Cross out in the notes the words or groups of words that stand for those subtopics so that you will not try to choose the same ideas again.

3. Repeat step 2 above to choose ideas to use as subtopics for each of the remaining main topics.

4. Think of a question which you expect the notes to answer about the

first subtopic under the *first* main topic. Then read all the words that are not crossed out in the notes to get answers to your question. Those answers are the ideas to use as details for the first subtopic under the first main topic. Cross out in the notes the words or groups of words that stand for those details so that you will not try to choose the same ideas again.

5. Repeat step 4 above to choose ideas to use as details for each of the remaining subtopics.

If you wish, test your choice of ideas for the first main topic, its first subtopic, and the details which tell about that subtopic. To do this, try to use each detail in turn with the subtopic, the main topic, and the *same* word or group of words in the subject to think a statement which makes sense. For example, you could think the statement *"Making furniture* which was *Windsor chairs* for the *living room* was an *occupation of colonial craftsmen."* For the expression *Windsor chairs,* can you substitute in that statement one at a time each of the three remaining details? You may want to think of other statements to use in testing your choice of other ideas.

In many schools, the teaching of social studies, science, and other content subjects often requires the pupil to gather from several different books information on a given subject or question and to take notes on that information as he reads. Sometimes he also has to outline ideas which his notes contain so that as he gives a report to the class or takes part in a discussion on the subject or question, he has at hand an aid which can help him present his information in a well-organized form. Such organizing of ideas is essential both to the pupil's digesting of the information he gathered and to his listeners' understanding of the talking he does.

Instruction in outlining ideas in a set of unorganized notes can be initiated in Grade 4 and should be expanded in each subsequent grade. At the fourth-grade level possibly the teaching should be limited to the choosing and stating of only main topics. The choosing and stating of subtopics may be added in Grade 5 and, if judged to be preferable, the choosing and stating of details may be reserved for sixth grade. Any instruction in outlining ideas in a set of unorganized notes should follow rather than precede instruction in outlining ideas in an informative selection that is well organized.

1. Introducing the Item

The material that follows this paragraph is addressed to the pupil and illustrates teaching him to outline ideas in a set of unorganized notes.

It is limited to the choosing and stating of only main topics and sub-topics. Its use assumes that the pupil has had instruction in outlining ideas in an article, as illustrated on pages 353–356, and in making notes on ideas which two or more books give on this or that subject or question. Presumably the instruction in making notes has taught him, among other things, (a) to make notes on only those ideas which tell about the subject or question, (b) to make each note in his own words without changing the meaning given by the book, (c) to use for each note as many words as are needed to enable him to recall later what the book said, (d) to write only notes that he understands, and (e) to number each note with the correct Arabic numeral.

To read and think over

Sometimes you need to get from different books ideas which those books give on some subject or question. Usually when you do this, you make a list of notes on the ideas that the books give you.

Often the notes in your lists are not well organized. Yet, just like an article, some of the ideas the notes give are main topics which tell about the subject. Other ideas are subtopics which tell about main topics. To understand all these ideas well, you can make an outline which shows which of them are main topics and which are subtopics. Later you can use the outline as you give a report or take part in a discussion on the subject.

Making an outline of ideas in a set of notes is much like making an outline of ideas in an article. Below is a list of notes that Jack made on the subject "Some Work Done by Pioneer Women." Can you decide which ideas are main topics and which are subtopics?

1. Preparing food by drying. Apples, pumpkins.
2. Cooking corn breads, meat. Also vegetables, pies, apple sauce, apple leather.
3. Used animal skins in making clothing. Jackets, leggings, moccasins.
4. Making candles by dipping. Wicks dipped into melted tallow in deep kettle many times.
5. Used salt in preserving meat.
6. Home made cloth used in making clothing. Trousers, skirts, dresses, jackets.
7. Churning butter. Churn like small barrel with handle through lid. Handle moved up and down. Dasher on bottom beat cream into butter.
8. Salt, vinegar, honey, maple sap used as seasonings.
9. Apple leather was good candy.
10. Some candles made by molding. Wick placed in tube. Melted tallow poured into tube. Allowed to set.
11. In making soap used lye water and grease. Lye obtained from wood ashes.

You can use the following steps to make an outline of ideas in a set of notes. Use them now if you are not sure that you already know what the main topics and the subtopics in Jack's notes are.

First, read the subject and think of a question which you expect the notes to answer about that subject. Remember that your question may ask *What, How, Why, Who, Where,* or *When.* Then read *all* the notes to get answers to your question. Those answers are the ideas to use for the main topics in an outline. Write now on a sheet of paper a word or group of words to stand for each of them. Use Roman numerals, periods, and capital letters where you need them. Then cross out lightly in the notes the words or groups of words that name the main topics so that you will not try to use the same ideas again in the outline.

Second, read the *first* main topic in the outline and think of a question which you expect the notes to answer about that topic. Then read in the notes *all* the words that are not crossed out to get answers to your question. Those answers are the ideas to use as subtopics for the first main topic. Write a word or group of words to stand for each of them in the outline. Indent each of them under the first main topic and use capital letters and periods where they are needed. Then cross out lightly in the notes the words or groups of words that name the subtopics so that you will not try to use the same ideas again in the outline.

Third, repeat the second step as many times as you must to choose ideas to use as subtopics to go with each remaining main topic in the outline.

Talking together

Help your class answer these questions:

1. Why may you need to make an outline of ideas in a set of notes?
2. What are the main topics in Jack's set of notes? What are the subtopics?
3. How can you decide which ideas in a set of notes should be used as main topics in an outline? How can you decide which ideas should be used as subtopics to go with a given main topic?

To do by yourself

Here is a set of notes that Mary made on the subject "Some Unusual Animal Helpers." On a sheet of paper, make an outline that shows what the main topics and the subtopics in the notes are.

1. The yak in Tibet. Carries loads. People, goods. A kind of ox. Tibet in Asia between China and India.
2. In India and Africa elephant piles teakwood logs.
3. Yak provides food. Meat, milk.
4. The carabao in Philippine Islands. Works in rice fields. A kind of ox.
5. The llama carries loads on mountain trails. Lives in South America. Something like camel. Much smaller.

6. Elephant carries hunters of wild animals.
7. Yak provides hair. Used in weaving cloth.
8. Llama gives milk for people. Sure-footed on mountain trails.
9. Carabao pulls two-wheeled cart. People ride in cart. Cart carries rice to market.
10. Elephant pulls farm machinery. Llama provides hair used in making clothing and blankets.

If you are asked to do so, read aloud one of the main topics and its sub-topics from your outline. If you made a mistake in choosing ideas to use for those topics, find out why it is a mistake.

2. Providing Practice in Using the Skill

The best opportunities for providing needed practice in outlining ideas in a set of unorganized notes appear in connection with the teaching of social studies, any other content subject, and English. As will be noted in Chapter 11, at least some of the reading assignments made in each content subject should stimulate the pupil to use several books rather than just one in gathering information on a given subject or question, to make notes on ideas provided by those books, and to outline the substance of his notes. Furthermore, class discussions should be of such a nature that they encourage the pupil to present in a well-organized form the information he contributes orally. Whatever instruction the teaching of English provides on the preparing and giving of reports should encourage the pupil (a) to make notes as he gathers from several books information to use in a report, (b) to make an outline of the ideas included in his notes, (3) to use that outline as an aid which tells him how many paragraphs he will have in his report, what one topic each paragraph is to tell about, and which ideas are to be put into each paragraph, and (4) to talk from his outline in giving the report instead of reading his composition aloud or reciting it from memory.

If necessary, special exercises in outlining ideas in a set of unorganized notes may be used. In general, the types of exercises described on page 359 will be satisfactory, if, of course, the words *unorganized notes* are substituted for the words *informative selection*.

Interpreting Graphs

Now and then in studying informative selections the reader encounters simple graphs. These are drawings which present numerical data, show relative sizes or quantities, are intended to make facts obvious rather than to report exact figures, and are supposed to be easier to read quickly than words stating the same facts would be. The commonest types of simple graphs are the line graph, the bar graph, the pictograph, and the circle or pie graph.

The line graph, the bar graph, or the pictograph shows quantitative data which report approximate amounts attained at given times or increases and decreases in those amounts over a period of time and which refer to such topics as income, taxes, trade, farm products, population, production of goods, school attendance, and the like. In a line graph, horizontal lines that stand perhaps for different amounts are crossed at right angles by vertical lines that stand perhaps for different dates or time periods. A heavy line connects points on or between the horizontal lines and the vertical lines which indicate amounts attained on the different dates or during the different time periods. Often in a bar graph, either horizontal lines or vertical lines stand for amounts, and wide black or colored bars indicate amounts attained at a given time or during a given time period. When the lines that stand for amounts in a bar graph are horizontal, the bars are vertical and are labeled at the bottom to indicate dates or time periods. When the lines are vertical, the bars are horizontal and are labeled at the left to indicate time. If a bar graph contains no lines that stand for amounts, usually each bar is placed to the right of a time label, and the amount that the bar represents is printed in figures on the bar itself. In a pictograph, amounts are shown by appropriate symbols such as coins, ships, human figures, animals, trees, bushel baskets, or labeled blocks that are placed to the right of names of dates or time periods. In a circle graph, the circle stands for a whole amount — the total taxes collected by the national government during a given year, for example — and the label and per cent printed on or near each of the wedges into which the circle is divided — such as income tax, inheritance tax, and excise tax — show the per cent which that part is of the whole. An example of each of the four types of simple graphs appears in the illustrative material which follows.

Graphs appear in the pupil's social studies and sciences textbooks, in more detailed informative books which should be available to him, and in encyclopedias intended for his use. That he should learn to read these drawings in order to get certain facts offered by his reading matter is beyond question. The instruction concerned with equipping him to interpret graphs can be initiated as soon as one such drawing appears in his reading matter and should be expanded later as this material places additional demands upon him.

1. Introducing the Item

The following material, addressed to the pupil, illustrates an introduction to the interpreting of simple graphs. Although the line graph, the bar graph, the pictograph, and the circle graph are included, it is understood that the use of any one reading period may be limited to a consideration of only one type of graph.

To read and think over

Sometimes, as you study an article, you will find there one or more drawings that are called graphs and that you need to read. Graphs show facts that tell about such topics as income, population, costs, school attendance, farm products, production of goods, and taxes. If you know how to read a graph, you can get the facts it gives more quickly than you could by reading sentences which tell those facts.

The graph shown below is a line graph. What does the title at the top say that the graph tells about?

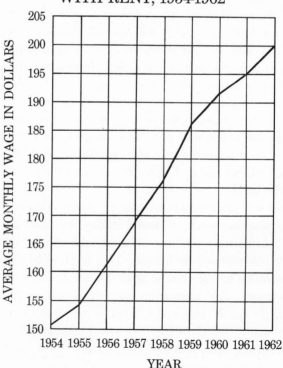

AVERAGE MONTHLY FARM WAGE
WITH RENT, 1954-1962

Notice the label "Year" at the bottom of the chart. It tells you that each number along the bottom line of the chart is the number of a certain year. It means also that the average farm wage for each year named is some point on the vertical line which runs from the number of that year to the top of the chart. We call the vertical lines in this chart the year lines.

What does the label "Average Wage in Dollars" at the left mean? It tells you that the numbers along the left of the chart stand for the dollars paid in average wages. The horizontal lines which begin at these numbers and run straight across the chart can be called wage lines.

The heavy crooked line that runs up and across the chart is the graph line. It is the points on that line which you need to read.

Notice that the graph line starts on year line 1954. At what point on that line? Somewhere between wage line 150 and wage line 155. This means that the average wage in 1954 was more than 150 but less than 155. To decide just how much more than 150, you must imagine wage lines that stand for 151, 152, 153, and 154. You can think that line 151 would be just a little above 150 and that line 152 would be just a little above 151 but not quite halfway up to line 155. Line 153 would be just a little more than half-way up to line 155, and line 154 would be just a little below line 155. The graph line meets year line 1954 just about where wage line 151 would be. That is why you know the average monthly farm wage in 1954 was $151.

Look now at year line 1961. Where does the graph line meet it? Exactly at the point where wage line 195 crosses year line 1961. This means that the average wage in 1961 was $195. What was the average wage in 1962? In 1955? In 1956?

The graph you see below is a bar graph. It shows the same facts that you read in the line graph.

AVERAGE MONTHLY FARM WAGE WITH RENT, 1954-1962
AVERAGE MONTHLY WAGE IN DOLLARS

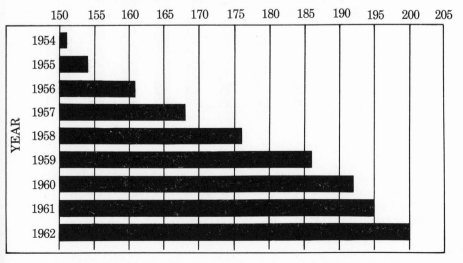

Notice that the vertical lines in the graph are wage lines. You can see too that instead of year lines, the graph has horizontal bars. That is why such a graph is often called a horizontal bar graph.

To read the graph, you must find the point where the right end of each bar is on the chart. When the end is exactly at a wage line, use the figure at the top of that line as the average wage. If the end of a bar is between two wage lines, you will have to imagine and use wage lines just as you did in reading the line graph. What was the average farm wage in 1957?

The graph you just read could have been drawn as a vertical bar graph like this:

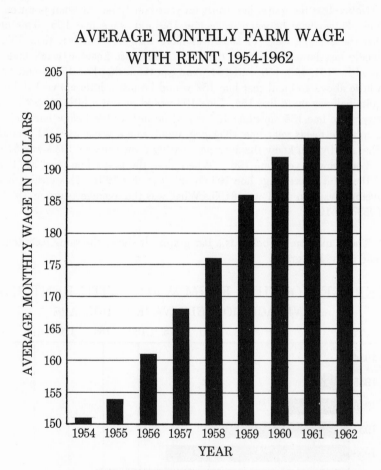

AVERAGE MONTHLY FARM WAGE WITH RENT, 1954-1962

In the vertical bar graph, the wage lines are horizontal and the bars stand for the years, but you can read the graph in the same way that you read the horizontal bar graph. You can see that the average monthly wage in 1961 was $195. What was the average wage in 1958?

The graph that comes next is called a pictograph. There are no lines or bars in it. The numbers of the years are shown at the left. Pictures of silver dollars and parts of dollars are used to show the average wages. By reading the label at the bottom, you can see that each whole dollar stands for fifty dollars.

AVERAGE MONTHLY FARM
WAGE WITH RENT, 1954-1962

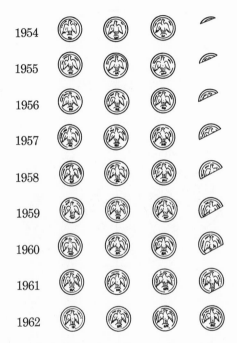

Each whole silver dollar stands for fifty dollars

Look at the pictures for the year 1962. There you see four whole dollars. Since each dollar stands for $50, you know that the average wage for 1962 was four times fifty or $200.

Look at the pictures for the year 1958. There you see three dollars and a part of another dollar, so you know that the average wage for 1958 was more than $150. Is the part of a dollar that is shown as much as a half? It is just a little more than a half. That is why you can think, "The average wage in 1958 was a little more than $175". What was the average wage for 1959?

Another kind of graph is called a circle graph. In such a graph, a circle stands for the whole amount of something. The circle is divided into **parts** or wedges that are shaped like pieces of pie. The size of each wedge **and** the figures printed on or near it tell how much of the whole that part is.

Here is a circle graph. What does the title at the top say the graph tells about? Did the Yankees win as many series as all the other teams put together?

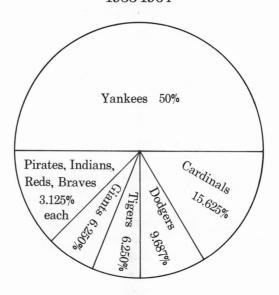

WINNERS OF WORLD SERIES,
1933-1964

Talking together

Help your class answer these questions:

1. What are the different kinds of graphs you have read about?
2. In what way are graphs easier to read than sentences which tell the same facts?
3. What is the difference between a line graph and a bar graph? What is the difference between a horizontal bar graph and a vertical bar graph?
4. What points about a graph should you keep in mind as you read it?
5. What was the average monthly farm wage in 1955? 1956? 1958? 1962?
6. What pictures might you expect to see in a pictograph that tells about the the number of trees lost in forest fires? The number of sheep raised? The amount of corn grown?

7. In what way is a circle graph different from other graphs?

To do by yourself

Number a paper from 1 through 5. After each number write the answer or answers to the following question which has that same number:

1. What was the average monthly farm wage in 1959? In 1960?
2. Did farm wages decrease between 1954 and 1962?
3. In what year did the average monthly farm wage increase most?
4. In what two years did the average monthly farm wage increase least?
5. What baseball team won the most world series? What team ranked second?

If you are asked to do so, read some of your answers aloud. If you find any of your answers are mistakes, find out why they are mistakes.

2. Providing Practice in Using the Skill

The pupil can get just about all the practice he needs in interpreting graphs simply by reading those which appear in the informative books that should be available for him to work with in social studies and other content subjects. To stimulate this reading, the teacher can remind him now and then to be sure to find out what facts are reported by whatever graphs are included in this or that selection to be read. In addition, some of the questions raised in class discussions of the content of assigned reading matter should pertain to facts supplied by graphs presented in that material. Further practice can be supplied by having the pupil make simple graphs which report contemporary numerical data of interest to him, including perhaps the progress he makes in learning the words that make up spelling lessons, the minimum daily temperatures for a week, or the daily school attendance of his class over a given period of time. Special exercises in interpreting graphs which appear in workbooks accompanying some basal readers may be used if the pupil needs the practice they offer.

A Concluding Statement

Chapter 8 and the present chapter have considered the teaching of fourteen insights and skills which pertain to coping with meaning difficulties included in reading matter and to studying informative selections effectively. Chapter 10 is concerned with the teaching of a few additional items of particular importance in evaluating informative material that has been read. The teaching proposed in these three chapters is a very significant part of this volume's program of instruction in reading in Grades 3 through 6. It is essential to the pupil's acquisition of the power to understand what his reading matter says, to study informative material skillfully, and to react critically to questionable statements he has read. As previously noted, all of this instruction is concerned with helping the pupil learn to use reading as a more effective vehicle for receiving meaning through language than listening is or can be and as a means of continuing his education independently long after his school days have passed.

Probably it is reasonable to say that in most schools approximately 170 periods are assigned each year to teaching reading in each of Grades 3 through 6. As mentioned in Chapter 7, it is not at all uncommon for the majority if not all of these periods to be used in (1) introducing this or that selection to be read in a basal reader, (2) having the pupils read the selection silently, (3) holding a group or class discussion of the content read, (4) having pupils read aloud parts if not all of the selection, and (5) having pupils work out one or more exercises bearing on the content of the selection. By no stretch of the imagination can this series of activities in itself be called the teaching of reading. It is hoped that some of the 170 reading periods will be used for introducing items discussed in Chapters 8, 9, and 10 and that sensible and appropriate opportunities for practicing the skills which those items include will be provided in other school work.

QUESTIONS TO BE ANSWERED

1. Chapter 8 gave one reason why reading in Grades 3 through 6 is more difficult than reading in the first two grades. What other reason does the present chapter give?

2. What are the items which this chapter suggests that pupils be taught? Of what two main teaching activities does the instruction in each item consist?

3. What is the purpose of the introductory teaching suggested for each item? What could keep a teacher from giving this instruction?

4. With what particular points would you expect the pupil to have the most difficulty in using the index of a book?

5. What procedure does the chapter recommend that the pupil be taught to follow in locating quickly on a page the information to which the index refers?

6. In what way or ways can reading for one purpose differ from reading for

another purpose? What should teaching the pupil to read for a given purpose include?

7. What is the difference between the topic of a paragraph and the main topic in a paragraph? Why should the pupil learn how to decide what the topic of a paragraph is? What procedure can he follow in deciding what the topic of a paragraph is?

8. What is the procedure that this chapter recommends the pupil be taught to follow in outlining an informative selection? Why may the outlining of unorganized notes be more difficult for the pupil than is the outlining of an informative selection?

9. What one thing would you do to provide in other school work practice in each of the following: (a) using the index of a book, (b) deciding what the topic of a paragraph is, (c) outlining an informative selection, (d) outlining unorganized notes, (e) interpreting graphs?

10. What, if anything, did you get from this chapter which you think will help you in your study of informative material?

MORE TO READ

Bond, Guy, and Eva Wagner, *Teaching the Child to Read,* The Macmillan Co., New York, 1950, Chapters 12, 13, 14.

Dechant, Emerald, *Improving the Teaching of Reading,* Prentice-Hall, Inc., Englewood Cliffs, N.J., 1964, Chapter 9.

Durrell, Donald, *Improving Reading Instruction,* World Book Company, Yonkers-on-Hudson, N.Y., 1956, Chapters 13, 14.

Gray, Lillian, and Dora Reese, *Teaching Children to Read,* The Ronald Press Company, New York, 1957, Chapter 13.

Harris, Albert, *Effective Teaching of Reading,* David McKay Co., Inc., New York, 1962, Chapter 12.

McKee, Paul, *The Teaching of Reading in the Elementary School,* Houghton Mifflin Company, Boston, 1948, Chapters 13, 14, 15, 16.

Preston, Ralph, and Morton Botel, *How to Study,* Science Research Associates, Chicago, 1956.

Robinson, Francis, *Effective Study,* Harper & Row, New York, 1961, Chapter 9.

Russell, David, *Children Learn to Read,* Ginn & Company, Boston, 1962, Chapter 11.

Spache, George, *Toward Better Reading,* The Garrard Press, Champaign, Ill., 1963, Chapter 18.

Yoakam, Gerald, *Basal Reading Instruction,* McGraw-Hill Book Co., Inc., New York, 1955, Chapter 12.

THINGS TO DO

1. Get any intermediate-grade basal reader, the accompanying teacher's guide, and the pupil's workbook. Examine these materials to find out what instruction they provide in skills needed for studying informative reading matter and in which book that instruction is provided.

2. Examine other books on the teaching of reading to discover what skills they suggest pupils be taught for use in studying informative material.

3. Choose any one of the seven items discussed in this chapter. Then make a list of things you would do to teach that item as completely as you think you should at any intermediate-grade level you choose.

4. Choose one of the seven items and make an exercise that gives pupils practice in using the skill.

5. Examine the teacher's guide for any intermediate-grade basal reader. Find out what its suggestions are for giving the pupil opportunities in other school work to use skills which have been taught for the study of informative material?

6. Examine intermediate-grade social studies and science textbooks, including geographies. Try to think of yourself as studying that material and make a list of skills which are not discussed in this chapter and which you think pupils should have in order to study informative material effectively.

chapter 10

Critical Reading

Chapter 8 considered the development of insights and skills which any pupil needs to cope with the meaning difficulties that he encounters in reading narrative selections and informative material. Chapter 9 proposed instruction which can equip the pupil with additional insights and skills essential to his effective study of informative reading matter. The present chapter offers suggestions for teaching the pupil how to read critically. The three chapters together describe the first of the three main teaching activities listed on page 228 in Chapter 7 and are devoted to helping the pupil to use reading as a means of educating himself during his school days and the years that follow.

The term *critical reading* is relatively new in the teacher's lexicon. It has evolved from an increasing awareness of the importance of the reader's reacting to or thinking about ideas expressed by the writer. Yet not just any such reacting or thinking is critical reading. *As used in this volume,* this term refers to the act — simple or complicated — of evaluating and judging printed, informative statements. According to this definition, limited in scope though it may be, decide which of the numbered items below describes the critical reading of the following statement:

The candidate has distinguished himself by his unstinting service to the people.

1. The reader makes correct meaning for the statement.

2. The reader makes correct meaning for the statement and reacts by thinking: "The candidate is a person who, if elected to office, will do much for the benefit of the people."

3. The reader makes correct meaning for the statement and, in addition, reacts by evaluating the author or his statement. In attempting to evaluate, the reader either (a) uses immediately appropriate and adequate information which he already has at hand or (b) finds such information over a period of time and then uses it in making his decision.

The act described by the first item is not critical reading of the statement. It is simply the act of thinking for the statement a meaning which is intended by the writer, and it is what some authorities call literal comprehension. It is also what most of the instruction proposed in Chapters 4, 5, 7, and 8 can equip the pupil to do well.

The act described by the second item is not critical reading of the statement. Here the reader, in addition to achieving literal comprehension, reacts by making an interpretation. Usually the term *interpretation* functions in this setting as a name for such reactions as (1) making an inference or drawing a conclusion which is based on but not expressed in the statement, (2) thinking an idea which is not expressed in the statement but which is either an implication or a ramification of what the statement says, and (3) thinking a relationship which, though not expressed in the statement, does exist between what the statement says and some other idea. Certainly any reader at times should engage in such reacting, and, as explained in Chapters 5 and 7, some of the questions asked of elementary school pupils relative to selections they have read should stimulate them to do this very thing. Yet two cautions are of particular importance here. *First,* there is little if any profit for the reader in making an inference, drawing a conclusion, or in thinking an implication or a ramification of the statement, unless the statement is true. *Second,* trying to think a meaning which is not expressed but which seems to be "between the lines" often can be one of the tempting snares that endangers communication between the writer and the reader.

The act described by the third item includes critical reading simply because the reader, after making correct meaning for the statement, and perhaps after making an interpretation, undertakes the task of trying to evaluate and judge that statement. Whenever the reader is sufficiently acquainted with the persuasive expressions that a writer can use and is well informed on the topic of the statement, his task is relatively simple. He calls to mind his fund of appropriate and reliable information and uses it as a measuring stick in judging the statement. However, since the reader is rarely so well equipped, usually his task is much more complicated. For example, in order to build a measuring stick for judging the validity of a given statement, he may need to determine whether the writer intends the statement to be one of fact or one of opinion. He may need to decide whether the statement is definite and clear rather than vague or ambiguous and whether it is straightforward or objective rather than biased or emotive, whether it follows logically from a prestated premise, whether it is a warranted generalization, or whether it is purely hypothetical. He may need to compare the statement with others made by the same writer on the same topic and with statements made by other writers on that topic in sources which he judges to be authentic. He may need to check the writer's background in order to get some idea of his competence to give accurate information on the topic of his statement. It is understood here that critical reading is carried on almost entirely with the use of reading matter that is supposed to be informative, and that usually it pertains to only those short or long statements which, for one reason or another, the reader questions or which are of much importance to his purpose. In the case of many statements, of course, it is impossible to get the information needed for judging their validity.[1]

Other aspects of reading could logically be called critical reading. For example, analyzing the literary merit of a work of fiction by examining the author's descriptive techniques, plot, and beauty of phrase involves processes which could be classified as critical reading. It has become customary, however, to classify these processes under the heading of literary appreciation and to reserve the term *critical reading* for the processes involved in judging informative statements as described here.

The need for critical reading increases as society grows more complex. Each day we are bombarded by printed matter which contains both obvious and obscure attempts made by others to get us to think as they think, to believe what they want us to believe, and to do what they hope we will do. Each day the quantity of printed matter that is supposed to be informative increases, and the necessity for judging its probable validity becomes more crucial. In a society which gives each person a share of the responsibility for charting its future course, it is imperative that everyone have not only the ability to understand printed matter but also the insights and skills required for evaluating the validity of the ideas it presents. The responsibility for helping people acquire

---

[1] For one discussion of the nature of critical reading, see Nila B. Smith, "What Is Critical Reading?" *Elementary English*, April, 1963, pp. 409–410. The term *critical reading* is used with different meanings by different people.

these insights and skills lies with the elementary school, the secondary school, and the college or university.

Most pupils enrolled in the later grades of the elementary school are poorly equipped to read critically. In the first place, they have acquired beliefs that make them unwilling to question statements in informative material. Two of these beliefs are as follows: (1) simply because an idea appears in print it must be true and therefore is not to be challenged, and (2) any printed statement on a given point is necessarily more valid than a spoken statement on the same point. Second, these pupils are unacquainted with even the most rudimentary ways of trying to determine the validity of a statement. For example, they know little about distinguishing a statement of fact from a statement of opinion. They do not even understand that often at the beginning of a statement a writer uses an expression such as *Apparently, It seems as though, Probably, It appears that,* or *In the author's judgment* to tell the reader that he is about to state an opinion. They are not aware of the difference between emotive language and factual language, the simplest earmarks of bias, or the techniques of even blatant propaganda. They do not know how to check a given statement by using other statements on the same topic by the same writer or statements by other writers on that topic. They have little if any idea how to determine a writer's competence to make a valid statement on a given topic. Thus they are far too ready to swallow passively almost any ideas presented in their reading matter and are at the mercy of many statements which can do little more than give them false notions.

Trying to judge the validity of a printed statement can be at times quite a complicated act, and no one can be expected to reach during his elementary school days his full potential to do it. Yet this condition does not mean that all appropriate instruction should be reserved for the secondary school and the college. On the contrary, the beginnings of such teaching should be initiated during the elementary school years. This proposal is based on two propositions which admittedly may be at odds with others sometimes voiced.

The first proposition is that pupils in the middle grades can develop certain basic insights and skills essential to critical reading and that it is appropriate to promote these at the elementary level. The fact that this *can* be done then has been established by the work of many good teachers, as illustrated in the remainder of this chapter. Whether the teaching *should* be done rests on three premises. First is the importance which critical reading has in developing people who are concerned about furthering their education independently and about the welfare of society. Second, since many students do not complete both elementary and secondary education, the instruction should not be withheld from intermediate-grade pupils. Third, the ability to read critically can be developed most adequately by introducing some of its basic aspects as soon as the pupil can understand and use them. More refined aspects which fit the pupil's continuing maturation should be reserved for later years of schooling.

The second proposition is that a reader can read critically to at least some degree without being already well informed on the topic. This does not imply that the degree of sophistication in critical reading will be the same whether he has a strong background of information or not. Obviously, he will be more likely to detect, for example, bias, inadequate evidence, and persuasive but misleading expressions in statements on topics about which he is well informed. However, although no one can be well informed about every topic on which he does or should read, he should read as critically as he can. Can you read critically the following statements?

> Today, in a speech delivered to the Society of Newspaper Editors, Charles Smith, National Chairman of the Do Something Party, assailed the record of the opposition and said that during the past four years they have not come forth with a single piece of forward-looking legislation.

> The barbarians who conquered Rome loved freedom.

These rather obvious examples indicate that there are some aspects of critical reading which you can apply in reacting to statements about topics on which you are not well informed. Since the first example is fictitious, although somewhat representative, it is impossible for you to be informed about the topic. You can, however, question the objectivity of Charles Smith, his acquaintance with and evaluation of the opposition's record, and the exactness of the reporter's indirect quoting of Mr. Smith. The second example is paraphrased from an elementary school social studies text. Even though you may not be acquainted with the true nature of the barbarians who conquered Rome, you do not want to assume, without analysis, that the term *freedom* as used in that statement means the same kind of freedom which you enjoy in your society. Making a "correct meaning" based on your own experiences may not accurately depict the individual freedom enjoyed by the barbarians at all.

There are two main ways in which intermediate-grade teachers can help pupils build the ability to read informative statements critically. One is to foster a realistic idea about the nature of informative reading matter as far as its validity is concerned. Probably this can be accomplished best through the manner in which social studies, science, and other content subjects are taught. Of prime importance here is to provide for the pupil several books — not just one — as sources of information on a given question that is part of an assignment. This provision, properly applied, can help the pupil to learn that sometimes different books do not agree on a certain point, that a printed statement can be out of date, that a writer can make misstatements, that consequently it is possible for a printed statement to tell something which is not true, and that it is all right for him to question calmly and seriously statements which he reads. In addition, the pupil should be encouraged to question during his study any statement which is of sufficient importance to him and to apply then whatever he has been taught to do in trying to check the validity of the statement. Finally, if the validity of a statement made by a given book becomes the subject of class disagreement, the statement should be evaluated further. The fostering of this realistic idea about the validity of informative reading matter should either prevent the pupil's developing the mistaken beliefs described on page 380 or supplant them.

The second way in which intermediate-grade teachers can help pupils build the ability to read informative statements critically is to teach certain definite skills which are essential to such reading and which, for want of a better term, can be called items. The four main sections which make up the remainder of this chapter are devoted to discussions of some of these items. The particular items considered are: (1) distinguishing statements of fact from statements of opinion, (2) recognizing assumptions and vague expressions, (3) recognizing propaganda techniques, and (4) judging the competence of the writer. As in Chapters 8 and 9, each main section first explores the nature of the item with which it is concerned and then offers suggestions pertaining to the teaching of that item. In each case the suggested instruction, which consists of introducing the item to the pupil and providing him with subsequent practice in its use, is applicable in teaching fifth- and sixth-grade pupils, although there is no particular reason why instruction in any of the items should not be initiated earlier with pupils who can begin to learn them. No claim is made that other items which are not included herein and which some persons may think appropriate and important should not be taught to intermediate-grade pupils.

Distinguishing Fact from Opinion

The information that a short or long printed statement gives can be presented either as fact or as opinion, and no skill required for critical

---

[2] Somewhat detailed explanations of statements made in this paragraph appear in Chapter 11.

reading is more vital than that of distinguishing statements presented as facts from those presented as opinions. Although a reader often accepts opinions as facts, there are relatively clear guideposts which can prevent him from making this mistake. Consider, for example, the following revised comments from a columnist's report:

> In a recent speech to a private group, Mr. Smith analyzed with precision and force the government's position in the war. His statement is the most complete and convincing argument that has been made for continuing the war. He went to the very heart of our nation's interests as the basis for his position and wisely ignored the carping of those who lack his vision.

Here the writer makes no effort to disguise the point that he is presenting his opinion of Mr. Smith's speech. He does not quote any of the statements which the speaker made but, instead, uses descriptive words such as *precision, force,* and *convincing* to lead the reader to conclude that the speech was a truly outstanding one. Having read this description, the reader could be expected to have a predisposition to accept a later factual report of the speech, provided he has no strong beliefs against the writer, Mr. Smith, or the war itself.

Consider the following statements taken from elementary school social studies texts. Pay particular attention to the italicized words and phrases:

> *Probably* most of the pans and cooking utensils in the kitchens of our homes are made from aluminum.

> The great forests of the north *may* some day be a valuable resource.

> The people of Switzerland have succeeded in overcoming their handicaps and *in making the best possible use* of the advantages they have.

The first two statements provide cues which warn us that they are statements of opinion. Children should learn to look for signals such as *probably* and *may.* In the third statement there is no cue word, but the italicized phrase is an obvious value judgment. The opinion offered there may be shared by many authorities, but it is still an opinion.

Newspapers and magazines generally carry in each issue several columnists' reports which follow the general style of the foregoing analysis of the speech by "Mr. Smith." Each contains the name of the person expressing the opinion and frequently supplies a picture of him. The guideposts which point out that the report is an expression of opinion are evident for anyone who has learned to recognize them. If all statements of opinion were as obvious as the ones just given, if the reader could always draw such a sharp dividing line between fact and opinion, the problem would be greatly simplified. Unfortunately, trying to provide a sharp cleavage is difficult, if not impossible.

Deciding whether a given statement is one of fact or one of opinion can be relatively easy when the reader must choose either of the extremes of a continuum, but dealing with the gray areas between those extremes may call for more sophisticated efforts. Consider first, for example, the two statements *Sam is six feet tall* and *Sam is very tall*. The first statement is given as a fact and as such can be verified or refuted. Sam can be measured, and if he is actually six feet tall, the first statement is one of fact. But what about the second statement? Would you say that Sam is very tall? Your conclusion regarding the validity of that statement depends on whether your idea of *very tall* agrees with the writer's. Since the second statement is given with a descriptive word expressing a judgment, it is a statement of opinion.

Compare now the following brief accounts of a battle in a fictitious war:

1

The forces of the Blue army clashed with those of the Green army again yesterday. Following the battle, the Blue army returned to the positions it had previously held.

2

The forces of the Blues vainly threw themselves against the solid lines of the Green army yesterday. Following the battle, the Blues hastily withdrew in disordered retreat.

3

The forces of the Blue army savagely attacked the Greens again yesterday. Following the battle, the Blue army withdrew its front lines into previously prepared positions.

These three accounts of the same battle demonstrate how opinion is frequently interwoven with fact in a way which is difficult to discern but effective in directing the reader's thoughts. In the first report, the actual facts of the battle are presented without the writer's opinion. In the second and third reports, however, the opinions of the writers have dictated the choice of words which create opposing impressions. Compare the effect of *vainly threw themselves against* with that of *savagely attacked*.

So far, in this discussion we have examined several statements which exemplify both fact and opinion. But determining whether a given selection or part of a selection presents statements of fact or opinion does not tell a reader whether one or another of these statements is true. An examination of the diagram below may help clarify the steps a mature critical reader takes after he has decided whether a given statement is one of fact or of opinion.

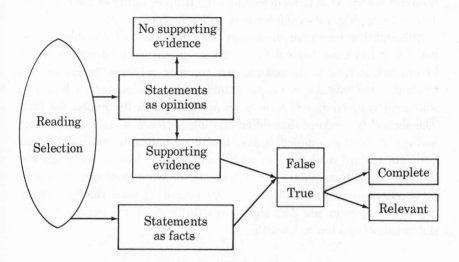

If the reader decides that a statement is given as fact — *The tallest building in the world is the Empire State Building* — his next step is to determine the truth or falsity of that statement. Sometimes, it is important for him to confirm the fact, in which case he would probably consult a standard reference such as an encyclopedia, the *World Almanac,* or some other source that he accepts as a final arbiter. If he finds there that the statement is false, he rejects it. If he finds that it is true, he accepts it.

In the case of longer, more complex statements than the above example, however, determining that they are true will still not settle the matter. For example, an author may conclude that all public utilities should be nationalized and cite several facts which have led him to this conclusion. Even though the facts presented may be true, a mature critical reader would still determine whether the author has examined a complete set of facts and whether the facts he has explored are relevant to the conclusion he has reached. Citing facts is inadequate if many others which are important are ignored, or if those which are given do not directly bear on the matter at hand.

Let us explore now the steps which a mature reader would take if he decides that the statements are expressed as opinions rather than as facts. The next step would be to analyze the presentation to determine whether the author has offered supporting evidence or not. If none is given, either through examples, logical reasoning, or some other procedure, the reader must analyze it through other methods, such as evaluating the author himself. If supporting evidence is offered, the reader then follows the same procedures that he would if statements of fact had been presented. That is, he determines the truth or falsity of the evidence, and, if true, judges its completeness and relevancy.

Although the foregoing discussion does not cover all possible contingencies, it has gone beyond the customarily cursory treatment in order to prevent anyone from making two common mistakes in his critical reading. One mistake is simply thinking that determining whether a statement is given as a fact or as an opinion settles the matter for him. The second is thinking that differentiating between a statement of fact and a statement of opinion is akin to differentiating between good and bad. No mature reader makes such a distinction. Instead, he notes the difference and then judges the statements for what they are. Similarly, no good teacher ever brushes off a statement of opinion simply because it is one of opinion, nor does she convey to the pupil the impression that statements of opinion lack worth.

1. Introducing the Item

The degree to which a pupil can explore the complexities of distinguishing between statements of fact and statements of opinion depends upon his maturity and the procedures used in teaching. The following material, addressed to the pupil, exemplifies one relatively simple approach. Its different parts and their purposes are much the same as those of the illustrative lessons included in Chapters 8 and 9.

To read and think over

Mrs. Smith's fifth-grade class decided to start a school newspaper. They planned to put it out every two weeks and to make enough copies for all the boys and girls in Grades 4, 5, and 6.

As the deadline for the first issue drew near, the news reports started to come in, the editors began to check the reports, and then — the trouble began. It concerned the following statement that Jim wrote to be used as a news item. Why do you think that the head editor felt that it should not be used as a news item?

Last year our school got an outside basketball court. Now it has been decided that the new rooms to be added to the school this summer will be built there. This means that we won't have a court to practice on during recess and noon hours next year.

It isn't fair to take our basketball court away from us. If we can't practice, we won't make the team when we get to junior high school.

A good news item sticks to facts and does not give opinions of the person who wrote it. It includes information which gives facts that help the reader make decisions for himself. It does not make decisions for the reader and then try to convince him that they are right.

Look back at Jim's news items to see that he started out by giving facts and then gave his opinions. In the first paragraph, he says (1) last year the school got a court, (2) new rooms will be built there this summer, and (3) next year the pupils won't have a court to practice on. He gives this information as facts. We don't know for sure that these facts are right — maybe the rooms won't be built this summer — but he states them plainly and without telling what he thinks about the matter.

But take a look at Jim's second paragraph. There he gives two of his opinions on what he is writing about. These are (1) it isn't fair, and (2) the boys won't make the junior high team if they don't have the court. Jim's saying *It isn't fair* is an opinion, simply because the question of fairness must be a matter of opinion. His saying *we won't make the team* is not a statement of fact. That tells only what Jim thinks will happen.

Sometimes you read things which seem to be facts but which are just the writer's opinions. The writer may or may not be trying to fool you into thinking that he is giving facts. Jim wasn't trying to fool his readers in his news item. He just got so carried away with his feelings about the court that he started giving his opinions instead of facts.

Sometimes a writer puts at the beginning of a statement a word or group of words such as *Possibly, Apparently, It seems that, It is probable that,* or *In the author's judgment.* Often, but not always, he does this to tell you that the statement he is starting to make is a statement of opinion.

Whenever you read anything which gives information, always check carefully to see whether that information is presented as facts or whether it is just the writer's opinion.

Talking together

Help your class answer these questions:

1. Why do you think the editor would not put Jim's news item in the newspaper?
2. What do we mean when we say that a statement gives information as facts? What do we mean when we say that it gives information as opinion?
3. Which words in the second paragraph of Jim's news item show that he is giving his opinions?
4. What could Jim have said in his second paragraph so that his opinions play a smaller part than they do?
5. What could you add in Jim's first paragraph so that it gives opinions as well as facts?

6. What statement can you make now about something so that you give information as facts? What statement can you make that gives information as opinion?

To do by yourself

Some of the following sentences are stated as facts, and others are stated as opinions. Write F in front of each sentence that gives information as fact. Write O in front of each sentence that gives information as opinion.

_____ 1. The average yearly temperature in Florida is higher than the average yearly temperature in Minnesota.
_____ 2. The weather in Florida is more enjoyable than the weather in Minnesota.
_____ 3. Telephone and electric poles are often placed beside the road.
_____ 4. The countryside would look much better if there were no poles beside the road.
_____ 5. Alaska, the largest state, has the smallest population.
_____ 6. Hawaii is the last state admitted to the Union.
_____ 7. Elementary school pupils should spend more time studying geography.
_____ 8. Probably pupils who save their allowances will also save much of their salaries when they grow up.
_____ 9. A football game is more fun to watch than a baseball game.
_____ 10. There are more players on a football team than there are on a baseball team.

If you are asked to do so, tell your class which sentences you marked F and why you think they are statements of fact. Tell also why you think each sentence you marked O is a statement of opinion.

2. Providing Practice in Using the Skill

Pupils should be encouraged to differentiate between statements of fact and statements of opinion in much of the informative reading that they do. For example, after that skill has been introduced to them, you can select appropriate short passages from their content books which contain statements that are basically opinion. Have the pupils read these statements to select the words or phrases which led them to conclude that they were statements of opinion, then discuss with them how such words and phrases serve as guideposts in indicating opinion. Pupils who are having difficulty may be asked to rewrite selected sentences from their books leaving out or rewording the parts which are basically opinion.

Pupils who are capable of going beneath the issue of opinion or fact, as suggested in the diagram on page 385, should be encouraged to do so in relation to some content area that they are exploring and that is of particular interest to them. For example, the entire class may be studying a social studies unit on communication, with some pupils working on the subtopic of television. As they search for information on television, they may come across an article contending that the United States should have nationalized television just as some other countries do. A pupil who is interested in pursuing this matter can be helped to see the importance of asking questions like the following: What is opinion and what is stated as fact in the article? Are the opinions backed by supporting evidence in the article? What else do I need to find out in order to determine whether the supporting evidence and statements of fact are true or false? Has the author left out any important points which should be considered in reaching a decision? Are the points that he has presented relevant to television in our country?

Other specific activities that you can use to give pupils needed practice include the following:

a. Write brief stories or descriptions like those in Jim's story and have your pupils indicate which sentences contain statements given as opinion.

b. Write sentences similar to the ten given under "To do by yourself" in the illustrative lesson and have pupils indicate whether each sentence is opinion or fact.

c. Have your pupils bring editorials from your local paper or the school paper and examine the style that differentiates them from news stories.

d. Bring selections written by different columnists and have your pupils note whether the writers express their opinions about issues. If possible, find columns which represent different opinions on the same issue or compare a columnist's comments on an event with a news report on the same event.

e. Have your pupils read and compare a biography of a famous person with a fictionalized story about that person.

Recognizing Assumptions and Vague Expressions

Sometimes, in reading a selection critically, the reader needs to determine just what if any assumptions serve as a basis for the writer's statements. Can you do that with the brief and hypothetical but rather representative passage which follows?

Since it has become evident that health care in this country is markedly inferior to that in many other countries, the need for medical reform has become increasingly evident. As we search for causes of the vast gap between medical knowledge and medical application, we should look first at the physicians' professional organization, which automatically rejects any ideas coming from outside.

Now examine each of the assumptions that the writer of the passage made:

1. Health care in this country is markedly below that in many other countries. The writer offers no evidence for this assumption. Instead, he states it offhandedly and then proceeds to build his arguments on this unsupported foundation. Although an author does not have to present background evidence for every statement he makes, he does have an obligation to support one from which additional generalizations are drawn.

2. There is a vast gap between medical knowledge and medical application. By focusing the reader's attention on supposed causes in the first part of the sentence, the writer attempts to distract him from noting that the writer, once again, is making an unsupported assumption.

3. The physicians' professional organization automatically rejects ideas. This assumption is glibly made but unsupported by the writer.

So where are you now? If you are unwilling to accept the assumptions, which are completely unsupported, you are left with only equally unsupported opinions of the author. It is surprising how many selections are replete with stated and unstated assumptions such as these. A pupil can and should be taught to watch for them in his reading of material which is supposed to be informative.

Sometimes a writer tries to convince a reader by using words and groups of words which are vague in the sense that they have no definite referents in the setting he depicts. Can you find such expressions in the following paragraph? (Please bear in mind that this example and others in subsequent sections of this chapter might well be expected to appear in larger context in conventional writing. For purposes of illustration, however, you should treat them as separate and complete entities with neither more nor less information available to the reader.)

> The progress we have made in recent years has made us the envy of the world. Not satisfied with resting on our well-earned laurels, we have dedicated ourselves to even more fantastic advances which are compatible with our way of life in the new era that dawns ahead of us.

The paragraph may be overloaded with vague expressions, but it is no more so than many you encounter. The cumulative effect of *progress, well-earned laurels, dedicated, fantastic advances, our way of life, the new era,* and *dawns ahead of us* is, in the setting depicted, a brief inspirational paragraph that could easily tempt a reader to make an incorrect conclusion and that could refer to almost anything. Do the vague expressions tempt you to support whatever the writer may be talking about? Is he talking about a company that manufactures soap? A service such as medicine, law, or education? Or, perhaps, the progress of a country? If so, what country? Far too many statements that are presented in informative reading matter are full of just such terms. The reader must learn to recognize them for what they are in a given setting rather than to accept them passively.

1. Introducing the Item

The following material, addressed to the pupil, exemplifies one way of showing him how to recognize assumptions. Introducing the recognition of vague expressions can follow the same general procedure.

To read and think over

Do you know what an assumption is? The word may be new to you, but the chances are that you have been making assumptions or reading assumptions for a long time without knowing it. An assumption is a statement that is taken for granted. It is something that is accepted as being true whether it is true or not. Let's look at a few sentences which contain assumptions and try to decide what those assumptions are.

1. Since the water must be cold, I will not go swimming.
2. Danny will not try out for the team because he can't learn to block.
3. The coach's mistakes lost the ball game for us.

In sentence 1 the assumption is stated and followed by a statement of fact based on that assumption. It says that I won't go swimming because the water must be cold. I am stating that the water must be cold, whether it is or not. It may or may not be, but I am accepting it as a statement of fact. I am *assuming* that the water is cold. This is the assumption that is made in the sentence.

Look now at sentence 2. Here, again, I have an assumption that is stated, but this one comes at the end of the sentence. I start out by stating that Danny won't try out for the team and then I make the assumption that he can't learn to block. The assumption is given as the reason that he won't try out, but the assumption may or may not be true. I am *assuming* that he can't learn.

In sentence 3, the assumption is not quite so clear. If you will look back at the first two sentences you will note that the assumptions were introduced with the words *since* and *because*, but sentence 3 doesn't have a word like that to help you see what the assumption is. Here the assumption isn't even stated. Can you tell what it is?

The assumption in sentence 3 is that the coach actually made mistakes. It might have been written, *Because of the coach's mistakes, we lost the ball game.* Then the assumption would have been more easily picked out. However, when a writer doesn't even state his assumption, as in sentence 3, there is a better chance that you may just go ahead and accept it without examining it. If this is what he wants you to do, he may hide it, as is done here.

Here are three more sentences which have assumptions. Can you decide what the assumptions are?

4. Since Sam can't learn Spanish, he says that he won't go to Mexico.
5. After our team wins the game, we will celebrate.
6. Having studied this carefully, you should be able to recognize assumptions.

Talking together

Help your class answer these questions:

1. What words make up the assumption in sentence 1? In sentence 2? In sentence 3?
2. Are the assumptions in the first three sentences true?
3. What would you say to make the assumption in sentence 1 a statement of fact?
4. What additional information would you need for sentence 3 to know whether the assumption was true?
5. What is the assumption in sentence 4? Can you tell whether the assumption is true? What would you have to know in order to tell whether it is false?
6. What is the assumption in sentence 5? Can you change that sentence so the assumption becomes a statement of fact?
7. What is the assumption in sentence 6? Can you tell whether this assumption is true or, instead, false?

To do by yourself

There is an assumption in each of the following sentences. On a separate sheet of paper, number from 1 through 5 and write after each number the assumption that has been made in the sentence which has the same number.

1. When we have finished these lessons, we will check our papers.
2. Jack will try out for the team after he gets his ball for Christmas.
3. Since it is going to rain, I will not go fishing this afternoon.
4. The interest you showed in your homework helped you to get that good grade.
5. After Mary practices fast reading next summer, she will be able to read faster in the fall.

If you are asked to do so, tell what the assumption in each of the five sentences is.

Look back at sentence 5 in the last part of the foregoing illustrative lesson. Do you see two assumptions in it? The most obvious one is that Mary *will* practice fast reading next summer. The second, which involves a cause-and-effect relationship, is that practicing fast reading will actually lead to faster reading later on. If a pupil points out the assumption in such statements, either of the two would be correct. Probably some of the faster pupils will note the existence of two assumptions in such statements. If those assumptions are not recognized but you believe your pupils are mature enough to find them, you should help them examine such statements more thoroughly.

2. Providing Practice in Using the Skill

Much informative reading matter contains both assumptions and vague expressions, yet not many of these are likely to appear in social studies, science, and other content textbooks. However, the chances are good that some may be found there. To help your pupils get needed practice in recognizing assumptions and vague expressions, go through some of the subject matter materials you use and select statements which should be examined for these features. When the pupils read these parts, call their attention to the statements that you have selected and discuss with them the assumptions and vague expressions.

Pupils are more likely to come across unsupported assumptions or vague expressions in their outside reading. For example, newspapers and newsmagazines are fruitful sources for such items. You can have the pupils copy statements from these publications and bring them to class for discussion. Some statements may be duplicated, and pupils can be asked to react to them on paper before they are discussed. This procedure insures that even the slowest members of the class will have a chance to give statements some thought before the correct answers are brought up.

In addition to the subject matter materials and the outside reading materials, you can devise statements of your own similar to those which were previously given in the introductory lesson. Making such statements is not difficult, and a collection, once made, can be modified and used year after year. This is a good way to tailor the statements to the maturity of your pupils. For example, slower-learning pupils may need statements written in a simpler vocabulary and containing more obvious assumptions than will fast learners.

Recognizing Propaganda Techniques

Propaganda techniques as elements to be observed in reading informative material critically seldom appear there unaccompanied by other elements explored in this chapter. For example, an article heavily loaded with propaganda may include opinions trying to masquerade as facts, unsupported assumptions, and vague expressions. Yet it is evident that propaganda does not have to include any of these other elements and that writings which are basically expressions of opinion or which are overabundant in either unsupported assumptions or vague expressions are not necessarily propaganda. Even though these various elements are not mutually exclusive, they can be examined individually.

Broadly conceived, any piece of printed propaganda is simply an attempt to persuade the reader to accept a given proposition or to engage in a given action. Sometimes the suggested proposition or action is a sensible and desirable one and is presented in a straightforward and objective manner. The term does not necessarily include deceit or recommend action which would be detrimental to the reader. Often, however, the proposition or action is highly questionable, one which could be detrimental to the reader and others, and its presentation is intended to be misleading if not deceitful. Hence, in common usage, propaganda has come to have rather unpleasant connotations, and when many people say that something is only propaganda, their intent is to discredit it and to imply that accepting the suggested proposition or following the suggested action will be detrimental.

There are several propaganda techniques designed to influence the reader. For example, testimonials, emotive language, repetition, and name-calling are generally classified as techniques of propaganda along with various kinds of half-truths and outright lies. Since propaganda takes so many forms, it is usually difficult to describe precisely. However, a reader who is bombarded with printed propaganda during a portion of each day can find many examples to aid him in learning to recognize it.

One means of sensing the propaganda intent of an article is to note some of the writer's descriptive words. Note the effect of the words printed in italics in the following passage:

> Joe Smith has been one of the most *fearless* and *determined* members of our state legislature. His *decisive, straightforward confidence* has often led him to *bold* actions. His *quick* and *aggressive* manner has also played a large part in his climb to power.

Do you have a mental picture of Joe Smith? What additional adjectives might apply to him in that picture? But take a look at Mr. Smith through the eyes of a different observer. All the words in this next description are exactly the same as those in the first except the eight which appeared there in italics. The eight new adjectives describe the same qualities but produce an effect that is somewhat different.

Joe Smith has been one of the most *foolhardy* and *inflexible* members of our state legislature. His *impulsive, brusque vainness* has often led him to *impetuous* actions. His *abrupt* and *arrogant* manner has also played a large part in his climb to power.

Is this the same Joe Smith that the previous paragraph described? It is, but the additional adjectives that you might use to describe him now would certainly differ from those that you would have used after reading only the first paragraph. Both writers have described Joe, but they have managed to give completely different pictures.

Certainly one of the most common and effective forms of propaganda is exemplified in most advertisements. Many people are conscious of the fact that they are propaganda and are probably aware of the techniques used in them to entice the reader to rush out and buy — almost anything. Nevertheless, some persons still are moved to foolish actions because of their inability to read as critically as they should. For example, the following numbered items are representative statements taken from a daily newspaper:

1. "Give them the taste they deserve," topped by the picture of two very appealing children, would certainly indicate that any parent who failed to provide this product for his children was depriving them of their just rewards.

2. "This is the name seen on the shoulder pad recommended by most coaches" is a good example of the prestige appeal which plays on the desire of people to be with the majority and at the same time provides an indirect testimonial. The testimonial is by *most coaches*, although this expression is vague and impossible to verify, and the implication is that most people use this product, so you should, too.

3. "Pay less for a new Suitzmobile" is so obvious that it may not be fair to use it. But since it and its many cousins such as "You get more miles with . . . ," "Our tire is safer," "For longer wear try . . ." appear so often one must assume that they get results and, if they do, the lack of a referent — less than what?, more miles than what?, safer than what?, and wear longer than what? — has not disturbed many readers. Of course,

a reader may just buy the product because it is a good one, but it would be comforting to know that he has learned to recognize the omission of such referents.

1. Introducing the Item

The following material, addressed to the pupil, illustrates one way of introducing him to the recognizing of propaganda techniques:

To read and think over

John Spencer looked carefully at the ads that were all around him on the floor. He had been reading them with care for almost an hour now, but he still had a puzzled look on his face.

"What's the matter, John?" asked John's father as he walked into the room.

"I'm trying to decide about my new bicycle, Dad," answered John. "I have saved enough money delivering papers to buy one, but I can't decide which one to get. The trouble is these ads. Sometimes they help, but two of these just sound good without saying anything. Here, Dad, look."

This is what was written on four of the bicycle ads that John had:

1. We sell more bicycles than any other dealer in the state.
2. This bicycle has a double headlight, a carrier, and an easy-to-use coaster brake.
3. Our bicycles are nationally shown in *Every Boy's Magazine*.
4. This week's special bicycle is a lightweight, with quick stopping hand brakes and a spotlight.

Suppose you were going to buy a bicycle and you were using these ads to help get information about different ones the merchants have. Which two ads sound good without saying anything?

The first ad is trying to get customers by saying that the merchant sells more bicycles than anyone else in the state. This doesn't really give you any information about his bicycles. The merchant is trying to get you to trade with him because a lot of other people do.

Now look at the second ad. Does that give any facts about the kind of bicycle you might buy there? It does, doesn't it? You know only that, if you want a bicycle with a double headlight, a carrier, and a coaster brake, you could find it there.

Look at the third ad. What does that tell you about the kind of bicycle you could get there? It only tells you that whatever bicycles this dealer carries are advertised in a national magazine, doesn't it? So you still don't know about the bicycles.

Look at the last ad. What does that tell you? It tells you about the kind of bicycle the merchant has as a special, doesn't it? And it tells you some of the things which that bicycle has on it.

Which of the two ads do you think John was talking about when he said they "sound good without saying anything"?

Sometimes people try to persuade us to do something through the things that we read. This is called propaganda. All four of the ads contained propaganda because all four of the merchants wanted people to buy bicycles from them. But two of them told things about their bicycles, and two of them told only about their stores or companies.

When you read you should try to recognize different kinds of propaganda. When you do that, you can decide what to do.

Talking together

Help your class answer these questions.

1. Which two ads did not tell anything specific about the bicycles to be sold?
2. What kind of person do you think the first ad would be most likely to appeal to?
3. What is the purpose of the words *easy-to-use* in the second ad? Would you ever expect to see an ad that says a bicycle has a coaster brake that is hard to use?
4. If the bicycles mentioned in the third ad are really nationally advertised, what does that tell you about the company?
5. In the fourth ad, look again at the words *This week's special.* What do you suppose the advertiser is trying to get you to think by using those words?

To do by yourself

When someone writes propaganda, he often uses words which are meant to get you to feel one way or the other about something without thinking. For example, instead of saying that something is large, he may write that it is huge if he wants you to think that it is bigger than it really is. Most of us think of something that is huge as being bigger than something that is called large. In the following list pick the one word after each number that would most likely be used in propaganda and draw a line around it. Then tell why you picked each word that you did.

1. small	tiny
2. wash	scrub
3. spotless	clean
4. cry	sob
5. struggle	fight
6. jump	plunge
7. tremble	shake
8. want	desire
9. horrified	frightened
10. now	immediately

2. Providing Practice in Using the Skill

Since there are many forms of propaganda and since pupils come into contact with them frequently, they should be able to collect many examples to be discussed in class. These could be filed under appropriate categories.

Discuss the various categories of propaganda with your pupils. Frequently used categories are (a) *common folks* ("Senator Brown rose from the position of a common laborer"), (b) *bandwagon* ("More people use X Brand Mouthwash than any other"), (c) *repetition* ("It leaves your mouth clean, clean, clean"), (d) *testimonials* ("The World Series hero smokes Chokies"), (e) *snob appeal* ("For the few who want the very best"), and (f) *emotional words* ("irresponsible"). Since there are no commonly accepted categories, the class could profitably make up some. The purpose of categorizing is to help the pupil become more conscious of techniques of propaganda, not to determine precise classifications.

Because they are frequently most obvious, you may want to concentrate initially on propaganda techniques exemplified through advertisements. However, pupils should also become conscious of propaganda techniques in newspapers and magazines. Those who are capable of doing so, for example, could compare news stories of the same event as described by different reporters. You may find it profitable to compose brief descriptive paragraphs similar to the paragraph describing Joe Smith in the first part of this section, underline selected words, and have the pupils rewrite the paragraph with different words which could have been used by someone having a different point of view.

When local and state elections are in progress, newspapers generally carry a wealth of political advertisements which are excellent exercises for practice in recognizing propaganda techniques. For example, a candidate frequently lists his marital status, his service record, and other similar facts which may have no value in determining his suitability for the office he seeks. A collection of actual examples from newspapers, edited by the teacher to create an impression of anonymity, can be used for years with different groups of pupils.

Judging the Competence of the Writer

In trying to judge the validity of an informative statement, the reader can use his ability to decide whether the statement is one of fact or of opinion, to note the use of unsupported assumptions and vague expressions, and to recognize techniques of propaganda. Further, he can attempt to check the competence of the writer to make a valid statement on the topic he is talking about. In general, this competence rests on both the writer's point of view and his background of knowledge on that topic.

When a reader who is well acquainted with the publications of a given writer reads a new informative statement made by him, he often expects to find there a point of view he noted time and again in the previous writings. Suppose you know the writer Mr. Smith as a strong supporter of the President and a member of the party in power and the writer Mr. Jones as an opponent of many of the President's policies and a member of the opposition party. Which of the following statements would you say was written by Mr. Jones about the President's buildup of troops in Gumgobia? Which by Mr. Smith?

1

The President has shown the world that we will not flee in the face of danger.

2

The President has shown the world that we cannot be trusted to keep our promise of non-aggression.

Would you expect either Mr. Smith or Mr. Jones to be a disinterested observer? One must be on guard, of course, against overgeneralizing about the probable viewpoints in an informative statement. Not all members of a political party adhere unwaveringly to a party line, and there are a few who may depart from party position more often than they follow it. Similarly, certain columnists occasionally step out of character by taking a stand that is not in line with expectations based on their previous writings. However, such exceptions prevent one from always predicting the view of a given writer, and they do not destroy the desirability of anticipating his position and using this anticipation as one basis for evaluating his statements.

Sometimes a writer has a predisposition to react in a certain way to an issue. For example, the training and experience of two newspaper columnists may be comparable, but on an issue such as increased taxation the past writings of one indicate his probable support while the past writings of the other indicate his probable opposition. The reader, then, can expect to find a selection of facts in the works of each columnist which will buttress his support or opposition, and he could not read either one and conclude safely that the whole picture was being presented without bias.

The same predisposition is frequently found in the presentation of news items in newspapers and magazines. A newsmagazine, merely presenting the facts as perhaps a reporter and an editor see them, may and generally does influence the reader's emotional reaction to those facts. For example, the following is paraphrased from one of the more objective newsmagazines. The italics are used by the author to call your attention to those particular words.

There is current concern *in responsible circles* for the present direction of the movement. Occasionally even government investigators speak *in whispers* of those who are close to the leaders. The movement's style is based on *mystic* faith in ultimate success.

The words in italics all appeared in the report, but none of them was necessary to convey the facts of the report. To check this for yourself, read the three sentences again omitting the italicized words completely.

To try to determine the background of knowledge which a writer has on a topic that he talks about, the reader can turn to many sources — a biographical dictionary such as *Who's Who in America* or *American Men of Science,* a card catalogue, or to the *Reader's Guide to Periodical Literature.* In a biographical dictionary he may find a short and limited biographical sketch of the writer. As he reads it he should note, not so much the writer's family background, the name of the college or university from which he was graduated, his place of residence, or his title or position, but rather the extent to which he has studied or worked on the topic which his statement talks about. In a card catalogue or the *Reader's Guide to Periodical Literature,* the reader can find the titles of books and magazine articles pertaining to that topic which the writer has produced, and then he can read them if he wishes. A writer whose training and experience or previous writings show that he has made a profitable and somewhat prolonged study of a given topic may present now and then false or misleading information about the topic, but in general the reader can expect more veracity from him than from someone without those qualifications.

1. Introducing the Item

The following material, addressed to the pupil, illustrates one way of introducing to him the judging of a writer's competence to make a valid statement on a given topic.

To read and think over

Sometimes when you read an article, you may want to check the ability of the writer to make true statements on the topic that the article tells about. For example, if you were reading about how wonderful it is to be a pilot, you would expect the writer to be someone who is a pilot. If you found out that he had never flown an airplane, you might be more likely to question his ideas than if you found out that he had been flying for many years.

There are two things that you want to try to find out about a writer when you are checking on him. First, you want to find out whether there is any reason to believe that he does or does not have accurate information on the topic that he is writing about. You can't always be sure, but sometimes you can learn whether he is likely to have it.

Second, you will want to find out whether the writer is known for complete reports which give a clear picture, or whether he is known for reports which just tell one side of a story. For example, suppose you knew that a certain sportswriter was known to have opinions which were always opposite to those of a certain coach. If you read this writer's report of the coach's direction of a game, you might expect the report to have a lot about the coach's mistakes in it. You would not expect to find many statements about the things that the coach did right. If you know this, then, you know that you are probably not getting a complete picture of the game.

You may not want to check on the writer of each article that you read or you may not always be able to, but you should know that you sometimes need to do so. If you read two articles that have opposite opinions or information, you may want to check on each writer to get a better idea of which one is probably right.

Talking together

Help your class answer the following questions about the material you just read.

1. What two things may you need to find out about a writer?
2. If you were reading an article on automobiles written by a racing driver, what things would you expect him to stress?
3. If you were reading an article on strikes and labor problems that was written by a union leader, what kind of opinions would you expect to find there?

To do by yourself

Following is a list of topics that you might read about and questions concerning those topics. After each, you will find some information about two writers. Which writer do you think would give the most accurate information about the topic?

1. Which writer would you expect to have the most up-to-date information on new governments in Africa?
   Writer 1: A man who had spent five years studying governments in different African countries.
   Writer 2: A man who has written books about African explorers.

2. Which writer would you expect to give the most helpful information about how to practice different baseball pitches?
Writer 1: A man who has been a sportswriter for ten years.
Writer 2: A former pitcher who now coaches.

3. Which writer would you expect to be most in favor of having our government build more ships?
Writer 1: A man who has spent most of his life in the Navy.
Writer 2: A former pilot who is now a government official.

4. Which writer would you expect to be most in favor of more money for education?
Writer 1: A former teacher.
Writer 2: A leader of a movement against taxes.

5. Which writer would you expect to know more about the ways that forest fires harm wild animals?
Writer 1: A man who is in charge of a zoo.
Writer 2: A man who is an official in the forest rangers.

If you are asked to do so, tell which writers you chose and why you chose them.

2. Providing Practice in Using the Skill

Although pupils can get a great deal of additional practice through the use of materials used in teaching the content subjects, it is also desirable for you to prepare and use with them exercises which are expressly written to provide that practice, such as that in the last part of the preceding illustrative lesson. Note that the items there ask the pupil to make judgments on both the probable information possessed by the writer and the affiliations of the writer which may cause him to favor one position over the other. If any pupils have difficulty with these concepts, you may want them to use exercises containing only items of one kind for awhile before requiring them to judge first on one criterion and then on the other.

Following the use of such exercises, you may have pupils gather information about the writers of some of the materials they use in their school work. Writers of texts are frequently listed in various kinds of references. If such references are available to the pupils, they should certainly have the opportunity to check them for themselves. If they are not available, you might gather the information yourself and have it duplicated for consideration by the pupils.

A Concluding Statement

This chapter has considered certain insights and skills essential to the critical reading of informative statements which are within the understanding of most intermediate-grade pupils. Quite possibly other appropriate items could be included in a school's offering in critical reading. It is important to keep in mind, however, that no one can teach any item to any pupil merely by admonishing him to read his informative material critically. The necessary instruction on each item has been exemplified in the illustrative lessons and the suggestions for subsequent practice which the chapter provides. Attention is called once again to the fact that the critical reading of a statement requires that the reader understand the statement. Critical reading may be either an act of immediate analysis based on experience and information already accumulated or a later collecting and applying of the needed information. Obviously, as the pupil should come to understand, the whole matter of being critical of informative statements applies not only to statements in reading matter but equally to those in discussions and speeches, whether heard directly, or indirectly, by watching television or listening to the radio.

QUESTIONS TO BE ANSWERED

1. What four items pertaining to critical reading were discussed in this chapter?
2. What is the relationship between critical reading and comprehension?
3. What two major reasons were given for including critical reading as an important learning for the elementary school?
4. Must a person have previous knowledge of the subject matter of a reading selection in order to read it critically? Why or why not?
5. What steps does a mature critical reader follow after he has determined whether statements are given as statements of opinion or as statements of fact?
6. How can content textbooks be used to give pupils practice in differentiating between statements given as facts and statements given as opinions?
7. What are examples of assumptions which children might encounter in their reading?
8. What are the different techniques of propaganda?
9. What two things do you want to find out about an author when you are checking his competence?
10. Specifically, how can you apply the information presented in this chapter in your own reading?

MORE TO READ

Gans, Roma, *Common Sense in Teaching Reading,* The Bobbs-Merrill Company, Inc., Indianapolis, 1963, Chapter 10.

Harris, Albert, *Readings on Reading Instruction,* David McKay Co., Inc., New York, 1963, Chapter 10.

Heilman, Arthur, *Principles and Practices of Teaching Reading.* Charles E. Merrill Books, Inc., Columbus, Ohio, 1961, Chapter 9.

Hester, Kathleen, *Teaching Every Child to Read,* Harper & Row, Publishers, New York, 1963, Chapter 16.

Russell, David, *Children's Thinking,* Ginn & Company, Boston, 1956, Chapter 10.

Schettler, Clarence, *Public Opinion in American Society,* Harper & Brothers, New York, 1960, Chapters 2, 3, 9, 10.

Smith, Nila, *Reading Instruction for Today's Children,* Prentice-Hall, Inc., Englewood Cliffs, N.J., 1963, Chapter 9.

Spache, George D., *Reading in the Elementary School,* Allyn and Bacon, Inc., Boston, 1964, Chapter 9.

THINGS TO DO

1. Use the intermediate readers of any basal series to locate instances in which critical reading skills could be applied. Develop plans for teaching the skills in connection with those materials.

2. In history, geography, social studies, science, or health textbooks designed for elementary pupils locate instances where pupils could be helped to apply skills of critical reading. Design the specific teaching procedures that you would use to help them make this application.

3. Prepare seatwork materials for each of the skills introduced in this chapter. You may use as guides the sections entitled "To do by yourself" in the illustrative lessons, but you should also devise different kinds of materials to provide the appropriate practice.

4. Start a collection of clippings from newspapers and newsmagazines which can be used to exemplify and provide additional practice in the skills introduced in this chapter. You may need to rewrite some of the stories so that they can be used by children.

chapter 11

Improving Reading Through
Instruction in the Content Subjects

That the pupil's achievement in social studies, science, and other content subjects in Grades 3 through 6 is dependent upon his reading ability has been demonstrated time and again and today is accepted by most teachers. But the contribution that skillful teaching of the content subjects can make to the improvement of the pupil's reading during these years is not understood in many schools. Neither is the damage that careless teaching of these subjects can do to his skill, interest, and attitude in reading given the critical examination to which it should be subjected.

Skillful instruction in any content subject is carried on with the teacher's full awareness of the nature of the topics or problems which the pupil is to study, of the fact that whatever ideas the pupil acquires on any topic are constructed by rather than given to him, of the sensible use of the different instructional media through which the pupil can do this constructing, and of the limitations of the background, interest, and reading ability which the pupil brings to his consideration of a topic. During any one school year, this teaching centers the pupil's attention on a relatively few topics or problems which he can attack with some degree of success and which the teacher's fund of knowledge and the available instructional media can illuminate in some detail. Highly focalized assignments arouse the pupil's interest in the topics to be studied, help him build background needed for reading on those topics, direct his reading of much appropriate and detailed material on each topic, and encourage him to make use of skills which, as described in Chapters 8 and 9, are required in studying any problem through reading. Class or group discussions place emphasis upon helping the pupil clarify and organize ideas encountered in studying a given topic and stimulate him to read further on that topic. Furthermore, every sensible effort is made to bring reality to objects, places, events, conditions, situations, and other items which the pupil needs to consider, and much care is devoted to insuring that the ideas he constructs about these matters are correct, clear, and organized rather than incorrect, vague and disconnected. Such instruction can increase the power to read independently, intensify concern for understanding what is read, develop willingness to think critically about what is read, and widen the scope of reading interests.

Careless teaching of a content subject exposes the pupil to a relatively large number of topics or problems, no few of which are much too complex for him to cope with, which the teacher herself does not understand, and for which needed instructional equipment simply is not available. Too often, assignments are nothing more than the teacher's naming of pages to be read by the pupil in a textbook, without even the direction or motivation that questions to be discussed later could supply. The purpose of class discussions is almost entirely that of getting from the pupil an expression of what the textbook says. At no point is much of anything done to make real the ideas which the pupil encounters and is supposed to construct. Such instruction, reflecting none of the awareness and the ingredients mentioned in the preceding paragraph, is quite likely to be so superficial, perfunctory, vague, and unorganized that it serves as a fertile breeding ground for verbalism. Once the pupil falls prey to using language symbols without getting the substance which they are intended to convey, he soon becomes a non-demander of meaning in his reading, develops a passive and negative if not rebellious attitude toward reading, and is in no position to build an interest in reading on topics that should become of some concern to him.

Three important matters that pertain to the nature of the process of reading and that are crucial to understanding the pupil's task in interpreting printed matter in the content subjects need to be emphasized here. *First,* there are no meanings on any printed page. The various words and groups of words shown there are merely symbols that stand for meanings intended by the writer. Consequently, reading is not and cannot be in any sense the getting of meaning from the page. It is fundamentally the reader's act of making or constructing meanings that are as close as possible to those which the writer had in mind when he wrote the lines. Each printed word or group of words serves as a sort of trigger which stimulates the reader to think whatever concept he has built through his experiences and has associated with that symbol. Whether or not the reader can and will think the concept he needs to think depends much upon his background of experiences, what he has learned from them, and his interest in understanding the writer's ideas. No person can read a word or group of words that stands for a concept with which his experiences have not provided him, nor will he read it, even though he can, unless he has some desire to find out what the writer is saying.

Second, the quality of the meaning which the reader makes for a given printed word or group of words is highly dependent upon the quality of the concept which his experiences have enabled him to build and which he has attached to that symbol. If the concept he has built is clear and correct, the meaning he makes for the symbol can be clear and correct. If the concept is vague or erroneous, the meaning he makes for the symbol will have either or both of these same characteristics. Thus concepts that are clear and correct lead to the making of meanings in reading which are sufficiently close to those intended by the writer. Concepts that are vague or erroneous lead only to misunderstanding or lack of understanding of the writer's ideas.

Third, if the concept the reader has built and attached to a given symbol is clear and correct, the thinking which he must do in order to make the writer's intended meaning is quite simple. All he must do is to call that concept to mind. But if the reader's concept is vague or erroneous, the thinking he must do is much more complicated. Here, by using context or a dictionary as explained in Chapter 8, by listening to the teacher's oral explanation, or by employing other means to be noted later, he must alter in the right way the particular concept he does have. If he has not yet built a concept or has not attached the concept he does have to the symbol, he must use the same means to acquire what he needs in order to make correct meaning for that symbol.

It is the purpose of this chapter to consider only those aspects of the teaching of the content subjects which are most likely to affect the pupil's reading. These aspects are (1) selecting topics or problems to be studied by the pupil, (2) making reading assignments, (3) conducting study periods, (4) conducting class or group discussions, and (5) providing reality. Although the discussions are concerned chiefly with instruction in social studies, all of them are applicable to the teaching of any content subject. Nothing proposed in the discussion implies that any content subject is in any sense merely a vehicle for improving the pupil's reading, and it is hoped that applications of included propositions to the teaching of a given content subject will enhance both the pupil's reading and the instruction in the content subject itself.

Selecting Topics or Problems

The scope of the elementary school subject commonly called social studies has not been clearly defined, and the content which is most important for the pupil to learn through his pursuit of that subject in Grades 3 through 6 remains to be determined. Today most if not all instruction in elementary social studies seeks to help the pupil develop some acquaintance with topics or problems in history, geography, economics, anthropology, sociology, and government — as overlapping as those disciplines may be — which are judged to warrant his serious study. Thus the offering presented by one school — possibly quite different from the programs of other schools — may include topics pertaining to pioneer life in western United States, the effect of climate on people's occupations, the relation between the division of labor and the production of desired goods, the development of written language, laws pertaining to civil wrongs, and services provided by government. As Ernest Horn implied years ago,[1] the extent to which the pupil can and will read vigorously on any given topic or problem depends upon certain characteristics of the topic itself, the authenticity and suitability of the instructional media available for the pupil's use in study, the mental equipment possessed by the pupil, and the teacher's ability to illuminate ideas which the pupil must construct and to equip him for the reading and study that he should do. All these factors are to be considered in deciding whether any particular topic is to be studied at least partially through reading in Grades 3 through 6.

Topics proposed as parts of a school's offering in social studies vary in their remoteness, difficulty, and complexity. A topic can be remote in time, in space, in both time and space, and in its relation to the situations, conditions, and activities which the pupil encounters in contemporary living. It can be difficult because, in acquiring even a minimum acquaintance with it, the pupil must construct at the outset and during his study a large number of concepts which he does not as yet possess.

[1] Ernest Horn, *Methods of Instruction in the Social Studies* (Charles Scribner's Sons, New York, 1937), pp. 125–141. Many of the ideas presented in this chapter originated in Dr. Horn's work. Whatever errors appear in the author's stating or applying of these ideas are to be charged to him and not to Dr. Horn.

It can be complex in the sense that it reaches into many facets of living and needs to be clarified through the sensible use of appropriate community resources and the helpful parts of various school subjects, some of which are not included among the social studies. As will be noted later, remoteness, difficulty, or complexity is relieved only insofar as the skillful use of excellent instructional media makes real to the pupil what he should encounter but cannot experience directly, relates the topic sensibly to his present-day living, enables him to build concepts required for gaining acquaintance with the topic, and brings to bear upon his consideration of the topic appropriate and enlightening parts of various school subjects. When such relief is not or cannot be provided as needed, his reading on the topic is almost inevitably unmotivated and quite barren of meaning.

In studying almost any topic the pupil must construct ideas pertaining to quite a variety of items: objects, events, places, personalities, conditions, customs, attitudes, movements, situations, and activities. The instructional media through which he is to do this constructing include, among other things, printed language, the teacher's oral explanations, pictures of various types, models, maps, and charts. In varying degrees, all these media are symbols of ideas to be constructed rather than the ideas themselves, and any one of them is helpful only to the extent that it represents the ideas faithfully and can be interpreted by the pupil. Judging by the prevalent use of language and the relatively small number of ideas which other media can represent, printed language and the teacher's oral explanations are the chief means of presenting the ideas that should be constructed. If the available printed language is limited to the condensed and summary expressions which can be interpreted only by persons who are already well acquainted with the topic and which necessarily make up most of the content of a textbook,[2] if the teacher's oral explanations are as inexact, vague, ambiguous, and unorganized as they are often found to be, and if statements in this printed language and spoken language are erroneous, the pupil has little chance of building correct and clear ideas. Furthermore, whatever fuzzy and mistaken notions he does acquire through these two media are — unless corrected — the very meanings he calls to mind later when he reads symbols which stand for the ideas he should have constructed. It is almost too obvious to mention that pictures of any type, models, maps, and charts which are not faithful representations of the ideas or which the pupil cannot or is not taught to interpret are also an invitation for him to resort to verbalism in his reading.

[2] Advantages and disadvantages of a textbook are considered later in this chapter.

Among the important ingredients of the mental equipment which the pupil can bring to a consideration of a topic are a background of experience relative to the topic, an interest in the topic, an ability to read and study informative material effectively, and skill in stating and organizing the ideas constructed. Any idea about a topic must be built out of the concepts already acquired through the direct and vicarious experiences the pupil has had in and out of school. If these experiences have been so meager or misleading that, as shown by investigations, even his present concepts of simple mathematical terms and operations, historical events and personalities, and geographical locations — basic to the study of many topics — are and remain foggy and unorganized, it is almost impossible for him to construct at least some of the ideas essential to becoming acquainted with those topics. When the pupil has no interest in a topic which he is expected to study and the teacher makes little or no effective effort to arouse such interest, whatever attempts he makes to become acquainted with the topic are quite likely to be perfunctory and fruitless. Without the ability to study informative material effectively, he is in no position to use that printed matter as the stimulation to constructing ideas which it can be. If he has serious difficulty in using language as a medium of thought and does not know or is not taught how to state and organize the ideas he constructs on a given topic, his study of it is likely to give him only ambiguous and isolated pieces of knowledge rather than the organized body of information which he should acquire. Each time he undertakes the task of becoming acquainted with a topic for which he does not have and is not supplied with the required background, in which he does not have and cannot generate sufficient interest, and in the pursuit of which he needs reading skills and language skills he does not possess, one can expect most of his reading on that topic to be desultory and loaded with verbalism.

To help the pupil develop through reading some acquaintance with a given topic in social studies, the teacher should possess certain assets which may be somewhat peculiar to that task. Knowledge of and enthusiasm for whatever subject matter included in the social studies and other school subjects is inherent in that topic are essential, plus an awareness of the problems, conditions, and customs in the pupil's environment. It is chiefly through this knowledge, enthusiasm, and awareness that the teacher can provide background that the pupil needs for reading on the topic, relate the topic to his contemporary living, and illuminate through oral explanations ideas which he is to construct. A thorough acquaintance with the pupil's reading matter and other instructional media available for his use and with devices for making ideas real is imperative if the teacher is to provide material the pupil can read, decide what background if any is necessary for doing that reading, help him make intelligent use of pictures, models, maps, and charts, and create an authentic atmosphere of reality for ideas which are remote to him. Awareness of and the ability to teach appropriate reading skills and language skills are required for improving the pupil's power to read and study informative reading matter effectively and to state and organize the ideas he constructs on a given topic. Last but not least, the ability to compose exact, clear, and well-organized English that the pupil can interpret is essential to the teacher's preparation and presentation of oral explanations.

At least four important questions can be raised in deciding whether a given topic or problem is one which pupils at this or that level should be expected to study. *First*, is its degree of remoteness, difficulty, or complexity sufficiently low so that the pupil, with whatever mental equipment he possesses at the time, can carry on his study successfully? Here one should remember that, as experience has demonstrated recently, some topics which at first thought appear complicated in one way or another to adults can be attacked successfully by the pupil who works under the direction of a well-informed and skillful teacher and that no attempt to teach everything about a topic should be made. *Second,* is the topic one through the study of which the pupil can acquire some understanding of conditions, situations, and activities that he encounters in his present-day living? *Third,* is the topic one on which the teacher is or can become well informed, about which she is enthusiastic, and in which she can arouse and foster the pupil's interest? *Fourth,* are the instructional media essential to effective study of the topic — including a large variety and amount of suitable and authentic reading matter — available? If the answers to these questions are in the affirmative, there is good reason to believe that the pupil's study of the topic will contribute to rather than handicap the development of his reading ability and interests.

In many schools, the number of topics presented to pupils at a given grade level during a school year, semester, month, week, or even a single class period is so large that effective teaching and learning are impossible. This crowded offering and the "hurry-up" attitude which it forces the teacher to adopt foster instruction that presents abstractions without providing through reading and other media the details required for making these abstractions intelligible. Under such teaching, ideas constructed by the pupil on a given topic are quite likely to be vague if not incorrect, the meanings he makes later for printed symbols that stand for ideas he should have constructed are misconceptions, and much of his reading on the topic becomes merely a means of resorting to verbalism rather than a search for substance. Since it takes time to make an idea clear to the pupil, since he does not and cannot construct an idea all at once, and since providing much illuminating detail is essential to his acquisition of most ideas, obviously the number of topics now presented during a given time period should be sharply reduced. If the teaching of social studies is to improve the pupil's reading, to help him build some real acquaintance with important topics, and to equip him with procedures to follow later in studying such topics on his own, is it not better to teach a relatively few topics well than to provide only superficial treatments of many topics?

Making Reading Assignments

Making a challenging assignment of the reading which the pupil is to do in his study of a given topic or part of a topic contributes much to developing his reading ability and interests. Such an assignment arouses the pupil's interest in the topic and often provides background for reading on it. It helps him state and organize questions on which information is to be gathered, which aid him in setting up purposes for reading, and which focalize his attention on ideas to be gained through his reading. It leads him to printed matter which he can read without too much difficulty and stimulates him to undertake his reading aggressively. Obviously the making of an assignment offering these advantages may consume one or more entire class periods.

Certain characteristics of textbooks in elementary social studies, as well as other matters of importance, should be considered before discussing in some detail the making of reading assignments. It is true that a good textbook does the following things, among others: (1) treats an array of topics which were chosen by people who are well acquainted with the content of the social studies and which the pupil can study with profit during a given school year or semester, (2) gives an overview of each included topic and supplies the pupil with authentic reading matter on that topic, (3) connects each topic with the immediately preceding topic and the topic that comes next, (4) provides a rather large number of useful pictures, maps, and other aids and connects these items correctly with the reading matter, (5) offers within itself and the accompanying teacher's guide valuable suggestions pertaining to the pupil's study, to helpful activities he may carry on and additional reading he may do, and to procedures and supplementary materials the teacher may use, and (6) serves as a means for reviewing or thinking in summary form ideas constructed on the topics studied.

Yet a textbook has at least four other characteristics which, if not recognized and compensated for by the teacher, can seriously hinder the improvement of reading. *First,* the textbook presents an excessive number of topics, many of them quite remote from the pupil, lacking in appeal to him, and insufficiently connected with conditions, situations, and activities in his contemporary environment. *Second,* the much too brief treatment of each topic is made up largely of summary statements that can be interpreted only by persons who know already the details on which those statements are based and which the pupil simply does not possess. *Third,* many statements included in the reading matter contain words and groups of words — perhaps, for example, *made fire with flint and steel, chinked the logs,* and *held husking bees* — which stand for concepts that are unfamiliar to the pupil and that are not explained by the reading matter itself. *Fourth,* treatments of topics now and then present other meaning difficulties — individual words which stand for strange meanings, strange figures of speech, unfamiliar uses of punctuation marks, difficult sentence structures, and poorly organized paragraphs — that the pupil is not yet equipped to overcome. Practically all publishers and authors of textbooks in elementary social studies are well aware of but do not condone these four characteristics, and they deplore the brief and abstract reading matter which lack of space makes almost mandatory. What accounts for the continued existence of the characteristics is largely the influence of persons who apparently believe it is better to supply superficial treatments of many topics than to teach a few topics well, who either ignore or minimize the amount of time and detail that the pupil requires for constructing ideas on a topic, who are not aware of the language limitations of the pupil, and who do not understand what reading is.

In most schools a basal textbook is about the only reading matter the pupil has. With its exclusive use the responsibility of the teacher to provide enough detailed oral explanation for the pupil to understand its summary statements is great indeed. In some schools, in addition to a basal textbook, the pupil is expected to read other textbooks which present topics included in the basal text. Since their treatments of topics are just as brief and abstract as those in the basal text, the additional texts contribute little if anything to either understanding of the topics or improvement in reading. Other schools base their instruction on a basal textbook and also provide detailed books and other materials which illuminate topics presented by that textbook. In a few schools no textbook is used;

the topics to be taught are outlined briefly in the social studies guide, and the pupil's reading matter is made up of detailed books and other materials pertaining to those topics.

The first six characteristics of a textbook as listed on page 412, the weaknesses inherent in limiting reading matter to that provided by a textbook, and the paucity and inappropriateness of much of the subject matter in social studies with which professional education has supplied most elementary school teachers are not to be ignored. Consequently, the author recommends that the pupil's reading matter consist of (1) only one good textbook and (2) much detailed matter on the topics included in that textbook. The textbook, to be chosen with great care, will indicate the scope of the topics or problems to be attacked and will give an overview of, a small amount of authentic reading matter on, and helpful visual aids pertaining to each topic. Thus it can serve first as a means of gaining a nodding acquaintance with a given topic and later — after this acquaintance has been broadened and deepened by digesting substance presented in detailed reading material, in class discussions, and in oral explanations by the teacher — as a résumé for reviewing ideas acquired on the topic. The nature, benefits, and selection of the detailed material which contains some but not all of the substance needed for extending acquaintance with the topic and for interpreting brief and abstract statements presented by the textbook are considered in the next three paragraphs.

The detailed material is composed of (1) general reference books, including encyclopedias, atlases, and yearbooks such as the *World Almanac*, (2) individual informative books, each of which supplies a wealth of detail on one or more aspects of a given topic, (3) appropriate poems, anecdotes, and lyrics of songs, (4) original sources such as documents, letters, diaries, and memoirs which for the pupil's use have been enlarged and vitalized without being made misrepresentative, (5) dependable magazines and newspapers, and (6) juvenile story books. Some of the story books are authentic in that they are faithful narratives pertaining to actual persons, events, customs, conditions, and the like that existed at a certain time in a certain place or that exist there now. The remainder are authentic in that, while they do not report about actual persons, events, and the like, they are true to the life of the time and place depicted.

Proper use of the detailed material offers several benefits for the pupil. It supplies much of the vividness, color, atmosphere, and feeling of reality which enables him to live in his imagination with the characters, events, customs, attitudes, and conditions in whatever environment he is studying. It arouses and fosters his interest in topics to be studied and in reading widely on those topics and, consequently, gives him the best sort of practice required for improving his reading ability. It furnishes specific and vitalized information which, as presented in sufficient space, combats the verbalism that would be almost inescapable if he were to use only a textbook. It allows him to become acquainted with general references in studying topics and with some of the periodical literature that can enable him to keep abreast of contemporary events and conditions. The extent to which these benefits are realized depends much upon possession and use of the skills discussed in Chapters 8, 9, and 10.

Considerable care should be exercised in selecting the detailed material. Each piece of reading matter must be authentic, and it must be intelligible to the pupils who are to use it. The range of reading difficulty of the total array of selections should correspond closely with the range of the pupils' reading ability. Some selections should be difficult enough to challenge the best readers in the class. Others should be sufficiently simple so that, no matter how easy and detailed their language and content may be, they can be read by the poorest readers. Few if any pupils should be expected to read all the selections which ought to be made available, and the teacher will need to advise each pupil on just which ones are suited to his use. Although titles of suitable detailed books are listed in some social studies textbooks, some professional books on the teaching of social studies, various guides to children's reading material, publishers' catalogues, and contemporary professional magazines, there is at present a great need for the publication of many detailed books which deal with various aspects of topics to be taught and which elementary school pupils can read with relative ease. It is unfortunate, too, that the funds most schools have set aside for purchasing detailed reading matter in the social studies are inexcusably low and that much of the meager material now at hand in many school and classroom libraries is obsolete.

The teacher's work in making a good assignment may and often should include (1) arousing the pupil's interest in learning about the topic or part of a topic to be studied, (2) helping him build whatever background he may need for reading on the topic, and (3) introducing certain strange words which he will encounter in his reading. Since the pupil should understand that what is to be studied is a topic or problem and that his reading is just a means of becoming acquainted with the topic, most certainly each assignment must include also (4) setting up questions on which the pupil is to locate, interpret, and organize information and (5) identifying references to be read on those questions. Now and then the attack to be made on a given topic may be so brief that only one assignment will be required, followed immediately by one or more study periods and one or more class or group discussions. Usually, however, the attack is of such length that it should be broken into parts, and an assignment, to be followed by one or more study periods and one or more discussions, should be made for each part.

The extensiveness of the teacher's work in performing acts 1, 2, and 3 in the preceding paragraph depends upon the nature of the topic to be studied, the pupil's present interest in that topic, the difficulty of the reading matter which he is to use, and his power to read independently. If the topic lies somewhat within his experience and is related to his present needs, if he has some interest in learning more about it, if his reading matter contains few if any strange concepts, and if he has acquired the skills discussed in Chapter 8, the time and effort to be spent on the first three acts may be meager indeed. However, if the topic is remote from the pupil in any sense, if he has at present no interest in learning about it, if his reading matter contains quite a number of strange concepts not explained therein, and if he himself is not equipped to overcome the reading difficulties he encounters, the first three acts may require much time, effort, and patience of the teacher. In any case, sometimes these acts may be performed in the sequences indicated or in any other sequence, at other times they may be interwoven and carried on simultaneously, and always, as immediately subsequent paragraphs imply, they should be completed before acts 4 and 5 are undertaken.

To arouse pupils' interest, the teacher may have the pupils read and talk over whatever so-called teasers the basal textbook supplies in introducing the topic. She can relate orally or read aloud a somewhat detailed treatment of a particularly enticing aspect of the topic. She can show and have the pupils talk over whatever appropriate sound film or set of film strips is available. She can raise questions about some contemporary event, condition, or situation which the pupils know well and which can serve as a springboard to the topic. Pertinent pictures and objects can be exhibited, explained, and discussed. Pupils may be asked to tell what, if anything, they know about the topic, or one or more problems referring to the topic may be raised and the pupils asked to tell what they think the answers may be. The most intriguing books which pupils are to read may be shown and introduced to them. It is obvious that in order to do these things the teacher must be well acquainted with the topic and the content of the books supplied for the pupils' use.

Helping a pupil build the particular background he needs for reading on the topic consists almost entirely in doing two main things. The first is to develop certain broad ideas such as events, conditions, and situations which lie behind and are essential to making correct meaning for printed matter on the topic but which are outside the pupil's experience and are not explained adequately in the reading material he is to use. The other is to construct specific concepts which are represented by individual words and groups of words in the basal textbook, which are strange to the pupil, and which are not clarified by either the textbook itself or the detailed material he is to read. The teacher's guides accompanying some basal textbooks in social studies identify broad ideas and specific concepts which the authors of those texts believe should be developed and offer suggestions pertaining to procedures to be followed. But since these identifications and suggestions are made with practically all pupils in mind, each teacher must be so well acquainted with the topic, her pupils' experiences, and the content of the textbook and the detailed material that she can decide just which broad ideas and specific concepts need to be developed for those particular pupils. Here it is easy to spend more time and effort than is necessary. Often there is no point in developing broad ideas and specific concepts which, although treated meagerly in the basal textbook, are explained adequately in the detailed reading material.

The four numbered paragraphs that follow describe briefly certain means of building background which pupils may need for reading on a given topic:[3]

1. Much can be contributed by the teacher's oral explanations. Many of these will necessarily be composed by the teacher from her fund of knowledge on the topic and the pupils' experiences and will be used by her in talking to the pupils. The remainder, appearing in detailed publications to which pupils do not have access or which for one reason or another cannot be read by them in the time available, will be read aloud by the teacher. Each oral explanation must contain considerable detail, and in composing any explanation, it is imperative that the teacher plan carefully just what is to be said so that vague expressions and ambiguous sentences are avoided and clear organization of ideas is guaranteed.

2. Some concepts, particularly those pertaining to objects and activities, can be developed by having the pupils observe critically pictures of all types, including illustrations in books, loose prints, film strips, and sound films. Care must be taken to use only pictures which are authentic in the sense that they present objects and activities as they really were

[3] Other means are taken up later in this chapter in connection with the discussion on providing reality.

or are, to prepare pupils for their observations, and to check through subsequent discussion their acquisition of the background the pictures offer.

3. One of the most fruitful ways of developing concepts of objects, activities, and conditions is critical observation of those items themselves. Examples are found in the direct observation of a copper mine, a pioneer fireplace, an Indian tepee, a covered wagon, a farm tractor in action, cloth being woven, fire being made by flint and steel, pom-pom-pullaway being played, refined sugar being manufactured, and wheat being threshed. Often direct observation requires excursions to places where the objects, activities, or conditions are to be seen. Such excursions, preferable only when they are more helpful than other available means, should be carefully planned and administered so that the pupil is made aware of what is to be observed, is led to make his observation intelligently, and takes part in a clinching subsequent discussion.

4. Probably the most effective means of helping the pupil construct concepts of activities and of objects inherent in them is to make it possible for him to engage in those activities himself. Typical construction activities, as they are sometimes called, are churning butter, parching corn, playing a pioneer play-party game, making fire with a drill, drying apples, making hominy, making paper, and drying skins. As will be noted later in some detail, each activity must be authentic in the sense that the pupil can get from it a correct or truthful concept. Insofar as possible the material and processes used in that activity in life outside the school must be duplicated. There is no place for the misleading artificial activities, such as making a tepee of paper, making a Pullman car of a shoe box, building a make-believe farm on the floor of the classroom, or making a castle of cardboard, any one of which shows the pupil what something is not or how something was or is not done.

Practically all of the strange words to be introduced before pupils begin to read on a topic or part of a topic are included in the basal textbook. Many of them are strange to the pupils only in print. Some are strange only in meaning. The remainder, including some proper names, are strange in form, meaning, and pronunciation. Surely, since pupils who have been taught competently will have acquired by at least the middle of the third grade the needed skill in unlocking independently words which are strange only in print, as described in Chapter 4, there will be no need for the teacher to introduce such words. If a given topic is presented after pupils have been taught, as explained in Chapter 8, how to use context and a dictionary to get the meaning of a word and how to use a dictionary or the glossary or pronouncing index included in the basal textbook to get the pronunciation of a word, there will be no need to introduce words which are strange only in meaning or words which are strange in form, meaning, and pronunciation. One should expect pupils to apply these acquired skills in attacking such words on their own as they read. Only when a topic is presented before pupils have acquired the skills just mentioned will the teacher need to introduce these words. Suggestions for introducing words that are strange only in meaning and words that are strange in form, meaning, and pronunciation were offered in Chapter 7.

Once the teacher has aroused the pupils' interest in learning about a topic, helped them build background needed for reading on that topic, and introduced whatever words should be introduced, the questions on which information is to be located, read, and organized should be set up. Here the teacher may begin by asking pupils to propose questions which they think need to be answered and which she will write and number on the chalkboard in whatever order they are given. To these she must add others which, from her knowledge of the topic, she knows the pupils certainly should consider but have overlooked in making their proposals. Then, as needed, some time should be spent cooperatively in eliminating duplicate questions and in restating questions so that they become more clearly worded and more highly focused than they were as given by the pupils. Finally, teacher and pupils should organize the questions in outline form so that main coordinate questions are indicated as such and subsidiary questions are placed where they belong. This stating and organizing of questions makes a reading assignment that defines sharply the points with which the pupils' reading is to be concerned, focalizes their attention on just what is to be studied through reading, and gives them criteria for selecting from their reading matter the particular information needed. Giving the pupils a large share in stating and organizing the questions strongly motivates the reading they are to do and helps them understand that it is the topic which is to be studied and that their reading is an important means to an end. The following material, composed by a fourth-grade class and the teacher during their attack on the topic "The Story of Travel in the United States," refers to one problem or part of that topic and illustrates the stating and organizing of questions on which reading was to be done:

Problem Four: What Were the First Railroads Like?

I. What trains were used before the first steam locomotives were built?
   A. How were the cars moved along the track?
   B. What were the cars like?

    C. On what railroad were these trains used and how fast did they travel?

    D. Why were these first trains unsuccessful?

  II. What were the first steam locomotives used?

    A. What locomotives were brought from England? What did they look like? Why were they not successful?

    B. Who built the Tom Thumb? What did it look like? What famous race did it have?

    C. What was the first locomotive built for regular use on a railroad? What happened to it?

 III. What were the first tracks and wheels like?

    A. What were they made of?

    B. What troubles did the tracks and wheels cause?

    C. What was used on the front of locomotives to push things off the track?

 IV. Why were the coaches uncomfortable?

    A. How were they heated and lighted?

    B. What was used to keep out bad weather?

    C. What caused the passengers to be tossed up and down in their seats and to be jolted about so much?

    D. What was the De Witt Clinton? Where was it used? What were its coaches like?

  V. What were the first sleeping cars like?

    A. What were the berths made of?

    B. What comforts did they not have that Pullman cars have today?

After the questions are stated and organized in final form for the study of a part of a topic, the teacher must supply the references to be read. They will include the basal textbook and whatever general references and other detailed materials are available and pertinent. It is important here to cite references in such a way that the pupils get to the appropriate reading matter in those sources as quickly as possible and at the same time acquire practice in locating such information independently through the use of the index, as discussed in Chapter 9. To this end, it is probably good procedure to list for each major question (1) the title of and the numbers of the pages to be read in each of the most useful references and (2) the titles of other references without naming the numbers of the pages to be read. In addition, it is good practice to cite no references for some minor questions and to encourage pupils to find relevant sources on their own and to locate independently within such sources the particular information needed. As stated previously, the range of the reading difficulty of the references which should be made available for pupils' use in attacking a part of a topic must fit well with the range of reading ability in the class. There must be some references to challenge the best readers and some which the poorest readers can interpret, and there is no sound reason for expecting every pupil to read all the references supplied. Indeed, it is often helpful but not always advisable to assign the study of each major question and its subsidiary questions to a different group or committee of pupils.

Conducting Study

Once the assignment has been built for a given topic or part of a topic, pupils may undertake their study of material bearing on the questions as stated and organized. It is understood that, depending largely upon the nature and number of the questions, the pupil's reading ability, and the amount of suitable material available, the time required for this study may consume either just one or two or more successive class periods. During this time, each pupil must understand that his task is to become acquainted with the topic rather than just to read pages, that he will need to locate, comprehend, think critically about, make notes on, and organize information pertinent to the topic, and that he should expect to work as independently as possible, using his last straw, so to speak, before asking for help. Obviously, the extent to which any pupil's study can be independent is determined much by the amount of control he has acquired over the skills described in Chapters 8, 9, and 10.

Some of the help that the teacher can and should give to any pupil during his study consists in offering certain suggestions relating to the material he is to read, his attitude toward this reading, and his preparation for taking part in subsequent discussion. *First*, often it is imperative that the teacher, with knowledge of the pupil's reading ability and of the approximate reading difficulty of each of the references listed for a given major question, recommend the particular sources which he should read. *Second*, every effort should be made to help the pupil realize that he should expect to understand what his reading matter says, that merely knowing what a group of words is without understanding its intended meaning is not the reading of the expression, and that whenever he suspects he has not made correct meaning for a given passage, he should make attempts to overcome the difficulty. Such attempts may include (1) interpreting whatever visual aids he has learned to interpret and the teacher has made available for his use in study, (2) reading another passage on the same point in another source which supplies detail he needs for understanding the original passage and which the teacher recommends, and (3) writing out questions which ask for explanations of what he does not understand and which he hopes will be answered in subsequent discussion. *Third,* the pupil should be encouraged to write out also other questions which come to his mind as he reads, which are not answered in the particular reading matter he uses, and which he wants answered in class discussion. *Fourth,* if the talking which the pupil does as he makes his contribution in class discussion on a given question is to be clear enough so that his listeners can learn from what he says, he must be encouraged during study to make notes on ideas he gains from reading and, as explained in Chapter 9, to organize those notes carefully.

Other help that the teacher can and should give as needed is directed at the solution of specific reading difficulties which the pupil may encounter and does not overcome immediately by himself. Among such difficulties are (1) unlocking words which are strange only in print, (2) getting the meanings of words which are strange in meaning, (3) interpreting unfamiliar figures of speech, (4) using the index of a book, (5) selecting from a page the particular information that is pertinent to a given question, (6) deciding what the topic of a paragraph is, (7) interpreting graphs and maps, (8) checking the validity of a statement, and (9) organizing notes. The nature of the help given depends largely upon whether or not the particular skill which, as explained in Chapters 4, 8, 9, and 10, is required for solving the difficulty has already been introduced. If it has, the teacher should never give the pupil the answer to his problem. Rather she should raise questions and make statements which stimulate him to recall what he needs in order to overcome the difficulty all by himself. If the required skill has not yet been introduced to the pupil, the teacher may need to give him the answer so that his study can proceed without unreasonable delay. Yet the fact that this baby-sitting is necessary surely emphasizes the need for the teaching of that skill.

All statements made in the three foregoing paragraphs apply to the pupil's study in almost any situation, whether he is working alone or as a member of a small group or committee responsible for reporting to the class information on a given major question. No statement in the immediately preceding paragraph condones the teacher's hopeful hunting for pupils to help. Neither does it support the interference which can result from the teacher's insistence upon helping the pupil when he is getting along all right by himself.

Conducting Discussions

Each group or class discussion that follows the completion of one or more study periods can do much to improve the pupil's reading. But to achieve this end, the discussion must be a learning activity — something quite different from a quizzing or checking in which the teacher merely raises questions to determine whether the pupil can recite words used in the textbook or express in his own words (whatever that may mean) ideas presented there. Surely the discussion, as the term itself implies, should be a considering of information on one or more of the major questions in the assignment with the purpose of clearing up difficulties and arriving at the truth. No doubt most of the available time should be devoted to appraising information given by pupils, correcting erroneous ideas, clarifying vague notions, and organizing correct and clear ideas about the question into the useful body of information which is essential to pupils' understanding of the topic and which subsequently will serve them well as background for reading further on the topic. The aspects of discussion that need to be considered here in some detail are the contributions to be made by pupils and the work to be carried on by the teacher.

During a discussion, individual pupils will give information which they have acquired through their reading matter and other aids and which is pertinent to this or that question included in the assignment. A pupil may or may not use the brief outline he made of ideas contained in the notes he wrote. Any piece of information that a pupil reports may or may not have been encountered by other pupils in their study, and at times a statement by one pupil may be in disagreement with a statement by another pupil on the same point. Whenever disagreement arises, each pupil should be expected to turn again to the source on which his statement is based, to read to the class just what that source says, and to help the group reach a decision about the controversy. In addition to giving information, the pupil should ask questions about items which he feels he does not understand or which were not told about in the particular reading matter he used. It is to be hoped that over a short period of time each pupil will become sensitive to the importance of giving information accurately, of presenting ideas in a well-organized form, and of asking for explanation whenever he does not understand a given statement or item. Since statements and questions which pupils speak expose erroneous or vague ideas that need to be corrected or clarified and can help the teacher think of things to say and do in order to make the needed corrections and clarifications, it is important for her to listen carefully to each pupil's talking.

During any discussion the teacher should raise useful questions that not only serve as means of judging the effectiveness of the pupil's study but also lead to the discovery of ideas which need to be cleared up, stimulate the pupil to explain this or that point further, help him to say clearly and exactly what he has just said vaguely, and enable him to recall what he already knows and needs to think now in order to answer a preceding question. Such questions are not concerned with checking the pupil's memory of expressions in the textbook, do not point up trivial or barren matters or require stereotyped answers, include no misleading or tricky suggestions, and place on no item emphasis which is out of all proportion to its significance. Instead, they stimulate the pupil's interest in learning, lead him to expand his ideas, encourage him to think critically about what he has read, enable him to feel some sense of achievement, make him aware of additional knowledge he needs, and invite him to read further on the topic. It is understood that each question will be stated clearly, that the pupil will be given sufficient time to do whatever thinking is required for answering the question, and that the total array of questions raised will ask the pupil for both facts and judgments and will be well distributed among all members of the class. Perhaps it should be added here that permitting any pupil to act as chairman of a discussion — to do the work which the teacher can and should do — is likely to be futile if not dangerous. There are ample data to show that even the most advanced pupil in a class lacks sufficient knowledge of the subject matter being considered and of the purposes of instructional questioning to undertake this task. Further, such substituting of pupil for teacher tends to discourage other members of the class from raising questions which they need to ask in order to resolve their difficulties.

A large part of the time devoted to almost any discussion must be used by the teacher in correcting the erroneous ideas and clarifying the vague notions which the pupils' talking and the teacher's questioning have exposed, in amplifying information that the pupils' reading matter supplied, in filling in gaps which this reading matter left, and in relating ideas gained through study to the pupils' contemporary living. As will be explained in the next and last section of this chapter, some of this work can and should be done through the use of appropriate visual and auditory aids of various types. But because of the unavailability or limitations of these aids, often much of it must be accomplished through the teacher's oral explanations. Sometimes such explanations are presented by her oral reading of detailed passages included in references that are too difficult for the pupil to read. Sometimes they are short comments that she offers on or adds to statements made by pupils. More often than is customary, they should be somewhat lengthy talks that are well planned and timed, that are composed of authentic and detailed substance, and that are intelligible to the pupil. There is no place in these talks for the incorrect ideas, vague language, and poor organization of thought that are not at all uncommon in much instructional talking and that make it almost impossible for the pupil to construct from oral explanations the ideas which he needs to build. This brief plea for the use of extended oral explanations by the teacher may not be viewed with sympathy by those persons who believe that most teachers talk too much in school. Yet there need be no great concern here. In the United States, the great trouble with most elementary teachers' talking is not its amount but its inclusion of incorrect ideas, its vagueness, its ambiguity, and its lack of clean-cut organization. One is tempted to wish that elementary teachers in the United States were as well versed in subject matter and as skillful in communicating ideas to pupils through talk as many elementary teachers in most European schools are.

No discussion of a major question included in the assignment can be considered complete until time has been spent in organizing the ideas which have been accumulated on that question in various ways, even though it requires an extra class period. Often this organizing should be done by teacher and pupils working together to state the various main ideas and subordinate ideas in an outline form which shows their interrelationships. Sometimes each pupil may make such an outline by himself. Or, assuming that he has been taught how to do so, he may write out a summary which presents the organization he needs to understand. The organizing recommended by this paragraph can prevent the pupil's thinking only a hodgepodge of isolated and unrelated ideas whenever he encounters the question or topic subsequently. It is essential to his acquisition of the well-organized body of information he needs as background for further reading on the topic.

The effectiveness of any discussion is necessarily conditioned by the extent to which the pupils are acquainted with and apply standards to be followed in talking with others. Such standards, which it is hoped the school develops probably through the instruction it provides in elementary English, include at least the following:

1. Keep to the problem or question of the discussion. Make each thing you say tell or ask something about that problem or question.

2. Talk only when no one else is talking.

3. Take part in the discussion by telling interesting things and by asking questions.

4. Give others a chance to talk. Do not talk too often or too long at a time.

5. Help others to take part by asking for their ideas or by raising questions which you know they can answer.

6. Listen to what others say. What they say can help you think of things to tell or ask.

7. If someone says something you do not understand, ask him to explain what he means.

8. Be polite when you say that you disagree with something that another person says.

9. Do not interrupt someone who is talking unless it is necessary to do so. When it is, do the interrupting politely.

10. When a boy and a girl begin talking at the same time, the boy should stop and let the girl finish what she started to say.

11. When a boy or a girl and an older person begin talking at the same time, the boy or girl should stop and let the older person finish what he started to say.

12. When two boys or two girls begin talking at the same time, both should stop and decide between them who should continue talking first.

13. When you talk, say what you have to say as clearly and exactly as you can so that others can understand just what you mean.

Providing Reality

As stated previously in this chapter, one of the major tasks faced by the pupil in his pursuit of almost any topic or part of a topic in social studies is the constructing of correct and clear ideas pertaining to objects, events, places, personalities, the situations, conditions, and great movements under which people once lived or live now, and the activities, customs, and attitudes of people. Thus in a very true sense the instruction to be provided on any topic should be concerned with helping the pupil live in the shoes, so to speak, of others. Necessarily much of this instruction must come through the medium of printed or spoken language, even though the marks that writers make or the sounds that speakers utter are entirely symbolic and have serious limitations. It is almost impossible for the well-informed and skillful writer or talker to present fully in words alone the ideas he wants to convey, and it is equally difficult for even the reader or listener who is quite skillful in interpreting language and who possesses much interest and appropriate background to construct fully from only words the ideas he needs to build. Since what words can say about any item — perhaps the stove that Franklin invented, the pioneers' making of soap, or the advantages of a democratic type of society — is much less than that item itself and since the pupil often lacks the background, interest, and skill to make language mean what it is intended to mean, additional media which supply a sense of reality that language itself cannot offer and which bring in their own right needed illumination of a given topic should be used appropriately and sensibly. Such use of these media can go a long way to help the pupil build correct and clear ideas during his attack on a topic, generate and maintain interest in the topic, and construct background essential in making correct meaning in his subsequent reading on the topic.

The additional media to be noted briefly in this discussion can be classified arbitrarily as (1) pictures of various types, (2) objects, models, and specimens, (3) maps, graphs, charts, and diagrams, (4) auditory aids, (5) excursions, and (6) construction activities. Rarely is the use of any of these media a substitute for either the reading which the pupil should do or the oral explaining which the teacher should undertake. Even with the phenomenal advance made in the production and use of visual-audio aids during recent years, there are still a number of items to which they do not refer or cannot be applied with profit. Almost all the media have certain values in common, and each of them offers benefits which only it can supply. Each is to be used at the most appropriate time and for the most useful purpose, whether that purpose be to build some of the background and interest required for reading, to illustrate the teacher's oral explanations, to aid either the individual pupil or the entire class during study, or to correct, clarify, and organize ideas during a group or class discussion. It is poor policy to use any one of the media just because it is available or to reserve its use as a reward for pupils after they have studied their reading matter well, listened attentively to the teacher's talking, and carried on a productive discussion.

All suitable pictures are intended to represent what the attentive pupil would sense upon encountering the reality itself. Insofar as a picture serves this function well, it can contribute meaning which enables the pupil to avoid verbalism, stimulate and give some degree of permanence to his interest in studying a given topic, and aid his retention of ideas on that topic. Motion pictures include 8 mm. and 16 mm. silent pictures and sound pictures, television and video tapes, and repetitive impact kits. Among projected still pictures are 2″ × 2″ and 2¼″ × 2¼″ slides, micro projection slides, 35 mm. film strips and sound film strips, and 10″ × 10″

overhead transparencies. Other still pictures, many of which can be used in an opaque projector, includes loose prints, stereographs, and photographs, drawings, and paintings presented in the textbook and other books the pupil uses. Since pictures which contain misrepresentations of items as they were or are can stimulate the pupil to construct erroneous ideas and to muddle correct ideas he has already built, it is imperative that each picture be authentic in the sense that it depicts the truth according to the most reliable information available. In addition, each picture should pertain to some important aspect of the topic being studied rather than to a trivial or minor matter, should emphasize the significant items to be observed and place unimportant items in their proper perspective, should be technically well made, and should have the attractiveness needed for arousing the pupil's interest and thought.

Certain points relative to the use of pictures should be stressed. To help the pupil build background for and interest in the reading he is to do, motion pictures, film strips, slides, loose prints, and pictures included in books can and should be used during the making of assignments. Loose prints, stereographs, and pictures included in books are particularly useful to the pupil in his individual study. Practically all pictures, with the possible exception of stereographs, can be helpful in correcting and clarifying ideas during discussions, and at times a picture used in making an assignment should be shown again during discussion to aid in the organizing and clinching of ideas. In general the teacher should acquaint the pupil with the fact that pictures as well as printed and spoken words are means of conveying ideas to him, that they tell part of the story he needs to get, and that they are to be observed attentively. Usually the teacher should view each picture first — particularly each motion picture, film strip, and slide — in order to plan comments which place the picture in its proper relationship to the topic being studied, point up items the pupil is to observe, and stimulate the raising of questions that the picture is to answer. To prevent the pupil's retention of erroneous ideas which he may build from his observing of a picture, just as he does in his reading, it is often necessary to provide for the discovery and correction of those ideas through critical questioning and detailed oral explaining after the picture has been shown.

The fact that the best use of even the most helpful pictures has a limitation must be recognized. Only a small part of what the pupil needs to learn about almost any topic is or can be depicted through pictures, and the service they can render is quite specialized. Even if all the available pictures on a given topic were at hand, they could not possibly supply all the instruction needed on that topic. Thus pictures are a supplement to or a co-worker with rather than a substitute for the pupil's reading, the teacher's oral explaining, and other media to be noted later. It is a serious error to use pictures when they are not needed, to use pictures which are irrelevant to the topic, or to permit the availability of or an ease of accessibility to a large supply of pictures to be the dominant factor in deciding what is to be taught about a topic or what topics are to be taught.

The use of actual objects, true models, and specimens can help the pupil gain a sense of reality in his consideration of some items and has approximately the same purposes as the use of pictures. In addition, the firsthand experience of observing, examining, and, when appropriate and advisable, using a loom or a pioneer spinning wheel, for example, can be more profitable than studying pictures of those objects. The same applies to study of a specimen, such as that of iron ore, raw rubber, or cotton, and to examination of a model, such as that of a harbor, a mountain range, or a cattle ranch, provided the pupil draws no wrong conclusions pertaining to the size of what the model represents. Each object, model, or specimen must have educational value which is much more fundamental than whatever appeal mere curios or relics offer. The teacher should be fully aware of just what items to be studied can and should be clarified by these aids, and both teacher and pupil should understand exactly what purpose any given aid is to serve. Usually the teacher will need to spend some time in helping the pupil realize his need for using this or that aid, in raising questions which the aid is to answer, and subsequently in having the pupil apply to the topic being studied what his use of the aid has made plain to him. Today in many school systems audio-visual centers house the total supply of these aids along with other instructional media and distribute them upon request to different buildings and teachers. In some communities officials of public museums encourage classes to visit the exhibits there and at times lend collections to schools. Often objects of historical value can be borrowed from residents of a community, and now and then the owner of an object can be persuaded to explain or demonstrate its use to a class. Some professional books on the teaching of social studies and some teachers' guides that accompany social studies textbooks list sources from which small objects and specimens can be obtained, including the names of manufacturers that provide samples of their products free or at nominal cost.

While an actual object or specimen is a reality, and a picture or a model represents a reality, any map, graph, chart, or diagram merely symbolizes and provides explanatory information about a reality. The use of maps is essential to understanding, among other things, spatial relationships, relative and exact location, size, and elevation, and the shapes of various areas. Graphs, charts, and diagrams present numerical data to explain relationships and developments in a form which usually can be read more quickly and easily than words supplying the same information. Since the use of these aids is almost indispensable to the avoidance of verbalism, it is indeed unfortunate that, as available data show, the ability of intermediate-grade pupils to read them is inexcusably low. That the pupil should be taught how to read different types of maps, their varying symbols notwithstanding, and different types of graphs, charts, and diagrams, as illustrated in Chapter 9, is beyond question.

The chief auditory aids which can lend reality to certain items that need to be clarified are (1) disc phonograph records such as some of the Caedmon records and some of those accompanying the Landmark books, (2) tape recordings, and (3) radio programs, whether they be predetermined or recorded broadcasts. These aids offer talks, songs, stories, and plays that depict some of the conditions, activities, attitudes, and atmosphere of former times and fit well with certain historical topics commonly included in the social studies curriculum. Each disc record, tape recording, or radio program to be used must be authentic, contribute to the learning of an item which is essential to understanding the topic being taught, supply help which other media do not provide, and should be considered as a supplement to rather than a substitute for those other media. As a rule, in connection with the use of any auditory aid, the pupil should be encouraged to listen attentively to and think critically about what he hears, and often a discussion should follow to clear up any misconceptions he may have built through that listening. Even though a disc record, tape recording, or radio program was carefully planned and spoken by experts, the pupil's difficulties in interpreting spoken language, as explained in Chapter 2, must be remembered. Furthermore, this talking has the same disadvantages which, the same chapter explains, are associated with that on television performances used as instructional aids.

Since some aids that are helpful in providing reality cannot be brought into the classroom or the school building, carefully planned and well-managed excursions are sometimes advisable. Thus a teacher and a class or group may take a trip to a farm, a museum, a store, a zoo, a creamery, a bakery, or a factory to observe or obtain direct contact with objects, pictures, models, and particularly the carrying on of activities or processes such as the manufacturing of beet sugar or the weaving of cloth. But to be of real benefit, any excursion must contribute to the pupil's understanding of the topic being taught, enable him to learn something he does not yet know, and supply insight unattainable through other media. Each excursion should be preceded by classroom work which establishes a need for and points up the purpose of that activity and followed soon by a discussion which applies the information gained to the topic being studied. It goes without saying that the permission and cooperation of the officials of whatever place is to be visited must be obtained, that plans must be made for the transportation and safety of pupils, and that the pupils themselves should have a large part in making these arrangements.

Engaging in certain so-called construction activities, including the making of objects and models and the carrying out of acts and processes, can develop a strong sense of reality for some items. Thus, for example, during the study of pioneer life in the early West, pupils may do things as the pioneers did them, including perhaps singing "The Sod Shanty," playing crack-the-whip, pom-pom-pullaway, or the play-party games "Skip to My Lou" and "Miller Boy," making a latch and string for a cabin door or a flail for threshing wheat by hand, oiling paper for cabin windows, making apple leather, hominy, butter, soap, candles, dyes, or a Betty lamp, parching corn, drying apples or pumpkins, curing a skin, and washing, carding, spinning, and weaving wool. By providing reality, such construction activities help pupils understand the topic being studied, stimulate their thinking, relieve verbalism, give life to items with which the topic deals, and enable the pupils to construct ideas which they will need for making correct meaning in subsequent reading they do on the topic. Yet one must remember that only a relatively small number of items to be taught in social studies can be presented through construction activities and that it is a mistake to use any such activity which is too difficult for the pupils to carry out, which requires more time than can be justified by what the pupils could learn, or which contributes nothing that cannot be learned just as well through other and more convenient media.

No matter what topic is being studied or whether that topic pertains to a historical period or to some aspect of contemporary living, the pupil should be led to think of each construction activity as a contribution to his learning of an item included in the topic rather than as an end in itself. Furthermore, both the teacher and the pupil should emphasize, not the manual, but the intellectual attributes and performance which lie behind and should be attached to the pupil's work. Above all, each construction activity must be authentic in the sense that what the pupil does supplies him with correct ideas about the item or items to be learned. Thus each object made must be true to the life and the time being studied, and each model, whether it shows only form and structure or is also usable in demonstrating function, should be built to scale and, when appropriate, illustrate the function correctly. Insofar as possible, each construction activity from which the pupil is expected to acquire an acquaintance with a process must make use of the same materials, follow the same steps, and produce the same product as the actual process that the activity is intended to depict. In addition, the significance which any process once used had in the lives of the people at that time should be pointed up, and when possible it should be contrasted with the modern process used for the same purpose in contemporary living.

From numerous construction activities carried on in some schools the pupil constructs false, fuzzy, or distorted ideas about objects and processes as they actually were or are. Such make-believe activities, supported by much loose talk and writing about the need for self-expression, the nature of creativity, the freeing of the imagination, and the development of initiative, are exemplified by the following: (1) "parching corn" by placing the grains in a shoe box and shaking them over a fireplace in which an electric light bulb burns under red paper, (2) making a "model" of the first Pullman car out of a shoe box in which paper or cardboard constructions represent the stove, the water tank, and the berths, (3) making with sticks and paper an "Indian teepee" that stands one foot high, (4) building a "castle" of cardboard or clay on a table and using silver Christmas wrapping paper to represent the moat, (5) building a "pioneer sod house" by molding a dome of clay, leaving an opening on one side, and placing pieces of sod on the top, (6) building the "layout of a farm" on the floor or a table and using paper or cardboard constructions for buildings, fences, animals, and fields, (7) making "Stone Age arrowheads and axes" of clay or cardboard, (8) making a "dugout canoe as the Indians made them" by using a pocket knife to dig out part of the middle of a short stick, (9) making "polar bears" by pasting cotton to paper or cardboard shapes, and (10) making "candles as the pioneers made them" by molding tallow by hand around a string. As implied earlier in this chapter, probably the best that such fanciful activities can do for the pupil is to make clear to him what a given object was or is not, or one way in which a process was or is not carried on. That they encourage him to engage in careless thinking, to disregard the need for learning the truth, to become interested in trivial matters, and to let his imagination run riot is beyond question. Of special import to the purpose of this volume is the fact that much of the misunderstanding which the pupil builds and the verbalism to which he resorts in his subsequent reading of social studies material can be traced to the false and distorted ideas he constructs through the use of such make-believe construction activities.

QUESTIONS TO BE ANSWERED

1. What particular aspects of the nature of reading need to be kept in mind in connection with the teaching of any content subject?

2. In what ways is the selection of topics to be taught in social studies related to the pupil's reading? What standards does this volume recommend for use in selecting such topics? Why is each of those standards important?

3. What things does a good reading assignment in social studies do? How can the pupil's interest in reading on a topic be aroused? How can background which he does not have and needs for reading on a topic be built? Why should the pupil have a part in stating and organizing the questions to be answered?

4. What are the advantages of a textbook? What are the disadvantages of using only a textbook? What different types of detailed reading matter should be used, and what benefits do they provide? What should be kept in mind relative to the selection of detailed reading matter?

5. In what way can the making of an assignment provide opportunity for the pupil to use skills described in Chapter 9?

6. What things should the teacher do to try to improve the pupil's work during the study period? What skills described in Chapters 8, 9, and 10 should the pupil be expected to use during study?

7. What do you consider to be the main purposes of the class discussion? How can erroneous ideas be corrected and vague ideas clarified? What should be done to help the pupil organize ideas presented in the discussion?

8. What should characterize the teacher's questioning in the discussion? Why should the pupil be encouraged to ask questions?

9. Why is it important to provide reality for the ideas that the pupil is to construct? What media can be used for this purpose? When should they be used?

10. What cautions should be observed in using pictures? Objects, models, and specimens? Maps, graphs, charts, and diagrams? Auditory aids? Construction activities?

MORE TO READ

Horn, Ernest, *Methods of Instruction in the Social Studies,* Charles Scribner's Sons, New York, 1937, Chapters IV–X.

Jarolimek, John, *Social Studies in Elementary Education,* The Macmillan Co., New York, 1959, Chapters 6, 7, 8, 9.

Michaelis, John, *Social Studies for Children in a Democracy,* Prentice-Hall, Inc., Englewood Cliffs, N.J., 1956, Chapters 9, 10, 12, 13.

Moffat, Maurice, and Hazel Howell, *Elementary Social Studies Instruction,* Longmans, Green & Co., Inc., New York, 1952, Chapters 11, 12.

Preston, Ralph, *Teaching Social Studies in the Elementary Schools,* Holt, Rinehart & Winston, Inc., New York, 1958, Chapters 10, 11, 13.

Ragan, William, and John McAulay, *Social Studies for Today's Children,* Appleton-Century-Crofts, Inc., New York, 1964, Chapters 10, 11, 12.

Smith, Henry, and Emerald Dechant, *Psychology in Teaching Reading,* Prentice-Hall, Inc., Englewood Cliffs, N.J., 1961, Chapter 13.

Spache, George, *Toward Better Reading,* The Garrard Press, Champaign, Ill., 1963, Chapter 16.

Wesley, Edgar, and Mary Adams, *Teaching Social Studies in the Elementary Schools,* D. C. Heath & Company, Boston, 1952, Chapters 17, 18, 19, 21.

THINGS TO DO

1. In one or more of the references above, read the particular chapter concerned with (a) reading in relation to the social studies, (b) the use of pictures, or (c) the use of construction activities. Then write out what you consider to be a fair evaluation of the suggestions given there.

2. Choose any grade level you wish from Grades 3 through 6 and examine a social studies textbook intended for use at that level. List major topics treated therein which you think should not be taught to a class you know in a school you are well acquainted with and explain why you think they should not be taught.

3. Choose any social studies topic commonly taught in the intermediate grades and write out in detail just what you would do and say in making an assignment for any part of that topic to a so-called average class.

4. Examine a social studies textbook and its accompanying teacher's guide to find out what reading skills, if any, those sources suggest be taught to pupils and what supplementary instructional media they recommend for use.

5. Choose any social studies topic you wish. Then in a school library make a list of the titles of detailed reading material you find there which you would make available to pupils at any grade level you choose.

6. Read the treatment that any social studies textbook gives on any one major topic. Then write out one or more of the following:
   (a) A statement of the background you would build in making assignments.
   (b) A statement of ideas you think you should and could amplify by means of oral explanations.
   (c) A statement of ideas you think you would amplify during discussions.
   (d) Questions you would raise in discussions.
   (e) A statement of ideas you would hope to clarify by means other than language and just what medium or media you would use in clarifying each idea.

7. Choose any social studies topic you wish. Then go to the audio-visual center in a school or school system and find out what aids are available there for use in teaching that topic.

8. Examine advertisements in magazines to get the names and addresses of manufacturers that supply free of charge or at nominal cost specimens or samples that could be used in making ideas clear to pupils.

chapter 12

Instruction in Children's Literature

As stated in Chapter 2, the program of instruction in reading which this volume offers has only two main objectives: (1) to help the pupil develop the power to read independently and (2) to stimulate him to construct an abiding interest in reading a variety of worthy material on a wide range of topics. Although most but, as will be recalled soon, not all of the content of Chapters 3 through 11 is directed at the attainment of the first objective, there must be no discounting of the importance of instruction devoted to the accomplishment of the second objective. Surely the extent to which any pupil reaps the benefits which reading can provide[1] depends much on the interest he builds in using printed matter as a means of gaining both pleasure and information, on the quality and amount of the material he does read, and on the significance and number of the topics he wants to read about. The pupil who builds little or no desire to read anything in addition to the meager materials which his school prescribes, who wants to read only material which lacks substance or is poorly written, or who is an avid reader of much material concerned with only one or two significant topics or any number of trivial matters cannot possibly realize many of these benefits and obviously has not acquired the selective and broad interest in reading that adequate

[1] See Chapter 2.

instruction can and should enable him to construct. Prominent among the results of the numerous investigations of the voluntary reading of both children and adults is the simple fact that this reading is by no means as large in amount, as selective in quality of content, or as broad in scope of topics as the school should expect it to be.

It is an interest in and a taste for the reading of much high-quality material of various types on many significant topics that the school should stimulate the pupil to build. A small amount of the stimulating that needs to be done is inherent in the proper use of basal readers and has been considered in brief passages in Chapters 5 and 7. Some of it is an important part of the teaching of social studies, science, and other content subjects and has been discussed in Chapter 11. The remainder is the main function of the teaching of children's literature, sometimes called the teaching of recreatory reading. Detailed suggestions for providing stimulation through the teaching of children's literature to first-grade and second-grade pupils were supplied by the last main section of Chapter 6. It is the purpose of the present chapter to discuss what the author considers to be the most important aspects of the teaching of children's literature in Grades 3 through 6.

Let it be noted at the very beginning that whether instruction in children's literature in Grades 3 through 6 stimulates the pupils in any given group or class to construct the needed interest depends a great deal upon the making of two basic provisions.[2] First, the needed worthy reading matter must be available. It contains not only the so-called children's classics but also old and new selections, non-factual and factual, including prose fiction, travel, history, science, myths, fables, legends, poetry, ballads, folk tales, fairy tales, drama, and nonsense passages. It is made up entirely of selections of high quality which have strong interest appeal for pupils, which pertain to many different topics of significance, and which cover a wide range of reading difficulty. Only with the use of much reading matter having all these characteristics can one hope to have pupils build a permanent interest in reading a variety of high-quality material on many different topics.

Second, it is imperative that children's literature be taught in such a way that the pupil experiences insofar as possible whatever a given selection, prose or poetry, has to tell. That is, the teaching or use of a selection should center upon helping him to experience once again whatever familiar incidents, sights, sounds, and feeling are portrayed therein and, as he reads, to combine, relate, or rearrange his concepts so that he makes new vicarious experiences for himself. Thus, for example, he

[2] These provisions are explained more fully later in the chapter.

sees mountains he has not seen, hears a waterfall he has not heard, or feels a pleasure he has not felt. Consequently, methods of instruction which prevent or do not enhance the pupil's experiencing of what a selection has to say should be eliminated. Procedures that require him to memorize poems which he cannot experience or does not like, the names of authors whose writings he does not enjoy, and the titles of those writings; to study such matters as style, the development of plot, the mechanical construction of poetry, and the lives of authors; and to look upon literature as something to be analyzed, are highly questionable. Only when the teacher realizes the import of the proposition that a given selection was written to be experienced by the reader, that instruction must move continually toward this experiencing, and that children's literature is to be read and enjoyed rather than regarded as subject matter to be studied or information to be retained can there be much hope for the pupil's construction of the interest in reading to which he is entitled.

The suggestions offered in the remainder of this chapter fall into two main sections: (1) choosing the reading selections to be made available to a given group or class and (2) providing the needed instruction. The former proposes and explains criteria to be applied in choosing reading selections for the pupils' use. The latter discusses certain principles to be followed and instructional activities to be carried on in doing the needed teaching. Certain other related matters are considered under each of these headings.

Choosing Reading Selections

Reading matter intended for children's use, including the thousands of selections now in print and those which come from the presses each year, is very large in amount, displays a variety of types of writing, and tells about many different topics. But by no means is all this material literature. Much of it is unquestionably shallow in substance, trivial in intent, and shoddy in composition. As used in the present discussion, the term *children's literature* is a name for all selections which are not textbooks or reference books, which can be read by boys and girls, and in particular which possess literary merit in the sense that their content is worth reading and is excellently written. These superior publications include juvenile books, narrative and factual, some so-called adult books that boys and girls can read at least in part, and certain passages in magazines and newspapers. Parenthetically, let the author express here both his belief that the writing of literature for children is a most worthy activity and his hope that really accomplished writers will produce soon for children's use much more material of unquestioned literary merit and high interest appeal than they have been inclined to offer during past years.

The selections to be made available in any class or group should feed the worthy immediate interests of pupils, introduce other valuable interests to be nurtured through reading, and entice them progressively through the year into reading literature that is more and more mature. That is why choosing the selections should be based on the application of discriminating standards and carried on with care. The following ten criteria are appropriate to this purpose.[3]

First, the total array of superior selections is composed of three main kinds of writings. Some of these writings are true in that they faithfully relate interesting events, conditions, and situations as they actually happened and, consequently, are significant portrayals of real experiences through which people passed. Other writings, particularly excellent prose fiction, poetry, and drama, while fictional in the sense that they do not depict actual events, are true to life as at least some people have experienced it and should constitute the bulk of the offering in children's literature. Additional excellent writings such as fairy lore, nonsense passages, and some humorous stories admit by their very nature that they are neither true nor true to life, nothing but pure fancy; they should hold a much larger place in children's literature than they do at the present time in most schools. It is to be noted here, as it was in Chapter 6, that children's literature has no room for the numerous selections which are poorly written and which are not but pretend — often somewhat slyly — to be true or true to life. Yet it is the author's contention that once someone who knows the difference between children's literature and cheap juvenile writings explains this difference in non-technical language to the pupil and he recognizes a given selection as an example of the latter, the harm which his reading of that selection can do to him is small indeed.

Second, each selection should have such a strong and sustained interest appeal that once the pupil has begun to read the passage — no matter how short or long — the enjoyment he finds there makes him want to continue reading to the end. True, a skillful teacher can arouse the pupil's interest in beginning to read a selection, but beyond this she can do little to supply him with the sustained interest he needs. The selection itself must carry its own interest-building load. Indeed, each line, paragraph, verse, scene, page, or any other part should be of such a nature

[3] Certain aspects of some of these criteria were considered briefly in Chapter 6.

that the pupil is motivated to read the next line, paragraph, or part. No one can expect a pupil to gain from reading a selection which is dull to him a feeding of an interest he already has, an introduction to an interest that is new to him, or a desire to read literature that is more mature.

Third, whatever new experiences are presented by a given selection must be within the range of the pupil's imagination. To acquire through reading a new experience such as the rush of a buffalo stampede, the rain on the roof of an attic, the aroma of burning leaves in the fall, or the fear of people on a sinking ship that a story tells about, the pupil must have had other experiences that allow him to sense, in the eyes, the ears, the nose, and the feelings of his mind, so to speak, the sights, sounds, odors, and emotions depicted. No person can experience any event, condition, or situation read about unless he has passed through it or has had other experiences which he can apply, alter, combine, or rearrange — and so imagine what the reading matter reports.

Fourth, the total array of selections should cover a variety of types of literature, including at least all those listed on page 437. A type may be represented by a single book, a part of a collection within a book, or a passage in a magazine or newspaper. Adherence to this criterion is essential if the pupil is to become acquainted with and interested in reading many kinds of children's literature and if classroom and school libraries are to become more satisfactory than they are today.

Fifth, the various selections must offer the pupil a wide range of wholesome and understandable experiences, no matter how remote those experiences may be in time or space from his immediate environment. What he reads about an experience he has already had can enrich and amplify the meaning and the significance he attached previously to that experience. All wholesome and understandable experiences portrayed that are new to the pupil allow him to extend his acquaintance with and interest in one or more aspects of life. Surely the degree to which children's literature can help enrich and extend experience and develop an interest in reading about a variety of significant topics depends much upon the range of the experiences offered therein.

Sixth, the various selections should enable the pupil to gain some acquaintance with life as it is lived by people of different races and countries. Thus through reading, he can acquire at least a little understanding of the struggles, customs, aspirations, culture, and outlook of different ethnic groups and nationalities. Actually, in the fifth and sixth grades the pupil should read translations of several selections from great literatures other than American and English. Quite probably, the applying of this sixth criterion provides a more realistic and satisfactory way for a pupil to come in contact with different ethnic groups than do the relatively minor attempts undertaken in any series of basal readers.

Seventh, selections should appeal to the different moods and satisfy the different purposes with which the pupil is likely to approach literature. Whether in a mood of cheerfulness, eagerness for adventure, loneliness, curiosity about a particular matter, discouragement or slight depression, boredom, lack of self-confidence, elation, or a desire to just loaf, he should be able to find a selection to fit that mood. He may be ready to experience a good story, rhythm and rhyme, humor or amusing nonsense, to get excitement, to mingle vicariously with the story characters or become one of them in his imagination, to find out about something of concern to him, to see how others live with a disadvantage or a handicap, to escape monotony, to see how others stand up to threatening situations, to relish the accomplishments of others, or to idle time away. That reading can feed a wholesome mood or interrupt the often insidious growth of one which could become harmful is hardly to be denied, but whether the pupil learns to take advantage of this function of reading depends largely on the breadth of offerings in children's literature available to him.

Eighth, through the portrayal of characters and events that are real and convincing, many selections should present examples of the operation of moral and spiritual values or attributes — such as gentleness, honesty, courage, kindness, sincerity, and perseverance — which generation after generation has become convinced are important for any individual to acquire and hold fast. But each such presentation should be made without moralizing and without being didactic, pompous, or self-righteous, should illustrate the natural and realistic fruits of the operation of a given attribute, and should be of such a nature that the pupil, with little if any pointing out, emphasizing, and certainly no belaboring by the teacher or anyone else sees the point for himself. None of this implies that simply reading about striking examples will endow the pupil with an attribute or value. It does mean that through reading he can become acquainted with at least some of the many different and often subtle expressions or applications of a given attribute and thus can be encouraged to behave in such a way as to make it one of his own dominant characteristics.

Ninth, all selections must appeal to worthy interests of the pupils. Not that pupils' whims or even their desirable interests are to be substituted for literary merit in choosing the selections. But among selections which possess this merit, those which appeal most to such interests are to be chosen. Many of the chosen selections will nurture interests which the pupils already have, and the remainder will appeal to new interests. Some selections, because of their high interest appeal and superior literary merit, can be used to entice pupils into reading literature which, in the sense that it is written with unusual skill, carries ample substance, and pertains to topics of much significance, is more mature than most of their reading matter.

To choose selections which fit well with the immediate worthy interests of the pupils in a given group or class, the teacher will first have to discover what those interests are. Here it can be quite helpful to interview each pupil, encouraging him to tell what he likes to do at various times and under different conditions, what his hobbies are, and what he thinks he would like to have, be, or do. Further, the teacher can carefully note the exposure of each pupil's interests over a period of time in his statements and questions in elementary English class as he takes part in conversations and discussions, makes reports of various types on topics of his choice, composes and tells stories, gives brief reviews of books, television programs, and plays he has enjoyed, and even gives directions and descriptions pertaining to matters of concern to him. In addition, one or more of the available inventories of children's interests can be administered to each pupil.[4]

Once the pupils' immediate interests have been identified, the teacher will need to decide whether this or that interest is worth fostering and, if so, whether suitable reading matter for fostering it exists. Since there are no objective standards to use in measuring the relative worth of an interest, the teacher will have to make here the best personal judgment possible. To decide whether suitable reading matter pertaining to a given interest exists, the teacher must have or acquire acquaintance with children's literature, confer with a librarian who has that knowledge, or consult sources to be noted later.

During the past forty-five years or more, scores of investigations have been concerned with the discovery of the kinds of material which elementary school pupils read voluntarily, the particular books, stories, and

[4] For examples of such inventories see Edward Dolch, *A Manual for Remedial Reading* (Garrard Press, Champaign, Ill., 1945), pp. 444–446; Albert Harris, *How to Increase Reading Ability* (Longmans, Green & Co., Inc., New York, 1956), pp. 479, 482–483; Albert Harris, *Effective Teaching of Reading* (David McKay Co., Inc., New York, 1962), p. 293; L. Thorpe, C. Myers, and M. Sea, *What I Like to Do* (Science Research Associates, Chicago, 1954); Paul Witty, *Reading in Modern Education* (D. C. Heath & Company, Boston, 1949), pp. 302–307; Paul Witty and David Kopel, *Reading and the Educative Process* (Ginn & Company, Boston, 1939), pp. 185–188, 316–321; Paul Witty, David Kopel, and Anne Coomer, *The Northwestern Interest Inventory* (Psycho-Educational Clinic, Northwestern University, Evanston, Ill., 1949).

poems they enjoy most, and the characteristics of selections they prefer.[5] Some of the generalizations which become apparent if not obvious when one considers these investigations together are the following:

1. Children read a larger amount and variety of material than many persons think. Some of this material is trash. Some of it is reasonably good writing, and the rest is literature. The important point here is not that children read some cheap writings, but that they do read some literature. No one can distinguish literature from trash unless he has had experience in reading both and learns in one way or another what the differences between the two are. It is a responsibility of teachers to accept the voluntary reading of pupils for what it is, to raise the level of their preferences, and to entice them into the reading of more and more literature.

2. Children's preferences in books and stories seem to be influenced by several factors, including ingredients of the selections, mental age, cultural background, sex, maturity, and the recommendations of other people. Boys and girls both prefer selections that contain excitement, action, suspense, adventure, humor, mystery, or surprise. The reading interests of children who are bright, mature, and come from cultured homes are rather wide and extend to selections which are somewhat mature, and pupils who have low intelligence, who are immature, or who lack cultural background turn to relatively simple and immature selections. Boys and girls both choose selections that are biographical, that tell about animals and nature, that relate adventure, and that contain humor and nonsense, and girls often read selections intended primarily for boys while boys seldom read those obviously written chiefly for girls. Selections preferred by girls more than boys tell about home and family life, school, careers, and early romance. Those preferred more by boys than girls tell about hobbies, science, history, and sports, explain how to do things, and appeal to hero worship. Exceptionally popular are the series books such as *Nancy Drew* and *The Hardy Boys*, read chiefly by only

[5] Results of what the author considers the best study of the reading preferences of children in Grades 3 through 6 appear in George Norvell, *What Children Like to Read* (Silver Burdett Company, Morristown, N.J., 1958). Examples of relatively recent and somewhat extensive investigations of the voluntary reading of pupils are Evelyn Thompson, "The Voluntary Reading of Children in Grades Four, Five, and Six in Houston, Texas," Doctor's dissertation, Colorado State College, 1956, and Annette Kelty, "An Investigation to Determine the Nature and Scope of the Voluntary Reading of Newspapers, Magazines, and Books by Intermediate Grade Pupils Attending the Public Schools of Rockport Centre, New York," Doctor's Research Study, No. 2, Colorado State College, 1958. An old but still important study of children's choices in poetry is Helen MacIntosh, *A Critical Study of Children's Choices in Poetry*, University of Iowa Studies in Education, Vol. VII, No. 4, Iowa City, 1932.

the appropriate sex, but also, even at this late date, are some of the old classics such as *Black Beauty* and *Heidi*. Among the books that children enjoy most are some but by no means all of those which have received the Newbery medal or the Caldecott award. A large number of the books that children prefer are obtained from public libraries, school libraries, book clubs, and friends and are recommended by teachers, parents, librarians, and friends.

3. Children read parts of juvenile magazines. While boys and girls both read some magazines in common, those publications obviously intended for one sex in particular are read primarily by members of that sex. Stories and jokes are the most popular parts of children's magazines, and the adult magazines read most often are basically picture magazines. Boys read most often magazines that tell about sports and mechanics, and girls prefer those which contain selections pertaining to home life, movies, and early romance.

4. The most popular parts of newspapers, regardless of sex, are comic strips, cartoons, front-page news items, sports, puzzles, crime news, and movie news.

5. Comic books are exceptionally popular and are read extensively, chiefly because, as pupils report, they contain light and entertaining material, relate humor and adventure, and can be picked up easily in various places at odd moments.

6. Prose is much more popular than poetry, and the most preferred type of prose is fiction. Yet many children read poems of various types and enjoy hearing them read aloud, particularly poems that tell stories.

7. The spread of children's reading preferences over different grade levels is wide, maturity is more indicative than sex as a factor which influences choice, and the great and varying individual differences in choices are more significant than differences associated with groups according to sex, age, intelligence, or cultural background.

In general, the results of investigations of children's preferences give the teacher some knowledge of what particular books, stories, and poems boys and girls liked best and of some of the characteristics of selections they enjoyed most at the time the studies were made. But they do not necessarily tell what particular literature, old and new, will appeal most today to the worthy immediate interests of any given class or of any member of that class. Consequently it is important for each teacher to determine the worthy interests of her pupils by means already explained and to provide literature which in her best judgment can feed those interests.

Each time the teacher undertakes to stimulate pupils to begin developing a worthy interest they do not yet have and can pursue through the reading of literature, it is imperative that she choose a topic about which she is now or can soon become well informed and enthusiastic and on which suitable literature is available for the pupils' use. Sometimes an interest is exposed by pupil statements and questions in class discussions, through reactions to what is observed during class excursions, or in responses to television programs seen in school. Sometimes the teacher herself thinks of a favorable possibility. To introduce any new interest, the teacher simply presents a topic about which, with her enthusiasm and fund of information, she believes she has a good chance of arousing and maintaining the pupils' curiosity. Usually this introducing includes making intriguing statements and showing objects and pictures that tell about the topic, getting from the pupils questions they want answered, and showing and telling just a little about at least some of the literature available for them to read on the topic.

To lead pupils into reading literature that is more mature than what they have read, it is necessary to provide for their use and to advertise to them selections which appeal to their interests, which they can read, and which, when considered together, represent what can be called a ramp of increasing maturity. Thus for the pursuit of any given interest through reading, there will be at hand a number of selections covering a range of literary maturity. As will be noted later, any selection of increased maturity can be advertised by one or more of several means, including a brief and teasing review given by a pupil who has read the selection with satisfaction and the teacher's introduction of the selection through showing it, telling a little about it, and reading an intriguing part aloud. Quite probably, in connection with this whole matter of trying to raise the level of pupils' taste for increasingly mature literature, the teacher, through referring to selections which the pupils have read, should point out the most obvious reasons why excellent writing is excellent. She should also explain in a simple way that some selections are true because they tell about events and conditions which occurred or are occurring, that others are not actual portrayals but are true to life because they depict how at least some people once lived or live now, and that some selections are purely fanciful, without pretending to be true in any way.

Tenth, and finally, the total array of selections to be made available to a given class must have a range of reading difficulty which fits the spread of reading ability among the pupils. The spread of reading ability is often quite wide, ranging, for example, in a fourth-grade class from Grade 2 through at least Grade 6. Thus there must be some selections which the poorest readers can read with satisfaction and some which will challenge the best readers.

To try to get some objective measurement of the reading difficulty of any selection intended for pupils in Grades 3 through 6, certain formulas can be used in examining samplings of its content.[6] All of them are concerned almost entirely with a few structural elements that characterize the composition of a selection and are at least somewhat related to children's comprehension in reading. No available formula is concerned with the background and the particular reading skills that pupils who might be expected to read a given selection possess or with the interest appeal which that selection has for them. Thus in applying a formula to a selection, one seeks answers to only such questions as the following: What is the number of different words included? How many of the words are polysyllabic? Are most of the words among those which word lists show are used with high frequency in reading matter? Are most of the sentences simple rather than complex or compound? How many prepositional phrases are included? Surely a selection judged to be difficult through the application of any formula can be relatively easy for pupils who are skillful at unlocking independently words which are strange to them only in print, who are equipped to cope with meaning difficulties as described in Chapter 8, who possess adequate background for understanding what the selection says, and for whom the selection presents strong interest appeal. The author recommends strongly that the teacher not spend precious time applying any formula to any selection, but instead read the selection herself, note the degree of interest appeal it carries and the difficult elements it contains, think whether she has already taught skills needed for overcoming those difficulties, and then decide whether the selection is or is not too difficult for this or that pupil. It is well to remember too that often the quickest and most satisfactory way to discover whether a selection is too difficult for a pupil is simply to let him try to read it.

Clearly no one selection can satisfy all of the ten criteria just described. Each selection should meet the first, second, third, and ninth criteria. Some selections will also satisfy some of the remaining standards. The

[6] See, for example, Edgar Dale and Jeanne Chall, "A Formula for Predicting Readability," *Educational Research Bulletin*, Ohio State University, Columbus, No. 27, 1948, pp. 11–20. Rudolph Flesch, "A New Readability Yardstick," *Journal of Applied Psychology*, 32: 221–233 (June, 1948); Irving Lorge, "Predicting Readability," *Teachers College Record*, 45: 404–419 (March, 1944); Carleton Washburne and Mabel Morphett, "Grade Placement of Children's Books," *Elementary School Journal*, 38: 355–364 (January, 1938); Gerald Yoakam, "Determining the Readability of Instructional Material," *Current Problems of Reading Instruction* (University of Pittsburgh, Pittsburgh, Penn., 1951), pp. 47–53.

important point is that the total array of selections to be made available to a given class during the year should as a group meet all ten criteria.

Preferably each elementary school should have a school library and each classroom should have a relatively small and changing classroom library. The school library should be under the direction of a children's librarian who knows children's literature well, who is aware of the nature of and sympathetic with the instructional activities that teachers need to carry on in teaching children's literature, and who can give each classroom teacher help from time to time in choosing selections for the classroom library. Each classroom will have selections borrowed for a period of time from the school library, the public city and county libraries, private libraries of pupils, and the teacher's personal collection. It is essential that the classroom library be changed from time to time during the school year as circumstances and the pupils' interests and progress demand.

Obviously, in order to provide satisfactory instruction, the teacher must have considerable acquaintance with children's literature. Let anyone who believes that his knowledge of such material is inadequate read a few books intended especially to relieve this condition.[7] Among the carefully prepared and suitable lists of children's books are *A Basic Book Collection for Elementary Grades*,[8] *Best Books for Children*,[9] *Good Books for Children*,[10] *Good Reading for Poor Readers*,[11] *Growing Up with Books*,[12] *Subject Index to Books for Intermediate Grades*,[13] *Adventuring with Books*,[14] *Catalogue of the Best Books for Children*,[15] and *Treasure for the Taking*.[16] Appropriate book clubs for children are Arrow Book Club,[17] Junior Deluxe Editions Club,[18] Junior Literary Guild,[19] Parents' Magazine's Read Aloud Book Club for Little Listeners and Beginning

---

[7] See, for example, May Arbuthnot, *Children and Books* (Scott, Foresman & Company, Chicago, 1957), Nancy Larrick, *A Teacher's Guide to Children's Books* (Charles E. Merrill Books, Inc., Columbus, Ohio, 1960), Ruth Tooze, *Your Children Want to Read* (Prentice-Hall, Inc., Englewood Cliffs, N.J., 1957).

[8] Compiled by Miriam Mathes and published by the American Library Association, Chicago, 1960.

[9] Compiled by Mary Turner and published by R. R. Bowker Co., New York. Revised each year.

[10] Prepared by Mary Eakin and published by University of Chicago Press, Chicago, 1959.

[11] By George Spache, published by Garrard Press, Champaign, Ill., 1960.

[12] Published by R. R. Bowker Co., New York. Revised each year.

[13] By Eloise Rue, published by the American Library Association, Chicago, 1950.

[14] Published by National Council of Teachers of English, Champaign, Ill., 1956.

[15] Prepared by Junior Reviewers, Wellesley Hills, Mass., 1956.

[16] By Anne Eaton, published by Viking Press, Inc., New York, 1957.

[17] Scholastic Magazines, Inc., New York.

[18] Garden City, N.Y.

[19] New York, N.Y.

Readers,[20] Young Folks Book Club,[21] Weekly Reader Children's Book Club.[22] Outstanding collections of poems for children[23] and valuable indexes to such poetry[24] are available. Appropriate children's magazines that contain some selections of literary quality are *American Girl*,[25] *Boys' Life*,[26] *Children's Digest*,[27] and *Children's Playmate*.[28] Weekly newspapers published for children in Grades 3 through 6 now and then contain selections that can be classified as literature.[29] To keep up to date on new books for children as they come from the press, the teacher can examine the catalogues of publishers who issue juveniles and read reviews in bulletins of the Center for Children's Books,[30] in the *Horn Book*,[31] *Elementary English*,[32] *Saturday Review*,[33] *School Library Journal*,[34] and in the children's book sections in newspapers such as the *New York Times* and the *New York Herald Tribune*.

Providing Needed Instruction

Year after year — for at least two generations — people interested in the teaching of children's literature have insisted that this instruction can greatly extend the pupil's experience, increase his taste for excellent writing, stimulate him to acquire high ideals and moral or spiritual values, and broaden the scope of his reading interests. Whether these and other worthy goals are achieved or even approached depends, not only on the

[20] Parents' Magazine Enterprises, Inc., New York.

[21] Brooklyn, N.Y.

[22] Middletown, Conn.

[23] See, for example, May Arbuthnot, *Time for Poetry* (Scott, Foresman & Company, Chicago, 1952), Ralph Henry and Lucile Pannell, *My American Heritage* (Rand McNally & Co., Skokie, Ill., 1949), Miriam Huber, *Story and Verse for Children* (The Macmillan Co., New York, 1959), Edna Johnson and Carrie Scott, *Children's Literature* (Houghton Mifflin Company, Boston, 1948), Louis Untermeyer, *The Golden Treasury of Poetry* (Golden Press, Inc., New York, 1959).

[24] See E. J. and Sarah Brewton, *Index to Children's Poetry* (R. R. Bowker Co., New York), the first supplement to the foregoing index, Violet Sell, *Subject Index to Poetry for Children and Young People* (American Library Association, Chicago, 1957).

[25] Published by Girl Scouts of the U.S.A., New York.

[26] Published by Boy Scouts of America, New York.

[27] Published by The Better Reading Foundation, Inc., New York.

[28] Published by Children's Playmate Mag., Inc., New York.

[29] See *News Trails*, *News Explorer*, *NewsTime*, and *Young Citizen*, published by Scholastic Magazines, Inc., New York, and for each grade level the appropriate issue of *My Weekly Reader*, published by American Education Publications, Columbus, Ohio.

[30] Issued by the Center for Children's Books, University of Chicago, Chicago.

[31] Horn Book Co, Inc., Boston.

[32] National Council of Teachers of English, Champaign, Ill.

[33] Saturday Review, Inc., New York.

[34] R. R. Bowker Co., New York.

nature of the selections which are made available for the pupil to read, but also on the particular matters to which his attention is directed in those selections and how the directing is done. In many elementary schools, particularly at the higher grade levels, pupils are still being asked to learn if not memorize facts about or mentioned in literature and to concern themselves with word study, rhythm, sentence structure, style, the names of figures of speech, and other structural elements. The author insists that emphasizing such matters is in no sense a part of the teaching of literature to elementary school pupils and that every aspect of instruction should center on helping them experience as fully as possible what selections say, use what they find there as means of deepening, broadening, and adding satisfaction to their own experiences, and by manipulating those experiences, live imaginatively in various times and places and under different conditions. It is the purpose of the remainder of this chapter to point out certain principles on which instruction should be based and to describe a number of suggested literature activities which can be carried on. Those principles and activities have always characterized good teaching of children's literature and today are important features of what is commonly called individualized or personalized reading.

1. Principles to be Followed

It is chiefly the fostering of the pupil's hearty enjoyment of selections and his pursuit of experiences portrayed therein that instruction in children's literature must continuously undertake. The passages that follow explain briefly four principles for achieving that end.

a. Instruction should be carried on in such a way that the pupil learns to approach a juvenile book, a short story, a poem, a nonsense passage, or any other type of selection as something to be enjoyed rather than as information to be studied or remembered. The attitude he should be encouraged to develop is much the same as that with which he watches an intriguing play or television show. It is understood that this recreatory attitude of enjoyment in no way implies frivolity or passive idleness. Indeed, his experiencing of what a given selection has to tell will require him to do the very active job of perceiving sounds, objects, actions, odors, feelings, and other matters presented in the selection and of drawing on his own experiences so that he constructs in imagination the events and conditions it portrays.

This proposition has several important implications. In the first place, it should be clear that in teaching or using a selection one should not insist upon the pupil's memorizing such items as the date of publication of the writing, any passage contained in the selection, the titles of other writings produced by the author, or events in the author's life. This does not mean that the pupil should be prevented from memorizing passages which have a strong appeal for him or from discovering interesting things about his favorite authors. On the contrary, skillful teaching will indirectly encourage him to memorize voluntarily passages to which he becomes closely attached and to build so much interest in his favorite authors that he tries to learn as much as he can about them.

Second, the hearing or reading of any selection should not be followed by questioning and answering concerned primarily with checking mere comprehension. However, a normal discussion of a selection may take place whenever the pupils are moved to the point of expression. Consequently they should be encouraged to make comments on the selection, to tell about things that caught their interest, to ask questions, and in other ways to share experiences gathered from the selection. If they have no comments to make or questions to ask, the matter can well be left as it is. One must get away from the idea that no learning can go on unless the teacher is asking questions and children are answering them.

Third, while memorization of poetry should be encouraged, it must never be forced or assigned. In fact, there is no good reason for insisting that a pupil memorize any particular poem. If a poem has become real, vivid, and delightful to him as an experience, he will choose to memorize it and thus make it a part of himself, just as he chooses to learn a melody which he can whistle, hum, or sing as he goes about his business. The point is that the teacher must make a poem so real and pleasant to the pupil that he wants to memorize it. Such a poem will be full of experience for him. In this one at least he can see the pictures and hear the sounds. He likes it and wants to be able to say it over and over.

Fourth, in teaching children's literature, there is no place for tests which ask pupils to match authors and titles or authors and passages taken from their writings, to describe objects or situations presented in selections, or in other ways to expose their mastery of unimportant matters. Desirable tests will seek to discover what the pupil experienced through his contact with a selection and to stimulate further realization of such experiences. The questions asked should deal with the definiteness of the mental pictures, the clarity of perceptions, and the interpretations the pupil makes. Consequently, appropriate questions for literature tests are concerned with what the child thinks about the characters, what he thinks about the value of behavior described, and how he reacts to the selection. Most tests should be taken with the selection at hand; that is, with books open. In addition, the test may well be followed by class discussion of the questions, which should do a great deal to make the experiencing of the selection more real.

b. The approach to a selection must never be analytical. This means, for one thing, that no attention should be given to such matters as style, structure, and the development of plot. Concern for these and similar matters should be reserved for more advanced students whose particularized talents tend to equip them for a consideration of the construction of literature. Furthermore, the idea that the pupil must catch a moral from exposure to a poem or story and be subjected to a quizzing or discussion on that moral needs to be discouraged. Of course, there can be no possible objection if the pupil senses — largely by himself — a moral value in a selection, but to insist that the essential purpose in his reading is to realize the moral values the selection supposedly presents is to miss the real value of literature.

Some teachers tend to use children's literature, not so much as something that has value in its own right, but as a vehicle for teaching other matters which seem to them more important. For example, they may teach a poem or a story as a means of developing an understanding of some social problem such as racial tolerance or participation in community affairs. While the author expects that good literature will make its contribution to the development of the pupil's social conscience, he insists that there is no more reason for using it fundamentally as a vehicle for the teaching of social studies than there is for using music, painting, or any other art for the same purpose, and that persistence in so using literature may easily cause the pupil to lose interest in reading literature. One must continually keep in mind the fact that practically all literature for children was written to be read and enjoyed in its own right rather than analyzed for any purpose whatever.

Often a background must be constructed before pupils are ready to read or hear a given selection. It will consist of specific concepts and broader understandings which are necessary for experiencing what the selection has to tell. These concepts and understandings can best be developed, perhaps, through the use of pictures, objects, and excursions. In situations in which such media cannot be used, the best help lies in the teacher's simple oral explanations and a cooperative discussion that explains the needed concepts. It is understood that no time will be taken for the construction of background if the pupils already possess the required concepts and understandings, and that the teacher will not mistake gushing about literature for the building of background.

In teaching a given selection there may be a temptation to dwell on allusions that are bypaths. Prolonged attention to allusions which require a consideration of historical or geographical facts, of character study, of events in the author's life, or of other matters having nothing to do with experiencing what the selection has to tell should be avoided. On the other hand, attention to allusions that need to be sensed in order to achieve that experiencing should be encouraged.

c. In taking part in many of the different literature activities described later in this chapter, children at times are confronted with particular reading difficulties such as the pronunciation or the meaning of a word. This blocking tends to break down experience-getting. Consequently, the teacher should not hesitate to give quickly whatever help is needed in order that the reading may go on immediately. She may, however, keep a record of such difficulties as they occur and take steps toward their eradication through the teaching of reading itself. All of this means that class periods scheduled for teaching literature should not be used for teaching reading skills.

d. The pupils must be given ample opportunity for free choice of selections to be read. For example, each pupil should be encouraged to browse, and to choose by himself one or more selections to read silently now or soon. He should be allowed also to introduce to the class now and then a new book he has read and to choose a short selection he has enjoyed which he believes others in the class have not read and which he can read well to them. While the teacher herself often will decide just what new books she should introduce to the pupils and what poems, short stories, nonsense items, and other types of selections she should read to them, certainly the class should be permitted to ask for introductions of new books they have seen or heard of but have not read and to request an oral rereading of selections they want to hear again. It is clear that little if any free choice can be provided unless there are at least a single copy and preferably several copies of many different juveniles and children's magazines rather than just sets of literary readers which supply a copy for each pupil. This is not to say that all pupils in a class or group should never read and talk over the same selection, much as adults discuss a play they have seen or a book they have read, but most if not all of this group consideration of the same piece of literature can be provided through the sensible use of selections in the basal reader as discussed in Chapter 7.

2. Suggested Literature Activities

The literature activities now to be described are not exhaustive, but the author considers them to be major ways of helping pupils develop an abiding interest in reading a variety of worthy material on a wide range of topics. In order of their appearance, these activities are (a) oral reading by the teacher, (b) free silent reading, (c) oral reading by pupils, (d) book introductions, (e) dramatizations, (f) panel discussions, and (g) providing for contributing factors. Each activity is a part of the instruction to be given at any grade level from 3 through 6. It is the author's recommendation that all of them rather than just one or two be used at each grade level and that at least one reading period each week be devoted to carrying on one or another of the first six activities.[35]

a. Oral Reading by the Teacher

Some class periods assigned to instruction in children's literature in Grades 3 through 6 should be devoted to the teacher's reading of choice selections to the pupils. When this oral reading is done well, pupils can gain considerable enjoyment of excellent writings and become aware of and interested in the types of content which literature offers. At times they can also add words to their listening vocabulary, hear different sentence structures with which they need to be more familiar than they are, and acquire background for their later silent reading of literature. The selection read aloud may be a short story, a poem the pupils have not heard or read or one they want to hear again, a piece of nonsense, a short play, or some other material particularly fitting at the time. It may be one relatively long selection, a part of a longer selection, or two or more short selections and often — but by no means always — should be typical of other selections available for pupils to read to themselves later. Now and then it is especially appropriate to introduce poems the pupils have not read or heard and to present once more poems they have learned to enjoy and now ask to hear again.

Sometimes before starting to read, the teacher may need to supply a little background that builds a favorable setting for the pupils' listening and explains items which, as presented in the selection, they would not otherwise understand as they listen. Only the teacher, with an awareness of the pupils' experiences and the ideas the selection offers, can decide just what this background should be. During the oral reading of any selection the teacher should feel free to point up a particularly intriguing part, to give any further explanation the pupils may need, to repeat the reading of lines as requested, and to laugh with the pupils over an especially humorous saying or incident. Whether or not a class discussion follows the teacher's oral reading depends much on the pupils' desire to converse about one or more features of what they heard. During discussion it must be remembered that the basic purpose of the talking back and forth is to let pupils express their reactions and to increase their enjoyment

[35] Some of these activities were described briefly in Chapter 6.

of what was read. Any questions the teacher raises should be concerned with achieving this purpose rather than with a mere checking of the pupils' comprehension.

Excellent oral reading of children's classics, other good stories, poems, and plays is presented by some recordings[36] and occasionally by television shows and radio programs. Such recordings should be a part of any school's offering in children's literature. If at all possible, provision should be made for pupils to see and hear the appropriate television shows and radio programs.

b. Free Silent Reading

Some periods assigned to the teaching of children's literature should be given over simply to each pupil's browsing through juveniles, magazines, and newspapers in the classroom library and then reading to himself at a table or at his regular seat one or more selections he has chosen, just as he reads to himself at home or in the school or public library. At the beginning of each such period the teacher, knowing the available selections and a pupil's interests and reading ability, may need to help that pupil choose a piece of literature which will appeal to him. During the silent reading the teacher may also need to give aid which relieves a particular reading difficulty a pupil encounters. If the difficulty is one which previous instruction has equipped the pupil to cope with independently, help consists almost entirely in asking questions and making statements that stimulate him to apply the appropriate skill or skills he has been taught. When the difficulty is one which previous teaching has not equipped the pupil to handle by himself, the teacher should tell him now exactly what he needs to know and thus enable him to continue his reading immediately.

Sometimes while free silent reading is going on, the teacher finds a pupil chuckling over a bit of humor or showing intense interest in some exciting incident. In this case, although as a rule the silent reading is not followed by a group or class discussion of what has been read, it may be advisable to reserve several minutes near the close of the period for pupils so inclined to tell a little about what they have enjoyed. Certainly during the silent reading any pupil should feel free to make comments privately to the teacher about what he is reading. In this situation often he and the teacher decide that the selection or part of a selection at hand is one he should prepare to read aloud later to the class or some other group

---

[36] See particularly the Caedmon records, distributed by Houghton Mifflin Company, Boston, and the records which accompany the Landmark books, published by Random House, Inc., New York.

c. Oral Reading by Pupils

In connection with the use of a basal reader in Grades 3 through 6, it is rather common practice to have pupils read aloud parts or all of at least some selections included in that book. Yet, as suggested in Chapter 7, much of this oral reading is often quite artificial in purpose and performance. Usually each pupil in the group or class has in hand a copy of any passage to be read aloud, has already read that passage to himself, has talked it over with his classmates, and now has little if any desire to hear it read aloud. Surely any pupil knows all this at the time he is asked to read aloud. Under such conditions, how can the class have any real motive for listening? How can the pupil who is asked to read aloud have any real motive for reading well? If this particular use of oral reading provides most of the practice that elementary school pupils get in reading to others, it is no wonder that by the time they complete the sixth grade their oral reading is poor.

It is a different use of pupils' oral reading that the author proposes as a vehicle of instruction in children's literature. Each of several individual pupils should read to his classmates or some other group a different literature passage — one which he has already read to himself and enjoyed, which he believes his classmates would like to hear and he wants to share with them, and which he has prepared himself to read aloud well. It is also one the others do not have in hand at the time and have not read to themselves or, having read, now want to hear read aloud. Such a passage may be a part of a story, a poem, an incident in a play, an anecdote, an entire very short story, a piece of nonsense, or any other suitable item. In this situation it is possible for the listeners to have an attentive audience attitude and for the pupil who reads aloud to be sensitive to his responsibility to convey to them the understanding and enjoyment he experienced when he read the selection to himself. The practice the pupil gets in reading aloud can thus contribute to the growth of his interest in and taste for literature and to the improvement of his ability to read well to others.

From the very beginning, the teacher must understand that reading a selection or a part of a selection well to others is something in addition to, rather than different from, reading the same material silently and that oral reading is more difficult than silent reading. Any word or sentence in a selection must be read silently before it is read orally, whether the silent reading is done a fraction of a second or a day or more before the oral reading is attempted. In fact, the reading itself is done before the reader proceeds through so-called oral reading to try to convey the author's intended meaning to his listener. Thus oral reading, a poor name for what is actually meant, is in fact oral expression of what has been read and requires the use of even more than what is needed for reading silently. Although this "more" includes such matters as posture, the holding of the book, and emotional adjustment to one's audience, it is largely a problem of transmitting the author's intended meaning to others. It requires the effective use of a pleasant voice, the correct pronunciation of words, and the phrasing and intonation needed to convey the author's meaning. For the pupil who reads silently with sufficient skill, reading orally to others is basically a speech problem rather than a reading problem.

Soon after the opening of the school year, probably the teacher and the pupils together should build a list of standards for reading well to others. Most pupils have heard enough good oral reading and poor oral reading so that they have some idea of differences between the two, can suggest items to be included in the list, and can use the standards they adopt to judge the quality of their subsequent oral reading. A list of standards that a class builds may include one or more of the following:

1. Read loud enough so that everyone in the room can hear.
2. Sit or stand in a comfortable position.
3. Hold the book below your face.
4. Hold your head up and look at the audience from time to time.
5. Read the lines so that they sound just as they would if you were saying them.
6. Use your voice to show feelings that the story tells about.
7. Pronounce words correctly.

During the school year, some periods assigned to teaching children's literature should be spent in having individual pupils read to the class passages they have chosen for that purpose. The passage any pupil reads aloud in this setting may be one he found during a free reading period in the classroom, or he may have come across it at home, in the school library, or a friend's private library. At any rate he has secured the teacher's permission to read his chosen passage to the class, and he has prepared himself to do that reading well. Any class discussion that follows either an individual pupil's reading of a passage or all the oral reading done during the period should spring from the pupils' desire to talk over the content of what they have heard. At the close of the period, it may be advisable occasionally (but not always) to ask the class to recall the standards they built for reading well to others and to apply those standards in evaluating the oral reading they heard. However, this evaluating should refer to all the reading heard rather than to the performance of any one pupil, and it should consist entirely of suggesting how all pupils can improve their oral reading.

Since poor oral reading of literature can easily prevent listeners from experiencing what that material offers, considerable emphasis should be placed on the pupil's preparation for reading aloud to his classmates. Surely the pupil will need to read again to himself whatever passage he has chosen, make sure he understands the meaning of each expression and pronounces each word correctly, decide what voice intonations he needs to use in saying each line, and practice reading the passage aloud to the teacher or to someone else who can aid him with any difficult part. Often the oral reading of a pupil who does not make such preparation contains much word-calling and several delaying attempts to unlock strange words. These inadequacies are almost certain to exasperate the listeners and to cause the pupil himself embarrassment that threatens his self-confidence.

At times what is often called group oral reading can be helpful, particularly in trying to care for individual differences in ability to read well aloud. This activity is essentially a matter of dividing the class into several small groups, giving each group a different selection to read, breaking the selection into parts so that each pupil in the group has a part, and having each group read its selection to the class or some other group. The following paragraphs tell how one teacher carried on group oral reading with a fourth-grade class:

At the opening of a reading period, the teacher proposed that the class prepare to read a few short stories to Miss Brown's third-grade pupils. The class readily agreed. Then the teacher divided the class into five groups of about six pupils each, appointed a leader for each group, and gave that group sufficient copies of a short story which no one in the class had read. Previously the teacher had divided each story into marked parts so that each pupil except the leader of each group had a part to read aloud later.

Each group formed a small circle in an assigned place in the classroom and worked there to prepare for the oral reading. First each pupil read the entire story to himself. Then as the leader prepared a brief introduction to the story, each of the other members made further preparation for the oral reading he was to do. During all this preparation, the teacher moved from group to group to give help as needed.

At the beginning of the next reading period, the entire class formed one circle and practiced their oral reading. The procedure followed was quite similar for each group. The leader gave the brief introduction to the story, and each member read aloud the part he had prepared himself to read. Comments were made and questions were asked by the class when the reading of each story was completed. The reading of one group followed that of another until all groups had read their stories. At the close of all the reading, the class made a few suggestions pertaining to further preparation needed before reading to Miss Brown's pupils.

During the reading period on the following day, each group read its story to Miss Brown's pupils.

Two additional uses of pupils' oral reading should be noted briefly. One is choral reading of poems by the entire class or a smaller group. Any poem used for this purpose should be one that the pupils enjoy and now want to learn to read aloud in concert. Many poems suitable for choral reading appear in the anthologies named in footnote 23 on page 448. The other use is the singing of poetry by the class, particularly ballads that hold strong appeal for pupils.[37]

d. Book Introductions

Now and then the teacher should use a literature period to introduce to the class or a smaller group a few juvenile books that apparently carry strong interest appeal for those pupils and that they have not read. Any such book may be a new one that is to be placed in the classroom library or the school library soon or that is now available in only the public library or a friend's private library. It may be an older book that for one reason or another the pupils have rejected or not encountered and can be borrowed from some library or the teacher's or a pupil's collection. In introducing any book, the teacher can show it and some of its pictures, tell its title, the name of the author, the names of main characters, the setting of the story, and just a little of what the story is about, read aloud an exceptionally interesting part, and explain where the book can be obtained. Probably any questions the pupils ask about the book should be answered, except those which ask for telling too much of the story itself. The purpose of a book introduction is not to review the book or to tell its story but to reveal just enough so that the pupil can decide whether he wants to read the book.

Soon after the opening of the school year, the teacher and the pupils together should set up standards for giving book introductions. The list may include one or more of the following items:

1. Tell the title of the book and the name of the author.
2. Show the book and a few of its pictures.
3. Tell who and what the story is about and where it happens.

[37] Poems set to music appear in S. B. Gould and H. F. Shepherd, *Songs and Ballads of the West* (Patery and Willis, London), H. E. Krehbiel, *American Folk Songs* (G. Schirmer, New York), J. A. Lomax, *Cowboy Songs* (Sturges and Walton, New York), H. Rodeheaver, *Plantation Melodies* (Rodeheaver Company, New York), and J. B. Radcliffe-Whitehead, *Folk Songs and Other Songs for Children* (Oliver Ditson, New York).

4. Tell or read aloud one short interesting part, but not so much that you spoil a surprise for others.
5. Tell whether you liked the book.
6. Tell where others can get the book.

During the school year, some literature periods should be given over to having individual pupils introduce books that others in the class have not read. Each introduction should follow the standards that the class has decided on. Listeners should be allowed time to raise questions they want answered about a book, but no question that asks for the exposure of a surprise or an explanation of how the story turns out should be answered.

Any pupil can be encouraged to write book introductions on 4" × 6" index cards. The title of a book is placed in the upper left-hand corner, the name of the author in the upper right-hand corner, the introduction itself under these items, and the pupil's name and the date at the bottom. All such cards can be filed alphabetically by book titles in a box labeled "Book Introductions." Thereafter any pupil who wishes to find out what others in his class think about a book he is considering as possible reading material can get those judgments by referring to the file.

e. Dramatizations

One good way to help pupils experience certain stories and plays and engage in good oral reading or speaking is to have them give and listen to dramatizations of those selections. Usually preparation for dramatizing a story or play gives each pupil who is to take part strong motivation to concentrate on the meaning of the lines he is to read aloud or speak, to select the voice intonations required for conveying that meaning to the listeners, and to read or speak his lines well. Often the pupil who cannot read aloud well a relatively long passage or who is particularly self-conscious when he attempts to do so as he stands alone in front of the class can read or speak without tension or embarrassment the short sets of lines assigned to him as a member of a performing group. Probably some pupils who listen to a good dramatization get from the performance some experiences depicted in the story or play that they overlooked or would overlook in reading the selection to themselves.

Many stories written for children, including some found in basal readers, lend themselves readily to what is often called dramatic oral reading. Usually a story to be dramatized is first read silently by the entire class or a smaller group. Then the children decide how many scenes are required and what each scene is to include, select the pupils who will read the parts of the story characters, determine what settings, scenery, and props if any are called for, and choose someone to read aloud whatever introductions are needed at the beginning and between scenes. Pupils chosen to take the parts of story characters and to give introductions then prepare to read those parts, and those who are not to read prepare stage settings and props. The actual dramatization consists in pupils' reading aloud the lines of story characters they represent, each omitting words not included within quotation marks in the story. Dramatizing a story as a make-believe radio broadcast in a corner of the classroom screened from the listeners permits pupils to read their lines without the self-consciousness they may have when performing before a group and gives other pupils a chance to participate by producing sound effects.

Pupils should be given ample opportunity to dramatize published plays that are literature. A few such plays are included in some basal readers. Others make up the content of juvenile books.[38] After the entire class or a smaller group have read a play silently and orally, pupils are chosen for character roles, and they proceed to memorize their lines. Pupils who enjoy doing art work but are not assigned roles can make murals or posters depicting scenes to announce or advertise the play. If the play is of a historical nature, other pupils can be encouraged to read additional material that describes the times, the setting, events, and characters of the play and to report their findings to the class. If songs and dances of the period are included in the play, still other pupils who have no speaking parts can participate in the performance. When the play is to be given in a somewhat elaborate rather than a simple form, committees of pupils can be responsible for such items as scenery, props, and costumes.

Several points on dramatizations should be emphasized. *First,* under the guidance of the teacher, the pupils must have a major responsibility in planning dramatizations. This includes the selection of stories and plays to be dramatized, the choosing of pupils to play character parts, the planning of stage settings, and the designing or selecting of whatever scenery and costumes are necessary. *Second,* dramatizations should be kept as simple as possible within the limits of providing sufficient reality. Many dramatizations can be given in the classroom without costumes and scenery. Much ado about elaborate costumes, stage settings, and the like may center the pupils' attention on physical properties and decoration to the point that the values of dramatizing are clouded if not lost. *Third,* no attempt should be made to produce a polished performance. Putting on a finished presentation frequently consumes more time and persistent effort than the polishing is worth and can easily defeat the basic purpose

[38] See, for example, *Tales from the Four Winds,* a four-book series of plays, and *They Helped Build America.* All these volumes were written by Fan Kissen and are published by Houghton Mifflin Company, Boston.

of getting the pupils to express what they experienced in reading the story or play. *Fourth,* all available help should be used in dramatizing a play. For example, the art teacher and interested pupils can do much to make the stage attractive in colors and properties. The music teacher can see that songs in the play are sung properly. Boys in shop work can be helpful in supplying props and sound effects. *Fifth,* any dramatization must reveal the pupils' own conceptions of the events and characters as they experienced them in reading the story or play. Under no circumstances should the performance attempt to present chiefly the teacher's conceptions of those events and characters. *Finally,* opportunities to have pupils present dramatizations before other children and adults should be welcomed. Among such opportunities are meetings of parents and teachers, school assemblies, special-day programs, visiting days, and programs given for another class. Here again, however, the teacher must see that eagerness to produce a polished performance does not force her into making a dramatization her own work rather than the pupils'.

f. Panel Discussions

Now and then a literature period may be devoted to a panel discussion carried on by a few pupils in front of the rest of the class or some other audience. The chief purpose of this activity is to allow members of the panel to exchange their ideas on books or stories they have all read and to introduce to the listeners selections they might like to read to themselves. The topic of any panel discussion may be a single book that only the panel members have read and are now introducing to the listeners. It may be several books written by the same author, favorite poems, books dealing with the same subject such as wild animals or seafaring adventures, or the contents of certain magazines for children. Usually the teacher or an appointed pupil should serve as a leader of the discussion so that members of the panel keep to the topic and do not repeat what others have already told. Furthermore, care must be taken to see that in any discussion concerned with introducing books or stories the listeners have not read, too much about their content is not divulged. Indeed, for the first few panel discussions to be held early in the school year, it may be necessary to decide beforehand just what each member of the panel is to tell and just what questions if any he is to raise.

g. Providing for Contributing Factors

Teachers who apply the principles explained on pages 449–452 and use the six literature activities just described do much to help the pupil develop an interest in reading a wide variety of worthy material. There are in addition, however, other factors which, insofar as they advertise juveniles to the pupil, can contribute to the achievement of this goal. The paragraphs that follow describe those factors the author believes are most helpful:

Near the classroom library should be a table displaying a few juveniles. Here the pupil may browse, discovering what the books tell about and choosing one to read at his leisure. Any book displayed may be a new one to be placed on a shelf of the classroom library later, an old one which for one reason or another has not yet attracted the pupils' attention, or one borrowed for a short time from the school library, the public library, the traveling bookmobile, or a friend. It is particularly important that the display be changed frequently and never become stale.

Juveniles can be grouped on shelves of the classroom library according to pupils' interests, topics being studied in other school work, special events, and seasonal activities. Thus, for example, as the situation or occasion suggests, the teacher can assemble books that tell about space travel, books that illuminate the history of transportation, books that pertain to this or that holiday or some other special day, and books that tell about winter sports. Usually signs of some sort should be used to call pupils' attention to the different groups assembled from time to time.

A large bulletin board should be used to advertise juveniles to pupils. Among the materials to be placed there are jackets of new books, book introductions written by pupils, printed book reviews, pupils' illustrations, photographs of authors, and lists of books the teacher or librarian recommends. It is important that the bulletin board be kept attractive, that it never be crowded, and that the items on it be changed frequently.

Some teachers find it advantageous to have each pupil keep a record of books he has read. One kind of record is quite simple, being merely a list of those books. Others are constructed in such a way that a book read is recorded as a point in a game. Records described in Chapter 6 are suitable for use in Grades 3 through 6.

More often than is commonly thought, informative television performances arouse pupils' curiosity about topics that can be pursued through reading. It can be helpful now and then to have pupils name events, people, objects, and activities they have observed on television and would like to know more about. Then the teacher can call attention to whatever suitable books, if any, they can read to find out what they want to know.

The pupils in any class can play a quiz game about books many of them have read. Each pupil chooses a book he has read and makes a list of statements that tell about the story itself or one of the story characters, without naming the book or the character. He arranges the statements in an order so that the one he thinks gives the weakest clue to the name of the book comes first and the one he thinks gives the strongest clue comes last. When his turn comes, he reads aloud the first statement in his list and waits to see if someone can guess from that clue the name of the book. If no one guesses the name, he continues with the remaining statements one after the other until someone names the book. Sometimes a group of pupils who have read the same book give one or more charades depicting events in that book, and the rest of the pupils try to guess the name of the book.

Almost any class can make and play a game called Authors. To begin making the game, the teacher should write on the board the names of authors the pupils give and place under each name the titles of books or short stories written by that author — four titles if possible. Then the name of an author and the titles of his four books or stories should be written on each of four cards to make a set. At the top of each card in a set the particular title the card stands for should be printed in capital letters. Below this title should come in order the author's name and the three remaining titles. A set of four cards for an author would look something like this:

COMANCHE OF THE SEVENTH

Margaret Leighton
Secret of Smuggler's Cove
Secret of the Old House
Judith of France

SECRET OF SMUGGLER'S COVE

Margaret Leighton
Secret of the Old House
Judith of France
Comanche of the Seventh

SECRET OF THE OLD HOUSE

Margaret Leighton
Judith of France
Comanche of the Seventh
Secret of Smuggler's Cove

JUDITH OF FRANCE

Margaret Leighton
Comanche of the Seventh
Secret of Smuggler's Cove
Secret of the Old House

The game can be played by two or more pupils. Four cards are dealt to each player, and the remaining cards are placed face down to form a stack. The purpose of each player is to get as many sets of four cards as he can. The player to the right of the dealer starts the game by looking at his cards to see whether he has four cards about the same author. If he has, he puts all of them face up in front of him and draws four more from the stack. If he hasn't, he draws one card from the stack, discards one from his hand to start a discard pile, and tells the title of the book listed at the top of the discarded card. The next player may take a card from the top of either the stack or the discard pile and must discard one from his hand. Whenever a player completes a set of four cards, he places that set in front of him and draws four more cards from the stack. When the first stack has been used up, the discard pile is turned face down to make a new one and the drawing and discarding continue. The game ends when there are no more cards in either the stack or the discard pile or when the players agree that no more sets can be made. The winner is the player who has made the most sets of four. In some classrooms small groups of pupils play this homemade game during recess periods and the noon hours.

Assembly programs on books and authors can be presented. During such a program, new books can be introduced to the audience and passages may be read orally by teachers, the librarian, and pupils who read aloud well. Interesting facts can be told about the lives of favorite authors. Pupils can dramatize scenes from books and tell about their favorite stories. Children's book clubs can be described, and when appropriate the awarding of the Newbery Medal and the Caldecott Medal can be explained.

Most teachers are acquainted with the nature and purposes of children's book fairs and Book Week. Any class should be encouraged to visit book fairs whenever and wherever they are held in the community and to examine the exhibits displayed there. Now and then a school blessed with a reasonable supply of juveniles can hold a book fair of its own to which pupils enrolled in other schools and interested adults are invited. Some activities that can be carried on during Book Week are the holding of a school assembly such as that just described, the dramatizing by different classes of scenes from favorite books and stories, the performing of pantomimes about incidents in books, and the displaying of posters and other art work pupils have made to tell about books. Other suggestions relative to Book Week appear in publications prepared and distributed by some state departments of education, the Department of Health, Education, and Welfare, Washington, D.C., the American Library Association, Chicago, Illinois, and the Children's Book Council, New York City.

QUESTIONS TO BE ANSWERED

1. With what main objective of instruction in reading is the teaching of children's literature chiefly concerned?

2. What are the ten criteria suggested for use in choosing selections to be made available to a given class? Why is each of them by itself important? Which criteria are to be applied in choosing any selection?

3. What are the three main kinds of writings which constitute children's literature?

4. What are some of the different types of children's literature?

5. How can a teacher try to determine what the immediate worthy interests of her pupils are?

6. How can new interests to be followed through the reading of literature be introduced to pupils? How can pupils' taste for literature that is more mature than what they have read be raised?

7. How wide may the spread of reading ability among the pupils of a given class be? What does this spread have to do with the choosing of selections to be made available to a class? How can a teacher try to judge whether a given selection is too difficult for a pupil to read?

8. Why, in your judgment, is it preferable for an elementary school to have both a school library and a library in each classroom? What things do you think should be kept in mind about a classroom library?

9. What are sources to which a teacher can turn to become acquainted with the realm of children's literature? Where can the teacher find lists of selected children's books? Of poems for children? How can the teacher keep informed on new juveniles as they come from the press?

10. What are the four principles on which literature activities should be based? Why is each of them important?

11. What are the different suggested literature activities? Which of these activities would you be least interested in carrying on with pupils? Why?

MORE TO READ

Barbe, Walter, *Educator's Guide to Personalized Reading Instruction*, Prentice-Hall, Inc., Englewood Cliffs, N.J., 1961, Chapter Six.

DeBoer, John, and Martha Dallmann, *The Teaching of Reading*, Rev. Ed., Holt, Rinehart & Winston, Inc., New York, 1964, Chapters 11A, 11B.

Gans, Roma, *Common Sense in Teaching Reading*, Bobbs-Merrill Co., Inc., Indianapolis, 1963, Chapter 13.

Gray, Lillian, and Dora Reese, *Teaching Children to Read*, The Ronald Press Company, New York, 1957, Chapters 14, 15.

Harris, Albert, *How to Increase Reading Ability*, Longmans, Green & Co., Inc., New York, 1956, Chapter XIII.

————, *Effective Teaching of Reading*, David McKay Co., Inc., New York, 1962, Chapter 13.

Hildreth, Gertrude, *Teaching Reading*, Henry Holt & Co., 1958, Chapters 18, 21, 22.

Robinson, Helen, *Developing Permanent Interests in Reading*, Supplementary Educational Monographs, No. 84, University of Chicago Press, Chicago, 1956.

Russell, David, *Children Learn to Read*, Ginn & Company, Boston, 1962, Chapters XII, XIII.

Smith, Henry, and Emerald Dechant, *Psychology in Teaching Reading*, Prentice-Hall, Inc., Englewood Cliffs, N.J., 1961, Chapter 10.

Spache, George, *Toward Better Reading*, The Garrard Press, Champaign, Ill., 1963, Chapters 9, 11.

THINGS TO DO

1. Go to a children's library and find there a few juveniles which you would like to have in the library of a classroom in which you might teach. For each book you choose, make a list of the criteria which you believe it satisfies.

2. Examine a basal reader for any grade level you choose to find selections which you classify as literature. Then read in the accompanying teacher's guide the suggestions given for using that selection with pupils. Decide what if any of the suggestions violate one or another of the first two principles on which literature activities should be based.

3. Think of a topic which you believe pupils at a grade level you choose are interested in reading about. Then go to a children's library and make a list of the titles of literary selections you find there and would use to help satisfy that interest.

4. Think of a topic which you believe you are informed and enthusiastic about. Then go to a children's library and make a list of literary selections you find there and would use in introducing that interest to pupils at any grade level you choose.

5. Think of a topic which you would expect pupils at any grade level you choose to be interested in reading about now. Then go to a children's library to find juveniles that you think could be used in improving the pupils' taste for literature. Make a list of the titles in the order in which you would introduce the books to the pupils.

6. Choose either (a) reading poems to pupils or (b) introducing new juveniles to them. Then go to a children's library to find selections you would use in carrying on that activity at any grade level you choose. Make a list of the titles of the selections you find.

7. Examine a few copies of a children's magazine or a children's newspaper to find selections you would use in teaching children's literature.

Selected Bibliography of Research on the
Teaching of Reading in the Elementary School

During the past eighty years, reports of at least five thousand investigations pertaining to the sociology, physiology, psychology, and teaching of reading have appeared in print. Unfortunately, much of this tremendous volume of research has been somewhat unfocalized, fragmentary, disorganized, and unrelated. Consequently, there exist today adequate and valid data on just a few problems, only partial and inconclusive data on innumerable problems, and no data whatever on some problems which are still particularly pressing. There is hope now that in the future, research in reading will be much more closely coordinated and highly focalized than was the research reported from 1884 to 1965.

Anyone who wants to become acquainted with the research published up to 1965 and to keep in touch with contemporary research reported from time to time should use at least the following sources:

1. Gray, W. S. *Summary of Investigations Relating to Reading,* Supplementary Education Monographs, No. 28. University of Chicago Press, Chicago, 1925. This book summarizes or notes the research reported during the years preceding 1925.

2. One or more articles by Gray, W. S., usually entitled "Summary of Investigations Relating to Reading," appearing in each of Volumes 26 through 32 of the *Elementary School Journal* and in each of Volumes 26 through 50 of the *Journal of Educational Research.* These articles summarize or note research reported from 1925 through 1957.

3. Traxler, Arthur, and Seder, Margaret. *Ten Years of Research in Reading,* Educational Records Bulletin, No. 32. Educational Records Bureau, New York, 1941. This article summarizes or notes research reported during 1930–1940.

4. ———, and Townsend, Agatha. *Another Five Years of Research in Reading,* Educational Records Bulletin, No. 46. Educational Records Bureau, New York, 1946. This article summarizes or notes research reported during 1940–1945.

5. ———. *Eight More Years of Research in Reading: Summary and Bibliography,* Educational Records Bulletin, No. 64. Educational Records Bureau, New York, 1955. This article summarizes or notes research reported during 1946–1953.

6. ———. *Research in Reading During Another Four Years,* Educational Records Bulletin, No. 75. Educational Records Bureau, New York, 1958. This article summarizes or notes research reported during 1954–1957.

7. Gray, W. S. "Reading," in the *Encyclopedia of Educational Research.* The Macmillan Co., New York, 1960, pp. 1086–1135.

8. Dussell, D. H., and Henry, R. F. "Research on Teaching Reading," in American Educational Research Association, *Handbook of Research on Teaching.* Rand, McNally & Co., Chicago, 1963, pp. 865–928.

9. Appropriate issues of the *Review of Educational Research,* usually one every third year from 1931 through 1958. American Educational Research Association, National Education Association, Washington, D.C.

10. Contemporary summaries prepared by different writers and reports of individual pieces of research presented from time to time in professional periodicals, including *The Reading Teacher,* the *Journal of Educational Research,* the *Elementary School Journal, Elementary English,* the *Journal of Educational Psychology,* the *Journal of Education, Educational Administration and Supervision,* the *Journal of Developmental Reading,* and bulletins of the U.S. Office of Education.

Only part of the reported research pertains to the aspect of reading to which this volume is devoted, the teaching of reading in the elementary school. A number of these appropriate investigations were concerned with problems or topics that are undoubtedly trivial. Some were poorly designed or controlled, some applied inadequate statistical treatment of data collected, and apparently, some were carried on by investigators who lacked insight into the teaching of reading when interpreting their data. This questionable use of time, effort, and money has led to the failure to solve crucial and persistent problems which research could and should have settled years ago, and to the accumulation of data which have little if anything to do with improving the teaching of reading in the elementary school. Nevertheless, many appropriate investigations have provided valid data, which, when applied sensibly, are very helpful in determining just what needs to be taught, the sequence in which important skills should be taught, and procedures to be followed in supplying needed instruction.

A partial bibliography of research on the teaching of reading in the elementary school is listed on the pages that follow. In using this bibliography, the reader should keep the following points in mind:

1. The bibliography is not intended to be exhaustive and is far from complete. Many items equal in merit to most of those included have been omitted, and the list is selective only in the sense that it is limited to some of the research which bears on topics discussed in this volume. Yet anyone who wants to identify many problems with which research on the teaching of reading in the elementary school has been concerned and to find out what the included research explains will find the bibliography useful.

2. Items included in the bibliography are arranged according to topics treated in the various chapters in this volume, except for Chapter 1, for which no literature is available. Thus, the items listed under the first heading, "General," are appropriate to topics discussed in Chapter 2; those under the second heading, "Readiness for Beginning Reading," are appropriate for Chapter 3; those under "Word Recognition Skills," for Chapter 4; "The Reading Program," Chapters 5 and 7; "Literature for Children," Chapters 6 and 12; "Comprehension in Reading," Chapter 8; "Reading–Study Skills," Chapter 9; "Critical Reading," Chapter 10; "Reading in the Content Subjects," Chapter 11.

3. Most of the bibliographical items are magazine articles, some are books, and a few are bulletins. Some items are quite old but still of considerable significance; others are relatively new. Many items are reports of individual pieces of research, a few are summaries of research on one or another phase of the teaching of reading, and some are a mixture of the writer's critical consideration of a problem and his reference to or evaluation of research on that problem.

4. Some items support the author's points of view as expressed here and there in this volume; others do not.

General

Anderson, Irving, and Hughes, Byron. "The Relationship Between Learning to Read and Growth as a Whole," *University of Michigan School of Education Bulletin*, No. 26. Ann Arbor, Mich., 1955, pp. 65–68.

Bogart, Leo. *The Age of Television*. Frederick Ungar Publishing Company, New York, 1956.

Buswell, G. T. "The Process of Reading," *The Reading Teacher*, Vol. 13, 1959, pp. 108–114.

Gray, W. S. *The Teaching of Reading and Writing: An International Survey*, Monographs on Fundamental Education, X. UNESCO, Washington, D.C., 1956.

————, and Rogers, Bernice. *Maturity in Reading*. University of Chicago Press, Chicago, 1956.

Hildreth, Gertrude. "Interrelationships Among the Language Arts," *Elementary School Journal*, Vol. 48, 1948, pp. 538–549.

Langman, Muriel. "The Process of Reading: A Descriptive Inter-Disciplinary Approach," *Genetic Psychology Monographs*, No. 62, 1960, pp. 1–40.

McDonagh, E. C., and others. "Television and the Family," *Sociology and Social Research*, Vol. 35, 1950, pp. 113–122.

Many, Wesley. "Is There Really Any Difference — Reading or Listening?" *The Reading Teacher*, Vol. 19, 1965, pp. 110–113.

Olson, Willard. "Reading as a Function of the Total Growth of the Child," in Gray, W. S., *Reading and Pupil Development*. University of Chicago Press, Chicago, 1940, pp. 233–237.

Waples, Douglas, and others. *What Reading Does to People*. University of Chicago Press, Chicago, 1940.

Winger, Howard. "Historical Perspectives of the Role of the Book in Society," *Library Quarterly*, Vol. 25, 1955, pp. 295–305.

Witty, Paul, and Sizemore, R. A. "Studies in Listening," *Elementary English*, Vol. 35, 1958, pp. 538–552. See also *Elementary English*, Vol. 36, 1959, pp. 59–70, 130–140.

Young, W. E. "The Relation of Reading Comprehension and Retention to Hearing Comprehension and Retention," *Journal of Experimental Education*, Vol. 5, 1936, pp. 30–39.

Readiness for Beginning Reading

Almy, Millie. *Children's Experiences Prior to First Grade and Success in Beginning Reading.* Teachers College, Columbia University, New York, 1949.

Ames, Wilbur. "The Understanding Vocabulary of First Grade Pupils," *Elementary English*, Vol. 41, 1964, pp. 64–68.

Artley, A. S. "Oral Language Growth and Reading Ability," *Elementary School Journal*, Vol. 53, 1953, pp. 321–328.

Barrett, T. C. "Visual Discrimination Tasks as Predictors of First Grade Reading Achievement," *The Reading Teacher*, Vol. 18, 1964, pp. 276–282.

Betts, E. A. "Factors in Readiness for Reading," *Educational Administration and Supervision*, Vol. 24, 1943, pp. 199–230.

Black, Millard. "Characteristics of the Culturally Disadvantaged Child," *The Reading Teacher*, Vol. 18, 1965, pp. 465–470.

Bradley, Beatrice. "An Experimental Study of the Readiness Approach to Reading," *Elementary School Journal*, Vol. 56, 1956, pp. 262–267.

Bruner, J. S. "On Perceptual Readiness," *Psychological Review*, Vol. 64, 1957, pp. 123–152.

Brzeinski, Joseph. "Beginning Reading in Denver," *The Reading Teacher*, Vol. 18, 1964, pp. 16–21.

———. "Reading in the Kindergarten," in *Teaching Young Children to Read*, U.S. Office of Education, Bulletin 19. Government Printing Office, Washington, D.C., 1964, pp, 50–58.

Burcham, Grace. *The Difference in Effect of Two Reading Readiness Programs as Revealed by Success in First Grade Reading.* Doctoral dissertation, Colorado State College, Greeley, 1961.

Duggins, Lydia. "Theory and Techniques of Auditory Perception as an Approach to Reading," in Causey, O. S., *The Reading Teacher's Reader*. The Ronald Press Company, New York, 1958, pp. 35–39.

Durkin, Dolores. "An Earlier Start in Reading?" *Elementary School Journal*, Vol. 63, 1962, pp. 146–151.

———. "Early Readers — Reflections After Six Years of Research," *The Reading Teacher*, Vol. 18, 1964, pp. 3–7.

———. "Reading Instruction and the Five-Year-Old Child," in *Challenge and*

Experiment in Reading, Conference Proceedings of the International Reading Association, VII. Scholastic Magazines, Inc., New York, 1962, pp. 23–27.

Durrell, Donald, and Murphy, Helen. "Reading Readiness," in "Boston University Research in Elementary School Reading: 1933–1963," *Journal of Education,* Vol. 146, 1963, pp. 3–19.

———. "The Auditory Discrimination Factor in Reading Readiness and Reading Disability," *Education,* Vol. 73, 1953, pp. 556–560.

Durrell, Donald, and others. "Success in First Grade Reading," *Journal of Education,* Vol. 140, 1958.

Edwards, Thomas. "The Language-Experience Attack on Cultural Deprivation," *The Reading Teacher,* Vol. 18, 1964, pp. 546–551.

Fast, Irene. "Kindergarten Training and Grade I Reading," *Journal of Educational Psychology,* Vol. 48, 1957, pp. 52–57.

Gates, Arthur. "The Necessary Age for Beginning Reading," *Elementary School Journal,* Vol. 37, 1937, pp. 497–508.

Harrison, Lucile. "Innovations in the Teaching of Reading," in *School Boards in a Changing Society,* Convention Proceedings of the National School Boards Association. The Association, Evanston, Ill., 1963, pp. 165–168.

Hildreth, Gertrude. "The Role of Pronunciation and Sounding in Learning to Read," *Elementary School Journal,* Vol. 55, 1594, pp. 141–147.

Hughes, Marie, and Cox, Vivian. "The Language of First Grade Children, I.," *Elementary English,* Vol. 26, 1949, pp. 373–380, 406.

Lloyd, Helene. "What's Ahead in Reading for the Disadvantaged?" *The Reading Teacher,* Vol. 18, 1964, pp. 471–476.

Loban, Walter. *The Language of Elementary School Children.* National Council of Teachers of English, Champaign, Ill., 1963.

Lynn, R. "Reading Readiness and the Perceptual Abilities of Young Children," *Educational Research* (London), Vol. 6, 1963, pp. 15–19.

McCarthy, Dorothea. "Language Development in Young Children," in Carmichael, Leonard, *A Manual of Child Psychology.* John Wiley & Sons, Inc., New York, 1954, pp. 492–630.

Mosbo, Alvin. *A Study of the Effectiveness of Certain Reading Readiness Materials in First Grade.* Doctoral Field Study, No. 2., Colorado State College, Greeley, 1951.

Noel, Doris, "A Comparative Study of the Relationship Between the Quality of the Child's Language Usage and the Quality and Types of Language Used in the Home," *Journal of Educational Research,* Vol. 47, 1953, pp. 161–167.

Piaget, Jean. *The Language and Thought of the Child.* Harcourt, Brace & World, Inc., New York, 1926.

Plessas, Gus, and Oakes, Clifton. "Prereading Experiences of Early Selected Readers," *The Reading Teacher,* Vol. 17, 1964, pp. 241–245.

Popp, Helen. "Visual Discrimination of Alphabet Letters," *The Reading Teacher,* Vol. 17, 1964, pp. 221–225.

Robinson, Helen. "Factors Which Affect Success in Reading," *Elementary School Journal,* Vol. 55, 1955, pp. 263–269.

Smith, Madorah. *An Investigation of the Development of the Sentence and the Extent of Vocabulary in Young Children,* State University of Iowa Studies in Child Welfare, No. 5. Iowa City, 1926.

Smith, Mary. "Measurement of the Size of General English Vocabulary Through the Elementary Grades and High School," *Genetic Psychological Monographs,* No. 24, 1941, pp. 311–345.

Sutton, Marjorie. "Readiness for Reading at the Kindergarten Level," *The Reading Teacher,* Vol. 17, 1964, pp. 234–239. See also, Sutton, Marjorie. "First-Grade Children Who Learned to Read in Kindergarten," *The Reading Teacher,* Vol. 19, 1965, pp. 192–196.

Sutton, Rachel. "A Study of Certain Factors Associated with Reading Readiness in the Kindergarten," *Journal of Educational Research,* Vol. 48, 1955, pp. 531–538.

Taylor, Christian. "The Effect of Training in Reading Readiness," in *Studies in Reading,* Vol. 2. University of London, London, England, 1950, pp. 64–80.

Templin, Mildred. *Certain Language Skills in Children: Their Development and Inter-relationships.* University of Minnesota Press, Minneapolis, 1957.

Triggs, Frances. "A Study of Visual Discrimination and Its Relationship to Success in Reading," in *Reading in a Changing Society,* Conference Proceedings of the International Reading Association, IV. Scholastic Magazines, Inc., New York, 1959, pp. 82–84.

Word Recognition Skills

Agnew, Donald. *The Effect of Varied Amounts of Phonetic Training on Primary Reading.* Duke University Press, Durham, N.C., 1939.

Anderson, I. H., and Dearborn, W. F. *The Psychology of Teaching Reading.* The Ronald Press Company, New York, 1952, Chapter 2.

Baker, Norma. "Confusion in Word Recognition," *Elementary School Journal,* Vol. 45, 1945, pp. 575–577.

Beltramo, Louise. *An Alphabetical Approach to the Teaching of Reading in Grade One.* Doctoral dissertation, State University of Iowa, Iowa City, 1954.

Betts, E. A. "Phonics: Practical Considerations Based on Research," *Elementary English,* Vol. 33, 1956, pp. 357–371.

———. "Phonics: Syllables," *Education,* Vol. 79, 1959, pp. 557–564.

———. "Visual Perception in Reading," *Education,* Vol. 73, 1953, pp. 575–582.

Bruner, Jerome, and Minturn, A. L. "Perceptual Identification and Perceptual Organization," *Journal of Genetic Psychology,* Vol. 53, 1955, pp. 21–28.

Brzeinski, Joseph. "When Should Phonics Instruction Begin?" in *Reading as an Intellectual Activity,* Conference Proceedings of the International Reading Association, VIII. Scholastic Magazines, Inc., New York, 1963, pp. 228–232.

Burrows, Alvina, and Lourie, Zyra. "When Two Vowels Go Walking," *The Reading Teacher,* Vol. 17, 1963, pp. 79–82.

Buswell, Guy. "Perceptual Research and Methods of Learning," *Science Monthly,* Vol. 64, 1947, pp. 521–526.

————. "The Relationship Between Perceptual and Intellectual Processes in Reading," *California Journal of Educational Research,* Vol. 8, 1957, pp. 93–103.

Byrne, Robert. "Effect of Word Form on Retention," *Reading as an Intellectual Activity,* Conference Proceedings of the International Reading Association, VIII. Scholastic Magazines, Inc., New York, 1963, pp. 134–136.

Catterson, Jane. "Inductive Versus Deductive Methods in Teaching Word Attack Skills," *Challenge and Experiment in Reading,* Conference Proceedings of the International Reading Association, VII. Scholastic Magazines, Inc., New York, 1962, pp. 121–123.

Clymer, Theodore. "The Utility of Phonetic Generalizations in the Primary Grades," *The Reading Teacher,* Vol. 16, 1963, pp. 252–258.

Coleman, J. C. "Perception Retardation in Reading Disability Cases," *Journal of Educational Psychology,* Vol. 44, 1953, pp. 497–503.

Cordts, Anna. "And Its All Known as Phonics," *Elementary English,* Vol. 32, 1955, pp. 376–378.

Downing, John. "The ITA Reading Experiment," *The Reading Teacher,* Vol. 18, 1964, pp. 105–110.

Durrell, Donald, and Murphy, Helen. "Reading in Grade One," in "Boston University Research in Elementary Education: 1933–1963," *Journal of Education,* Vol. 146, 1963, pp. 11–25.

Dvorine, I. "What you Should Know about Sight: Parts I and II," *Education,* Vol. 78, 1958, pp. 381–382, 471–475.

Elwell, C. E. "Phonics Indeed — But When?" *Changing Concepts of Reading Instruction,* Conference Proceedings of the International Reading Association, VI. Scholastic Magazines, Inc., New York, 1961, pp. 127–130.

Fleming, C. M. "What's Happening in Reading in Great Britain?" *The Reading Teacher,* Vol. 12, 1959, pp. 176–180.

Forgays, D. G. "The Development of Differential Word Recognition," *Journal of Experimental Psychology,* Vol. 45, 1953, pp. 165–168.

Gates, Arthur, and Russell, David. "Types of Materials, Vocabulary Burden, Word Analysis, and Other Factors in Beginning Reading," *Elementary School Journal,* Vol. 39, 1938, pp. 27–35, 119–128.

Goins, Jean. *Visual Perception Abilities and Early Reading Progress,* Supplementary Educational Monographs, No. 87. University of Chicago Press, Chicago, 1958.

————. "Visual and Auditory Perception in Reading," *The Reading Teacher,* Vol. 13, 1959, pp. 9–13.

Harrington, Sister Mary, and Durrell, Donald. "Mental Maturity Versus Perception Abilities in Primary Reading," *Journal of Educational Psychology,* Vol. 46, 1955, pp. 375–380.

McDowell, Rev. John B. "A Report on the Phonetic Method of Teaching Children to Read," *Catholic Education Review,* Vol. 51, 1953, pp. 506–519.

Mills, Robert. "An Evaluation of Techniques for Teaching Word Recognition," *Elementary School Journal,* Vol. 56, 1956, pp. 221–225.

Morris, Joyce. "Teaching Children to Read," *Educational Research,* Vol. 1, 1958, pp. 38–49. See also, Morris, Joyce. "Teaching Children to Read," *Educational Research,* Vol. 1; 1959, pp. 61–75.

Mulder, R. F., and Curtin, J. "Vocal Phonetic Ability and Silent Reading Achievement," *Educational Digest,* Vol. 21, 1956, pp. 46–47.

Oaks, Ruth. "A Study of the Vowel Situation in a Primary Vocabulary," *Education,* Vol. 72, 1952, pp. 604–617.

Olsen, Arthur. "Phonics and Success in Beginning Reading," *Journal of Developmental Reading,* Vol. 6, 1963, pp. 256–260.

Roberts, R. W., and Coleman, J. C. "Investigation of the Role of Visual and Kinesthetic Factors in Reading Failure," *Journal of Educational Research,* Vol. 51, 1948, pp. 445–451.

Robinson, H. A. "A Study of the Techniques of Word Identification," *The Reading Teacher,* Vol. 16, 1963, pp. 238–242.

Robinson, Helen. "Special Difficulties in Word Perception as Revealed in Clinical Studies," in *Basic Instruction in Reading in Elementary and High Schools,* Supplementary Educational Monographs, No. 65. University of Chicago Press, Chicago, 1948.

Rudisill, Mabel. "Interrelationships of Functional Phonic Knowledge, Reading, Spelling, and Mental Age," *Elementary School Journal,* Vol. 57, 1957, pp. 264–267.

Smith, Henry. "The Perceptual Nature of the Reading Process," *University of Kansas Bulletin of Education,* Lawrence, Kans., 1962, pp. 60–69.

Smith, Nila. "What Research Tells Us About Word Recognition," *Elementary School Journal,* Vol. 55, 1955, pp. 440–446.

Solomon, R. L., and Postman, L. "Frequency of Usage as a Determinant of Recognition Thresholds for Words," *Journal of Experimental Psychology,* Vol. 43, 1952, pp. 195–201.

Tate, Harry, and others. "Nonphonic Primary Reading," *Elementary School Journal,* Vol. 40, 1940, pp. 529–537.

Vernon, Magdalen. *A Further Study of Word Perception.* Cambridge University, Cambridge, England, 1954.

————. "The Perceptual Process in Reading," *The Reading Teacher,* Vol. 13, 1959, pp. 2–8.

Witty, Paul. "Phonic Study and Word Analysis," *Elementary English,* Vol. 30, 1953, pp. 296–305, 373–383.

————, and Sizemore, Robert. "Phonics in the Reading Program: A Review and an Evaluation," *Elementary English,* Vol. 32, 1955, pp. 355–371.

The Reading Program

Allen, Robert. "Better Reading Through the Recognition of Grammatical Relations," *The Reading Teacher,* Vol. 18, 1964, pp. 172–178.

Anderson, I. H.; Hughes, B. A.; and Dixon, W. R. "The Relation Between Reading Achievement and the Method of Teaching Reading," *University of Michigan School of Education Bulletin,* No. 27. Ann Arbor, Mich., 1956, pp. 104–108.

Austin, Mary, and Morrison, Coleman. *The First R: The Harvard Report on Reading in Elementary Schools.* The Macmillan Co., New York, 1963.

Balow, I. H., and Ruddell, A. K. "The Effects of Three Types of Grouping on Achievement," *California Journal of Educational Research,* Vol. 14, 1963, pp. 108–117.

Bateman, Barbara, and Wetherell, Janis. "A Critique of Bloomfield's Approach to the Teaching of Reading," *The Reading Teacher,* Vol. 18, 1964, pp. 98–104.

Betts, E. A. "Developing Basic Reading Skills Through Class Organization," *Education,* Vol. 78, 1958, pp. 561–576.

Blanchard, Marjorie. "Adjusting Learning Activities and Reading Materials to Individual Differences: In Grades Four to Six," in *Improving Reading in All Curriculum Areas,* Supplementary Educational Monographs, No. 76. University of Chicago Press, Chicago, 1952, pp. 32–36.

Bohnhorst, B. A., and Sellars, Sophia. "Individual Reading Instruction Versus Basal Textbook Instruction," *Elementary English,* Vol. 36, 1959, pp. 185–190, 212.

Bonney, Jill, and Hannigan, L. B. "Individualized Teaching of Reading," *National Elementary Principal,* Vol. 35, 1955, pp. 76–82.

Botel, Morton. "We Need a Total Approach to Reading," *The Reading Teacher,* Vol. 13, 1960, pp. 254–257.

————. "What Linguists Say to This Teacher of Reading and Spelling," *The Reading Teacher,* Vol. 18, 1964, pp. 188–193.

Byers, Lorella. "Pupil Interests and the Content of Primary Reading Texts," *The Reading Teacher,* Vol. 17, 1964, pp. 227–233.

Cammarota, Gloria. "Word Groups in Speech and Reading," *The Reading Teacher*, Vol. 18, 1964, pp. 94–97.

Canfield, James. "Flexibility in Grouping for Reading," *The Reading Teacher*, Vol. 11, 1957, pp. 91–94.

Carlson, Esther, and Northrup, Joyce. "An Experiment in Grouping Pupils for Instruction in Reading," *National Elementary Principal*, Vol. 35, 1955, pp. 53–57.

Crosby, Muriel. "Organization for Reading Instruction," *Elementary English*, Vol. 37, 1960, pp. 169–173.

Cyrog, Frances. "Self-Selection in Reading: Report of a Longitudinal Study," in *Reading in a Responsible Society*, Twenty-sixth Yearbook of the Claremont Reading Conference. Claremont College, Claremont, Calif., 1962, pp. 106–113.

Dale, Edgar, and Razik, Taher. *Bibliography of Vocabulary Studies*. Ohio State University, Columbus, 1963.

Davis, David. "Phonemic Structural Approach to Initial Instruction in Reading," *Elementary English*, Vol. 41, 1964, pp. 218–223.

Dolch, E. W. "Groups in Reading," *Elementary English*, Vol. 31, 1954, pp. 477–484.

Durrell, Donald, and Murphy, Helen. "Reading in Grades Two and Three" and "Reading in the Intermediate Grades," in "Boston University Research in Elementary School Reading: 1933–1963," *Journal of Education*, Vol. 146, 1963, pp. 26–35, 36–53.

———, and Palos, Viola. "Pupils Study Teams in Reading," *Education*, Vol. 76, 1956, pp. 552–556.

Edmiston, R. W. "The Relationship Between Group Achievement and Range of Abilities Within the Groups," *Journal of Educational Research*, Vol. 42, 1949, pp. 547–548.

Edward, Sister Mary. "A Modified Linguistic Versus a Composite Basal Reading Program," *The Reading Teacher*, Vol. 17, 1964, pp. 511–515, 527.

Floyd, Cecil. "Meeting Children's Reading Needs in the Middle Grades," *Elementary School Journal*, Vol. 55, 1954, pp. 99–104.

Fox, L. K., and McCullough, Constance. "Individualized Reading," *NEA Journal*, Vol. 47, 1958, pp. 162–163.

Fries, Charles. "Linguistics and the Teaching of Reading," *The Reading Teacher*, Vol. 17, 1964, pp. 594–598.

Gates, Arthur. "Vocabulary Control in Basal Reading Material," *The Reading Teacher*, Vol. 15, 1961, pp. 81–85.

Gray, W. S. "Role of Group and Individualized Teaching in a Sound Reading Program," *The Reading Teacher*, Vol. 11, 1957, pp. 99–108.

Green, D. R., and Ripley, Hazel. "Interclass Grouping for Reading Instruction in the Middle Grades," *Journal of Experimental Education*, Vol. 31, 1963, pp. 273–278.

Groff, Patrick. "Comparisons of Individualized and Ability-Grouping Approaches as to Reading Achievement," *Elementary English*, Vol. 40, 1963, pp. 258–264.

―――. "Comparisons of Individualized and Ability-Grouping Approaches to Teaching Reading: A Supplement," *Elementary English*, Vol. 41, 1964, pp. 238–241.

Hildreth, Gertrude. "Linguistic Factors in Early Reading Instruction," *The Reading Teacher*, Vol. 18, 1964, pp. 172–177.

Jenkins, Marian. "Self-Selection in Reading," *The Reading Teacher*, Vol. 11, 1957, pp. 84–90.

Jones, Daisy. "An Experiment in Adaptation to Individual Differences," *Journal of Educational Psychology*, Vol. 39, 1948, pp. 257–272.

Keislar, Evan. "Conference on Perceptual and Linguistic Aspects of Reading," *The Reading Teacher*, Vol. 18, 1964, pp. 43–49.

Lazar, May. "Individualized Reading: A Dynamic Approach," *The Reading Teacher*, Vol. 11, 1957, pp. 75–83.

Lofthouse, Yvonne. "Individualized Reading: Significant Research," *The Reading Teacher*, Vol. 16, 1962, pp. 35–37, 47.

Moorhouse, William. "Interclass Grouping for Reading Instruction," *Elementary School Journal*, Vol. 64, 1964, pp. 280–286.

Parkin, Phyllis. "An Individualized Program in Reading," *Educational Leadership*, Vol. 14, 1956, pp. 34–38.

Powell, William. "The Joplin Plan: An Evaluation," *Elementary School Journal*, Vol. 64, 1964, pp. 387–392.

Ramsey, Wallace. "An Evaluation of Three Methods of Teaching Sixth Grade Reading," *Challenge and Experiment in Reading*, Conference Proceedings of the International Reading Association, VII. Scholastic Magazines, Inc., New York, 1962, pp. 151–153.

Rittenhouse, Gloria. "An Experiment in Reading by Invitation in Grades One Through Four," *The Reading Teacher*, Vol. 13, 1960, pp. 258–261.

Robinson, Margaret. "Differentiating Instruction to Provide for the Needs of Learners Through Organizational Practices: In Grades Four Through Six," in *New Frontiers in Reading*, Conference Proceedings of the International Reading Association, V. Scholastic Magazines, Inc., New York, 1960, pp. 29–32.

Ruddell, Robert. "The Effect of Oral and Written Patterns of Language Structure on Reading Comprehension," *The Reading Teacher*, Vol. 18, 1964, pp. 270–275.

Russell, D. H. "Interclass Grouping for Reading Instruction in the Intermediate Grades," *Journal of Educational Research*, Vol. 39, 1946, pp. 462–470.

Safford, A. L. "Evaluation of an Individualized Reading Program," *The Reading Teacher*, Vol. 13, 1960, pp. 266–270.

Sarten, H. W. "The Roseville Experiment with Individualized Reading," *The Reading Teacher,* Vol. 13, 1960, pp. 277–281.

Sheldon, W. D. "Differentiating Instruction to Provide for the Needs of Learners," *New Frontiers in Reading,* Conference Proceedings of the International Reading Association, V. Scholastic Magazines, Inc., New York, 1960, pp. 23–26.

Smith, Nila. "Classroom Organization: An Age-Old Problem with New Slants," *The Reading Teacher,* Vol. 11, 1957, pp. 73–74.

Strickland, Ruth. "The Contribution of Structural Linguistics to the Teaching of Reading, Writing, and Grammar in the Elementary School," *Bulletin of the School of Education, University of Indiana,* Vol. 40, No. 1. Bloomington, Ind., 1964.

Talbert, Dorothy, and Merritt, C. B. "The Relative Effectiveness of Two Approaches to the Teaching of Reading in Grade V," *The Reading Teacher,* Vol. 19, 1965, pp. 183–186.

Veatch, Jeanette. "In Defense of Individualized Reading," *Elementary English,* Vol. 37, 1960, pp. 227–234.

Walker, Clare. *An Evaluation of Two Programs of Reading in Grades Four, Five, and Six in the Elementary School.* Doctoral dissertation, New York University, New York, 1957.

Whipple, Gertrude. "Good Practices in Grouping," *The Reading Teacher,* Vol. 7, 1953, pp. 69–74.

Williams, Pauline. "Some Group Reading Results," *Chicago School Journal,* Vol. 31, 1949, pp. 90–94.

Witty, Paul. "Individualized Reading — A Summary and Evaluation," *Elementary English,* Vol. 36, 1959, pp. 401–412, 450.

Literature for Children

Addy, Martha. *A Study of Children's Choices in Poetry.* Doctoral Field Study No. 2., Colorado State College, Greeley, 1943.

Amatora, Sister M., and Edith, Sister M. "The Age Factor in Children's Interests in Free Reading," *Education,* Vol. 71, 1951, pp. 567–571.

American Association of School Librarians. *Standards for School Library Programs.* American Library Association, Chicago, 1960.

Austin, Mary, and Morrison, Coleman. *The First R: The Harvard Report on Reading in Elementary Schools.* The Macmillan Co., New York, 1963.

Avegno, T. Sylvia. "Intermediate Grade Children's Choices of Poetry," *Elementary English,* Vol. 33, 1956, pp. 428–432.

Bernstein, Margery. "Relationship Between Interest and Reading Comprehension," *Journal of Educational Research,* Vol. 49, 1955, pp. 283–288.

Celestine, Sister Mary. "A Survey of the Literature on the Reading Interests of Children of the Elementary Grades," *Catholic Education,* 1940.

Corliss, William. "Elementary School Libraries," *Elementary English*, Vol. 38, 1961, pp. 494–496.

Frank, Jossette. *Your Children's Reading Today*. Doubleday & Company, Inc., New York, 1954.

Gaver, Mary. *Effectiveness of Centralized Library Service in Elementary Schools*. Rutgers University Press, New Brunswick, N.J., 1963.

————. "Research on Elementary School Libraries: A Bibliographic Essay," *ALA Bulletin*, No. 56. American Library Association, Chicago, 1962, pp. 117–126.

Getzels, J. W. *The Nature of Reading Interests: Psychological Aspects*, Supplementary Educational Monographs, No. 84. University of Chicago Press, Chicago, 1956, pp. 5–9.

Gray, W. S. *Characteristics of Effective Oral Reading*, Supplementary Educational Monographs, No. 82. University of Chicago Press, Chicago, 1955, pp. 5–10.

Henne, Frances. "The Basic Need in Library Service for Youth," *Library Quarterly*, Vol. 25, 1955, pp. 37–46.

————, and Spain, Frances. "The School and the Public Library," *The Annals of the American Academy of Political and Social Science*, No. 302, 1955, pp. 52–59.

Herminghaus, E. G. *The Effect of Bibliotherapy on the Attitudes and Personal and Social Adjustment of Elementary School Children*. Doctoral dissertation, University of Washington, Seattle, 1954.

Hockett, J. and Forry K. "Interest in Reading Expressed by Pupils in Grades Three to Seven," in Dean, R. B., and Others, *Children's Interests*, Twelfth Yearbook of the California Elementary School Principals Association. The Association, Sacramento, Calif., 1940, pp. 89–95.

Horn, E. "Poetry for Primary Children," *State University of Iowa Extension Bulletin*, College of Education Series, No. 40. Iowa City, 1961.

Huber, M.; Bruner, H,; and Curry M. *Children's Interests in Poetry*. Rand McNally & Co., Chicago, 1927.

Humphrey, P. "The Reading Interests and Habits of Six Hundred Children in the Intermediate Grades," in the *Twentieth Yearbook of the Department of Elementary School Principals*. National Education Association, Washington, D.C., 1941.

Huus, Helen. "Interpreting Research in Children's Literature," in *Children, Books, and Reading*. International Reading Association, Newark, Del., 1964, pp. 123–245.

Jefferson, B. F. "Some Relationships Between Children's Preferences in Juvenile Literature," *Elementary School Journal*, Vol. 58, 1958, pp. 212–218.

Johnson, Lois. "Children's Newspaper Reading," *Elementary English*, Vol. 40, 1963. pp. 428–432.

Kelty, Annette. *An Investigation to Determine the Nature and Scope of the Voluntary Reading of Newspapers, Magazines, and Books by the Intermediate Grade Pupils Attending the Public Schools of Rockville Center, New York.* Doctoral Field Study, No. 2., Colorado State College, Greeley, 1958.

Kennedy, Ruth. *A Study of Children's Choices in Poetry.* Master's thesis, Colorado State College, Greeley, 1936.

Lazar, M. *Reading Interests, Activities, and Opportunities of Bright, Average, and Dull Children.* Teachers College, Columbia University, New York, 1937.

Leary, Bernice. "Meeting the Needs of Children Through Literature," in *Current Problems of Reading Instruction,* Report of the Seventh Annual Conference on Reading. University of Pittsburgh, Pittsburgh, Pa., 1951, pp. 36–39.

MacIntosh, Helen. *A Critical Study of Children's Choices in Poetry,* State University of Iowa Studies in Education, Vol. VII, No. 4. Iowa City, 1932.

Norvell, G. W. *What Boys and Girls Like to Read.* Silver Burdett Company, Morristown, N.J., 1958.

Public School Library Statistics, 1958–1959, U.S. Office of Education. Government Printing Office, Washington, D.C., 1960.

Rankin, M. *Children's Interests in Library Books of Fiction.* Teachers College, Columbia University, New York, 1944.

Robinson, Helen. "What Research Says to the Teacher of Reading: Reading Interests," *The Reading Teacher,* Vol. 8, 1955, pp. 173–177.

Rogers, Helen, and Robinson, H. A. "Reading Interests of First Graders," *Elementary English,* Vol. 40, 1963, pp. 707–711.

Rudman, H. C. "Informal Needs and Reading Interests of Children in Grades IV Through VIII," *Elementary School Journal,* Vol. 55, 1955, pp. 502–512.

Shrodes, Caroline. *Bibliotherapy: A Theoretical and Clinical-Experimental Study.* Doctoral dissertation, University of California, Berkeley, 1949.

Taylor, Marian, and Schneider, Mary. "What Books Are Our Children Reading?" *Chicago Schools Journal,* Vol. 38, 1957, pp. 155–160.

Terman, L. M., and Lima, Margaret. *Children's Reading.* Appleton-Century-Crofts, Inc., New York, 1935.

Thompson, Evelyn. *The Voluntary Reading of Children in Grades Four, Five, and Six in Houston, Texas.* Doctoral dissertation, Colorado State College, Greeley, 1956.

Thorndike, R. *Children's Reading Interests.* Teachers College, Columbia University, New York, 1941.

Vandament, W. E., and Thalman, W. A. "An Investigation Into the Reading Interests of Children," *Journal of Educational Research,* Vol. 49, 1956, pp. 467–470.

Witty, Paul. "Children's Interests in Comics, Radio, and Motion Pictures," *Educational Administration and Supervision,* Vol. 38, 1952, pp. 138–147.

————, and Sizemore, Robert. "Reading the Comics: A Summary of Studies and An Evaluation, I," *Elementary English*, Vol. 31, 1954, pp. 501–506. See also *Elementary English*, Vol. 32, 1955, pp. 45–49.

Wolfson, Bernice. "What Do Children Say Their Reading Interests Are?" *The Reading Teacher*, Vol. 14, 1960, pp. 81–82.

Comprehension in Reading

Addy, Martha. *The Development of a Meaning Vocabulary in the Intermediate Grades.* Doctoral Field Study, No. 1., Colorado State College, Greeley, 1942.

Arbuthnot, Sue. *An Investigation of the Use of Bold Face Type to Indicate Emphasis in Reading Matter.* Doctoral dissertation, Colorado State College, Greeley, 1961.

Betts, E. A. "Reading Is Thinking," *The Reading Teacher*, Vol. 12, 1959, pp. 146–151.

————. "Research on Reading as a Thinking Process," *Journal of Educational Research*, Vol. 50, 1956, pp. 1–15.

Bradbury, Helen. *The Ability of Fourth Grade Pupils to Construct the Meaning of a Strange Word from Context.* Master's thesis, Colorado State College, Greeley, 1943.

Cook, Luella. "Language Factors Involved in Interpretation," *The Reading Teacher*, Vol. 12, 1959, pp. 152–157.

Davis, F. B. "Fundamental Factors of Comprehension in Reading," *Psychometrika*, Vol. 9, 1944, pp. 185–197.

Dewey, Joseph. *A Case Study of Reading Comprehension Difficulties in American History*, State University of Iowa Studies in Education, Vol. X, No. 1. Iowa City, 1935.

Dolch, E. W. "Vocabulary Development," *Elementary English*, Vol. 49, 1949, pp. 341–347.

Dumas, Enoch. *The Effect of Controlling Vocabulary Upon the Understanding of Sentences in Reading.* Doctoral Field Study, No. 1., Colorado State College, Greeley, 1941.

Fennema, Elizabeth. "Mental Imagery and the Reading Process," *Elementary School Journal*, Vol. 59, 1959, pp. 286–289.

Gibbons, Helen. *The Ability to See Relationship Between the Parts of a Sentence.* Doctoral Field Study, No. 1., Colorado State College, Greeley, 1940.

Godfrey, Grace. *A Study of Context as a Means of Explaining the Meaning of Strange Words in Certain Children's Books.* Master's thesis, Colorado State College, Greeley, 1941.

Gray, W. S. "Reading and Understanding," *Elementary English*, Vol. 28, 1948, pp. 148–149.

————, and Holmes, Eleanor. *The Development of Meaning Vocabularies in Reading.* University of Chicago Press, Chicago, 1938.

Groesbeck, Hulda. *The Comprehension of Figurative Language by Elementary Children.* Doctoral dissertation, University of Oklahoma, Norman, 1961.

Guilfoile, Elizabeth. "Training Pupils to Cope with Language Difficulties in Interpreting What Is Read: In Grades Four to Six," in *Promoting Growth Toward Maturity in Interpreting What Is Read,* Supplementary Educational Monographs, No. 74. University of Chicago Press, Chicago, 1951, pp. 96–101.

Hollingsed, James. *A Study of Figures of Speech in Intermediate Grade Reading.* Doctoral dissertation, Colorado State College, Greeley, 1958.

Horn, Ernest. *Methods of Instruction in the Social Studies.* Charles Scribner's Sons, New York, 1937, Chapters IV and V.

Jan-Tausch, James. "Concrete Thinking as a Factor in Reading Comprehension," in *Challenge and Experiment in Reading,* Conference Proceedings of the International Reading Association, VII. Scholastic Magazines, Inc. New York, 1962, pp. 161–164.

Johnson, Marjorie. "Factors in Reading Comprehension," *Educational Administration and Supervision,* Vol. 35, 1949, pp. 385–406.

Lane, Wilson. *A Study to Determine the Effects of Bold Face Emphasis on the Reading Comprehension of Fifth Grade Pupils.* Doctoral dissertation, Colorado State College, Greeley, 1957.

Lofton, Lucille. *Use of Punctuation Marks in Certain Fourth Grade Readers.* Master's thesis, Colorado State College, Greeley, 1944.

McCullough, Constance. "Context Aids in Reading," *The Reading Teacher,* Vol. 11, 1958, pp. 225–229.

————. "What Does Research Reveal about Practices in Teaching Reading?" *English Journal,* Vol. 46, 1957, pp. 475–490.

McKee, Paul. *The Teaching of Reading in the Elementary School.* Houghton Mifflin Company, Boston, 1948, pp. 46–58.

Muehlhausen, Edward. *An Experimental Study to Determine the Effect of Typographical Emphasis on the Reading Comprehension of Sixth Grade Pupils.* Doctoral Field Study, No. 2, Colorado State College, Greeley, 1954.

Piekarz, Josephine. "Getting Meaning from Reading," *Elementary School Journal,* Vol. 56, 1956, pp. 303–309.

Research in Reading for the Middle Grades, U.S. Office of Education, Bulletin 1963, No. 31. Government Printing Office, Washington, D.C., 1963. (See annotations of appropriate studies.)

Russell, David. "The Dimensions of Children's Meaning Vocabularies in Grades Four Through Twelve," *University of California Publication in Education,* Vol. 11. Berkeley, 1954, pp. 315–414.

Shaw, Philip. "Rhetorical Guides to Reading Comprehension," *The Reading Teacher,* Vol. 11, 1958, pp. 239–243.

Springman, John. *Sixth Grade Pupils Understanding of Passages in Social Studies Textbooks.* Doctoral Field Study, No. 1., Colorado State College, Greeley, 1942.

Stolte, Helen. *The Ability of Fourth Grade Children to Comprehend Certain Geographical Concepts.* Master's thesis, State University of Iowa, Iowa City, 1935.

Sutton, Rachel. "The Effect of Vocabulary Building on Reading Skills," *Elementary School Journal,* Vol. 54, 1953, pp. 94–97.

Thorndike, E. L. "Reading as Reasoning: A Study of Mistakes in Paragraph Reading," *Journal of Educational Psychology,* Vol. 8, 1917, pp. 323–332.

Werner, H., and Kaplan, Edith. *The Acquisition of Word Meanings: A Developmental Study,* Monograph of the Society for Research in Child Development, No. 51. The Society, Chicago, 1950.

Wozencraft, Marian. "Word Meaning Difficulties," *Elementary English,* Vol. 41, 1964, pp. 44–46.

Yoakam, G. A. "The Development of Comprehension in the Middle Grades," in *Current Problems of Reading Instruction,* Report of the Seventh Annual Conference on Reading. University of Pittsburgh, Pittsburgh, Pa., 1951, pp. 28–35.

Reading–Study Skills

Barton, W. E. *Outlining as a Study Procedure.* Teachers College, Columbia University, New York, 1930.

Germane, C. E. "The Value of the Controlled Mental Summary as a Method of Studying," *School and Society,* Vol. 12, 1920, pp. 591–593.

————. "The Value of the Corrected Summary as Compared with the Rereading of the Same Article," *Elementary School Journal,* Vol. 21, 1921, pp. 461–464.

————. "Outlining and Summarizing Compared with Rereading as Methods of Studying," in the *Twentieth Yearbook of the National Society for the Study of Education,* Part II. Public School Publishing Company, Bloomington, Ill., 1921, pp. 103–112.

Grayum, Helen. *An Analytic Description of Skimming: Its Purpose and Place as an Ability in Reading.* Indiana University, Bloomington, 1952.

Hollingsworth, Paul. "Can Training in Listening Improve Reading?" *The Reading Teacher,* Vol. 18, 1964, pp. 121–123, 127.

Howell, Wallace. "Work Study Skills of Children in Grades IV to VIII," *Elementary School Journal,* Vol. 50, 1950, pp. 384–389.

Kelty, Annette. *A Report of an Experimental Study to Determine the Effect of Listening for Certain Purposes Upon Achievement in Reading for Those Purposes.* Doctoral Field Study, No. 1., Colorado State College, Greeley, 1956.

Lewis, Maurice. *The Effect of Training in Listening for Certain Purposes Upon Reading for Those Purposes.* Doctoral Field Study, No. 1., Colorado State College, Greeley, 1953.

McCullough, Constance. "Responses of Elementary School Children to Common Types of Reading Comprehension Questions," *Journal of Educational Research*, Vol. 51, 1957, pp. 67–70.

McDivitt, William. *Reading Skills Being Taught to Children in the Elementary School.* Doctoral dissertation, Colorado State College, Greeley, 1956.

Malter, M. S. "Children's Ability to Read Diagrammatical Materials," *Elementary School Journal*, Vol. 49, 1948, pp. 98–102.

Marsden, W. W. *A Study of the Value of Training in Listening to Achievement in Reading.* Doctoral Field Study, No. 1., Colorado State College, Greeley, 1952.

Moore, Walter. "Research on the Skimming Process in Reading," *University of Kansas Bulletin of Education*, No. 17. Lawrence, Kans., 1962, pp. 20–28.

Newlun, C. O. *Teaching Children to Summarize in Fifth Grade History.* Teachers College, Columbia University, New York, 1930.

Robinson, Francis. *Effective Study.* Harper & Brothers, New York, 1961.

Rushdoony, Haig. "Achievement in Map Reading: An Experimental Study," *Elementary School Journal*, Vol. 64, 1963, pp. 70–75.

Smith, Nila. "Utilizing Reading Opportunities in the Entire Curriculum," *Education*, Vol. 72, 1952, pp. 579–589.

Yoakam, G. A. "The Reading-Study Approach to Printed Materials," *The Reading Teacher*, Vol. 11, 1958, pp. 146–151.

———. *Reading and Study.* The Macmillan Co., New York, 1928, Chapters VIII, IX.

Critical Reading

Anderson, H. R.; Marcham, F. G.; and Dunn, S. B. "An Experiment in Teaching Certain Skills of Critical Thinking," *Journal of Educational Research*, Vol. 38, 1944, pp. 241–251.

Betts, E. A. "Research in Reading as a Thinking Process," *Journal of Educational Research*, Vol. 50, 1956, pp. 1–15.

Crossen, H. J. "Effect of Attitudes of the Reader Upon Critical Reading Ability," *Journal of Educational Research*, Vol. 42, 1948, pp. 289–298.

Engel, G.; O'Shea, H. E.; and Mendenhall, J. H. "Projective Responses to a News Article: A Study in Aspects of Bias," *Journal of Psychology*, Vol. 46, 1958, pp. 309–319.

Fay, Leo. "Promoting Growth in Ability to Interpret When Reading Critically: In Grades Four to Six," in *Promoting Growth Toward Maturity in Interpreting What Is Read*, Supplementary Educational Monographs, No. 74. University of Chicago Press, Chicago, 1951, pp. 144–148.

Gans, Roma. *Study of Critical Reading Comprehension in the Intermediate Grades*. Teachers College, Columbia University, 1940.

Grener, N., and Raths, L. E. "Thinking in Grade III," *Educational Research Bulletin*, Vol. 24, 1945, pp. 38–42.

Groff, P. J. "Children's Attitudes Toward Reading and Their Critical Reading Abilities in Four Content-Type Materials," *Journal of Educational Research*, Vol. 55, 1962, pp. 313–318.

Johnson, Marjorie. "Readiness for Critical Reading," *Education*, Vol. 73, 1953, pp. 391–396.

Maney, E. S. "Literal and Critical Reading in Science," *Journal of Experimental Education*, Vol. 27, 1958, pp. 57–64.

Miller, J., and Weston, G. "Slow Learners Improve in Critical Thinking," *Social Education*, Vol. 13, 1949, pp. 315–316.

Nardelli, R. R. "Some Aspects of Creative Reading," *Journal of Educational Research*, Vol. 50, 1957, pp. 495–508.

Sochor, Elna. "The Nature of Critical Reading," *Elementary English*, Vol. 36, 1959, pp. 47–58.

Thayer, L. O., and Pronko, N .H. "The Effect of Conceptual Stereotypes in an Ambiguous Situation," *Journal of General Psychology*, Vol. 60, 1959, pp. 269–273.

Reading in the Content Subjects

Arnsdorf, Val. "Readability of Basal Social Studies Material," *The Reading Teacher*, Vol. 16, 1963, pp. 243–246.

————. "The Influence of Indefinite Terms of Time and Space on Comprehension of Social Studies Material," in *Challenge and Experiment in Reading*, Conference Proceedings of the International Reading Association, VII. Scholastic Magazines, Inc., New York, 1962, pp. 159–161.

Artley, A. S. "The Appraisal of Reading Comprehension," *Journal of Educational Psychology*, Vol. 34, 1943, pp. 50–60.

Brownell, W. A., and Hendrickson, C. "How Children Learn Information, Concepts, and Generalizations," in the *Forty-Ninth Yearbook of the National Society for the Study of Education, Part I*. University of Chicago Press, Chicago, 1950, pp. 92–128.

Carner, R. L., and Sheldon, V. D. "Problems in the Development of Concepts Through Reading," *Elementary School Journal*, Vol. 55, 1954, pp. 226–229.

Christensen, Clifford, and Stordahl, Kalmer. "The Effect of Organization Aids on Comprehension and Retention," *Journal of Educational Psychology*, Vol. 46, 1955, pp. 65–74.

Dolch, E. W. "Reading Pictures," *Eleventh Yearbook of the Claremont Reading Conference*. Claremont College, Claremont, Calif., 1946, pp. 183–186.

Fay, L. C. "Responsibility for and Methods of Promoting Growth in Reading in Content Areas," in *Better Reading for Our Times,* Conference Proceedings of the International Reading Association, I. The Association, Newark, N.J., 1956, pp. 88–92.

———. "The Relationship Between Specific Skills and Selected Areas of Sixth Grade Achievement," *Journal of Educational Research,* Vol. 43, 1950, pp. 541–547.

———. "What Research Has to Say About Reading in the Content Areas," *The Reading Teacher,* Vol. 8, 1954, pp. 68–72.

Feldman, Shirley; Merrill, Kathleen; and MacGintie, W. "An Effective Aid for Teaching Reading," *The Reading Teacher,* Vol. 13, 1960, pp. 208–211.

Friedman, Kopple. "Time Concepts of Elementary School Children," *Elementary School Journal,* Vol. 44, 1944, pp. 337–342.

Gorman, H. "Adventure with Film Readers: How Motion Pictures Correlated with Film Story Books Help Young Readers Read," *Education Screen,* Vol. 30, 1951, pp. 13–15.

Harris, T. L. "Making Reading an Effective Instrument of Learning in the Content Fields," in the *Forty-Seventh Yearbook of the National Society for the Study of Education, Part II.* University of Chicago Press, Chicago, 1948, pp. 116–135.

Johnson, Mary. "The Vocabulary Difficulty of Content Subjects in Grade Five," *Elementary English,* Vol. 29, 1952, pp. 277–280.

Robinson, H. A. "Reading Skills Employed in Solving Social Studies Problems," *The Reading Teacher,* Vol. 18, 1964, pp. 263–269.

Russell, D. H. *Children's Thinking.* Ginn & Company, Boston, 1956.

Serra, Mary. "How to Develop Concepts and Their Verbal Representations," *Elementary School Journal,* Vol. 53, 1953, pp. 275–285.

———. "The Concept Burden of Instructional Materials," *Elementary School Journal,* Vol. 53, 1953, pp. 508–512.

Vinake, L. C. "Concept Formation in Children of School Age," *Education,* Vol. 74, 1955, pp. 571–576.

Wagner, Louise. "Measuring the Map Reading Ability of Sixth Grade Children," *Elementary School Journal,* Vol. 53, 1953, pp. 338–344.

Whipple, Gertrude. "Changing Concepts of Reading Instruction in the Content Areas," in *Changing Concepts of Reading Instruction.* Conference Proceedings of the International Reading Association, VI. Scholastic Magazines, Inc., New York, 1961.

Witty, Paul. "Reading of Social Studies Material," *Elementary English,* Vol. 27, 1950, pp. 1–8.

Young, William. "Recent Research on Reading in the Social Studies," *Education,* Vol. 57, 1941, pp. 18–26.

Index